Photography

Third Edition

Phil Davis

University of Michigan

Photography

wcb   **Wm. C. Brown Company Publishers**   **Dubuque, Iowa**

Book Team

Robert Nash
Executive Editor

David A. Corona
Designer

Julie Kennedy
Production Editor

Marla Schafer
Design Layout Assistant

Mary Heller
Visual Research Editor

Cover photo: James L. Ballard

Cover props courtesy of **Hoo's Photo,**
Evanston, Illinois and **Standard Photo
Supply,** Chicago, Illinois

Reviewers

Professor James Alinder
Executive Director
Friends of Photography
Carmel, California

Professor Loren Cockrell
San Jose State University

Professor Walter Craig
The Ohio State University

Professor Bernard Freemesser
(deceased)
University of Oregon

Professor Eric Kronengold
Arizona State University

Professor Rosalind Kimball Moulton
Stephens College, Columbia, Missouri

Professor Gary B. Pearson
Ricks College, Rexburg, Idaho

Professor David Read
University of Nebraska, Lincoln

Professor Bob Smith
Mercy College, Dobbs Ferry, New York

Professor Dick Stevens
University of Notre Dame

Professor Ralph Talbert
California State University, Sacramento

Professor Samuel Wang
Clemson University, Clemson, South Carolina

Revision Focus Group Participants

Professor David Read
University of Nebraska, Lincoln

Professor Dick Stevens
University of Notre Dame

Professor Jean Locey
New School for Social Research, New York

Professor Jaromir Stephany
University of Maryland, Baltimore County

Professor Martha A. Strawn
University of North Carolina, Charlotte

Introductory Photography Course
Focus Group Participants.

Professor James Alinder
Executive Director
Friends of Photography
Carmel, California

Professor Richman Haire
Minneapolis College of Art and Design

Professor Wayne R. Lazorik
University of New Mexico

Photography

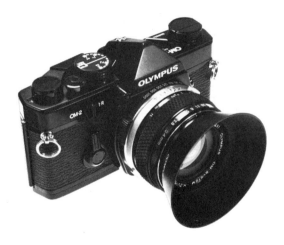

Contents

Preface

My intent in writing *Photography,* in its original version, was to provide students with some background in the history of the medium, to present the necessary technical information in a logical sequence, and to stimulate student interest in photography as a craft, an art, and a medium of personal expression. Although the third edition has been thoroughly reworked and changed in many ways, the original purposes have not been modified. I believe this book, as it now stands, represents a significant improvement over previous editions.

Photography begins with expanded coverage of the history. After a brief introduction to the photographic process, three chapters are devoted to fundamental information and instruction in black-and-white photography—cameras, lenses, and related equipment (emphasizing the use of the popular small cameras), film processing, and printing. The next two chapters, "Working with Light" and "Color Photography," discuss the principles of light control, filtration, and color, with detailed instruction in color printing. Chapter 8, "Special Camera Techniques," presents the basics of view camera operation, exposure-development controls, the Zone System, and close-up photography. The next chapter discusses several procedures for technical manipulation of the image in the darkroom, plus step-by-step instructions for two "nonsilver" processes—cyanotype and gum-bichromate printing. The final chapter is a revised attempt to cope with the knotty problem, "What Is a Good Photograph?," leading to a selection of what I consider to be good photographs, in the "Portfolio."

A number of new features have been added as reference aids. Each chapter begins with a list of main topics, which correspond with the major heads that appear throughout the chapter. The popular marginal notes have been retained to highlight the main points of the chapter's content, paragraph by paragraph. Most of the illustrations are new and many have been added to clarify and enhance the text. A new feature, the synopsis, appears at strategic places throughout the book. The synopses are helpful step-by-step reviews of various procedures. A summary at the end of each chapter will also facilitate review. A bibliography lists by categories other books and periodicals that may be of interest. In addition, the appendix, new in this edition, contains a great deal of helpful technical data and useful reference information.

I am indebted to a number of individuals and organizations for supplying me with information or illustration material, among them—Richard Rideout, Kenneth T. Lassiter, and Dr. Warren H. Jones of the Eastman Kodak Company; Edmund W. Lowe of Edwal Scientific Products Corporation; and Paul Graf and Sam Fox of Ethol Chemicals, Inc. I am especially grateful to Bob Chapman of Unicolor Corporation for his generous donation of materials and his patience in supplying technical advice, and to John Wilson, manager of the photo division of Home Appliance Mart in Ann Arbor, Michigan, for supplying product information and loaning equipment for illustration purposes.

I would also like to thank David Travis, director, Nancy Thrall, and Linda Cohen of the Museum Photography Department of the Art Institute of Chicago; Michael Kamins of International Museum of Photography, George Eastman House; and Brett Waller, director of the Museum of Art at the University of Michigan, for their cooperation and assistance in supplying photographs.

Bob Nash and others at Wm. C. Brown Company Publishers deserve credit for their persistence in adhering to schedules and their patience in dealing with my lack of organization. My appreciation to my son Jon for his help with some of the illustrations, and affectionate gratitude to my wife Martha, without whose typing skill and moral support this book might never have been finished.

Outline

1 A Survey of the History of Photography

Photography wasn't just invented, it evolved

It is almost impossible to imagine what the world would be like if photographs and photographic processes were suddenly taken from us. We take television for granted and accept motion pictures, photographic magazines, and newspaper illustrations as a matter of course, but these are only the more obvious signs of the influence of photography on our lives. It is involved, directly or indirectly, in almost everything we experience.

It wasn't always like this. Newspaper and magazine reproduction of photographs was still a novelty at the beginning of this century. Color photography was in its infancy in 1910. Sound-on-film recording was in-troduced in the motion picture industry in the 1920s. And television, which seems to have made the whole world picture-conscious, was still new to most people in 1950.

Considering the fascination that image-making has always held for people, it sometimes seems surprising that it took so long for photography to be invented. In fact it wasn't just invented, it evolved; and that evolution was a long and painful process.

The Discovery and Evolution of Photography

The camera came into being long before there was any real use for it. It was probably inspired by the observation of some naturally formed image. Aristotle mentioned the images of a solar eclipse formed on the ground by sunlight passing through little gaps in tree foliage, and his comments indicate that he had some grasp of the principles involved.

No one knows when the first camera was constructed, but in view of Aristotle's obvious recognition of the principles, it could have been done by some unknown Greek. It's more likely, though, that it came more than a thousand years later. Roger Bacon discussed the camera obscura knowledgeably about 1267 and is presumed to have learned about it from the writings of tenth-century Arab scholars.

Figure 1.1
Camera obscura. From an early print.
(Courtesy of the IMP, GEH)

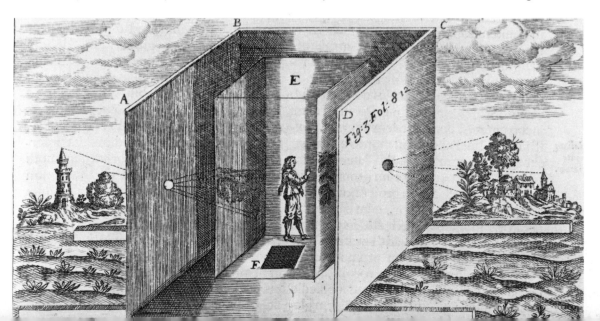

In its earliest form the camera obscura was what the name implies, a dark chamber or room. Leonardo da Vinci described one in some detail in about 1490, pointing out that the image was viewed through the back of a screen of paper which "must be very thin." He also specified that the hole "should be made in a piece of very thin sheet iron."

In 1558 the camera obscura was described fully by Giovanni Battista della Porta who, in the first edition of his *Magiae Naturalis,* specified that a conical hole be installed in the shutter of a darkened room and that the image be shown on a white screen. He mentioned that the image will appear upside down and reversed from left to right and that the image size is proportional to the distance from the hole to the viewing screen— all of which are equally valid observations for the cameras we use today. Porta recommended that the camera obscura image be used as a guide for drawing and then went on to invent a method for producing an erect image using lenses and curved mirrors. With this apparatus, he astounded viewers with the images of elaborate theatrical productions staged outside and is even supposed to have been accused of sorcery for his trouble.

The application of lenses to the camera obscura after 1550 was a significant step. The image could then be made both sharper and more brilliant because a lens can admit much more light than a simple hole and also focuses the light rays to finer points. Cameras began to be refined in design and construction as more and more people became interested in them, and by about 1575 the first movable cameras appeared. They were, at first, wooden huts or tents, still completely enclosing the viewer and viewing screen. Later more elaborate models, such as sedan chairs, were constructed.

From that point on, the evolution was rapid. Smaller models were designed which permitted the operator to view or trace the image from outside the main enclosure, and finally completely portable cameras appeared. A *reflex* camera, one in which the image is reflected up onto a top-mounted viewing screen by an inclined mirror behind the lens, was built in 1676; a *ball-and-socket* mount (like some modern *tripod heads*) appeared in 1680; and a *telephoto* lens was installed in a camera obscura in 1685. The camera was ready, but for what?

Photographic chemistry started late and proceeded slowly. In 1614 Angelo Sala noted that silver nitrate, when exposed to the sun, turned black, but apparently saw nothing significant in the change and did not ascribe it to the action of light.

The first discovery of importance was made in 1725 by Johann Heinrich Schulze, a professor of anatomy at the University of Altdorf. He had mixed powdered chalk into a solution of nitric acid in an attempt to make a phosphorescent material (the "luminous stone" of the alchemist, Balduin) and was amazed to discover that the mixture turned dark violet in sunlight. He traced the discoloration to a contaminant in the acid, silver, and eventually proved that silver compounds were visibly changed by the action of light, rather than heat or exposure to air, as had been previously suggested. Schulze made numerous stencil prints on the sensitive contents of his bottles but apparently never applied the solutions to paper or made any attempt to record natural images.

In 1777 Carl Wilhelm Scheele, the Swedish chemist, investigated the properties of silver chloride and made some interesting discoveries. Like Schulze, he established that the blackening effect on his silver salt was due to light, not heat. He also proved that the black material was metallic silver and noted that ammonia, which was known to dissolve silver chloride, did not affect the blackened silver. If Scheele had realized the importance of this last discovery, he could very well have become the inventor of photography, for now the essential processes were known. Silver chloride could be reduced to black metallic silver by exposure to light; ammonia could serve to preserve the image by dissolving the silver chloride without harming the image tones; and, of course, the camera was still waiting in the wings. But Scheele's investigations were only noted in passing. The world was not yet ready for photography. The fantastic possibility of producing images by the action of light had simply not occurred to anyone as a serious thought.

Wedgwood and Davy could not fix the image

Niépce experimented with silver chloride

In 1826 Niépce made the world's first camera image

Daguerre wrote to Niépce in 1826

They formed a partnership

This essential idea finally came to Thomas Wedgwood, the youngest son of the famous potter Josiah, who, in addition to being an outstanding craftsman and artist, was a brilliant and respected member of the English scientific community. Thomas was familiar with the camera obscura because his father had used it as an aid in drawing scenes for use on his pottery. The Wedgwood family also owned the notebooks of William Lewis, who had described in 1763 Schulze's and his own experiments with the silver compounds. These circumstances and natural curiosity prompted young Thomas to begin experiments of his own, probably about 1795. Thomas Wedgwood narrowly missed becoming the inventor of photography for two reasons. He gave up attempts to make pictures with the camera obscura (his exposures were not sufficient), and he was not able to fix the silver images he did produce by direct printing.

It's strange that he failed to take note of Scheele's experiments with ammonia and silver chloride, particularly in light of his father's familiarity with things scientific and his own close friendship with Sir Humphry Davy, a famous young English chemist. Wedgwood's experiments with prints on paper and leather were published in 1802 with Davy's wistful summary, "Nothing but a method of preventing the unshaded parts of the delineation from being coloured by exposure to the day is wanting, to render the process as useful as it is elegant." This same problem continued to frustrate experimenters for the next thirty years. It was as if Scheele's work had never been done at all.

In France, meanwhile, Joseph Nicéphore Niépce and his son Isidore were busy experimenting with lithography at the family estate near Chalon. Then Isidore, who had been copying drawings onto the stones for his father, joined the army, and Nicéphore began to explore light-sensitive varnishes, hoping to find a coating for the stones which would record the drawings by exposure to light. He must have made some progress because, in 1816, he set out to take pictures from nature using a camera and paper sensitized with silver chloride.

He had limited success almost immediately, but he was not pleased that the image tones were reversed from nature (they were negative), nor could he make the image permanent. He realized that the tonal reversal was an inherent part of the silver process and tried to produce a positive print by reprinting one of his negatives but was unsuccessful. He also found that nitric acid helped to preserve the image for a while, but it only postponed disaster and could not prevent it. He began to experiment with other materials.

Finally, in 1822, he produced a copy of an engraving by exposing through the original onto a glass plate coated with bitumen of Judea, a type of asphalt. Light hardens this material, and when Niépce washed his exposed plate with the usual solvents, the unexposed portions were floated away, leaving the image in permanent lines. He called his process heliography (sun-writing). He made a number of similar heliographs in the next few years and continued his efforts to record a camera image. At last, in 1826, he succeeded. The world's first permanent camera image shows the view from Niépce's second floor window and is little more than an impression. It is a bitumen image on pewter, showing only masses of light and dark tones. The exposure is supposed to have taken about eight hours.

In January 1826 Niépce received a letter from a Parisian painter, Louis Jacques Mandé Daguerre, who mentioned that he was also working with light images and inquired about Niépce's progress. Niépce was initially cautious, but after visiting Daguerre on a trip through Paris, his suspicions were somewhat allayed. After occasional correspondence, he finally suggested to Daguerre in 1829 that they form a partnership to do "mutual work in the improvement of my heliographic process." Daguerre accepted and visited Niépce to work out the details. They became friends and corresponded frequently but they never met again.

Until the time of their partnership, Daguerre had not produced a useful light image, although he had implied that his work was rather well advanced. The agreement with Niépce seemed to spur him on. He became a tireless experimenter and mentioned in a letter of May 21, 1831, his growing interest in silver iodide. "I think after many new tests that we ought to concentrate our researches on 20," he wrote, "this substance is highly light-sensitive when it is in contact with 18." They were writing in code; "20" meant iodine, "18" meant silver plate.

Niépce could not contribute much in this direction. His early experiments with silver compounds had left him prejudiced against them. Finally, impoverished and discouraged, he died. Daguerre was saddened but resumed his work with Isidore Niépce as his partner. He was now completely committed to working with the silver compounds.

In 1835 Daguerre discovered (quite by accident, if the story is true) that treatment with mercury vapor would produce a visible image on an iodized silver plate which had been briefly exposed to light. He also managed to stabilize the image with a strong solution of salt. In spite of the fact that Isidore had contributed nothing to the discovery, Daguerre included him in a new contract and set about trying to find a market for his process. He did not have much luck.

Finally, late in 1838, he contacted a group of leading French scientists, among them François Arago, and solicited their help. Arago was immediately impressed with the invention and made a brief announcement of it at the Academie des Sciences in January 1839.

Daguerre had supported himself quite handsomely during most of the period of his research with the proceeds from his Diorama, a kind of light show which combined enormous paintings on translucent screens with some real objects, controlled light effects, and music to create illusions of famous scenes or ceremonies. It was a disaster for him, then, when the Paris Diorama was totally destroyed by fire in March 1839.

Arago immediately sprang to his aid and succeeded in convincing the government that French national honor was at stake. A bill was passed granting life pensions to Daguerre and Niépce, and the details of the process were announced to a frenzied public in August 1839. Although the French government had announced that the process was now public property, this was not entirely true. Daguerre had secretly patented it in England just a few days before the formal French announcement.

News of the daguerreotype process spread like wildfire. Enthusiastic experimenters, French and foreign, were soon happily engrossed in the new technique. But there was dismay in England. A respected member of the Royal Society of London, William Henry Fox Talbot, saw the new process as a threat to his own investigations and, in an attempt to establish priority, had written Arago on January 29, 1839, to claim that he had been the first to find a method for taking pictures with the camera obscura and for fixing them. He overstated his case. He had not accomplished much more than Niépce had in his experiments with silver chloride, and his method of fixation was far from satisfactory.

Talbot was not an artist, but he was a brilliant, well-educated man. He apparently conceived the notion of capturing camera obscura images while trying to draw some landscapes in Italy and later wrote in his famous picture book, *The Pencil of Nature,*

> And this led me to reflect on the inimitable beauty of the pictures of nature's painting which the glass lens of the camera throws upon the paper in its focus—fairy pictures, creations of a moment, and destined as rapidly to fade away. It was during these thoughts that the idea occurred to me—how charming it would be if it were possible to cause these natural images to imprint themselves durably, and remain fixed upon the paper!

On returning to England in 1834, Talbot began experimentation. Having heard that silver nitrate was light-sensitive, he made his first attempts with silver nitrate-coated paper. He quickly found it unsatisfactory and turned to silver chloride, at first coating paper with the prepared salt, then producing it in the paper by successive washes of sodium chloride (common salt) and silver nitrate. He soon found that too much salt reduced the sensitivity of the paper and turned, as Daguerre had done, to the use of a strong salt solution for fixing the image. Before long, Talbot ran across the accounts of the experiments of Wedgwood and Davy and investigated them fairly thoroughly, apparently without discovering much of real value. He had not yet heard of the work of either Niépce or Daguerre.

Although his early experiments were confined to making prints of objects laid directly on the paper surface, Talbot had succeeded, by the summer of 1835, in taking pictures with a tiny camera obscura fitted with a microscope lens (his wife called his little cameras "mouse traps"). The pictures were only about an inch square, but he had found larger ones impossible to make due to the length of the exposure required.

Talbot made little progress in the next three years. His attention was diverted to other things. His interest and concern were apparent, however, when he received word of Arago's announcement of Daguerre's fantastic discovery.

The news which stunned Talbot also greatly intrigued Sir John Frederick William Herschel, son of the famous German-born English astronomer, and a prominent mathematician, astronomer, and chemist in his own right. Within a week, Herschel was at work in his laboratory near London, investigating the various known processes and keeping careful notes of his procedures.

It is an indication of Herschel's intelligence and acuity as an investigator that in less than two weeks he successfully tested several silver salts for sensitivity, took several successful pictures, printed a negative to make a positive paper image, and fixed the images with a chemical he had described twenty years previously, that he called "hyposulphite of soda."

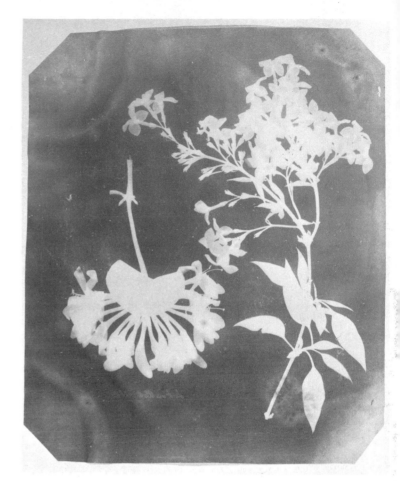

Figure 1.2
William Henry Fox Talbot (1800–1877).
Silhouette of Leaves. (Courtesy of the
Art Institute of Chicago)

5   A Survey of the History of
Photography

At the height of this investigation, less than two weeks after hearing about Arago's momentous announcement, Talbot visited Herschel at his laboratory, bringing with him samples of his work. Talbot begins to appear, at this moment in history, as a somewhat unlovely character. His treatment of the frank and generous Herschel was rather shabby. Herschel showed Talbot his results and described them in full detail, including his use of *hypo* for fixing. Talbot, on the other hand, revealed nothing. He referred airily to his own method of fixing the image, without explaining how it was done, and convinced Herschel that he should not mention the use of hypo until Talbot had announced his process. Herschel agreed, later writing admiringly that Talbot's method of fixing "must be a very chemical jewel," and gave Talbot permission to announce the use of hypo with his own process.

In fairness to Talbot, it must be acknowledged that he credited Herschel with the application of hyposulphite of soda. In his letter of disclosure to a member of the French Academy, he outlined his own methods of fixing, then described Herschel's hypo as being "worth all the others combined." Daguerre immediately applied it to his own process.

Niépce, Daguerre, and Talbot can each be called the "inventor of photography" with certain justification, but so can a fourth man who is less well known, Hippolyte Bayard. Bayard lived in Paris and was a minor employee of the Ministry of Finance. His experiments with light-sensitive materials probably began about 1837 and, initially, seem to have paralleled Talbot's. His first images were negatives on silver chloride-treated paper. On learning of Daguerre's discovery, he set out to produce direct positive images. Within a few months he succeeded with a process that involved blackening a conventional silver chloride paper in light, then coating it with a solution of potassium iodide and exposing it in the camera. The exposing light bleached this paper, producing a direct positive image, which was then fixed in hypo.

Bayard was apparently a very quiet, retiring man of modest means. Many of his pictures are still-life arrangements or details of his house and garden. In some of these views he appears seated in a doorway or in his garden, surrounded by flowerpots and garden tools. Although he did make a few tentative attempts to gain recognition and support, they were not very successful. Perhaps, too, he was unlucky in his choice of consultants. He showed some prints to Arago in May 1839 and asked for his help, but Arago, who was very interested in Daguerre's career at that point, arranged for a token grant of six hundred francs to help Bayard finance his experiments and counselled him to remain quietly in the background until Daguerre's process had been publicly revealed. After that revelation, of course, Bayard's work seemed anticlimactic and insignificant, and he was virtually ignored by the public and the government alike.

Understandably bitter at this callous treatment Bayard expressed his hurt by photographing himself as a half-naked corpse and explained, in a long and piteous caption, that this was the dead body of the unhappy Bayard who, unrecognized and unrewarded, had thrown himself into the water and drowned.

Although in his lifetime he was never given the credit he deserved, he did eventually receive a little prize of three thousand francs. Now he is remembered as a significant figure, a victim of circumstances who might have been as well known as Daguerre if things had worked in his favor.

Photography, a name which is generally credited to Herschel, languished in England. The daguerreotype process was patented, and Talbot began immediately to secure his own processes by patents so restrictive that even amateur experiments were inhibited. Talbot improved his original paper negative process by subjecting the exposed paper to development in gallic acid and silver nitrate solution, thus shortening the necessary exposure time considerably. He called the new process *calotype* (also later referred to as *talbotype*) and included in its patent the use of hypo for fixing—blatantly appropriating Herschel's discovery.

Talbot must receive credit for inventing the photographic process as we now know it, but he also must be remembered as a stumbling block in its evolution. As new procedures were announced, Talbot promptly laid claims to them on the grounds that they were only modifications of the basic principles of his patented processes. Although these tactics created a great deal of antagonism and various suits were threatened, Talbot was generally successful in controlling photography in England until 1855.

The two decades following the invention of photography were years of rapid technical evolution and experimentation. The daguerreotype process was sufficiently refined to permit studio portraiture by about 1841. Talbot's calotype process was improved by Louis-Désiré Blanquart-Evrard; Gustave LeGray went a step further by sensitizing waxed paper to produce negatives of greater sharpness and translucency, and Claude Niépce de St.-Victor's glass plates, sensitized with an albumin emulsion, gave photographers still another alternative. All of these processes were in use in 1851 when Frederick Scott Archer announced the details of his collodion process and gave it freely for all to use.

The process was not free for long. Talbot, with typical lack of scruple, claimed that it was covered by his patents and announced that he would prosecute anyone who used it without his license. A number of challenges were made to this outrageous claim. Finally in December 1854 the courts found Talbot's claims illegal and his tyranny ended.

By the 1850s photography was well established as a commercial enterprise. As early as November 1839 Noel Lerebours, a French optician and entrepreneur, had dispatched several crews of painters and photographers to various exotic places, such as Greece, England, America, and Egypt. The views that they collected, while "daguerreotyping away like lions,"—as one group reported—were copied by skilled engravers and Lerebours published them as *Excursions Daguerriennes.*

In England, Talbot had sold "sun pictures" of landscapes and other scenes and eventually set up a "glass house" at Reading where his several employees printed editions of photographs and sold calotype materials to Talbot's license-holders. In 1844 the "Reading Establishment" began turning out the calotype illustrations for Talbot's famous *Pencil of Nature,* the first book ever published with photographic illustrations. Several years later, Blanquart-Evrard opened a similar, but larger, printing establishment in France, where, using his improved process, his employees were able to produce several hundred prints per day. He also produced several booklets and albums illustrated with actual paper prints.

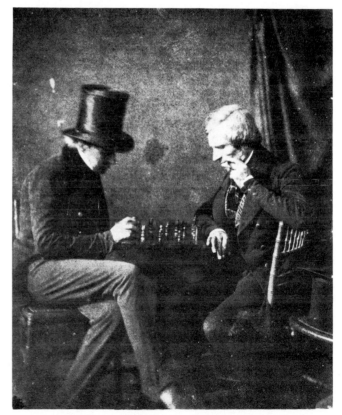

Figure 1.3
William Henry Fox Talbot. *Chess Players.*
(Courtesy of the Art Institute of Chicago)

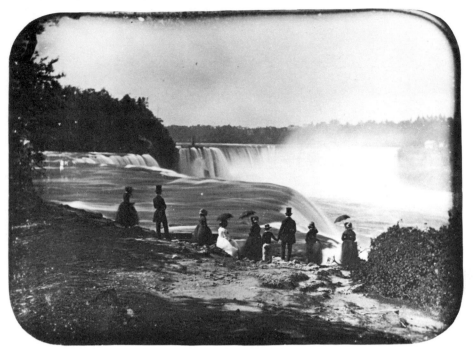

Figure 1.4
Platt D. Babbitt. *Group at Niagara Falls.*
(Courtesy of the IMP, GEH)

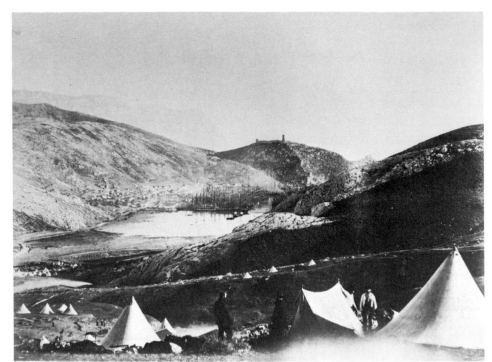

Figure 1.5
Roger Fenton. *Balaklava.* (Courtesy of
the Art Institute of Chicago)

**In America, Morse and Draper
experimented with the daguerreotype**

**American photographers worked with
the daguerreotype process**

The paper processes were never popular in America, although various experimenters had worked with them unsuccessfully prior to the announcement of the daguerreotype. One of these men, Samuel F. B. Morse, had visited Daguerre in Paris (he was demonstrating his telegraph to Daguerre in the hour that the Diorama burned) and was enchanted by the image that Daguerre had shown him. After returning to America, Morse had a camera built and soon joined forces with John W. Draper in attempting to master the process. Morse and the other pioneers soon became enthusiastic teachers and many of their students, among them Mathew Brady and Albert Southworth, ultimately became famous as portrait photographers.

The American daguerreotypist was not confined to the studio by any means. The Langenheim brothers of Philadelphia produced a panoramic view of Niagara Falls in 1845 by mounting five separate pictures edge to edge. An even more spectacular panorama of the city of Cincinnati, eight feet long, was assembled by Fontayne and Porter in 1848. A daguerreotypist named Platt Babbitt specialized in photographing tourist groups in front of Niagara Falls and, in St. Louis, J. H. Fitzgibbon photographed riverboats, frontier scenes, and Indians, as well as maintaining a conventional portrait studio. A number of adventurous men, such as Britt, Vance, McIntyre, and Carvalho, daguerreotyped the Far West, including the Rocky Mountains, the California gold fields, and San Francisco, a number of years before the better-known expeditions of Carleton Watkins, Timothy O'Sullivan, and William Jackson.

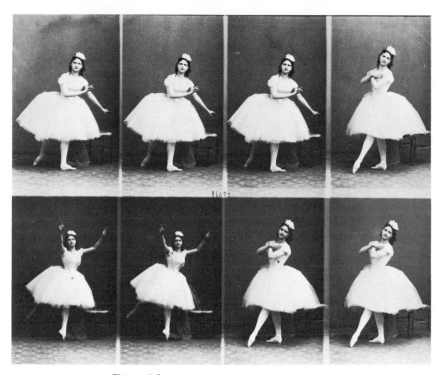

Figure 1.6
Adolphe-Eugène Disdéri. Carte-de-visite, uncut sheet. (Courtesy of the IMP, GEH)

Development in pyrogallic acid or a solution of ferrous sulfate had to follow immediately before the plate dried. For obvious reasons, it came to be known as the wet-plate process.

Roger Fenton was one of the first to use it for reportage, by covering the Crimean War in 1855. In spite of almost insurmountable difficulties, Fenton managed to produce a series of photographs which, although curiously unwarlike, do record the terrain and the camp life impressively.

J. A. Cutting's invention of the ambrotype (collodion on glass) and André Adolphe-Eugène Disdéri's popularization of the photographic carte-de-visite (albumin emulsion on paper), both in 1854, doomed the daguerreotype and disrupted the studio portrait business. Although the ambrotype was markedly inferior to the daguerreotype in clarity and brilliance, it was cheap and relatively easy to make. The carte-de-visite images, usually made eight-to-a-plate, then cut into individual pictures, were even cheaper. They became a world-wide sensation and were sold, traded, and collected by the hundreds of thousands.

The tintype (collodion on metal), also called ferrotype and *melainotype,* was patented by Hamilton Smith in 1855. It, too, became a quick, cheap and easy way to produce portraits and views and, although the image quality was poor, tintypes became popular. These cheap, mass-produced images were viewed with hostility and alarm by many "high-class" portrait photographers, but they had little choice; they could follow the trend or lose business. Most of them began producing the new, cheap images.

Stereoscopic views were also exceedingly popular. Although the principle of the stereoscope had been known for a long time, it was not adapted for photographic use until Charles Wheatstone suggested it in 1841. His early stereo viewer was effective but required careful adjustment and was rather clumsy to use. Sir David Brewster replaced the mirrors in Wheatstone's design with lenses in 1849, an improvement which allowed the paired images to be mounted on a single card, side by side. Before long, stereoscope

European photographers favored the paper processes and albumin

Fenton used "wet plates" to photograph the Crimean War

The ambrotype, carte-de-viste, tintype, and stereoscope

For somewhat similar work being done at about the same time, European photographers favored the various paper processes or albumin-coated glass plates. The calotype and the waxed-paper process were popular there until about 1855, and proof of their refinement is seen in the works of Charles Nègre, Henri Le Secq, John Shaw Smith, Roger Fenton, and others. Their landscapes, architectural views, and archeological records of Egypt, in particular, are frequently larger than one would expect and startlingly beautiful.

The collodion process offered photographers a negative material of greater sensitivity and better quality than paper, but the process was a demanding one. A glass plate had to be cleaned, then flooded with iodized collodion to form a uniform, blemish-free coating. It then had to be immersed in a bath of silver nitrate and rushed into the camera for exposure while still wet.

views, both prints and transparencies, were being produced and sold in great numbers. By 1860 every well-furnished American parlor featured an ornate album of carte-de-visite and tintype pictures and a stereo viewer, complete with dozens of slides.

Portrait photographers were doing a brisk business as the Civil War threatened. Mathew Brady, internationally famous as "Brady of Broadway," saw the impending conflict as a momentous historical event. Brady's sense of history was already well demonstrated. For years he had made it a practice to photograph famous people and had published *The Gallery of Illustrious Americans* in 1850. Now he felt impelled to document the war.

President Lincoln gave Brady his consent, but no financial backing. This was enough. Brady was a moderately wealthy man and he was willing to spend his own money for such a significant purpose. He assembled a staff of several men, outfitted them with the materials and equipment needed to make wet-plate photographs, and went to war. The pictures they made, under the most awkward and dangerous conditions imaginable, form a remarkable document of that desperate struggle.

Brady emerged from the enterprise practically destitute. There was little market for his war pictures and their historical value was overlooked. His plates were stored in warehouses and eventually auctioned off. Ironically, one lot of them was bought by the government for storage charges. Brady, heavily in debt, was forced to sell his portrait studio. Except for a belated government grant of $25,000, he went unrewarded for his labors and died penniless in 1896.

The mid-nineteenth-century market for pictures of famous buildings, picturesque landscapes, and exotic foreign scenes kept many photographers employed. They were a hardy lot. The wet-plate process was difficult and awkward and was complicated considerably by the demand for larger and larger images. Francis Frith, one of the most enterprising travel photographers,

journeyed more than 800 miles up the Nile River in Egypt in 1856, carrying several cameras, the largest of which accepted 16″ × 20″ plates. Flowing an even coat of collodion over such a plate is difficult under the best conditions, but Frith, and others like him, managed to do it in desert heat and mountain cold, in spite of blowing dust, biting insects, and dripping rain. The fact that their pictures turned out at all is amazing; in fact, many of them are of excellent quality even by modern standards.

In 1860 the Bisson brothers, Louis and Auguste, photographed Mt. Blanc. Climbing to more than 15,000 feet with cameras as large as 12″ × 17″, they battled below-zero cold, which threatened to freeze the collodion on their plates, and made a number of spectacular views of the windswept peaks and glaciers.

In America after the Civil War the exploration of the West began again in earnest and photographers were in the vanguard. Timothy O'Sullivan, who had been one of Brady's photographers during the war, joined an expedition exploring the 40th parallel in 1867 and was soon photographing the deserts and mining areas of Nevada. Three years later he travelled to Panama with the Darien Expedition and, in 1871, joined the Wheeler Expedition. O'Sullivan's photographs are technically fine and frequently display considerable artistic sensitivity.

William H. Jackson's work is probably better known than O'Sullivan's, if only because Jackson's photographs of Yellowstone helped to persuade Congress to establish that region as the first National Park. As a child, Jackson was encouraged to draw and paint and was introduced to photography by his father. He served with the Vermont infantry during the Civil War, then—after being jilted by his fiancee—headed West with an ex-army buddy. They travelled with a wagon train to Montana where Jackson struck out on his own. After two years of wandering from job to job, he arrived in Omaha where he was hired by a local photographer.

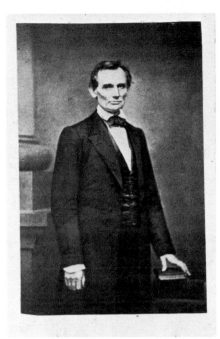 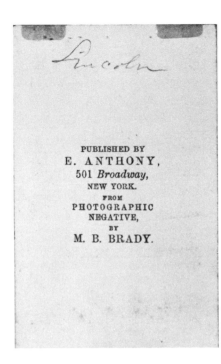

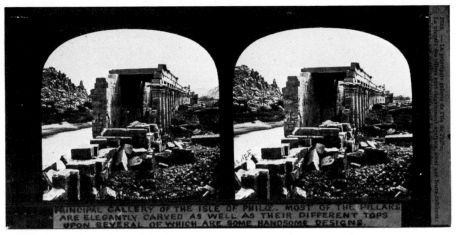

Figure 1.7 ◄
Mathew Brady (1823–1896). *Portrait of Lincoln,* carte-de-visite (obverse and reverse). (Courtesy of William A. Lewis)

Figure 1.8 ▲
Francis Frith (1822–1899). Stereo transparency on glass. (Courtesy of William A. Lewis)

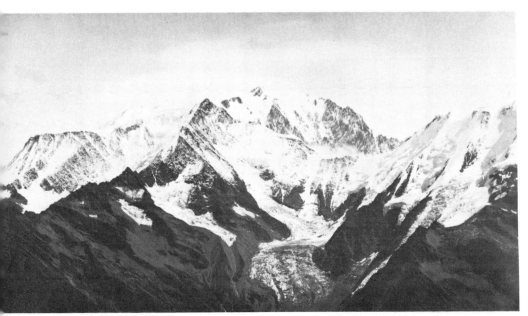

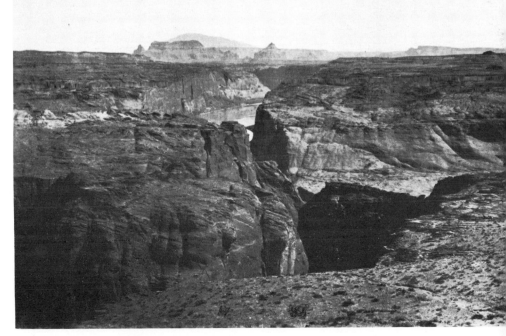

Figure 1.9 ▲
Auguste Bisson. *Savoie 46—Mont Blanc, vu de Mont Joli.* (Courtesy of the Art Institute of Chicago)

Figure 1.10 ►
Timothy O'Sullivan (1840–1882). *Cañon of the Colorado River near the Mouth of the San Juan River, Arizona,* 1873, Wheeler Expedition. (Courtesy of William A. Lewis)

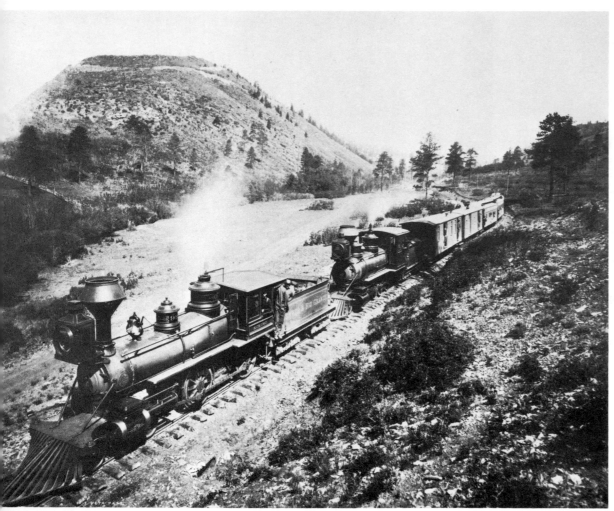

Figure 1.11
William H. Jackson (1843–1942). *The Rocky Mountains, Scenes Along the Line of the Denver and Rio Grande Railway.* (Courtesy of William A. Lewis)

In 1869 he met Dr. F. V. Hayden who was conducting a U. S. Geological Survey of the Territories, and was persuaded to join him. During the nine years that he worked on the Survey, Jackson produced thousands of magnificent negatives of both scientific and scenic value. An extract from his diary gives us some inkling of the difficulties of working in the mountains with the wet-plate process:

> Aug. 2, (1878) Upper Wind River Lake. Returned to upper lake. Wilson, Eccles, his man Payot and Richardson going with me. Fine morning and got good 11 by 14 exposure first trial. There were two or three small defects but impossible to take it over and get as good a lighting. Time 9 m. with Portable Symmetrical, single lens, at F. 32. Made 5 by 8 of same subject. Came up too thin, but intensifying made it as much too dense. Took camera up high for a general view. Exposed 2 m., F. 16, Portable Symmetrical, with some over-exposure. In packing up to return, I forgot to remove the two 11 by 14 plates that I had put in the bath holder to bring the solution up to its proper depth. Hoggie, the pack mule carrying the outfit, traveled so roughly that when I opened up the bath holder later I found the plates smashed to pieces and one side of the bath holder punched full of holes. It is going to bother me now to replace it. Was two or three hours making general repairs. I don't think I ever had so inconvenient an outfit.

In 1879 Jackson moved to Denver, set up a studio, and returned to his earlier interest, photographing the railroads. For twenty years he travelled through every state in the Union and from Montreal to Mexico City, often in "Jackson Special" cars supplied by the railroads, making photographs of all sizes from 20″ × 24″ to the popular stereo views. In 1898 he established the Detroit Publishing Company, specializing in views and postcards printed in color, derived from his vast store of negatives. When he "retired" in 1924, he took up painting again and did a series of pictures for the National Park Service. Still vigorous in his nineties, Jackson continued to tour, paint, and photograph the West each summer until his death in 1942.

Before long he owned his own studio but his wanderlust was still strong. Outfitting a horse-drawn wagon as a portable darkroom, he began to roam the country around Omaha photographing the prairies and the Indians who inhabited them. Soon he was attracted by the dramatic expansion of the railroads and, redesigning his equipment to fit on packmules, he began to travel in earnest.

Jackson joined the Hayden expedition

Edward Muggeridge thought his name was really Eadweard Muybridge

He photographed Leland Stanford's horses

And showed motion pictures with his zoopraxiscope

Another Western photographer was English-born Eadweard Muybridge (who thought that this strange spelling was the correct Anglo-Saxon version of his real name, Edward Muggeridge). Muybridge was well known in the 1860s as a fine landscapist and industrial photographer but his fame now stems from his research in motion photography.

Almost from the beginning photographers were intrigued by the possibility of taking "instantaneous photographs." In 1851 Talbot used an electric spark to record the image of a page from the *Times* which he had fastened to a rapidly revolving wheel, and by 1860 several other photographers had managed to take outdoor views which showed walking figures caught in midstride.

Muybridge was the first to attack the problem seriously though, when he was commissioned by Leland Stanford—one-time governor of California—to photograph a running horse. Stanford financed this experiment, so the story goes, to settle a bet he had made with a friend. Stanford claimed that all four of a trotter's feet leave the ground at some point in his stride; his friend insisted that at least one foot is always on the ground. Although his first attempts were failures, Muybridge finally managed to prove that Stanford was right.

In 1874 Muybridge was tried and acquitted for murdering his wife's lover. He left the country for a time, returning to resume his work in motion photography with Stanford in 1877. By 1880 he had refined his procedures considerably and was able to project a crude motion picture sequence with a device he called the *zoopraxiscope*. In 1883 he was invited to continue his experiments at the University of Pennsylvania, an invitation that the painter Thomas Eakins may have influenced. In 1887 a set of his motion sequence photographs, analyzing both animal and human activities, was published under the title *Animal Locomotion.*

Although his work was denounced by a number of influential painters and photographers as "inartistic" and "untrue," Muybridge clearly influenced men like Étienne Jules Marey and Thomas Eakins, both of whom

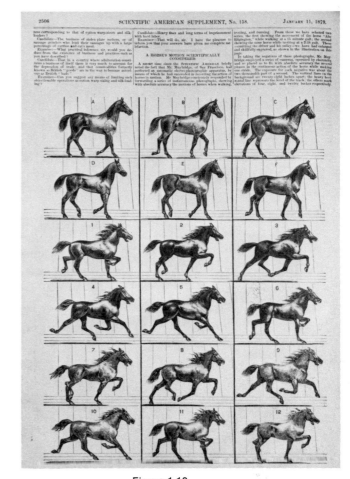

Figure 1.12
Eadweard Muybridge (1830–1904). *A Horse's Motion Scientifically Considered,* engravings after photographs. (From a copy of the *Scientific American Supplement,* no. 158, January 11, 1879, in the collection of the University of Michigan Library)

Nonsilver photographic materials were investigated

Poitevin's research led to the carbon and collotype processes

The woodburytype was an ingenious process

Art photographers favored photogravure and platinotype

devised cameras for making multiple exposures of moving figures. Their work, in turn, clearly foreshadows the Futurist paintings of Duchamps, Balla, and others.

While most of the prints made for commercial purposes after 1850 were done on albuminized paper, the albumin process was not entirely satisfactory. The color was not altogether pleasing, and, like the other silver papers, the image was likely to fade or discolor, especially if the photographer was less than meticulous in his processing. For these and other reasons, considerable attention was devoted to the perfection of nonsilver photographic materials.

This was not a new thought. In 1839 Mungo Ponton discovered that a solution of potassium dichromate spread on paper would be insolubly stained by exposure to light and had used this principle to produce simple images. Edmond Becquerel pointed out, shortly thereafter, that the reaction was largely due to the effect of the dichromate on the starch size in the paper. This soon attracted the attention of the ubiquitous Talbot, who, in 1852, patented *photoglyphic drawing,* based on the tanning effect of dichromates on a number of organic colloids, including glue, gelatin, starch, and various gums.

The honor of applying this technique to the production of photographic prints belongs to Alphonse Louis Poitevin, a French chemist and engineer. His research led to the eventual discovery of several methods of printing, including the carbon and the collotype processes. In the carbon process, a layer of gelatin containing powdered carbon and dichromate is spread on paper, dried, and exposed under a negative. The image, composed of hardened gelatin and carbon, remains on the paper after the unexposed (still soluble) portions of the gelatin area are washed away in hot water. This first form of the technique produced a black-and-white image without gradation, but later modifications resulted in a complete range of tones, making it one of the best of the nonsilver processes.

The collotype process also uses a dichromated gelatin layer, often on glass, but without the carbon pigment. Exposure tans the gelatin making it less absorptive to water, and therefore capable of holding a coating of greasy ink. When properly dampened and inked, the collotype plate can be used for printing like a lithograph stone. The exposed portions, holding ink, print dark, while the unexposed portions, holding water and repelling the ink, print light in tone. When competently done, the process is capable of a complete range of tones, and is, in fact, still considered to be one of the finest methods of printing known, although it has practically disappeared as a commercial process.

Another interesting and ingenious process, which was used for production runs of a few thousand printed impressions, was the *woodburytype.* Making use of the fact that the image on an exposed dichromated gelatin film is in low relief, Walter B. Woodbury, an English photographer, devised a method that pressed the relief image onto a lead plate to form an intaglio image. The depressions thus formed were filled with liquid pigmented gelatin which was then impressed on paper. The image was formed by the varying thicknesses of the pigment. The woodburytype process is without a doubt the most faithful method of mechanical reproduction of images ever devised. In many cases, woodburytype prints are indistinguishable from actual carbon prints; there is no artificial grain or texture, and the original tonal scale and sharpness of detail are preserved.

Although albumin paper continued to be used into the 1900s, the gelatin-coated papers, introduced before 1880, gave amateur and professional photographers a more versatile and stable print material. The "art" photographers, however, were not so easily pleased. The Naturalists, especially, sought a quality of surface and tone that the silver emulsions could not provide and began to look for alternatives. Two processes that suited them were photogravure and the platinotype.

Photogravure, which became popular in the 1890s derived from another early patent of Talbot's. In this process a positive transparency is printed on gelatin-coated paper, sensitized with dichromate. The paper is then soaked briefly and rolled onto a grained copper plate. Warm water rinses dissolve the unexposed gelatin, leaving the image in low relief on the copper surface. When dry, the copper is etched in ferric chloride to produce an intaglio image which can be inked and printed like an aquatint etching. While this procedure is a handcraft process, it was modified by Karel Klic, a Czechoslovak, for use on rotary printing presses in 1895.

Herschel's early investigations led to various photographic processes based on the light-sensitive properties of iron salts. These included numerous variations on the blueprint or cyanotype, the chrysotype, kallitype, and most importantly the platinotype, which was first made practical and patented by Willis in 1873. The platinotype image is composed of platinum metal and is considered to be one of the most permanent photographic prints. It is typically neutral gray to brownish in tone, although bluish grays are occasionally seen, with excellent, delicate highlight and midtone gradation. Platinum paper was manufactured and sold in Europe from about 1879 until World War I. It was still available in America as late as the early 1930s.

For almost thirty years after its introduction by Archer, the collodion process reigned supreme in spite of its obvious shortcomings. It was not sensitive enough, it had to be used wet, and the large glass plates were fragile and bulky to handle. In the mid-1870s gelatin began to be used, first as a coating for printing papers and then for camera materials.

The first of these required elaborate handling. The emulsion was coated on a paper base for exposure in the camera, then developed and stripped off the paper to another support material, such as glass, for printing. Glass plates were also coated directly for camera use, but the growing public desire for smaller, lighter cameras spurred experimenters in their search for glass substitutes.

The first commercial production of flexible film is credited to John Carbutt in 1888, but the Reverend Hannibal Goodwin had independently invented a similar film and applied for patent rights the previous year. Goodwin did not have enough money to produce his film and his patent application was so vague that it had to be revised several times.

By the time his patent was finally granted in 1898, the Eastman Company had also devised a flexible film, patented it, and gone into production. At Goodwin's death in 1900, his patent was taken over by Edward and Henry Anthony, who filed suit against Eastman for infringement. The litigation continued for twelve years, during which time the firms of Anthony and Scovill merged to form Ansco. In 1914 the courts found in favor of Ansco, and Eastman settled the claim for $5 million.

By this time the Eastman Kodak Company had captured the amateur market with a simple, portable camera that could be purchased, loaded with one hundred exposures of rollfilm, for $25. Eastman selected the name *Kodak* for it quite arbitrarily. He wanted a name that was easy to remember, one which was not liable to be mispronounced in any language and one which could be registered in the patent office without confusion. Additionally, he is supposed to have admired the firmness of the letter *K*.

In practically no time, the name Kodak and the slogan which accompanied it, "You press the button; we do the rest," were household words. The slogan was no idle boast. When the one hundred pictures were taken, the owner simply mailed the entire camera back to the company; where, for $10 the film was removed and processed, prints made, the camera reloaded and returned with the finished pictures, ready for the next one hundred shots.

With the formation of large manufacturing corporations like the Eastman Kodak Company, technical research in photography spurted ahead. The heyday of the amateur kitchen-chemist was definitely over. A significant step in this direction was the publication in

1890 of a paper by Dr. Ferdinand Hurter and Vero C. Driffield, entitled "Photochemical Investigations and a New Method of Determination of the Sensitiveness of Photographic Plates." This was the first serious attempt to analyze the effects of exposure and development and to organize the findings into useful form. This effort was not lost on the pictorialist leader, Henry P. Robinson, who in a magazine article in 1892 said:

> Two very clever scientists, whom I much respect, Dr. Hurter and Mr. Driffield, have proved to everybody's unsatisfaction that photographers have no control over the gradations; but this does not alter the fact that—to put the simplest case— he (sic) knows when a negative is over- or underexposed or developed too dense or too thin to properly represent his idea of nature. . . .

Robinson, like most of his contemporaries, was under the impression that image density and contrast could be controlled equally well by modifying either exposure or development and that exposure errors could be corrected by suitable development. Hurter and Driffield's work was not accepted fully by many amateurs for almost fifty years.

The techniques of photography by 1910 were similar to those used today. Cameras of all shapes and sizes were available; films were sensitive enough to make action pictures possible; lenses of large relative aperture and good correction existed; and color photographs, long a theoretical possibility, became a practical reality with the commercial production of *Autochrome* film by the Lumière brothers, Auguste and Louis, in 1907.

From the earliest days of photography, fixing the colors was an intriguing problem. Color theory was still in a primitive state in 1839 and, of course, the simple silver compounds which formed the sensitive surfaces of the daguerreotype and calotype were almost totally blind to half of the visible spectrum.

It was generally believed that color was an intrinsic quality of a material's surface and that the different hues were due to differences in the molecular structure.

Because of this, the early researchers spent a great deal of time compounding various mixtures of the silver salts known to be light-sensitive, coating them on paper and other materials, and observing their reaction to colored light. They were encouraged, occasionally, by the formation of colored compounds which seemed to relate to the light color which formed them. In a few cases, daguerreotypes were reported to have recorded traces of color, frequently reddish tints.

Robert Hunt, one of the more reliable and perceptive chemists of the time, reported one instance, in 1843, when he photographed (on calotype paper) a scene containing "a clear blue sky, stucco-fronted houses and a green field." After a fifteen-minute exposure in the camera he obtained

> a very beautiful picture . . . which held between the eye and the light, exhibited a curious order of colours. The sky was of a crimson hue, the houses of a slaty blue, and the green fields of a brick red tint.

In 1851 the Reverend Levi Hill, of Westkill, New York, announced that he had perfected a special daguerreotype process with which he claimed to have made

> a view containing a red house, green grass and foliage, the wood-color of the trees, several cows of different shades of red and brindle, colored garments on a clothes-line, blue sky, and the faint blue of the atmosphere, intervening between the camera and the distant mountains, very delicately spread over the picture, as if by the hand of a fairy artist.

The excitement that this announcement generated was sufficient to bring ordinary daguerreotypy to a virtual standstill, and, according to a contemporary photographer, Marcus A. Root, "injured the heliographic artists to the amount of many thousand of dollars." Hill seems to have convinced many of his contemporaries that the process was genuine. However, as time went by and he failed to release details of the procedure, explaining that he was having difficulty with the color yellow and referring to the "invisible goblins" which were plaguing him, their suspicions grew.

Maxwell and Sutton produced "a sort of photograph . . . in natural colours"

du Hauron confused the color primaries

Autochrome film employed a screen of dyed starch grains

The one-shot camera

Root, who had at first believed Hill's claim, ultimately discounted it as a trick and suspected that the few examples that Hill had actually shown were "probably common daguerreotypes, carefully colored by hand." One that he examined revealed "dry colored powder . . . distinctly visible on the face and hair," and, he concluded, "As his endeavor succeeded but partially, if at all, and as there appears to have been deception in the matter, I shall meddle with it no further."

The idea that color is a characteristic of light rather than surface and the concept of *color separation* of white light were demonstrated in 1861 by Maxwell and Sutton. Sutton had photographed a colored ribbon through red, green, and violet filters (he also prepared a yellow separation which was not used) and made positive transparencies of the negatives. Using the same filters and three separate projectors, Maxwell projected the colored images in register on a screen to produce what Sutton described as "a sort of photograph of the striped ribbon . . . in natural colours."

Theoretically this shouldn't have worked, since the collodion plates used were not sensitive to red at all, but Ralph Evans, a hundred years later, proved, by recreating the experiment, that the red image had actually been produced by fluorescence of the particular dye used in the red stripes.

In 1869 Louis Ducos du Hauron described a method of producing color images by making a negative and viewing the subsequent positive through a screen covered with tiny dots or lines of red, yellow, and blue. This was an ingenious idea and the one which was eventually used in the very successful Lumière process. However, du Hauron mistakenly recommended the *subtractive* (pigment) primaries instead of the correct *additive* (light) primaries, red, green, and blue. He did, however, present a workable plan for making color prints or transparencies by using colored carbon tissues.

In 1873 Dr. Hermann Vogel made the initial discovery of dye-sensitizing, which extends the sensitivity of silver emulsions into the green, yellow, and red regions of the spectrum. This discovery was soon improved by Becquerel, Waterhouse, Eder, and others.

The first panchromatic gelatin plates, sensitive to all the visible colors, were marketed in 1906 by Wratten and Wainwright.

Panchromatic sensitivity finally made color photography possible. The Lumière brothers' Autochrome film, marketed in 1907, employed a screen of minute dyed starch grains coated with a panchromatic emulsion. The film, exposed through the screen, was developed to form a black-and-white negative which was, in turn, bleached out. Reexposure and development produced a positive transparency which, when viewed through the screen, appeared as a full color image of the original scene. Several other films subsequently appeared, based on a similar principle but using screens of ruled lines rather than the dyed starch grains. One such material, Dufaycolor, was available in both roll and sheet sizes until the 1940s.

The screen processes, good as they were, had their faults. They were relatively insensitive—Autochrome required fifty times more exposure than comparable black-and-white film—and the image could not be enlarged to any great degree without revealing the screen texture.

One solution to these problems was sought in the one-shot camera design. Three films were exposed simultaneously, each through its appropriate filter, by an ingenious arrangement of semitransparent mirrors. When developed, the negatives could be printed by any of several methods, such as *carbro* or *wash-off relief* (later called *dye-transfer)*, to produce a full color print. Although these cameras could take color photographs of fine quality under ideal conditions, they were clumsy and slow.

As early as 1912 Siegrist and Fischer had devised a process for producing color by chemically forming dyes in the emulsion during development. This is the method most modern color films employ but it was not reliable enough to be useful until about 1936. The early difficulties were largely due to the tendency of the dyes to migrate or bleed in the emulsion layers.

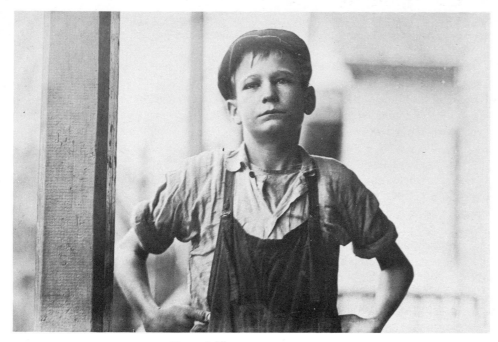

Figure 1.13
Lewis Hine (1874–1940). *Young Mill-worker.* (Collection of the author)

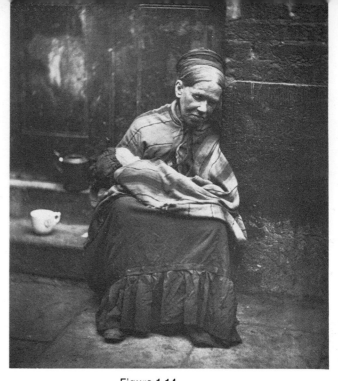

Figure 1.14
John Thomson (1837–1921). *The Crawlers,* from *Street Life in London,* woodburytype. (Courtesy of the University of Michigan Museum of Art)

Kodachrome, Ektachrome, and color negative films

Gasparcolor

The SX-70

Kodachrome film, which was introduced in 1935, avoided this difficulty by omitting the color couplers from the emulsions and introducing them during processing.

With the appearance of Ektachrome film in 1942, positive reversal color film became both practical and convenient. Kodacolor, released for general use in 1941, and Ektacolor, in 1947, were designed to produce color negatives. With their introduction color became a relatively simple process and successive improvements, by various manufacturers, have brought color printing within reach of everyone.

A quite different approach to color was described by Christiansen in 1918 and by Gaspar in the early 1930s. Gasparcolor and the modern refinement of it, *Cibachrome* (see chapter 7), employed the principle of dye-destruction. In this process the image dyes are incorporated in the emulsion during manufacture and are bleached selectively as the silver image is removed during processing. This process results in images of relatively great stability and exceptional sharpness.

An almost incredibly complex and ingenious color film and camera system was announced in 1972 by the Polaroid Corporation. Called the SX-70, the camera features automatic exposure control and produces "instant" color prints which process themselves after ejection from the camera. The film, containing no less than sixteen layers of emulsion material, incorporates its own darkroom in the form of an opaque chemical layer which protects the developing image from light.

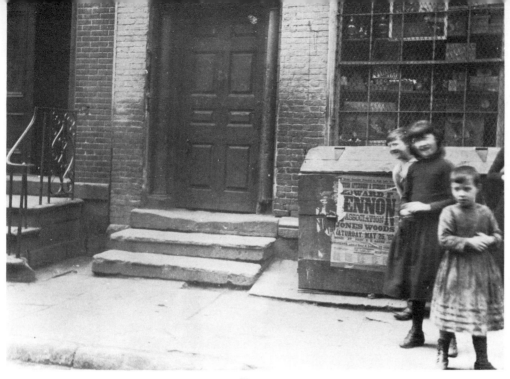

Figure 1.15
Jacob A. Riis (1849–1914). *Old House in Cherry Street, The Cradle of the Tenement.* (Jacob A. Riis Collection, Museum of the City of New York)

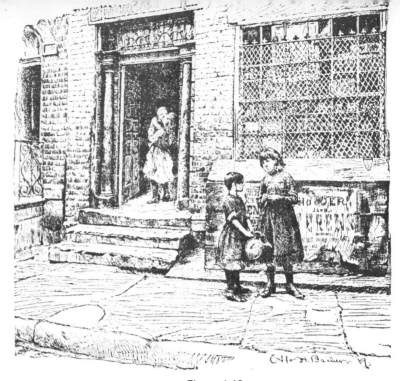

Figure 1.16
Before about 1900, Riis's book, *How the Other Half Lives,* was illustrated with engravings like this one. The artists apparently felt free to "improve" the compositions, as has been done here.

Hine saw photography's potential for social documentation

So had some earlier workers

At the end of the developing action and as the image becomes stable, the opacifier gradually disappears, leaving the image sealed under a plastic cover clearly visible against a pure white ground.

SX-70 cameras and film have proven to be extremely popular. Recently a somewhat similar system has been announced by Eastman Kodak.

By 1900, halftone reproductions of photographs were appearing frequently in magazines, books, and newspapers, and the photograph was beginning to be appreciated as an effective means of communication and persuasion. Lewis Hine, a trained sociologist, saw its potential for effecting social change and, teaching himself to use a camera, began to document the callous treatment of immigrants at Ellis Island and their painful entry into the melting pot of New York City's tenement district.

Hine was not the first photographer to work in this vein. Mayhew and Beard had collaborated on a major social study *London Labour and the London Poor* in the early 1850s; Adolphe Smith and John Thomson had published a similar report, in words and pictures, called *Street Life in London* in 1877; and Jacob Riis had produced a series of books aimed at social reform, the first of which, *How the Other Half Lives,* was a scathing indictment of New York's slum lords and the festering conditions in their tenements in the 1880s.

Street Life in London was an important book for two reasons. It was a notable early attempt to use the camera editorially, and it was illustrated with woodburytypes, which gave Thomson's photographs authenticity and power. Beard's daguerreotypes for the *London Labour and the London Poor* were copied and published as wood engravings and Riis's photographs were similarly translated into print by a hand-engraver. In both cases the pictures suffer from a kind of esthetic distance. They lack credibility and take on a stylistic prettiness which contradicts their real message.

Hine's photographs undoubtedly benefitted from being published as convincing halftones, but they are also well-seen, well-crafted images which invite attention. Thomson's pictures, superb as they are, have a theatrical quality, occasionally flawed by clumsy retouching. Riis photographed with obvious passion and sincerity but the camera and the subject conditions were frequently too much for him to handle. His pictures are harsh in gradation, frequently out of focus or blurred, and rather haphazardly composed. It's probably remarkable that he managed to get any pictures at all, considering the awkwardness of the circumstances. On at least two occasions the flame from his flash powder set fire to the buildings he was photographing, and once he managed to ignite his own clothing. Regardless of his technical ineptitude, Riis's pictures accomplished their purpose. They awakened public sympathy and started a program of reforms which brought about real improvements. Hine's first work with the immigrants, then, continued the campaign that Riis had begun some twenty years before.

In 1908 Hine began a series of pictures of Pittsburgh miners. He also worked for the Child Labor Committee to expose the exploitation of children in various industries. These are some of his most powerful pictures and they helped to bring about new laws and reforms designed to protect children. During World War I, Hine served as a photographer with the Red Cross in Europe. Later he returned to devote himself to a series called "Men at Work," in which he documented the construction of the Empire State Building, climbing among the girders with the construction workers to capture both the spirit and the details of the project.

In April 1906 San Francisco was virtually destroyed by a violent earthquake and the devastation was carefully recorded by Arnold Genthe, a resident portrait photographer. Genthe was well known for his idealized portrait studies and romantic landscapes, but his most significant early work was his extended document of San Francisco's Chinatown. The first tremors of the earthquake destroyed Genthe's studio but he coolly borrowed a little box camera and proceeded to document the disaster as it occurred, displaying the courage and instincts of a true news photographer. This was probably the high point of his career. In later years he reverted to his pictorial style and his work, although competently done, was undistinguished.

After World War I, news photography was no longer a novelty. The unique power of the photograph to communicate ideas was just beginning to be appreciated.

Dr. Erich Salomon, sometimes called the father of modern photojournalism, was one of the first to concentrate in this field. Like many of the earlier workers, he began taking pictures rather late in life (at the age of about forty-two) and almost out of necessity rather than real interest. Employed by a German publishing house, he found that working with hired photographers was a time-consuming and expensive business, so he bought a camera and set out to learn to use it.

The camera that made him famous was the Zeiss Ikon (Dresden) Ermanox, which was introduced in 1927. It took 4.5 cm $\times$ 6 cm glass plates in individual holders and featured an amazingly fast f/1.8 Ernostar lens of 85mm focal length. (Salomon's own camera was equipped with an f/2.0 lens, according to his son.)

Salomon experimented briefly with artificial lighting, but soon gave it up in favor of the more natural and pleasing effect of available light. Using the little Ermanox on a tripod because of the long exposures required (usually from about $\frac{1}{5}$ second to one full second), he specialized in photographing political notables, usually unposed, at their meetings and conferences. He had an uncanny knack for catching his subjects unaware in the midst of some characteristic or expressive gesture, somehow managing—in spite of the relatively long exposure times—to avoid excessive blurring of the image.

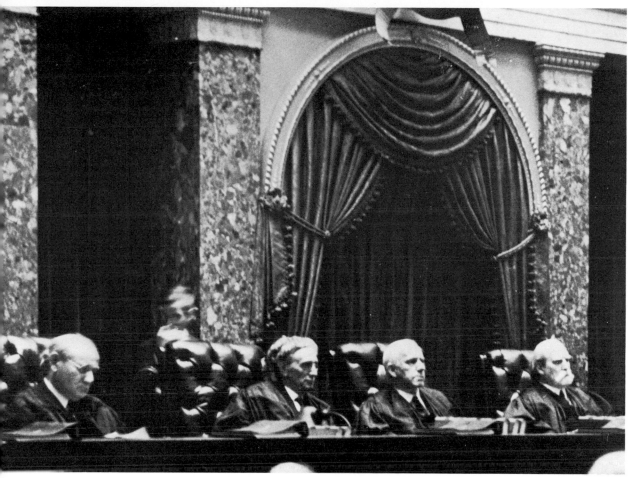

Figure 1.17
Erich Salomon (1886–1944). *Supreme
Court, Chief Justice Hughes Presiding,
1932.* (Courtesy of the IMP, GEH)

He was a master of persuasion and subterfuge when it was required to get the picture, often concealing his camera in a flower vase, in a briefcase, in a stack of books, or in his own clothing. He once smuggled a camera into the Supreme Court, where pictures were strictly forbidden, by putting his arm in an enormous sling and concealing the camera in the wrappings of the cast. He was so successful in these efforts that he eventually became accepted in international political circles; so much so that a famous diplomat was once heard to remark, "Where is Salomon? If we begin without him people will think this conference is not important!"

Like Mathew Brady, Salomon had a great sense of the historical significance of his work. It is ironic that he died in a German prison camp, a victim of a political system that he had watched, documented, and opposed. Characteristically, he managed to conceal his precious negatives from his captors. Just before he was arrested, he arranged for some of them to be left with the librarian of the Dutch parliament and was able to bury the rest, safely wrapped and sealed, in a friend's garden.

The 1930s were significant years in the history of photography. *Fortune* magazine was launched in late 1929 and did well in spite of the great stock market crash and the subsequent depression. *Life* magazine began in 1936, starting a whole new trend in journalism, based on the concept of the picture story. *Life's* Alfred Eisenstadt, who had worked beside Salomon in covering the Geneva League of Nations conferences, and Margaret Bourke-White were original staff photographers whose names soon became familiar to everyone. It was not long before other publishers got on the bandwagon. *Look* appeared in 1937, followed closely by a number of others, such as *Pic* and *Click*. Pictorial supplements were also added to Sunday newspapers and suddenly the nation was picture-conscious.

Advertisers were relatively slow to employ photographic illustration. Although articles and stories in magazines like *Vanity Fair* were illustrated almost entirely with photographs before 1900, their ad illustra-

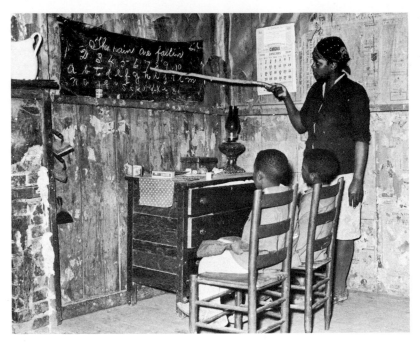

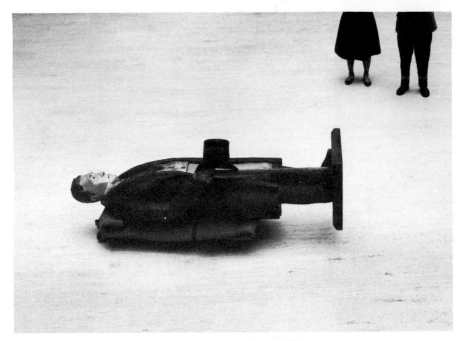

Figure 1.18
Russell Lee (1903–   ). *Sharecropper
Mother Teaching Children, Transylvania,
La.,* 1939. (Library of Congress)

Figure 1.19
André Kertész. *Utica, New York.* (Courtesy of Magnum Photos, Inc.)

**Photo-illustration quickly became
sophisticated**

Stryker and the FSA

tions were rarely photographic before about 1910, and
advertising photography, as we think of it now, was
not practiced until the 1920s. It quickly reached a high
degree of quality and sophistication, however, in the
work of Steichen, Beaton, Outerbridge, Hiller, and later
Horst, Rawlings, Blumenfeld, Matter, Penn, and a great
many others.

The earliest advertising photographs were often
simply pictures, frequently of unrelated subject matter,
which presumably attracted attention because of their
novelty. It was not long, however, before photographs of
the products themselves appeared, then the now-
familiar pictures of models, frequently pretty girls and
babies. Before World War I though, exotic typography,
art nouveau decoration, and outrageous verbal messages were the major elements of successful advertising.

The stock market crash of 1929, and the depression which followed it, left millions of Americans impoverished. Various government agencies were established to provide employment and stimulate economic
recovery. One of these, now known as the Farm Security Administration, included a photographic unit
headed by Roy Stryker. Stryker was not a photographer
himself, but he was appreciative of good pictures. He
was also sensible enough to hire good people and let
them work more or less in their own styles. The project
began in 1935. Arthur Rothstein, Dorothea Lange,
Walker Evans, Russell Lee, Ben Shahn, John Vachon,
and Marion Post Wolcott were among the dozen or
so photographers employed and, by the time America
entered World War II, when the project was ended, they
had amassed more than 250,000 negatives. These pictures, which are now filed in the Library of Congress

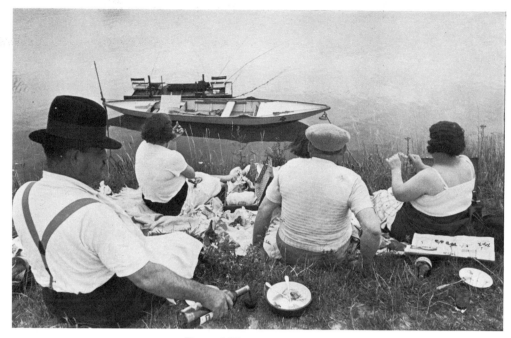

Figure 1.20
Henri Cartier-Bresson (1908–). *Sunday on the banks of the Marne, 1938,* from *The Decisive Moment.* (Courtesy of Magnum Photos, Inc.)

Kertész was one of the first to use the Leica

Brassaï's work is impressively varied

magazines. He was one of the first to buy and use the newly introduced Leica and immediately fell in love with it. By the mid-1930s he was successful and famous.

In 1936 he came to the United States to work for a commercial studio, a move which turned out to be a near-disaster. Unable to return to France because of the war in Europe, he found himself overwhelmed by the pressures of commercial photography and his natural sensitivity was stifled. He settled into semiobscurity for more than twenty years, supporting himself with competently done, but uninspired work, until illness forced him into temporary retirement in 1960. It gave him time to reflect and in 1962 he gave up commercial work to return to his own expression. Once again the wry humor and economy of design, which had characterized his work in Paris, appeared in his pictures and he has now been rediscovered as one of the most innovative of the pioneers of journalistic photography.

Brassaï (a name derived from his native Transylvanian town, Brasso) was a young painter, fresh out of art school, when he arrived in Paris in 1923 and immediately fitted himself into the community of artists. He soon met Kertész, who helped stimulate his interest in photography by lending a camera to him. He immediately began a series of pictures that eventually became a book, *Paris by Night.* An unusually versatile and talented artist, Brassaï has alternately worked as a painter, sculptor, photographer, cinematographer, author, and stage designer and has done them all well. This same restless capability is evident in his photographs. They are impressively varied in style, from the Atget-like views of streets and parks and the candid vignettes of cabaret life, reminiscent of Lautrec's lithographs, to penetrating portraits and abstract compositions based on graffiti. Brassaï's work wears well and, although well known, he deserves more attention than he has been given.

Henri Cartier-Bresson dabbled in painting as a child before taking up photography. His first photographs were taken with a little wooden camera without a shutter, in a style inspired by Atget's pictures. He discovered the Leica in the early 1930s and said of

Archives, are a stunning document of the suffering of the American poor during those dreadful times. The FSA project was successful in eliciting sympathy and support for the homeless and destitute victims of the depression and proved again, as the work of Thomson, Riis, and Hine had done, the persuasive force of the photographic image.

Among the many photographers working in the photojournalistic style of the 1920s and 1930s, three names stand out—André Kertész, Brassaï (Gyula Halász), and Henri Cartier-Bresson.

Kertész, born in 1894 in Budapest, travelled to Paris in 1925 to make his way as a photographer. He had had virtually no previous training and only an amateur's experience but his determination was strong. Before long he was selling some of his pictures to friends and managing to get a few assignments from local

Cartier-Bresson's Leica "became the extension of my eye"

Photography brought the reality of war home to the people

Television and death of the picture magazines

The technical evolution of photography has accelerated

it, "It became the extension of my eye. . . ." An adequate allowance made it possible for him to travel extensively and he began to work in the style that was to make him famous. He was, he said, "determined to 'trap' life . . . to seize the whole essence . . . of some situation that was in the process of unrolling itself before my eyes."

In 1947 Cartier-Bresson and four other free-lance photographers formed Magnum Photos, a cooperative organization which distributed their work. Since then Cartier-Bresson's photographs have appeared frequently in publications around the world, including more than twenty books—the most famous of which, *The Decisive Moment,* was published in 1952 and is now a rare and expensive collector's item. Although he is an avowed "photo-reporter," committed to the concept of the published picture story, Cartier-Bresson's work shows a greater sensitivity than is typical in photojournalism. His compositions are always based on the full frame dimensions of the 35mm format and are typically taut and graceful. He has a masterful sense of organization and pattern and his pictures frequently feature dramatic effects of light and shade. But the identifying characteristic of his work is suggested by *The Decisive Moment,* his ability to "preserve life in the act of living."

World War II brought tremendous advances in technology. Photography played a vital part in every phase of the war effort and was extensively employed for aerial reconnaissance. But its greatest value may have derived from the work of the news photographers who, moving into combat with the front-line troops, brought the grim reality of war home to the people with unprecedented immediacy. The work of these photographers, Robert Capa, Eugene Smith, Carl Mydans, Margaret Bourke-White, Gordon Parks, and many others, raised photojournalism to a new level of effectiveness as a medium of communication.

Until about 1960 the photojournalists were major interpreters of the world's news. At the same time the photoillustrators played a major part in moulding public taste and controlling buying habits. It was a serious blow to both groups when that lusty young medium,

television, began to usurp their functions. *Look* magazine died rather quietly in 1971, a victim of increased costs and reduced advertising income, the same factors which previously eliminated *Colliers, Saturday Evening Post,* and others. *Life* struggled gamely on but the handwriting was on the wall. In spite of a brave editorial policy of "more picture emphasis," waning public interest in the magazine picture story and loss of advertising revenue finally took their toll. The magazine published its last regular issue in December 1972.

As the flow of advertising money began to shift from magazine space to television, a similar, but less traumatic readjustment was forced on the illustrators. While some of the well-established photographers were relatively unaffected, a great many saw their profits dwindle. By 1970 it was clear that photographic journalism and illustration would never be the same again. Television has the public firmly in its grip and has become a frighteningly effective influence on our lives.

Since World War II the technical evolution of photographic equipment has gradually accelerated. The single-lens reflex camera, exemplified before the war by the Graflex and the 35mm Exakta, was considerably improved by the addition of a pentaprism viewing system which corrected the lateral reversal of the image and increased its magnification and brightness. The first prism-reflex camera, the Contax S, was manufactured soon after the war by the East German half of the Zeiss Company and the new design quickly became a model for the industry.

In the early 1950s the Japanese camera industry began to compete in the world market with cameras which were rather obvious copies of the highly respected pre-war German cameras, Leica, Contax, and Rolleiflex. These designs evolved rapidly, however, and in a very few years the Japanese were producing quantities of excellent, relatively inexpensive cameras of original design. Their industry has continued to excel and dominates the world market today in numbers of camera models and lenses. Much of this success has been due to an aggressive research program. Japanese designers have consistently led the way in introducing

But the outlook is not entirely reassuring

The early nineteenth century brought
rapid changes in science and industry

The arts were in a similar state of flux

Delaroche:
"From this day painting is dead"

such technical refinements as the instant-return mirror, automatic diaphragm, various forms of exposure automation, commercial production of multicoated lenses, and the metal blade focal plane shutter.

Improvements in lens design have been dramatic, too. Computers now do in seconds the optical calculations that used to take years of human figuring. New glasses, new construction techniques, and new testing procedures have resulted in a generation of lenses which are more versatile, more precise, and, in some cases, less expensive than comparable models of twenty years ago.

There seems to be no end in sight, either. Although recent improvements in design features, lens quality, miniaturization, and automation seem almost revolutionary, it seems likely that the cameras we admire today will seem primitive to the photographers of the next generation.

The changes in photographic materials over the years have not all resulted in obvious improvement, however. Certainly black-and-white films have become more sensitive, sharper and finer-grained, and are less easily damaged in processing than were pre-war films. Color materials, too, have improved in most respects, although there are some people who will argue that the quality of color reproduction is no better, and perhaps worse, than that of Lumière's Autochromes. Polaroid materials, especially the SX-70 color film, are technical miracles, and Cibachrome has brought a new standard of image sharpness and brilliance within reach of the amateur printer.

But the improvements in color materials seem to have been made at the expense of the black-and-white, which, deliberately or not, the manufacturers appear to be deemphasizing. Large sheet films are increasingly difficult to find and some have been discontinued entirely. A good variety of rollfilms are available in most sizes but printing paper manufacturers offer fewer and fewer options. The outlook is not reassuring either. Silver is becoming scarce and expensive, as is high-quality paper itself. The resin-coated papers, introduced a few years ago, are convenient and will serve for most commercial applications, but "art" photographers view them with despair. If the few remaining fine-quality fiber-based papers are phased out in favor of the resin-coated materials, it will certainly alter our perception of the "fine print" and may endanger the future of photography as a collectible art.

The Art of Photography

In the early years of the nineteenth century, rapid changes were beginning to take place in science and industry. In the entire history of chemistry, for example, only about thirty elements had been identified before 1800 and by 1839 twenty-five new ones had been discovered. Fundamental electrical theory was being formulated by Ohm, Faraday, Ampere, Henry, and others. The steam engine, which had supplied power for the beginning of the industrial revolution, was being refined and installed in ships and railroad engines. Iron was being rolled into sheets and bars for structural uses. The inventors were busy, too. The telegraph, the Colt revolver, Portland cement, McCormick's reaper, the electric pile battery, the electromagnet, and vulcanized rubber, to name a few, were all invented between 1800 and 1839.

The arts in France, especially painting, were in a similar state of flux. The neoclassic influence still lingered, with Ingres at its head. Delacroix, as the leading Romanticist, was enthusiastically painting harem scenes and trading insults with Ingres at every opportunity and the open air painters of Barbizon were setting their easels in the fields and forests to paint directly from nature.

The formal announcement of the daguerreotype process on August 19, 1839, and the sudden concentration of public attention on the photographic image, was shocking to at least some of the artists of the day. When Delaroche saw his first daguerreotype he exclaimed, "from this day painting is dead!" but later he described photography as "an easy means of collecting studies" and decided that Daguerre had "rendered an immense service to the arts."

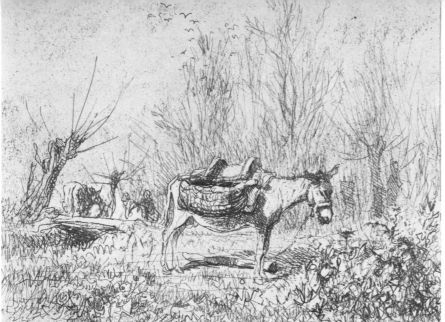

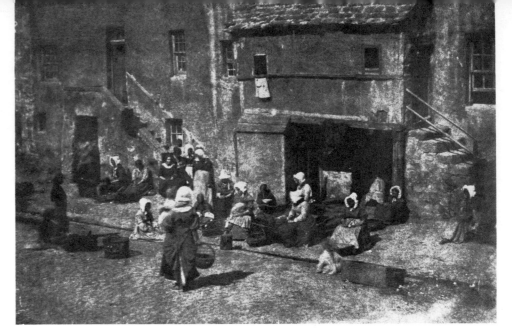

Figure 1.21
Charles F. Daubigny (1817–1878). *L'Ane au Pre,* 1862, cliché-verre. (Courtesy of the University of Michigan Museum of Art)

Figure 1.22
D.O. Hill (1802–1870). *St. Andrews,* calotype. (Courtesy of the University of University of Michigan Museum of Art)

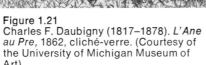

Painting and photography influenced each other

Notable work was done by Hill and Adamson

This ambivalence was typical. Ruskin, who was initially charmed by the daguerreotype, later became one of photography's sternest critics, and Ingres, who professed to despise photography (possibly because Delacroix was enthusiastic about it), is said to have worked rather frequently from photographs made for him by Nadar.

This uproar and confusion affected both painting and photography for many years. Many early photographers patterned their photographic compositions after the prevailing painting styles, while the painters, acutely conscious of the unique visual character of the photograph, were undoubtedly influenced by photography's incredible rendering of detail, its characteristic interpretation of light and shade, its informal compositions, and its curious blurring of out-of-focus scenes and moving objects.

Although photography was probably a factor in the brief revival of interest in such meticulously detailed painting as that of the pre-Raphaelites, it was even more obviously an influence toward Impressionism and the freely composed snapshot vision of Daumier, Lautrec, and especially Degas. In this sense, painting profited tremendously from photography, while the early photographers were hindered in their search for a genuinely photographic esthetic by the generally hostile art establishment.

It's hardly surprising, under the circumstances, that many of the early photographers were painters. Some of them, Delacroix, Corot, and Daubigny, for example, experimented a little with photography but remained essentially painters. Others, like Oscar Rejlander and Henry Peach Robinson, turned away from painting and concentrated on photography.

Some of the most notable work produced by an early painter-photographer was done by David Octavius Hill in partnership with Robert Adamson. The pair began their work in 1843 by making calotype portraits which Hill intended to use as reference material for a huge painting, depicting a conference of some four hundred Scottish churchmen. They soon began to photograph

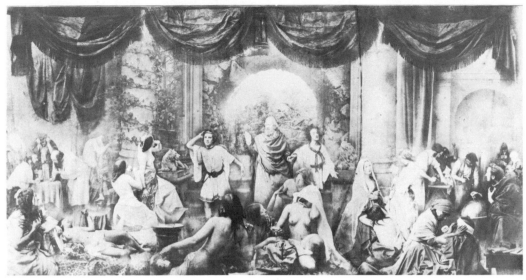

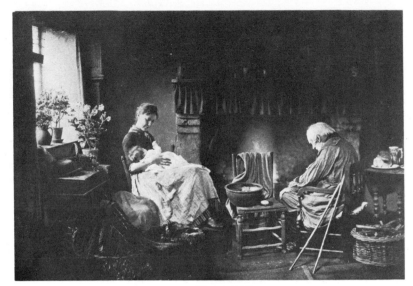

Figure 1.23
Oscar G. Rejlander (1813–1875). *Two Ways of Life*. (Courtesy of the Royal Photographic Society, London, and the IMP, GEH)

Figure 1.24
Henry Peach Robinson (1830–1901). *Dawn and Sunset*. (Courtesy of the Art Institute of Chicago)

Rejlander's *Two Ways of Life* was controversial

Robinson as spokesman for pictorial photography

other people and scenes as well. Hill became so preoccupied that his painting was not completed for more than twenty years. Although they worked together for only about four years (Adamson became terminally ill in 1847), Hill and Adamson produced more than 2500 calotypes, many of which were portraits of enduring charm. Hill continued to work sporadically after Adamson's death but neither his later photographs nor his painting can be compared to the work done during their brief collaboration.

Oscar Rejlander is best known for his large composite photographic composition, *Two Ways of Life,* done in 1857. Assembled from more than thirty separate photographs, this picture was an heroic allegory in the romantic style. Although it was a considerable success, it was highly controversial. The Photographic Society of Scotland refused to exhibit the photograph until it was agreed that the "offensive" half, depicting Dissipation, would be covered with drapery, leaving "respectable" Industry in view.

Rejlander made other composites but eventually turned toward "straight" photography and portraiture. Some of his work was remarkably inventive and advanced for his day and he deserves to be better known.

Robinson, like Rejlander, achieved immediate recognition for his montages. He was an extraordinarily prolific photographer and an extremely skillful one. He was also convinced that photography could be called an art, as long as it was governed by the same rules that had traditionally applied to painting. In promoting this view he wrote almost a dozen books and numerous articles and established himself as the spokesman for pictorial photography. His influence was enormous. So, apparently, was his ability to rationalize. Caught between the popular belief that "truth was beauty" and the obvious fact that the camera recorded much truth that was not beautiful, Robinson solved the dilemma by declaring, in effect, that beauty was truth, and contended that combination printing (photomontage) permitted the photographer "greater facilities for representing the truth of nature."

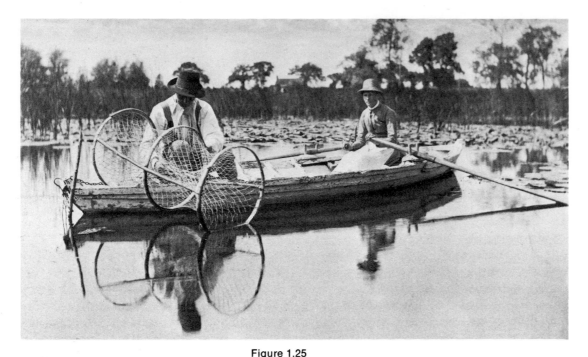

Figure 1.25
Peter Henry Emerson (1856–1936). *Setting the Bow Net,* platinum print. (Courtesy of the University of Michigan Museum of Art)

Emerson advocated naturalistic photography

Cameron was an amateur but an artist of significance

Davison challenged Emerson's leadership

Robinson's views continued to dominate photography well into the 1880s until he was challenged by Peter Henry Emerson, an avid amateur photographer, naturalist, and physician. Emerson and Robinson disliked each other's work intensely and Emerson, in particular, made no effort to be polite about it. Of combination printing he said: "this process is really what many of us practised in the nursery, that is, cutting . . . and pasting . . . though such 'work' may produce sensational effects in photographic galleries, it is but the art of the opera bouffe." Emerson advocated a return to nature and referred his readers to the work of the Barbizon painters. A naturalistic photograph, he declared must be

1. True in natural sentiment
2. True in appearance to the point of illusion
3. Decorative

To achieve these qualities he thought it necessary to use a slightly undercorrected lens, of relatively long focal length, at moderate aperture. Naturalistic focus was achieved when the background of the picture was thrown out of focus to an extent which did not produce "destruction of the structure," the principal object of the picture being either "sharp or just out of sharp."

Emerson's tremendous ego shows in his references to other photographers. Even in mentioning the three he most admired—Rejlander, Adam-Salomon, and Julia Margaret Cameron—he was careful to point out their limitations: Rejlander he thought of as a "trained painter (of) very second rate artistic ability"; Adam-Salomon, a sculptor "without first-rate ability"; and Cameron he described as "not an artist" and an "amateur."

Julia Margaret Cameron was an amateur, certainly, but we now recognize her as an artist of significance. She was forty-eight years old when she began photographing in 1863 and within a year she had taught herself the rudiments of the craft. Using a rapid-rectilinear lens of 30″ focal length, she was a ruthless person to sit for, sometimes subjecting her subjects to extraordinarily long exposure times (in dim light) if she felt the visual effect was pleasing. Her portraits were her best work. They introduced a new directness and sensitivity to photography which was ahead of her time. On the other hand, she was fond of illustrating biblical and literary themes and it's tempting to agree with Emerson's opinion of these, as "puerile and amateurish."

If the Impressionist painters were influenced by photography's treatment of atmosphere, soft-focus, movement blur, and halation (as it seems certain they must have been), some of the naturalist photographers were, in turn, affected by Impressionism. One of them, George Davison, carried Emerson's naturalistic focus principles much farther than Emerson approved and, by promoting the virtues of soft-focus work, challenged Emerson's position as spokesman for art photographers. Emerson's reaction was immediate and spiteful.

And was scolded

The Linked Ring Brotherhood

Emerson awarded prizes to Stieglitz and Fraprie

Stieglitz and Fraprie were poles apart

In a vitriolic renunciation of his previous views—as explained at great length in his book, *Naturalistic Photography for Students of the Art,* he declared that photography was not, and could never be, an art. The term *photographic impressionist,* which Davison was fond of, he called "a term consecrate to charlatans, and especially to photographic imposters, pickpockets, parasites and vanity intoxicated amateurs." He then described Davison as "an amateur without training, and with superficial knowledge (who took) my old ideas . . . freely and impudently handed (them) about with no credit given me." Finally, he said, "when I have fully reconsidered the limited art possibilities of photography . . . I will write another book; in the meantime, let students avoid all spurious imitations."

Emerson was clearly a difficult man to get along with but he was also a fine photographer of landscape and genre studies and an excellent craftsman. He worked almost exclusively in platinotype and photogravure.

In 1892 a little group of rebel pictorialists broke away from the Royal Photographic Society and formed The Linked Ring Brotherhood. This group, which included most of the naturalists, led now by Davison, was devoted to advancing the art of photography and included such notables as J. Craig Annan, Horsley Hinton, and Frederick Evans. Interestingly, H. P. Robinson was also a member, but Emerson, after his *Death of Naturalistic Photography* tirade, had returned to the venerable and conservative Royal. The Linked Ring lasted until 1910.

In 1887, while judging a photography contest, Emerson awarded the first prize to a young American, Alfred Stieglitz, and told Stieglitz that his picture, *A Good Joke,* was the only "truly spontaneous picture" in the exhibition. Similarly, in 1903 he gave first prize to a young American college student, Frank Fraprie. Fraprie eventually became a driving force in the pictorialist movement in America, as editor of several photographic publications including *The American Annual of Photography,* while Stieglitz was soon to assemble a little group of dedicated photographers who would call themselves the Photo-Secessionists.

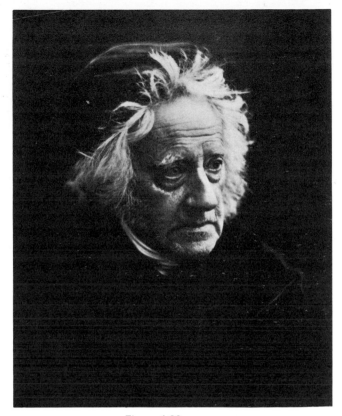

Figure 1.26
Julia Margaret Cameron (1815–1879). *Sir John Herschel.* (Courtesy of the Art Institute of Chicago)

Although Fraprie and Stieglitz were poles apart philosophically (Fraprie later referred disparagingly to "Stieglitz and his crew" and the "Photo-Secession clique" in one of his articles), both remembered Emerson's appreciation of their work with satisfaction. It's interesting to note that Stieglitz carried on Emerson's philosophy of naturalism into straight photography, while Fraprie fixed superficially on Emerson's naturalistic focus and truth in sentiment recommendations and, with the other pictorialists of the 1920s, 1930s, and 1940s, let those noble aims degenerate into out-of-focus images and contrived situation photographs of the most cloying sentimentality.

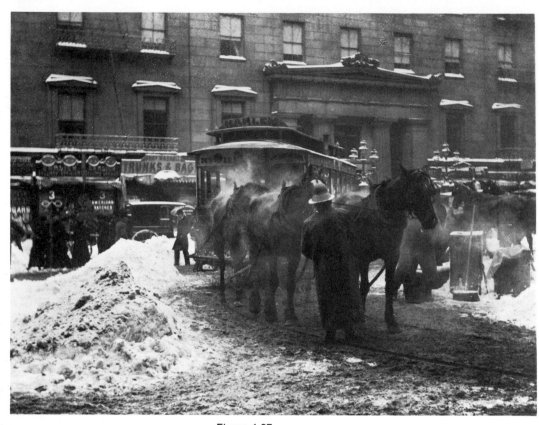

Figure 1.27
Alfred Steiglitz (1864–1946). *The Ter-minal.* (Courtesy of the Art Institute of Chicago)

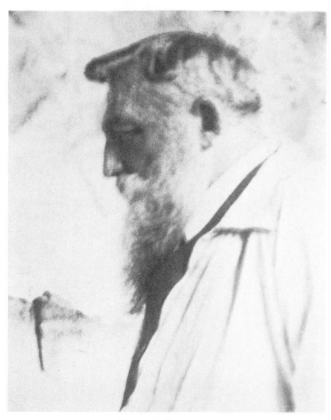

Figure 1.28
Gertrude Käsebier (1852–1934). *Portrait of Rodin.* (Courtesy of the Art Institute of Chicago)

Stieglitz formed the Photo-Secession

Alfred Stieglitz was born in New Jersey in 1864. He spent his student years in Europe and was introduced to photography in 1883 during his first year as an engineering student at the Berlin Polytechnic. He became obsessed with photography almost at once and experimented constantly while studying chemistry under Vogel. He spent nine years in Europe, during which he studied and travelled on a modest income from his family, apparently leading a life which any young man would envy, and taking pictures incessantly. By 1890 he was internationally famous as an exhibitor of photographs.

He returned to New York in 1890 and was fascinated by the city. An abortive attempt at business occupied him briefly, but he was soon out of it and devoted himself to photographing and promoting interest in photography by publishing *Camera Notes,* a quarterly for the Camera Club of New York. The group of sympathizers which soon surrounded him could have been called the "who's who" of American photography: Clarence White, Gertrude Käsebier, Alvin Langdon Coburn, Edward Steichen, Frank Eugene, Joseph Keiley, and others. In 1902 they formed their own informal group which Stieglitz, on impulse, named the Photo-Secession.

In 1903 Stieglitz published the first quarterly issue of *Camera Work,* a lavishly printed magazine devoted to the promotion of photography as an art form. The magazine and the Photo-Secessionists flourished for some time and their gallery, three rooms at 291 Fifth Avenue next to Steichen's room, became a meeting place for artists of all kinds.

The arts were united by Stieglitz as by no other individual. Although he was a photographer himself—and an extremely sensitive one—his passion transcended photography. He encouraged all artists who met his high standards of perception and dedication without caring what medium they chose to work in. As a seasoned traveller (and a member of the Linked Ring Brotherhood) he was thoroughly familiar with European photography and, with Steichen's advice and assistance, became acquainted with the work of many new talents in painting and sculpture, as well.

Together, he and Steichen began to import European work which seemed to them to be vital and significant. As a result many of the artists recognized as outstanding today were discovered and shown in America for the first time at 291; among them—Cezanne, Picasso, Braque, Matisse, Picabia, Toulouse-Lautrec, and Brancusi. He was equally supportive of promising American talent. The work of John Marin, Marsden Hartley, Arthur Dove, Max Weber, and Georgia O'Keeffe (whom Stieglitz later married) was shown frequently.

For the first three years, photographs dominated the walls of 291 but Stieglitz was discovering that the Photo-Secessionists were less vital than the young painters. During the year 1909 only three of the eleven shows presented were photographic. In the following years through May 1917, only three photographers were shown at 291: Steichen in 1910, Stieglitz himself in 1913, and Paul Strand in 1916. The other forty-seven exhibitions included paintings, drawings, children's art, sculpture, ceramics, lithographs, and caricatures.

Stieglitz's efforts to promote photography as a fine art culminated in a monumental exhibition of photographs in the Albright Museum of Art in Buffalo, New York, in 1910. In spite of the opposition of Frank Fraprie, who denounced the Photo-Secessionists as a ''reac-

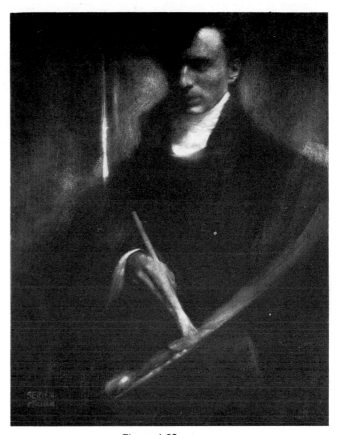

Figure 1.29
Edward Steichen (1879–1973). *Self Portrait.* (Courtesy of the Art Institute of Chicago)

tionary force of the most dangerous type,'' the exhibition (designed and hung by Max Weber) was a great success and a very significant step toward the acceptance of photography by the art establishment.

For fifteen years Stieglitz's strength and vision had brought the arts together and photography and painting had co-existed in an atmosphere of mutual respect. But it was painting that profited most immediately. The majority of photographers after World War I, as if in reaction to Stieglitz's influence, reverted to the fuzzy Victorian silliness of the 1890s. Photography did not become a vital art again, with a few notable exceptions, for more than thirty years.

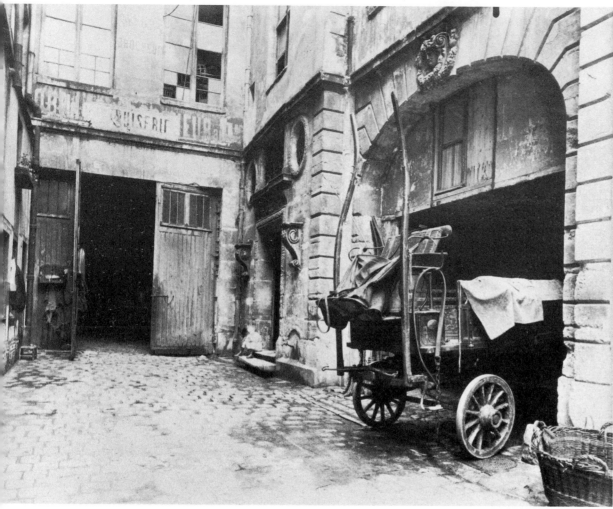

Figure 1.30
Eugène Atget (1856–1927). *Un Coin de la Rue Reynie*. (Courtesy of the University of Michigan Museum of Art)

In every period there seem to be a few photographers whose work is difficult to classify and Eugène Atget is one of them. Born in France in 1856, he was raised by an uncle and went to sea as a cabin boy. Later he became an actor and toured the country playing minor roles until he was about forty-two. He began to photograph in 1898 and was self-taught. Using an old view camera and a simple set of lenses, he spent most of the rest of his life recording the city of Paris and its environs. Although he made a meager living by selling his views (many of them to local artists), he apparently knew very little about the work of other photographers and was, himself, similarly unknown during his lifetime. Much of his work was saved from discard after his death by the efforts of Berenice Abbott—herself a fine photographer—who obtained a large number of his plates and published a book of his images. Atget was a lonely figure but an important one in the history of photography. His work was a personal, direct, intense, and unusually honest product of the photographic process.

At about the same time, another unknown photographer was beginning to exercise his unique vision. The absolute opposite of Atget in almost every respect, Jacques Henri Lartigue was seven years old when he took his first picture, a snapshot of his family. Lartigue's family was wealthy and they appear in his photographs as a very lively, fun-loving group of people. He recorded them in all sorts of activities but specialized in sports and action shots—swimming, jumping, attempting to fly, touring and racing wheeled bobsleds. His other major interest was photographing fashionable women, usually strolling along the avenue, resplendent in silk and lace and feathers. These pictures have an immediacy and intimacy which suggests that the ladies considered the boy with the camera harmless, if not actually invisible. They could hardly have suspected that their images would hang in the Museum of Modern Art fifty years later, nor that they would become well-known visual symbols of the secure and affluent society of "La Belle Epoque."

The new freedom of thought and vision, which inspired painters to break away from the representation

Eugène Atget was a lonely but important figure

Lartigue began photographing at seven

Coburn experimented with Vortographs

Dada—the anti-art of the irrational and absurd

Heartfield attacked Nazism with photomontage

of subject matter, also affected a few photographers. Again, it appears that the two media fed on each other: the Futurists' attempts to express speed and motion obviously derived from the photographs of Muybridge, Marey, and Eakins, while the Futurists and Cubists, in turn, inspired Alvin Langdon Coburn to experiment with mirror-multiplied photographic images which he called *Vortographs*. Coburn, who had been a member of the Photo-Secession and the Linked Ring Brotherhood, was very interested in portraiture during most of his early career, but later turned to more diverse subject matter. He was a skilled printer in photogravure and personally made and proofed the plates used to illustrate four of his books.

Coburn was not the first man to experiment with distortions of the photographic image; Ducos du Hauron, at least, had preceded him by almost thirty years. Coburn was, however, the first photographer to work with distortion in a deliberate attempt to create a new visual direction for photography. Although his Vortographs were clearly limited, his exploration of new viewpoints and perspectives was ahead of his time.

The appearance of the Dada movement in art, just before World War I, was a direct attack on traditional values of all sorts. Dada proclaimed itself the anti-art of the irrational and absurd and produced such un-settling objects as a urinal displayed as *R. Mutt's Foun-tain*, a flat-iron studded with carpet tacks, and Marcel Duchamp's saucy distortion of a color reproduction of the Mona Lisa, to which he added a pencilled beard and moustache and the title, *L.H.O.O.Q.,* which spoken rap-idly in French sounds like the phrase "Elle a chaud au cul" (she has hot pants).

The Dadaists and Surrealists were not interested in photography as such, but they frequently made use of photographic images in their collages. George Grosz, John Heartfield, and Hannah Höch were particularly adept at this art form and Heartfield, especially, used photomontage effectively to attack the rising Nazi menace in Germany. Dada eventually evolved into Sur-realism and Constructivism, which, in turn, influenced some of the members of the Bauhaus in Germany in the early 1920s.

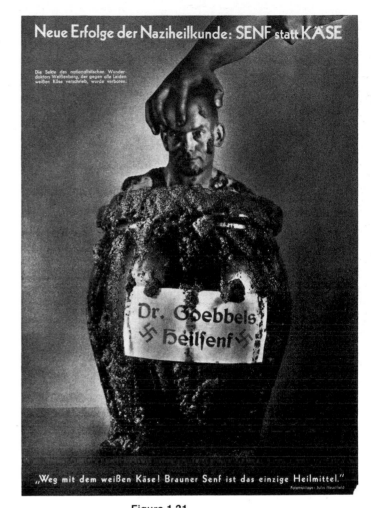

Figure 1.31
John Heartfield. *Dr. Goebbels Heilsenf,* photomontage. (Courtesy of the IMP, GEH)

When the Nazis closed the Bauhaus in 1933, one of its members, László Moholy-Nagy, started the New Bauhaus (which later became the Institute of Design) in Chicago. Moholy-Nagy was convinced that photography was indispensible, not only as a scientific tool or means of expression, but fundamentally as an extension of vision. Like Christian Schad and Man Ray, Moholy-Nagy had reinvented the technique of shadow-printing which Talbot had called "photogenic drawing." Schad's prints were called *Schadographs,* Man Ray called his *Rayograms,* while Moholy-Nagy named his *photograms,* the term we usually use today.

Moholy-Nagy did not neglect straight photography but he was an experimenter and investigator by nature. Like Coburn he explored the visual effects of optical distortion and unusual viewpoint; but he went beyond Coburn by applying these techniques to graphic design and by pointing out the beauty to be found in photomicrographs and other types of scientific photographs. Moholy-Nagy, like all the other Bauhaus artists, was committed to order, structure, and, to a degree, formula, but he was also a brilliant innovator whose teachings had a great deal to do with photography's acceptance as a visual language.

Meanwhile, photography was also evolving as an expressive medium. The final double issue of *Camera Work* in 1917 was devoted to the work of a young protégé of Stieglitz, Paul Strand. Strand had been introduced to Stieglitz while on a field trip to the 291 gallery with his teacher, Lewis Hine, and they formed an immediate friendship. Strand quickly worked his way through the soft-focus pictorialist style and concentrated on straight photographs of New York and its street people, which Stieglitz described as being "brutally direct . . . devoid of trickery . . . devoid of any attempt to mystify. . . . These photographs are the direct expression of today."

Strand worked as an X-ray technician and as a member of a medical movie crew during World War I. In the mid-1920s, after having supported himself for several years as a cinematographer, he returned to still photography and nature, first in Colorado, then in Maine

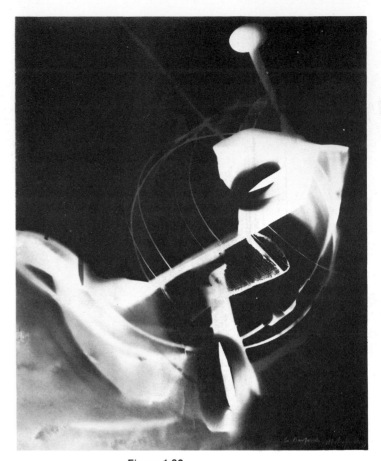

Figure 1.32
László Moholy-Nagy (1895–1946). *Photogram.* (Courtesy of the Art Institute of Chicago)

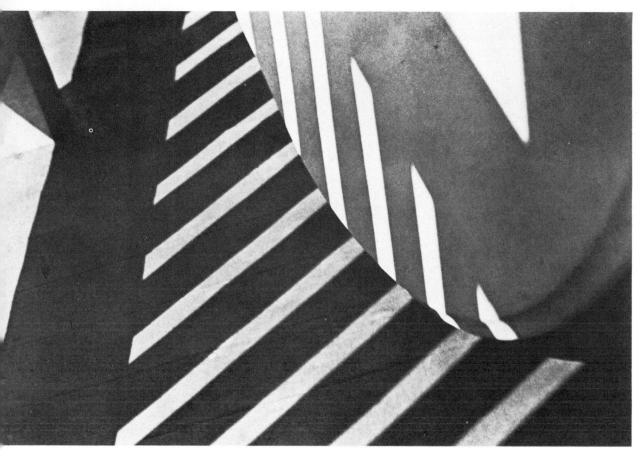

Figure 1.33
Paul Strand (1890–1976). *Shadows*.
(Courtesy of the Art Institute of Chicago)

and the Atlantic coast. Later, in Mexico, Strand collected the images that ultimately comprised his gravure *Mexican Portfolio*. Alternating still and motion picture photography for several years, Strand did a number of documentary films and had a major exhibition in the Museum of Modern Art. Then, in 1948, he moved to France. He devoted the rest of his life to travel and photographing, producing several books in collaboration with various authors. He died in 1976.

After the dissolution of the Photo-Secession group and the closing of 291 in 1917, Alfred Stieglitz withdrew to a more private existence for a while, but his crusade went on. He continued to encourage O'Keeffe and Marin especially, almost as symbols of an attitude in art that had to be protected and preserved. In 1921 he prefaced a retrospective exhibition of his own work with a statement that ended, "I was born in Hoboken. I am an American. Photography is my passion. The search for Truth my obsession."

Later, in response to a comment that the power of his photographs resulted from his influence over the sitters, Stieglitz produced a series of cloud photographs "to show," he wrote, "that my photographs were not due to subject matter—not to special trees, or faces, or interiors . . . clouds were there for everyone—no tax as yet on them—free." These pictures, according to Stieglitz, inspired the composer, Ernest Bloch, to exclaim, "Music! music! Man, why that is music!" In an exhibition the next year, he showed another series of small cloud pictures entitled "Songs of the Sky." These two groups of photographs, which are very abstract and evocative, he called *equivalents,* meaning that they were intended to be seen not just as pictures of clouds, but as incitements to perception analogous to other experiences.

Although Stieglitz was not universally loved, by any means, no one can contest the fact that he was one of the most influential men in the history of art. Both painting and photography owe him a considerable debt. His final gallery, An American Place, opened in 1929 and continued to be a mecca for artists of all persuasions until his death in 1946.

On the West Coast, out of Stieglitz's immediate influence, the photography scene was less tempestuous. The pictorialist influence was strong and, in 1906, when Edward Weston opened his first studio in California, he was completely committed to making soft-focus romantic portraits. He married and had four sons, but the marriage was not a happy one. He became increasingly dissatisfied with having to cater to the tastes of his clients, too, and in 1922 he travelled to New York where he met Stieglitz, O'Keeffe, Strand, and Sheeler. The meetings encouraged and stimulated him and, anxious to concentrate on a personal expression in photography, he travelled to Mexico with his oldest son Chandler and Tina Modotti, an artists' model. He lived there for almost two years, producing portraits, nudes, and cloud studies and working in quite close contact with Mexico's leading artists.

He returned to California in 1926 and in 1929 settled in Carmel where he spent most of the rest of his life. He worked with minimal equipment, an old 8 × 10 view camera and a primitive darkroom, but there is no hint of this in his photographs. They are still exceptional for their glorification of natural forms in light, their sharpness of detail, and their delicacy of texture.

Weston kept a diary during most of his productive life and it has been published in two edited volumes, _The Daybooks of Edward Weston._ It is a revealing and inspiring record of the life and creative struggles of one of the major artists of this century. He was the first photographer to receive a Guggenheim Foundation Fellowship and was given a major retrospective exhibition in the Museum of Modern Art in New York in 1946. He died in Carmel in 1958.

In 1932 a little group of West Coast photographers banded together informally in reaction to pictorialism. Calling themselves Group f-64 they worked to achieve sharpness and brilliance in their prints by careful selection of subject, camera position, light conditions, and focus. The title suggested their use of small lens apertures for greatest depth of field and good definition. Weston was a charter member of the group, as were Imogen Cunningham and Ansel Adams.

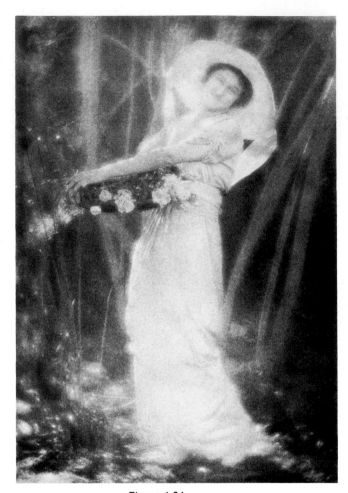

Figure 1.34
Edward Weston (1886–1958). _Roses and Sunshine,_ from the _Platinum Print,_ vol. 1, no. 5 August 1914.

Adams had begun photographing only a few years earlier and was initially influenced by the prevailing pictorialist style. He was a trained musician and photography was only an absorbing hobby until he happened to see some of Paul Strand's photographs in 1930. He was tremendously impressed and immediately decided to make photography his career. Within a very short time he was getting international recognition and in 1936 his work was shown in Stieglitz's gallery, An American Place.

Adams has spent much of his professional life photographing nature, concentrating on the Southwest and especially Yosemite. His photographs display a rare mixture of visual sensitivity and technical excellence and are notable for their dramatic effects of light, rich textures, and brilliant tonality.

He has been extremely productive and has published several books of photographs as well as a number of textbooks, the first of which, *Making a Photograph,* was published in 1935. He has also worked commercially and has been a consultant to the Polaroid Corporation for many years. As the acknowledged leader of the West Coast landscape photographers, Adams has influenced a generation of students, many of them through his frequent workshops, but his fame as a teacher is due largely to his Zone System, a procedure for controlling the translation of subject tones into print values. Adams's place in the history of photography is secure, probably no other photographer has been more highly respected, more widely known, or more materially successful.

Edward Steichen, whose name had been intimately associated with photography since before 1900, became the director of photography for the Museum of Modern Art in New York in 1947. He brought to the post a variety of experience as painter, pictorialist, secessionist, aerial reconnaissance during World War I, portrait, advertising, and fashion photographer, and director of photography for the Navy in World War II. During his directorship at the Museum of Modern Art, Steichen expanded and diversified the collection of photographs and put on more than forty photographic exhibitions, culminating in 1955 in a massive display of more than

five hundred prints from photographers all over the world. He called it "The Family of Man." Assembled from more than two million prints submitted, the exhibition was a notable success. In 1964 the museum established the "Edward Steichen Photography Center" in his honor and conferred on him the title of "Director Emeritus," which he held until his death at the age of 94 in 1973. Steichen's career in art and photography is almost without parallel. No other individual has combined so many talents, devoted so much energy, and achieved such success in so many branches of the medium.

In spite of its enthusiastic acceptance by viewers around the world, the "Family of Man," seen in retrospect, was impressive more for the statistics of its presentation than for its artistic significance. It told its story and was persuasive, but it used photography conservatively. Its real power lay in the sheer size and number of prints and the magnificence of its installation. It probably had to be done, if only to complete the era of the picture story in a grand manner but it was primarily a tour-de-force of photojournalism and had little to do with the "modern art" of photography in the 1950s. New, more personal and creative expressions were soon to appear.

The end of World War II brought sweeping social changes. With the post-war prosperity and the flood of consumer goods came the sobering realization that the world's last frontiers had been explored and that—for the first time in history—man had the physical capacity to exterminate himself with one grand gesture. To many young people of the 1950s and 1960s these factors combined into a ghastly paradox. They saw ahead of them lives full of comfort and plenty, but devoid of purpose, empty of human value, and threatened by atomic disaster, runaway population growth, and resource depletion. Their initial unease, heightened by the Korean War, became anguished rebellion with our involvement in Vietnam. Some of them looked at this new, crazy world with suddenly sharpened perception, and, while many were caught up in waves of semiorganized protest and demonstration, a few expressed themselves through their art, including photography.

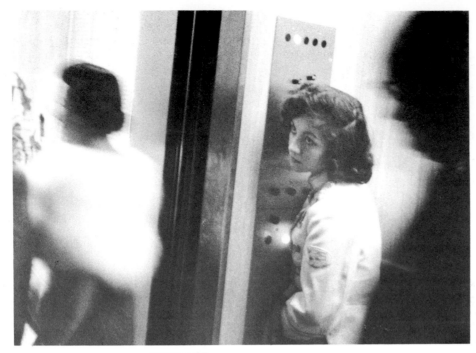

Figure 1.35
Robert Frank. *Elevator Girl*. (Courtesy of
Robert Frank, from *The Americans*.)

Modern photography of the fifties still had some link with the past, however. The creative spark that Stieglitz passed on to Weston, Strand, and Adams persisted after World War II to inspire Harry Callahan, Minor White, and many others.

Callahan, under whose later direction the Chicago Institute of Design's photography program became nationally known, first displayed an interest in pattern and design. Since the late 1940s he has worked in a variety of styles including experimental multiple exposure abstractions, nudes, street photographs, and formalistic patterns, all of which are characterized by an obvious interest in organization and structure, but which represent for him an intensification of the essential qualities of his subjects. Callahan has been an important force in photography as both artist and teacher for more than thirty years, but in a modest way. He has seldom written or lectured on photography, but his numerous exhibitions attest to his continuing productivity and his appreciation by an ever-widening audience.

Minor White became interested in photography as a boy but put it aside during his college years in favor of writing. At the age of thirty, in 1938, he took up photography again and, resisting the prevailing pictorialist influences, studied the work of Stieglitz, Adams, Weston, and Abbott. He quickly became a masterful technician and in 1938–39 completed documentary projects on the iron-front buildings and the waterfront areas of Portland, Oregon.

He returned to writing during his army service and developed an interest in religion and philosophy which preoccupied him increasingly for the rest of his life. After World War II, he became interested in the concept of "reading" photographs and, after meeting Stieglitz, Strand, Callahan, Adams, and Weston in 1946, he began working with Stieglitz's idea of the *equivalent* and images in series.

In the following years, he taught at the California School of Fine Arts, the Rochester Institute of Technology, and, finally at the Massachusetts Institute of Technology. He was, meanwhile, a very active exhibitor, writer, critic, lecturer, and workshop instructor. Addi-

Frank's *The Americans* was startling

Minor White's early interest was in writing

Robert Frank's book, *The Americans,* gave us a first shocked look at ourselves in 1959. The pictures seem quite ordinary now because Frank's work started a style which is still popular. In 1959, however, it was new and startling, direct, artless, and often irritating. It confronted us with things we had trained ourselves not to see and we reacted with gut feelings of alienation, dislocation, and a dismayed recognition of life's overwhelming trivia. Frank's work was a new, raw descendant of the social commentary approach to imagery, traceable through the Farm Security Administration documentary of the depression to Hine, Riis, and Thomson. However, it had a new roughness of style which seemed to deny, or at least ignore, the older traditions of compositional elegance and the concept of the fine print. *The Americans* leads more or less directly to the work of Lee Friedlander, Gary Winogrand, Danny Lyon, and others, who have come to be known as the social landscape photographers.

He worked with equivalents and images in series

The stylistic shift of the 50s resembled Dada

By 1960 photography was well established in the schools

Academic education of photographers is having unprecedented effects

tionally, he found time to join the staff of George Eastman House and edit the magazine *Aperture*. His interest in religious experience, philosophy, and psychology eventually embraced various Far Eastern religions and astrology and these principles became inseparable from his artistic expressions in photography and poetry.

White's *sequences,* photographs in series, frequently with accompanying poems, are some of his best work. He had a masterful command of technique and his prints are rich and luminous. His images are always evocative, usually ambiguous, and frequently involve forms which are poetically suggestive of religious and erotic ideas. White was not without his critics. He inspired either admiration or scorn without much middle ground, but on the whole he was a genuinely constructive force and a powerful one.

The stylistic shift in the late 1950s, represented by Frank, Winogrand, and others, had some of the characteristics of the Dada movement in the teens and 1920s. Like Dada, it rejected the prevailing esthetic standards, involved subject matter which had been considered unfit, vulgar, trivial, and banal, and displayed a fine lack of concern for technical polish. Unlike Dada, which was a violent outburst by a militant few, this photographic revolution was a relatively genteel reaction which spread widely and resulted in a gradual and progressive change. Although it inspired a great deal of interest in the street photograph and the snapshot, the major effect of Frank's efforts was not so much in establishing a new style as in repudiating an old one. By finally disposing of the restrictive and ritualistic esthetic formula of the pictorialists, the young rebels of the 1950s opened the door to experimentation and gave photographers a new freedom of expression.

By 1960 photography had begun to find widespread acceptance in the high schools, colleges, and universities. It spread rapidly. In 1963 a group of teachers founded the Society for Photographic Education (SPE) to establish formal lines of communication between teachers of photography, to encourage the growth of photography in the schools, and to cooperate with other organizations, such as the Professional Photographers

of America (PP of A), also interested in education. The SPE has grown slowly but steadily and now has about 1600 active members widely distributed over the United States, as well as a few members in foreign countries.

Although it is a fairly recent phenomenon, this academic education of photographers is having unprecedented effects. One of these has been a dramatic increase in interest in photography as a respectable art form and its consequent appearance in galleries, art museums, and extensive private collections. Until recently much of this professional interest was centered around vintage prints, work done personally by photographers who are no longer living. These prints are becoming rare and are, therefore, valuable. This market will probably stabilize within a few years as the majority of these prints find their way through various dealers' hands, becoming more expensive with each transaction, and eventually settle in the archives of museums or the files of wealthy private collectors. There is also substantial traffic in the work of some of the better-known contemporary photographers. This trend seems to be increasing. Whether this will continue or not is a question still to be answered.

A hopeful sign is the increase of color prints in museum exhibitions, especially in the Museum of Modern Art. Previously, collectors, both public and private, have generally considered color photographs to be a risky investment because of the notorious instability of their dyes. Improvements in color permanency will undoubtedly lead to a wider acceptance of color and we can probably expect to see color prints made, exhibited, and collected with increasing frequency in the near future.

Marie Cosindas's subtle Polacolor still-lives and portraits were some of the first contemporary color photographs to be taken seriously as collectible art, although there had been some previous traffic in dye-transfer prints by masters of scenic landscape, like Eliot Porter. Subsequent exhibitions in major galleries and museums of the work of William Eggleston, Stephen Shore, Joel Meyerowitz, and Mark Cohen have emphasized the potential of color in contemporary photographic art.

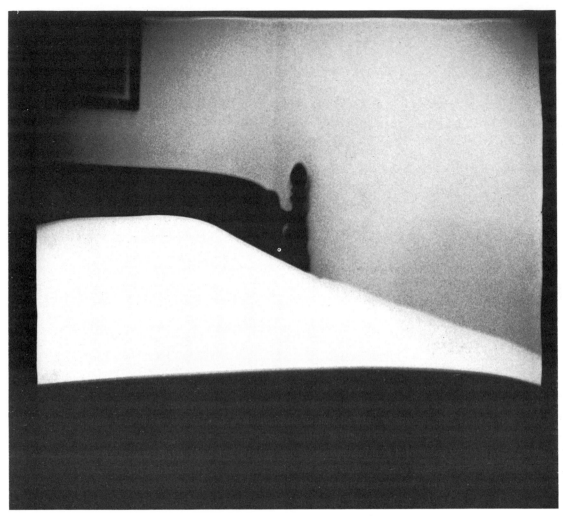

Figure 1.36
Nancy Rexroth. *A Woman's Bed, Ohio 1969.* (Courtesy of the photographer)

However, black-and-white photography is still healthy and is used in a variety of ways. Technically, one extreme is represented by Nick Nixon, who combines a social documentary approach with the exquisite quality of the large format contact print; the other may be Nancy Rexroth's ethereal essay, "Iowa," done with the $1.50 "Diana" plastic camera. Between these two extremes, the majority of contemporary photographers seem to prefer 35mm cameras and the prevailing style, in straight photography at least, seems to be casual, personal, informal, direct, and, not infrequently, pretentiously unpretentious.

There is still a considerable interest in manipulated and mixed-media imagery. Jerry Uelsmann continues to produce his amazing surrealistic montages. Todd Walker's off-set publications of delicately multi-hued solarized nudes are still esoterically intriguing. Robert Heinecken's work is still unpredictably varied in material and style but is predictably shocking to conservative tastes. Betty Hahn is still exploring historic processes and embellishing them with handwork; and there are many others who combine photographic imagery with other techniques such as drawing or painting, for example, James Henkel, Patty Carroll, and Marcia Resnick. The Polaroid SX-70 images provide Lucas Samaras, Les Krims, and Ardine Nelson, among others, with raw material for bizarre transformations, and Jill Lynne is one of a number of workers who are investigating machine art with the Xerox color copier. (See the "Portfolio" for examples of the work of some of these artists.)

We can only speculate about future trends but a few possibilities are apparent. The present materials of photography are in short supply and will become more expensive. It seems likely that new processes, based on more readily available materials, will have to be devised if the steadily increasing interest in photography is to be satisfied. It also seems likely that our attitude toward making and consuming photographs must change, if only because our physical world, our culture, and we, as individuals, are changing. But

Black-and-white photography is still healthy

We can only speculate about future trends

But man will continue to express himself in photographic imagery

of one thing we can probably be sure: man has a fundamental need to express himself in imagery and photography, no matter what form it may take in the future, will continue to be used to satisfy that need.

Summary

The camera obscura was invented long before there was any real use for it. At first it was a curiosity, then an aid for drawing. Niépce is credited with producing the first camera image in 1826. He later formed a partnership with Daguerre to work toward an improved process. At the same time others, such as Talbot and Bayard, worked independently toward the same goal.

After the announcement of the daguerreotype process in 1839, the evolution of photography was rapid. Archer's invention of the collodion wet-plate process in 1851 established the basic procedures that are used today. Numerous methods were devised for producing photographic images in pigments and inks. Eventually this experimentation led to the introduction of such processes as carbon, collotype, woodburytype, and photogravure. Flexible film was introduced commercially in 1888 and in a few years George Eastman began to sell Kodak cameras with the slogan "You press the button; we do the rest." The introduction of Autochrome film in 1907 marked the successful end of a long search for a practical color material, a search which began almost as soon as photography was invented.

The popularity of photography has grown as rapidly as its technical advancements. Photojournalism had its roots in the documentation of the Civil War by Mathew Brady, the explorations of the West by Timothy O'Sullivan and William H. Jackson, and the studies of the immigrants and child laborers by Lewis Hine. By 1900 halftone illustrations were beginning to appear in books and magazines. This enabled the development of the picture story magazines and fields of photoillustration and advertising photography.

Almost from the beginning art and photography had a tremendous influence on each other. At first photographers followed the current painting styles, which were undoubtedly influenced by photography's unique visual characteristics. Photographers, such as Alfred Stieglitz and Edward Steichen, encouraged many young photographers and promoted photography as an acceptable art form. Exhibitions of photographs in major museums, especially the Museum of Modern Art, have given the medium new status.

Technical advances in photography have been astounding. However, a crisis may result as raw materials become increasingly scarce and as the medium's popularity increases daily. Photography will continue to fulfill the fundamental human need to communicate visually.

Outline

Light-Sensitive Materials

Image Formation
Pinhole
Lens

2 Introduction to the Photographic Process

Light is a form of energy

Direct-positive and negative images

An image can be printed-out or developed-out

Light-Sensitive Materials

Light is a form of energy. It affects many materials in various ways. Sunlight bleaches dyes, darkens freshly sawn pine, turns plants green, makes some plastic materials disintegrate, and reddens or tans human skin.

Photography takes advantage of this property of light. By shielding part of a sensitive surface and allowing light to act on the uncovered portion, a simple *photogram* can be produced. If the material is bleached by the action of light, as dyes are, the shaded portion of the surface will remain relatively dark and the illuminated area will be lighter in tone. This results in a *direct-positive* image, one in which the light produces light and shadow results in dark image tone. A *negative* image results when the light effect is reversed; that is, when the illuminated area turns dark in tone and the shaded area remains light-toned. This is the photographic process that sunbathers unwittingly use to print photograms of bikinis on their bare skins.

In these examples the image is formed gradually, but directly, by the action of light alone. An image formed this way is said to have been *printed-out*. Some modern photographic materials can be used to produce printed-out images, however, it's more satisfactory to *develop-out* the image by treating the exposed material with a chemical developer solution.

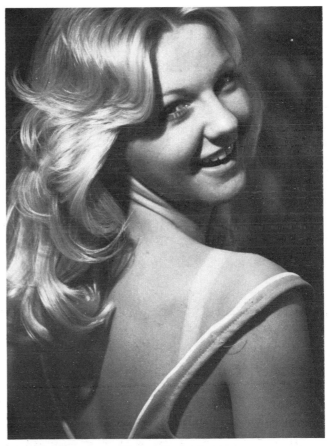

Figure 2.1
Suntan pattern on bather (Photo by Jim Terry)

The latent image is invisible

Gelatin is uniquely suitable for photographic emulsions

Common halides are silver chloride, bromide, and iodide

Silver images must be fixed

A pinhole will form a useful image

It takes a relatively short exposure to form a developable image; in fact, the image is *latent* (invisible) until the developer makes it appear. A developed image is also stronger than a printed-out image; that is, its dark tones are darker and the contrast of the image is higher. Generally, a developed image is also more neutral in color. Printed-out images are usually brownish, pinkish, lavendar, or slaty-blue, depending on what material they have been sensitized with.

Virtually all photographic films and papers currently used are coated with emulsions of silver compounds suspended in hardened gelatin. Gelatin has a number of unique properties which make it suitable for this purpose. It is easy to apply to the base material during manufacture. It absorbs the developing solutions quickly and evenly but is not dissolved. It protects the sensitive silver compounds, improves their image-forming efficiency, and, when dry, forms a tough, durable, uniform surface.

A great many silver compounds are sensitive to light but most modern photographic emulsions employ the halogen salts or halides of silver. (The halogens are the chemical elements fluorine, chlorine, bromine, and iodine.) Silver chloride, bromide, and iodide are most commonly used and they are blended in various proportions to produce emulsions of widely diverse characteristics. In general the *slower* (less sensitive) materials, such as *contact printing papers,* are sensitized with emulsion mixtures rich in silver chloride. *Faster* papers, such as those designed for *projection printing,* are likely to be coated with *chlorobromide* emulsions. Film emulsions contain higher proportions of silver bromide and iodide, as a general rule.

It's a curious fact that the chloride emulsions, which are the least sensitive of the developing-out papers, are most satisfactory for printing-out experiments. They form a relatively rich and contrasty printed-out image quickly in strong light. Film emulsions, on the other hand, do not form satisfactory printed-out images under any conditions of exposure, although they are thousands of times more sensitive to light than papers are, when used in the conventional developing-out process.

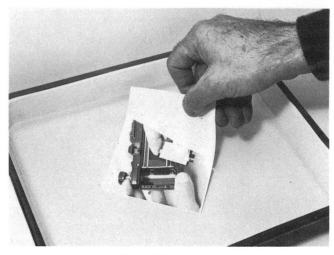

Figure 2.2
Half-image appearing in developer

Regardless of how they are formed, silver images are not stable until they have been *fixed* by a chemical treatment which dissolves the unused halides from the emulsion. If not removed these still-sensitive compounds will gradually discolor and darken, degrading the highlights of the image and eventually ruining it. There are a number of chemicals which can dissolve the unused halides without harming the silver image. They are all referred to commonly as *hypo,* in honor of Herschel's discovery of the chemical he mistakenly called "sodium *hypo*sulphite." Actually it should have been named sodium thiosulfate; perhaps, if Herschel had named it correctly, we'd call the fixing bath "thio" now, instead of "hypo."

Image Formation

Photogram images are the shadow records of objects placed on or close to the paper surface. Camera images result from light patterns projected onto the sensitive film surface by the lens. Actually, it's possible to form a useful image in a camera without any lens at all; a simple pinhole will do the job.

Only those light rays which are aimed at the pinhole can pass through

The image will be upside down and backwards

Pinhole images are not very sharp; diffraction is a problem

A pinhole will not transmit much light to the film

A pinhole forms images by allowing only a single, thin ray of light from each object point to reach the film surface. This is an easy concept to visualize if you consider, for example, photographing the stars in the Big Dipper constellation. Stars can be considered to be *point sources* of light because they are so far away that they have no measurable dimension. They are, however, radiating countless rays of light in all directions so that each star illuminates the entire earth's hemisphere that faces it. If you point a pinhole camera at the Big Dipper, only those light rays which happen to be aimed straight toward the pinhole can pass through to the film. Therefore, each star in the constellation can contribute only a single ray of light to the image, and, since light travels in straight lines, the star images on the film surface form a miniature duplicate of the constellation.

Because the entering rays must cross each other at the pinhole, the image they form is upside-down and backwards. This is easily remedied, however. When the film has been developed it can be turned right-side-up and, when viewed from the back, is seen unreversed.

As a device for forming images, a pinhole has two major drawbacks: its images are not really very sharp and it works very slowly. The image points can never be smaller than the pinhole itself, so, if the image is to be usefully clear and adequately defined, the pinhole must be very small. In practice, however, it cannot be made extremely small or image sharpness will actually be reduced by *diffraction,* a kind of turbulence in the light rays, induced by the edges of the aperture and somewhat similar to the water spray that results from a faulty hose nozzle. It is impossible, therefore, to produce a truly sharp pinhole image; image quality is degraded if the hole is either too large or too small.

Even the largest useful pinhole is tiny and the amount of light it transmits to the film is correspondingly small. A pinhole camera, therefore, would not be suitable for actually photographing the Big Dipper. The light from the constellation is extremely dim. After being attenuated by the tiny pinhole, there would be virtually nothing left to affect the film.

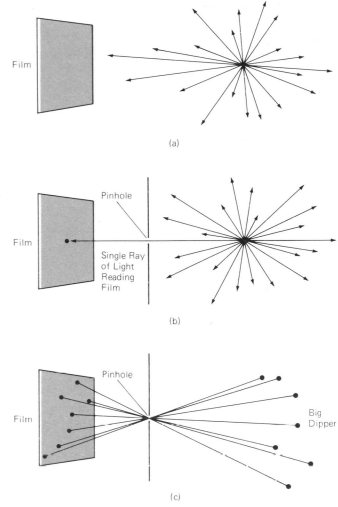

(a)

(b)

(c)

Figure 2.3
a. If film is exposed directly to light from a single point source, such as a star, the uncontrolled rays affect the entire surface equally and the film is simply fogged without forming a useful image.

b. If the film is shielded from most of the starlight and only a single ray is allowed to strike the film surface, only a tiny area of the film is exposed and an image of the star is formed.

c. Each of the seven stars of the Big Dipper constellation projects a single light ray through the pinhole to the film surface to form an image of the constellation.

A lens can transmit more light and form a sharper image

But it must be focused

Nearby objects may not fall within the useful depth of field

Films are generally faster than papers

Camera lenses were invented to solve these problems. A good lens can focus light rays to much finer points than any pinhole can form and, because of its much larger aperture, a lens admits a great deal more light, possibly several thousand times more.

Consider the Big Dipper again and imagine that you have pointed a regular camera at it. If the effective diameter of the lens opening is one inch, for example, the lens will admit a cylindrical beam of light one inch in diameter from each star within its field of view. These cylinders of light do not reach the film directly. The lens converges each one into a cone, and, if the camera is properly adjusted, just the tip of each light cone touches the film surface to form the star image. If the camera is not focused properly, the light cones fail to converge precisely on the film surface, and the resulting star images are visible as *circles of confusion,* rather than points.

When photographing stars, or any other objects which are very far away, the lens is focused on *infinity,* and the image light cones all converge neatly on the surface of the film. When the objects are closer than infinity, but at different distances from the camera, the image points are formed at different distances from the lens. Under these conditions, if the camera is focused on a nearby object, its image will be sharp, but distant objects will be imaged as blurred shapes. In this situation a pinhole may be better than a lens. Although no portion of a pinhole image is critically sharp, it does not have to be focused and is, at least, uniformly sharp for objects at all distances. A lens can produce more precisely defined image details for objects at some specific distance, but may not, at the same time, be able to include closer or more distant objects within its *depth of field* (range of acceptable sharpness).

Although some cameras can be hand-loaded with sensitized paper, if you have any reason to do so, they all normally use film. In either case the image formed, after exposure and development, is negative. For camera use, film is preferable to paper for two reasons: we seldom have use for a negative print on paper, and most films are much faster than papers, and, therefore, require much less exposure to form a useful image.

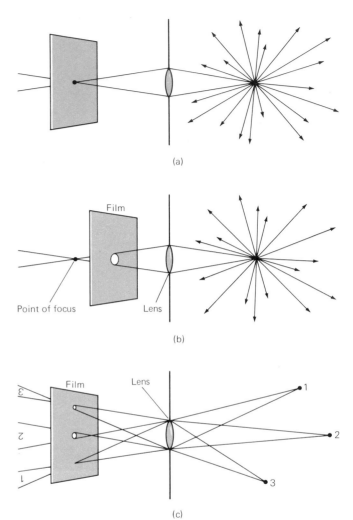

(a)

(b)

(c)

Figure 2.4 ◄
a. A very large pinhole will admit a bundle of rays and form a blurred image area (rather than an image point) on the film. A lens can concentrate these light rays to focus at a point. If the film is positioned accurately at the focus point, it can record a precise image of the star—much brighter than the image formed by a pinhole.

b. If the film is not placed precisely at the focal plane, the converging rays will form blurred circles of confusion rather than sharply defined points and we say the image is out-of-focus.

c. Light rays from very distant objects will focus on a single plane and will all be recorded sharply when the camera is focused at infinity. Objects closer than infinity, however, form images at different points behind the lens. No single adjustment of the camera focus will render them all equally sharp.

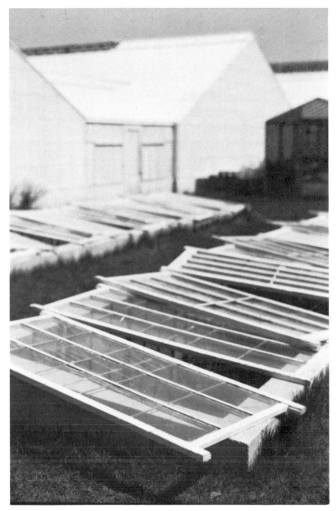

Figure 2.5
In this photograph the camera lens was focused on the glass frame in the foreground. At maximum aperture the lens renders the foreground sharply but depth of field is shallow and the background greenhouses are badly blurred.

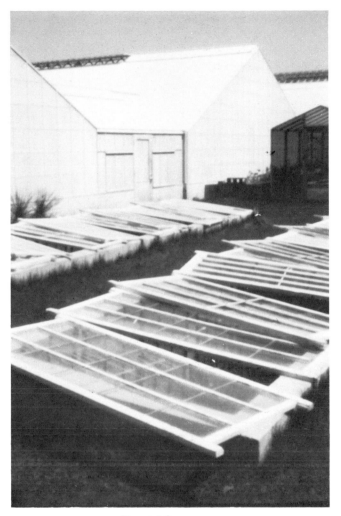

Figure 2.6
Although contrast in the shadows is reduced and fine details are blurred, this pinhole image is uniformly sharp from front to rear.

Negatives can be printed by contact or projection

A positive print is a negative of the negative

Xerox prints are examples of a direct positive process

The term "negative," when used alone, almost invariably refers to a film negative image. Film negatives are generally not useful as finished images, but are intended to be printed on sensitized paper, either by contact, which means that the negative is placed in contact with the paper emulsion and exposed to light, or by projection. A machine called an *enlarger* is used for projection printing and, as the name implies, the projected image is usually, but not necessarily always, larger than the negative itself. Most enlargers can also be adjusted to project images of the same size or smaller than the negative, but this is rarely necessary or desirable.

The term "print" usually means a positive image on paper. Strictly speaking, a print is a negative of the negative, which means, of course, that the subject tones, which were reversed in the film negative, are re-reversed in the print. A positive image, therefore, resembles the original subject.

If, for some reason, we needed a negative image on paper, we would normally refer to it as a *negative print*. Similarly, if we wanted to produce a positive image on film, we might describe it as a *positive* or a *film positive* or a *positive transparency*. A more precise term, diapositive, which is popular in Europe and occasionally used here, refers to a positive transparency intended to be viewed directly or by projection like an ordinary color slide. The term "direct positive," which was mentioned previously, also has a specific meaning. It refers to a positive image which has been produced without having gone through a separate or identifiable negative stage. Xerox prints are good examples of direct positive images. In conventional photography direct positive materials are rare and specialized.

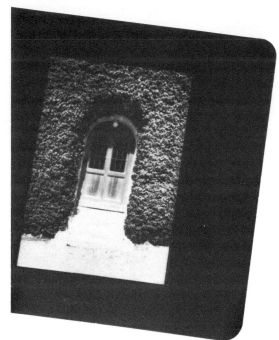

Figure 2.7
a. Positive transparency

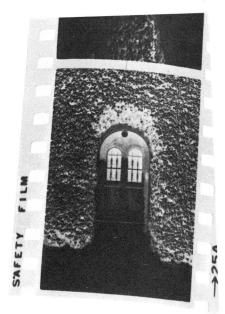

b. Negative

Summary

In photography, light rays reflected from an object enter the camera through the lens and are focused onto the film surface. This surface is coated with a light-sensitive emulsion of silver halides, which absorb the light to produce a latent or invisible image. The film is then developed into a visible silver image and then fixed to remove the unused halides. The developed film, called a negative, is then washed and dried.

The negative is printed either by placing it in direct contact with the paper or by projecting it onto the paper through an enlarger. This forms another latent image which is also developed and fixed. The result is a positive image which resembles the original object in tonality.

Outline

3 Cameras, Lenses, and Related Equipment

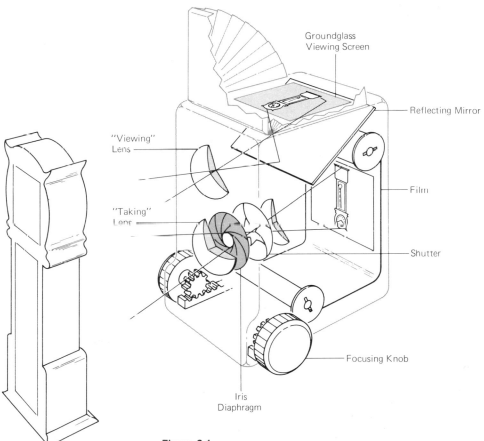

Groundglass
Viewing Screen

Reflecting Mirror

"Viewing"
Lens

Film

"Taking"
Lens

Shutter

Focusing Knob

Iris
Diaphragm

Figure 3.1
Camera function diagram

Cameras: Types and Features

All cameras are basically alike. Regardless of its other features every useful camera must be a lighttight box, equipped with a lens on one side and a film-holding device on the other. It must provide a viewfinder function which allows pointing the camera and composing the image with some accuracy, and it must have a shutter mechanism which can be opened to admit light through the lens and closed to restrict light when it is not wanted. Additionally, most cameras will provide some means of adjusting the lens-to-film distance so the image can be focused accurately. They will also include an *iris diaphragm* or other device, to constrict the lens aperture and thus reduce the light intensity on the film surface, when that is desirable.

In addition to these essentials, modern cameras may incorporate a bewildering array of convenience features which make them easier to operate, enhance their various abilities, and, unfortunately, make them very expensive. Before you buy a camera, you should try to decide which features are important to you and which you can get along without. Then you can select, from the group of cameras which have the features you want, the one that feels best in your hands, is most convenient for you to operate, and gives you the best viewfinder image for focusing and composing.

The simplest cameras have open-frame or small optical finders

They suffer from parallax and other things

Some may not focus; others may permit scale focusing

The very simplest camera types may have either *open-frame* viewfinders or small optical finders like miniature reversed telescopes. In both cases you look *through* the finder at the subject. The finder image covers approximately the same area that the camera lens will record and provides a good indication of the picture shape. Finders of this type cannot be used to focus the camera, nor do they provide any indication of *depth of field*—the region of the subject from front to rear which will be acceptably sharp in the picture. They also suffer from *parallax error* because the lens and the viewfinder "see" the subject from slightly different points of view. Although *parallax* is usually insignificant for subjects more than a few feet from the camera, it can, in some cases, lead to miscalculation of the exact boundaries of the image area or, for example, let you photograph someone with a tree growing out of his ear, despite the fact that the viewfinder image may have shown tree and ear to be safely separated. An extreme example of parallax error is the possibility that you might forget to remove the lens cap and take a lot of pictures of nothing, assuming, because the viewfinder image was visible, that the lens was functioning normally.

Very simple cameras of this type may not have any focusing adjustment. If not, they will have been set at the factory to focus most sharply somewhere in the middle distance and will usually take acceptably sharp pictures of any subject more than a few feet from the camera. They may not have adjustable lens openings or shutter speeds either. In this case they will be restricted to use in normal daylight conditions with general purpose films, although some of them will accept *flashcubes* or *electronic flash* units to permit their use in poor light conditions.

A few viewfinder-type cameras permit *scale focusing,* which means that you must measure or estimate the distance from camera to subject and adjust the focusing control manually. In some cases, especially on the small *pocket cameras* which use the 110-size film cartridges, the focusing scale is calibrated with visual

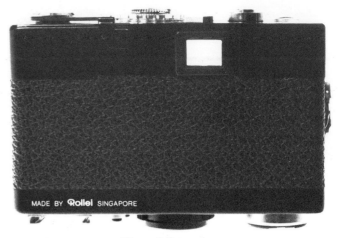

Figure 3.2
Frame or optical finder

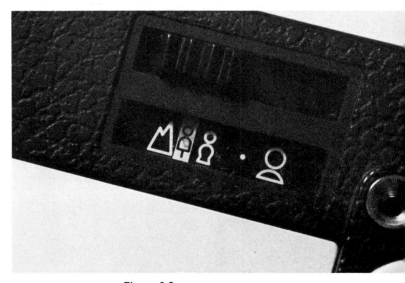

Figure 3.3
Scale focus on 110 camera

Rangefinder cameras focus quickly and accurately

Some will accept interchangeable lenses

symbols rather than specific distance numbers. For example, a stylized silhouette of a mountain may indicate the proper focus setting for distant objects; a full figure silhouette may indicate the setting for mid-range subjects; and a stylized head or head-and-shoulder silhouette may indicate the proper setting for close-up focusing. Although this may seem rather imprecise, these small cameras provide great depth of field and absolute accuracy of focus is not essential.

The better cameras of this type include *rangefinders* for faster and more accurate focusing. A rangefinder consists of a pair of mirrors or prisms, placed two or three inches apart, and arranged so the eye, in looking through one of them, sees a double image of the subject. The other mirror can be pivoted to make the images converge and is connected to the focusing control of the camera so, as the lens is moved in focusing, the two images are always superimposed on the subject point of focus.

Rangefinder cameras, when well-designed and constructed, provide an excellent finder image, partially corrected for parallax error, and very brilliant. Focusing is fast and very accurate, and cameras of this type are particularly suitable for use in poor light conditions or in situations which require accurate framing of rapidly moving objects. The better rangefinder cameras will accept interchangeable lenses, automatically presenting the appropriate viewfinder field for (usually) one wide-angle and one telephoto lens, in addition to the normal field of view. In general, extreme *wide-angle* or *telephoto* lenses require accessory finders, and the inherent advantages of the rangefinder camera—operating speed, accuracy of focus, finder brilliance, and accuracy—may be compromised or lost.

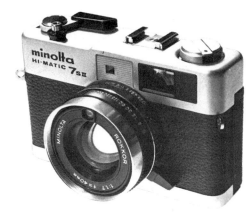

Figure 3.4
Rangefinder camera

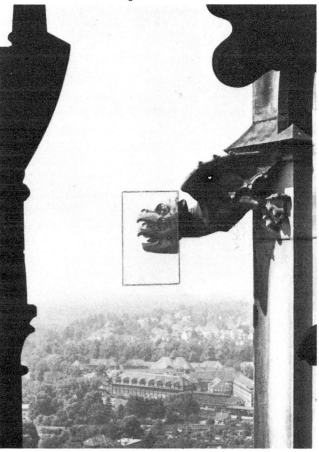

Figure 3.5 ►
When a rangefinder camera is not focused properly the image will appear something like this. When the double image blends into one—as you can make it do by turning the focusing control—the image is in focus.

Many are equipped with built-in exposure meters

Reflex cameras form groundglass images

The TLR is really two cameras in one

The TLR viewfinder image is laterally reversed

SLRs combine viewing and taking functions in one lens

The pentaprism finder system has many advantages

In many instances, cameras of this type are equipped with built-in *exposure meters.* If the meter is coupled to the lens and shutter, matching the meter pointer (visible in the viewfinder) with an index mark of some sort can be accomplished by adjusting the camera controls, and when this is done, the camera is set to expose the film properly. The light-sensitive photocell, which actuates the meter pointer, is usually built into the camera body and is designed to "see" about the same area of the subject that the lens will cover.

Reflex cameras reflect the viewfinder image onto a groundglass screen as two-dimensional images to be looked *at* rather than *through.* This tends to simplify the problems of visualizing what the finished camera image will look like, makes composition easier and more precise (for most people), and makes it possible to appraise the sharpness of the image visually as the camera focusing controls are manipulated.

In the *twin-lens reflex* (TLR) design, the lens which forms the viewfinder image is optically similar to the camera lens itself and the two lenses are mounted as close together as possible to reduce parallax. The TLR is really, therefore, two cameras operating as one; the upper unit serving merely to form the viewing image, while the lower unit contains the film and records the image. An inclined mirror, angled down behind the viewing lens, reflects its image up to the groundglass screen set into the top of the camera and, because the viewing and taking lenses focus together, the film image is in focus when the image on the groundglass appears sharp. The TLR is usually held at waist level and, looking down into the finder, the image is seen upright but laterally reversed, a characteristic which takes some getting used to. The groundglass image is partially shielded from outside light by a folding metal hood. A simple lens, built into the hood, can be flipped up to magnify the image and when the eye is placed close to this magnifying lens the image can be seen larger and more clearly for focusing and composing at eye-level.

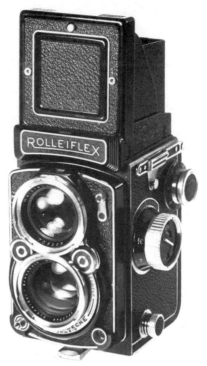

Figure 3.6
Twin-lens reflex

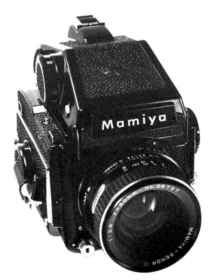

Figure 3.7
Single-lens reflex

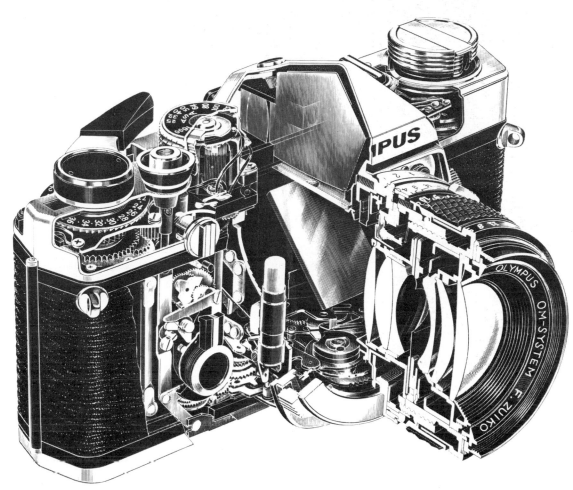

Figure 3.8
Cutaway view of the Olympus OM–1, a
typical prism reflex 35mm camera.
(Courtesy of Olympus Camera Corp.)

Single-lens reflex (SLR) cameras have become much more popular than TLRs. SLR design combines the viewing and taking functions in one lens so there is no parallax error at all and the image seen in the viewfinder is, in most respects, identical with the image that the film will record. The mirror which reflects the image upward to the viewing screen is hinged in the SLR and flips up out of the way when the shutter release is pressed, allowing the image light to reach the film plane. During the actual interval of film exposure the visual image in the finder is lost but, in almost all SLRs, the *instant return mirror* drops back into position as soon as the shutter closes, and the viewfinder image is restored. In practice the brief loss of the visual image at the critical instant of exposure is usually only a minor annoyance. In some cases, however, the image blackout is troublesome and, in situations such as following erratically moving objects, a rangefinder camera is generally more convenient.

The lateral reversal of the viewfinder image, which is characteristic of simple reflex cameras, can be corrected by the addition of a *pentaprism* to the viewing system. *Prism reflexes* are necessarily bulkier and heavier than cameras without prisms but the prism system has many advantages. In addition to the fact that the image is oriented correctly, the prism assembly provides eye-level viewing of a magnified, brilliant image. Because the viewed image is formed by the same lens that takes the picture, it will show the effects of focus changes, depth of field, and any other factor that will influence the final picture. Wide-angle or telephoto lenses can be used without major difficulty. Very long telephoto lenses may crop off the top of the viewfinder image in some cameras, but the film image is not affected and will be complete.

In spite of the fact that the SLR groundglass image is well shielded from outside light and is brightened (especially in the corners) by a built-in *fresnel lens,* it is not always easy to focus. The groundglass texture tends to obscure very fine image details and the concentric rings of the fresnel lens, although minute, contribute to this problem. In poor light the image becomes

Microprisms cause an out-of-focus image to shimmer

Rangefinder prisms displace the halves of an out-of-focus image

Special focusing screens are available

Far-sighted people will have trouble with some SLR finders

Most small cameras are equipped with coupled exposure meters

Aperture priority; shutter priority

too dim to see clearly and things become even worse if the lens in use is slow (does not admit much light) or if filters or other lens attachments which absorb light are being used. To make focusing simpler under these conditions, most SLR groundglass screens incorporate some type of *focusing aid,* usually a *microprism grid* or a *rangefinder prism* assembly, or some combination of these.

The microprism grid usually occupies a small circular area in the center of the groundglass and consists of dozens of minute pyramids of plastic. When the image is not in focus the pyramid faces disperse the image light so the image seems to shimmer, especially when the camera is moved slightly. A well-focused image appears rather coarse-grained, but intact, and no shimmer is visible.

The rangefinder prism consists of two shallow wedges of glass or plastic laid side by side, pointing in opposite directions. Like the microprisms, the wedges refract light and react only to image light from the margins of the lens. These marginal rays are bent most sharply in focusing so the image they form appears to go in and out of focus abruptly. The out-of-focus image appears divided with each half displaced along the intersection of the prism wedges. Focusing the image brings the image halves into alignment, and the image form appears whole.

Neither device is as accurate as a real rangefinder but both are usually better than a plain groundglass. Unfortunately, when used with a lens of inappropriate focal length or when used with any lens at a small aperture, one or both halves of the rangefinder prism will appear black. Under the same conditions, the microprism grid simply darkens into a mealy-looking area of texture and refuses to fracture the image or shimmer. For this reason, most manufacturers offer separate prism-equipped screens for use with wide-angle and telephoto lenses. If you plan to specialize in working with one of these lenses, the special groundglass screen will be a good investment.

In some SLR finders the image appears to hang in space quite close to the eye. Other camera designs provide apparent image distances of up to several feet. If you are far-sighted, you will discover that you can't use some camera finders easily, but will have no trouble with others. Investigate several brands; they are not all alike.

If you wear glasses but prefer to photograph without them, dioptric correction lenses can be added to most viewfinders to correct near- or far-sightedness and special correction lenses, ground to your personal prescription, are offered by some manufacturers. You can, of course, wear your glasses while photographing but they may keep you from placing your eye close enough to the finder eyepiece to see the whole image area. Camera finders differ in this *eye relief* characteristic. Try several varieties. You may find one that allows comfortable full-field vision even with your glasses on.

Most cameras which take 35mm or smaller size film are equipped with built-in exposure meters and, almost without exception, they are coupled to the camera lens and shutter controls. In the *match-needle* or *match-pointer* design (common in SLRs), a paddle-shaped pointer (lollipop) situated near one edge of the viewfinder, is controlled by the shutter speed dial and moves in a gentle arc as the dial is adjusted. The meter pointer, which is also visible, responds to changes in subject illumination and movements of the aperture control. When the aperture is adjusted to superimpose the pointer over the lollipop, the camera controls are set to expose the film properly.

In some cameras the lollipop is missing and the meter pointer can be matched to some fixed index mark by adjusting either lens or shutter, or both. In a number of designs the moving pointers have been replaced by patterns of *light-emitting diodes* (LEDs) which glow brightly to indicate proper exposure or, in a different sequence or arrangement, to indicate various degrees of under- or over-exposure. As an added feature, some viewfinders also display the actual lens and shutter settings in illuminated windows in the dark margins of the image area.

Figure 3.9

a. This SLR viewing screen contains a central rangefinder prism focusing aid, diagonally divided; the next ring is a microprism grid; next is a ring of fine-textured groundglass for visual focusing; the rest of the screen area is a fresnel lens, whose concentric line pattern shows in the corners of this detail. This picture shows the image focused on the crest of the snow-covered hill in the middle distance; the building corner is slightly out-of-focus.

b. When the camera is focused for close-up, both the building corner and the hill are out-of-focus.

c. Stopping the lens down renders both focusing aids useless and groundglass grain shows strongly.

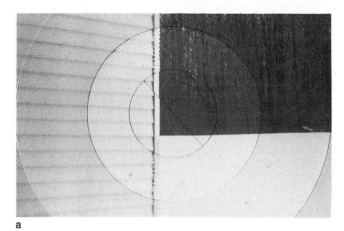

a

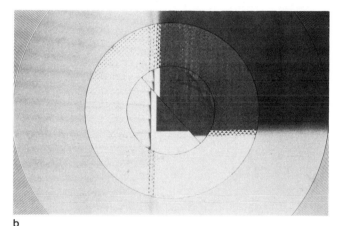

b

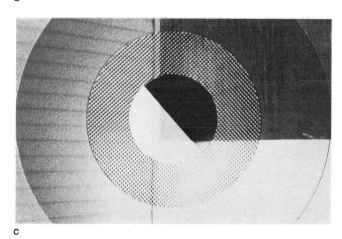

c

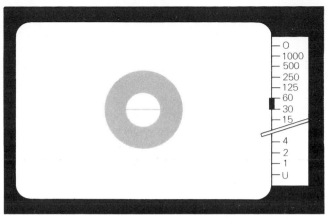

Figure 3.10

Typical viewing screen illustrating aperture-priority automatic metering system. The pointer indicates that the camera has selected a shutter speed of ⅛th second. The groundglass screen is equipped with a rangefinder prism (central divided circle) and a microprism grid (larger textured circle). The mark between 30 and 60 is an index for checking the meter battery.

There are quite a few cameras on the market which offer automatic exposure control. In many cases this really means semiautomatic because you must do part of the work manually. In *aperture priority* (or *aperture preferred*) systems, you select and set the lens aperture, and the camera will then select the appropriate shutter speed. *Shutter priority* systems are the reverse; you set the shutter speed and the camera adjusts its aperture to match. There are arguments in favor of both systems but, in my opinion, the aperture priority is more versatile, since it provides a greater range of automatic operation.

Programmed exposure automation is featured in a number of inexpensive 35mm cameras and 110-size pocket cameras. In this system the camera selects both lens and shutter settings automatically in response to changes in subject illumination. The two adjustments are rather closely matched throughout the total automated range; that is, the camera will select its maximum aperture and longest exposure time in dim light, ad-

Photocells:
CdS, SPD, GPD, SBC, GAP (GaAsP)

The trend is toward more electronics in camera design

The camera shutter controls the duration of film exposure

BTL shutters are part of the lens assembly

FP shutters are built into the camera body

just to a medium aperture and moderately fast shutter speed in normal light, and *stop down* to its smallest aperture with its highest shutter speed in very bright light. In the automatic mode you have no choice of settings; you take what the camera gives you. However, some models will permit switching off the automatic function for manual operation.

New types of light-sensitive cells, introduced within the last few years, have revolutionized exposure meter design. The cadmium sulfide cell (CdS), which made built-in meters and automated exposure systems practical, is commendably sensitive but suffers from slow response time, memory effects, poor color response, and temperature sensitivity. It is now being replaced by the *silicon photo-diode* (SPD) or the *gallium-arsenide-phosphide* (GaAsP or GAP) cell, commonly known as the *gallium photo-diode* (GPD). Both silicon and gallium photo-diodes have extremely fast response time, excellent sensitivity, good stability, and freedom from memory. Silicon photo-diodes, when blue-filtered (*silicon-blue cells* or SBCs), have good color response. Gallium cells do not normally require filtering.

CdS cells function satisfactorily on simple battery power. SPDs and GPDs require complex electronic circuitry to amplify and stabilize their response. Although this sounds risky and expensive, both systems have proven to be reliable. Modern integrated circuitry techniques are so sophisticated that their costs have been kept low. In fact, the trend is toward more electric and electronic emphasis in camera design. This should lead to smaller, lighter cameras of greater precision and reliability, and eventually to lower cost. The major drawback is their increasing dependence on battery power, but that is a small price to pay for the convenience and versatility of the new designs.

The purpose of the camera *shutter* is to control the time, or duration, of film exposure. Except for the actual period of exposure, the shutter is closed to protect the film from light. When the *shutter release* is pressed to make an exposure, the shutter snaps open, allowing light to reach the film surface. It remains open for a selected interval, then snaps closed to terminate the exposure.

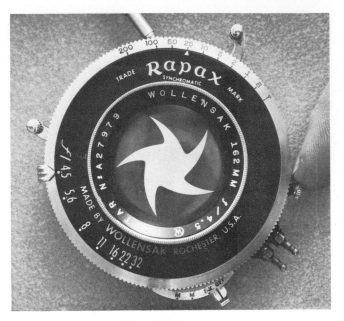

Figure 3.11
BTL shutter with blades partly open

There are two general types of shutters in common use, *between-the-lens* and *focal plane*. Between-the-lens (BTL) shutters are part of the lens assembly and operate in a space between the lens elements. The thin metal leaves of the shutter are arranged coaxially with the lens axis and are pivoted so they can swing out to open and admit light, or swing in to overlap and restrict it.

Focal plane (FP) shutters are part of the camera body and usually operate just in front of the film surface. There are two types, *curtain* shutters and, recently, *leaf* or *blade* shutters. Curtain shutters may be made of either thin metal foil or cloth. Two curtains are actually involved. In the closed position, their edges meet or overlap slightly to cover the film completely. During the exposure, the curtains separate and travel across the film surface in tandem, the space between their edges permitting light to reach the film.

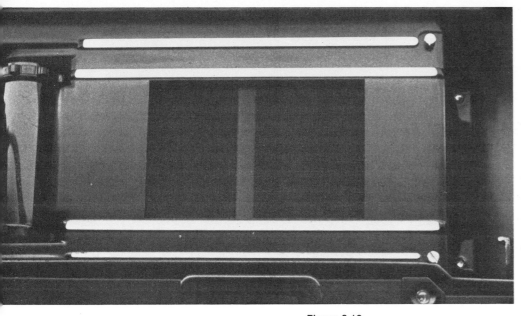

Figure 3.12
Focal plane curtain shutter

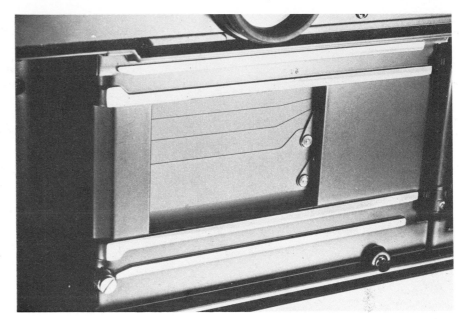

Figure 3.13
Focal plane blade shutter

BTL shutters expose the whole film area at once

FP shutters expose the film area progressively

FP blade shutters are becoming popular

Leaf or blade shutters typically consist of several thin metal leaves in each of two groups, one at the top of the film gate and the other at the bottom. In the closed position, one group of leaves is fanned out to cover the film, with the other group remaining folded. During the exposure cycle the first group of leaves retracts to its folded position, exposing the film. The second group then fans out to cover the film and terminate the exposure.

Because of its location near the optical center of the lens, the BTL shutter illuminates the entire film area uniformly throughout the complete exposure cycle, although the illumination is dimmed during the opening and closing phases. Focal plane shutters, on the other hand, expose the film progressively, wiping the image light across the film surface like a paint roller. BTL shutters, therefore, are more suitable for use with *synchronized flash*. FP shutters cannot be used successfully with electronic flash at high shutter speeds because only a narrow portion of the film surface is exposed at any instant during the exposure interval.

Focal plane shutters provide higher speeds, up to 1/2000th second in some models, but sometimes distort rapidly moving objects. BTL shutters are limited to a maximum speed of about 1/500th second or more and rapidly moving objects are undistorted but may be blurred. BTL shutters are relatively quiet and vibration-free and expose the film evenly. FP shutters, especially at higher speeds, may travel erratically and leave stripes or bands of uneven exposure on the film. Although this effect is usually insignificant, it may show up occasionally in otherwise uniform areas of image tone such as clear skies. FP shutters, by separating lens and shutter functions, permit a wide variety of interchangeable lenses to be used with the camera body and simplify the design of aperture priority shutter automation.

Although the curtain type of FP shutter is the traditional form, the blade shutter is becoming increasingly popular. The newest types are fairly quiet and vibration-free but their main advantages are higher flash synchronization speed of up to about 1/125th second and compact physical dimensions which permit their use in a new generation of smaller, lighter SLRs.

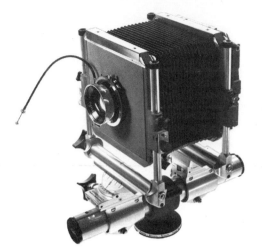

Figure 3.14
View camera

View cameras, in contrast with modern SLRs, are simple in design, unautomated, heavy to carry, clumsy and slow to operate, and expensive. Their lenses and shutters are relatively limited in speed. Their major virtue is their ability to make pictures of incomparable technical quality.

The terms view and field cameras are rather arbitrary. Both types are basically bellows enclosures with spring backs (which accept the film holders) and removable lensboards. Both must be used on a tripod, or similar support, and are focused by inspection of the image, which is formed by the taking lens on a groundglass screen built into the back. The view camera design is usually sturdier and heavier, includes more adjustments, and permits greater interchangeability of parts. Field cameras usually feature light wooden construction, have somewhat limited adjustments, and can be folded into rather compact dimensions for carrying. Both cameras will accept a wide variety of lenses in BTL shutters.

There are quite a few special purpose cameras on the market. The Widelux, for example, uses a unique moving-lens mechanism to make very wide-angle pictures which feature (or suffer from, depending on your point of view) obvious perspective distortion. The Nikonos is a special waterproof camera to be used under water or in other wet or dusty environments which might damage a normal camera. The Gowlandflex is a limited production TLR which uses $4'' \times 5''$ sheet film. The Minox (about the size of a short, fat cigar) can be carried anywhere and takes fine snapshots on miniature rollfilm. There are many others.

In this category, the Polaroid cameras, and the somewhat similar Kodaks, deserve special mention. The newest models of these cameras take color pictures which develop themselves outside the camera. They feature automatic exposure control and, in some models, motorized print ejection and film advance. Unlike the older Polaroid films, these newer materials are litter-free and, Polaroid prints, at least, are relatively stable and colorfast.

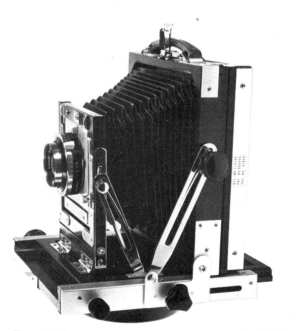

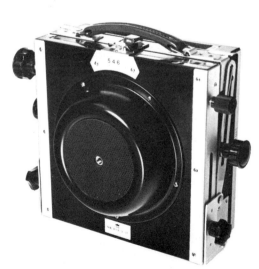

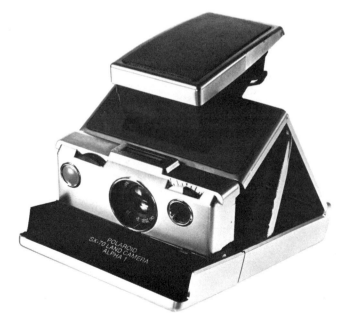

Figure 3.15
a. Field camera (unfolded)

b. Field camera (folded)

Figure 3.16
SX-70 camera

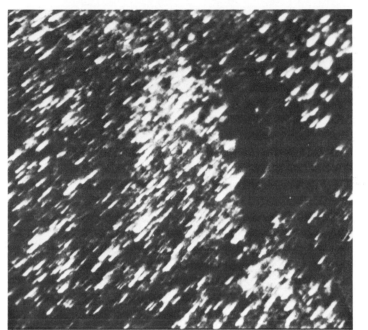

a

A good general purpose lens must form a sharp image

b

Lenses: Features, Function, and Calibration

A good general purpose camera lens must, first of all, form a sharply defined image, free from *color fringes* and other optical blurring effects. It must form this fine image on a reasonably flat plane so the film can record it, and the image should be free from obvious linear distortion. The image should be fairly uniformly illuminated, even in the corners (absolutely uniform illumination is theoretically impossible), and should not be marred by *flare* spots or streaks. Finally, the lens should be capable of covering a fairly wide field of view and should have a large usable aperture to admit a lot of light. No lens does all of these things perfectly but many modern lenses come satisfactorily close.

Lenses form less-than-perfect images because inherent defects in material, design, and construction show up as *aberrations.* Some aberrations are natural characteristics of simple lenses. For example, a simple lens tends to form its best image on a saucer-shaped plane. This *curvature of field* is identified as a problem

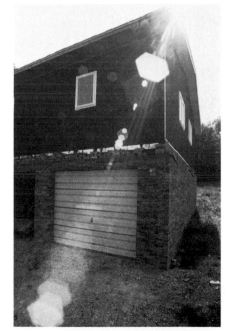

c

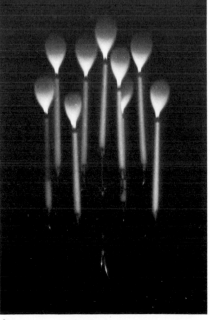

d

Figure 3.17
a. Spherical aberration is responsible for the soft-sharp quality of this photograph. This picture was made at the lens maximum aperture (f/2.9). When stopped down to f/4, or farther, it is quite sharp.

b. This enlarged detail from the corners of a transparency shows how the lens focused blue light. Some of the blue streaking is probably due to ultraviolet light and could have been reduced somewhat by using a skylight (Wratten 1A) filter over the camera lens. In the color transparency, and prints made from it, the streaks show as red-yellow blobs with sharp blue tails.

c. You have to try hard to produce this kind of flare with modern coated lenses, but it's possible. The smaller spots, spaced randomly around the flare pattern, are caused by dust spots on the front surface of the lens, glowing in the sunlight. To avoid problems like this, keep the lens free from dust particles and always keep the lens shaded so direct light cannot strike it.

d. Here coma is used purposely to form these decorative candle flames.

Correcting lens aberrations requires special glass and careful design and construction

Lens correction is extended by floating elements

Lenses are coated to reduce flare

Important lens characteristics, focal length and relative aperture

because the image doesn't fit neatly onto the flat film surface. Simple lenses also disperse light into its component colors, forming the different colored images on different planes and in different sizes. We dislike color-fringed images and refer to the several varieties of this defect as *chromatic aberration. Spherical aberration* and *coma* result in image blurring because light rays striking the lens surface near its center don't focus precisely with the marginal rays or with rays entering the lens obliquely. *Astigmatism,* another troublesome aberration, causes image lines which are radial to the image circle to focus differently from the tangential lines. *Distortion,* still another problem, turns square shapes in the subject into *barrel* or *pincushion* shapes in the image.

Correcting these aberrations to a useful degree requires the use of at least two different kinds of glass and, frequently, several different lens *elements* of different shapes, very carefully assembled into a single functioning compound unit, the camera lens. The possible combinations of material, shapes, number of elements, and arrangement are almost infinite. Before the age of electronic computers, a new lens design might occupy mathematicians for months or years as they struggled through endless calculations. Now, with many new types of exotic glass and sophisticated computers to do the calculating, very complex lens designs can be completed in hours or days.

Many of the aberrations are related to the fact that lens elements are usually ground and polished with surfaces of spherical form. A few lenses, however, make use of one or more *aspheric* elements. Although they can simplify design and improve lens corrections, aspherical surfaces are difficult to manufacture and are consequently very expensive. Except where maximum performance is required and cost is no object, aspheric lenses are seldom worthwhile.

A lens can be well-corrected for the various aberrations when focused on distant objects, but not perform well at close range. At one time this was unavoidable, but some modern lenses have been designed to work very well at all distances from close-ups to infinity. *Floating elements* within the lens structure accomplish

this by adjusting themselves automatically to optimize lens correction as the lens focusing control is turned. The improvement is most noticeable at close range and is significant enough so that floating-element lenses are usually specifically identified as such by their manufacturers.

Some of the light entering the lens is lost by multiple reflections between the various glass surfaces. Frequently some of this wayward *flare light* reaches the film, not as part of the useful image, but in streaks, geometric patterns, or *fog,* unrelated to the image. To reduce flare and increase the effective intensity and contrast of the image, modern lenses are *coated* with very thin layers of a hard, transparent material. A single layer of coating will absorb a large proportion of flare light, but not all colors are absorbed equally. *Multicoating,* adding several specially controlled layers of coating, can reduce flare of all colors satisfactorily and is a technique used in many lenses today. Multicoating is necessary only on certain types of lens elements. In some cases, a single coating is adequate or even preferable. Don't feel that a single-coated lens is necessarily inferior. Most manufacturers apply multiple coatings only where they are needed to improve lens performance, saving the expense of multicoating, where it is not necessary, by applying the cheaper, but effective, single coatings.

Two of the most important characteristics of a lens are its *focal length* and its *relative aperture.* The focal length is the approximate distance from the center of the lens to the film when the lens is focused on infinity. There is no obvious center measuring point in most modern camera lenses; in fact, in some instances, the measuring point is not even contained within the lens structure. Fortunately, all lenses are clearly marked with their focal lengths, which makes actual measurement seldom necessary.

The focal length is important because it indicates something about the function and purpose of the lens. The normal lens for most cameras has a focal length approximately equal to the diagonal of the film image and will photograph objects in about the same way that the

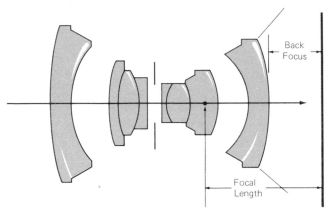

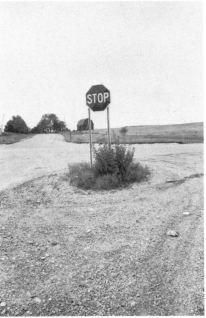

Figure 3.18
In this lens formula the second principle point, from which the focal length is measured, lies approximately in the position shown. There is no way to determine its exact location without special measuring equipment.

Figure 3.19
a. Image size and angular coverage is determined by lens focal length; perspective is determined by subject-to-camera distance. Here the camera is close to the stop sign so the barn appears far away and small. The 24mm lens covers a large expanse of road and farmland.

b. A 50mm lens, twice as far from the sign as the previous picture, enlarges the barn and shows less of the road and fields, but leaves the sign the same size.

c. Doubling both the subject distance and the lens focal length keeps the sign the same size as before. The 100mm lens field angle is much narrower and the barn appears larger and closer.

d. Here a 200mm lens, at twice the previous distance, leaves the sign size unchanged. The coverage angle is again cut in half and the barn looms large in a shallow space.

e. Distance and focal length again doubled, this 400mm lens appears to compress the background space still further, and the lens coverage angle barely includes the barn width.

a

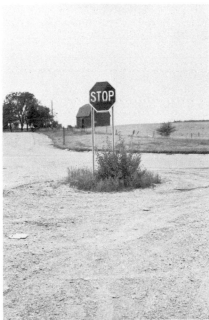

b

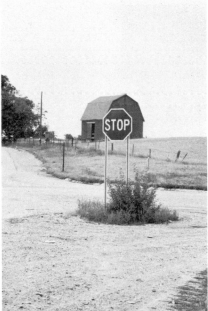

c

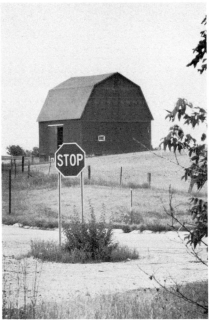

d

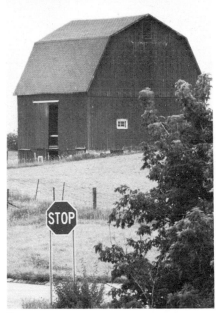

e

Figure 3.20
a. Taken with a 24mm lens, this picture covers a wide field but makes house, in center, insignificantly small.

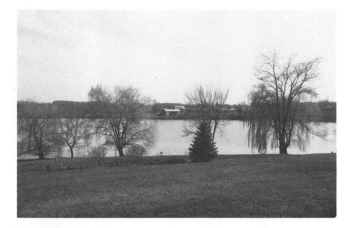

b. Picture taken from identical spot, this time with a 400mm lens, magnifies the house to full-frame size, and shows it in sharp detail.

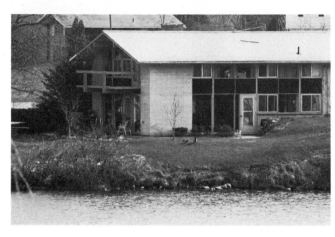

c. Center of 24mm negative, enlarged about 16 diameters, covers the same area and displays the same perspective shown in the 400mm image. Camera position governs perspective; focal length determines image size and angular field.

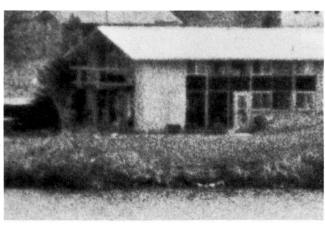

eye sees them, including about as much of the subject area as is perceived from the camera position.

A *long lens* has a focal length appreciably greater than the film diagonal. It will form an image of larger scale than the normal lens but will cover a narrower field of view. *Wide* lenses (*wide-angle* lenses or *short* lenses) have focal lengths appreciably shorter than the film diagonal. Their images are small in scale but the subject area covered is substantially greater than normal. The advantage of wide and long lenses relates to their coverage. The wide lens simply includes more of the subject area in the picture; the long lens records a narrow field of view but permits clear, magnified images of distant objects without excessive enlargement of the negative.

The other important lens characteristic, relative aperture, is an indication of the amount of light the lens can transmit to the film. It derives from the calibration of the *stops* that were used in the late nineteenth century to adjust lens aperture size.

Stops were usually thin metal plates, each pierced by a single central hole, and designed to be inserted into the lens system through a slot in the lens barrel. The hole sizes were calculated so replacing one stop with the next larger one would effectively double the exposure. Although the aperture size is now adjusted by using a variable iris diaphragm instead of individual metal stop plates, the aperture is still referred to as a stop and changing from one aperture to a smaller one is called *stopping down*. Increasing the aperture size is referred to as *opening up;* the obvious term, "stopping up," is never used.

Relative apertures are identified by *f/ numbers* which are found by dividing the focal length of the lens by its aperture diameter:

$$f/ = \frac{\text{Focal Length (F)}}{\text{Aperture Diameter (D)}}$$

For example, if a lens with a 4″ focal length is found to have an aperture diameter of 2″, the relative aperture, or f/ number, is f/2.0.

$$f/ = \frac{F}{D} = \frac{4}{2} = 2, \text{ or } f/2.0$$

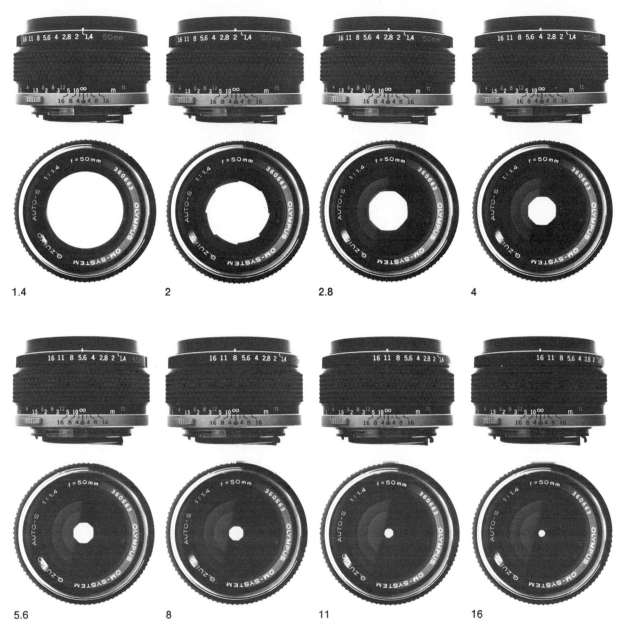

1.4 2 2.8 4

5.6 8 11 16

Figure 3.21
Lens openings front and top with
calibrations

If the diaphragm of this lens is stopped down to a diameter of one inch, its f/ number becomes f/4.

$$f/ = \frac{F}{D} = \frac{4}{1} = 4, \text{ or } f/4.0$$

These f/ numbers are engraved on the aperture scale of the lens.

Although the wide open aperture of a lens may be some unusual f/number like f/1.7, f/2.5, or f/3.2, the rest of the aperture scale will follow a standard sequence such as this:

f/ . . . 2, 2.8, 4.0, 5.6, 8.0, 11, 16, 22, 32, 45 . . .

Notice that every second number in the ascending sequence is approximately doubled.

The smaller numbers (f/2, 2.8) represent stops of large diameter relative to the focal length and indicate *fast* apertures which will transmit a great deal of light to the film. The larger numbers (f/16, f/22) indicate *slow* stops (smaller apertures) which transmit only a little light and thus require longer exposure times.

In the standard sequence of f/ numbers, each higher number transmits just half as much light as the stop preceding it. For example, f/8 is only half as fast as f/5.6 and f/4 is only half as fast as f/2.8. But f/16 is twice as fast as f/22. This is usually expressed as f/8 is *one stop slower* than f/5.6 or f/16 is *a stop faster* than f/22.

The term "stop" also commonly describes any factor or condition which influences exposure. If the sun goes under a cloud, we say the light "has dropped a couple of stops," or one film might be described as being "a stop faster" than another, or we might even consider resetting the shutter speed as a way of changing the exposure "a stop or two." This terminology is clearly colloquial, but it is firmly rooted in practice and is universally understood. Some authorities would prefer "steps" instead of "stops" in these applications, but most of us will continue to say "stops" in the belief that being understood is better than being correct but incomprehensible.

Telephoto and retro-focus lenses feature special construction

Macro-lenses are specially corrected for close-up work

Shift lenses can sometimes help control perspective

Very long lenses are awkward to carry and use because of their physical length. Therefore, most long lenses are built as relatively compact *telephoto* designs, which implies that the effective focal length of the lens is greater than its physical length would appear to permit. Similarly, very wide-angle lenses for SLRs are *reversed telephoto* or *retro-focus* design, which means that their effective focal lengths are substantially shorter than their *back focus,* the actual space between the rear element of the lens and the film surface. This construction is essential in SLRs to allow the reflex mirror space in which to move. A short lens of normal construction would block it.

There are several types of lenses designed for special applications. *Macro-lenses* (one manufacturer calls his product a *micro-lens)* are specially corrected for close-up photography, but will also work satisfactorily with subjects at any distance. These lenses come in several focal lengths, most commonly about 50mm, for 35mm cameras, and can be focused in a range from infinity to about 6″ or 8″ by simply turning the focusing ring. Most of them are supplied with an accessory life-size adapter or a special *extension tube* which can be fitted between the camera body and the lens to permit even closer focusing, so life-size images can be made directly on the film.

Some manufacturers offer specially corrected macro-lenses for different subject distances, each designed to work within a very limited range. Usually these special macros come in plain, nonfocusing barrel mounts and must be used with accessory bellows units for focusing.

A few manufacturers offer *perspective control* (PC) lenses, which are also sometimes called *shift* lenses because they can be shifted laterally in their mounts about one-half inch or more in each direction. PC lenses for 35mm SLRs are usually of fairly short focal length, making them moderately wide-angle lenses when used in the normal, unshifted position. They are corrected for a much wider field, though, so even when the lens is displaced as far off-axis as possible, the image quality is maintained at a satisfactory level.

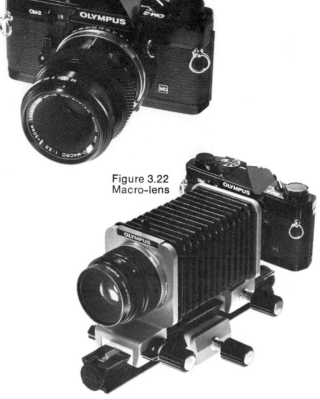

Figure 3.22
Macro-lens

Figure 3.23
Super macro-lens on bellows

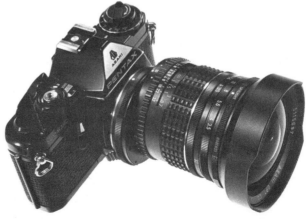

Figure 3.24
PC lens

Figure 3.25
Zoom lens

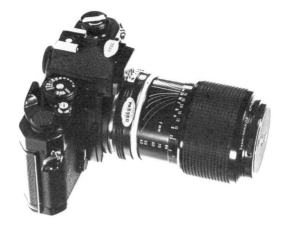

Figure 3.26
a. Camera with a
mirror lens

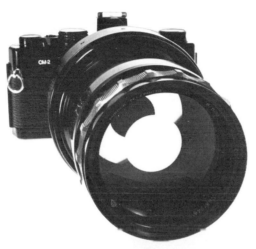

b. These light doughnuts are typical out-of-focus image points formed by a mirror lens. Because the light rays from the edges of the subject area pass through the lens system slightly obliquely, the circles near the image margins are deformed into pointed ellipses.

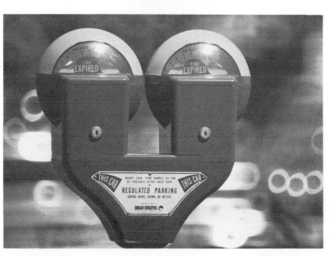

PC lenses are especially suitable for architectural photography because the shift feature makes it possible to rectify, or at least reduce, the apparent convergence of parallel lines in perspective, and buildings can usually be photographed without objectionable distortion.

From a given camera position the focal length of the lens in use will determine the size of the image and the area of the subject recorded. If the camera cannot be moved and if the image must be very precisely composed, it is frequently convenient to use a *zoom* lens. The focal length of a zoom lens can be varied over a rather wide range by merely turning or sliding a collar on the lens barrel. *Zooming* can effectively magnify (or minify) the image so it can be fitted neatly into the compositional space of the film frame, an especially valuable feature for color slide work. Although zoom lenses are typically not quite as well corrected as fixed-focal-length lenses, many of them are very good. Because the zoom feature necessitates floating elements, a number of manufacturers have doubled their function to include a measure of close-up correction in their designs. Zoom lenses are somewhat larger and more expensive than the longest fixed-focal-length lenses they replace, but they are extremely versatile and convenient to use.

Some very long focal length lenses include spherical mirror elements, as well as lenses, in their design. These *catadioptric* lenses (referred to familiarly as *cats*) are more compact than regular telephotos of similar focal length and frequently have a greater range of focus adjustment. They do not have adjustable apertures. Light transmission through the lens must be reduced, when necessary, by the use of *filters*. A *mirror lens* appears to have a very large aperture, but its effective aperture is reduced considerably by an opaque disc, which is actually a small mirror cemented in the center of the front element. This construction causes the out-of-focus images of bright points of light in the subject to be formed as doughnut shapes rather than the usual *circles of confusion* formed by a regular lens.

Fisheye lenses emphasize distortion

Cats typically produce images of slightly lower contrast than regular telephotos do, but the best ones can compare very favorably in image sharpness. They are very convenient to use, most are not excessively expensive, and they are available in extremely long focal lengths.

Most lenses are carefully corrected to eliminate linear distortion but *fisheye* lenses emphasize it. They are usually of very short focal length and cover an extremely wide field. The image they form resembles the world as seen in the familiar mirror-surfaced garden balls; nearby objects are grossly distorted and straight lines appear as sweeping arcs. Some fisheye lenses form images which cover the entire film area, the corner-to-corner coverage approximating 180°. Others form a smaller, circular image with equal or even greater angular coverage. In either case the image is bizarre, and, although the "fisheye effect" is no longer novel, the lenses are occasionally useful for very wide-angle shots or dramatic distortions.

Figure 3.27
Extreme barrel distortion is a characteristic of fisheye images.

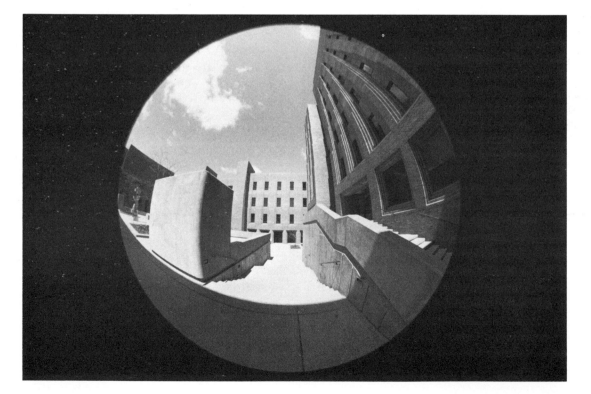

Camera and Lens Accessories

Camera and lens accessories are expensive. Even though some of them are more trouble than they're worth, there are a few items that you should have. A *lens cap* is one. If you have more than one lens, keep one with a front cap on the camera and provide caps for both front and rear elements of the other lenses so that they are never uncovered except when actually in use. You should always use a good *lens shade* (*lens hood*) too. Buy shades deep enough to exclude side light but not so deep that they cause *vignetting* (shading) of the image corners. If you have an SLR or view camera it's easy to check for vignetting. Focus the camera at infinity and check the extreme corners of the finder image as you stop the lens down to its smallest aperture. If the corners darken with the shade in place and lighten when it's removed, the shade is too deep for that lens. Try a shallower one.

You may not need a tripod for most of your photography, but when you do, you'll need it badly. Buy a sturdy one that will hold the camera steady at at least head height, even in a moderate breeze. It should have rubber feet to protect finished floors. Some also provide handy retractable metal spikes for use on rough or slippery surfaces. Some models provide extendable center columns to facilitate minor height adjustments, which is a desirable feature. Gear-operated columns are the best; they should operate smoothly and have a positive locking arrangement.

Most tripods intended for use with hand cameras have two or three leg sections which can be extended and secured in position by means of threaded locking collars. Check the collars for smooth operation and positive locking. Avoid any that bind, feel gritty as they're turned, or fail to hold the leg firmly in position. View camera tripods must be exceptionally strong and stable. Don't economize here; a flimsy tripod is worse than useless.

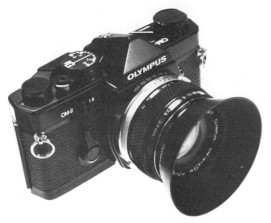

Figure 3.28
a. Lens shade

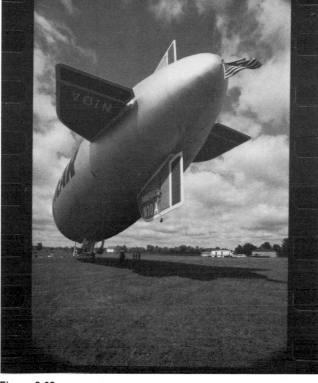

Figure 3.29
Vignetted corners result from the use of a too-deep sunshade, in this case a 24mm lens with a 35mm sunshade.

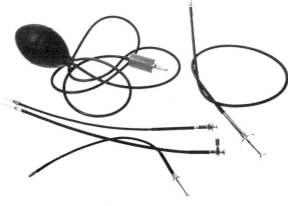

Figure 3.30
Cable releases

b. Tripod

A *cable release* is another important accessory. Buy a good quality, flexible *cable* that is at least 10″ long. For view camera use, an even longer one is preferable. Some cable releases are provided with locking devices, which can be used with the camera shutter set on its B (*Bulb*) setting to make manually-timed exposures of any length. This is a useful feature if your camera shutter does not provide a T (*Time*) exposure setting, as most focal plane shutters do not. There are several types of locking devices. The best type has a knurled set screw, which can be turned in against the cable plunger to hold it firmly in any position.

There are many lens accessories, including caps, sunshades, filters, and close-up lenses, that are designed to clamp over or screw into the front of the lens mount. If you have several lenses in mounts of the same inside thread diameter, you can interchange screw-in accessories among them with a minimum of fuss. If some lenses are larger than others, buy threaded accessories to fit the largest one and use threaded *adapter rings* to match these accessories to the smaller lenses. Most of these accessories are double threaded so they can be stacked. This will allow you to use two or more at a time, but there is some risk of vignetting the image and increasing diffusion and flare.

Years ago several standard sizes of filters were established and intended to be used in slip-on adapter rings. These so-called "series" filters are not threaded and are normally less convenient than the screw-in variety, but they are valuable for use with lenses in unthreaded mounts or in mounts of nonstandard size.

Some view camera lenses, especially the larger sizes, are difficult to fit with either screw-in filters or series-sized adapter rings. Usually these big lenses use gelatin filter holders and gelatin filter squares instead of the glass filters normally used on small cameras. Actually, many view camera users simply tape the flexible gelatin filters in place over the lens. They are relatively inexpensive and can be discarded when they become scratched or badly soiled.

A lens extender may be useful

For poor light conditions, consider flash

Electronic flash units are versatile and convenient

But bulbs can give more light and may be less expensive to use

If you only occasionally need a moderately long lens for your SLR, you might consider buying an *extender* or *converter* rather than a separate lens. Extenders attach between the camera body and the camera lens and effectively double (or triple, in some cases) the lens focal length. Most of them cause some deterioration in the lens performance, but this is usually tolerable. More seriously, they reduce the lens speed substantially and must be used at relatively small apertures for best results, which may limit their usefulness in poor light conditions.

If you work frequently in poor light conditions or are interested in some control over light effects, you may want to investigate *flash* units. Some small 110-size pocket cameras have built-in sockets for *flashcubes* or *flipflash* bars and most can be purchased with matching, plug-in *electronic flash* units. Many 35mm and larger cameras, which have *hot shoe* flash brackets, will also accept small, self-contained slip-on units but, for greater light output and versatility, larger and more powerful units are preferable.

Many modern electronic flash units have built-in *photocell sensors,* which can be set to monitor the light reflected from the subject and adjust the exposure automatically, by limiting the duration of the flash. Thyristor circuits are useful in conserving battery power and in speeding up the recycling time under some conditions. Some units offer *bare bulb* attachments for more uniform distribution of light and some permit tilting the flash head for *bounce light* effects. Accessory filters, diffusion screens, and reflectors are also available.

Unless you plan to do a lot of work with flash, *flashbulbs* may be better for your purposes than electronic flash. Although bulbs are relatively expensive per actual flash, the equipment cost is low. Bulbs can also provide more total light output than any portable electronic flash unit can, and they won't deteriorate during prolonged storage. Electronic units have a fairly high initial cost but their operating cost is low if they are used frequently and regularly. Intermittent or infrequent use may reduce their efficiency, especially if they have rechargeable *ni-cad* (nickel cadmium) batteries. Elec-

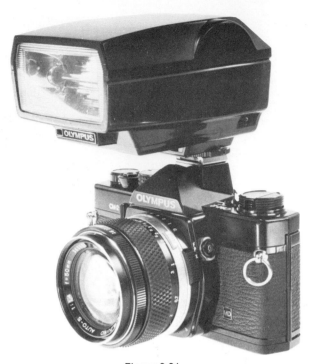

Figure 3.31
Flash on hot shoe

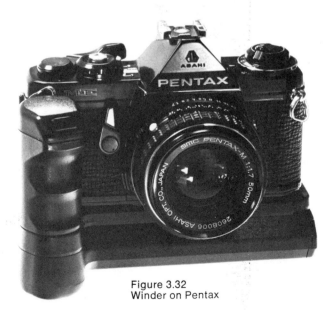

Figure 3.32
Winder on Pentax

**If you decide to buy
an electronic flash unit, get a good one**

**Motor drives and winders are useful—
sometimes**

**But don't buy one
unless you really need it**

**If your camera doesn't have a meter,
buy a handheld one**

tronic flash is certainly more convenient, provides a considerable degree of automation, produces little heat, and requires very short exposure times. Consider both options; then, if you decide to buy an electronic flash unit, be sure it is powerful and versatile enough to do what you want. The smallest ones are little more than toys.

Motor drives, which replace the camera base-plate and permit automatic sequence photography at the rate of several pictures a second, have been around for a long time. Recently, simplified versions, called *winders,* have become popular. Many of these winders, for 35mm cameras, permit automatic operation at about two frames-per-second but some simply advance the film and wind the shutter after each manual exposure. Lighter, smaller and less expensive than regular motor drives, winders are useful in sequence photography and in special situations where manual winding would be difficult or impossible. Most of them can be electrically operated from a considerable distance, as for nature work, sports photography, or scientific purposes. Don't buy one unless you really need it. For ordinary work, a winder is an expensive luxury which almost doubles the size and weight of your camera.

If your camera is not equipped with a meter you will probably need to get a separate, handheld meter. These, like the newer built-ins, are now using silicon instead of CdS cells and, as a result, are faster acting and more stable under extremes of temperature. CdS meters, however, are not necessarily any less accurate or reliable, if used knowledgeably under normal conditions.

There are three general methods of taking light readings: *incident* readings are measurements of *illumination,* taken at the subject position; *reflectance* readings measure *luminance* light reflected toward the camera from the subject surfaces; and *spot* readings are reflectance readings taken from very small areas of the subject. Most modern meters are capable of making incident and reflectance readings and some, with accessory attachments, can make semi-spot readings of from about 7½° to 15° fields. True spot metering, how-

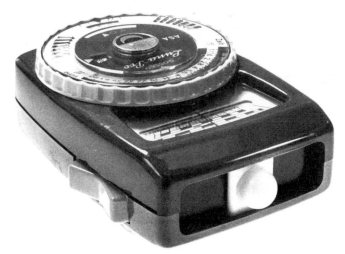

Figure 3.33
a. Meter in incident mode

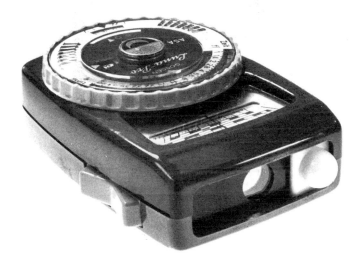

b. Meter in reflectance mode

**A spotmeter is best for
Zone System work**

**The road to better pictures is *not* paved
with money**

**Shop sensibly for good, used equipment;
avoid duplication**

**Test the equipment thoroughly
before the warranty expires**

ever, is done best with a specialized *spotmeter*. These instruments read a subject field of only about 1° and are relatively expensive, especially some recent models which feature electronic digital readout. A spotmeter is a good investment if you are a serious worker in black-and-white, especially if you use a view camera and want to work with the Zone System of exposure control.

Before You Buy

Before you buy a camera, try to decide what sort of pictures you want to make and what your standards of image quality are. Small cameras are easy to carry around and convenient to use. However, their negatives will have to be enlarged considerably, for most purposes, and their prints will consequently be somewhat less sharp than prints made from larger negatives. Very large cameras, on the other hand, can provide superb image quality, but will be correspondingly difficult to carry and less convenient to use.

Small cameras, especially the better rangefinder types, are excellent for quick, spontaneous snapshooting. View cameras, the other extreme, must be used methodically and are best for pictures that require planning and thoughtful refinement. Medium-size cameras are intended to be universally useful, and some of them, at least, combine fairly convenient operation with fine image quality.

Although the medium-size cameras, most of which use 120 rollfilm, would seem to be the best choice for a beginner, the 35mm SLR is, in my opinion, a better one. First, there are many more models to choose from and most of them are less expensive to buy and operate than are rollfilm cameras of similar capability. Second, they are more convenient to use and offer a much greater variety of accessories. Third, there are more types of film available for 35mm cameras (135-size) than are available in rollfilm sizes. Finally, although the larger film size is inherently capable of producing prints of better quality, the differences in practice are frequently not great. If you are a careful craftsman, you can do fine work with a 35mm SLR.

Photographers are notorious gadget-lovers and and most of us own more equipment than we need or use. It's easy to convince ourselves that the road to better pictures is paved with money, but it simply isn't true. Hardware doesn't produce good photographs; people do! The moral is clear—buy only what you need; buy good quality equipment; and buy matched equipment, if possible, to permit interchangeability of parts and to avoid unnecessary duplication of accessories.

New camera equipment is becoming almost prohibitively expensive but, good used equipment is frequently reasonably priced. If you're in the market for a camera and have limited funds, you should consider "last year's models" of the better brands, particularly those whose newest models have been changed appreciably. Many photographers trade perfectly good cameras merely to get their hands on the "latest thing," and you can profit at their expense. SLRs with match-needle CdS cell meters are a good example. Recently replaced by silicon and gallium cells, these meters are still functional, but not popular. Similarly, the new, compact 35mm SLRs have made the older, larger models look like dinosaurs, although, for picture-making purposes, they are just as good as the newer models. As their popularity declines, so will their prices.

If possible, buy from a reputable dealer and get some sort of warranty from him. Test the equipment thoroughly under your normal working conditions and inspect the results critically. If there is any hint of mechanical or optical defect in the equipment, return it with the pictures and ask the dealer to correct the problem. Don't make any repairs yourself or have them done by anyone else, as long as the equipment is under warranty.

Films: Types and Characteristics

Before you take pictures, you'll have to buy some film. There are many varieties and you'll need to know a little about them before you can make a choice. It would probably be wise to begin with black-and-white.

Film grain is inherent and unavoidable

Film speed is indicated by its ASA number

Black-and-white films record colors as shades of gray

Ortho films are not sensitive to red light

Black-and-white films are sensitized with an emulsion of silver halide crystals suspended in gelatin. After exposure and development, some of these crystals are reduced to particles of opaque metallic silver to form the image. Although the individual particles are too small to be seen with the unaided eye, they overlap randomly to form visible clumps which, distributed more or less uniformly, give the film image a granular visual texture. When a *grainy* negative is enlarged in printing, the print image reproduces the film grain clearly as a pepper-and-salt texture, most apparent in the areas of middle tone.

Although grain is inherent and unavoidable, some films form a coarser grain structure than others do. In general, highly sensitive films (*high speed* or *fast* films) are relatively coarse-grained; *slow* films are typically fine-grained. These terms are relative. Whether grain is coarse or objectionable, or even noticeable, depends on your personal perception and taste. Some photographers like grain and use fast films purposely to achieve it. Others are displeased by grain. They are likely to select slow films and use large film sizes to avoid having to enlarge their images.

It's generally true that slow films are capable of resolving very fine detail with excellent sharpness. Fast films are somewhat less capable in these respects but, barring extreme examples, the film images must be magnified considerably before any real differences are apparent. For most purposes, therefore, you can select films from the middle speed range without too much concern about differences in image quality.

The speed of a film is indicated by its *ASA film speed* number. These numbers are arrived at through testing procedures which follow a method suggested by the American National Standards Institute, the ANSI. When the test method was first formulated, the ANSI was known as the American Standards Association (ASA) and those initials have survived.

Film speed numbers are selected from a series which goes like this:

. . . 10, 12, 16, 20, 25, 32, 40, 50, 64, 80, 100, 125, 160 . . .

As you can see, every *third* number in the ascending sequence is doubled so adjacent numbers relate to each other by a factor of about 1.26 (the cube root of 2). The series can be extended in both directions; for example, the number following 160, in this list, can be found by doubling 100, or by multiplying 160 by 1.26 and rounding off to 200.

The higher numbers in the series refer to faster films. A film rated at 100 ASA is twice as fast as a 50 ASA film, for example. Kodak's Panatomic-X 135-size film, which is rated at ASA 32, requires 10 times more exposure than does Tri-X Professional sheet film, which is rated at ASA 320.

ASA numbers are printed on the information sheets packaged with films and are usually printed on the outside of the cartons as well. A recent trend (in Kodak color films, at least) is to include the film speed in the film title. Kodachrome 25, Ektachrome 64, and Kodacolor 400, for example, have ASA speeds of 25, 64, and 400 respectively.

Although black-and-white films don't produce color images, they do respond to color in the subject by recording the different hues in various shades of gray. The natural color sensitivity of the simple silver halide emulsion is restricted to the blue, violet, and ultraviolet region of the spectrum. The emulsion is effectively blind to red, orange, yellow, and some of the green. Ordinary or noncolor sensitized (NC) emulsions of this sort produce images which, in final print form, render blues and violet shades as almost white. Reds, oranges, and yellows show up in the print as black or dark gray tones. This effect is apparent in daguerreotypes and in prints from collodion negatives. Pale eyes in nineteenth-century portraits of blue-eyed individuals and blank white skies demonstrate the relatively great blue-sensitivity of these early negative materials.

Orthochromatic films have had their sensitivity extended into the green region. Their reproduction of the *cool* colors appears more natural, but red objects are still photographed as if they were black. Further extension of sensitivity into the red region of the spectrum has given us *panchromatic* emulsions. Their reproduction of

Figure 3.34

Following the rule that colors to which the film is very sensitive will appear in the print as light tones, and colors to which the film is not very sensitive will appear dark in the print, see if you can determine the colors of the plastic chips and the rooster in these photographs. Figure *a* was taken on an "ordinary" blue-sensitive film, figure *b* was an orthochromatic film, and figure *c* was made on a popular panchromatic film of type "B" sensitivity. The fourth picture, figure *d,* was made on Polaroid film, type 52. Its color response verges on type "C" panchromatic balance.

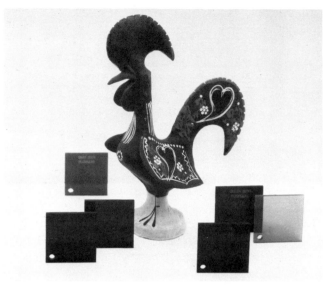

a

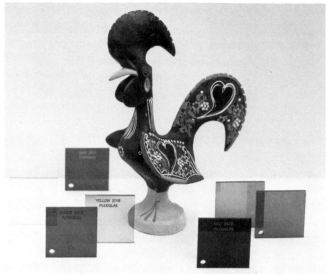

b

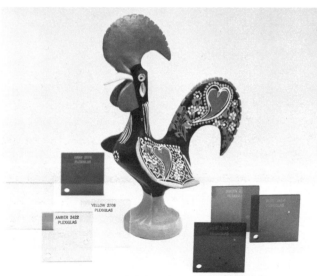

c

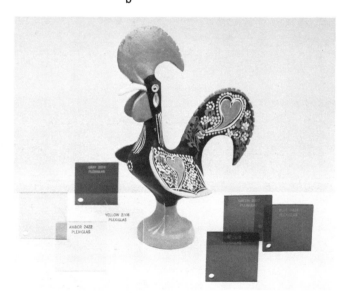

d

**Pan films are sensitive to
all visible colors**

Read the film instruction sheet

First clean the camera

***Don't* touch the mirror surface**

the spectrum colors in various shades of gray is quite balanced and believable, and generally preferable to *ortho* or *ordinary* rendition. Most *pan* films match the color sensitivity of the human eye quite satisfactorily and are occasionally designated as *type B* materials. *Type C* pan films are even more sensitive to red than the eye is and tend to lighten red objects so they appear in the print as unnaturally light gray or even white. These type designations are rarely used any more and there are very few type C emulsions available for general use.

In selecting a film type for use, consider what you want to use it for and what sort of quality you expect in the prints. In both color and black-and-white films, low speeds are likely to indicate fine-grained, high-resolution materials which are appropriate for use in situations where the light is good and the pictures must be exceptionally clear and sharp. Very fast films will permit more freedom of operation in dim light conditions but will produce grainier images which are somewhat less crisply delineated. Medium-speed films, logically enough, represent a compromise between these extremes. See the film chart in the appendix, page 294.

When you have made your selection and bought the film, you are almost ready to begin photographing; but first, open the film package in subdued light and remove the information sheet. Read it. It contains valuable information about the exposure and development of the film, which is up-to-date and valid for that particular roll. Save the sheet for reference until the film has been developed, then throw it away. Manufacturers change their recommendations from time to time and handling data from reference books (like this one) or old information sheets may be inappropriate for new film.

Loading the Camera

Before loading the film into your camera, inspect the camera to be sure it is clean and operating properly

Open the back and examine the interior for film chips and other particles. Remove any that you see with a soft brush or gentle blasts of compressed air. Be careful of the focal plane shutter leaves or curtain; a direct air blast may damage them and excessive pressure on the brush can deform the thin metal foil of some curtain shutters. Most canned air, although very convenient and effective, should not be used; it is pure freon, an environmentally unsafe substance.

The mirror chamber should be inspected too. Take the lens off and peer inside, but *don't touch* the mirror surface. A few specks of dust on the mirror will cause no harm, but if it seems excessively dusty or linty, use a rubber squeeze-bulb (ear syringe or aspirator at your drugstore) to blow it clean—gently. The mirror will need only very occasional cleaning if you are careful to keep the camera body opening covered, either with a lens or a *body cap,* at all times. Again, *don't touch* the mirror. The surface is very fragile and easily damaged. Now inspect the lens surfaces, front and rear.

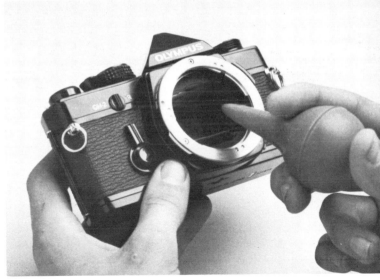

Figure 3.35
Camera cleaning

Figure 3.36

a. Clean loose dust particles from the lens surfaces with a soft brush.

b. Or blow them off with a rubber syringe. Don't use canned air; it's an environmental hazard.

c. Moisten a clean, crumpled piece of lens tissue with a drop of liquid cleaner.

d. And rub the lens gently, with circular strokes, until the soil is loosened; then polish the surface dry with a fresh piece of lens tissue, crumpled into a soft wad. Be gentle!

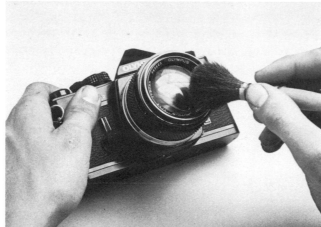
a

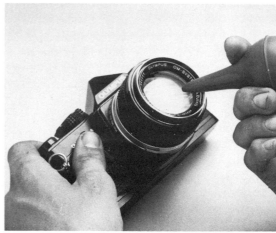
b

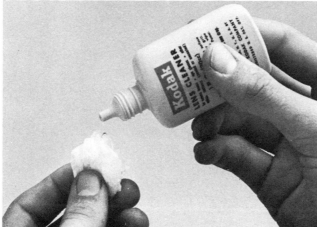
c

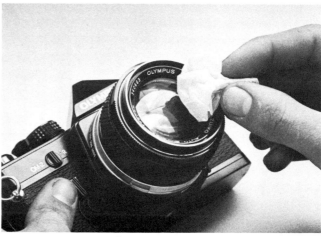
d

Don't clean the lens unless it really needs it

But, if you must, do it carefully

Like the mirror surface, the lens glass surfaces are delicate. Don't clean them unless they are obviously dusty or soiled. When cleaning *is* necessary, first dust the lens surface lightly to remove abrasive particles, using jets of air from the aspirator or a soft, clean brush. This is frequently all the cleaning that is necessary, but if obvious soil remains, put a drop or two of lens cleaner fluid on a softly crumpled wad of *lens tissue* to moisten and soften it, and wipe the lens surface gently with a circular motion. Polish the surface with a fresh piece of dry, crumpled lens tissue and inspect the lens by breathing on it and observing the pattern of condensed vapor. Residual soils will show up clearly as irregular patches or streaks, as the vapor film evaporates.

If necessary, repeat the cleaning procedure, once. Two applications of lens cleaner will probably remove any soil that can be removed by this treatment. Blemishes that remain are probably so embedded in the lens coating that they are permanent. Leave them alone. Prolonged scrubbing is very likely to damage the lens coating or scratch the glass.

In an emergency, if no lens tissue or cleaning fluid is available, you can blow dust from the lens yourself, but be very careful not to spit on the glass. Saliva will leave smudges when it evaporates. Blow through a drinking straw, if one is available; it's safer and more effective. Then, breathing on the glass will supply moisture for cleaning. Wipe off the condensed vapor very gently, with the softest, most absorbent, clean material available. A clean, well-washed cotton handkerchief will do. Surgical cotton is very good for dusting and for cleaning; use separate, clean wads, of course.

When you are satisfied that the lens is clean, replace it on the camera body and put on the lens cap.

Protect the lens surfaces so they won't need cleaning.
Always remove dust before wiping or polishing the lens surfaces.
Never simply wipe a dry lens surface with a dry tissue or cloth—moisten the tissue or cloth first, to soften it.
Don't clean a lens unless it obviously needs it, but do remove fingerprints or greasy soils or dirty water spots immediately.
Never touch, wipe, or use cleaning solvents on the SLR mirror surface.

Now load the film. If you have a 35mm SLR, you can proceed as follows (in the absence of more specific instructions): Open the camera back and lay the camera facedown (be sure the lens is capped) on your lap or on a convenient table surface, with the camera base closest to you. Pull up the rewind knob as far as it will go, so the film cartridge can be placed into the rewind chamber, and slip the cartridge into the chamber with its protruding spool end pointing toward the camera base and the cartridge light trap on the right. Push the rewind knob down so its forked end engages the cartridge spool. It may be necessary to turn the knob slightly as you push, in order to get the knob down all the way.

Now insert the end of the film tongue into one of the slots on the take-up spool on the right-hand side of the camera. (With some cameras it is easier to do this *before* putting the film cartridge into the rewind chamber.) Be careful not to poke or press on the shutter curtain as you do this. Be sure that the film tongue is firmly attached to the take-up spool, that it meets the spool squarely (not at an angle), and that the bottom edge of the film is touching the lower flange of the spool. Press the camera shutter release and advance the film with the winding lever once, to be sure the film is tracking smoothly and the teeth of the sprocket wheel are properly engaged with the perforations on the edge of the film tongue.

Now release the shutter and advance the film until the film tongue is wound onto the take-up spool and both sets of sprocket teeth have engaged the film perforations. Turn the rewind crank or knob until the film lies flat and you feel slight tension (don't overdo this; there is danger of *cinching* the film in the cartridge and scratching it); then close the camera back. Release the shutter and advance the film twice to dispose of the fogged leader and to provide fresh film for the first exposure. Watch to see that the rewind knob turns as the film advances. (If it doesn't, the film may not be loaded properly; check it in the dark.) The exposure counter should now read 1 (some cameras may indicate 0). You are almost ready to take your first picture. First, you should set the appropriate ASA film speed. On most cameras the ASA window is near the shutter speed dial or on the speed knob itself. If in the latter position, set the ASA speed by lifting the shutter speed knob up and turning it until the appropriate ASA number appears in the window. Tear off one of the end flaps from the film box and insert into the film identification frame on the back of the camera, if your camera has one. This will keep you from forgetting what kind of film is in the camera.

Figure 3.37

a. Open the camera back. On this camera the back latch is released by pulling up on the rewind knob.

b. Be sure the camera interior is clean, then insert the film cartridge and push the rewind knob down to engage the cartridge spool.

c. Insert the film tongue into the slotted take-up spool and be sure it is fully engaged and straight.

d. Wind the film by working the advance lever and releasing the shutter until both rows of perforations are mated with the teeth of the sprocket wheels; then take up the slack film in the cartridge, gently, by turning the rewind knob until the film is under slight tension. Close the camera back and wind off two exposures to get rid of the exposed film leader.

e. Set the film speed into the camera ASA dial before you forget it.

f. If your camera is equipped with a reminder frame of this sort, insert the end flap from the film box in it so you won't forget what kind of film you have in the camera.

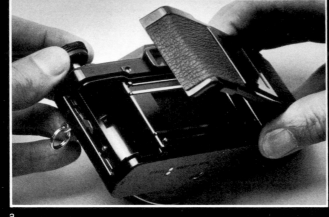

a

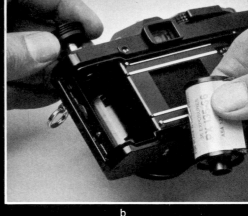

b

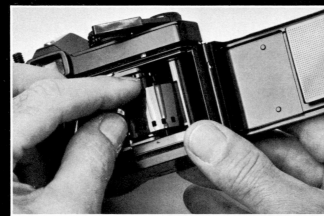

c

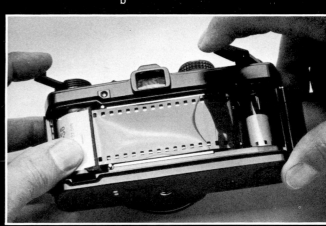

d

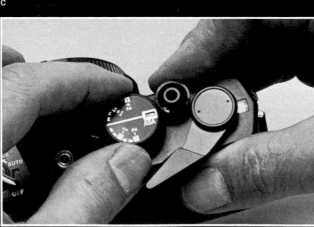

e

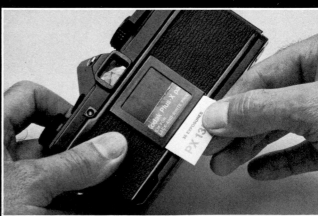

f

**Remember—
large aperture, short exposure;
small aperture, long exposure**

**Aperture affects depth;
shutter affects motion**

The Camera Settings

If you plan to use a handheld meter, instead of the one built into your camera (or if your camera doesn't have one), be sure to set the ASA speed into the meter dial before you use it. If the film speed is not set properly, either type of meter will give you bad advice and your pictures will probably be over- or under-exposed.

Setting the ASA speed into the meter, in effect, tells the meter how much light the film needs in order to form a good image. The meter can then measure the subject reflectance to see how much light is available to work with. With these two bits of information it recommends several possible pairs of aperture and shutter speed settings. Any pair should result in a well-exposed film. For example, using Plus-X film (ASA 125)

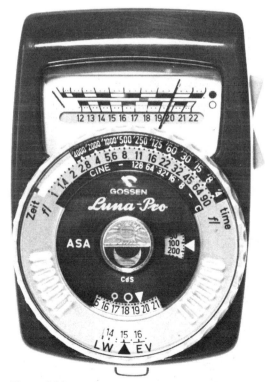

Figure 3.38
Luna-Pro dial

on a typically sunny day (Luna-Pro meter reading 19⅔), the meter suggests the following pairs of camera settings:

    f/4   @ 1/2000th sec.
    f/5.6 @ 1/1000th sec.
    f/8   @ 1/500th sec.
    f/11 @ 1/250th sec.
    f/16 @ 1/125th sec.
    f/22 @ 1/60th sec.

Practically speaking, these pairs are all alike, as far as film exposure is concerned, because the largest lens openings are paired with the shortest exposure times and the smallest lens opening is matched with the longest exposure time. Be sure you understand this relationship; if you wish to change from one lens aperture to a larger one without changing the film exposure, you must shorten the exposure time to compensate for the increased light intensity on the film surface. Remember—large aperture, short exposure; small aperture, long exposure.

Depth of Field and Subject Motion

If all these settings provide the same exposure, you may ask, why use one in preference to any other? Well, because the aperture size affects the appearance of the image by altering the depth of field and the various shutter speeds affect the way moving objects are pictured.

At its widest aperture a lens produces relatively shallow depth of field, which means that, although the subject focused on may be sharp and clearly detailed, its immediate foreground and background may be obviously out-of-focus. At smaller lens apertures, depth of field is increased, normally extending about twice as far beyond the subject plane of focus as it extends forward toward the camera. At its smallest aperture the lens with which a 35mm SLR is normally equipped may, under certain conditions, be able to record sharply everything from about 8′ to infinity, a rather extensive depth of field.

In addition to increasing depth of field, stopping down the lens affects image quality, because the lens aberrations are reduced at small apertures. Unfortunately, however, the increased sharpness and contrast which should result are partially negated by the increasing effects of diffraction. In practice a typical lens will produce its sharpest images at moderate apertures, usually about two or three stops down from wide open. This is not a serious concern unless you are striving for absolute maximum performance from your lens. The images formed at all apertures, by almost all modern lenses of reputable manufacture, are respectably sharp and satisfactory for most ordinary purposes.

The shutter speed can affect the appearance of the image, too. Obviously, a long exposure will record moving objects as blurs, and a high shutter speed will freeze moving objects and record them as relatively sharp. Blurring of the image is likely if you handhold your camera for exposure times of 1/30th second or longer, but this is not a hard and fast rule. Short lenses are less likely to produce objectionably blurred images than long ones are, at least until you enlarge the images. As a rule of thumb, set your shutter speed on the number which is closest to the focal length of your lens in millimeters. For example, with the normal 50mm lens on your camera, a shutter speed of 60 (which really means 1/60th second) should be a safe speed. Your 28mm wide-angle lens can probably be held still at a shutter speed of 1/30th second and your 500mm *cat* telephoto is likely to give you fuzzy images at speeds of longer than 1/500th second, unless you've put it on a tripod.

There are four factors which influence exposure. They are (1) the luminance of the subject (2) the film speed (3) the aperture or f/ number, and (4) the duration of the exposure interval or shutter speed. Additionally, any adjustment of the aperture will affect depth of field and any adjustment of shutter speed may affect the sharpness of the image if either the subject or the camera is moving.

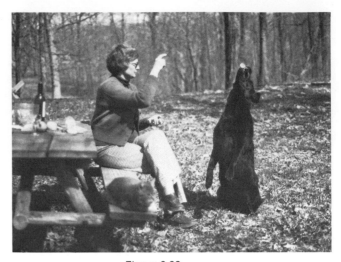

Figure 3.39
A high shutter speed, necessary to stop the motion of the dog catching potato chips, requires a correspondingly large lens opening for proper film exposure. This large aperture, in turn, reduces depth of field. Here the dog is caught in mid-gulp but both the foreground cat and trees in background are out-of-focus.

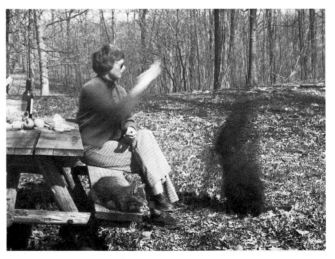

Figure 3.40
Stopping the lens down to a small aperture increases the depth of field sufficiently to get everything sharp but, because proper exposure now requires a slow shutter speed, all motion is blurred.

Now, pick your camera position, frame your subject, and focus. Focusing an SLR is usually as simple as turning the large focusing ring on the lens barrel until the image in the viewfinder appears to be sharp. This is not *always* satisfactory, however, because the viewfinder image is normally formed by the lens at maximum aperture and does not give an accurate indication of the depth of field that will result when the lens stops down to make the exposure.

You can get a fairly good idea of what the final depth of field will be if you stop the lens down manually (most cameras will permit this), but the image will darken considerably at the smaller aperture and may become too dim to appraise. If you need to include a specific zone of the subject within the useful depth of field, or if you want to obtain the greatest possible depth of field, you will have to rely on the distance scale and the matching depth of field scale, both of which are engraved on the lens barrel, usually at the top, close to the camera body.

To achieve the greatest possible depth that your lens can provide, at any given aperture, simply turn the focusing ring to align the *infinity* mark (∞) on the focusing scale with the *far limit* mark which corresponds to the aperture you intend to use. The distance indicated opposite the *near limit* mark now represents the front plane of acceptable sharpness and the depth will extend to infinity. The distance indicated by the normal focusing mark, incidentally, is called the *hyperfocal distance* (it is just twice as far away as the near limit) and this adjustment of the focusing control is called *hyperfocal focusing*. If you own lenses of more than one focal length, notice that the longer lenses appear to provide less depth of field than the short ones do, at any given aperture setting.

Zone focusing is a convenient method of preparing some cameras for fast snapshooting. Most small camera lenses have depth of field scales which indicate the near and far limits of depth (approximately) for any combination of lens aperture and subject distance. If one of these scales is well calibrated, it is possible to use it to prefocus the lens on a selected zone of the

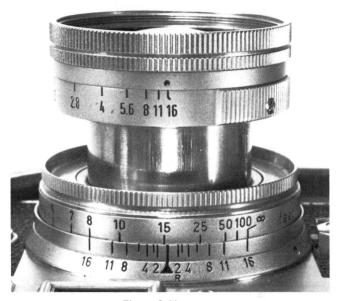

Figure 3.41
Lens set for hyperfocal distance

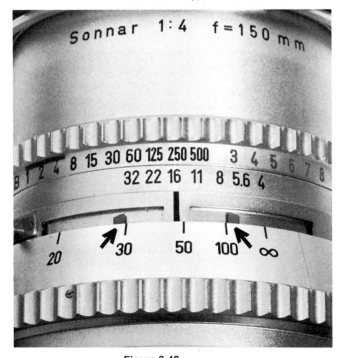

Figure 3.42
Lens set for Zone focus

subject and be assured that any object that appears in the zone will be within the depth of field. For example, assume you want to prepare for some action that will occur somewhere between 30' and 100' from the camera. Using a 150mm Sonnar telephoto lens for the Hasselblad camera (for purposes of illustration), turn the focusing ring until 30' and 100' straddle the focusing index mark and align them with the movable markers which define the near and far limits of depth of field. This has been done in the illustration, which shows the 150mm lens, zone focused for 30' and 100' and indicates that the required aperture is f/16. The shutter speed is shown as 1/250th second but, in practice, it would be dictated by the film speed and the light condition.

Zone focusing some small camera lenses is more of a guessing game. In some cases the marked distances are widely spaced and their exact positions are ambiguous. This is probably deliberate on the part of the manufacturer, to avoid the implication that depth of field can be controlled with real precision.

Since depth of field defines the portion of the subject from front to rear that is acceptably sharp, it depends partly on personal perception and taste. A very small image, like a contact print from a 35mm negative, for example, will seem to exhibit great depth of field because, with the naked eye, it's difficult to distinguish between the in- and out-of-focus areas. Enlarging the image will make the distinction easier and the effective depth of field will seem to be reduced. Similarly, a print of any size, viewed from a great distance, will seem to have great depth of field. Seen from close-up, some of the area previously seen as acceptably sharp can be recognized as definitely fuzzy, and depth of field is reduced.

People will tell you that, when used at the same aperture and subject distance, long lenses produce less depth of field than short ones do. This is true at the same *relative aperture* (f/ number), but the short lens's advantage is not great at normal distances. The smaller image formed by the short lens will have greater depth until it is enlarged to match the long lens's image size.

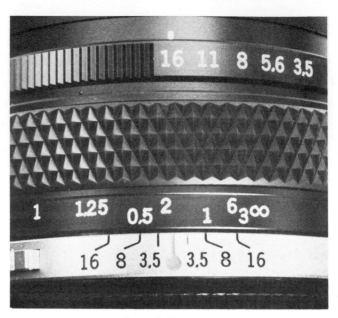

Figure 3.43
Small lens scale

When that is done, the two images will be quite similar. If used at the same aperture *diameter,* the long lens will work effectively at a smaller relative aperture and will provide substantially greater depth.

Rule 1—In general any factor (short lens focal length, great subject distance, small print size, great viewing distance, etc.) which tends to make the image small or difficult to see will increase the effective depth of field.

Rule 2—Depth of field is greatest at small apertures, regardless of the lens used.

Hint—The most effective way to increase depth of field is to stop the lens down. Also consider using a lens of longer focal length and backing away from the subject to preserve image size. Because long lenses frequently provide smaller minimum apertures than short lenses do, an increase in focal length is more than compensated for by the smaller relative aperture (larger f/number) and increased subject distance.

Select aperture or speed,
then match the needles

Pointing the camera is critical

The meter will assume the subject is
average

You may have to override it

Using the Meter to Determine Exposure

When you have set the film speed, selected the subject area, focused, and considered the depth of field and motion requirements of the subject before you, you are ready to determine the camera settings. Assuming that your camera has a match-needle metering system, you must select either a lens aperture or a shutter speed. If you want to use a particular lens opening, set it first, then match the needles in the viewfinder by turning the shutter speed dial. If you have selected a desired shutter speed, you can superimpose the pointers in the viewfinder by turning the aperture ring. In both cases the proper exposure should result if you have pointed the camera toward the correct area of the subject while working the meter.

Pointing the camera is a critical part of the metering procedure because the meter will respond to the *average luminance* of the subject within its field of view. In the ideal subject the average luminance, including highlights, shadows, and all the intermediate gray values, is equivalent to *middle gray,* a value of gray which, by definition, reflects about 18% of the light which strikes it. Meters are designed to provide exposure settings which will translate this ideal 18% subject gray into a print gray of approximately the same value.

The meter, poor dumb thing, has no way of knowing whether the subject you're pointing it at is really "average" or not, but it will assume that it is and will do its best to expose it as if it were. If you point the meter at a black wall, for example, it will think, "my goodness, it certainly is dark out there," and proceed to compensate for what it sees as a middle gray subject in very dim light. If it is a good meter it will overexpose the wall enough so it will print as a middle gray. Similarly, it will underexpose a white or light gray subject to make it middle gray in the print, unless you specifically instruct it not to.

Practically speaking, this characteristic of the meter must be considered when pointing the camera at any subject of other than average luminance. If you want to preserve the somber gloom of a deep forest

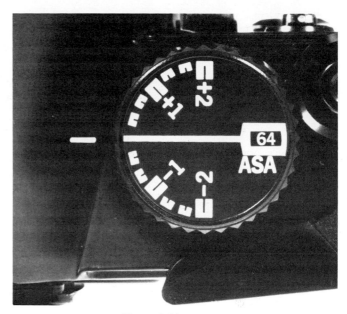

Figure 3.44
Override dial

scene, for example, you'll have to *override* the meter by modifying its recommended setting to underexpose somewhat. Similarly, snow scenes must usually be given more exposure than the meter recommends because you know (but the meter doesn't) that snow is supposed to be white.

There are at least two convenient methods of making the necessary override adjustment. On some cameras it can be accomplished by turning a calibrated override control knob, which is combined with the ASA film speed control, thus effectively changing the film speed. This will modify the meter reading so it will give corrected lens opening and shutter speed recommendations. Although this is a very convenient and direct method, it's easy to forget that you've made the film speed change, and subsequent pictures may be improperly exposed. Some cameras flash a warning light in the viewfinder to alert you when the override dial is not in its neutral position, a convenient feature.

Another easy and effective technique involves a form of *substitute metering.* Simply take the meter reading and make the necessary lens and shutter adjust-

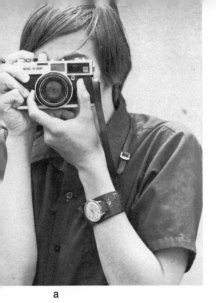

a

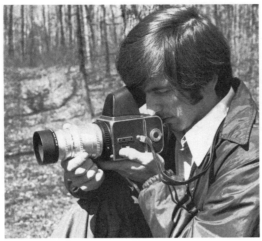

b

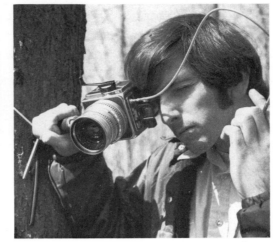

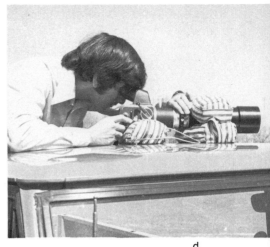

c

d

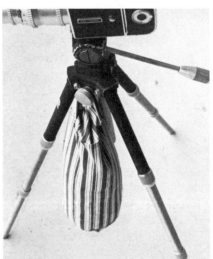

e

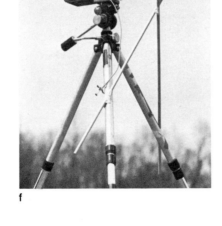

f

Figure 3.45

a. This is good form for shooting with a small camera: the right hand holds the camera body, releases the shutter, and advances the film; the left hand supports the camera and operates the focusing and aperture controls. Keep your elbows braced firmly against your body for good camera support.

b. Bracing your arm on your knee will help provide firm support for the camera.

c. A small table-top tripod, braced against some solid support, will help steady the camera for fairly long exposures.

d. Bean-bags or shot-bags make a fine camera support and dampen vibration very effectively.

e. A shot-bag hung on the tripod will help stabilize it.

f. Brace a long telephoto with sticks, as shown, to reduce vibration.

ments while pointing the camera at some area, whether part of the desired subject or not, which contains an approximately average blend of light and dark tones. Obviously the area selected for metering must be representative of the subject in value and must occupy a similar position relative to the light. With a little practice you'll find this an easy way to deal with the problem. In most cases the camera will only have to be moved slightly. For landscapes, for example, you can position the horizon line across the middle of the finder area, giving the meter equal areas of light and dark tone to work with, and make the indicated settings for proper exposure. After determining the exposure, tilt the camera down a little and shoot (without changing the settings) to emphasize the dark foreground if you want to, or raise it slightly to feature the sky. In either case the exposure is likely to be better than it would have been if calculated from the preferred subject area.

You'll have to experiment with your own camera to determine the best technique for substitute metering, when it becomes necessary, because meters, even those described as *full field averaging,* are not uniformly sensitive to light in different regions of the image area. Most meters, in fact, are designed to favor the central or low-central area of the visual field, under the apparent assumption that the most important area of the subject will be centered. In fact, these

Experiment with your own camera

Center-weighted meters are surprisingly effective

Hold the camera steady and press the release

EV numbers are sometimes a convenience

The reciprocity law can fail

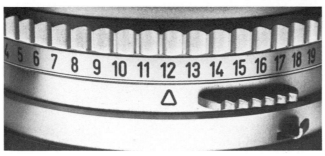

Figure 3.46
EV scale on camera

center-weighted meters are surprisingly effective under most circumstances, and their advice can usually be taken without significant modification.

Now you've taken care of everything. The film speed is set properly; the camera is focused; the lens is set on an f/ number that will provide enough light and also give adequate depth of field; the shutter speed is sufficiently long to give good exposure, but short enough to control subject motion; and you've framed and composed the subject comfortably in the viewfinder. Hold the camera steady and press the shutter release to make the exposure. Good luck!

Some cameras may have a series of exposure value (EV) numbers inscribed on the lens mount or shutter speed scale, instead of or in addition to the regular shutter speed and aperture numbers. EV numbers are intended to simplify camera operation by combining light intensity and film speed values into a single number. An EV number really stands for a certain potential exposure rather than any specific camera setting. For example, EV 10 represents a light and film combination for which any of the following pairs of lens and shutter settings would be appropriate:

1/1000th sec	@ f/1.0
1/125th sec	@ f/2.8
1/15th sec	@ f/8.0
1/4th sec	@ f/16
2 seconds	@ f/45

Although the EV system is sometimes a minor convenience because it allows the correct exposure settings to be made with only a single camera adjustment (on some cameras), it ignores motion and depth of field requirements. For control of these important factors the actual lens and shutter settings must still be considered and selected individually.

Under normal light conditions film exposure is governed by the *reciprocity law,* which states that exposure will vary uniformly with changes in either time or intensity. For example, changing a camera setting of ¼ sec @ f/11 to ½ sec @ f/11 will double the exposure. Similarly, changing a setting of ¼ sec @ f/11 to ¼ sec @ f/8 will double the exposure. Likewise, according to the law, camera settings of 1 sec @ f/16 and 1/100th sec @ f/1.6 should result in the same effective exposure on the film. Unfortunately, if the exposing light intensity on the film surface is either unusually dim or bright, the film does not respond normally and effectively loses speed. Under these conditions we say the reciprocity law has failed.

Films vary in their susceptibility to *reciprocity failure* but, in general, if the light conditions permit exposure times between 1 second and 1/1000th second, reciprocity failure can be ignored. At exposure times of longer than 1 second, the reduced light intensity on the film surface will necessitate *more* than normal exposure, and *less* than normal development for black-and-white films. (See reciprocity failure compensation chart in the appendix, page 306.) Color films will similarly require extra exposure and may also need corrective filtration to prevent color shifts.

Abnormally bright film illumination will also cause loss of effective film speed and color films will again require corrective filtration. Black-and-white films lose contrast, as well as speed, under these conditions, and will need both extra exposure and extra development.

Taking Care of Cameras and Lenses

Cameras are precision instruments, but they can stand a fair amount of wear and tear. They should be protected from dust, moisture, and excessive heat, however, and don't expect one to survive being dropped from any height onto a hard surface. Lenses are more delicate.

Protect your camera and lenses

And store them carefully

Keep them capped at all times when not in use and carry them in padded cases to guard against hard knocks.

Don't simply carry your camera around in your hands when you're out photographing, equip it with a neckstrap, and use it. Most neckstraps are much too long. The camera will be safer and more convenient to use if it hangs high on your chest. While you're not actually photographing, sling the strap over one shoulder and the camera should lie snugly against your side, high up behind your arm. When transporting your equipment it should be packed in protective cases, but camera cases, even the (n)ever ready types, are usually more of a hindrance than a help when you're trying to work.

If you are working in rainy weather, it makes sense to keep the camera covered as much as possible. Keep it under your shirt or jacket while it's hanging around your neck and cover it with a coat or plastic sheet if it has to stand out on a tripod. Use a good deep lens shade and put a *skylight filter* or clear glass cap on the lens to protect it. When you get inside, wipe the outside surfaces of the camera as dry as possible, and leave it out of its case for at least several hours so it can dry out thoroughly.

If you aren't going to use your camera for several weeks or months, remove the batteries, if it has any, release tension on the shutter, and tuck the camera away in a reasonably cool, dry place. Don't wrap it tightly in plastic, because moisture may condense inside. Wrap it in cloth if you want to, or keep it in a *gadget bag* or equipment case. It's probably a good idea to exercise a stored camera occasionally. Take it out every few weeks and work all the controls a few times, or, better yet, go out and take some pictures!

Summary

Every camera is basically a lighttight box, equipped with a lens, film chamber, viewfinder, shutter, and some provision for controlling light intensity, such as an iris diaphragm. Cameras vary greatly in size, design, and convenience features. The simplest types require manual adjustment of all controls; more complex designs may provide automatic operation of most essential functions.

Viewfinder and rangefinder cameras are easy to use, lightweight, and quiet in operation. SLR cameras provide accurate viewfinder images, but are less quiet and more complicated mechanically. Prism-reflex cameras provide excellent viewfinder image quality, are usually equipped with some sort of focusing aid, and frequently feature built-in exposure meters with either semiautomatic or automatic exposure control.

View and field cameras provide groundglass focusing. They are intended for use on a tripod, have almost no automatic features, and are slow and clumsy to operate. They are very versatile, however, and are capable of producing exceptionally fine image quality.

Modern lenses are carefully designed and constructed to minimize the aberrations and provide good image quality. Most are coated or multi-coated to avoid or minimize flare.

There is quite a variety of lenses designed for special applications. Very long focal length lenses are usually built as telephoto lenses to keep them as compact as possible. Similarly, retro-focus design permits the use of very short wide-angle lenses on SLR cameras. Macro-lenses are specially corrected for close-up work; PC or shift lenses permit some control of image perspective. Zoom lenses permit adjustment of focal length and image size. Mirror lenses offer some advantages over conventional telephotos. Fisheye lenses feature extremely wide-angle coverage and extreme distortion.

Among the many camera accessories are lens caps and lens shades, tripods, cable releases, filters, lens extenders or converters, flash units, and motor drives or winders. Handheld exposure meters are also available in several types for making incident, reflectance, or spot readings of subject light. Consider your needs carefully before you buy.

Select an appropriate film type; high speed if you will be working in poor light and handholding the camera; slow film if fine grain and maximum sharpness are of paramount importance; medium or fast film for general purposes.

Before loading film into your camera, inspect the camera body and lens and clean them if necessary. Be very careful not to damage the lens surfaces, or the very fragile surface of the reflex mirror. After loading the film, set the film speed into your meter and identify the film type if the camera provides some method for doing so.

Setting the film speed into the meter tells the meter how much light the film needs to form a good image. Then the meter measures the light which is available to work with and suggests camera settings which will provide useful exposure.

Built-in meters must be used with care if the subject itself is unusually light or dark in tone. Automatic cameras usually provide some way to override the meter when desired. Most built-in meters now favor the center area of the image field and are surprisingly effective.

When you've set the camera controls properly to produce the image effect you want, hold the camera steady and make the exposure. When you're through shooting, check your equipment to be sure it's clean and dry before storing it away. Keep your exposed film protected from direct sunlight and store it in a cool, dry place until you're ready to develop it.

Outline

4 Black-and-White Film Processing

Exposed film must be treated with chemicals to form the negative

Film must be protected from light until it is fixed

Films can be developed in tanks or trays

Exposed film must be treated with a chemical developer solution to make the latent film image visible. It is then rinsed briefly in a stop bath (short-stop) solution and placed in the fixing bath (fixer or hypo). The fixing bath dissolves the undeveloped silver halides from the emulsion, leaving the developed silver image as a pattern of dark tones on the transparent film base to form the negative. After brief treatment in a *hypo-clearing bath,* the negatives are washed in running water and dried.

Because the film is extremely sensitive to light until it has been fixed in the hypo bath, the first few steps of the process must be carried out in complete darkness. Development must, therefore, be controlled by careful adjustment of *time,* developer *temperature,* and *agitation* (stirring of the developer or movement of the film through the developer during development) to avoid under- or over-development, either of which will produce negatives of poor quality.

Since development can't be watched anyway, it's customary to load exposed rollfilm (in total darkness) onto a spiral reel, and place the reel into a lighttight tank for processing. A light trap opening in the tank cover permits the various processing chemical solutions to be poured in and out without admitting light, so after the film is loaded and the tank cover is in place, the lights can be turned on and the actual processing carried out in full light.

Sheet films can be processed either in special *tank and hanger* equipment or by hand in trays. In either case the process must be done in total darkness.

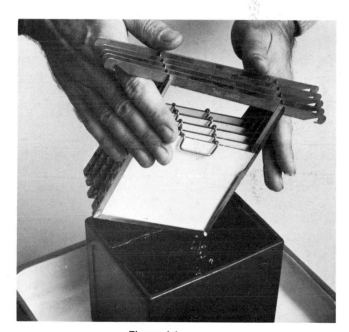

Figure 4.1
Tank and hanger

The work is done by the reducing agent

It must be accelerated, preserved, and restrained

The stop bath halts developer action

The fixer dissolves the unused silver halides

Processing Solutions: Ingredients and Their Functions

A developer, to be satisfactory, must possess several special characteristics. It must actively *reduce* the exposed silver halide crystals of the latent image to visible particles of metallic silver but it should not affect the unexposed halides. In other words, it should produce a useful image without excessive *chemical fog.* It should work predictably, have a long useful life, be relatively economical to use, and be relatively non-staining and nontoxic. No single known chemical, in solution, can fill these requirements but there are literally hundreds of published formulas for mixtures and blends of chemicals which will serve as useful developers.

In a useful formula the work is done by the reducing agent or developing agent, the most common of which are Metol, hydroquinone, and Phenidone. Metol (also known as Elon, Pictol, Rhodol, Photol, etc.) or hydroquinone are occasionally used alone in developer formulas, but more frequently you will find both Metol and hydroquinone (MQ or MH developers) or Phenidone and hydroquinone (PQ or PH) specified. These pairs of reducing agents are sometimes called *super additive* because their mixtures are uniquely effective.

Most reducing agents are inactive, or only weakly active, in neutral or acid solutions and must be activated or accelerated by some alkaline material. Almost any alkaline chemical will do, but the usual ones are borax (sodium tetraborate), Kodalk (Kodak's proprietary version of sodium metaborate), and sodium carbonate.

A simple mixture of a reducing agent and an accelerator would be an active developer, but it would oxidize and spoil very rapidly. The solution must, therefore, contain a preservative chemical, usually sodium sulfite.

In some cases a solution containing a reducing agent, an accelerator, and a preservative would serve as a practical developer, but there is some danger that it might attack the unexposed silver halides to produce chemical fog. The addition of small amounts of a restrainer chemical, usually potassium bromide or benzotriazole, will minimize this difficulty and produce a *clean working* developer.

Although most practical developers contain at least one chemical ingredient for each of the four basic functions just described, some successful formulas require only two or three. Kodak's D–23 developer, for example, contains only Elon and sulfite and functions satisfactorily because Elon (Kodak's brand of Metol) is inherently an active and easily accelerated reducing agent, and sulfite, being mildly alkaline, can serve as both preservative and accelerator. Elon needs no restrainer in this formula, partly because it is such a mild solution and partly because some of the natural by-products of the film developing action are bromide salts which are effective as restrainers in the solution.

When the film has been developed sufficiently, the action of the developer can be arrested by placing the film into the short-stop solution or stop bath. Although some photographers feel that this solution is unnecessary (or even harmful) and can be replaced with a simple water rinse, most authorities now agree that a mildly acidic stop bath is preferable to plain water. It is typically about a 1% solution of acetic acid. This stop bath, by neutralizing the alkaline accelerator, halts development almost immediately. It also serves to rinse away the developer chemicals which might, under some extreme circumstances, cause staining of the film, and, by leaving the film in a slightly acid condition, helps to preserve the essential acid balance of the fixing bath.

The *fixing bath* is another mixture of chemicals dissolved in water. The major ingredient, in the ordinary fixing bath, is sodium thiosulfate, traditionally called *hypo.* In the so-called *rapid-fixing baths* ammonium thiosulfate is used, but all fixing baths are familiarly known as hypo and all are capable of dissolving the unused and still light-sensitive silver halides, without harming the silver image.

Sodium or ammonium thiosulfate and water alone will work as a fixer but the useful life of the solution is short and it is likely to decompose. Again, sodium sul-

Most fixers contain a hardener

Hypo and the halides form complex compounds

The wetting agent can help prevent water spots and scums

Replenishment is intended to restore developer strength

fite acts as a preservative, extending both the storage life and the working capacity of the solution. When preserved with sulfite, the hypo solution can also be acidified slightly to help neutralize any developer alkali that might escape the action of the short-stop. This is usually accomplished by adding an acid sulfite such as sodium bisulfite or potassium metabisulfite to the solution. These three chemicals—hypo, sulfite, and bisulfite—make up a satisfactory *nonhardening fixer.*

It is, however, generally a good idea to harden film by toughening or tanning the gelatin emulsion. This helps to protect it from physical damage and improves image quality by reducing swelling during processing and hastening the drying of the finished negatives. The hardener usually employed is potassium alum and, since it must be in acid solution to work well (it may precipitate out of an alkaline solution), it is customary to include some acetic acid with it, instead of the bisulfite used in the nonhardening formula.

The hypo bath hardens more efficiently, is made more stable, is less likely to throw down a sludgy precipitate in use, and is less malodorous with the addition of some borax or metaborate. Without this ingredient the fixer develops a sharp, highly penetrating, sinus-torturing odor after standing a while, especially in the stuffy confines of the typical home darkroom.

Hypo contains a considerable amount of sulfur and produces some very complex sulfur compounds as it combines with and dissolves the undeveloped silver salts in the emulsion. The hypo itself (and these sulfur compounds) must be removed from the emulsion after its work is done to prevent eventual tarnishing, staining, or fading of the silver image. Because some of the sulfur products of fixation are relatively insoluble, they are not removed from the emulsion easily by simple washing in plain water. Under ideal conditions plain washing is adequate if done long enough and if the water circulates around the films freely; but films wash faster and more efficiently if they are treated before washing with a *hypo-clearing bath.*

There are a number of proprietary hypo-clearing baths on the market and any one of them is probably better than none at all. Presumably they all work when their instructions are followed, but some of them sound rather too magical to be believed. It would probably be wise to overdo the recommended treatment a little with most of them, since very little harm can result from *moderate* over-treatment, and the penalty for insufficient treatment is the probable, eventual deterioration of your negatives.

After the films have been washed, they should be treated briefly in a weak solution of *wetting agent,* which, by reducing surface tension, causes the water on the film to flow off evenly instead of forming droplets or beads (which might cause spots or scum deposits when they dry) on the film surfaces. There are a number of brands, all effective when used as directed, but some may produce a stronger solution than is necessary to do the job. Experiment with the brand you select and use the weakest solution that effectively prevents scum spots. Too strong a solution may leave greasy streaks on your negatives, especially if it is made with hard tap water. Distilled water is best, if available.

Developers: Types and Characteristics

There are several ways to use developers. One type is intended to be mixed in rather small volume, used, and then *replenished* by the addition of a small amount of developer concentrate. Replenishment is intended to restore the used developer to full strength, make up for the normal deterioration due to oxidation, and keep the solution at full volume. In practice, replenished developers can rarely be maintained at a uniform strength throughout their working lives, but the change in characteristics is so gradual that it can easily go unrecognized. An old solution usually works slowly and produces negatives of relatively low contrast, whereas a new solution is full of "fire" and works rapidly and vigorously. To avoid problems when an old solution is replaced with a freshly-mixed one, most authorities recommend adding several ounces of the old used solution to the fresh new one to temper it.

Replenished developers are not entirely reliable

One-shot developers are reliable and convenient

D-76 is an excellent general purpose developer

Almost any developer will do if it is used wisely

Some developers can cause contact dermatitis

My recommendation is to avoid replenished developers entirely unless you are shooting enough film to wear the solutions out from use before they gradually deteriorate from sheer old age. Even then they're risky. Contamination from improperly cleaned tanks or reels (which, of course, should *always* be clean) can weaken the solution; oxidation rate is unpredictable; replenishment itself is based on average rather than actual requirements; and, although proper replenishment might possibly be adequate to replace actual chemical loss, it can't compensate for the gradual build-up of restraining bromide in the used solution.

Some of the same criticisms can be levelled at any developer that is intended for repeated use, including the two-solution compensating types and the monobaths which combine the functions of developer and fixer in one solution. Although all of these developer types have their unique advantages and will certainly produce negatives of excellent quality under ideal conditions, they're likely to be more trouble than they're worth, especially for beginners.

In my opinion, the simplest and most reliable way to develop film is to use a *one-shot* developer. Although almost any developer can be used this way, one-shots are usually supplied in highly concentrated stock solution, a small volume of which is diluted for use with a much larger volume of water. The resulting working solution is used once and then discarded.

This procedure has many advantages: storage problems are minimized; the concentrated stock solutions are extremely stable and resistant to oxidation and will maintain their full strength for a very long time. The working solutions, therefore, are likely to be very consistent in strength, which makes it relatively easy to produce negatives of uniform quality. The procedure is quick and easy, too. Developer temperature is easy to adjust before use because the working solution will assume the temperature of the water used for dilution. After use, the exhausted developer is simply poured down the drain.

One-shots typically produce good image quality, too. Because of their high dilution they tend to be *compensating* in action; that is, they automatically restrain development in the areas of heaviest image density so that unprintable extremes of contrast are less likely to occur. They also tend to enhance the apparent sharpness of the image, separating contrasting areas of image value with unusual crispness. They also emphasize the sharpness and contrast (but not necessarily the size) of the image grain structure, giving the image a snappy pepper-and-salt texture, which some photographers dislike but others admire. Unfortunately, some one-shots are rather expensive.

If you are a beginning photographer, you will probably find that the old standard Kodak formula D-76 (identical with Ilford's ID-11) is an excellent general purpose film developer to start out with. It is available packaged in powder form at any photo store or, if you prefer to mix your own developer from bulk chemicals, the formula is given in the appendix, page 297. Another good general purpose developer is Kodak's HC-110. It is available only in highly concentrated, syrupy-liquid form, and the formula is not available.

Although D-76 can be used *straight* (undiluted) as a replenished developer, many photographers like to use it diluted with an equal volume of water as a one-shot. Used this way, a gallon of D-76 stock solution will develop up to about 32 rolls of 35mm film. HC-110, diluted to make a one-shot solution of similar strength (dilution B), is slightly less expensive to use at current prices, but both developers are at least as economical to use as any of the replenishment-type name brands.

There are many other developers to choose from. If you prefer not to use either D-76 or HC-110, start out with any developer you like, but stick with it and learn to use it before changing. The name of the developer you use is less important than the care with which you use it.

Although most people can tolerate the chemicals involved in black-and-white photography, some individuals are susceptible to contact dermatitis or *Metol poisoning*. Metol affects sensitive skin the way poison ivy does, causing swelling, itching, scaling, blisters, and, in severe cases, cracking and open sores. Even if you are not sensitive to Metol now, you can become sensitized, so it's prudent to take some precautions. Avoid

Whether you're sensitive or not, use chemicals with caution

And keep your darkroom clean

Wash everything, then wash your hands

You'll need a film tank; there are several kinds

unnecessary contact with *all* reducing agents, especially in dry form, and don't let developer solutions dry on your hands. Most people are able to handle developer solutions in normal darkroom use without any trouble at all, but an unfortunate few may have to use protective hand creams or rubber gloves. Some people become so sensitive to Metol that they can hardly walk through an active darkroom without breaking out in a rash. If you discover any sign of skin irritation after a few sessions in the darkroom, stay away from developers for a few days. If the problem clears up but recurs when you go back to work, you should give up Metol developers entirely. A list of developers, which are relatively safe alternatives to conventional Metol formulas, is included in the appendix. Try one or more of these if Metol is causing you discomfort.

Whether you are affected by developers or not, you should treat all chemicals with respect. Some of them can stain or bleach your clothing; others can corrode metal or dissolve your plastic watch crystal. Some give off suffocating or unpleasant vapors and a few can irritate or burn your skin. Ordinary care in handling will avoid all these problems; photography does not need to be hazardous to your health.

It will take a little more than ordinary care to avoid problems of chemical contamination while you're working. You will soon discover, if you're careless, that spilled chemical solutions, dirty utensils, and unclean hands will cause lots of trouble. If you are serious about photography you will have to become a careful craftsman. Try to keep your darkroom clean; be sure your chemicals are fresh and uncontaminated; wash all utensils immediately after use; keep all chemical solutions in the *wet area;* and never, *never* set trays or bottles or chemical containers on the *dry area* table surfaces where you'll be handling film or paper. Become a compulsive hand-washer. Never touch anything with developer (or especially hypo) on your fingers, and don't just wipe chemicals off your hands with a towel—rinse your hands first.

Cleanliness is particularly important if you're working in a school situation or community darkroom. In this case you should also wash trays and other utensils

routinely *before* use, whether they look clean or not. Wipe up spilled liquids, then wash the spots with several changes of water to prevent possible chemical scums. Be particularly wary of white powdery stains which will probably indicate dried hypo; wash them up wherever they appear! It's impossible to get a darkroom too clean. Wash everything. Then wash your hands.

Rollfilm Processing Equipment

To develop rollfilm conveniently and efficiently you'll need a darkroom space, a sink with hot-and-cold running water, and a few items of equipment. First, a rollfilm tank. There are several varieties on the market. The best ones, in my opinion, are made of stainless steel, but some photographers prefer plastic. Most tanks will work well enough, but don't get one that has lots of sculptured plastic shapes and many small parts—it will be hard to clean. The Nikor plastic tank with adjustable reels is especially suitable for 110 and other sub-miniature film sizes. Buy a good quality tank; there are some inexpensive stainless steel models that are rather flimsy and their film reels are not always accurately constructed. Avoid them.

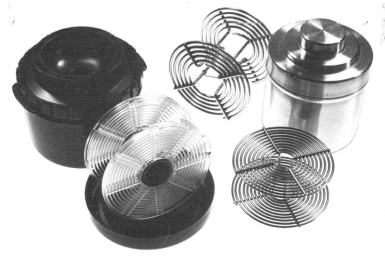

Figure 4.2
Tank and reels

Buy a good thermometer

And an interval timer

You'll need utensils for mixing and storing solutions

Buy or make a film washer

You'll need film clips

Clean-up materials are essential

You'll need a good thermometer for accurate control of solution temperatures. If you can afford a dial-type thermometer, buy it. If not, get a good quality glass one. Even though the dial thermometers are more expensive, they will outlast several glass ones in ordinary use. They are also likely to be at least as accurate, much faster in reacting to temperature changes, easier to read, and easier to use in bottles and tanks.

You can use your watch or a clock to time the various processes, but an interval timer is much more satisfactory. The spring-wound models are cheaper and perfectly satisfactory if you keep hypo out of them. The electric models will probably last longer. They're larger and easier to read in the dark (be sure to get one with a luminous dial) and can also be used as time switches for controlling lights or other electrical devices.

You'll need some utensils for mixing, measuring, pouring, and storing the various solutions. Plastic is a satisfactory material for graduates or measuring cups, stirring rods, and funnels; it is also fine for storage bottles for most of the solutions you'll use. Developers, particularly replenishment-types, should be stored in brown glass or plastic bottles and kept full and tightly capped. One-shot developers (stock solutions) should be stored in several small bottles, rather than one large one, to avoid the large airspace that will appear in the larger container as the solution is used. Regardless of how they're stored, try to protect developers from excessive exposure to air and bright light.

You can wash rollfilm in the developing tank, but, if you can afford it, a special film washing tank will do the job faster. You can also make a good washing tank out of an old plastic jug; cut off the top and punch a few holes around the bottom edge. Stack the film reels in it and set it under the faucet. Water flowing in at the top will leak out at the bottom, taking the hypo with it—a cheap and effective solution to the problem.

You will need some film clips. You can buy stainless steel clips or plastic ones, or you can use ordinary spring clothespins. Stainless steel clips are the best and most expensive; clothespins are cheap but select them with some care. They should grip the film tightly.

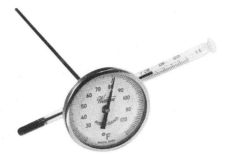

Figure 4.3
Thermometers

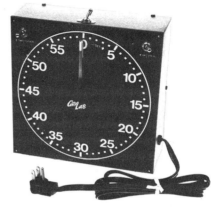

Figure 4.4
Timer

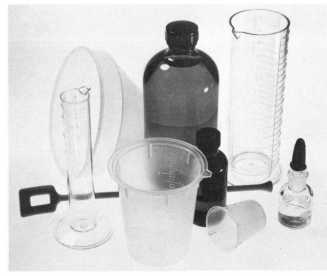

Figure 4.5
Darkroom utensils

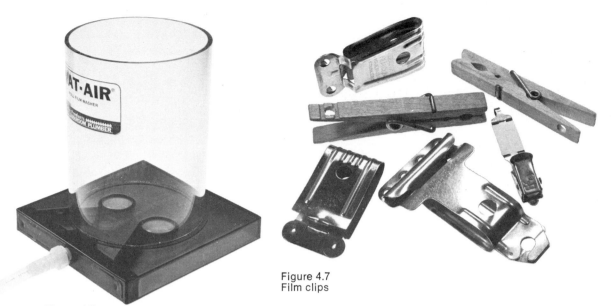

Figure 4.6
Film washer

Figure 4.7
Film clips

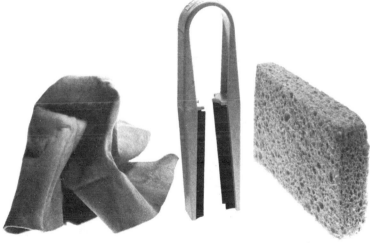

Figure 4.8
Sponge and chamois

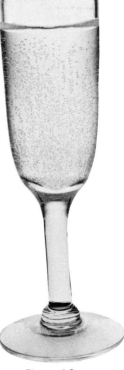

Figure 4.9
Air bubbles in water

Don't use any that are warped or weakened or they may let your film slip to the floor. Drill a hole through one of the flat wooden handles of each of the clothespins so they can be hung up conveniently.

You may want to have a clean, soft viscose sponge, chamois, or a soft rubber squeegee to wipe film with, if the wetting agent fails to leave it clean and free from streaks. The chamois is the better material, by far, but a good, photo-grade chamois will be expensive and hard to find. Ordinary car-washing chamois skins are a cheaper, coarser grade but you may find a section of one that is soft enough to use. Don't use one that has been previously used for car washing, window washing, or household cleaning. Before you use a utility grade chamois for photographic purposes wash it thoroughly in mild detergent and warm water, rinse it well several times and squeeze (don't wring) it dry.

Finally, you should have a large, coarse sponge for general clean-up purposes and a couple of old towels. Use one of them for wiping up the various darkroom surfaces, and use the other as a hand towel. They'll get badly stained but that's no real problem. Just launder them periodically to get rid of accumulated chemicals.

Water for Chemical Mixing

General purpose developers can be mixed with ordinary tap water in most areas of the country without harmful effect, but fine-grain developers and replenishment-type developers may require distilled water if your tap water is excessively hard or chemically treated. If there is any doubt in your mind, use distilled water. It's cheap and the quantities required are small.

Tap water sometimes contains dissolved air and air is detrimental to developers. Check your water supply by letting a freshly-drawn glassful of water stand quietly for a few hours. If a film of air bubbles forms on the inside of the glass, you should probably not use the water to mix developer stock solutions until it has either been boiled and cooled or allowed to stand loosely covered for a day or two. The water can be used right from the tap for diluting stock solutions for use or for making small volumes of developer that will be used within a few days. It will also probably be safe to use for mixing hypo or any of the other normal black-and-white film processing solutions.

Chemical Mixing and Preparation

Mixing packaged developers is simply a matter of following the instructions on the package. Usually the instructions call for a partial volume of warm or hot water and these temperature recommendations should be heeded. Too cool water will make the chemicals dissolve with difficulty; too hot water may hasten oxidation or decomposition of the solution. Chemicals should usually be poured into the water with moderately vigorous stirring and the stirring should be continued until the solution is complete. Don't overdo it, though; whipping the liquid into a froth will mix air into it and encourage oxidation. Finally, the warm solution is brought to proper volume with cool water and poured into a clean brown glass or plastic bottle for storage.

If the developer is a stock solution which will be used gradually, store it in several smaller bottles, each completely full, and keep them in a cool, dark place until needed. A small volume of developer in a large bottle will oxidize fairly rapidly. Most developers turn to a rich dark brown color when thoroughly spoiled and develop a kind of rotten garlic odor. Some developers have a rather pronounced tan color, even when fresh, but a distinctly yellowish or orangish tint almost always indicates the beginning of oxidation. Don't use any normal MQ developer which is approaching the color of weak tea.

If you decide to mix your developer from bulk chemicals, the routine is slightly different. Use the volume and temperature of water that is specified in the formula, but add each chemical ingredient separately and stir each until completely dissolved, unless otherwise instructed. The ingredients should normally be dissolved in the order given in the formula; if the proper order is not followed the chemicals may not dissolve or, in some cases, they may decompose. See formulas in the appendix, page 297.

You can buy the stop bath stock solution already prepared, or you can buy glacial acetic acid and prepare your own stock solution. Stop bath stock is simply 28% acetic acid and is strong-smelling, but relatively harmless. Glacial acetic is 99% pure and should be handled with caution. It is fairly mild, as acids go, but still potent enough to burn the skin painfully, corrode some metals, and act as a powerful solvent for some plastics. It also has a breathtakingly sharp and penetrating odor. Mix it only in a well-ventilated area, close to a source of running water, in case you spill it or splash some on your skin.

Contrary to popular belief, the rule "always pour acid into water" (which is vitally important with sulfuric acid) does not necessarily apply to acetic acid, but following it is probably good practice and will certainly do no harm. Treat it with respect, but don't panic; acetic acid is a friendly sort of acid, relatively speaking.

To prepare the 28% short-stop stock solution, add three parts of the glacial acetic acid to eight parts of water. A *part,* of course, can be any volume you choose. If you want to make approximately a quart of stock, for example, you will need a total of eleven parts (three acid plus eight water) to make a total volume of about 32 ounces. Divide 32 by 11 to get about 3 ounces for the volume of each part. Then:

```
add:   3 parts acid (times 3 ounces)  =  9 ounces acid
  to:  8 parts water (times 3 ounces) = 24 ounces water
total: 11 parts (times 3 ounces)      = 33 ounces stock
                                          solution
```

Add the acid to cool tap water, stir until blended, and store in a plain glass or plastic container. The solution is stable and will keep indefinitely. Label the bottle "stop bath stock solution" and add the words, "28% acetic acid," if you want to.

Commercial short-stop stock solutions frequently contain a yellow dye, called an "indicator." The stop bath itself, prepared from an indicator stock, is yellow as long as it remains in a useful acid condition, but when

Fixers are sensitive to mixing conditions

Prepare separate volumes for film and paper

Clearing baths can be used as one-shots

Distilled water is preferable for wetting baths

Film tank loading is an acquired skill

it becomes exhausted or neutralized, the yellow dye turns to purple as a visual signal that the bath should be replaced. Indicator stop baths are convenient for some purposes, but they are more expensive than plain acetic acid and are not suitable for use in some formulas (other than stop baths) which call for acetic acid. Plain acetic acid stop bath is perfectly satisfactory for film processing.

Although the fixing bath can be mixed from bulk chemicals, there is no particular advantage in doing so. Regular powdered fixer can be purchased readily and cheaply and it is convenient to mix. Rapid fixers are even easier. They usually come as liquid concentrates. Fixers are quite sensitive to mixing conditions, however, and the instructions should be followed carefully. Two things are especially important. Be sure not to have the mixing water too hot; and be sure, when mixing the liquid concentrates, not to add the hardener solution (smaller bottle of clear liquid) until the thiosulfate solution has been adequately diluted with water and thoroughly blended. Failure to observe these precautions will probably cause the solution to form a milky precipitate.

Although this precipitate will not completely destroy the solution (in mild cases it may disappear after standing for a day or two), it will make it unsuitable for use with films or papers which you plan to keep for any appreciable length of time. You shouldn't use milky fixer for any purpose, actually. It's bad craftsmanship. Learn to mix it properly.

Regular fixing bath (not rapid) is generally used at the same strength for both films and papers. Rapid fixers are much more active and, if made too strong, will bleach the silver image from the delicate paper emulsions. Rapid fixers are, therefore, mixed in two strengths—the stronger solution is used for film processing; the weaker solution is reserved for print processing. Regardless of the type you use, you should prepare separate volumes of fixer for films and papers. A fixing bath which has been used for film fixing should not be used for paper. Mix the film fixer according to the package directions, and store it in a plain glass or plastic bottle labelled "film fixer" or "film hypo." The solution is quite stable and will keep for a long time.

Hypo-clearing baths (also called hypo-neutralizing baths or washing aids) are sold as liquid concentrates in most cases, but the Kodak product comes in powder form which must be mixed to make a stock solution. Follow the instructions that come with the product you select; they are not all alike. In general the unused solutions keep fairly well, but some brands do not keep well after use. Although it's a slightly wasteful practice, it's convenient to mix the working solution in small volume just before use and discard it after one use, like a one-shot developer. This will avoid uncertainty about the condition of the solution and simplify your storage problems.

The wetting agent does not ordinarily require any preparation except dilution to a working solution, just before use. In hard water areas, however, it may be necessary to use distilled water in preparing the wetting rinse and, in this case, the bath can be saved and reused. Be sure that the film is thoroughly washed before being treated in the wetting bath and discard the bath after just a few rolls of film have gone through it. Discard it after a week or so, whether it's been used or not; old wetting baths sometimes develop strange algae-like growths. Freshly prepared solutions are best. No storage is required.

Processing Rollfilm

Loading the film onto the tank reel is a skill that you'll have to acquire with practice. If possible, get a roll or two of spoiled or developed film and practice loading it in the light so you can see what the problems are. When you feel confident, take the practice film into the darkroom and load it a few times. Then, if things are going well, load your good exposed film in total darkness. Put the reel into the tank and put the cover on securely before turning on the lights. Figures 4.10 and 4.11 show the critical steps in loading various film sizes. Study them carefully while you're practicing.

Figure 4.10

a. Open the film cartridge with Kodak's special gadget or a hook-type can opener.

b. Cut off the film tongue. Some films will tear, some won't. Scissors are recommended.

c. Palm the spool and squeeze the film edges together lightly to keep the extended end from rolling up.

d. Locate the end of the spiral film guides with your forefinger. They should be at the top of the reel, pointing toward the hand that holds the film.

e. The reel hub may be equipped with a clip to hold the film end or it may simply have a wide slot, as shown. Insert the film into the slot and center it between the reel flanges with thumb and finger of the left hand. This is important.

f. The start is critical; keeping the film slighly curled with the right hand and centered between the reel flanges with the left, pull on the film lightly and turn the reel counterclockwise so the film is bent sharply around the hub. It should slip smoothly into the spiral track. Let your left forefinger ride lightly on the back of the film to check for bulges and continue rotating the reel, feeding the film with the right hand.

g. If you detect any irregularity as you wind the film, go back at least a full turn and find the trouble; don't just try to force it. Correctly loaded film will feel loose in the reel grooves. When the reel is loaded cut off the film spool, tuck the film end into the tank. Be sure the cover is on snugly before turning the lights on.

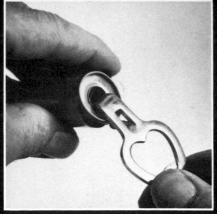
a

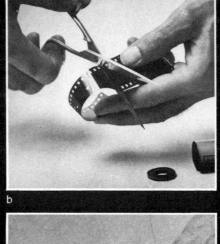
b

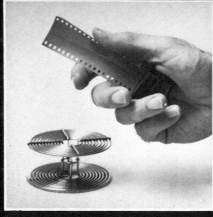
c

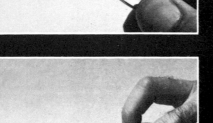
d

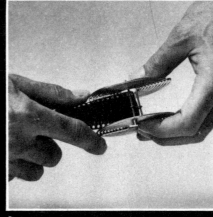
e

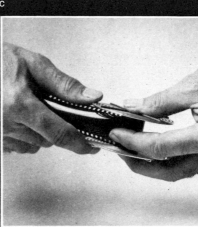
f

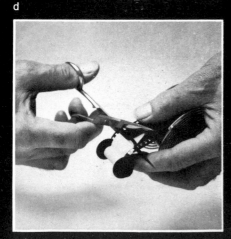
g

Figure 4.11

a. Open the 110 cartridge (in the dark!) by breaking it in two, as shown.

b. Pull out the paper leader; the film will appear and can be pulled out. It is not fastened. Handle it carefully to avoid kinking or fingerprinting it. The emulsion side is inside the natural curl.

c. Align the flanges of the film reel, as shown, and insert the film end into the starting slot. Push it straight in for at least two or three inches. If the reel is dry and clean, you may be able to push the whole length of film into the tracks but usually you'll feel some resistance after the first few inches.

d. "Walk" the film the rest of the way by depressing the locking tabs with your thumbs, alternately, and twisting the reel flanges back . . .

e. . . . and forth, as shown. Practice this motion in the light, first, with a strip of spoiled film. It's not difficult, but it will take some coordination. Some types of reels don't have the locking tabs; you simply hold the edge of the film down with your thumb as you turn the flange.

f. Put the loaded reel into the tank and replace the lid before turning on the lights. This tank features an adjustable reel. The flanges can be spread apart to accommodate 35mm film as well as the 110 size shown here.

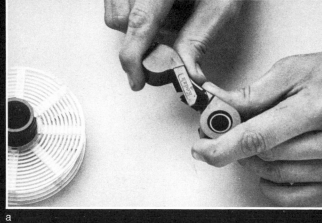
a

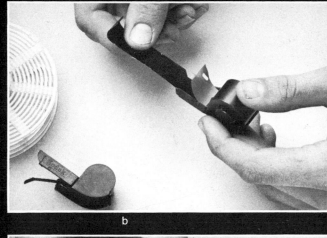
b

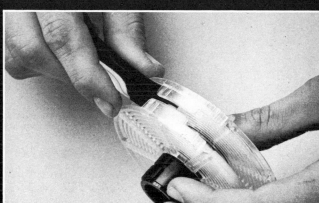
c

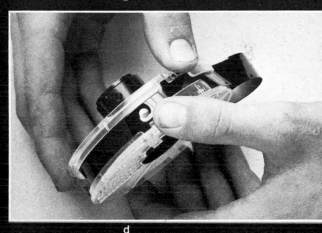
d

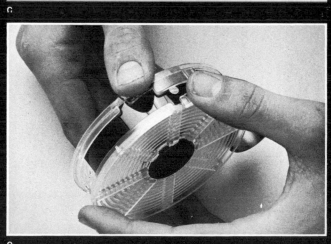
e

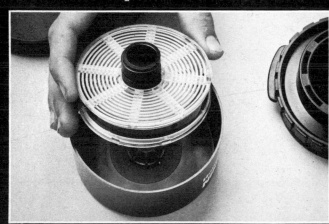
f

Figure 4.12

a. Check solution temperatures and set the bottles in a water bath if they need adjustment. If much change is necessary, pour the solution into a stainless steel film tank and set the tank in the water bath. Stir the solution with the thermometer stem, gently, until the temperature is satisfactory.

b. You can pour the developer into the loaded tank, like this, or you can fill the tank with developer before you load the film and place the loaded reel into the tank in the dark. Be sure to cover the tank before turning on the lights. In either case, start the timer as soon as the film is covered with developer.

c. Agitate continuously for the first fifteen seconds or so, then start a routine agitation procedure as described in the text.

d. When the developing time is almost up, pour the developer back into the storage jug if it's to be replenished. If it's a one-shot, dump it out. Time this operation so you can complete it before the timer rings.

e. Immediately pour in the stop bath. Ideally the tank should just be filled with stop as the timer goes off to signal the end of the developing step.

f. Agitate.

g. You can save the stop bath if you like. Some people do. I prefer to mix it fresh each time and throw it away after use.

h. Pour in the fixing bath and notice the time so you can determine the film clearing time.

i. Agitate for fifteen seconds or so.

j. Then remove the tank cover and inspect the film to see if it's clear. If not, replace it in the fixer and agitate it occasionally by lifting the reel out of the solution and replacing it. When it appears to be clear, note the time that clearing has taken and return the film to the fixer, with occasional agitation, for another similar time interval. (See text).

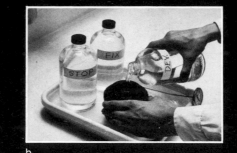
a

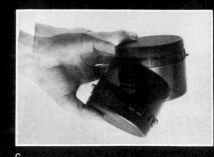
b

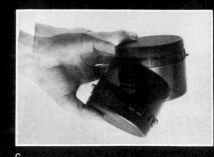
c

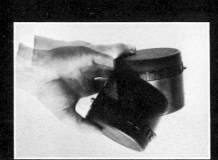
f

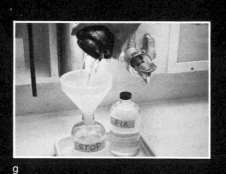
g

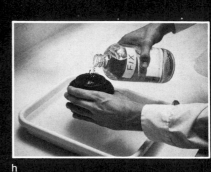
h

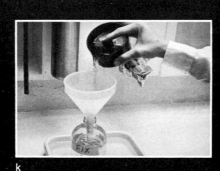
k

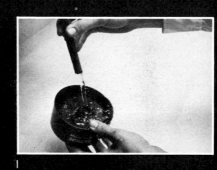
l

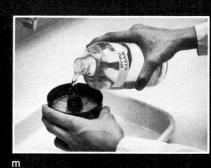
m

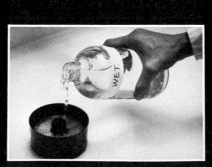
p

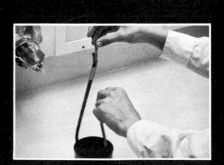
q

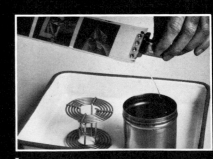
r

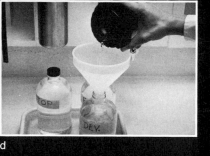

d

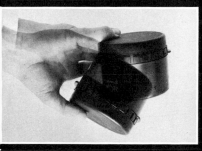

i

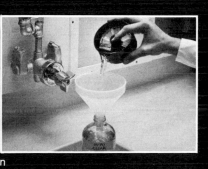

n

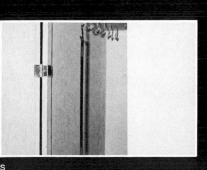

s

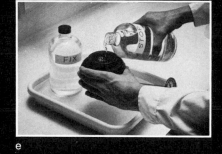

e

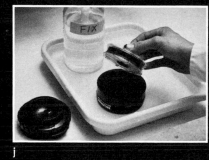

j

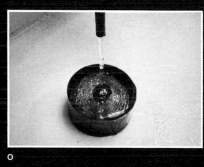

o

k. Pour the fixer back into the storage jug. It can be reused until it fails the hypo test. (See text.)

l. Rinse the film briefly under running water, to remove the surface fixer.

m. Pour in the hypo-clearing bath and agitate by picking the reel out of solution and replacing it periodically. Follow manufacturer's instructions for clearing bath use and storage.

n. You can save some clearing baths for immediate reuse, but they do not all keep well. I prefer to mix it fresh for each use and discard it afterward.

o. Wash the film in running water. If you use the film tank for this operation, as shown, empty it completely several times during the washing process to insure complete water changes. Follow washing instructions given for the clearing bath you use.

p. Treat the film with a wetting solution such as Photoflo diluted in distilled water. Let it soak for a few seconds, then . . .

q. . . . attach film clips to the film ends and see-saw the film through the wetting solution a few times and hang it up to dry.

r. Films larger than 110 will dry cleaner if they are held like this for a few seconds so the wetting solution can drain off to one edge. This will help to keep possible scums and spots out of the picture area. If the film strip is too long to handle this way conveniently, just hang it up.

s. Hang the film in a drying cabinet if you have one, otherwise find a dust-free place with adequate ventilation.

Development must be controlled carefully

Work at a standard temperature; 20°C is recommended

Initial agitation should be fairly vigorous, but brief

Then agitate briefly at intervals. Be consistent

Development should be timed; see the film information sheet

Fix for twice as long as it takes the film to clear

Film development must be controlled quite carefully. If the developer is too strong or too warm, or if the film is agitated too vigorously during development, or if the developing time is excessive, the film will be overdeveloped and the negatives will be too contrasty and probably too dense, also. On the other hand, underdevelopment will result if the developer is too weak or old, or too cool, or if the agitation is insufficient, or if the developing time is too short. Underdeveloped negatives will probably be *thin* (pale and transparent) and *flat* (low in contrast).

Although any temperature between about 18° and 24° Celsius (about 64° to 75° Fahrenheit) can be used satisfactorily with most developers, you should try to standardize. The generally recommended temperature for film development is 20°C (68°F). Although films and developers are not all alike in their sensitivity to changes in development temperature, the chart on page 306 of the appendix will help you estimate a satisfactory developing time for temperatures other than the normal 20°C.

Whatever temperature you elect to use (remember, 20°C is recommended), be sure that the three main processing solutions (developer, short-stop, and fixing bath) are all about the same. Try to keep the developer within one degree of the desired temperature; the other solutions can vary by about two degrees without significant danger.

An extreme *difference* in temperature between solutions should be avoided or you run the risk of *reticulation,* a fine net-like pattern of cracks or folds in the emulsion gelatin which coarsen the image texture and may destroy it. Extreme cases of reticulation are very rare with today's tough emulsions, but a mild case can appear as an emphasized grain pattern and may pass unrecognized.

Sheet film, developed in a tray, is given *constant agitation;* that is, it is moved through the solution continuously during the developing interval. Sheet film, developed in tank and hanger equipment, and rollfilms, developed in tanks, are given *"intermittent agitation,* brief periods of agitation, separated by longer periods of rest.

Films should be agitated fairly vigorously when first immersed in developer to insure complete wetting of the emulsion and to dislodge any air-bells which might be clinging to the surface. Rollfilm tanks of the stainless steel variety can be agitated initially by picking them up, turning them over and back several times with a swirling motion, and then rapping them smartly a time or two against the heel of your hand or the sink surface. This initial agitation should not be prolonged more than ten or fifteen seconds, then the tank should be allowed to rest quietly for twenty or thirty seconds before beginning the intermittent agitation routine.

If the total developing time is to be more than about six or seven minutes, the film should be agitated briefly at one-minute intervals. If the total developing time is to be less than about six minutes, it is better to agitate briefly every thirty seconds. These brief agitation periods involve simply turning the tank over and back two or three times, with a final swirling motion. This can be accomplished in two or three seconds and should not be prolonged beyond about five. Do it gently, too.

Excessive agitation or too vigorous agitation will increase negative density and contrast and may cause development streaks, usually along the margins of the film strip. Too little agitation can also cause problems: lowered contrast and density, and streaks that usually run across the width of the film. Try to be consistent with your agitation procedure. It is a critical part of the developing process.

Development should be timed from the moment the tank is *filled* with developer (or the film immersed in it) until the moment the tank is *filled* with the short-stop solution. Or, if you prefer, from the moment you *start to pour* developer onto the film until the moment you *start to pour* the short-stop. The actual time of development will depend upon the film type, the developer type and strength, developer temperature, agitation procedure, and the degree of development desired. The developing times recommended on the information sheets packed with the film are based on "normal" conditions and assume that you want "normal" contrast in your negatives. Normal is a good place to start.

Figure 4.13
If you don't load the tank properly or if you handle the film roughly, your negatives and prints may suffer, as shown here. On the negative strip (seen from the emulsion side) the irregular black blob resulted from improper loading; adjacent layers of film touched, preventing the processing liquids from doing their work. The raw emulsion material, neither developed nor fixed in this case, appear on the negative as a milky-gray area which is virtually opaque to transmitted light. It prints as a totally white shape. The little black crescent shapes I call "fingernail marks" because they resemble nail trimmings. They result from kinking the film; they print white or light gray.

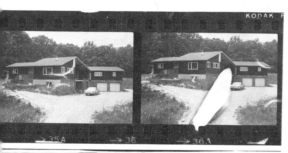

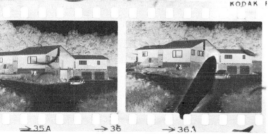

We'll talk about abnormal conditions later.

The working solution of short-stop is prepared from commercial stock solution or the 28% acetic acid stock solution, by diluting one part of the stock with about 25 to 30 parts of water. Don't make the stop bath stronger than a 1 to 20 dilution nor weaker than about 1 to 50. One ounce per quart of water (1 to 32) is a good ratio for rollfilms, and it's easy to remember. Be sure it is at about the same temperature as the developer.

Immediately after the developer is poured out of the tank, pour the short-stop in and give it continuous agitation for at least ten seconds. The total treatment in the short-stop should last from about 30 seconds to a minute but, if necessary for some reason, the film can remain in the short-stop bath for up to several minutes without harm. Agitate it periodically, then dump it out and pour in the fixing bath.

The fixer needs no further preparation, but its temperature, like that of the other solutions, should be approximately 20°C (or whatever the developer tem-

perature is). Agitate the tank for about ten or fifteen seconds immediately after filling it with fixer; then let it stand for a minute or so. This is a good time to wash the utensils you've used so far.

After the film has been in the fixer for a minute or so, it is safe to remove the tank cover. Lift the reel out of the solution part way and inspect the film. If the film has not been fixed yet, it will still contain undissolved silver salts which may appear as a solid or blotchy, creamy-white coating. The image may or may not be visible as a dark pattern, but it will gradually appear as the fixer dissolves the undeveloped halides. Let the film soak in the fixer for another half-minute with occasional gentle agitation, and check it again. If the film now looks totally dark with no visible trace of the whitish emulsions, it is *clear,* but not yet safe to remove! To be certain that all the silver halides are completely gone, leave the film in the fixer for two more minutes, or (*rulc*) leave the film in the fixer for *twice* as long as it takes to clear.

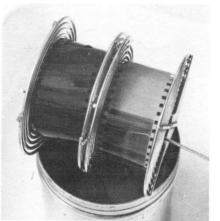

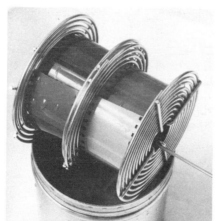

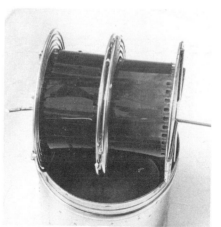

Figure 4.14
a. After 30 seconds in fixer, Plus-X film (left) and Infra-Red (right) are both still milky and opaque. Infra-Red appears lighter because it is on clear base material without antihalation dye.

b. After one minute the Plus-X is almost clear. The Infra-Red image areas are clearing but the leader is still milky and opaque.

c. After three minutes, Plus-X is clear and fully fixed. Infra-Red film is still showing traces of milkiness on the leader, particularly around the sprocket holes, but the image areas are clear. It cleared completely after another minute and was given four more minutes to insure complete fixing.

Don't overfix

Test the fixing bath occasionally

Clean up the darkroom

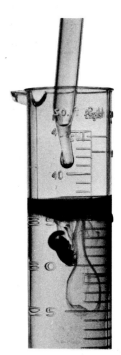

Figure 4.15
Hypo test and sulphur cloud

Beginners seem to have trouble with this concept, so let's go over it again. If the film clears (looks black with no trace of white emulsion) after one minute in the fixer, give it another minute for a total of two. If it first appears clear after five minutes, give it another five. If you don't open the tank for four minutes after pouring in the fixer and the film is clear when you look at it, assume that it *just* cleared, and give it another four minutes. Overfixing the film by five or ten minutes is not likely to hurt it, but don't leave it in the fixer (especially rapid-fix) for more than ten or fifteen minutes, since there is some danger that some types of film might be slightly bleached.

Some films require considerably longer to clear than others. Panatomic-X, for example, will probably clear in fresh rapid-fix in less than a minute and should be taken out after a similar period. Type 2475 recording film, on the other hand, may not appear to be clear for five or more minutes, especially if the fixer is nearing exhaustion. If the clearing time for a given film is normally, say, two minutes, in fresh fixer, you can reuse the fixer until the clearing time for that film is twice normal or four minutes. Total fixing time will then be eight minutes (in this example) and the fixer should be discarded and replaced with fresh solution.

It is important not to use exhausted fixer for films (and even more important for printing papers) because the products of fixation formed by old, used fixing baths are relatively insoluble and cannot be removed from the emulsion easily by normal washing procedures. You can check the condition of your fixing bath with a commercial *hypo test* solution, following package instructions. Alternatively, you can make your own test solution by dissolving 2.0 grams of potassium iodide in 100 milliliters of water. A drop of this solution, introduced gently into a small volume of the fixing bath, will cause a dense yellowish-white precipitate to form if the fixer is exhausted. Throw it away and mix a fresh bath. No precipitation will occur in a fresh or still usable solution. Return this fixer to its storage bottle.

After pouring the fixer from the tank, fill the tank with fresh water, adjusted to match the temperature of the fixer within a degree or two. Agitate the film briefly.

Pour the water out of the tank and pour in the hypo-clearing bath, mixed according to individual package instructions. It, too, should match the temperature of the previous processing solutions within a degree or two. Treat the film for at least the length of time and with the agitation specified for the product, and then wash the film in running water, at about the same temperature, for at least as much time as is recommended by the clearing bath manufacturer.

If you do not use a hypo-clearing bath, films should be washed for at least half-an-hour in slowly running water and agitated periodically to be sure the water circulation is reaching all areas of the film. Check for frothy coatings of tiny air bubbles on the film surface and rinse them off if they form. If running water is not available, or if water is in short supply, you can wash film satisfactorily by soaking it for periods of two minutes, with occasional agitation in each of ten changes of water, draining the tank thoroughly each time before refilling it with fresh water.

The final rinse bath consists of a wetting agent solution, mixed no stronger than is recommended in the package instructions. Distilled water is preferable to tap water for this bath; in fact, if your tap water is unusually hard or chemically treated, it is probably a good idea to agitate the film for a couple of minutes in a tankful of plain distilled water before treating it with the wetting solution. The preliminary rinse water should be discarded, but the wetting solution can be used for several rolls of film if they are done within a few days time. Don't reuse a wetting solution which has treated inadequately washed film; it will contaminate subsequent rolls. If there is any doubt in your mind about the condition of the solution, throw it away and mix a fresh bath.

Soak the film, still on the reel, in the wetting solution for about a minute, then remove the film from the reel, attach a film clip to each end of the film strip, and seesaw the film back and forth through the wetting solution, as shown in the illustration, to remove bubbles and surface particles. Then drain the wetting solution from the film, as shown, and carefully hang it in a dust-free environment to dry.

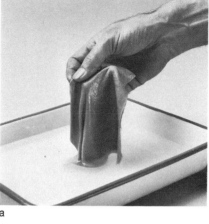
a

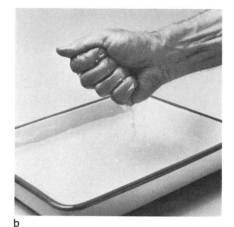
b

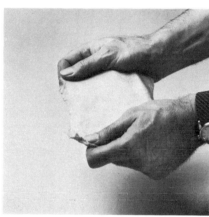
c

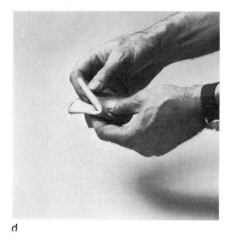
d

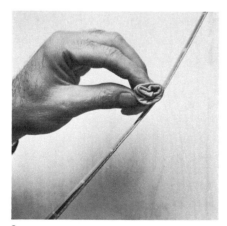
e

Figure 4.16
Soak the chamois thoroughly in clean water, then squeeze it dry, stretch out the wrinkles, fold it into a flat pad and wipe the film gently.

If you have not used a wetting solution, you will have to remove the water droplets from the film surfaces by wiping them. A dampened viscose sponge is better than nothing, but a folded piece of damp chamois skin is much more effective. Soak the chamois thoroughly to soften it, then *squeeze* it as dry as possible. Don't *wring* it or it is liable to shed its surface fibers and cover your film with tiny shreds of leather. Fold the chamois into a flat pad and, using moderate pressure, stroke the film from top to bottom, once on each side. It should be completely free from water droplets and visible moisture. If it is not, squeeze the chamois skin again, and repeat the wiping procedure *gently!* Alternatively, wipe the film surface dry with one stroke of a soft rubber squeegee such as a new (not used) windshield wiper blade. Although these are effective ways to treat film, there is some danger of scratching it. They are, therefore, not recommended unless the wetting agent treatment alone is ineffective.

Gentle circulation of warm, dry air will hasten the drying process, but avoid excessive heat and watch out for airborne dust. Commercial film dryers are available but you probably don't need one unless you have no suitable drying area or unless you're doing lots of processing on a daily basis.

If you have not already done so, now is the time to clean up the darkroom mess. Rinse developer-soiled articles with used or leftover short-stop, then rinse again with several changes of water. Rinse the tank cover under running water, paying particular attention to the light trap. Rinse the wetting solution out of the tank and off the reel until the water stops frothing, then set them in place to dry. Check the sink edge, light switches, and timer controls for chemical stains from unwashed fingers and wash them if necessary. Be very careful not to let water get into the light switches or the timer mechanism. Rinse off the outside of the storage bottles and flush out the sink with water. Dry your hands. Turn off the water and turn out the lights before leaving the darkroom.

When the film is dry, remove the film clips carefully so any water drops that they might be retaining will not fall on your new negatives. Cut 35mm negatives into

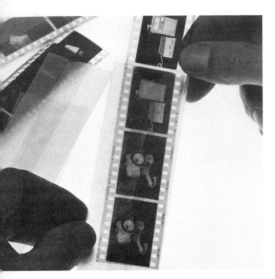

Figure 4.17
Cutting and filing negatives

Underexposure produces thin negatives; overexposure makes them dense

Underdevelopment produces low contrast; overdevelopment produces high contrast

Learn to recognize good negative quality

strips of six to fit most standard negative envelopes or sleeves (some types take strips of five). Rollfilm negatives are usually cut into strips of two to four, depending on the image format. Buy negative envelopes to accommodate the strip lengths you find most convenient and cut the film to fit them.

Handle the dry negatives with great care. They will scratch easily and are susceptible to damage from fingerprints and water spots. Slip each strip of negatives into its own separate envelope or sleeve (don't double them up). There are negative storage sheets available which are punched to fit into a standard three-hole notebook, each sheet capable of holding a full roll of negatives. Investigate them; they are convenient, offer good protection, and make the problem of locating a particular negative fairly simple.

Appraising Negative Quality

The quality of the negative image is influenced by both film exposure and development. In general, if development is normal and exposure is varied, the density of the negative will vary. Underexposure of the film will produce a thin, pale image, typically lacking in *shadow detail* because the shadow areas of the subject will have provided the least light for film exposure. Normal exposure will result in a negative of rather luminous quality, transparent enough to see some light through even the most dense areas, but retaining well-defined details in the thinnest shadow areas. Overexposure will result in heavy density overall; the highlight areas of the image may be virtually opaque in extreme cases and the image shadows will be well detailed but obviously dense.

Exposure, therefore, is said to control density. The other significant image characteristic is contrast. It is influenced strongly by development conditions.

If film exposure is normal, underdevelopment (caused by insufficient temperature or time or excessive dilution) will result in a *weak* negative image which will appear thin (as an underexposed image would) but will contain visible traces of shadow detail. The image

contrast (density difference between highlight and shadow areas) is low. Normal development will result in a negative of normal contrast and density, as described. Overdevelopment will produce dense highlights and relatively thin shadows; the negative will have a harsh appearance and contrast will be high.

Exposure and development are not entirely separate influences. Both control image density to some degree and, with some film types, both also influence contrast. Underexposure is easy to identify, however. If the negative highlights and midtones are thinner than normal and the shadow areas are transparent without useful image detail, the film exposure was insufficient. If, on the other hand, the shadows are unnecessarily dense and heavily detailed, the film exposure was overdone.

Development errors are not quite so easy to identify, but excessive contrast in the negative is an indication of more-than-necessary development for that particular subject condition. Low contrast, on the other hand, indicates that longer or more vigorous development would have been a good idea. Normal development will produce normal negative contrast when the subject contrast itself is normal. Abnormal subject contrast can be compensated for by modified development to produce normal negative contrast.

Good negative quality is essential if you want to make good prints. Expose and develop your film with care and treat the negatives tenderly. You'll soon learn to recognize "good quality" negatives, if you understand the effects of exposure and development and make an effort to analyze and correct your technical blunders.

Summary

Exposed film must be developed in total darkness. Development is controlled by adjustment of time, temperature, and agitation, and is usually carried out in a tank.

The developer typically contains chemicals which fulfill the functions of reducing agent, accelerator, preservative, and restrainer. Development is halted when

Synopsis **Rollfilm Developing Process Steps**

Total Darkness

1. Load the film onto the appropriate tank reel and place in tank. Put cover on tank. Turn on lights.

Normal Room Light

2. In three clean containers prepare appropriate volumes of developer, stop bath, and fixing bath (of film strength). Adjust temperatures of all solutions to 20°C (68°F). Set an interval timer for the appropriate developing time for the film and developer in use (see developing charts, page 306).
3. *Developer:* Pour developer into tank until it starts to overflow. Start the timer, replace top cap on tank, and agitate vigorously for 10 to 15 seconds. Thereafter, agitate by turning tank over and back two or three times, at intervals of thirty seconds (use one-minute intervals if total developing time will exceed about six minutes). About 30 seconds before end of developing time, pour developer out.
4. *Stop Bath:* Immediately pour stop bath into tank so tank is full just as the developing time is up. Agitate the stop bath continuously for 10 or 15 seconds, minimum. Pour out after about 30 seconds.
5. *Fixer:* Set timer running and note time. Pour fixer into tank and agitate for 10 or 15 seconds, then let it rest for a minute or so while you wash the used utensils. Remove tank cover and wash it thoroughly. Inspect film. If film is not clear, replace it in fixer and check it at 30-second intervals until it clears, then replace it in fixer and leave it for another interval equal to the total clearing time. Then pour fixer back into storage jug. Check fixer strength periodically.
6. *Water Rinse:* Fill open tank with clean water at about 20°C, agitate briefly, and pour out.
7. *Hypo-Clearing Bath:* Pour clearing bath at about 20°C into tank and agitate it two or three times. Repeat at frequent intervals during clearing time recommended by manufacturer.
8. *Wash:* Allow slowly running water at about 20°C to flow into the center of the open tank for time recommended by manufacturer of clearing bath. At frequent intervals empty tank and allow it to refill to insure complete water changes. Alternatively, use film washer following manufacturer's instructions.
9. *Wetting:* Fill tank with wetting agent solution at about 20°C preferably prepared with distilled water. In hard water areas, precede this bath with a thorough rinse in plain distilled water.
10. *Dry:* Drain wetting agent from film and hang the film strip to dry in a dust-free place. Avoid violent air movement or excessive heat. Wipe film surfaces only if necessary to avoid surface scums, but careful wiping with a clean, soft chamois, thoroughly soaked and squeezed very dry, is advisable if wetting agent is not used.
11. *Store:* Cut film into convenient lengths and store the negative strips in negative envelopes or sleeves to protect them from dust and fingerprints. Keep them away from heat and protected from moisture or high humidity.

---

the film is immersed in an acid stop bath and the fixing bath removes the unused light-sensitive material and hardens the film emulsion. To avoid eventual image deterioration, the film must be washed thoroughly.

Developers can be used and replenished or they can be used as one-shots and discarded. One-shots provide good image quality and some are mildly compensating. Pick a developer and learn to use it well.

Photographic chemicals should be treated with reasonable caution. Some individuals are susceptible to Metol poisoning. Keep your darkroom and utensils clean and wash your hands immediately after contact with any dry chemical or chemical solution.

For rollfilm processing you should have a darkroom equipped with a sink and hot-and-cold running water. Necessary or desirable equipment items include a tank, thermometer, timer, mixing and storage utensils and containers, a wash tank, film clips, and a soft sponge, chamois, or squeegee.

Most chemicals can be mixed with tap water. Follow mixing and storage instructions carefully. Some solutions are stock solutions, others are working solutions; don't confuse them.

Tank loading is a skill you'll have to acquire with practice. Use spoiled film while you're learning. When you are ready to develop, follow the process steps carefully. Time, temperature, and agitation are important and should be controlled quite precisely for best results. Film clearing time in the fixer is variable; learn to recognize cleared film. Don't use exhausted fixer; test it if in doubt. Use a hypo-clearing bath to speed washing and treat the washed film with a wetting agent. File the dry negative strips in separate sleeves.

Exposure is largely responsible for negative image density. Development is largely responsible for negative image contrast. Learn to recognize good negative quality.

Outline

5 Printing

Facilities and Equipment

Printing, like film processing, is easiest in a darkroom space with hot-and-cold running water. It's convenient to have a large sink to work in but a large table surface will do if it can be waterproofed so spilled solutions won't damage it or leak onto the floor. If you're building a darkroom, you can make an excellent sink out of plywood waterproofed with fiberglass cloth and acrylic or epoxy resin. These materials are available from boat dealers, who can also supply instructions for applying them. You can hardly make the sink too big; it should be at least six inches deep, two feet wide, and as long as possible. You'll find a six-foot sink cramped and, if you start making really big prints or getting involved in advanced color or nonsilver processes, you'll soon wish you had twelve feet of length.

Divide your darkroom space into two well-defined areas, *wet* and *dry,* and keep them separate. The sink and an associated table space constitute the wet area. Do your chemical mixing, film and print developing, washing, and any other procedure that involves use or storage of liquids in this area. The dry area should include the printing area, film and paper storage, space for film tank loading, a paper cutter, negative filing folders or cases, and space for any other dry, clean operations you'll be involved in. Be sure to provide plenty of electrical outlets for timers, safelights,

enlarger, and other needs. Don't neglect the ventilation —a closed darkroom can be very stuffy and unpleasant if you can't get fresh air into it.

You'll need lots of storage space, too. Cabinets with doors are preferable to open shelves because shelves collect dust. Try to provide a specific place for every item of equipment. It will simplify your housekeeping and make darkroom operations more efficient. A floor drain may come in handy but shouldn't be necessary unless you're a careless worker. If you enjoy comfortable working conditions, consider covering the floor with padded outdoor carpet and pipe in some stereo music. An extension phone is a real convenience, too.

Much of your film processing equipment will also serve for printing. The various measuring and mixing utensils (graduates, funnels, stirring rods, bottles, etc.) can do double duty. The thermometer and interval timer will occasionally be useful too, but a special timer for the enlarger is desirable. There are several varieties. The cheapest ones are spring wound, similar to inexpensive oven timers. They provide timed intervals of up to about one minute and turn the enlarger light off when the time interval has elapsed. Better models have electric clock-motor drive and frequently provide switched electrical outlets which can control both the enlarger light and a safelight. Some also provide automatic reset of the selected time interval so any given exposure time can be repeated by simply pressing a

You'll need at least two safelights

Paint the darkroom walls yellow

button. The best and most expensive are electronically controlled. They provide all the switching and convenience features of the mechanical and electric timers but offer a greater range of times and also permit accurate exposures of fractions of a second.

Films, because they are extremely sensitive to light of all colors, must be handled and developed in total darkness. Papers are not nearly as sensitive, even to white light, and they are practically insensitive to red, orange, and yellow light. Consequently, light of any of these colors is considered *safe* for papers and a light source, suitably filtered to produce only safe light, is called (reasonably enough) a *safelight*.

You will need at least two safelights in your darkroom; one near the enlarger and one suspended over the sink to illuminate the processing trays. Buy the largest ones you can afford and equip them with the orange-brown filters which are safe for variable-contrast papers. The Kodak designation is Wratten series OC, but equivalent filters of other brands will do as well. Other safelights can be placed strategically around the room to provide general room illumination and, if each is equipped with a bulb of the recommended wattage, the light will still be safe to work in. Don't economize on safelights. You'll enjoy your darkroom a great deal more if it is as light as possible.

If you have a large darkroom space it may be worth considering a sodium vapor safelight. Although they are quite expensive, they are very bright and will replace several smaller conventional models. There are also special fluorescent tubes available which are said to be both safe and bright. Regardless of the type of safelight you buy, you can increase the apparent illumination level in the room if you paint the walls and ceiling bright yellow. In yellow safelight illumination, the yellow walls will appear white or very light gray. Don't use white paint though. White light which may leak from the enlarger will reflect dangerously from a white surface, but its reflection from the yellow paint will be safely yellow. Black paint is safe for the walls but it will make the darkroom a dingy place to work in. You

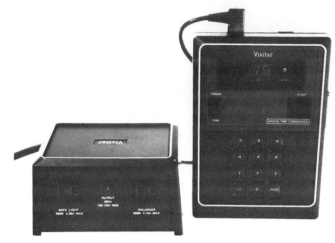

Figure 5.1
Enlarging timer and power supply

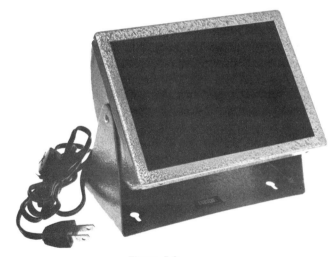

Figure 5.2
Safelight

Buy the best enlarger you can afford; some things to check

There are two general types: condenser and diffusion

Buy the best quality lenses you can afford

may, however, want to paint the wall area close to the enlarger black to subdue all reflections and protect panchromatic materials which you might occasionally want to use there.

The major equipment item in the darkroom is usually the enlarger. Shop carefully for your enlarger; a flimsy one that doesn't work well will be a continual source of frustration. There are many models and styles to choose from but there are certain features you should look for. The entire machine should be solidly built and as free from vibration as possible, even when raised to full height. The illumination on the baseboard should be bright and uniform over the entire area, without obvious *hot-spots* or patterns. The light source should remain cool during prolonged exposure times. The negative stage, the lensboard, and the baseboard should be absolutely parallel.

The negative carrier should be designed to hold the negatives flat without scratching them and should be arranged so it can be turned to straighten a tilted image or change from a horizontal to a vertical format. The enlarger head should be counterbalanced so it can be raised and lowered easily and it should lock firmly in the desired position. The focusing control should operate smoothly without backlash and the range of adjustment should be great enough to permit projection prints of reduced size. Some enlargers can be tilted for horizontal projection and some provide a calibrated tilting lensboard for distortion control; both are convenient features, but not essential.

Until a few years ago enlargers could be classified easily into two groups, condenser or diffusion. Condenser enlargers provide even illumination for the negative by employing a system of large condensing lenses to collimate the light from the lamp into a parallel beam and then converge the beam into a cone of light directed toward the enlarger lens. This system provides *specular* illumination for the negative and results in a projected image of relatively high intensity and contrast. Diffusion enlargers illuminate the negative evenly by scattering the light from the lamp through one or more layers of

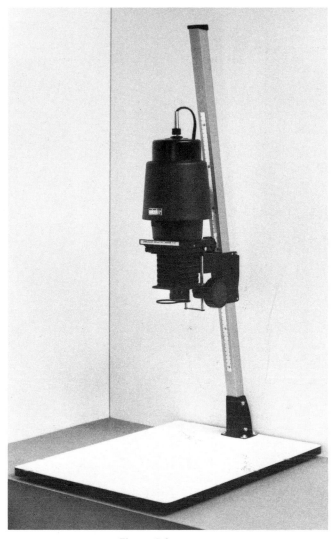

Figure 5.3
Black-and-white enlarger

Figure 5.4
a. In a condenser system the light from the lamp is not diffused. The condensers focus the light through the negative and into the enlarger lens, with a minimum of scattering, producing a brilliant, contrasty image.

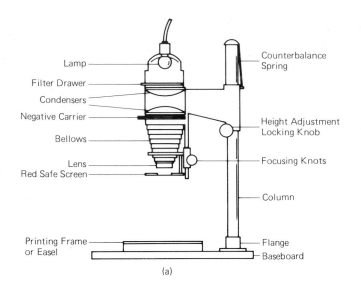

- Lamp
- Filter Drawer
- Condensers
- Negative Carrier
- Bellows
- Lens
- Red Safe Screen
- Printing Frame or Easel
- Counterbalance Spring
- Height Adjustment Locking Knob
- Focusing Knots
- Column
- Flange
- Baseboard

(a)

b. Diffusion enlargers provide a large source of light and diffuse it further by one or more layers of groundglass. The negative illumination is directionless, resulting in a relatively low intensity and low contrast.

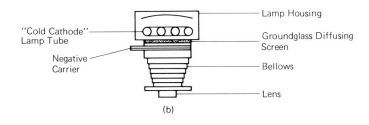

- "Cold Cathode" Lamp Tube
- Negative Carrier
- Lamp Housing
- Groundglass Diffusing Screen
- Bellows
- Lens

(b)

c. Modern dichroic enlargers frequently combine the diffused light from an integrating chamber with a condenser system, to provide negative illumination of relatively high intensity and moderate contrast. The dichroic filters control light color and protect the negative from IR radiation. Dichroic heads are a great convenience in color printing and are also useful for controlling contrast of black-and-white variable-contrast papers.

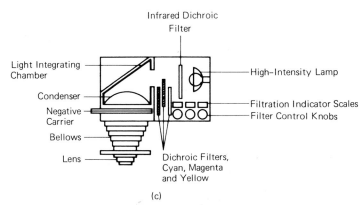

- Light Integrating Chamber
- Condenser
- Negative Carrier
- Bellows
- Lens
- Infrared Dichroic Filter
- High–Intensity Lamp
- Filtration Indicator Scales
- Filter Control Knobs
- Dichroic Filters, Cyan, Magenta and Yellow

(c)

opal glass or groundglass, by multiple reflection within an integrating chamber, or by using a light source of large area such as the cold-light heads which combine a grid of fluorescent or mercury-vapor tubing with some other diffusion. This diffuse illumination provides a projected image of somewhat lower intensity and lower contrast.

Photographers have rather strong prejudices and opinions about these two systems, but either one is capable of excellent results if it is used competently. In general, condenser enlargers have been thought to print faster and produce higher contrast, and some say they produce sharper images. Their critics say they emphasize image grain and surface blemishes and are likely to produce mottled images at very small lens apertures because of dust spots on the various condenser lens surfaces. Diffusion enlargers have been criticized for generating excessive heat (although not all do), providing relatively dim illumination, giving images of low contrast, and tending to soften both grain structure and image details. These arguments are not as appropriate as they used to be because many modern enlargers combine the virtues of both designs.

If you intend to do any color printing at all, and if the added expense is not too serious a problem, buy your enlarger equipped with a *color head*. Color heads incorporate a system of filters which can be introduced into the light beam in any combination to tint the light color, a feature which is highly desirable for color printing and also useful in black-and-white printing with variable-contrast papers. Modern enlargers use *dichroic* filters, which are much more heat- and fade-resistant than the older gelatin or acetate filter materials.

Color heads usually provide a printing light of high intensity and excellent uniformity, but don't feel that you can't manage with a regular black-and-white enlarger. A color head is a convenience, not a necessity, even for color work. Lots of photographers have worked very successfully in color by using acetate or gelatin filters with a black-and-white enlarger, and you can too, if you want to.

You obviously can't enlarge big negatives in a small enlarger but you can convert a big enlarger to accept small negatives. If you have more than one negative size to deal with, buy the enlarger to fit the largest one and convert it to work with the smaller negatives as required.

The normal enlarging lens focal length for 35mm negatives is about 40 to 50 mm; for 2¼″ × 2¼″ and 4.5 × 6cm negatives, about 75 to 80 mm; for 2¼″ × 3¼″ negatives, about 100 mm; and for 4″ × 5″ negatives, about 135 to 160 mm. Unless you need to make prints of maximum possible size, you can use somewhat longer-than-normal focal length lenses for your negatives (an 80mm lens for 35mm negatives, for example). You'll still be able to make enlargements of moderate size and the image quality is likely to be even better than that produced by the normal lens, because you'll be using only the center portion of the lens field, where both lens correction and image illumination are at their best. Well-corrected enlarging lenses are essential for fine work; buy the best ones you can afford.

A good enlarging easel is almost a necessity, too. Again, buy top quality. With reasonable care it will last for a lifetime. In my experience the solid metal easels with adjustable margins on all four sides have proven to be most satisfactory. One model permits adjustments of margins on prints smaller than 11″ × 14″, but will also hold 14″ × 17″ paper for full-area prints when the adjustable mask assembly is removed. This size is big enough for most purposes. Don't buy the 16″ × 20″ size unless you make these big prints frequently. They're much more expensive and are awkward to use for the usual smaller print sizes.

Focusing an enlarger sharply is even more difficult than focusing a camera. If you have trouble, buy a *grain focuser* magnifier. There are many models and the price range is surprisingly great. Price is not necessarily an indication of efficiency, either; some of the least expensive types work very well (although you may have to adjust them yourself for best performance) and some of the most expensive models are not significantly

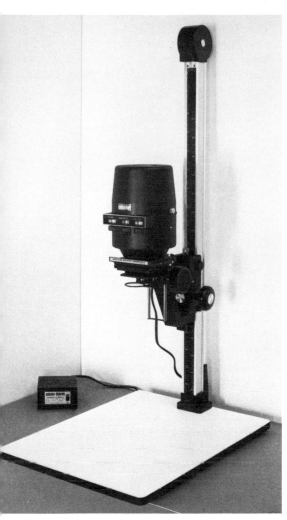

Figure 5.5
Color enlarger

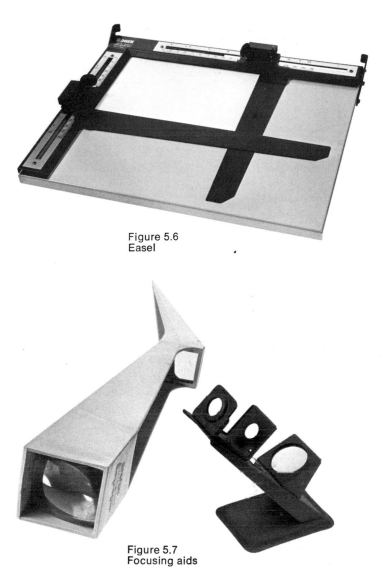

Figure 5.6
Easel

Figure 5.7
Focusing aids

A printing or proofing frame is useful; you can improvise

Make your own dodging tools

better. Check out several types to find one that you can work with comfortably. If you wear glasses, you may find some grain focusers less convenient to use than others.

You'll need a printing frame or something similar, for proofing your negatives and making contact prints. If you have enough room in your darkroom and can find a war-surplus contact printer at a real bargain price, buy it. Don't even consider a new one, though, unless you'll be specializing in contact printing large negatives. If you will make only occasional contact prints or proofs, you can get along with a homemade printer; cover a piece of smooth plywood or Masonite, about 8½″ × 10½″, with felt or thin foam plastic and provide it with a matching cover of double-strength glass. Hinge them together along one edge with plastic tape and you'll have a serviceable proofing frame. Look at the commercial proofing frames, too; they're neat, convenient, and not terribly expensive.

Dodging refers to the practice of shading part of the image area from the exposing light to prevent it from printing too dark. *Burning-in* the image is just the reverse; a portion of the image is given more light to make it darker in the print. You can make dodging tools easily, using music wire or any other thin, stiff wire for the handles and bits of black paper, cut to any desired shape and size to produce the necessary shadow. For some purposes a little tuft of absorbent cotton, instead of the black paper shape, will produce good results. It will give a soft-edged shadow with some slight fogging and diffusion of the image. A sheet of black paper or cardboard with a small hole cut in it, near the center, will make a useful burning tool. You can improvise tools for special purposes as you need them.

Print processing is done in open trays. You'll need three trays for the basic chemicals—developer, short-stop, and hypo. It's convenient to have at least two others, for a water rinse and hypo-clearing bath; and you'll need either a special print washer or a larger tray for the final wash.

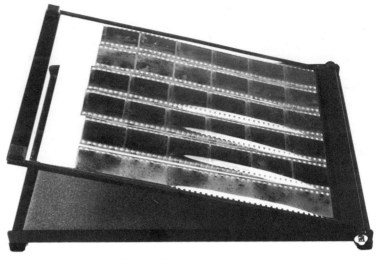

Figure 5.8
Proofing frame

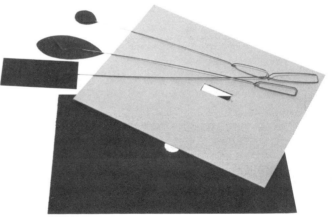

Figure 5.9
Dodging and burning tools

Trays come in several sizes and styles. The best ones are made of heavy white or yellow, slightly flexible plastic with large rolled edges and well-formed pouring lips. The cheaper, hard plastic trays usually have more angular contours and sharper edges. They will serve for light-duty use but they are brittle and more likely to crack. They usually have ridged bottoms too, which, in my opinion, is an undesirable feature.

Trays come in nominal print sizes. Get at least four, but preferably six 8″ × 10″ trays as a basic set, then buy at least four trays in each of the other print sizes you're likely to work with frequently. The washing tray should be at least one size, but preferably two sizes, larger than the prints you wash in it. Equip it with a *tray siphon* for automatic control of water level and good circulation. If you plan to do a lot of printing, it may be worth your while to buy a print washer, but consider this purchase carefully. Good print washers are expensive and bulky and will be neither economical nor convenient for only occasional use.

Many photographers like to handle prints with *tongs* or *paddles* during processing. These tools do have at least one advantage; they keep your hands out of the chemical solutions. They don't offer reliable protection from Metol poisoning, however, and they don't reduce the risk of print stains or physical damage significantly. In fact they are more likely to bruise the print emulsion than your fingers are, especially when handling large paper sizes. In my opinion, tongs are occasionally useful for small print processing of up to about 5″ × 7″ size. For larger sizes they are a nuisance. If you prefer to use them, get the kind that have soft plastic or rubber tips and are clearly color coded so you won't confuse them. You'll need at least two, one for the developer tray and one which can serve for short-stop and hypo. Some photographers prefer to use three, one in each tray, to avoid any chance of contamination.

After the prints have been washed, they must be dried. Prints on *resin-coated* (RC) papers can simply be sponged surface-dry and hung up with clothespins to

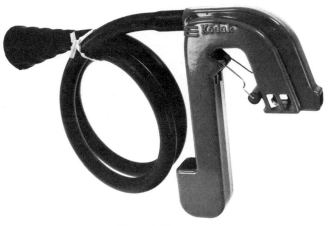

Figure 5.10
Print siphon

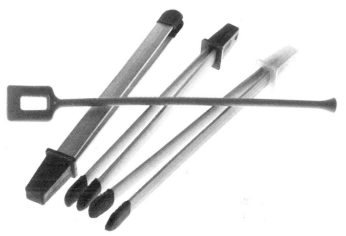

Figure 5.11
Tongs and paddles

Plastic screens make good print drying frames

If you want to dry-mount your prints, you'll need a press

Matting and mounting require miscellaneous tools

There are two general types: fiber-based and RC

RC papers are not considered archival

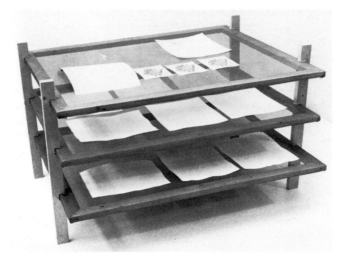

Figure 5.12
Plastic drying screens

air-dry. Alternatively, they can be laid out on plastic screens (aluminum-framed window screens are fine). Conventional *fiber-based* papers can be dried in blotter books or rolls, laid out on the plastic screens, or heat-dried in electric print dryers. Unless you are interested in *ferrotyping* fiber-based papers to produce a high-gloss print finish, or unless you do a lot of printing every day, a commercial heat dryer is probably an unnecessary expense. For most purposes, screen frames are entirely satisfactory. They are cheap, convenient, easy to store, and easy to keep clean.

Finished prints are usually mounted or matted for presentation. *Dry-mounting* has been a preferred method because it is fast, neat, and permanent. A dry-mounting press is required. There are several models, all expensive, but this is another one-time purchase which should last for years. Buy a big enough press to accommodate the largest print size you'll use frequently. You will also need a *tacking iron,* a small electrically-heated hand tool used for attaching the dry-mount tissue adhesive sheet to the print and mount board before heating them in the press. For some other methods of presentation, such as the use of pressure-sensitive tissues or art corners, a mounting press is not necessary.

Matting involves measuring and cutting the mount and mat boards and requires miscellaneous tools. A *print-trimmer* or *paper cutter* is a convenient accessory for cutting prints and tissue, but mat and mount board should be cut to shape with a *mat knife* and heavy metal *straightedge*. A special *mat-cutter* is essential if you want bevelled edges on your mats and you'll find a T-square, ruler, and a large draftsman's triangle (30°–60°) useful for measuring and marking the boards. You should also have a soft pencil (#2 or 2B), an eraser (art gum, kneaded, or Pink Pearl), and some fabric or plastic tape. Don't use ordinary masking tape; it will dry out and discolor with age.

Printing Papers: Types and Characteristics

Until a few years ago printing papers really were paper. Now the variety of fiber-based papers has diminished considerably and manufacturers are supplying more and more resin-coated (RC) papers. For commercial purposes and for prints which will be used and discarded, RC papers are usually satisfactory; in fact they offer real advantages in ease of processing. But for art purposes and for pictures which are intended for very long-term storage, such as in museum archives, fiber-based papers are preferred.

Although this is a matter of individual preference, a great many photographers feel that RC papers look plastic and cheap. The image lacks depth and quality, and the variety of surfaces, tones, and weights is very limited. On the other hand, there are photographers who feel that the paper should be as neutral and unobtrusive as possible to avoid any competition with the image itself. You can make your own decision. Both groups recognize the advantage of fiber-based papers for long-term storage, however. RC papers are not yet considered stable enough to be archival.

This is not as serious as it sounds. Despite the continuing interest in archival processing techniques, the most carefully pampered prints will survive only if they are stored properly, a factor which is out of the

But most prints shouldn't be saved anyway

RC papers simplify processing

Projection papers are more sensitive than contact papers

Papers come in a variety of sheet and package sizes

Many different surface textures are offered

photographer's control. Further, it's probably true that a very sizable proportion of all prints, archivally processed or not, have little long-term value or significance and shouldn't be kept anyway. For almost all uses then, RC papers can be considered to be adequately permanent and, if you find a surface and image color you like in an RC paper, use it with no regrets.

RC papers are literally plastic-coated paper and because of this they are almost waterproof. The processing chemicals affect only the gelatin emulsion and can only penetrate the paper itself along the cut edges of the sheet. This penetration is negligible if the processing steps are carried out normally. RC prints can be completely processed and dried in the time it takes to wash a fiber-based print thoroughly. The prints dry flat and remain flat, too, unlike paper prints which warp severely while drying, unless they're dried very slowly or covered under light pressure.

Most commonly available papers are designed for projection printing and are sensitive enough to respond to the relatively dim light produced by the enlarger. Contact papers are much less sensitive because they were originally intended to be used (in contact with the negative) either in subdued daylight or strong artificial light. Contact printing is not very popular anymore and many photographers, who do still make contact prints, make them on projection paper, using the enlarger as a light source. Contact papers, therefore, are now fairly rare and difficult to obtain; the only variety generally available is Kodak's Azo.

Although Azo is a fine paper, it is *only* useful for bright light contact printing. Don't buy it for use under the enlarger, even in a printing frame; it is much too slow to be practical. You should, however, try contact printing at least once. There are many photographers who believe that a good contact print represents the ultimate in photographic quality and elegance.

Printing papers come in sheet sizes from about 2″ × 3″ to 20″ × 24″, and in uncut rolls 20″ or 40″ wide. The most common sizes are probably 8″ × 10″, 11″ × 14″, and 16″ × 20″. Paper is commonly sold in pack-

ages of 10 sheets (for larger sheet sizes) to 500 sheets and is, of course, somewhat less expensive per sheet in the larger quantities. The two most common package sizes for 8″ × 10″ paper are 25-sheet double envelopes and 100-sheet boxes.

Although we don't usually think of black-and-white papers as having any color, they are available in several subtle tints, such as white, warm white, natural, cream white, etc. Additionally, some papers contain a brightener which fluoresces in daylight or ultraviolet light and makes the paper appear more brilliantly white than untreated paper. The silver image itself varies in color to some extent, too. Warm-tone papers produce a brownish image, while cold-tone papers give a bluish-black image. Most papers are neutral in tone. Their images appear uncolored or very slightly warm black. Image color is influenced by development conditions also and can be altered after development by special chemical *toning* treatment.

The thickness, or weight, of the paper stock is indicated on the package by terms such as single weight, double weight, medium weight, etc. Single-weight papers are less expensive than the heavier grades and are generally satisfactory for prints of normal size. Some photographers prefer double-weight papers because they are less easily creased or wrinkled in processing and drying and because they feel more substantial in the hand. This is largely a matter of choice. There is no significant difference in image quality.

The surface texture of printing paper is also specified on the package by some descriptive phrase, such as smooth, glossy; fine-grain, lustre; silk, lustre; rough; etc. In Kodak papers, the stock tint and surface characteristics are also symbolized by a letter designation, such as F for white, smooth, glossy or G for cream-white, fine-grain, lustre. Agfa paper packages display a combined letter and number code which expresses most of the essential information. BEH 1, for example, stands for Brovira, extra-hard, single-weight, white, glossy. BW 111 indicates Brovira, soft, double-weight, white, glossy.

Figure 5.13
Printing paper contrast is indicated by number. The low numbers indicate low contrast; high numbers indicate high contrast. These prints, all made from the same negative, show the range of a typical enlarging paper.

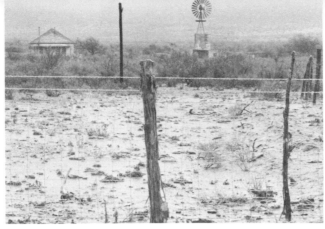

a. Kodabromide number 1

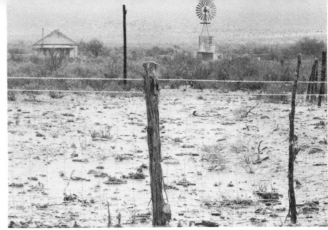

b. Kodabromide number 2

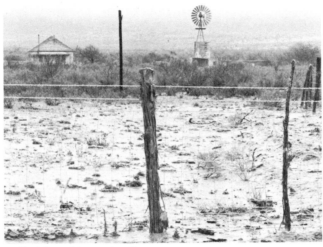

c. Kodabromide number 3

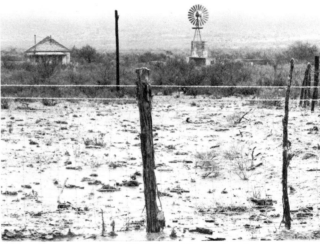

d. Kodabromide number 4

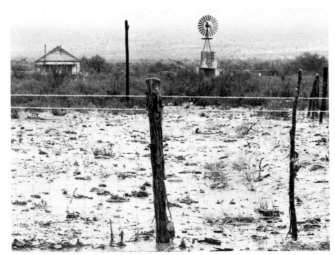

e. Kodabromide number 5

The descriptions extra-hard and soft refer to the inherent contrast characteristic of the paper emulsion (see p. 295 in the appendix). *Hard* papers produce images of high contrast; *soft* papers produce low contrast. In addition to the letter symbols, Agfa papers indicate the paper contrast grade by another number series, from 1 through 6, in which the lower numbers stand for low contrast and the higher numbers indicate grades of increasing contrast. Number 4 (Brovira) is considered normal contrast, but number 3 papers are preferred for general use by some workers. Number 3 is the normal grade of Agfa Portriga paper. Ilford papers and some Kodak papers designate contrast grades similarly but their number series runs from 0 through 5 and the normal contrast grade is considered to be number 2. Kodak's Kodabrome projection paper carries word descriptions only—soft, medium, hard, etc.

Kodak's Polycontrast paper is a variable-contrast material. Coated with a mixture of high-contrast and low-contrast emulsions, the effective contrast of the print image can be controlled by varying the color of the exposing light. Green light (transmitted by a yellow filter) affects the low-contrast emulsion and will produce a low-contrast image. Blue light (transmitted by a magenta filter) affects only the high-contrast emulsion and the paper produces a hard image. Mixtures of green and blue light produce intermediate grades of contrast.

In use, the desired contrast is produced by inserting a filter of the appropriate color into the enlarger light path. The filters are numbered to correspond with conventional paper grades, with the number 2 filter being considered normal. The paper also reacts with approximately normal contrast to the unfiltered incandescent enlarger light but cannot be used satisfactorily with some cold-light enlargers whose light is deficient in green. Polycontrast Rapid is similar to Polycontrast, but it is faster and yields a more neutral image tone. Polycontrast RC is the resin-coated version of regular Poly, and Ektamatic SC is a fast, variable-contrast material, featuring white paper stock and a neutral image tone. It is intended for *stabilization processing* but also works very well in trays.

Stabilization papers, like Ektamatic SC, include a reducing agent in their emulsion mixture. After exposure they can be processed in seconds by running them through a motorized stabilization processor which first spreads a coating of strongly alkaline *activator* solution on the emulsion (developing the image almost instantly) and then coats the emulsion with a *stabilizer* solution which effectively renders the silver halides inert but does not fix the image in the usual sense. Stabilized prints emerge from the processor in about 10 seconds, thoroughly contaminated with chemicals, but damp dry and ready for immediate use. In this condition they are not suitable for long-term storage, nor should they be allowed to contact conventionally processed prints, for fear of contaminating them, but they can be made permanent, if desired, by 10-minute treatment in the fixing bath, followed by the usual clearing bath and wash. When processed in trays in the normal manner, Ektamatic SC reacts like any ordinary paper, producing fine image quality with rather exceptionally rich blacks. Because of its versatility, it is an excellent paper for student use.

Preparing the Printing Chemicals

Most print developers are either Metol-hydroquinone or Phenidone-hydroquinone formulas, accelerated with sodium carbonate. They are usually mixed into a stock solution for storage and diluted with one or more parts of water to make the working solution. The solutions have considerable reserve strength and are normally used for a number of prints, one after the other, without replenishment; although in a few instances, replenishment is suggested as a means of extending their working life. Print developers, especially after dilution, oxidize fairly quickly and working solutions should not be saved for more than a few hours whether they have been exhausted by use or not. Stock solutions are fairly stable and will keep for several months under ideal conditions.

There's not much reason to experiment with brands

Develop prints normally; there's no sensible alternative

You can use an indicator stop with papers, if you want to

Keep print fixer separate and test it frequently

Don't overfix prints

Developing time recommendations vary from brand to brand of developer and will be different for different dilutions of the same developer. There's not much reason to experiment with different developers though, until you've learned the process fairly thoroughly. Get a good standard brand and use it according to the recommendations on the package.

If you have no other guide, develop prints for about twice as long as it takes the image to become completely visible. This will be somewhat longer than absolutely necessary, but slight overdevelopment is far better than slight underdevelopment. Most importantly, once you've established a workable development time, don't change it, regardless of what the print image is doing. *Development variations cannot be relied on to correct for improper print exposure.* If you're serious about fine print quality, expose the print so it can be developed normally, whatever you find that to be. There is simply no sensible alternative.

A stop bath, similar to the one used for film, is also satisfactory for use with papers, but it may be made a little stronger, if desired. The working solution should not normally exceed about 1½% acid strength (slightly more than 1½ ounces of 28% acetic acid stock solution in 32 ounces of water). The yellow indicator stop bath is more appropriate for use with prints than for films because it is designed to be used in yellow safelight conditions. An indicator bath in good condition appears clear and colorless in the yellow light but will turn dark and appear almost opaque when exhausted. Although adding acetic acid to the exhausted bath will restore its clarity, it is better to throw the used bath away and mix a fresh one to avoid possible contamination.

The stop bath serves the same function in printing that it serves in film developing; it rinses the developer chemicals off the print surfaces, halts the action of the developer, and, most importantly, neutralizes the developer alkalinity so the essential acidity of the fixing bath will be preserved. The neutralizing action of the acetic acid on the sodium carbonate from the developer is sometimes accompanied by a high-pitched whining or whistling sound as tiny streams of carbon dioxide gas bubbles are forced out of the paper fibers. This sound (if it occurs at all) usually begins 10 or 15 seconds after the print is put into the short-stop and may continue for another 15 seconds or so. Leave the print in until it stops. You may not hear any sound at all. If you don't, don't worry about it. It only occurs with fiber-based papers anyhow. RC prints take their treatment in the short-stop without a murmur.

Prints will fix satisfactorily in either regular or rapid-fixing baths. The regular bath, made with sodium thiosulfate, is used at the same strength for both film and papers. Rapid-fixer should be mixed at half-strength for papers to avoid possible bleaching of the relatively delicate print image. Regardless of the kind of fixer used, films and papers should not be fixed in the same volume of solution. Film fixers rapidly accumulate complex silver-sulfur compounds which can be washed out of the film emulsions without too much difficulty, but which are extremely difficult to wash out of papers. Keep film and paper fixing baths separate and test them frequently; an exhausted fixing bath will eventually kill your prints.

Prints don't "clear" obviously in the fixing bath the way films do, so there's no way to know for sure when fixing is complete. For this reason we usually leave prints in the fixer for longer than is probably necessary. Actually, most papers fix very rapidly and there is more danger of overfixing them than there is with films. Don't let them soak in the fixer for extended periods of time or they may begin to bleach out. This is especially important if you are using a rapid-fixing bath. Projection papers will fix adequately in a fresh fixing bath in 5 minutes or a little less.

Contact papers require even shorter times, try 3 to 4 minutes. RC papers need only about 2 minutes. In all cases these times apply only if there is an adequate volume of fixer and the prints are given frequent agitation. Discard the fixer after treating about one hundred 8″ × 10″ prints per gallon.

Two-bath fixation will extend fixer life and give better results

Hypo-clearing baths are important for fiber-based papers, not RC

Processing temperature is not critical, but standardize

With clean, dry hands, prepare the printing frame

The negatives will usually curl toward their emulsion side, but check

You can extend the fixing times to about twice the normal length to compensate for partial exhaustion of the bath, but don't exceed that and don't overwork the solution. For maximum economy and best results with fiber-based papers (not RC) you should really use two fixing baths in sequence. Agitate the prints in the first bath for 3 to 5 minutes, then transfer them to the second bath, and repeat the treatment. The first bath will do most of the work and wear out first, but it should be adequate for about two hundred 8″ × 10″ prints per gallon of solution. Discard it then and replace it with the second bath. Mix a fresh volume of fixer for the new second bath. This pair will be good for another two hundred prints and this cycle can be repeated once or twice more. Then both baths should be thrown out and new ones prepared. Don't keep a used pair of solutions for more than a week, whether they are exhausted from use or not.

Hypo-clearing or neutralizing baths are especially important for use with fiber-based papers, but are not recommended for RC papers. Follow mixing and use instructions for the product you select. Don't attempt to store and reuse a working solution of hypo-clearing agent unless the instructions suggest it. The stock solutions will keep indefinitely.

Set up your processing solutions in trays in the darkroom sink. From left to right the trays should contain working solutions of developer, short-stop, and fixer. If space permits and if you have enough trays, you can add a water rinse, hypo-clearing agent, and finally, of course, the washing tray or print washer. Prepare enough of each solution so you have a working depth of at least ½″ in the trays. An 8″ × 10″ tray will require about a quart. This much developer at standard working strength is sufficient for ten or more 8″ × 10″ prints. Smaller volumes can be used if you have only a print or two to make, but don't be stingy with chemicals. A quart of developer costs less than one 8″ × 10″ sheet of paper. Ruining paper to save chemicals is clearly false economy.

The temperatures of the various processing solutions should, ideally, be about 20°C, plus or minus a degree or so. The actual temperature, within reasonable limits, is not terribly important in printing because the development goes to completion and the image characteristics are not changed much after the first minute or two in the developer. You should, however, try to establish a working routine and stick to it. If your darkroom maintains the solutions at a reasonably constant 21°C, then work at 21°C. If 18°C is easier to maintain, work at 18°C. Two or three degrees variation will not cause any serious problems, but excessively high temperatures increase the risk of fog and stains and may soften the print emulsion. Extremely low temperatures will certainly slow down the action of the developer and may change its contrast characteristics also.

Proofing Negatives by Contact

When the chemicals have been prepared, wash your hands and dry them thoroughly before handling negatives or printing paper. Check the printing frame glass for dust and fingerprints and clean it if necessary. Lay the frame facedown on the table and arrange the negatives on the glass, emulsion side up. The emulsion side is the side that appears least glossy and the film usually (but not always) curls toward the emulsion. As a further check, you can look through the negatives and check the orientation of the images. When viewed from the emulsion side the images will be backwards. Dust the negative strips lightly on both sides but don't handle them any more than necessary. They'll have to be cleaned more thoroughly before they're enlarged.

Turn out the white lights and work, from this point on, in the yellow safelight illumination. Open the paper package and remove one sheet of paper, then close the paper package securely so the contents will be protected from accidental exposure to white light.

Figure 5.14

a. Clean the printing frame glass.

b. Dust the negatives. Handle them carefully by the edges to avoid fingerprints.

c. There are several ways to identify the emulsion side of negatives—it is usually, but not always, on the inside of the natural curl; it is usually dull or matte compared to the more glossy back; the edge frame numbers are backwards when seen from the emulsion side; and the image itself is reversed, left to right, when viewed from the emulsion side. Here the left strip shows the emulsion side; the right strip is facedown and the back is showing.

d. Arrange the negatives on the glass, emulsion up, that is, with the backs touching the glass surface. Turn out the room lights and work from here on in safelight.

e. Remove a sheet of paper from its lighttight package and identify the emulsion side. It is usually, but not always, on the inside of the natural curl; it is usually, but not always, more lustrous than the paper back. Resin-coated papers may be especially confusing. When in doubt, expose a little strip and develop it.

f. Lay a sheet of paper over the negatives, emulsion down. Remember the printing rule, the materials should face each other, emulsion to emulsion.

g. Expose, using the enlarger as a light source, as explained in the text. The negative carrier has been removed here to provide a large area of illumination on the baseboard.

h. Develop the print, following the text instructions. The image will appear gradually after about 15 seconds in the developer. Be sure to agitate efficiently.

i. After the developing time is up, pick the print up with the developer tongs, transfer it to the stop bath, and handle it there with the stop tongs. Agitate.

j. After the stop bath, transfer the print to the fixing bath. Keep the tongs separate to avoid possible contamination.

k. The print can be placed directly into the clearing bath after it has been fixed, but the clearing bath will last longer and be more efficient if the prints are rinsed briefly before they are cleared. From here on you can handle the print with your fingers. Actually, I prefer fingers for all the operations. Don't clear RC prints.

l. Leave the print in the clearing bath for the recommended time, then wash it in running water. RC prints wash quickly without having been cleared. See text.

m. Squeegee RC prints lightly or wipe them with a dampened viscose sponge to remove surface droplets. Fiber-based prints can be wiped or blotted to remove surface moisture.

n. Hang RC prints or lay them out on some clean surface, faceup, to air-dry. Drying screens are excellent for both print types but fiber-based prints should be dried facedown to reduce their tendency to curl.

o. Alternatively, fiber-based prints can be dried between blotters or in blotter books or rolls. Don't dry RC prints this way.

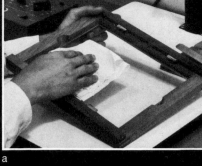

a

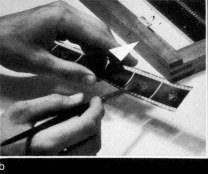

b

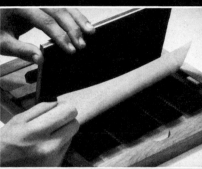

f

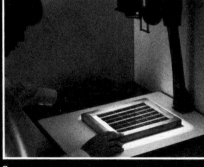

g

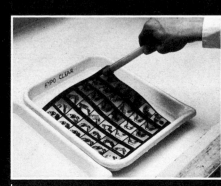

k

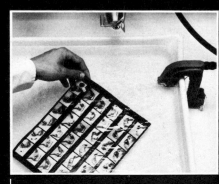

l

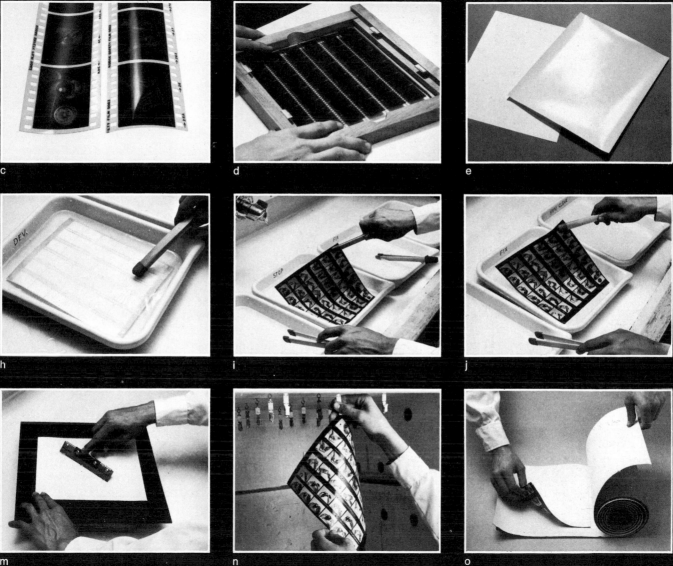

c

d

e

h

i

j

m

n

o

Expose contact printing paper, like Azo, to bright light

Expose other papers under the enlarger

Don't **vary development time**

Agitate the print in the stop bath

Then slip it into the fixing bath and agitate

Place the paper sheet in the printing frame so the emulsion side of the paper (usually the shinier side, inside the natural curl) is in contact with the emulsion side of the negatives. Clamp the hinged back of the printing frame securely in position and you are ready to make the exposure.

If you are using a contact printing paper, such as Azo, you can make the exposure by simply turning on the white room lights for an appropriate length of time (be sure your paper package is closed securely first, though). It's better to use a single light bulb without any reflector, about 3 or 4 feet away from the frame, however. The exposure time, using a 100-watt bulb at about 4 feet, should be about a minute. A medium-speed projection paper, such as Polycontrast, exposed under the same conditions, would need only about ½ second, an impractically short exposure time for accurate measurement.

If you want to use projection paper for proofing or contact printing, it's better to use the enlarger as a light source. As a rough guide to exposure, if the enlarger is set up to make an 8-diameter enlargement (8″ × 10″ print from 35mm negative) and the lens is stopped down to f/8, the exposure time for normal negatives will be somewhere around 15 to 30 seconds. Don't take this estimate too seriously; enlargers vary considerably in their effective light output and you'll have to determine your own best time by trial. The enlarger lens should be focused as if a negative were actually in the negative carrier, and for maximum working area the carrier may be removed from the enlarger when making proofs or contacts.

After exposing the proof, remove the paper from the printing frame and, immediately after starting the interval timer or noting the time on a clock, slip the sheet into the developer solution with one smooth motion. Alternatively, you can flop the sheet into the developer facedown and immediately wiggle it back and forth in the solution as you pat it under the surface. As soon as it's submerged, lift it out by one corner and replace it in the solution, this time faceup. Push it under the surface again by patting it down lightly with your fingertips (or tongs, if you insist) and continue to agitate it in the solution by rocking the tray. Keep the print submerged during development. It will tend to float to the surface and will have to be patted back down fairly frequently.

The time of development will depend on the kind of paper in use, the developer type and dilution, and your personal preference. In general, using commonly available papers and a developer, such as Kodak Dektol or Ektaflo, appropriately diluted, contact papers should develop in 45 seconds to a minute and projection papers, such as Polycontrast, should receive from 1½ minutes to 2 minutes minimum. My recommendation is to use *1* minute for contact papers and *2* minutes for projection papers, unless the manufacturer's instructions specify a *longer* time. A slightly longer development than is absolutely necessary will insure against brownish, mottled tones and incompletely formed shadow details in the print. Again, don't vary the developing time in an attempt to save the print. If the image is not satisfactory at the end of the normal developing time, make another print and change the exposure or the paper grade to correct the problem. *Don't* change development.

When development time is up, lift the print from the developer by one corner and let it drain briefly into the developer tray. Then place it in the short-stop and immerse it quickly with agitation. If you are using print tongs, it's considered good practice to avoid touching the short-stop with the developer tongs; handle the print in the short-stop with the stop bath-hypo tongs. There is no need to worry if you are using your fingers; in fact, the short-stop will rinse your fingers clean in the same way it cleanses the print. Agitate the print in the stop bath for 15 seconds or until it stops sizzling. Then place it in the hypo. Immerse it quickly and agitate it periodically, to be sure it stays submerged, for about 5 minutes (RC papers should stay in the short-stop bath for only about 5 seconds and in the fixer for 2 minutes with constant agitation). Rinse the hypo off your fingers before handling another print in the developer (or anything else, for that matter).

RC papers should be washed for 5 minutes, immediately following treatment in the hypo, and then dried. Ordinary prints should be given a brief rinse in plain water to remove most of the surface fixer, then treated in the hypo-clearing bath, following the instructions given by the manufacturer. Those same instructions should be followed in washing the print after treatment. If no hypo-clearing bath is used, single-weight prints should be washed for an hour in running water, at a temperature between 15°C and 25°C. Double-weight prints should wash for 2 hours. The water should be running fast enough to change the water in the wash tray every 5 minutes or so. The prints must be kept separated and moving so both surfaces are exposed to the water flow. Hypo-clearing treatment is highly recommended. It saves water and time and contributes to more efficient washing. Don't add unwashed prints to a trayful of partially washed prints. Wash them in batches. One unwashed print will contaminate a whole trayful of clean ones.

RC prints, after washing, should be sponged surface-dry and either hung by one corner or laid out on plastic screens or a clean cloth, faceup, to air-dry. Gently circulating warmed air will hasten drying but avoid strong drafts or excessive heat. In conditions of low to moderate humidity the prints should be dry in 30 minutes or less. Keep the prints from touching each other and protect them from airborne dust during drying. The emulsion is soft and tacky for the first few minutes and can be easily damaged.

Fiber-based prints should not be hung up or laid out faceup to dry because they will curl excessively. They should be dried facedown on the screens or a clean cloth-covered surface. If they tend to curl, they can be sandwiched between two screens or covered lightly with a layer or two of clean cloth. They can usually be dried satisfactorily between photographic blotters or in a special blotter book or blotter roll, but they may pick up lint from the blotters or become marked from the cover papers of the blotter book if the emulsion is soft. If this is a problem, it can some-times be cured by treating the prints longer in the fixing bath to harden the gelatin emulsion more completely. In extreme cases, a separate hardening bath may be used but excessive hardening will make the print emulsion so brittle after it is dry that it may crack in ordinary handling. Air-drying on screens is safest.

Prints can also be dried in any of several varieties of electrically heated dryers. Glossy fiber-based (not RC) papers can be given a mirrorlike surface if they are *ferrotyped* on a drum dryer. The wet prints are laid faceup on a moving canvas belt or apron which carries them into the machine where they are pressed between a rubber roller and the polished surface of a chromium-plated (or stainless steel) drum. As the heated drum slowly rotates, the prints dry and the soft gelatin emulsion is literally moulded smooth by the drum surface. After several minutes the prints emerge and drop off the drum surface into a basket.

Ferrotyping produces an immaculate surface, if all goes well, and gives prints the greatest possible brilliance and contrast. It is not always successful, however, and when it does not work well the prints may refuse to leave the drum or come off with a mottled or blotchy surface which is unacceptable. For best results the drum surface must be spotlessly clean and the prints must be properly hardened and well washed. The print emulsion must also be completely covered with a film of water as it meets the drum surface or tiny bubbles of air will be trapped between the surfaces and the print gloss will be freckled.

Ferrotyping can also be done by rolling wet glossy prints onto chrome-plated ferrotype tins or sheets of acrylic plastic, such as Lucite or Plexiglas, but unless drying conditions are ideal the prints may dry unevenly and become *oyster-shelled*. This can be avoided by covering the prints with two or three layers of clean, wrinkle-free cloth and drying the prints on the tins under moderate pressure. This will prolong the drying period considerably, but the results are usually good. RC glossy papers do not need this treatment. They will dry to a high gloss finish naturally in open air.

Figure 5.15
Gloss drying

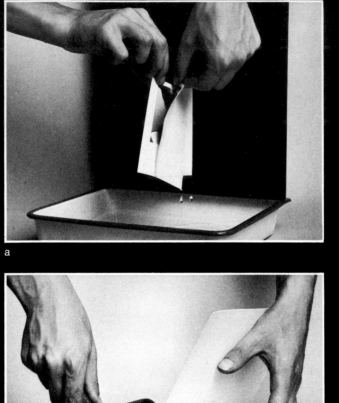

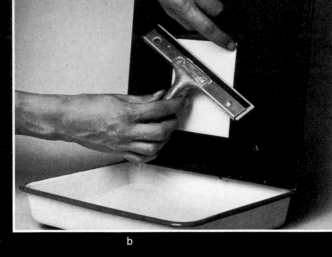

a

b

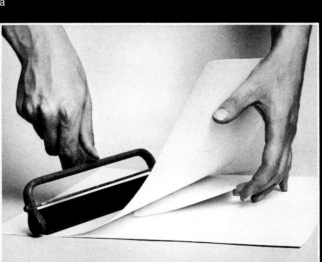

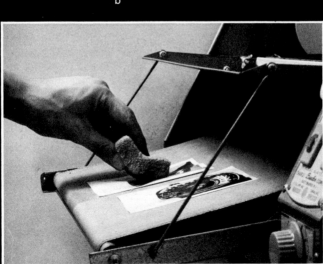

c

d

Heat-drying is not essential

Inspect the enlarger and adjust it for the correct negative size

Clean your negatives but don't use canned "air"; Freon is harmful to the environment

Drum dryers can also be used to dry nonglossy fiber-based papers, or to dry glossy papers to a semi-gloss finish, if the prints are laid on the dryer apron facedown rather than faceup. The print emulsion then faces the canvas apron as it dries and its normal texture is undisturbed. In some cases, if the print emulsion is too soft or the apron presses on it too firmly, the dry print may show signs of the canvas texture or it may be marred by bits of lint from the canvas. Usually resoaking the print thoroughly, wiping its wet surface with a soft sponge, and air-drying it will restore its natural surface.

For most purposes heat-drying is not essential. Unless you are making more prints than you can handle conveniently on screens, you don't need a heat dryer and shouldn't buy one. They're energy hogs, they require good ventilation, and they must be cleaned frequently to avoid contamination. Plain air-drying is cheaper, more appropriate for archival prints and the image quality is at least as good. In fact, some photographers insist that air-dried prints are better.

After the negatives have been proofed, study the contact sheet to see which negatives are suitable for enlargement. This is a good time to consider composition, too. The basic forms and value patterns are often easier to recognize in small scale than they are in the full-size print. Try to decide how you want to crop

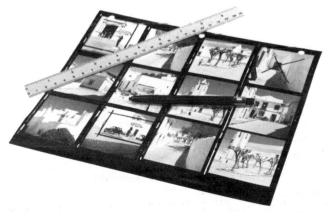

Figure 5.16
Proof sheet with images marked

the image and you may find it useful to mark the outlines right on the proof sheet with grease pencil or ball-point pen for future reference.

Making Prints by Projection

Before you begin to print, give the enlarger a routine examination and select a lens focal length appropriate for the negative size. A 50mm lens is normal for 35mm negatives; a 75mm to 80mm lens for 2¼″ × 2¼″ negatives; a 100mm to 105mm lens for 2¼″ × 3¼″ negatives; and a 135mm to 160mm lens for 4″ × 5″ negatives. If you'll be making prints of only moderate size, you may want to use the next-longer-than-normal focal length for best results. Be sure the lens is clean and essentially free from dust.

If you have a condenser enlarger, be sure the condensers are adjusted to match the lens focal length. A mismatch may cause uneven illumination or a hot spot in the center of the image area. Be sure the condensers are reasonably clean. Any significant spots of dust or flakes of paint from the lamphousing, which may appear on either surface of any of the condensers, may show up in the image as light-toned blobs, especially if you stop the lens down to a very small aperture. If your enlarger has a glass negative carrier, clean it carefully.

If you have processed your film competently and protected the negatives in envelopes or sleeves, they should not need more than a light dusting. Dust them gently with a clean, soft brush before you insert the strip into a glass carrier. You can dust them in the glassless carrier itself; in fact, in some designs, it's possible to get at them after the carrier has been inserted into the enlarger. That's the best way if it's possible. Turn the enlarger light on so the dust spots will show up clearly and pick them off, one by one, with the tip of a small brush. Wipe the brush across your forehead or the side of your nose to pick up a little "nose-oil." That will help dispel static electricity and make the brush slightly tacky so it will hold the

Figure 5.17

a. Inspect the enlarger, adjust it for the negative size in use, and clean the lens if necessary.

b. Insert the negative into the negative carrier and dust it carefully, using the enlarger light to show up the dust spots. If your enlarger permits it, raise the condensers and clean the negative after inserting it into the enlarger.

c. Open the lens to maximum aperture to provide maximum light for focusing and composing the image. Turn out the white lights; work in safelight from here on.

d. Adjust the image size and composition.

e. Focus carefully.

f. Stop the lens down to printing aperture.

g. Turn the enlarger light off. Cut a sheet of paper into test strips and return all but one to the paper package. Close the paper package to protect the paper from light.

h. Make a test strip as described in the text. Process it as previously described.

i. Inspect the test strip for density and contrast. If the contrast is not satisfactory, try another paper grade or change filters if you're using variable-contrast paper. It's best to make another test if you change contrast.

j. When you have determined the proper exposure and paper grade, make a full print, process it, and inspect it critically in good light.

k. If the print needs local control of density you can make another and dodge . . . .

l. . . . or burn, as indicated.

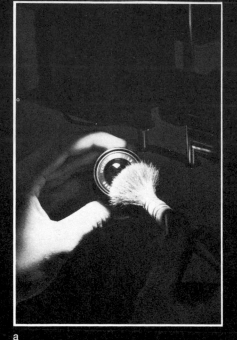

a

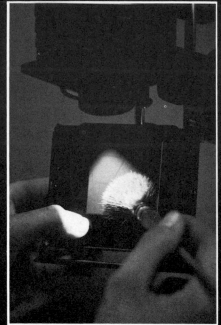

b

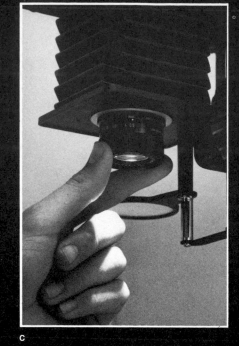

c

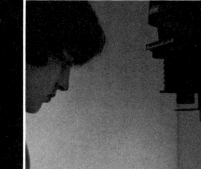

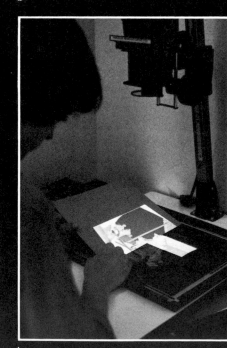

g

h

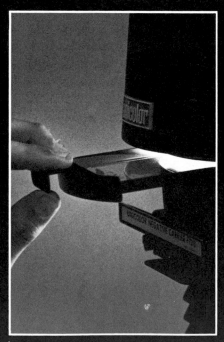

i

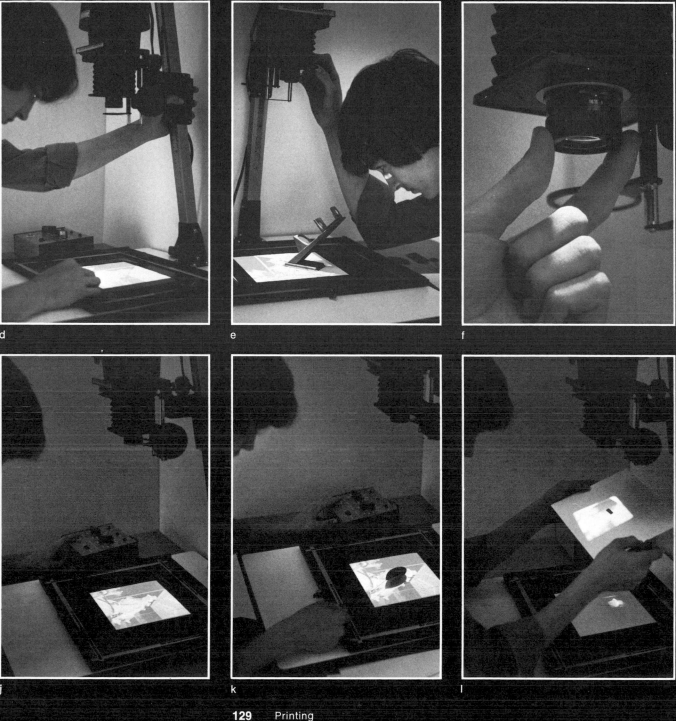

Under safelight conditions, focus and compose the image

Stop the lens down and make a test strip

There are at least two methods; the simplest first

Process the test strip normally

dust particles better. If money is no object and dust is a real problem to you, you can buy a static-neutralizing gun, such as the Zerostat. It will be particularly valuable in the wintertime when humidity is low. It will work well on your phonograph records, too.

When everything is tidy and the negative is safely in place, turn on the yellow safelights and turn off the white room lights. Turn on the enlarger light and open the lens diaphragm to its maximum aperture. Set your easel margins to the desired size and proportions of the image and put a piece of plain white paper in the easel to focus on. Bring the image into approximate focus and check it for orientation and size. If it is not right side up and correct from left to right, remove the negative carrier and correct it. You may have to dust the negative again. Then raise or lower the enlarger to adjust the image size. You will have to focus it in order to do this with precision because focusing changes the size slightly. But with a little practice you should be able to control it easily. Adjust the focus with your grain focuser, if you have one, stop the lens down to f/8 or f/11, and turn off the enlarger light.

The next problem is to determine the proper exposure time and the correct paper grade for the negative you're using. Temporarily, assume it's normal in contrast and work with normal paper. The exposure must be determined by trial and there are several ways to go about it. The most direct and economical way is to make a *test strip,* a strip of paper bearing several different exposure areas. In the yellow safelight illumination, open the package of projection paper, remove one sheet, and cut it into several strips, each about 1½″ to 2″ wide and 8″ long. Put all but one back into the paper package and close it to protect the paper from possible white light spills.

If your enlarger has a red safelight screen built into it, swing it into the light path and turn the enlarger on. Remove the white focusing paper from the easel (don't let the easel move) and position the paper test strip in the image area so it will record the most important areas of the subject. The red light image will

be dim and hard to see, but you should be able to discern the image details well enough. Be sure the emulsion side of the paper is facing up. Turn out the enlarger light and swing the red screen out of the way.

The simplest way to make the sample exposures is to start with some time increment which you're reasonably sure is too short to be useful and repeat it several times, covering a section of the strip after each exposure so the step exposures vary progressively. For example, suppose you decide to use an exposure of 2 seconds. Expose the whole strip for 2 seconds, then cover about one-sixth of it and expose it for 2 seconds again. Cover another sixth of the strip and repeat the 2-second exposure. Repeat this operation until the whole strip has been exposed. The first step, resulting from the initial exposure of the entire sheet, is a 2-second exposure; the second step had two 2-second exposures for a total of 4 seconds; the third step received three 2-second exposures for 6 seconds, etc. The steps, in other words, increase in 2-second increments.

Develop the test strip, just as you developed the proof sheet, for 2 minutes (or your own standard time), regardless of what it appears to be doing. Rinse it in the short-stop for 15 seconds or so and place it in the hypo. After a minute or so (check your paper package to be sure it's closed) turn on the white lights and inspect your results. If your exposure estimate was correct, you should see image details on all the steps; the 2-second step will be obviously too light in tone and the 12-second step too dark. One of the intermediate steps should be almost exactly right. If so, the test was successful. Determine the exposure of the satisfactory step and proceed to make a print. If not, try again, correcting the exposures.

This *fixed increment* method of test exposure is generally a quick and effective way to determine exposure, if you have some idea what the exposure is going to be. It is not a very good method if the probable exposure is in doubt, because it doesn't sample a very great range of possibilities. There is a danger, too, that the visual interval between adjacent steps may become

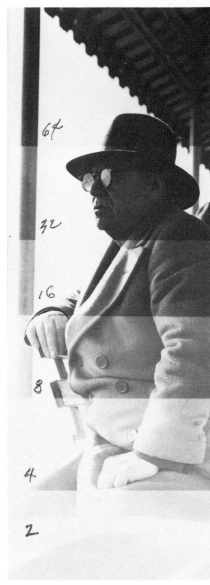

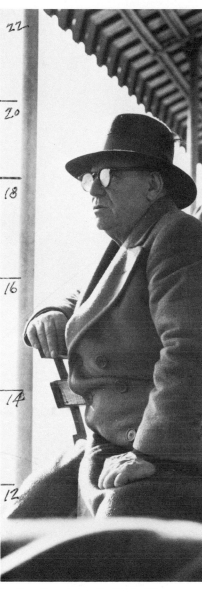

Figure 5.18
a. Geometric test strip.

b. Fixed increment test strip. The steps are practically invisible.

too subtle to be perceived. The 2-second interval between the 2-second and the 4-second exposure represents an exposure change of a full stop (doubled exposure), but the same 2-second interval between exposures of, say, 16 and 18 seconds is almost negligible. To be usefully visible the steps should all be separated by similar *geometric* intervals; in other words, the exposures should be increased by multiplying, rather than by simply adding, a constant factor.

Geometric test strips are simple enough to make, but there is a little trick involved, so pay attention. Each exposure (after the first) should be equivalent to the *accumulated total* exposure. In other words, if we give the whole sheet a 2-second exposure, the accumulated total is 2. Cover about a sixth of the strip and give it 2 seconds. Now the accumulated total is 4 (2 + 2). Cover another sixth of the strip and give it 4 seconds. The total now is 8 (2 + 2 + 4), so give it 8 seconds; then 16, then 32. The six exposures given, 2, 2, 4, 8, 16, and 32 seconds, have accumulated to yield steps of 2, 4, 8, 16, 32, and 64 seconds. Regardless of the actual exposure time used, each step will always double the previous one and the last step will be equal to twice the last exposure given.

After you've done it a few times, you will find this method of testing just as easy as adding a fixed increment repeatedly, and it will be more useful for unknown or unusual exposure situations. The fixed increment method will be best for subtle adjustments of exposure, once you get the general range. Use either one, but learn how to use them both.

Changes in print density or darkness are easy to make by varying the exposure time. Contrast adjustment is made by changing paper grades or, in the case of variable-contrast papers, filters. In either case it's a good idea to start with normal contrast and see what happens to the test image. If the test is harshly contrasty, with opaque blacks and bald whites without detail, the negative is much too contrasty for that paper grade and you should make a drastic change to a softer paper, which means a *lower* contrast number,

Remember, most prints will darken a little when they dry

Make a full print and examine it carefully in good light

It may require dodging or burning

Plan these controls with some care

like 1 or 0. If, on the other hand, the image turns out to be murky and gray without either black or white accent tones, it means that the negative is too *flat* (low contrast) for the paper and you should shift to a higher number, like 3, 4, or 5.

Changing paper grades or filters will probably change the exposure time at least slightly and you will be wise to make another test strip, varying the exposures around the best test exposure on the normal paper. Check this test for both density and contrast and, if either one is unsatisfactory, make another adjustment and test again. Remember that prints on most papers will appear to darken a little as they dry.

When the test strip image seems good, make a full-size print on the selected grade of paper, using the best test exposure but no other controls. This test is to confirm the exposure and paper contrast decision and also to see how the image tones relate to each other and to the basic composition. Again, develop this print for your normal developing time, regardless of what it appears to be doing in the developer. If the density and contrast are satisfactory, examine the print carefully in good light to look for areas of undesirable local tone. Try to visualize the image as it would look if certain dark areas were lightened slightly or certain highlight areas were darkened for richer texture. Possibly whole sections of the image should be modified. The sky in a landscape, for example, might not record clouds that are apparent in the negative. Extra sky exposure should bring them out. On the other hand, your concept might call for a totally white sky; less exposure will then be required to eliminate all tone and texture. These changes call for selective exposure, controlled by dodging or burning the image under the enlarger.

If the changes are extensive or elaborate, it will be wise to make separate test strips of the individual areas and make a little sketch of the image forms, labelling the areas you plan to modify, with the exposure times each should receive. The basic exposure will be the time appropriate for the largest area of the

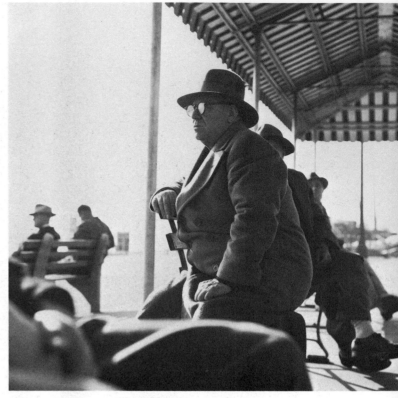

Figure 5.19
First print: 16 seconds, #2 filter.

image. Areas which require less time will have to be *held back* or dodged for part of the time while the exposure is in progress. Then areas which require more time can be burned in by allowing beams of image light to fall on them through appropriately shaped holes cut in opaque cards. These techniques will require some practice but they are not particularly difficult if you work systematically. Beginners almost always fail to test and plan sufficiently before picking up their dodging tools and punching the timer button. Don't trust to luck this way or you'll waste a lot of time and paper and still not get good pictures.

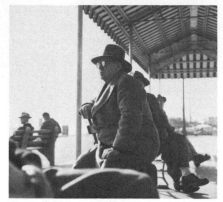

Figure 5.20
a. Polycontrast filter #1

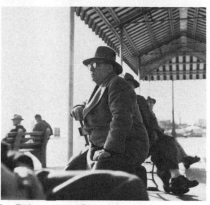

b. Polycontrast filter #2

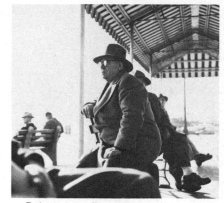

c. Polycontrast filter #3

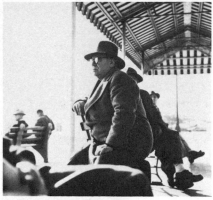

d. Polycontrast filter #4

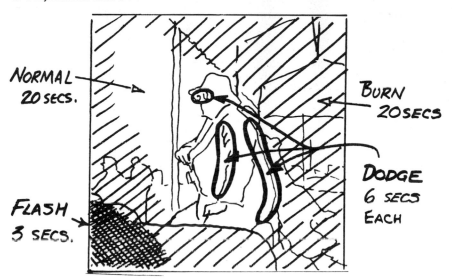

NORMAL
20 SECS.

BURN
20 SECS

DODGE
6 SECS
EACH

FLASH
3 SECS.

Figure 5.21
Dodging and burning diagram

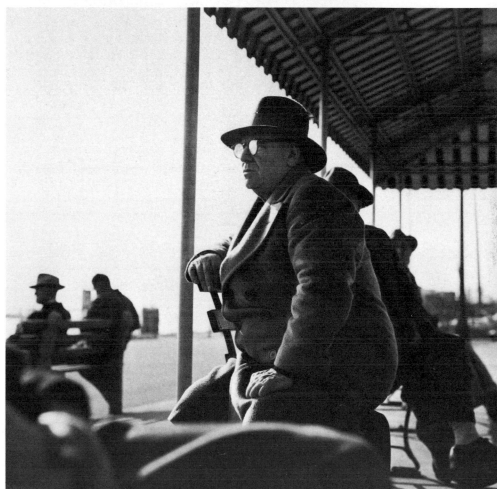

Figure 5.22 ▶
Final print 20 seconds, with dodging,
burning, and flashing as indicated in
figure 5.21.

133   Printing

For maximum print permanence, archival processing

Avoid contamination; use fresh chemicals

Eliminate hypo and tone the image

Hypo-eliminator will soften the emulsion; use care

Prints processed conventionally (as previously described) will probably last for many years without fading or discoloring, but they are not totally free from harmful chemicals and the silver image is not well protected from atmospheric contaminants such as gaseous compounds of sulfur. *Archival processing* attempts to correct these problems as completely as possible by more efficient fixing procedures, by better washing, and by protecting the silver image with some sort of coating or by converting it, wholly or partially, to a more stable material—a process called *toning*.

The procedure is not basically different from the normal one but there is greater emphasis on the use of fresh chemicals, control of times and temperatures, general cleanliness, and avoidance of contamination. There are also a few extra steps in the process.

The developer and short-stop baths need not be altered but the chemicals themselves should be renewed more frequently than usual to avoid possible staining or contamination. It is important to develop the image fully; the usual 2 minutes is adequate (in Dektol, at least). Short-stop treatment should be sufficiently long to neutralize the developer alkali; 30 seconds is adequate with agitation. Make the prints a little lighter than normal. They will darken after they've been toned in either selenium or gold (most other toners will lighten the image, however). The two-bath fixer should be used but Kodak's 200-print cycles seem excessive; my recommendation would be to limit each bath to one hundred 8″ × 10″ prints per gallon for archival purposes. After fixing, Kodak recommends placing the prints directly into a normal-strength solution of Kodak hypo-clearing agent (prepared according to package instructions) to which Kodak Rapid Selenium Toner concentrate has been added at the rate of 2 ounces of toner per gallon of clearing bath. Agitate single-weight prints in this solution for at least 2 minutes (double-weight prints for 3 minutes), then wash for 20 minutes in running water with frequent periods of agitation to insure good water circulation. Dry the prints on clean screens after sponging them to remove surface moisture.

Prints treated this way should last for a very long time under good storage conditions but they may still contain traces of dangerous sulfur compounds. Their life expectancy can be improved if they are given an additional hypo-elimination treatment and a final 10-minute wash. The formula for Kodak's hypo-eliminator, HE-1, is given in the appendix.

Some photographers object to the use of a combined hypo-clearing and toning bath because the degree of toning is not very controllable and because the selenium toner produces a rather sickly purple-brown color on some papers. An excellent alternative procedure, using gold rather than selenium as the protective toner, is as follows.

Develop and fix the prints as described above, then rinse them briefly and treat them in any good hypo-clearing bath, following package instructions. Wash them also, as instructed. Then treat the prints, one at a time, in the hypo-eliminator bath (HE-1) with gentle agitation for six minutes at not more than 20°C. Handle the prints very gently in this and following operations, because the gelatin emulsion will become very soft in the HE-1 bath. Then wash the prints in running water for 10 minutes at not more than 20°C, and treat them, one at a time, in the gold protective solution given in the appendix.

Toning proceeds slowly at the recommended 20°C but the temperature should not be raised. Keep the print immersed in the solution with gentle agitation. Because of the subtlety of the color change, it is difficult to tell when toning has proceeded far enough. It will help a great deal to have an identical print, untoned, in a tray of plain water beside the toning bath so you can compare the images. The first visible effect of the toner (either gold or selenium) is a slight intensification of the deep blacks of the image. The print should be removed from the toner after this intensification occurs and before there is an obvious change in image color.

Dry the prints on screens

You can lighten the silver image with Farmer's reducer

Presoak the print before treatment

Local reduction is possible too

The toning action will continue for a little while in the wash tray, so don't overdo it. Gold-toned prints which have been treated too long will look distinctly bluish after they've dried. This is no problem if you like the effect, but it may come as a surprise to you if you are not familiar with the process. Wash the toned prints for at least 10 minutes in running water, sponge them surface-dry (gently!), and lay them out on clean screens or cloth facedown to air-dry. Don't use screens if the dry prints show any sign of the screen mesh texture; resoak the prints thoroughly and dry them on clean, lintfree cloth.

Post-Development Controls

Occasionally the normal dodging and burning techniques are not adequate to adjust the image values to your complete satisfaction. Very small image areas, like highlights, or areas of unusual shape or sharp outline, are almost impossible to control during the print exposure. Occasionally, too, a print which looked great in the wash tray will *dry down* (look too dark when dry). Post-development chemical treatment may be helpful in these cases.

Usually it isn't feasible to *intensify* (darken) a print image area, but *reducing* (lightening) an area of tone is relatively easy. There are several chemical solutions that can be used for this purpose but Farmer's reducer (formula in appendix) is one of the best and most reliable. Farmer's reducer is made from potassium ferricyanide and hypo, and it works in a kind of two-stage process. The ferricyanide converts the silver image back into a compound which is both light-sensitive and soluble in hypo, and the hypo dissolves it away in the normal fixing action. The solutions can be used separately, if desired, but the action of the ferricyanide alone is difficult to appraise. It's better, in my opinion, to use the combined solution.

The reducer must be fresh. Its useful life is fairly short once the ingredients have been combined but the separate solutions will keep indefinitely if protected from strong light and air.

For use on prints the reducer should be diluted with water for slower, more controllable action. It's a good idea to try it on a scrap print first before attacking a choice one. Reduction is effective for prints which have turned out to be a little too dark overall. Soak the print in plain water for several minutes to soften it, then slip it into a tray of reducer that has been suitably diluted, and agitate it vigorously until it shows some signs of change. Get it out of the reducer and flood it with running water *before* it reaches the desired lightness. A print can always be given more treatment in the solution, but a too-light image can't be restored. Since the reducer contains hypo, follow it with a rinse, then use hypo-clearing agent, and the usual washing procedure.

It's quite possible to reduce the image locally, too. Soak the print first, then flatten it out on the bottom of an inverted tray or a sheet of glass or plastic. Prop it up at a slight angle in the sink, close to a source of running water, and wipe the emulsion surface-dry with the edge of your hand or a dampened sponge. Saturate a ball of cotton or a small sponge in moderately strong reducer and squeeze it quite dry. It must not drip when handled. Rub the area of the image to be lightened with the cotton, in a random pattern of strokes, covering the entire area as quickly and uniformly as possible. Be very careful not to let drops of reducer stand on the emulsion surface for more than a second or two at most. Then, at the first sign of change, flood the print surface with water and inspect the result.

The change in image density should be barely perceptible and the treated area should be free from mottle, streaks, or spots. If there are signs of uneven reduction, it may be due to poor technique. Perhaps the cotton dripped reducer, perhaps it was too small to cover the area uniformly, or perhaps you missed part of the area. It could also result from a too-strong mixture of reducer. If the problem is not too severe, further treatment may resolve it. Otherwise you may have to make another print. Be careful.

Avoid iron to prevent blue stains

Bleach baths can remove the image entirely

Iodine is a good bleach for small areas or spots

Hypo will remove the iodine stain

The bleached marks may have to be spotted

If the reducer is the right strength and your technique is good, it should take three or four cycles of wiping, reducing, and flooding to complete the job. But when completed, the area should be improved in value without obvious flaws. Be careful of light-toned areas or areas which contain light accents. The reducer will etch through light grays very quickly leaving yellowish white paper.

There may be tiny areas of the image which need lightening. These can be treated in similar fashion but the reducer should be applied with a cotton swab (Q-tip) or a brush. Be very careful if you use a brush with a metal ferrule. The ferricyanide may react with some metals to form a very intense and permanent blue dye (Prussian blue) which may stain the print and is very difficult to remove. For this same reason, Farmer's reducer should never be mixed, stored, or used in a metal container or in a chipped enamelled iron container.

For some purposes it is useful to remove the silver image from the emulsion entirely, which can be done with any of several *bleaches*. One of the best for this purpose is composed of potassium permanganate and acid (formula given in the appendix). Although the solution itself is not dangerous to handle, the concentrated acid is. Be very careful and prepare the solution near a source of running water so you can flood the acid off your skin if it happens to splash or spill. The permanganate bleach must be mixed fresh and used within a few minutes. It spoils quickly, whether used or not. It is best for removing large areas of the image, either by careful local application with a swab or by immersing the print in the solution. Portions of the image that you wish to preserve can be protected with a brushed-on layer of Maskoid or thinned rubber cement.

The bleach works quickly and will stain the paper reddish brown. Remove the print from the solution when the image shows no further traces of black and wash it in running water until the water runs clear, without any obvious pink stain. Then immerse the print in ordinary fixer or a nonhardening fixer (preferably), where the brownish-red stain and remains of the image

will both disappear, leaving the paper pure white. Treat the print in hypo-clearing bath and wash it as usual.

Small areas of the image, and especially the occasional black blemishes that occur, can be bleached more conveniently with an iodine solution. Ordinary tincture of iodine, available at any drugstore, is effective. Using a toothpick or match stick, deposit a drop of iodine solution on the spot and allow it to stand for a minute or so. Then pick it up carefully with the tip of a moistened blotter or a wisp of tissue and inspect the spot. Occasionally the iodine will penetrate the paper and produce a bright blue stain in the paper itself. Don't worry about it. If any trace of black or gray remains, treat it again with iodine. The spot will be heavily stained with brown but, when the blackish appearance is gone, deposit a heaping drop of fixer on the spot and both stains and image should disappear. A second application of (or total immersion in) fixer may be required to complete the action. The bleached area should be pure white, without any tinge of stain. Treat the print with hypo-clearing bath and wash as usual.

If your first attempt is not completely successful and some silver remains in the bleached area after treatment with the hypo, you will have to rinse the area thoroughly to remove the hypo before it can be treated with iodine again. Iodine will not work if there is much hypo present in the emulsion.

Almost every print will have a few image flaws that will have to be corrected before it is fit to exhibit. Dust or abrasions on the negative will show in the print as white spots or lines, and scratches or cuts in the negative emulsion will probably show as black marks. Bleaching the black marks will make them white marks and white marks will have to be *spotted*.

There are spotting colors and spotting dyes. The dyes are better for prints that are to be exhibited because they are invisible on the print surface. Spotting colors are really pigments which lie on the emulsion surface and are distractingly obvious. They are fine, though, for prints that are to be reproduced.

Spotting will take practice and you'll need to experiment to find the method that works best for you.

Figure 5.23
a. Saturate the brush in the appropriate dye mixture and stroke it almost dry on tissue. Rotate it as you stroke, to keep the point well formed.

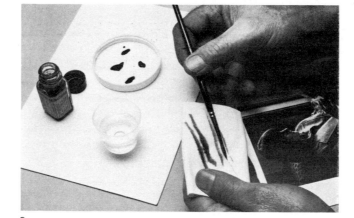
a

b. Greatly magnified view of a lint mark on a medium gray area of a moderately grainy image. Notice how fine the brush point is. A smaller brush will form no better point and will dry out much sooner, shifting the dye color and laying dry dye on the print surface.

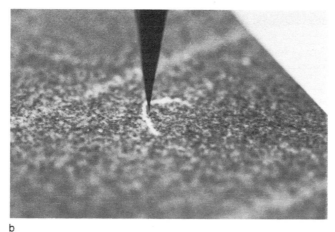
b

c. Here the lint mark is partly spotted. Use a stipple stroke to match the grain texture and break the line into sections first, to avoid the possibility of simply reinforcing the linear appearance if your technique is not perfect.

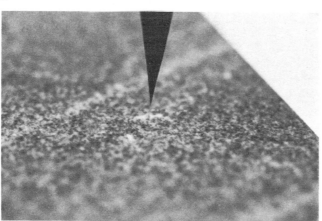
c

Provide yourself with a bottle of neutral spotting dye (Spotone is one brand), a small container for water, a white saucer or plastic palette for dye mixing, some facial tissues or paper towels, and a good, red sable watercolor brush about size #4. Most authorities recommend much smaller brushes, like #00 or even #0000, but I can't believe they're serious. If you get a #4 sable that forms a good point (test it in the store before you buy it), it will make as delicate a mark as any smaller brush. Furthermore, because it holds a great deal more dye mixture, it will allow you to spot faster, longer, and more consistently, which will result in a superior job. Small brushes dry out very rapidly as you work and the dye changes tone and consistency. Spotting is tough enough when everything is working right; don't make it any more difficult than it has to be.

Practice for a while on spoiled prints. The easiest spots to deal with are dust spots on a grainy image in an area of medium-light tone. The most difficult spots to eliminate are fine, sharp white lines on black areas. After you've labored over one of these, you'll learn to clean your negatives before you print them.

Place the dry print in good light, either flat on a table or on a slightly tilted surface, and arrange your equipment around it conveniently. Dip the brush into the dye and deposit a brushful on the saucer, dividing it into three or four separate puddles. Then dip the brush into the water and, without rinsing it, deposit several blobs of "dirty" water on the saucer. Now stroke the brush on the tissues, holding the handle low and pulling it across the tissue surface so the brush hairs are straightened and brought to a point. Rotating the handle in your fingers as you stroke will help to form the fine point you need. Continue stroking the tissue until the brush leaves only a faint line of moisture and appears to be surface-dry. It now contains a light-toned dye mixture, suitable for use on a light gray image area.

Holding the brush almost vertically, bring the tip hairs into contact with the white margin of the practice print and draw a thin line. Notice that the dye color is pale when the brush moves rapidly and becomes darker when the brush moves slowly. Also, notice that going over the line twice darkens the color. Practice brush control by making thin lines in various directions and try stippling an area of the practice print image with tiny dots. Be careful not to bear down on the brush; just use the tip hairs. You'll probably find that little stroking motions which make little apostrophe-shaped marks are easier to control than poking motions, which will tend to split the brush tip. Most spotting will require a gradual build-up of tone. Practice a blended-dot technique and avoid long linear strokes when working on a good print.

After two or three minutes you will notice that the dye marks are getting darker and that they have a granular appearance (this will happen much sooner with a small brush). The brush is too dry. Stop and recharge it with dye. *Don't* simply touch the tip to a dye puddle, blend the dye and water on the palette to the desired tint, then saturate the brush with the mixture and stroke it dry on tissue. Failure to do this will result in uncertain dye color and improper wetting, and you'll regret it. Practice until you feel confident, then charge the brush with a very light tint and tackle a good print, beginning with the lightest areas.

RC papers will spot a little easier if the dye mixture contains a little acid and some wetting agent. Add one drop of Photoflo and one drop of plain 28% acetic acid (*not* indicator short-stop) to about 2 ounces of water. Stir with the brush, until blended, and proceed as usual.

Beginners have a lot of trouble with dye spotting because they think of it as painting and assume that the dye is being deposited on the surface like pigment. Wrong! The dye is *absorbed* by the gelatin and will only work well if it is applied in the right consistency, neither too wet nor too dry. If too wet, it will be hard to control and leave visible liquid traces on the print surface; if too dry, it will not take easily and will look coarse and ragged on the surface of the print like pigment. It will also wipe off. When the dye is right it flows into the gelatin without a visible surface trace and simply becomes part of the image tone. It won't do this for you at first, but it will if you practice.

The neutral dye color may not match the image color of your paper. Other colors of dye are available and you can blend them to match just about any image color that a black-and-white paper can be made to produce. Be careful not to work too dark too soon. The dye will naturally darken in the brush as you progress toward the darker print tones. If you make a mistake and overdo it, the dye can be lightened but rarely removed completely by rewashing the print. Try soaking it in a weak solution of sodium carbonate or water to which a few drops of ammonia have been added. Be careful, this treatment will soften the gelatin somewhat.

When you are through spotting, rinse the brush thoroughly in clear water and shake it dry. Form the hairs into a perfect point. It may be necessary to dampen them again slightly to get them to hold together. Then store the brush in some location where it will not be deformed and where it will be protected from dust and dirt. Use this brush only for print spotting and preferably only for dyes. Pigments will eventually grind off the fine tip hairs which form the delicate point you need. For long-term storage wrap the brush in a paper cylinder and seal it; moths love red sable hair.

Mounting and Matting Prints

Prints to be exhibited should be mounted in some way to hold them flat and give them some body. There are several ways to do this. There are spray adhesives, liquid adhesives, adhesive sheets that can be stuck on the back of the print (Luminos S-ST RD paper is sold with an adhesive backing already applied), and various thermoplastic adhesive sheets. Of these, the thermoplastic materials are best, in my opinion, at least for fiber-based papers. Adhesive sheets are fine for RC prints. The thermoplastic sheets are universally referred to as *dry-mount tissue.*

Dry-mount tissue becomes adhesive when it's heated and sets when it cools. In normal use, a sheet of tissue is stuck to the back of the print with a light

Fiber-based prints can tolerate more heat than RCs can

Dry out the press pad. *Don't use the press to dry wet prints*

Always use a cover sheet over the print

The press platen must be kept clean

stroke of an electrically heated *tacking iron,* then a loose corner of the tissue is similarly stuck to the mounting board to hold the print in position. Finally, print, tissue, and board, protected from surface damage by a heavy paper or card-stock cover sheet, are all inserted into a heated *dry-mounting press* and held under pressure for several seconds, during which time the tissue softens and cements the print firmly to the mount board. After cooling for a minute or two, the bond is complete and virtually permanent.

Fiber-based prints can tolerate more heat than RC papers or color prints can, so it's important that you use the right materials and set the press at the correct temperature for the kind of prints you're mounting. Press thermostats are not accurately calibrated, but the proper heat for fiber-based papers is about 250°F (121°C) and for RC papers and color prints it's about 190°F (88°C). If you're using a press for the first time, with RC paper, try a spoiled print before you commit a good one. If the temperature is too low, the mounting tissue will not stick well; if the press is too hot, your print may be damaged. For best accuracy you can calibrate your press thermostat using Temperature Indicator Strips, manufactured by Seal, Inc., and available through photo stores.

Other than temperature control there are three features of the dry-mounting process which may give you trouble if you're not careful. Prints may not stick to the mount well if either the mount board or the foam-rubber press pad is damp. If the press platen (the flat metal plate that presses down on the print) is dirty, the print surface may be embossed or indented. If dirt particles are trapped between the print and the mount board, they will surely show on the print surface as little pimples.

The dampness problem is cured by heating the press in the closed position so the press pad is warmed thoroughly and then opening it from time to time so any moisture can evaporate. Dry out the mounting board the same way; alternately heat it and air it until it feels reasonably dry when it is first removed from the press.

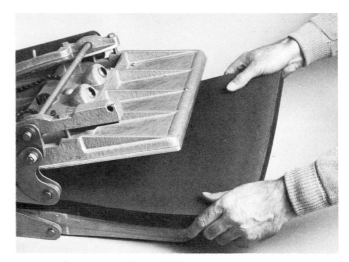

Figure 5.24
Drying press pad

Dampness will probably not be a problem in the wintertime when humidity is low, unless, in a community darkroom situation, someone has thoughtlessly used the press to dry some wet prints (a *thoroughly* antisocial thing to do!).

A community-used press is also likely to acquire a dirty platen and you should check it every time you use the press. The most common problem results from fragments of dry-mount tissue which adhere to the metal. They should never touch the platen in the first place because you should *always* cover the print with a clean paper cover sheet before closing the press. RC papers and color prints should be covered with special silicone-treated paper (available from photo stores) which will not stick to the prints even if they soften excessively from a too-high press temperature. Don't *ever* mount a print without using a cover sheet.

A dirty platen surface is very difficult to clean, but if the material is not baked on too thoroughly, it may dissolve in alcohol or ethylene dichloride or some similar solvent. Use these solvents with great care to avoid breathing the fumes; they are very toxic. If you must resort to using one of them, take the press outside and work upwind of it. If the material is insolubly charred,

Flush- or bleed-mounting

Smooth the edges of the print

Problems of too much or too little heat

Exhibition prints are frequently matted and framed

Establish border proportions with cropping Ls and paper strips

it will probably have to be polished off, but this is a last resort. Use fine steel wool (#000 or #0000) and rub the whole platen surface lightly, concentrating on the dirty spots. When the surface seems clean, wash it thoroughly and dry it. A spray coat of silicone lubricant, rubbed dry, will help protect it from future abuse.

High-temperature dry-mount tissues (for fiber-based prints) and most low-temperature tissues (for RC and color prints) are paper-based. To repeat, a sheet of either of these materials is attached to the print by laying the tissue sheet on the back of the print and stroking it lightly (to avoid marring the print), near center, with the flat surface of the hot tacking iron. Then, any tissue which extends beyond the print edges must be trimmed off to protect the press and to prevent the print from sticking to the cover sheet. If the print is to be *flush-mounted* or *bleed-mounted* (trimmed without borders), the tissue can be tacked to the mount board; just raise a corner of the print out of the way so you can touch the tissue directly with the tacking iron. After heating in the press, the print and mount can be trimmed to size, preferably with a mat-knife and straightedge.

A print, trimmed flush, will probably look a little untidy until the cut edges have been smoothed. Using fine sandpaper (200 grit or so) and a small block, sand the edges on both faces of the print, stroking away from the image area to avoid flaking the emulsion. When the edges are nicely smoothed and rounded, rub them with paraffin or a china-marking pencil (black or white) and polish the edges with a folded facial tissue. After this treatment, people will enjoy handling your prints whether they like your images or not!

If the print is to be trimmed without borders, but mounted in some specific location on a large board, the tissue should be tacked to the back of the print before they are trimmed together to the final image dimensions. Then, hold the print in position and, lifting a corner of the print only, tack the tissue to the mount. Protect the assembly with a cover sheet and clamp it in the press. The time required to complete the bond will have to be found by experimentation but somewhere around 15 to 30 seconds is a good place to start. Heavy mount board or a heavy-weight cover sheet will necessitate longer-than-normal times.

Insufficient time in the press or too-low temperature will produce a weak bond and the print may pop off the mount or loosen if the board is bent or twisted. Sometimes it's possible to lift a corner of the poorly mounted print and strip it partly or completely off the board. Reheating in the press at a higher temperature or for a longer time generally cures this problem. Overheating is rare with fiber-based papers. Overheated RC papers or color prints may be warped or their surfaces marred. There is no cure.

Small- and medium-size prints can be held in place on a mount board or in an album with gummed art corners. Slip the "corners" onto the corners of the print first, then moisten them, and press the print into position. After a minute or two the corners will be secure and the print can then be removed and replaced easily, if desired. Some photographers like to use corners to mount prints which will be matted (or over-matted) but dry-mounting is more common.

Exhibition prints are frequently dry-mounted, matted, and sometimes framed. The choice is yours. If you plan to mat a print, whether it will be framed or not, first decide the exact dimensions of the image area by establishing the outlines of the image with cropping Ls and measuring the composition boundaries. Then decide on the width of the mat borders. It is conventional, but certainly not obligatory, to make the side margins equal, the top margin equal to the side or slightly wider, and the bottom margin slightly wider than the top. The best guide is visual. Lay strips of paper or mat board around the print to simulate the finished mat and look at it critically. Then pick border proportions which seem most attractive.

Determine the size of the mat board by adding the print width dimension to the width of *both* side margins of the mat. Similarly, add the print image height dimension to the combined widths of the top and bottom mat margins. Cut a piece of mat board to these dimensions, being careful to keep the corners square and neat.

Figure 5.25

a. Lay the print facedown on a clean surface and attach a sheet of dry-mount tissue to it with a light touch of the hot tacking iron. Tack it in only one spot, preferably near center.

b. Trim off any tissue that extends beyond the edges of the print. It's easiest to do this if you take a narrow strip of the print margin with the tissue but be careful not to cut into the image area. The mat-knife and straightedge technique shown here is generally more satisfactory than using a print trimming board or paper cutter. When using a mat-knife, *always* keep a sheet of heavy cardboard under the work to serve as a cutting surface. *Never* cut on an unprotected tabletop or desktop.

c. Lift a corner of the print and tack the tissue to the mount board. Again, tack the tissue in only one spot to avoid creating folds or wrinkles in the tissue when it's pressed. The tissue which overhangs the mount board (right corner in the illustration) will have to be trimmed off before the board can be put into the press; otherwise it will stick to the press pad and make a mess.

d. Cover the face of the print with a clean cover sheet and slip it into the press. Time and temperature will depend on the type of paper in use and the mat board weight. See the text for details.

e. Trim the mounted print to finished size with mat-knife and straightedge. You can use a plastic triangle to keep the corners square and protect the print surface, as is shown here, but don't use it as a cutting guide; the plastic nicks easily.

f. Smooth the edges of the trimmed print on both faces with fine sandpaper and a block. Stroke away from the print face to avoid chipping the edge of the image gelatin. Then wax the smoothed edges and polish them with tissue. You can use wax crayons if you want toned borders; paraffin will finish the edges without leaving any visible trace.

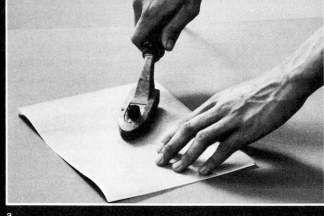

a

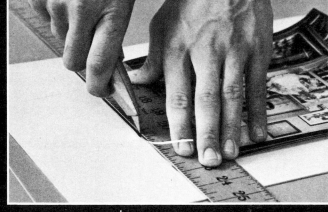

b

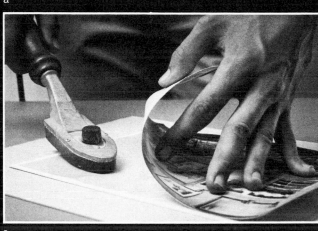

c

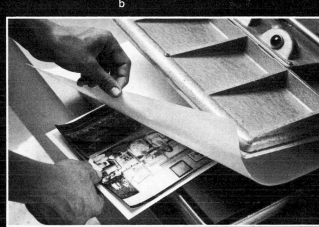

d

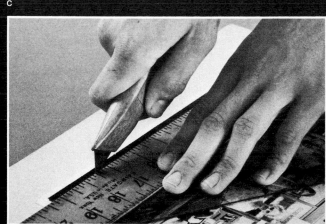

e

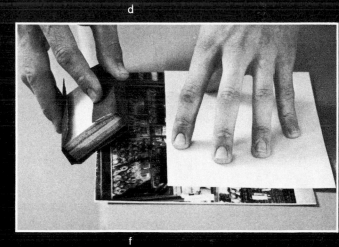

f

Figure 5.26

a. If you want your print mounted with borders, but not matted, you'll have to trim it to finished size and place it carefully on the mount board. The actual procedure will depend on the mounting technique used, but in any case you'll have to determine the image dimensions and mark the print position carefully and lightly on the mount board face. Use soft pencil and light pressure so the marks can be erased.

If you plan to dry-mount the print, attach the tissue and trim both print and tissue to finished size. An alternative drymounting method, using Scotch brand adhesive sheets #567, is shown here. Lay the adhesive sheet dull-side down on a clean surface and carefully peel back the adhesive tissue from the release paper. Lay the print facedown on the release paper.

c. Lay the tissue back down to cover the print and squeegee firmly to attach the tissue to the back of the print.

d. Lift a corner of the adhesive backing paper and slowly peel it away from the print. The adhesive film adheres to the print back as it leaves the backing paper. It is self-trimming.

e. The print will stick to your fingers now but it can be moved around on the board without adhering. Position it carefully on the guide marks and press it down lightly with your fingers.

Now cover the print with a clean paper, preferably a silicone-release paper, and squeegee firmly. This pressure bonds the print securely to the board.

g. If traces of the adhesive show around the print edges, they can be removed easily with a rubber cement lifter or a kneaded eraser. This mounting adhesive is claimed to be safe for photographs, long lasting, and nonstaining. Prints can be removed from the mounts, if necessary, with rubber cement thinner.

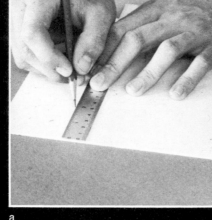
a

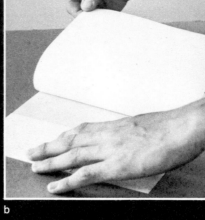
b

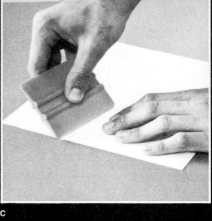
c

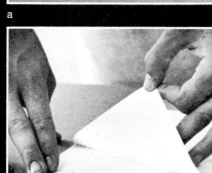
d

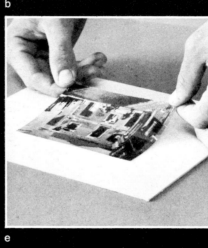
e

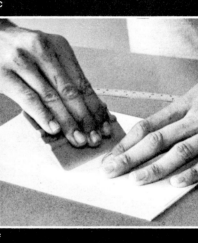
f

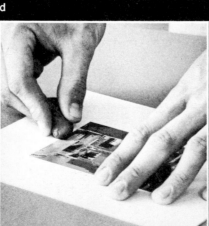
g

Figure 5.27

a. Tack a piece of dry-mount tissue to the back of the print, then trim off any tissue which extends beyond the edges of the print. A print to be matted should not be trimmed to exact size before mounting but final image dimensions must be known. Determine the composition with L-shaped cardboard strips (cropping Ls) laid over the print. Then measure the image dimensions and jot them down.

b. Determine the mat and mount board size by adding the desired margin widths to the print dimensions. Cut the mount board very slightly smaller than the mat so the mat will cover it completely. Mark the image corner positions on the front of the mat board. Some mat boards will not tolerate erasure so make the marks as light and inconspicuous as possible.

c. Using a metal straightedge as a guide, cut the mat opening with a sharp mat-knife or utility knife. Always cut on the "waste" side of the straightedge so, if the knife wanders off line, it won't damage the mat itself. Cut just past the corner marks so the mat corners will be clean and free from tufts of uncut fibers.

d. Place the print on the mount board; place the mat board over it; and align the mat and mount boards carefully. Then slide the print into satisfactory position in the mat opening. Check to be sure the boards are still in exact alignment.

e. Holding the print in position on the mount, lift the mat carefully and, lifting a corner of the print, tack a corner of the dry-mount tissue to the mount board.

f. Protecting the print face with a cover sheet, insert the mount board into the press and heat the print to bond it to the board.

g. Align the top edges of the mount and mat boards; the mount board should be faceup, the mat board facedown. Tape the intersection together to form a hinge. Use fabric library tape for archival quality prints; plastic or paper tape for temporary use. Ordinary masking tape is not desirable; it will dry out and discolor with age and may damage the print itself if it comes into contact with it. You can, of course, dry-mount or glue the mount and mat together permanently, if you want to.

h. The finished print is neatly presented. Select mat boards in any color or texture that pleases you.

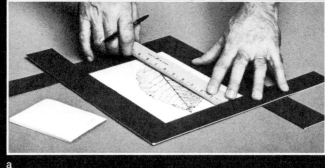
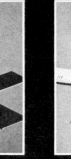
a

b

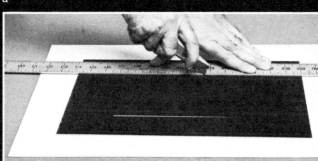
c

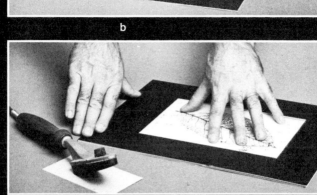
d

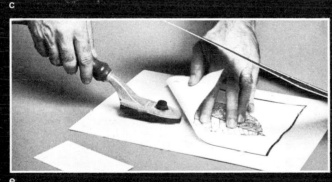
e

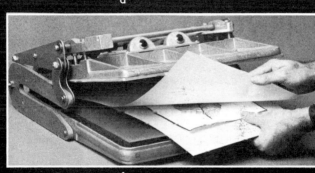
f

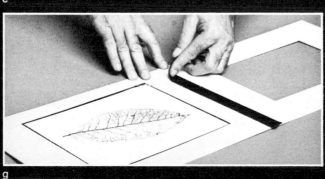
g

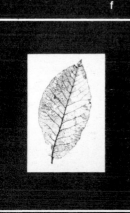
h

143 Printing

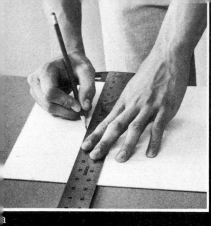

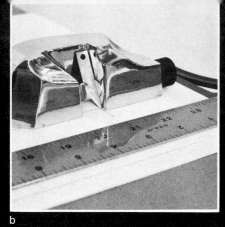

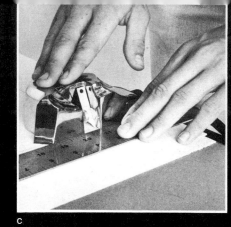

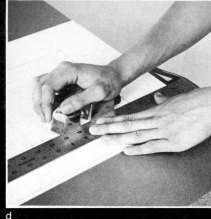

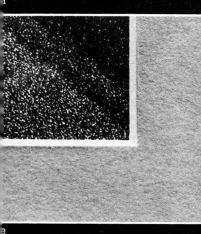

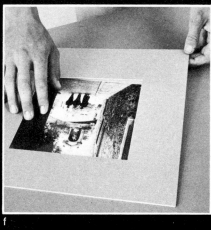

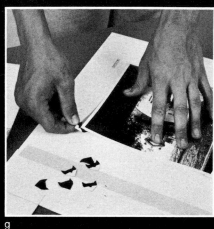

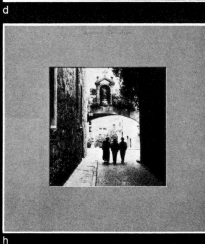

Figure 5.28

a. Cutting bevelled mats is not much different from cutting ordinary ones but a special mat-cutter makes the job easier. Here's one method, using the familiar and relatively inexpensive Dexter mat-cutter. Determine the mat opening dimensions and mark them on the *back of* the mat board. You can be bold with these lines and draw them well past the corners.

b. Place the mat board, facedown, on a sheet of expendable cardboard to serve as a cutting surface, and align both boards with the edge of your work table or drawing board. This allows you to use a metal T-square, both to keep the lines straight and to use as a cutting guide. The T-square is much easier to hold steady than an ordinary straightedge. Align the edge of the mat-cutter with the drawn border line and insert the knife point just behind the cross line, as shown. Press it down firmly.

c. Slide the T-square over to the cutter and allow it to square the cutter if it's slightly out of line. Check the board alignment again to be sure it is snug against the "T" of the T-square.

d. The Dexter mat-cutter is a strictly right-handed instrument. Place your hand on it naturally and, holding the T-square down firmly, push the cutter along the metal guide. If the knife blade is in good shape it should cut cleanly and easily without any tendency to wander away from the guide. Cut about ⅛-inch past the cross line to insure a clean corner. One authority suggests pinning the mat board down to help hold it in place—a good idea. Use a couple of pushpins in the waste center area of the board.

e. A finished mat corner.

f. Align mat and mount boards, as previously described, and center the print in the mat opening.

g. Some people like to use gummed art corners for mounting. If you want to try this method, it's helpful to hinge the mat and mount boards before positioning the print. Then hold the print in position and open the mat. Moisten the gummed backs of the art corners, one at a time, slip them over the print corners and press them down firmly. They stick almost immediately. You can lick them if you like, but I suggest using a dampened sponge (the glue tastes terrible).

h. Art corners are fine for small prints and especially for RC paper, which lies quite flat. Large prints may need more support if you want them to stay in place without bulging or warping as the weather changes.

Synopsis **Print Processing Steps**

1. In three clean trays prepare appropriate volumes of working solutions of print developer, short-stop, and print fixer, adjusted to about 20°C (68°F). If available, add a fourth tray of clean water and a fifth containing hypo-clearing bath, prepared according to manufacturer's instructions.

   No white lights: Safelight color, yellow (series OC or equivalent)

2. *Developer:* Immerse exposed paper in developer and note time. Agitate continuously, keeping print submerged, for standard developing time (my recommendation: 2 minutes in Dektol, diluted 1 : 2 with water, for projection papers; 1 minute for Azo). Drain briefly from one corner and transfer to short-stop.

3. *Short-Stop:* Immerse print in short-stop with continuous agitation for 15 to 30 seconds, then drain, and transfer to fixer.

4. *Fixer:* Immerse print in fresh fixer with continuous agitation for about 15 to 30 seconds and periodic agitation for 4 or 5 minutes more. Increase time as the fixer ages, but do not exceed about 10 minutes. *Note:* RC prints get 2 minutes in fresh fixer (to maximum of 5) with frequent agitation. Drain regular fiber-based prints and transfer to water rinse. RC prints go directly to wash tray.

5. *Rinse:* Agitate fiber-based prints in plain water for about a minute then transfer to hypo-clearing bath. Change rinse water frequently or use running water rinse.

6. *Hypo-Clearing Bath:* Treat fiber-based prints according to manufacturer's instructions. *Note:* RC prints don't need hypo clear.

7. *Wash:* Wash fiber-based prints as directed by manufacturer of clearing bath. *Note:* Wash RC prints for 5 minutes in running water. Wash prints in batches; don't add unwashed prints to partially washed batch.

8. *Dry:* Sponge or squeegee prints surface dry and lay out on plastic screens or clean cloth; fiber-based prints facedown, RC prints faceup. RC prints can also be dried by hanging them by corners with clothespins. Fiber-based prints can be ferrotyped on heated drum dryer or on plastic sheets, or dried to natural finish in blotter books or rolls.

9. *Cleanup:* Discard developer, short-stop, and clearing bath (unless manufacturer suggests saving it). Save fixer until it has treated about twenty-five 8″ x 10″ prints per quart or until it tests negative. Wash all utensils thoroughly and wash up chemical spills and traces on timers, switches, door handles, etc. Rinse off chemical storage bottles and store away. Return trays to racks. Wash your hands and dry them. Turn off the water and the lights.

Cut square-edged mats from the front of the board; bevelled edges from the back

Use sharp tools and cut on a firm surface for clean edges

If you want the mat opening to have ordinary square edges, draw a very light outline shape of the image area, in exact position, on the *face* of the mat board, using pencil, T-square, and triangle. Lay the mat board, faceup on a sheet of clean, smooth cardboard and, using a metal straightedge and mat knife, cut the mat opening by following the lightly pencilled image outline. If you prefer a bevelled mat opening, draw the image outline on the *back* of the mat board. Lay the mat board *facedown* on clean, smooth cardboard and use a mat-cutter with an angled blade to cut the mat opening.

Regardless of the tools used, always place the straightedge guide on the mat so it covers and protects the margins. Then, if the knife should slip, it will simply wander off into the unwanted center of the board. Always use a sharp blade and cut slightly past the corners of the image area so the cut-out piece will fall out cleanly without leaving little fuzzy tufts of uncut fibers in the corners. It is important to have a firm, smooth surface, like cardboard, under the mat while cutting

it. If the surface is rough or soft, the cut edges are likely to be ragged and uneven. If the surface is too hard, like glass or metal, the knife point may become dulled or broken. This is particularly serious with a mat-cutter; if the blade tip is damaged, the mat edges will probably be ragged. Finally, be careful. Stay in control and watch your fingers; blood is very difficult to remove from mat board.

When the mat is ready, brush the back of the print to remove dirt particles, tack a sheet of tissue to it, and trim off the excess. Cut a piece of mount board to the exact size of the mat board (or very slightly smaller) and lay the print on it faceup in the chosen location. Align the top edges of mat and mount boards and, holding them slightly apart, reach through the mat opening and position the print precisely in the mat opening. When it is correctly placed, reach under the mat board and hold the print in position while the mat is removed. Then lift a corner of the print and tack the tissue to the mount. Heat the board and print in the dry-mount press, protecting the surface with a cover sheet.

When the mat is placed over the mount board and the top edges are aligned, the image should be precisely framed by the mat opening. Tape the mount and mat together along their inside top edges or fasten them together in some other way. Look over the mat face carefully and remove any smudges or marks with an eraser (kneaded eraser or art gum for minor marks, Pink Pearl eraser for stubborn marks). If the print is to be framed under glass, be sure the inside dimensions of the frame are large enough to permit the mat to expand a little.

This is your reward for all those hours in the darkroom. If you handled the camera well and followed the various process steps effectively, you should have a print you can show with pride.

Summary

Printing is easiest in a darkroom equipped with a large sink, running water, electricity, good ventilation, and lots of storage space. In addition to the usual darkroom equipment and utensils you'll need timers, safelights, and an enlarger. Enlargers come in several sizes and designs; condenser or diffusion systems are available, with or without color heads.

Buy a good lens for your enlarger. You will also need an easel and you may want to buy a focusing aid or grain focuser. Other necessary or desirable equipment items include a proofing or printing frame, dodging tools, trays, a tray siphon, print tongs or paddles, print dryer or drying frames, dry-mount press and tacking iron, a print trimmer, and mount- and mat-cutting tools.

Fiber-based papers are still available in some surfaces and grades and are preferred for archival storage. Resin-coated papers are becoming more popular. They offer processing convenience but are not considered archival. Both types are available in a variety of sizes, weights, image tones, base tints, surfaces, and contrast grades. Some papers provide a variable-contrast characteristic, controllable by varying the color of the exposing light. Some papers are designed for stabilization processing.

Print developers are usually strong solutions, mixed and stored as stock solutions and diluted for use. The stop bath for papers is similar to that used for film, but paper fixer is usually less concentrated. Papers don't clear in the fixing bath. They should be treated carefully and not overfixed. For best results, use two fixing baths in sequence.

Temperature of processing solutions is not critical in printing, within reasonable limits, but try to standardize for consistent results.

You can use either contact or projection paper for proofing or contact printing. Working under safelight conditions, place the negatives on the paper surface, emulsion to emulsion, and hold them in position in a printing frame. Expose through the negatives under an appropriate light source. Develop for the standard time and follow the other process steps carefully. Fiber-based and RC papers require different washing and drying treatment; follow the separate instructions.

Select images to be enlarged by examining the contact proof sheet. Be sure your enlarger is properly adjusted for the negative size and clean the negative, lens, and carrier, if necessary. Under safelight conditions, adjust the image size and focus; then make a test strip. Image density can be adjusted by changes in print exposure; contrast is adjusted by changing paper grades or filtering the enlarger light.

Make a full test print and decide what adjustments are necessary. Dodging, burning, and flashing techniques are helpful for refining tonal balance.

For archival permanence, prints can be given special fixing, hypo-eliminating, and washing treatment, and the image can be further protected by toning. This treatment tends to soften the print emulsion; handle the prints carefully.

Print tones can also be adjusted by chemical reduction. Farmer's reducer can be used to lighten the entire print image or to treat small areas selectively. Bleaches remove the image completely. Permanganate bleach is recommended for large areas; iodine is effective for small areas. Bleached prints must be hypoed and washed thoroughly.

Spotting will remove small white blemishes in the print image. Use spotting dye and a fine-quality sable hair brush, and proceed carefully. Dyes can be blended to match almost any print image color and diluted to adjust the intensity of the tone.

Prints are usually mounted or matted for exhibition. Dry-mounting is one method; separate materials and press temperatures are required for fiber-based and RC papers. Dry out the mount board and the press pad. Always use a cover sheet over the print.

Mounted prints can be trimmed without borders, left with borders, or matted. Use cropping Ls to determine composition, then measure boards carefully and cut with mat knife and straightedge. Bevelled mats can be cut with a Dexter mat-cutter. Clean up the finished mat with art gum if necessary.

Outline

Light, Color, and Filters
The Spectrum Colors
How Light Is Controlled
Important Qualities of Light

Artificial Light Sources

Using Flash

Fluorescent Light

Ultraviolet and Infrared

Principles of Lighting
Lighting for Form
Lighting for Texture
Lighting for Color
Lighting for Effect

Available Light

Controlling Artificial Light

Working with Light

No single, simple theory explains light action

Visible light occupies a relatively minute portion of the electromagnetic spectrum

Light, Color, and Filters

There is no single, simple way to explain all the effects of light. The photochemical effects (dye bleaching, latent image formation in films, etc.) are best explained by the theory that a luminous body sprays out streams of particles called photons which transmit energy and are capable of doing work on sensitive surfaces. Optical effects of light (color, lens action, etc.) are easier to visualize if light is considered to travel through space in somewhat the same way that ripples travel across a pond, in waves. However, unlike ripples, which vibrate only up and down as they move, light waves, and other electromagnetic waves, are thought of as normally vibrating in all directions perpendicular to their direction of travel.

Waves in water can vary in size from the mammoth ground swells in the Pacific, a hundred feet or more from crest to crest, to tiny ripples less than an inch long. The electromagnetic spectrum, by comparison, contains waves which must be measured in kilometers or miles (low-frequency radio waves) as well as waves so incomprehensibly tiny that they must be measured in millionths and billionths of a millimeter.

The visible portion of the spectrum, which we call light, is a relatively minute band of wavelengths ranging in extent from only 700 nanometers (millionths of a

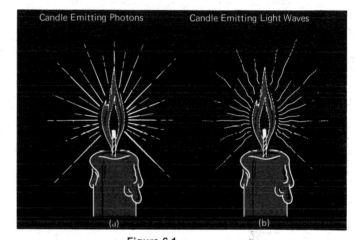

Figure 6.1
Candles emitting photons and light waves

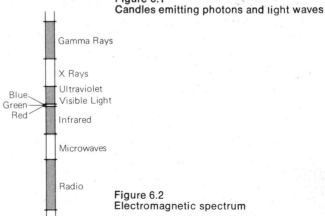

Figure 6.2
Electromagnetic spectrum

Light can be absorbed, reflected, transmitted, diffused, diffracted, refracted, or dispersed

In nature, dispersed colors can form rainbows

Colors can also be produced by interference

The light primary colors are red, green, and blue

Pigments don't have any color of their own

This is how filters work

millimeter), or the limit of visible red light, to 400 nanometers, or the last visible shade of deep violet. Above the 400nm boundary of the visible spectrum lies the region of ultraviolet (UV) radiations, which are invisible to the human eye but which tan skin, bleach dyes, and affect photographic emulsions strongly. Below 700 nm lies the extensive region of infrared (IR) radiations, which are invisible to both the eye and most films but are capable of affecting some exposure meters to a troublesome degree. We perceive the longest wavelengths of infrared as heat.

A light ray travelling through the air will continue to zip along in a straight line until it hits something or until its energy is gradually dissipated (in a perfect vacuum, presumably, it would go on forever). If it encounters an object of any sort, any of several things may happen to it. Almost certainly some of the light will be absorbed by any surface it touches. Part of it may be reflected, part may be transmitted if the material is transparent or translucent, and, if the material is cloudy or milky, the light may be diffused or scattered. Light can also be diffused by reflection from a rough or matte surface, and, if a ray is forced through a tiny aperture or made to graze a sharp edge, some of it will be diverted or disturbed and a special kind of diffusion, called *diffraction,* will result.

When a light ray travelling in air strikes a plain glass surface at somewhat less than 90°, the transmitted ray will be *refracted,* or bent, more steeply into the glass (or toward the perpendicular). When leaving the glass at another surface, the ray will be bent away from the perpendicular.

When white light is refracted in this way it is also *dispersed* into its component colors, because the various wavelengths of light are bent to different degrees. The shorter visible wavelengths (violet and blue) are refracted to the greatest degree; red and orange are least affected. In nature, dispersed rays display their colors when sunlight is refracted by falling raindrops to form a rainbow. (See plate 1.) In photography the effect of dispersion is less attractive when poorly corrected lenses form color fringes around image details in color

transparencies. Lens designers work hard to select special kinds of glass and to shape lens elements precisely so dispersion effects are minimized without compromising the desirable effect of refraction.

Light can also be split into its component colors by *interference.* Lens coatings, thin oil films on water, and soap bubbles operate on this principle, by trapping light between their closely spaced reflecting surfaces so certain wavelengths (colors) are folded back on themselves and cancelled. Varying the spacing between the surfaces will change their color absorption so, by controlling the thickness of the lens or filter coating, for example, any color of the spectrum can be eliminated from the reflected light.

In a somewhat similar manner, *dichroic* filters manage to separate the colors without actually destroying them; a portion of the light color is reflected back toward the source while the remaining color is transmitted.

In photography we are mostly concerned with the visible spectrum. Taken as a whole, we see it as white light. If portions of the spectrum are missing, we see the remaining mixture of wavelengths as color. Narrow sections of the spectrum, seen alone, we perceive as relatively pure color, and if the spectrum is divided roughly into thirds, they are seen individually as red, green, and blue. We call these the *light primary* colors, and sometimes *additive primaries,* because they are basic colors (not mixtures of more fundamental hues) and because blending them together (adding them) makes *white.*

If the pairs of light primaries are mixed together, they form the *secondary* colors. Thus, red and green light (not pigment) blended together make yellow; green and blue make cyan (greenish-blue); and red and blue make magenta. In every case, mixing light colors together increases the brightness of the light. (See plate 2.)

Pigments or dyes don't have any color of their own. They appear colored because they absorb portions of the light spectrum and reflect the rest. Thus a dye, which absorbs blue light, reflects red and green and will be

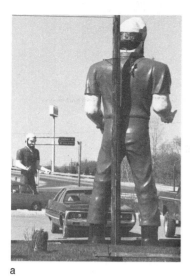
a

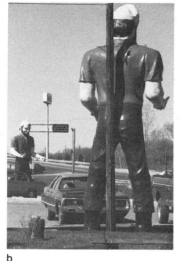
b

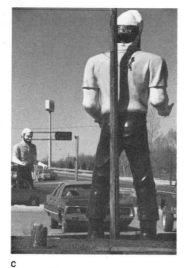
c

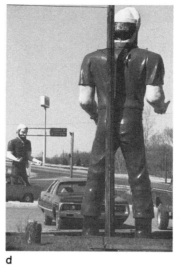
d

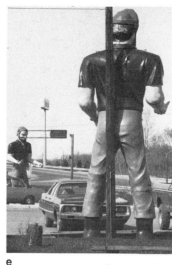
e

Figure 6.3
a. These figures have black hair and are wearing yellow caps, red shirts, blue trousers, and dusty black boots. The grass is brownish green and the sky is hazy blue. In this picture no filter was used; this is the natural color response of Plus-X film.

b. A light yellow filter darkens the sky, the trousers, and the shadows slightly.

c. A red filter darkens the blue sky and trousers dramatically, darkens the grass somewhat, increases contrast, and lightens the red shirts to a light gray.

d. A strong green filter darkens shirt and trousers, lightens the grass slightly, and leaves other areas practically unaffected.

e. A blue filter turns the sky almost white, lightens the blue trousers to gray, and darkens both the red shirts and the yellow caps. (See appendix, page 305.)

seen as yellow. A dye or pigment which absorbs green will be seen as magenta and a material which absorbs equal amounts of red, green, and blue will simply reduce the brightness of the light and appear gray. Because pigments absorb light color, they are called *subtractive colors,* and the pigment or dye primaries are *subtractive primaries.* Mixtures of the three subtractive primaries, if properly balanced, absorb virtually all the incident light and make *black.* (See plate 3.)

If a dye or pigment color completely absorbs some other light color, the colors are called *complementary,* or *complements* of each other. Thus, magenta dye, which totally absorbs green light, is the complement of green; blue is the complement of yellow; and red is the complement of cyan.

We use these principles, even in black-and-white photography, to control the pictorial quality of colored objects. A red filter placed over the camera lens, for example, will transmit only red light to the film, absorbing both blue and green light. Therefore, blue or green objects in the subject will be pictured in the print as black, because none of their light reaches the film. Red objects, on the other hand, will appear as bright as white objects in the print because red light passes through the filter as easily as white light does.

Filters lighten their own color and darken their complement in the print. If the filter color is intense and saturated, the effect on the image will be dramatic. If the filter is a pale tint, or an impure color, the filter effect will be less pronounced.

Most film exposures are based on white light and therefore must be increased, when a filter is used, because the filter absorbs some of the image light. This necessary exposure compensation is called the *filter factor* and is usually expressed as a number by which the exposure must be multiplied. For example, the Kodak Wratten #8 is a yellow filter which has a factor of 2x in daylight. When it is used, the normal (white light) exposure must be doubled, either by doubling the exposure time or by opening the lens up one stop. Similarly, the Wratten #25, a red filter, has a daylight factor of 8x and a tungsten light factor of 4x. When used in daylight, with panchromatic film, the exposure must be increased 8x, or 3 stops. In tungsten light (ordinary tungsten-filament light bulbs) the exposure must be increased only 4x or 2 stops. The difference in factors in the two light conditions is due to the color of the light. Daylight is relatively blue, while tungsten light is orange. The red filter restricts a large proportion of the bluish daylight but transmits the orange tungsten light with relatively little attenuation.

151 Working with Light

Light sources can be filtered

Neutral density filters simply reduce light intensity

Reflected light is frequently polarized

Some areas of the clear blue sky are strongly polarized

Obviously, there's no point in trying to use a red filter with either orthochromatic or non-color sensitized films, because neither film can respond usefully to red light—the only light the filter can transmit. It would be equally pointless to use a blue filter with blue-sensitive film, for example, because the film is sensitive only to blue and will form the same image, essentially, in either white or blue light. For most purposes, if you want to use filters to change the normal response of the film, you should work with a panchromatic film. You don't have to worry about this too much; practically all the rollfilms you're likely to find at your local camera shop are panchromatic.

It isn't always necessary to put a filter over the camera lens to achieve a filtered effect on the image. Filtering the light source will do as well. Thus, covering your studio lights with blue *gels,* for example, will make blue objects photograph as very light in tone, just as using a blue filter over the camera lens would do. Caution—although, in theory, you should not have to apply any filter factor when the meter reading is taken in colored light, most meters are a little colorblind and it would be wise to bracket the indicated exposure by deliberately overexposing and underexposing an extra few frames. Bracketing is also a wise precaution when reading your SLR meter with a strongly colored filter in place over the lens.

The filter effect on the film image is greatest on subject colors of high purity and is diminished for *tints* (colors diluted with white) and *shades* (colors diluted with black). Color filters have virtually no effect at all on black, white, and shades of gray. The filter factor must still be applied to the exposure, however, because the filter will absorb some of the image light whether its action alters the image tonality or not.

Finally, the filter effect depends to some extent on exposure. In general, underexposure tends to empha-size filter action and overexposure tends to reduce it.

Neutral density (ND) filters absorb all colors equally and appear gray. They are intended simply to reduce light intensity. Although they are not used as frequently as color filters are, they come in handy when it is de-sirable to change exposure without altering the camera settings, or when you wish to maintain normal exposure, but use a large lens opening or a very slow shutter speed in bright light with fast film. Neutral density filters come in thirteen accurately calibrated densities, from .1 (re-quiring a ⅓ stop exposure increase) to 4.0 (which re-quires an increase of 13⅓ stops, or 10,000x).

When a light ray is reflected from a smooth surface (except polished metal), its normal multidirectional wave vibration is likely to be more or less restricted to one plane and the light is said to have been *polarized.* This is practically an invisible effect; polarized light looks just like unpolarized light to the camera, the film, and to most people (some individuals can detect it under certain conditions). Polarization is a useful effect, however, because it provides us with a unique method of filtering one sort of light from another with-out distorting colors.

Polaroid filters (sometimes called Pola-screens) are capable of polarizing transmitted light; that is, they are transparent to light waves vibrating in one plane but are more or less opaque to waves vibrating in other planes. This characteristic permits the filter to reduce, or sometimes eliminate, the effect of reflected "glare" light. If you view a reflecting surface through a Pola-screen and slowly rotate it until its transmission axis is perpendicular to the vibration plane of the reflected light, the glare will magically disappear, without affect-ing the rest of the light at all.

By removing glare light from various areas of the subject, Pola-screens often seem to improve subject contrast and enhance the purity of colors. Since they are neutral gray in color, they do not affect color, as regular color filters do, and can be used with color films as well as with black-and-white materials.

Since the light from some areas of the clear blue sky is polarized, a Pola-screen can often be used to darken the sky dramatically. (See plate 4.) The greatest effect occurs in a broad arc of sky, 90° from the sun position; point your forefinger at the sun and your ex-tended thumb will point to the sky belt of most com-plete polarization.

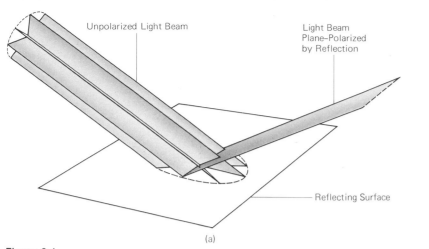

Unpolarized Light Beam

Light Beam
Plane-Polarized
by Reflection

Reflecting Surface

(a)

Unpolarized light beam

Filter Plane of
Polarization

Polarizing Filter

Plane-Polarized
Light Beam

(b)

Figure 6.4
Polarized light, reflection, transmission

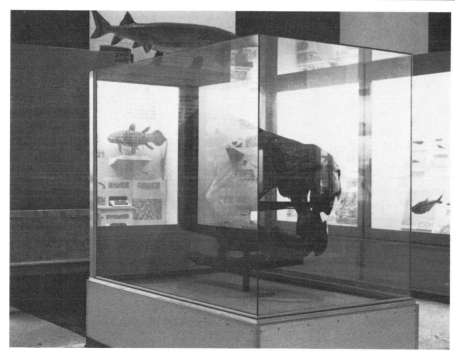

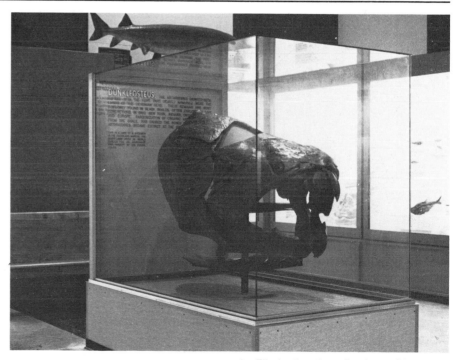

Figure 6.5
a. Surface reflections from surrounding displays almost obscure the fossil in this museum case.

b. Eliminating the reflections with a polarizing filter over the camera lens reveals this ferocious-looking fish skull and its descriptive caption.

Under some conditions white light can be dissected into its component colors by selective polarization. This effect can be demonstrated easily with a pair of polarizing filters and some scraps of cellophane (other plastic sheet materials may not work well). Place the cellophane scraps on one of the filters and cover them with the other one. When viewed against the light, the cellophane scraps will appear as brilliant colors which can be varied dramatically if one of the filters is slowly rotated. The effect is caused by cellophane's ability to rotate the plane of polarized light and is related to wavelength. Some plastic materials have a similar ability; when they are strained or bent in polarized light, they form color patterns which indicate the distribution of the internal stresses. This technique is sometimes used by engineers to test models of machine parts or building structures to see where potential structural weaknesses may exist.

Pola-screens do not have a single, constant filter factor because their absorption depends upon the amount of polarized light coming from the subject and the orientation of the filter axis relative to the polarity of the light. If no polarized light exists in the subject area, the filter factor for a typical Pola-screen amounts to about 3x, due entirely to its gray neutral density color. That same factor is approximately correct if the light is polarized in a plane parallel to the filter polarization axis. However, if much of the subject light is polarized and *not* parallel to the filter axis, the filter transmission will be greatly reduced and the necessary filter factor may amount to 6x, 8x, or even more. It is a good idea, when using a polarizing filter, to make several exposures of any subject that is likely to be reflecting polarized light. Start with the 3x factor, or a little less, then increase the exposures by a stop or two, just to make sure.

Synopsis **Filter Effect**

For greatest filter effect, use a filter of pure, saturated hue on a subject whose colors are equally strong and pure, then underexpose slightly. For minimal filter effect, use a pale filter on a barely tinted subject with more-than-normal exposure.

Filters will lighten their own colors in the subject and darken their complements, as rendered in the final print image. Filtering the light source is just as effective as placing the filter over the camera lens. An exposure based on a white light meter reading will have to be increased when a filter is used because the filter will absorb some of the image light. This increase is called the filter factor. The usual filter factor will not have to be applied if the meter reading is taken in filtered light or if an SLR through-the-lens meter is used to read through a filter on the lens. However, some compensation may be required; test your own meter by bracketing the settings it suggests.

Neutral density filters simply reduce light intensity without affecting color. Polarizing filters can reduce the intensity of glare from most reflecting surfaces without affecting the rest of the image substantially, in either value or color balance.

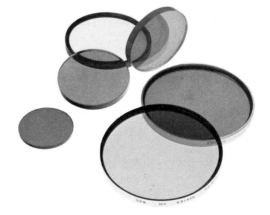

Artificial Light Sources

Sooner or later, at least some of your photographs will be taken in artificial light and, as you will discover, it exists in a great variety of forms. *Incandescent* light, the light produced by the hot tungsten filament of an ordinary light bulb, is common. So is *fluorescent* light. Occasionally you may have to cope with light from some *gas-discharge* source, like mercury-vapor or sodium vapor lamps which are often used for street lighting or industrial lighting. In the studio, tungsten-filament bulbs are universally used. Conventional flashbulbs are occasionally used, too, but electronic flash units are much more common.

One major difference between these various types of lights is in their color. Incandescent bulbs, including conventional flashbulbs, produce a *continuous spectrum* light, which implies that all the colors (wavelengths) of the spectrum are present in some amount. Gas-discharge bulbs, on the other hand, produce *discontinuous spectra,* from which certain light wavelengths are missing.

The light produced by all incandescent bulbs is apparently orange in color (compared with daylight) but the actual color of the light is determined by the temperature of the glowing tungsten filament. If the bulb is designed for long life, as ordinary household lamps are, the filament burns at a relatively low temperature and its light is brownish and low in intensity. If the filament temperature is increased (as by raising the line voltage, for example), the light output is increased, the light contains more blue and appears "whiter." At this higher temperature the filament deteriorates faster, too, and the life of the lamp is considerably shortened.

Incandescent bulbs intended for photographic use are designed to burn at either 3200° Kelvin (equivalent to 3200° above absolute zero in the Celsius scale) or 3400°K. The 3200°K varieties are now the most common and are standard for professional work; 3400°K bulbs are brighter, but much shorter lived, and were originally intended for amateur use. Ordinary light bulbs, by comparison, burn at about 2700°K.

Incandescent bulbs give a slightly more blue light when they are new than they do after a few hours of burning time, and near the end of their lives, their light is comparatively brownish. Their light output decreases, too, as the burning filament metal is vaporized and deposited as a dirty film on the inside surface of the glass bulb. An improved bulb, which avoids these problems to a useful degree, is made of fused quartz, instead of glass, and is filled with a halogen vapor (bromine or iodine). During use the halogen gas prevents darkening of the quartz envelope and prolongs the filament life so the bulb burns at a more uniform color and intensity and has a longer useful life than a conventional bulb does. Bulbs of this type were originally called *quartz-iodine* or *quartz-bromine* bulbs (quartz light) but they are now generally referred to as *tungsten halogen* or *halogen-cycle* bulbs. They are available in a wide variety of shapes and sizes and are generally much smaller, but more expensive, than conventional bulbs of the same wattage.

Flashbulbs give a continuous spectrum light of relatively high color temperature (about 3800°K). Unlike more conventional incandescent lamps, however, they are designed to burn out almost instantaneously, producing a tremendous blast of light for a very brief period of time. Flashbulbs are valuable for work on location, where ordinary lights would be difficult or impossible to use, because they are easily carried, can be fired by small batteries, and produce a great amount of light for their size. Most of them now, including the popular flashcube, flipflash, and flashstrip units for amateur use, are covered during manufacture with a blue filter layer which raises their effective color temperature sufficiently to make them useful with daylight color film (approximately 5500°K).

Using Flash

Although the flash from a flashbulb seems to be instantaneous, it actually takes several milliseconds (thousandths of a second) for the light to reach useful

Flashbulbs can be used in open flash technique

Or synchronized with the camera shutter

BTL shutters synchronize easily at all speeds

X synch is intended primarily for use with electronic flash

Strobes have no firing delay of any consequence

intensity after the firing voltage is applied. This delay is typically from about 5 to about 15 milliseconds for M (medium peak) and FP (focal plane) bulbs, and about 20 to 25 milliseconds for S (slow peak) bulbs. The useful flash duration for M bulbs is typically between 10 and 20 milliseconds, and these bulbs produce a very high peak intensity. FP bulbs have an effective flash duration of 25 ms or more and, because they burn slower, produce a less intense light for the longer time. Type S bulbs are designed for maximum light output; they produce extremely high intensity at peak output and burn usefully for 20 ms or more. They are most effective when they are used in *open flash* technique; the camera shutter is opened on *Time* or *Bulb,* the flashbulb is fired manually, and the shutter is closed.

Open flash provides the maximum possible amount of light for the film exposure, but it is a clumsy way to work with a small camera. Usually, we use flash to permit instantaneous exposures in dim light so most flash pictures are taken with *synchronized flash,* which means that the shutter and the bulb are timed so the shutter is open only during the actual flash. Most cameras now are equipped with built-in synchronizers for this purpose; it is only necessary to plug the flash unit into the proper socket on the camera and set the synchronizer switch for the type of flashbulb in use, and the camera will fire the bulb at the right instant so it will reach peak intensity while the shutter is open.

Cameras equipped with between-the-lens leaf shutters are easiest to synchronize with flashbulbs because the flash will illuminate the full film area at any shutter speed if the timing is correct. M-type bulbs, with their short peak of high-intensity light, are best for use with BTL shutters. Focal plane shutters, especially the curtain types, open completely only at their slower speeds. At speeds above 1/60th second (1/125th for some metal blade shutters), the shutter exposes the film progressively through a relatively narrow opening. M-type bulbs may not burn long enough or evenly enough to expose the film fully and uniformly at these speeds, and it is safer to use FP bulbs (with the synchronizer set on FP) under these conditions.

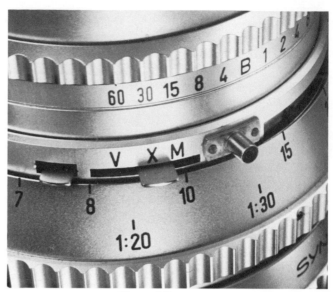

Figure 6.6
Camera synch controls

Before using any sort of flashbulb with your SLR, you should check your instruction manual carefully for instructions. If you don't have a manual for your camera, or if the instructions are not clear, you will probably be safe to use M-type bulbs on the M setting (if the camera has one) at speeds up to 1/60th second or so.

The X synchronizer setting is intended primarily for use with electronic flash. When set at X the synchronizer does not make firing contact until the shutter is fully open. If bulbs are used at the X setting, the shutter must remain open long enough to allow the bulb to kindle, flare up, and reach peak intensity, a minimum of perhaps 20 ms, or 1/50th second. Actually, because the useful flash persists for another 10 ms, or so, it is much better to use a shutter speed of 1/15th second or longer when M bulbs are fired at the X synch setting.

Electronic flash units (frequently referred to as *strobes*) produce their light by passing a brief pulse of high voltage electric current through a glass or quartz tube filled with a mixture of gases, such as krypton, argon, and xenon. There is no firing delay of any consequence, so electronic flash units are always X syn-

They synch at all BTL speeds and some FP speeds

Flash can be combined with ambient light for special effect

Special flash meters are required for exposure determination

Or you can estimate the exposure by using guide numbers

Electronic flash, although discontinuous, approximates daylight

chronized. Typical small units for on-camera use usually provide an effective flash duration of about 1/500th second. Most of the more expensive and more powerful models contain *thyristor* circuits which can be set to quench the flash current automatically when sufficient light has been produced to make the exposure, or when reduced output is desirable. These flash units are capable of producing flashes of as little as 1/50,000th second duration, under some conditions.

Because of the very brief duration of the flash, electronic flash units synchronize easily at all speeds with BTL shutters, and with all speeds which provide a fully open shutter with focal plane types. In almost all cases the electronic flash duration determines the exposure time and, if there is no ambient illumination (light existing at the subject position), the effective exposure on the film is not affected at all by the camera shutter speed.

If there is any significant amount of ambient illumination, it will supplement the flash and if the subject is moving, a double image or "ghost" image may be formed—one by the very brief pulse of the flash, the other by the longer exposure provided by the ambient light and slow shutter speed. This effect is particularly likely to occur with focal plane shutters because of their relatively low-speed X-synch, but it may occur at any speed if the ambient light is bright enough. It can be induced deliberately, if desired, by purposely setting the camera shutter at a low speed, or even opening it on Time or Bulb. Even when no subject motion is likely, this technique can be used to combine existing light with the electronic flash (or flashbulb) light for special effects.

Because of its very brief duration, the light produced by any sort of flash device cannot be measured with an ordinary exposure meter. Many electronic flash units now provide automatic exposure control and special flash meters are available for use with the larger, nonautomatic units. The exposure for flashbulbs is usually determined by consulting a chart of *guide numbers,* such as can be found on the information sheet which is packed with individual rolls of film.

A guide number represents the product of the lens f/ number multiplied by the distance in feet from flash to subject and can be found, for any given film speed, by matching a chosen shutter speed with the bulb type in use. Then, if the distance from flash-to-subject is known, the necessary aperture can be determined; if some specific aperture is desired, the necessary flash distance can be found. For example, if you are using Tri-X 35mm film, with a 25B bulb in shallow reflector, and you want to use a shutter speed of 1/60th second with M-synch, the published guide number is 220. If the flash-to-subject distance is 10 feet, divide 220 by 10 to find the necessary f/ number,

$$220 \div 10 = 22 \text{ or } f/22.$$

If you would prefer to use f/11, for example, divide 220 by 11 to find the proper flash distance,

$$220 \div 11 = 20, \text{ or } 20 \text{ feet.}$$

A similar chart is provided for use in estimating exposure for nonautomatic electronic flash, if you know the rated power of the unit in *beam-candle-power-seconds* (BCPS). For a flash unit rated at 1000 BCPS and Tri-X film, Kodak recommends a guide number of 140, for example. (See guide number charts in the appendix, page 304.)

Guide numbers are intended for use under "average" conditions and may not be accurate for use in highly reflective rooms or totally nonreflective areas (outdoors at night, for example). Also, they apply only to direct flash from near the camera position and can't be relied on, without some educated guesswork, if the flash unit is pointed away from the subject or "bounced" from a wall or ceiling.

Strictly speaking, electronic flash tubes are discontinuous spectrum sources and, as such, do not have a real Kelvin temperature rating. Because of the mixture of gases used, however, the light they produce includes enough of the spectral colors in the proper proportions to appear, and photograph, as a slightly purplish "white," which normally requires only a little yellow or amber filtration to work well with "daylight" color films. Many small flash units are equipped with built-in filter

Most ordinary luminous-gas sources are strongly colored

Fluorescent light looks white but photographs pea-green

It can be partially corrected by magenta filtration

Learn to cope with them; they're here to stay

UV and IR can be troublesome but UV is easily filtered

screens which serve this purpose and obviate the need for any other color correction. For black-and-white work electronic flash light is perfectly satisfactory, whether filtered or not.

Fluorescent Light

Most other light sources, which derive all or part of their light from luminous gas, concentrate all of their radiant energy into a relatively few bright lines of the spectrum, omitting large bands of color entirely. These lights can appear obviously colored, as the familiar red-orange neon tubes, the strong yellow sodium-vapor streetlights, and greenish-lavender mercury-vapor industrial night-lights do, or they can occasionally masquerade as "white." Without exception, however, they photograph as strongly colored, and because of their spikey spectral characteristics, they are almost impossible to filter back to anywhere near "normal." Rather than wasting your time trying to correct lights of this sort, make the best of the bizarre effect and try to use the color creatively. (See plate 5.)

Fluorescent lights are a little better, but generally not much. The gas with which fluorescent tubes are filled is designed to radiate strongly in the UV region of the spectrum, but produces very little visible light. The visible light results from the brilliant glow of *phosphors,* which coat the inside of the tube and which are excited into fluorescence by the ultraviolet radiation. The color of the light can be controlled over a wide range by selection of the phosphors used, and some special combinations will produce a light which both looks and photographs like daylight. Unfortunately, these tubes are rarely encountered. The more common cool white, warm white, and daylight tubes tend to photograph in some shade of sickly pea-green and are poor sources of light for color photography, even when filtered as effectively as possible. (See plate 6.)

If you must include fluorescent light in your color photographs, and if reasonably normal color balance is important, you can try one of the special *fluorescent filters* marketed by several companies. Two types are

available; one is intended for use with tungsten film, the other with daylight film. Another alternative is to use filters from the *color-compensating* (CC) series, marketed by Eastman Kodak in the form of dyed gelatin squares. Some authorities recommend combining magenta and blue filters in various strengths. My experience indicates that plain magenta, or even red, is preferable. In any case, filtering fluorescent lights is strictly a trial-and-error business and you must find your own solution. Color films of various types and speeds do not all require the same amount of filtration, even in the same light condition. I'd suggest starting out with daylight film and a CC 30M or 40M filter. Look over the resulting transparencies and go from there. Fluorescents are usually satisfactory for use with black-and-white films, without any filtration at all.

If you're wondering why gas-discharge and fluorescent lights are so widely used, despite their color problems, it's because they are much more efficient than incandescent lamps. Fluorescent lamps, for example, produce two or three times as much useful light as incandescents do, for the same amount of electricity consumed. They also last much longer and generate less heat so they are an obvious choice for applications which don't require daylight color quality. As energy consumption becomes more and more of a national problem, you can expect to find these, and other "energy efficient" sources, becoming more and more popular. Learn to cope with them; they're here to stay.

Ultraviolet and Infrared

The invisible radiations (ultraviolet and infrared), which lie just outside the boundaries of the visible spectrum, can be troublesome at times. All silver-sensitized films and papers are strongly sensitive to ultraviolet and will record it as if it were blue light. This effect is most apparent in scenic views taken at high altitudes (where the percentage of ultraviolet is relatively high) and shows as an emphasized distance haze and an abnormally bright blue color in nearby shadow areas. It may also cause overexposure, because most meters don't react as strongly to UV as films do. These problems are easy to avoid, however; UV filters are available in several very light tints of pink (*skylight* filter) or yellow (*haze* filter) and can be used with either black-and-white or color films without any exposure increase.

Infrared light, on the other edge of the visible spectrum, does not affect most films to any appreciable degree. This is a blessing because IR is almost impossible to control with ordinary glass or gelatin filters. When it is necessary to exclude it, as for example, from enlarger light when color printing, a special dichroic or interference filter is the most effective type.

For some special photographic purposes an ultraviolet light source can be used to illuminate the subject, if a very dark blue filter is used, either over the camera lens or over the light source, so as to exclude visible light from the camera completely. When used this way the results are occasionally similar to ordinary photographs, but contrast is usually low and the subject colors are likely to be translated into strange relationships of value. Frequently though, surface patterns and details which are normally invisible will appear, and this characteristic of UV photography is useful in such fields as medicine, science, and criminal investigation.

Ultraviolet can also be used to stimulate certain materials into fluorescence—another method of displaying surface patterns or material differences which are invisible in ordinary illumination. In this application the material is illuminated by UV, but the UV itself is excluded from the camera by a filter over the lens. The filter should be selected to absorb UV while transmitting the color of the fluorescence freely. Ordinary visible light should not be used unless background details are needed to relate to the fluorescing material.

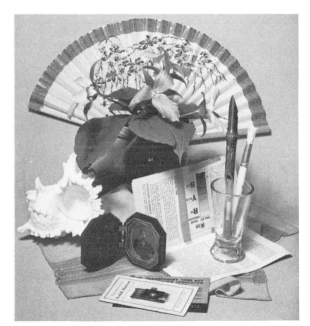

Figure 6.7
a. This still-life was shot with normal tungsten illumination.

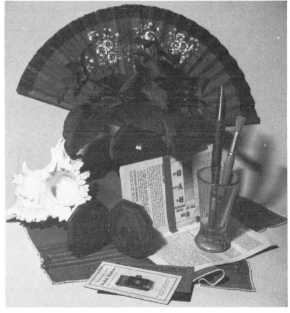

b. Ultraviolet light alone produced this result.

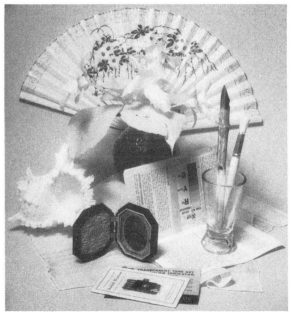

Figure 6.8
Same still-life taken on infrared film filtered with a Wratten #25 to exclude UV and blue light. Heavy grain and misty quality are typical of IR materials.

Infrared photography is also capable of displaying details and patterns which cannot be seen. However, ordinary film cannot be used. Special IR films are available in 35mm and sheet film sizes and they should be exposed through dark red or special IR filters to exclude visible light—especially blue and violet, to which the films are very sensitive. Infrared film is characteristically very grainy and occasionally the negatives are marred by blemishes, streaks, or pinholes which occur for no apparent reason, but it is an interesting material which can produce images of great beauty as well as pictures of practical value.

Taking photographs by UV or IR causes some unusual problems. Since most lenses are corrected and calibrated for use with visible light, neither UV nor IR will focus with the visual image in the camera. In general, the UV image is formed closer to the lens and the IR image is formed farther away from the lens than the visible image. Most small camera lenses have a reference mark on the lens mount to which the focusing scale can be turned to correct the visual focus for IR light, but there is no similar mark for UV. If you have no other guide, when using either of these invisible lights, try focusing a little in front of the subject in UV light and a little behind the subject when using IR film; then stop down at least two or three stops to increase the depth of field.

Exposure determination is equally haphazard. Since most meters are not affected much by UV and their sensitivity to IR is almost never known with any precision, regular meter readings will not be much help. Exposure suggestions are published in technical literature for UV, and the IR film data sheet contains some useful recommendations; but here again, experimentation is the best guide. Bracket rather extensively at first and keep a record of the conditions.

Ordinary color film is sensitive to UV, but there is no advantage in using it because the filtration which is necessary for the UV effect will exclude all color from the camera. Color film *is* useful for recording fluorescence, but it must be filtered to exclude UV and

transmit the fluorescent color, just as black-and-white film should be. Infrared does not affect ordinary color film usefully, but a special false-color IR film is available which, when properly filtered, produces unusual and gaudy distortions of the normal color relationships.

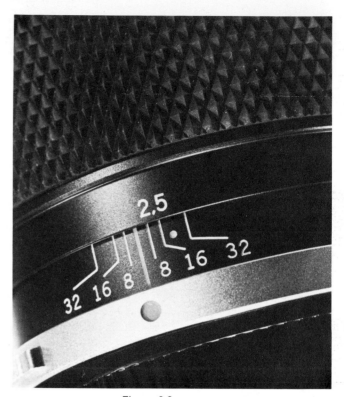

Figure 6.9
Focusing index for infrared light is the small dot between f/16 and f/32 lines.

Synopsis **Artificial Light Sources**

Incandescent lamps give continuous spectrum light and are suitable for color photography when appropriately filtered; gas-discharge lamps produce discontinuous spectrum light and most are unsuitable for color work. They cannot be corrected by filtration. There are several types of flashbulbs; they are usually synchronized to reach peak intensity with the full opening of the camera shutter. Electronic flash units must also be synchronized. They provide light of very short duration, high intensity, and near-daylight color balance. Flash exposure can be estimated by consulting a table of guide numbers for the film and flashbulb type in use. Most fluorescent lamps photograph as a yellowish-green but their light can be partially corrected by filtration. Ultraviolet and infrared light can be used for special photographic purposes and effects; exposure and camera focus must be estimated.

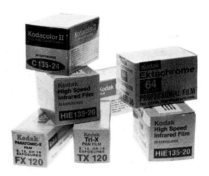

Beginners are concerned with light quantity

Light quality is much more important

Principles of Lighting

When appraising scenes they wish to photograph, beginning photographers—preoccupied as they are apt to be with the technicalities of film speeds, f/ numbers, shutter settings, and meter readings—are concerned primarily with light *quantity*. If there is enough light to produce a good meter reading and a clearly visible viewfinder image, they are likely to be satisfied. Sooner or later, though, the mere production of an image ceases to be a challenge, and light *quality* begins to assume real importance. At this point photography can begin to become at least a craft and perhaps an art.

Light quality is not easy to define, but we use the term to refer to the way light affects the appearance of the subject. In the simplest case we consider the light quality to be satisfactory if the subject can be seen clearly against its background and if its form and texture are well-rendered. More specifically, light quality is good if it contributes to a personal interpretation of the subject, displaying it in a way which best suits our purposes, whatever they may be.

There are several characteristics which determine the quality of light. They are intensity, color, degree of diffusion, evenness, direction, and duration.

Intensity is not a particularly important consideration as far as the image itself is concerned. Moderate variations in light intensity are easily compensated for by adjustment of the camera controls or selection of film speed and, barring extreme cases, the appearance of the finished image does not have to be dependent on the level of subject illumination.

Light *color* is obviously important in color photography because the subject colors will be tinted by light which is not white and the image colors may appear stained or distorted. In black-and-white work, light color is significant only if it is fairly obviously not white. Even then the image may not be seriously affected unless the subject colors are strong and saturated and their value relationships must be preserved.

The *degree of diffusion* of light is one of its most important characteristics and one which is almost always ignored by beginners. As much as any other single factor, the degree of diffusion affects subject contrast, surface appearance, color saturation, and mood. In general, a diffuse light source is one which radiates more or less uniformly from a large area. Diffuse light produces low contrast, soft-edged shadows, muted colors, and dull surface appearance. Small-area or point

Duration is only occasionally critical

Evenness can be controlled

So can direction

Direction can influence the illusion of space and form

Daylight analysis: Intensity, color degree of diffusion

sources, on the other hand, produce high subject contrast, sharp shadows, bright and saturated colors, and high surface sheen.

Except for rather special purposes the *duration* of a light is not particularly important. If the light persists for long enough to make an exposure possible, and if its intensity, color, and degree of diffusion are tolerable, it can be considered satisfactory.

Intensity, color, diffusion, and duration are all characteristics of the light source itself. Two other factors which affect light quality, evenness and direction, are related to the manner in which light is used or manipulated and apply to any light source.

Evenness refers to uniformity of illumination level at the subject position. In the studio it is affected by "beam spread" (a spotlight illuminates a small area intensely, but a floodlight covers a wide area with relatively uniform illumination), and by the proximity of the light source to the subject (a distant light will provide more uniform illumination than a close one will). Indoors or out, uneven illumination can be caused by local areas of shade at the subject position.

Light *direction* is another very important characteristic which, like degree of diffusion, affects subject contrast and mood and also strongly influences the rendering of subject forms and textures. Light which grazes the subject surfaces from any direction will tend to emphasize surface texture and subject contours. Direct frontlight tends to subdue both form and texture, tends to reduce contrast, and may make the subject space appear shallow and flat. Toplight usually appears natural and so does sidelight; light from below eye level may appear theatrical or bizarre. Backlight will minimize subject details and tend to produce silhouette effects, rim light, and glare.

Light direction affects the illusion of depth and space, too. In real-life situations we rely mostly on perspective and our binocular vision for depth perception. In photographs we read deep space by looking for perspective clues, but subject form and surface contours must be interpreted from the pictured effects of light and shade. If the light direction cannot be determined from inspection of the image, or if several lights of approximately equal strength illuminated the subject from different directions when the picture was made, our perception of subject form and space is hampered and the forms may be ambiguous. This is particularly true if the subject matter is not readily identifiable, but it is a bothersome factor in the interpretation of any image forms.

Any light condition can be analyzed and its probable effects predicted by determining its characteristics as just described. Daylight is no exception; on a sunny day with no clouds you can expect the following photographic effects:

Intensity will be high. The sun is very bright and you can use slow film with fairly small apertures or high shutter speeds. Fast films may not be useful unless image light is reduced by filtration (either color or neutral density filter).

Color. Two colors are involved. The direct sunlight is distinctly *warm* (yellow) while the skylight is strongly *cool* (blue). In color photography this may show up as a noticeable contrast between the warm highlights (illuminated mostly by direct sunlight) and cool shadows (which receive most of their light from the blue sky). This is a natural and familiar effect and will probably not be unpleasant. In black-and-white photography it will pose no problem and may even be useful, since, by filtering, the contrast can be either increased (yellow, orange, or red filter) or decreased to some extent (blue or green filter) if desired.

Degree of diffusion. Again, at least two sources are involved. The sun is apparently small and can be considered almost a point source. Its light is harsh and contrasty and will tend to form glaring highlights, sharply defined shadows, and crisply rendered textures. Color saturation will be high. The sky, on the other hand, is a very large source and provides extremely diffused light, but it is so much less intense than sunlight that its effect will only be visible in areas of shade or shadow. There it will produce very low contrast illumination, minimizing the effects of form and texture, and subduing color saturation.

Evenness, direction, duration

Available light is the light you find existing

Figure 6.10
Available light shot (Photograph courtesy of the University of Michigan Press)

Evenness. Daylight is inherently a very uniform light but there are frequently local variations of illumination to deal with. Areas of shade or cast shadows will be the chief problems.

Direction. Daylight is toplight, sidelight, or backlight and is completely believable. It will produce a single set of highlights and shadows which will describe the subject form unambiguously.

Duration is not a factor to be concerned with; daylight is continuous.

You can "control" daylight, for photographic purposes, by selection of the time of day (or season of the year) and by orienting your subject in the light and choosing your camera position to achieve the desired qualities of form and texture. Wait for passing

clouds to obscure the sun if contrast is too high, or place your model close to a light-colored wall (or snowbank or sandpile or something) so reflected light can cause *fill light* in the shadows and reduce the harshness of the illumination. Watch your subject carefully as the light changes and wait for the best effect. Don't forget to monitor the exposure, too; a cloud passing over the sun will probably reduce the light intensity by one or more stops.

If you pay attention to the way light works on things at various times of the day and in various weather conditions, you'll be amazed at the subtlety and variety of visual effects that are produced. (See plate 7.) Practice noticing light effects and analyzing them. Light is the raw material of your craft; as you become more conscious of it your work will become easier and your pictures will certainly improve.

Available Light

The term available light usually refers to light conditions, other than normal outdoor daylight, which are not arranged specifically for the purpose of taking pictures. Usually this implies indoor daylight, or artificially illuminated conditions, indoors or out, which you can't adjust or control.

Available light is frequently difficult to work with. The intensity may be very low, requiring fast film, slow shutter speeds, and large apertures. The color will probably not be a problem in black-and-white, but may require filtration for color photography. The illumination will probably contain a haphazard mixture of direct and diffuse light and will typically be uneven. It may come from any direction or directions and multiple shadows and confusing patterns are typical. Finally, you may sometimes encounter intermittent or flickering lights of very short duration (illuminated theater marquees, flashing signs, or television images are a few examples).

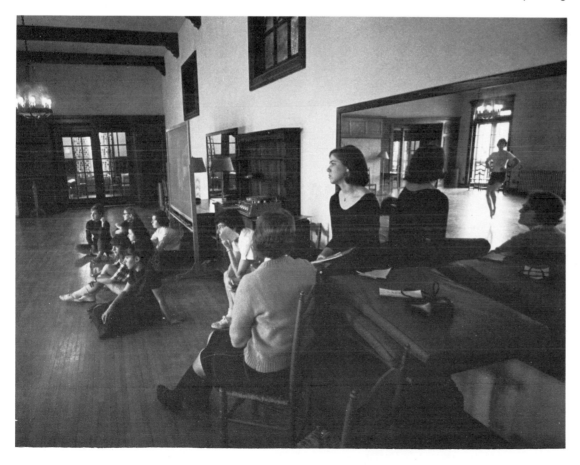

There are no rules for dealing with these conditions but a few guidelines are worth considering. Contrast will probably be high; if it is, be sure to expose the film fully and develop for a little *less* than normal. (This advice is contrary to the normal practice of *pushing* film to some unrealistic "speed.") Don't filter in very dim light unless it is really necessary; the longer exposure required may result in reciprocity failure and even further color distortion. Pick your camera position with particular care to achieve the best compromise between uniformity of illumination, clarity, description of form and texture, and mood. If glaring reflections or flare streaks are apparent, work with them for best visual effect; they are not necessarily "bad." Brace the camera firmly (or use a tripod) to avoid camera shake; or consider deliberate camera movement if the subject matter is suitable and some blurring would enhance your interpretation. Focus carefully; depth of field will be fairly shallow but out-of-focus forms can work well in your composition if they are placed carefully. You can use the shallow depth to subdue distracting background details or even to create interesting patterns in some situations. The relationship between subject and background is often awkward in this sort of photography; you may find that a change of lens focal length will improve the visual effect. Finally, bracket your exposures somewhat to be fairly sure you're covered and take a lot of pictures.

Not all "available light" is bad or difficult to deal with. Room interiors illuminated by skylights or large windows can provide a beautiful quality of light, excellent for portraiture or figure studies, and often equally useful for still-life subjects. A good skylight is almost the ideal light source for many purposes. It combines good intensity, good direction, and a good compromise between direct and diffuse illumination (direct enough to model form strongly but diffuse enough to retain delicacy and softness of surface). Color can be a problem (skylight is frequently very blue), but it is usually possible to filter it successfully.

A very large window, not exposed to direct sunlight, can also be used to good advantage for portraiture or small still-life setups. The light will tend to be rather uneven and will fall off rapidly across the width of the subject, but if the subject is not too large the effect is controllable. If the room interior is light in tone, or if some other source of reflected light can be provided to fill in the shadow side of the subject, the contrast will not be excessive. Beware of small windows, though; they will tend to give higher contrast especially if the subject is placed close to them and room reflectance is low.

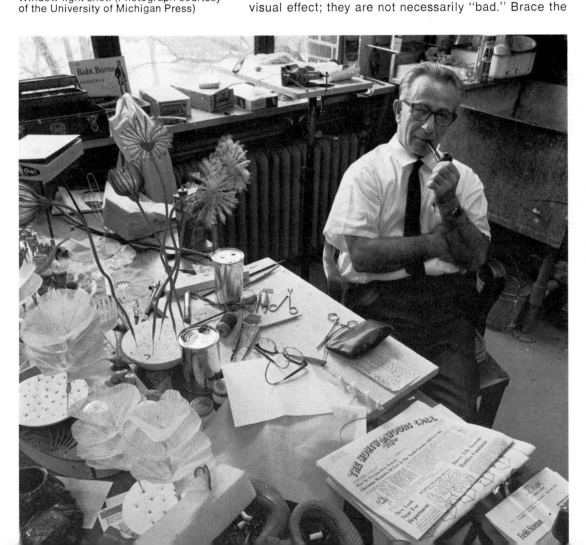

Figure 6.11
Window light shot. (Photograph courtesy of the University of Michigan Press)

Beginners typically make three mistakes

Figure 6.12
In this picture the photographer has used the limited range of a small electronic flash unit to illuminate the foreground strongly, allowing background details to fade out into black. The effect is stark and surreal—an emphatic visual interpretation of what is probably a rather unexciting subject in daylight. (Photograph courtesy of George Schietinger.)

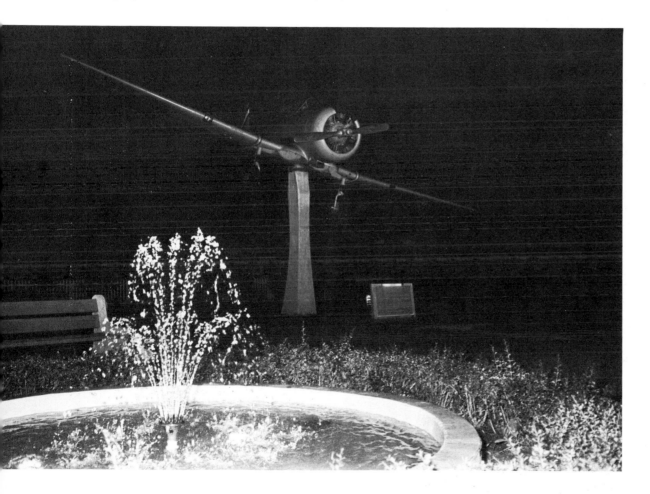

You can control the appearance of the subject in both skylight and window light by your choice of camera position and subject placement relative to the light source. Additionally, you can use available materials for backgrounds and reflectors; a sheet pinned to the wall behind the model will serve as a neutral, light-toned ground (watch out for obvious wrinkles) and a large towel or a sheet of newspaper can be used to reflect some light into the shadow side of the subject, if it seems necessary. With a little ingenuity you can produce beautiful light effects with these simple materials. Best of all, this light consumes no energy, and it's free!

Controlling Artificial Light

Sooner or later you will probably have to work with some form of artificial light. This doesn't mean, necessarily, that your pictures will look different (artificial light can be made to resemble daylight if you want it to) but it does pose different problems of handling and arrangement. In natural light it is only necessary to recognize the quality of illumination you're after and take advantage of it; in artificial lighting you must first visualize the effect you want, then select and arrange light sources and reflectors to produce it. There is another difference, too. The sun is a single, very bright light source, very far away, so the light is powerful and uniform in intensity. Artificial light sources are relatively weak, are frequently used in multiples, and must be used fairly close to the subject in a confined space; their illumination varies perceptibly across the subject space and must be adjusted with great care to appear uniform and coherent.

Beginners typically make three immediate and serious mistakes when they attempt artificial lighting. They tend to use lights raw (small sources, direct and without diffusion) and they place them too close to the subject (for maximum intensity). This will inevitably produce a harsh, glaring effect with burnt-out highlights and black shadow areas, which leads to the third mistake—adding more lights to "kill" the shadows. This rarely improves the picture and frequently makes it visually confusing.

A raw light will produce high intensity at close range but the intensity falls off rapidly at greater distances, according to the Inverse Square Law of illumination, which states that illumination decreases in intensity with the square of the distance from the source to the illuminated surface. Simply stated, this means that if you double the distance from the source to the surface the light intensity will be reduced by a factor of four; triple the distance and you'll have only one-ninth of the light left.

The Inverse Square Law is not as serious as it sounds

But you can't ignore it

Keep daylight quality in mind

Experiment with a single light

Enlarge the source by diffusion

Don't confuse diffusion with area

In practice the problem is not quite that serious. The Inverse Square Law is only completely effective for point light sources, like candle flames, electric arcs, and small clear glass light bulbs, used in an otherwise dark and unreflecting environment. Light from large sources, like fluorescent tubes, *umbrella* reflectors, or skylights, is much less seriously affected and they can be used at relatively close distances with good results. Further, most photographs are taken in at least moderately reflective environments where some light, bouncing back at the subject from nearby surfaces, is returned to help illuminate the shadows. For these reasons the Inverse Square Law is not as fearsome as it sounds at first, but don't think you can ignore it entirely; light intensity definitely *will* diminish with distance.

Although lighting can be controlled almost completely in the studio, it is not unusual, even there, to simulate a natural light condition. Frequently this turns out to resemble a kind of diffused daylight with one main light serving to establish the predominant pattern of light and shade, and other subdued sources arranged to keep the overall contrast within bounds and assist in defining edges and accenting forms and textures. At first, daylight is an excellent model to follow because it is both familiar and believable. Furthermore, it will tend to keep you from blundering into the confusion of too many light sources if you remember the basic characteristics of daylight—one relatively small, intense source (the sun) and one very large, less intense source (the sky).

The simplest possible lighting setup consists of a single bulb, usually placed above, in front of, and somewhat to one side of the subject. Try this arrangement and observe the results. If the bulb is bare, without a reflector, and if the surroundings are dark in tone, the light on the subject will probably look harsh and contrasty and the shadows will be fairly hard-edged and distinct. If the bulb is close to the subject, the illumination will be intense but will appear to fall off rapidly across the subject, increasing the effect of glare and harshness.

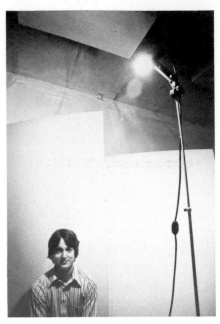

Figure 6.13
a. A single raw light in a moderately reflective environment gives this harsh effect. The subject contrast is lowered somewhat in this case by a large circular flare spot which covers the model's face and neck.

Probably the easiest and most dramatic improvement you can make in this arrangement is to enlarge the source by simply diffusing it. Hold a two-foot-square sheet of tissue paper between the bulb and the subject and observe the result. The glowing paper is now the light source. First, you will notice the loss of light intensity; then you should see a considerable improvement in the evenness of the illumination, a softening of the shadow edges, and a considerable reduction in contrast. If you can overlook the fact that the light is dim, you'll probably be pleasantly surprised by the quality of this softer light condition. It may even be good enough to use as is.

Now move the tissue paper close to the bulb. The shadow edges should become more distinct, the subject

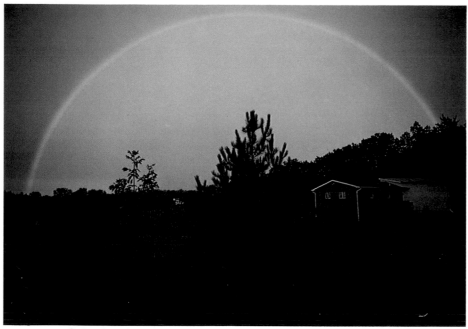

Colorplate 1

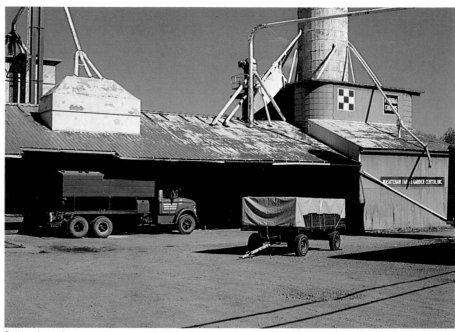

Colorplate 4   a

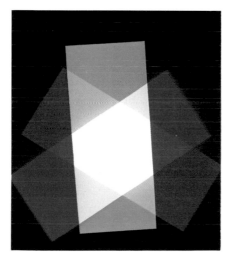

Colorplate 2
Light primary colors blend additively, producing secondaries which are brighter and more pastel than the primaries themselves. Mixtures of the three primaries, in proper proportion, yield white.

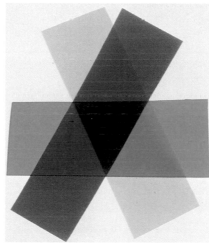

Colorplate 3
Pigment or dye primary colors are pure and bright. Their mixtures become less bright and more neutral, approaching black.

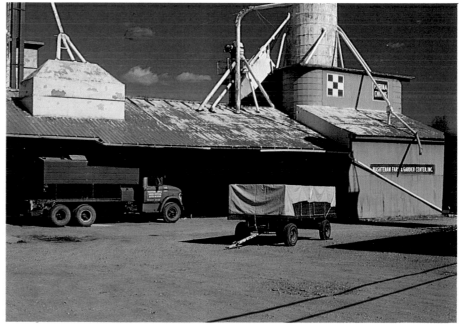

Colorplate 4   b

Colorplate 5
Mercury vapor streetlights appear greenish when compared to ordinary tungsten
light. Filtration can't correct a situation
like this.

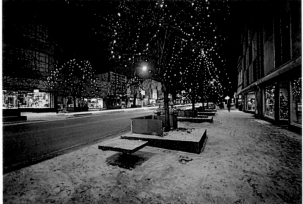

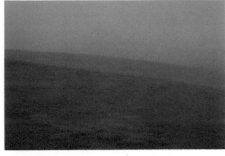

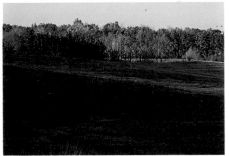

Colorplate 6 (Right)

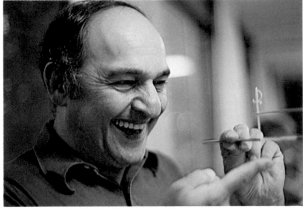

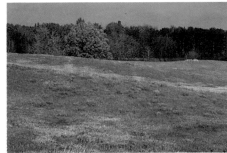

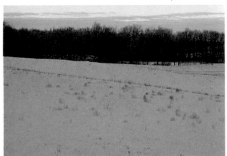

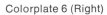

Colorplate 7 (Far right)

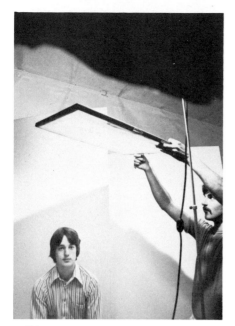

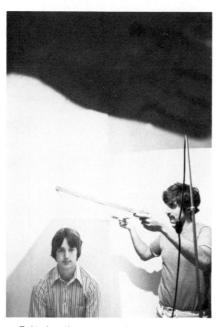

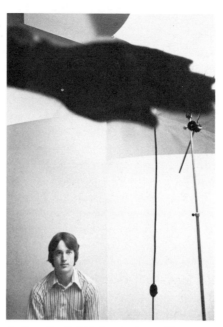

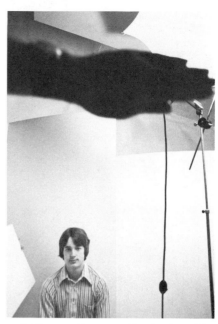

b. When the light source is covered (with my hand) to prevent lens flare effects, and a diffusing screen is used to enlarge the effective area of the source illuminating the model, the result is a soft, pleasing quality of light.

c. Bringing the screen closer to the model makes it effectively larger and reduces contrast still further.

d. Here the light is backed up with a white umbrella. It effectively enlarges the source and gives a result similar to the diffusing screen effects. Contrast is somewhat higher here because the umbrella is relatively far from the model.

e. Adding a reflector on the shadow side lightens the shadow and reduces contrast. The effect is overdone here, giving the model's face a "pinched" appearance. But careful placement of the reflector can result in very satisfactory lighting. You can use this basic approach to almost any lighting problem, adjusting and refining it as required.

contrast will increase, and the light may appear to get brighter. By varying the position of the diffusing tissue between the bulb and the subject, you can exert considerable control over the subject contrast because, as you move the tissue, you are changing the effective *area* of the light source.

Most beginners (and quite a few experienced photographers) think that a diffuser works because it scatters the light. Wrong. It scatters light all right, but the scattered light is largely wasted, which accounts for the drop in intensity; the reduction in contrast and increased evenness are due entirely to the increase in the effective area of the source. Don't confuse "diffusion" with "area"; they are not the same. A small source is a contrasty source whether it is supposedly diffused or not.

If, in your experiments with the tissue paper diffuser, you find the light too soft for your taste, you can combine direct and diffused light by eliminating the diffusing tissue screen and substituting for it a large, white card placed *behind* the bulb as a reflector. This arrangement will retain the sharp shadow edges, characteristic of a small light source, with the reduced contrast and greater evenness of a large one. This is what the bowl-shaped metal reflector of a flood lamp accomplishes, but more effectively, because it captures more of the light from the bulb and directs it toward the subject with less waste. This makes for higher light intensity, but focuses the light somewhat and may cause a hot spot.

The shadows may need some fill

You can use reflectors freely but beware of specular reflections

To light a surface, light the environment

You can demonstrate with a teaspoon

The best solution is a compromise

A single light source, small or large, may not illuminate the subject evenly enough to be satisfactory and it will frequently be desirable to fill in the shadow side of the subject with enough light to preserve shadow detail and avoid excessive subject contrast. At first you'll find it easiest and best to simply bounce some of the main light back into the shadows with one or more reflectors. Sheets of white cardboard or foam-core board are fine for this purpose, and they can be propped up as close to the subject as necessary and braced or taped in position.

You can use reflectors freely and place them almost anywhere (outside of the actual field of the camera) without having to worry too much about disrupting the lighting pattern. Reflected light from a matte-surfaced white card is necessarily less intense than the main light source and is highly diffused so there is almost no danger of forming secondary shadow patterns. Stay away from shiny metal foil, or actual mirror reflectors, at least until you've gained some experience, because they reflect a hard *specular* light, which can look unreal and distracting if not used with discretion.

Although it would seem obvious that the way to illuminate a surface is to direct a light beam at it, that isn't always the best way to get results. In fact, you'll find your lighting problems are simplified if you assume that the subject surfaces are mirrors in which you see (and photograph) light reflected from the walls, ceiling, floor, and furniture in the room. The direct light from the source, falling on the subject, serves mainly to define form and provide bright, specular highlights. Put another way, it's sometimes more important to illuminate the environment than it is to shine light directly on the subject.

While this explanation is a little overdramatic for most sorts of subject matter, it is completely accurate for mirror surfaces, such as polished metal, glass, and liquids. You can demonstrate the principle quite easily—find a brightly polished silver (or plated) teaspoon and lay it faceup on a sheet of white paper in front of you. In normal room light you should be able to see much of the room reflected in the concave spoon bowl,

and the details of windows, picture frames, other objects on the table, and so forth, should be clearly distinguishable. A photograph of the spoon would show the same details, but the contours and texture of the spoon would be poorly described, confusing, and irritating to the eye.

Now stand a sheet of white paper beside the spoon and notice the result. The confusing details of the room are replaced by a smooth gray tone where the paper is reflected, and the metal surface appears matte and dull, but clean and subtly modelled. By covering the spoon almost entirely with the paper sheet and looking in under one edge of the paper, you will probably be able to see the spoon completely "cleaned up" and totally free from distracting detail reflections. It will also be unnaturally dull and will look like paper or white plastic rather than polished silver.

To complete the experiment, try to illuminate the spoon satisfactorily without the paper cover, by bathing it with direct light from one or more sources, either raw or diffused. You will find that the raw, small sources make the silver look brilliant and polished, but produce glaring highlights and excessive contrast. There is no way to achieve the smooth gradation and subtle modelling, produced by the paper *tent,* without shielding the spoon from its room environment. In other words, any lighting setup you can contrive, which provides *tent lighting,* will in fact be a tent.

In practice, neither the smooth, lifeless modelling of the plain tent lighting nor the harsh confusion of direct light in an uncontrolled environment will be satisfactory for most purposes. The best solution will probably be some compromise. Working with the spoon again, enclose it in its white paper tent and shine a light on the tent from above. The spoon should appear brighter, but not any less matte than before. Now lay a strip of black paper across the top of the tent and observe the effect. By moving the strip you can "draw" a sharply defined gray stripe almost anywhere on the spoon surface. Raising the paper strip above the tent a little will soften the edges of the gray stripe on the spoon; putting the black strip inside the tent will make the spoon stripe black and crisp. By combining cast

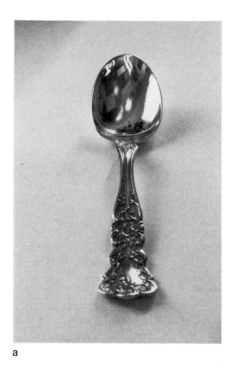

a

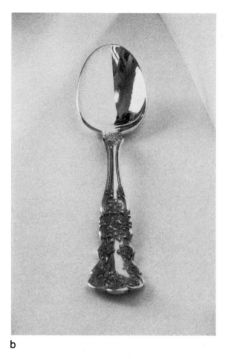

b

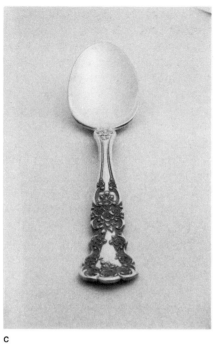

c

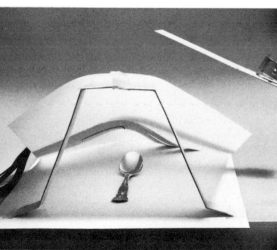

d

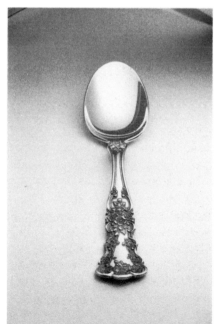

e

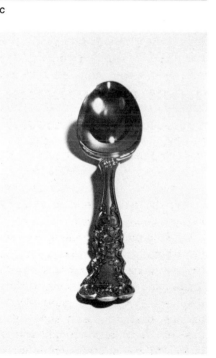

f

Figure 6.14

a. Although dull-surfaced objects seem to be easier to light than shiny ones, all objects are affected by their environments. When you learn to light shiny surfaces well, you'll find matte surfaces easier to deal with, too, and the results will be better. Here a polished silver spoon, illuminated by diffused window light, reflects the room interior in confusing patterns.

b. Simply standing a white card beside the spoon "cleans it up" by blocking off part of the room reflections.

c. Here the spoon is completely "clean." Covering it with a translucent tent of tracing paper has eliminated the reflections but left the surface featureless and formless. The polished surface appears matte and gray.

d. To restore some of the form and surface quality, necessary to express the character of silver, controlled reflections are produced by applying black paper strips to appropriate areas of the tent, both inside and out. The cast shadow from the cardboard strip at upper right produces a soft gray reflection; the small black strip inside the tent adds a sharp black accent.

e. Here is one possible effect. The variations are endless.

f. Here is the spoon as it would appear with the tent removed. Simply directing a light at a shiny object (or any object) is rarely a good way to handle it.

shadows on the top of the tent with bits of dark or colored paper strategically placed inside the tent itself, you will find that you can define the spoon contours and express its shiny quality without the confusion of its normal random reflections. This is the sort of game that professional illustrators play in order to produce the dazzling product photographs you see in the magazine ads. You can learn to do it too, if you want to work at it.

In all situations, keep in mind the fact that the subject must be groomed and adjusted to look right *from the camera position.* You can't judge any surface effect from off-camera, and if the camera must be moved, the whole process of "tickling" surfaces must begin again. You'll find it convenient to have a helper to hold reflectors and move things for you while you examine the image in the camera, especially for large setups.

Although matte surfaces will not show actual reflections of objects around them, they are affected by their environment to some degree. If you remember the principles involved, you can usually provide a satisfactory lighting condition for any sort of subject without too much wasted motion. As a rule, shiny objects will need a tent; matte objects will probably not need one. Lustrous objects, or arrangements containing a variety of surfaces, will probably be easiest to handle in a partially controlled space or open tent.

Tents can be constructed in many ways. You'll have to decide the best way to solve each problem. In many cases it's a good idea to begin by creating a *limbo* background; that is, a background which does not show any horizon line or any indication of a junction between floor and wall. This is easy to do—suspend a roll of paper on a crossbar between two light-stands (or other supports) two or three feet above a suitable table surface, and pull the paper down to cover the table. Tape the paper down at its front edge and adjust it so that it hangs in a smooth curve from roll to table surface. Objects placed on the paper and viewed from the front in uniform illumination will appear to "float" in the space, and surface reflections will be partially controlled by the smooth background tone.

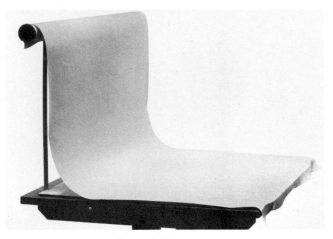

Figure 6.15
A limbo background, or *sweep,* of paper.

If a simple limbo background is not adequate, it may be necessary to enclose one or both sides. If the set is large, you can use large sheets of cardboard or painted canvas flats for this purpose, but for small, table-size still-lifes, it is usually preferable to use paper sheets hung from more crossbars constructed as before. If further enclosure is required, the paper background sheet can be extended forward across the top, over another crossbar and down the front to complete the cube. The camera lens can be poked through a small hole cut in the front wall of the tent, and adjustments of the subject can be made by lifting one of the sides temporarily. You can light the subject by illuminating areas of the tent walls from outside.

The basic cube tent will handle many kinds of subjects very adequately but occasionally you'll encounter some object, usually a very shiny, convex thing, which will show distressing reflections of the tent structure, its crossbars, and wall intersections. These problems will tax your ingenuity, but analyze the reflection problem and try to devise a structure which avoids it.

Sometimes the object can be placed in a paper cylinder and photographed through a hole cut in one side; perhaps you can build a paper cone and set it

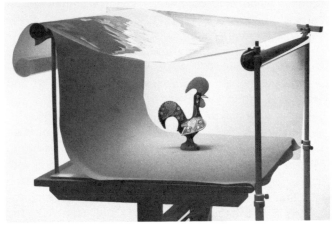

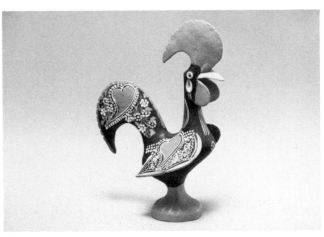

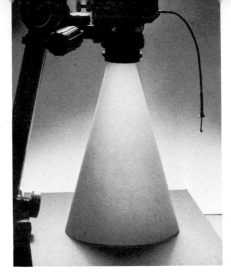

Figurer 6.16
a. A simple tent made by adding one side of tracing paper and a top of matte acetate to a limbo background.

b. Basic tent lighting. Accents can be added as desired.

Figure 6.17
An effective tent for small objects, made from translucent paper.

Provide a dominant light source

Then add accents

down over the object with the camera lens peering through a hole at the apex. If the camera lens shows in the surface of the subject as a black spot, try to position it so the reflection occurs on a corner or edge of the object where it will be relatively tiny and inconspicuous. Sometimes you can enlarge the lens reflection into a useful and decorative contour by surrounding the lens itself with black paper in some appropriate shape or pattern.

Frequently you will find that the object's own shadow causes unpleasant reflections in its surfaces or "ties it down" to the ground plane in an awkward manner. You can avoid this by supporting the object on some sort of concealed structure—a stiff wire or stick, for example, poked through the background paper. If the object is too heavy to be supported this way, you may be able to turn the whole setup (tent, lights, and all) over on its back and shoot down on the object as it rests on a solid floor stand protruding through the background wall. As a rule, don't enclose a tent any more completely than you have to to control the surfaces, because it's harder to light a closed tent than an open one.

Regardless of the construction, remember that good modelling of forms requires one dominant light source; provide that first. Even a partial tent will provide a great deal of internal reflection which will keep lighting contrast comfortably low and "open up" the shadows; but a single source may not be adequate to separate all the forms and edges, nor is it likely to provide those little accents of light which glorify surfaces and delight the eye.

By all means try to provide these accents, but do it without turning on any more lights than you need to. It's safer and generally more satisfactory to provide the necessary lighting emphasis by reflecting the main light where you want it with little mirrors or reflectors made from aluminum foil. For relatively hard and bright reflection use cosmetic mirrors, propped up or taped into position inside the tent. Aluminum foil can be cut into any desired shape and held with tape in almost any position, even concealed between objects in the still-life if a little extra light is necessary to emphasize the space or accent some area of texture or color. In cases where extra drama is appropriate, you can make the subject glow or radiate light by concealing small light bulbs here and there, and running the wires through the paper walls of the tent, out of camera view.

Again, there are no rules for this sort of work; do whatever you have to do to make the picture sparkle and sing. Just don't get carried away. You can ruin a good basic setup with too much tickling, just as too many bay leaves or too much pepper can ruin a good stew.

Summary

Light sources may be thought of as transmitting energy in particles called photons or in waves of electromagnetic energy. Visible light occupies a very small band of wavelengths in the spectrum and is bordered by invisible ultraviolet and infrared. Light normally travels in straight lines but can be absorbed, reflected, transmitted, diffused, diffracted, refracted, or dispersed when entering media of different density or encountering surfaces. White light can be dispersed into the visible spectrum as primary colors or reformed by their combination. The light secondaries are pigment primaries; the light and pigment primaries are complements of each other.

Color filters transmit their own color and absorb its complement. The absorption light loss necessitates an increase in exposure called the filter factor. Filters cannot be used effectively with colorblind films. Filtering the light source is as effective as using a filter over the lens. The filter effect is diminished by overexposure. Neutral density filters simply absorb light without changing its spectral characteristic.

Light reflected at some angles from most surfaces is polarized and can be absorbed by a properly oriented polarizing filter. Polarizers can eliminate surface glare and darken blue skies in either black-and-white or color photography. Their factor is variable.

Artificial light sources vary greatly in spectral characteristic and in apparent color. Incandescent tungsten-filament bulbs emit continuous spectra containing all the visible colors; fluorescent and luminous-gas bulbs emit discontinuous spectra from which some visible colors may be missing entirely. Tungsten-filament bulbs are generally best for indoor color photography; they are available in two standard whites, 3200°K and 3400°K. Blue flashbulbs and electronic flash units are balanced for daylight color film, rated at about 5500°K.

Flashlight must be synchronized with the camera shutter. Synchronization is easiest with BTL shutters; FP shutters cannot be synchronized at all speeds with all flash units. Modern electronic flash units are capable of automatic or semiautomatic exposure. If the ambient light is bright enough when a flash is used or if the exposure time is prolonged, a ghost image may be formed.

Flash exposure calculation requires a special flash meter or the use of guide numbers. Electronic flash guide number charts are frequently based on the BCPS rating of the flash unit.

Luminous-gas sources cannot usually be filtered satisfactorily for use with color films. Some fluorescent lights can be filtered sufficiently to be useful but you will have to experiment.

Films are highly sensitive to ultraviolet light but special emulsions are required to photograph by infrared light. Both UV and IR have useful photographic applications but require special techniques for good results. Exposures must usually be established by trial.

Beginning photographers pay more attention to light quantity than quality. The important light characteristics are intensity, color, degree of diffusion, evenness, direction, and duration. Any light can be analyzed for potential effect by considering these characteristics. Daylight and available light can be controlled by selection of time, place, angle, lens focal length, and exposure. Available light is frequently contrasty; pushing film speed is not very effective and may be detrimental to image quality. Some available light, such as skylight and window light, may be very satisfactory and give excellent results.

Arranging artificial lights in the studio is easiest at first if you visualize normal daylight as a model. Consider the Inverse Square Law. Try some exercises with a single bulb, a diffusing screen, and some reflectors. Direct light from a small source is seldom the best way to get good results. Think of the subject surfaces as mirrors in which the room environment is reflected, then light the environment.

A polished silver spoon makes a good subject for experimentation. Build a tent around it for complete control, then add decorative reflections as desired. Tents can be constructed in many ways. Matte-surfaced objects may not require any sort of tent but shiny objects will almost always need one. Start with a limbo background, then add sides and top if necessary. It's helpful to have an assistant adjust the lighting while you watch the groundglass image. Use your ingenuity but don't get carried away.

Outline

7 Color Photography

The light and pigment primaries

Subject colors are separated into light primaries

Then translated into the complementary dye colors to form a negative

How Color Films and Papers Work

It's a practical fact that light of any tint or shade of any color can be produced, quite satisfactorily, by blending together various proportions of the light (additive) primary colors, red, blue, and green. Similarly, if dyes or pigments of sufficient purity can be obtained, any paint color can be produced by mixing together various proportions of the pigment (or subtractive) primaries, cyan, magenta, and yellow. (See colorplates 2 and 3.)

The absence of all *light* color we recognize as black. Adding light colors to black (no light) produces color of increasing brightness until, when all three primary light colors are present in the proper proportions, we perceive "white"—a color of greater brightness and less obvious hue than any of its components.

The absence of all *pigment* color we perceive as white. Adding pigment colors to a white surface produces color of increasing darkness until, when all three pigment primaries are present in the proper proportions, we perceive "black"—a color of less brightness and less obvious hue than any of its components.

The light and pigment primary colors are complements of each other, or opposites, just as black is the opposite of white and a photographic negative is the opposite of the positive (print) image made from it.

In color photography the appearance of full, natural color is achieved by separating the complex shades and tints of the original subject colors into their basic components, the light primary colors. Color film consists, essentially, of three separate black-and-white emulsion layers, coated one over the other on a common base. Each of the emulsions responds to a single primary color—the top layer to blue light, the middle layer to green light, and the bottom layer to red light. After exposure in the camera, color negative film is developed in a special color developer which, in one operation, produces a black-and-white negative image in each of the emulsion layers and forms, with each silver image, a negative dye image. The top film layers, in other words, contains a silver negative image plus a yellow dye image (the complement or "negative" of blue); the middle negative layer consists of silver plus magenta dye (the complement of green); and the bottom negative layer consists of silver plus cyan dye (the complement of red). Then a bleach bath removes all three silver images, leaving the three dye images superposed to form a color negative image of the original subject. In practice, controlled amounts of dye are allowed to form a color-correcting mask. This mask layer gives color negatives their typical orange or straw-colored overall tint. (See plate 8a.)

Reversal films go through a preliminary black-and-white developer

Then the color is developed

Black-and-white film is tolerant of errors

Color films are less so

Neither exposure nor development can be varied drastically

Printing a color negative simply repeats the process (without forming a mask layer) on a paper base. The positive image is formed in silver and dye in each of the three layers; the silver is removed in a bleach step and the remaining dye layers, superposed, re-create the subject colors with commendable accuracy.

The familiar color slides, or transparencies, are positive images formed on the original film base rather than being printed on paper. Their reversal processing procedure is a little different from negative color processing. Three similar superposed emulsion layers are exposed in the camera, but treatment in the *first developer* produces only a negative silver image in each layer, as in the ordinary black-and-white process. This leaves, in each layer, a residue of unexposed and undeveloped emulsion which constitutes a potential positive image. When this remaining emulsion material has been fogged (either by exposure to white light or by chemical action), the film is developed in a color-forming solution which produces positive silver and dye images in all three layers simultaneously. The film now contains three negative silver images, three positive silver images, and three positive dye images and is totally opaque. After a bleach bath, which removes all the silver, only the positive dye images remain. Viewed against the light, the sandwiched dye layers blend together to present a reasonably faithful reproduction of the subject colors. (See plate 8b.)

The Polaroid and Kodak instant-print films produce their images by much more devious and remarkable processes than those just described. Each sheet of Polaroid SX-70 film, for example, is a sealed packet which contains all the ingredients required to produce a stable color print. Exposed through a clear plastic cover sheet, the image light is color-separated, as usual, on three emulsion layers. Development begins when the film packet is ejected from the camera, passing between a pair of steel rollers which rupture a capsule of activating chemicals and spread the mixture evenly between the plastic cover sheet and the film surface. An *opacifier* ingredient in the chemical mix protects the still-sensitive film from light while the developers

are at work in the emulsion; then, as the image is formed and the alkalinity of the developer diminishes, the opacifier gradually lightens and recedes, allowing the image to be seen. The image is positive because the developed silver image in each emulsion layer suppresses its complementary dye color rather than producing it, as in the case of conventional negative color film. This entire chemical miracle is accomplished in minutes, without a darkroom and without litter or waste. The dyes used are described as *metallized* and are said to be more stable and less subject to fading than those employed in ordinary color materials.

Black-and-white films are comparatively tolerant of mistakes in exposure and development. Overexposure of two or three stops or underexposure of a stop or two is not always disastrous and may not even be serious in some cases. Development variations of 20% or 30% from normal can often be compensated for without much difficulty and the print results are usually tolerable, if not perfect.

You will find that there is much less latitude for error in handling color materials. Although modern films will produce an image of some sort, and occasionally an unusual or dramatic one, under less than ideal conditions, best results will usually follow correct exposure and accurately controlled processing. This is true because the three emulsion layers that are necessary for color reproduction do not react in quite the same way under abnormal conditions, and when one of the layers is out of balance with the other two, or when none of them match, the resulting image color will be unnatural and frequently unpleasant.

Color negative films will usually tolerate a little underexposure (perhaps as much as one stop) and somewhat more overexposure (perhaps one or two stops). Contrast can be varied to some extent by changing development times. Negative contrast increases with increased development just as in black-and-white, but negative contrast cannot be varied greatly from normal, nor should it be, because there is very little possibility for contrast compensation in color printing.

Reversal films have somewhat less latitude than negative films. Overexposure is likely to produce bleached-out highlights and pastel colors; underexposure increases color saturation and, if overdone, will block up the shadow details and make the colors murky. Most films will also exhibit some color shift in extreme highlights and shadow areas if the film exposure is not near-normal. Unlike negative films, reversal materials are more tolerant of underexposure than overexposure and, if the first development is extended, they produce lower-than-normal maximum density and reduced contrast. Substantial changes in development will result in color shifts.

As is true with black-and-white films, high-speed color materials are grainier and less sharp than the slow films. This is less of a problem than it was a few years ago because improvements are being made constantly and even the high-speed materials now provide good enough quality for most ordinary purposes. The sharpest, least grainy transparency film available for general photography, however, is still Kodachrome 25. Its special emulsion design and special processing procedure apparently permit a degree of image precision which some new films have approached closely but have not yet matched.

Film Color Balance and Filtration

When you first begin to work with color films, especially transparency materials, you'll probably be surprised by some of the results you get. Light conditions that seemed quite normal and ordinary while you were photographing may appear in your slides as distinctly off-color, as if the pictures had been tinted or toned. Actually, the pictures may be a fairly accurate record of the real light color, and you simply didn't notice the color cast.

This problem arises because the human eye and brain are remarkably accommodating and the film is not. We see color *comparatively,* to a large extent, and can identify rather subtle distinctions between hues, seen side-by-side, under widely varying conditions of illumination color and intensity. We do not have the ability to identify color accurately without some reference, however, and in these respects our color perception is similar to our ability to judge the pitch of musical tones. Most of us can distinguish a high note from a lower one or sing simple melodies without straying off-key, but very few individuals can tell that an automobile horn is playing an A-flat major chord, for example. The few who are blessed with this ability are said to have perfect pitch. It's doubtful that anyone has perfect color pitch (as film does), and that's probably a good thing; if familiar objects apparently changed color every time the light color shifted, it would be unsettling, to say the least.

In almost any condition of illumination we can recognize and identify white objects, even though the entire scene may be strongly tinted with color. This perception of white provides us with a reference for judging both color and value of other areas in the scene. Interestingly enough, if a brighter white of more neutral color is introduced into the scene, we immediately perceive the first reference white area as tinted and degraded in value, but we may still be able to think of it as white. In other words, our perception of the color of familiar objects and surfaces is almost independent of illumination color, especially if the light contains representative amounts of all three of the primary colors in some reasonable proportion.

Color film doesn't have this ability. It is "balanced" during manufacture for a white light of very specific color, as indicated by its color temperature rating in degrees Kelvin (see discussion in chapter 6).

To review briefly, color temperature refers to the color of the light radiated by a *black body* (a hypothetical, nonreflecting object) which has been heated to incandescence, and relates the light color to the actual temperature of the black body in degrees Kelvin (degrees Celsius above absolute zero). At the lowest temperature which will produce visible light, about $1000°K$, the apparent color is a dull red. As the temperature is increased, the radiation increases in brightness and its color shifts gradually through orange and yellow toward an apparent white color. In theory, if the black body could be heated to about 6000° or 8000°K without vaporizing, its color would appear to be bluish white and, at still higher temperatures, would become increasingly blue.

Normal sunny daylight is considered to have a color temperature of about 5500°K, and most daylight reversal color films are balanced during manufacture for that white standard. If daylight film is used in light other than 5500°K, some color shift or tint may be apparent in the pictures—a blue shift if the light color temperature is higher than 5500°K, a yellow shift if it is lower than 5500°K.

If this color shift is not too severe, it can be corrected by a filter of the appropriate color placed over the camera lens. The filter, if correctly chosen, converts the off-color light back to daylight, as far as the film is concerned. The filter will absorb some of the incident light, of course, and some increase in exposure will be required as indicated by the filter factor.

While daylight film can be used in light of almost any reasonable color temperature, the filtration required to use it in tungsten illumination is rather excessive. It's preferable to use tungsten film under these conditions. There are presently two varieties—type A tungsten films were introduced originally to take advantage of the high-intensity 3400°K light output of photoflood bulbs, widely used by amateurs; type B films are balanced for 3200°K to match the standard professional tungsten spot and flood lamps. The 3200°K balance is now the most common.

With both daylight and tungsten films to work with, it is possible to get good color results in most light conditions by appropriate filtration. It isn't always easy, however; selecting the right filter even most of the time will require some understanding of the principles involved and considerable experience.

Eastman Kodak manufactures the Wratten filters in an extensive line which includes *conversion, light-balancing,* and *color-compensating* filters for color photography. In practice, the conversion and light-balancing filters are both used for making adjustments in color temperature, which means, of course, that they function

Table 7.1
Wratten Filters Chart

Color	Wratten Filter Number	Filter Factor	Mired Shift Value
bluish	82	⅓ stop	−10
	82A	⅓	−21
	82B	⅔	−32
	82C	⅔	−45
blue	80D	1 stop	−56
	80C	1	−81
	80B	2 stops	−112
	80A	2⅓ stops	−131
yellowish	81	⅓ stop	9
	81A	⅓	18
	81B	⅓	27
	81C	⅓	35
brownish	81D	⅔	42
	81EF	⅔	52
orange	85C	⅓	81
	85	⅔	112
	85B	⅔	131

in the yellow-blue range. Although there isn't any firm distinction between them, the term *conversion* is usually applied to filters in the 80 (blue) and 85 (orange) series and the term *light-balancing* is used to describe filters in the 81 (yellow-tan) and 82 (bluish) series. You will frequently hear the terms used interchangeably, but light-balancing is probably the most common.

As shown in table 7.1, each of these filters is capable of changing the color temperature of a light from one value to another. This color shift can be described in degrees Kelvin—the 80A conversion filter, for example, will adjust 3200°K tungsten light to 5500°K for use with daylight film. But this is a deceptive method of calibration, because the extent of the color shift in Kelvin degrees depends upon the color of the existing light. The 80A conversion filter produces a shift of 2300°K when used with a light source of 3200°K, but it will shift 5500°K daylight to almost 20,000°K—a correction of 14,500°K! On the other extreme, it will raise the color temperature of candlelight (about 1900°K) to only about 2530°K—a shift of only about 630°K.

Use mireds instead

Positive filters warm the light; negative filters cool it

Subtract what you've got from what you want

The filter numbers are confusing

It is possible, however, to calibrate filters in such a way that their shift value is a constant for all light colors. If the color temperature in Kelvin degrees is divided by 1,000,000 and then inverted, a number is obtained which expresses the light color in *"micro-reciprocal degrees"* or mireds (pronounced "my-reds"). A color shift expressed in mireds *is* constant for all light color temperatures and this simplifies the selection of conversion and light-balancing filters considerably. For example, suppose you are using daylight color film (5500°K balance) with an old model electronic flashgun which produces light with a color temperature of 6200°K. This will require *warming* the light source by some 700°K and indicates one of the yellowish light-balancing filters; but which one? If you consult the chart (see table 7.1) to find a filter which will produce a yellow shift of 700°K, you might be tempted to select an 81EF which will convert 3850°K to 3200°K; not quite 700°K, but the closest you can come with the information provided. This would not be proper correction for your flashgun, however. Working with mireds will give you the right information. First, convert the color temperatures, 5500° and 6200°, to mired values:

$$\text{Mireds} = \frac{1}{\frac{\text{Kelvin}°}{1,000,000}} \quad \text{or} \quad \frac{1,000,000}{\text{Kelvin}°}$$

$$\frac{1,000,000}{5500°} = 181.8 \quad \text{and} \quad \frac{1,000,000}{6200°} = 161.3$$

Subtracting 161.3 from 181.8 gives 20.5, the desired color temperature shift in mireds. Consulting the mired values in the chart shows that the most appropriate filter is the 81A; its 18 mired rating is a little less than desired, but may be preferable to the 81B whose 27 mired rating would overcorrect the light and make it noticeably yellowish. The 81EF, which seemed to be the logical choice for a shift of 700°K, is obviously much too strong for this purpose. Its 52 mired rating would shift the 6200°K light of the flashgun down to about 4700°K, much too yellow to be satisfactory with daylight color film.

Working with mireds or decamireds (one decamired equals ten mireds) is a great convenience but it has one confusing aspect: the *direction* of shift (toward blue or yellow) is indicated by the *sign* of the mired number; that is, a *positive* number indicates a yellow or orange filter which will warm the light, and a *negative* number indicates a blue filter which will cool the light. Thus, the 85B, with a rating of 131 mireds, is orange in color; the 80A, rated at −131 mireds, is blue.

If you keep your wits about you, you can usually figure out the filter color you need without worrying about the plus or minus signs of the mired numbers, but in some cases it can get confusing. For example, if you're using tungsten film, type B (3200°K) and photoflood lamps rated at 3400°K, what do you do? The color shift required is 18 mireds, but is it positive or negative—warm or cool? In the absence of any other clues, remember *subtract what you've got from what you want*. In other words, subtract the mired value of the existing light (294) from the mired value of the light color you want in order to match the film balance (312).

$$312 - 294 = 18$$

The number 18 is positive, therefore the required filter is yellowish. The chart indicates the correct filter is the 81A.

If the conditions were reversed and you were trying to use a 3400°K film (type A) with 3200°K lamps, subtracting 312 mireds ("what you've got") from 294 mireds ("what you want"), will give you a minus number of −18. The chart indicates that this is most closely approximated by the 82A, a bluish filter, with a rating of −21 mireds. Kodak has not made the situation any simpler with their numbering system, either. The warming filters are in the 81 and 85 series; cooling filters are listed in the 80 and 82 series. Furthermore, the 80s, 81s, and 82s all get stronger as the letter designations increase (the 80C is a stronger blue color than the 80B or the 80A, for example). But the 85B and the 85 are both a stronger orange than the 85C.

Decamired filters are more logical

A color temperature meter is helpful

Color-compensating filters are valuable

Either CC or CP filters can be used in color printing

Reciprocity failure affects color materials too

Reversal films should be filtered, if necessary during camera exposure

Some negative films are designated S and L

Developing color films is not difficult

In a laudable attempt to simplify this nomenclature, a number of manufacturers offer light-balancing filter sets calibrated in decamireds with the colors indicated by letter. Hasselblad's CR 1.5 filter, for example, is a conversion red filter of 1.5 decamired (15 mired) strength, roughly equivalent to the Wratten 81A. In that same series, the CB 12 is a blue filter of 120 mired strength. It is intended to convert tungsten light to daylight quality and would fall between the Wratten 80A and 80B filters in strength. In filter sets of this type each color, warm and cool, is represented by decamired values of 1.5, 3, 6, and 12. By using the filters singly and in various combinations it is possible to obtain any strength up to 22.5 decamireds, in increments of 1.5. Although the 1.5 decamired will produce noticeable steps of adjustment in color, it is almost always possible to arrive at satisfactory color balance using these sets, and their convenience is certainly obvious. For the rare occasions when more accurate color balance is necessary, the Wratten gelatin filters offer more subtle control and greater precision.

Although it's sometimes possible to estimate the filter color required for light-balancing, it's obviously not the best way. The problem is considerably simplified if you have a way of measuring light color, and this can be done with a color temperature meter, such as the Gossen Sixticolor. Meters of this type work by measuring the relative amounts of warm and cool light present in the illumination and are quite accurate and useful for continuous spectrum light from about 1500°K or 2000°K to about 20,000°K. They are not reliable for measuring lights of discontinuous spectra; if this is necessary, better results, at much higher cost, will be obtained with a three-color meter, such as the Spectra.

For controlling colors in tints and shades other than those covered by the light-balancing series, a complete spectrum of color-compensating (CC) filters is available in an extensive range of strengths or color densities.

These filters are valuable for use over the camera lens to compensate for minor variations in film color balance which occur during manufacture. They can also be used to compensate for unusual color shifts in illumination or to produce interesting distortions of color for creative purposes. They are also effective in the darkroom for controlling the balance of color prints.

By contrast with the haphazard nomenclature of the light-balancing filter series, the color-compensating filters are described logically and effectively. Each filter is identified by the prefix *CC* followed by a number which represents its density (actually its density multiplied by 100) for light of its complementary color and, finally, a letter indicating the dominant color of the filter itself. For example, CC 20R identifies a color-compensating filter of red which has an average effective density of .2 for cyan light; CC 05M describes a magenta filter which has an effective density of .05 for green light.

Color-compensating filters are available in the light primary colors, red, green, and blue, and their complements (the pigment primaries), cyan, magenta, and yellow. Densities of .05, .1, .2, .3, .4, and .5 are available in each color, and all colors except green and blue are also available in .025 density.

All six colors are useful and desirable for camera work, but for color printing applications it is only necessary to have magenta and yellow, and occasionally, cyan. The other colors can be produced easily by employing these three filters in various combinations and, although the mixed colors are not quite as pure as the individual primary colors are, the mixtures are very satisfactory. In using these (or any other) filters, it is wise to use the minimum number required to produce the desired color and density, especially when they are used in front of the lens. If more than two are required, as is sometimes the case in printing, it is best to use the larger acetate CP (color printing) filters some distance above the negative in your enlarger, rather than sandwiching a number of CC gelatins below the lens in the actual image path. Better yet, if you can afford it, buy a color enlarger equipped with dichroic filters as an integral part of the head assembly. Color heads of this sort provide color densities of up to as much as 2.0 (200) in each of the three colors and permit stepless control of color and density mixtures in all combinations.

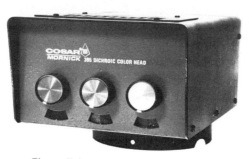

Figure 7.1
Color head

CC filters can be obtained in glass for camera use, but they must be specially ordered and are expensive. It is much more usual to use the gelatin squares mounted in metal frames or holders, or simply held in place over the lens with bits of tape. Although they are fragile and virtually impossible to clean, gelatins will last for a long time if they are given normal care and are protected from moisture and physical damage. With use they will gradually become abraded and soiled and when they begin to show obvious wear they should be replaced.

As is true with any filter, a CC filter will absorb some light which should be compensated for by an increase in the camera exposure. The filter factors are not the same for all the CC colors and many of them are awkward fractions of a stop (see table 7.1). Practically, for camera use, they can be rounded off to the nearest half-stop without serious effect on film exposure.

Color films suffer from the effects of reciprocity failure even more dramatically than black-and-white films do because each emulsion layer is affected separately. As a result, the normal color balance of the film is disrupted and a significant color shift occurs, accompanied by the usual loss of effective film speed. If the color shift is not too severe, it can be corrected by CC filtration and an exposure increase which must include the filter factors. Professional color films are tested during manufacture for color balance and reciprocity failure characteristics and come with an instruction sheet which gives the effective speed and filter recommendations for their particular emulsion batch. This is useful information, but not always accurate; age and storage conditions will change the film characteristics and, for critical applications, it is best to test the material yourself. This is especially true if the film is nearing expiration or has been subjected to heat or humidity during storage.

Reversal films must be filtered during camera exposure if any sort of color adjustment is required. The newest negative films for amateur use, on the other hand, combine fine quality and high emulsion speed

with a universal color balance which works well under most conditions of light color and simplifies correction in printing. Negative films for professional use are still supplied in two forms, but they are designated as types S and L rather than by a specific color temperature balance. In effect, type S (*short* exposure) is a daylight film and type L (*long* exposure) is intended for use in artificial light, but the exposure *time* is a more important consideration than the color of the illumination for these films. Type S film should be used for exposures of less than about 1/10th second, even in tungsten light, and type L is the right film for exposures of longer than 1/10th second, even in daylight. In both situations the appropriate light-balancing filter should be used. If type S film is used for long exposures, or type L for short ones, reciprocity failure will cause a color shift which may not be correctable in printing.

As a general rule, if the negative film you are using does not specify a color balance, assume it is balanced for daylight and, for best results, filter it accordingly if you use it in tungsten light. If you plan to have the negatives printed by a commercial photo-finisher, however, it may be wise to use the film without any camera filtration, because commercial printers sometimes guess at the proper printing filter packs by inspecting the subject matter of the pictures. If the subject looks like an indoor one, they may filter it for tungsten light whether it needs it or not.

Color Film Processing Outline

Developing color films is not much more difficult than processing black-and-white materials but in some processes there are more chemical steps involved and control of temperature is more critical. There is somewhat greater danger of chemical contamination, too, and you should be extra careful to wash the various containers and utensils thoroughly after each use. Color chemicals are somewhat more hazardous to handle than the normal black-and-white chemicals. The developers, especially the color-forming developers, are relatively strong sensitizers and strongly alkaline and should be

Table 7.2
Kodak Flexicolor Process C-41

Solution or Procedure	Time in Minutes	Temperature °F	Temperature °C	Agitation Initial	Agitation Rest	Agitation Agitate	Remarks
1. Developer	3¼	100 ± ¼	37.8 ± 0.15	30 sec	13	2	Total darkness
2. Bleach	6½	75 to 105	24 to 40.5	30 sec	25	5	Total darkness

Remaining steps can be done in normal room light.

3. Wash	3¼	75 to 105	24 to 40.5				Running water
4. Fixer	6½	75 to 105	24 to 40.5	30 sec	25	5	
5. Wash	3¼	75 to 105	24 to 40.5				Running water
6. Stabilizer	1½	75 to 105	24 to 40.5	30 sec			
7. Dry	10 to 20	75 to 110	24 to 43.5				See instructions

Reproduced with permission of the Eastman Kodak Company.

Table 7.3
Kodak Process E-6

Timing: Includes time required to drain tank.

Solution or Procedure	Time in Minutes	Agitation	Temperature °F	Temperature °C	Time Remaining at End of Step
1. First Developer	7	Initial & Subsequent	100 ± ½	37.8 ± 0.3	30
2. Wash	1	Initial & Subsequent	92–102	33–39	29
3. Wash	1	Initial & Subsequent	92–102	33–39	28
4. Reversal Bath	2	Initial	92–102	33–39	26

Remaining steps can be done in normal room light.

5. Color Developer	6	Initial & Subsequent	100 ± 2	37.8 ± 1.1	20
6. Conditioner	2	Initial	92–102	33–39	18
7. Bleach	7	Initial & Subsequent	92–102	33–39	11
8. Fixer	4	Initial & Subsequent	92–102	33–39	7
9. Wash (Running Water)	6	Initial & Subsequent	92–102	33–39	1
10. Stabilizer	1	Initial	92–102	33–39	0
11. Dry	Film removed from reels; temperature not higher than 140° F (60° C)				

Reproduced with permission of the Eastman Kodak Company.

handled with care. You should wear protective gloves when handling all the color chemicals, either in dry powder or liquid form. If you find gloves restrictive, at least consider using a barrier hand cream before contact. These silicone-based lotions, massaged into the skin and wiped dry, will leave your hands unencumbered while offering considerable protection. Get into the habit of washing your hands after every chemical contact. Dipping your hands into a regular short-stop bath (1% acetic acid) before rinsing them in water will help to neutralize the developer alkalis and make the rinse more effective.

Color chemicals have relatively limited life, too. The developers, particularly, need protection from air and light and should be stored in a cool place. Avoid really cold storage conditions, however, to prevent the solutions from crystalizing. Although this will not usually affect the activity of the chemicals, they will have to be warmed and stirred to redissolve the crystals before they can be used effectively, and this is sometimes difficult.

Although the various manufacturers' chemical systems for color negative film developing are not all alike, most of them now combine the bleach and fixing baths into one solution and specify fairly high temperature processing to keep the total time short. The Eastman Kodak Company, however, takes a typically conservative approach. Their procedure, although it involves more chemical steps than some competing systems, is reliable and predictable and produces excellent results. The Kodak C-41 process for Kodacolor II and Vericolor II film is given in table 7.2.

A 30-second agitation is recommended at the beginning of each chemical step; after this initial agitation period the film should be agitated for 2 seconds every 15 seconds during the developing period and 5 seconds every 30 seconds in the other chemical baths. As is true in all high-temperature processing, you should handle the film very carefully to avoid damage to the soft emulsion. Notice particularly that the film should *not* be washed after the stabilizer.

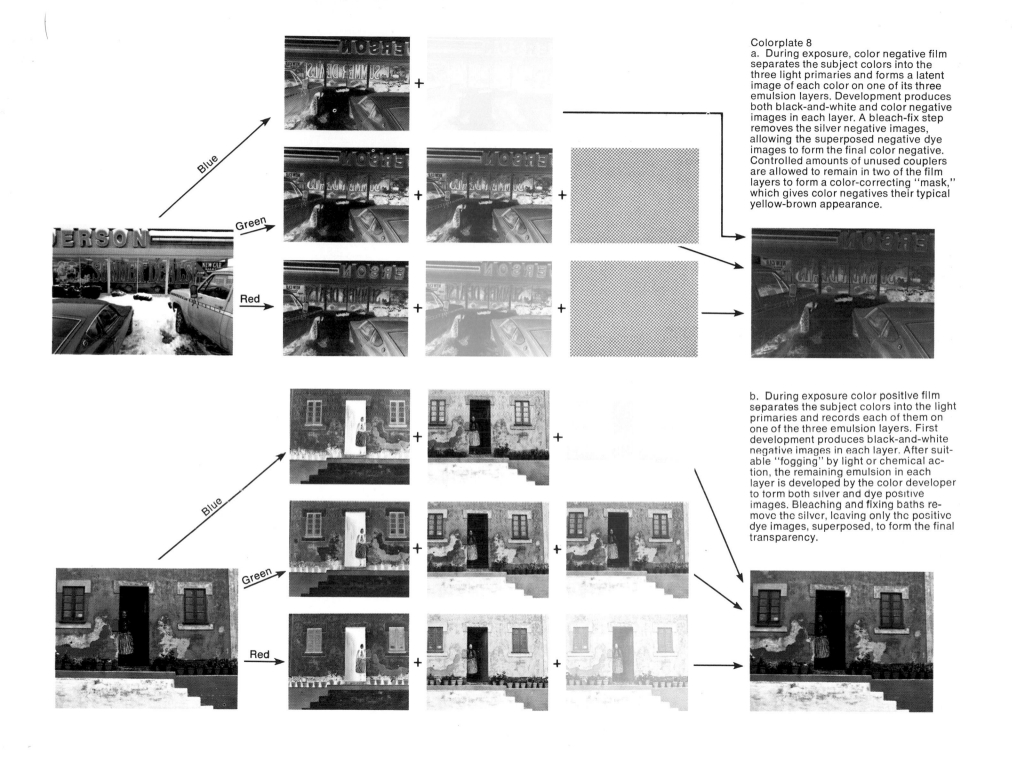

Colorplate 8

a. During exposure, color negative film separates the subject colors into the three light primaries and forms a latent image of each color on one of its three emulsion layers. Development produces both black-and-white and color negative images in each layer. A bleach-fix step removes the silver negative images, allowing the superposed negative dye images to form the final color negative. Controlled amounts of unused couplers are allowed to remain in two of the film layers to form a color-correcting "mask," which gives color negatives their typical yellow-brown appearance.

b. During exposure color positive film separates the subject colors into the light primaries and records each of them on one of the three emulsion layers. First development produces black-and-white negative images in each layer. After suitable "fogging" by light or chemical action, the remaining emulsion in each layer is developed by the color developer to form both silver and dye positive images. Bleaching and fixing baths remove the silver, leaving only the positive dye images, superposed, to form the final transparency.

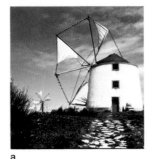
a

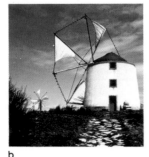
b

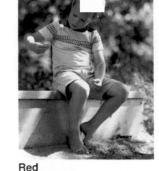
c

Colorplate 9

If you live in an area where there are frequent and severe variations in the power line voltage, you should probably get a voltage regulator. Under normal conditions, however, the line voltage rarely varies more than a few volts from the nominal value of 117 vac, and the problem is not usually very serious. This example shows the very slight exposure difference and negligible color shift resulting from 5-volt variations from normal: print (a) was exposed at 112 vac; print (b) at 117 vac; and print (c) at 122 vac. No compensation was made in exposure time, aperture, or filtration. These prints are on Cibachrome, which is relatively tolerant; negative print papers are affected more obviously but, except for critical work, voltage variations of this magnitude are no great cause for alarm.

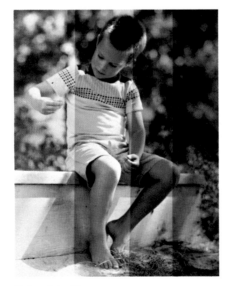

Colorplate 10

The simplest way to judge exposure and filtration is to make a test strip, using the manufacturer's recommended filter pack as a starting point. This test, using 30Y + 10C filters and exposures of 3, 6, 12, and 24 seconds, indicated a need for more yellow. Final print was made with 50Y + 10C at 7 seconds.

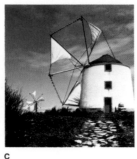
Red

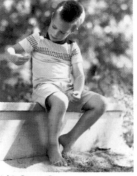
1/2 Stop Over

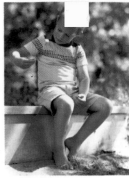
Magenta

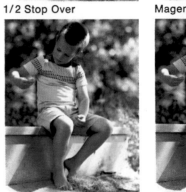
Yellow

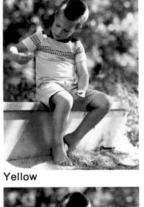
Normal

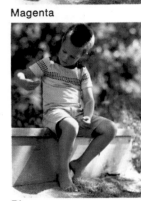
Blue

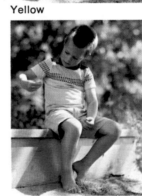
Green

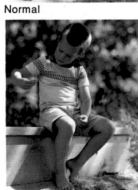
1/2 Stop Under

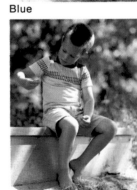
Cyan

Colorplate 11

The central image in this array matches the original transparency quite closely and is, therefore, considered "normal." The dark and light prints represent the effect of one-half stop under- and overexposure. The six color variations represent the effect of 10CC filtration in each of the six CC colors: Red, Green, Blue, Magenta, Yellow, and Cyan. The print material is Cibachrome.

Colorplate 12

a. "Normal" exposure of 4 seconds @ f/5.6 produced this print.

b. Supposedly equivalent exposure of 32 seconds @ f/16 causes slight underexposure and a very slight shift toward blue.

c. An exposure of 4 minutes and 15 seconds @ f/45 should also be equivalent to "normal" but the reduced illumination causes serious reciprocity failure. Resulting print is distinctly dark (underexposed) and bluish.

Colorplate 13

a. Normal Cibachrome print from contrasty transparency produces harsh effect with serious loss of both highlight and shadow details.

b. Diluting Cibachrome developer 1:1 with water improves detail rendering in shadows but the contrast is still excessive.

c. Substituting D-76 for Cibachrome developer causes a green shift and reduces contrast still further. Four-minute development time is barely sufficient to keep whites adequately clean. Yellow tint in bright mirror reflection is due to solarization—reversal due to extreme overexposure. Cibachrome solarizes rather easily and is difficult to use with contrasty transparencies.

d. Reducing D-76 development time to 3 minutes results in low contrast but highlights have not cleared up and whites are putty-colored. No attempt was made to adjust filtration; the greenish shift could be compensated for by red added to, or green subtracted from, the filter pack.

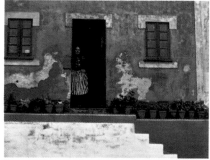
a

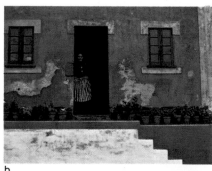
b

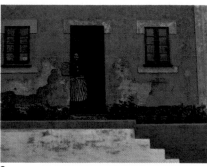
c

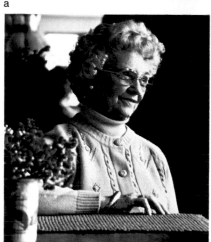
a

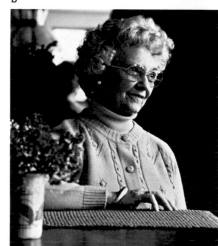
b

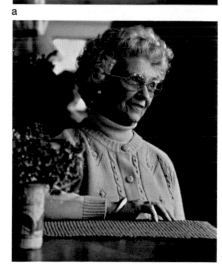
c

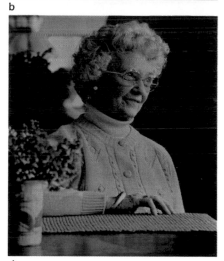
d

Colorplate 14
After your filter pack is approximately
adjusted you can proof the slides you
want to print. This will give you a rough
idea of both exposure and filtration requirements as well as providing a convenient record for your files. The step-
tablet image is helpful but not necessary.

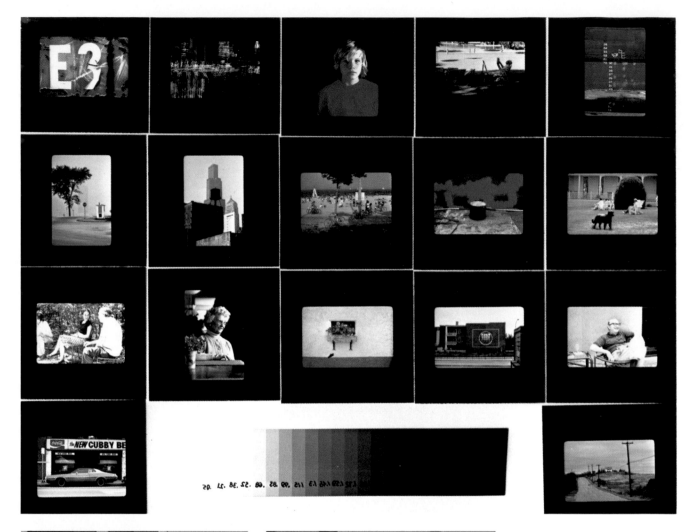

Colorplate 15

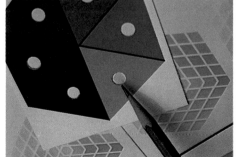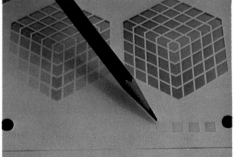

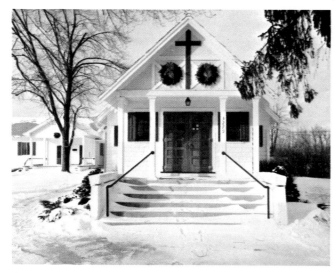

Colorplates 16 and 17
"Color-negative" prints seem to be much more affected by exposure and filtration changes than "positive" prints are. These Unicolor prints represent exposure variations of one-half stop from normal, and filtration variations of 10CC in each of the six colors. Notice that filter color is *subtracted* from these prints and that increased exposure makes the prints *darker*. Compare this test group with the Cibachrome array in colorplate 11.

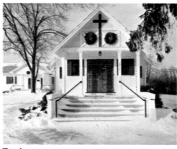

Red

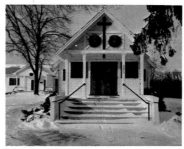

1/2 Stop Over

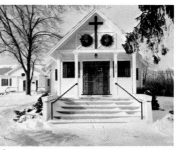

Magenta

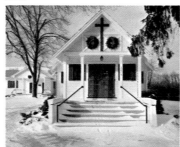

Yellow

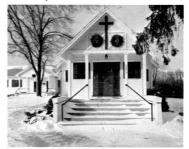

Normal

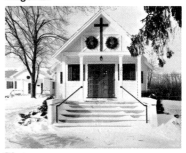

Blue

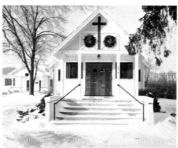

Green

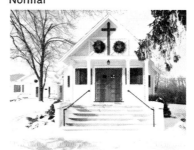

1/2 Stop Under

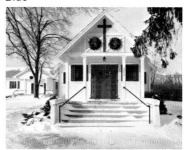

Cyan

Colorplate 18
The final print, properly exposed and
filtered for satisfactory color balance.

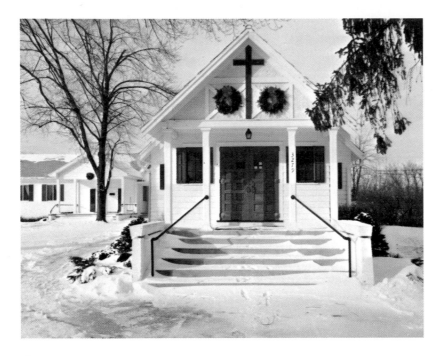

Colorplate 19
Reproduced by permission of Eastman
Kodak Company.

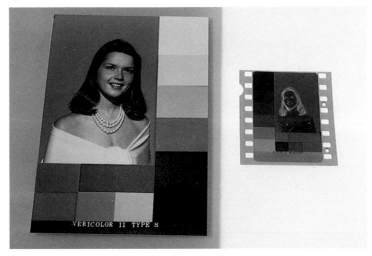

VERICOLOR II TYPE S

Color film processing is rather tedious

Color printing, on the other hand, is worth your while

You'll need a good basic darkroom

You should have a plastic drum

Reversal film processing involves more steps because the film must be developed twice—once to a negative, then again to form the positive image. The Kodak E-6 process for Ektachrome films is summarized in table 7.3.

Color film processing is a straightforward procedure which you will probably find rather tedious after the novelty wears off. There is very little advantage in doing it yourself usually, because the chemical cost is quite high, the capacity of the solutions is not very great, and their life is fairly short. Unless you have enough film to process so you can use up the chemicals completely within a week or so, you will not save much money by doing your own. You can, of course, control the effective speed of the film to some extent by varying the developing times, and this option is one of the best reasons for home processing. However, if you have only a roll or two to process, you'll save time and money and get good results (if you have a good commercial processor in your area) if you let the professionals do your film processing for you.

Color Printing

Color printing, on the other hand, *is* worth your while, and it is now remarkably simple. Whereas just a few years ago "doing color" was thought to require expensive equipment and professional skills, it is now within reach of any serious amateur and, in some respects, is less demanding than black-and-white. There are, of course, advantages in having a dichroic color head on your enlarger, a programmable electronic color analyzer, and an automatic color processor of some sort, but none of these lovely gadgets is really necessary; you can make perfectly satisfactory prints without any of them. All you really need is a good basic darkroom, adequately equipped for ordinary black-and-white printing, a reasonably good, color-corrected lens on your enlarger, and a set of filters. With this minimal equipment you'll not be very efficient but you *can* "do color."

A *little* extra hardware will make the process a lot easier and more efficient, however. Tray processing color prints is, in my opinion, rather tedious and uncertain, especially for beginners. Several manufacturers now offer plastic drums for print processing and these have several advantages. They are lighttight so, after loading the exposed paper into the drum in the dark (or in the recommended dim brown safelight, which you don't need), all the process steps can be done in full room light. They permit economical one-shot use of the processing chemicals which helps to insure uniformity of results and also simplifies temperature control.

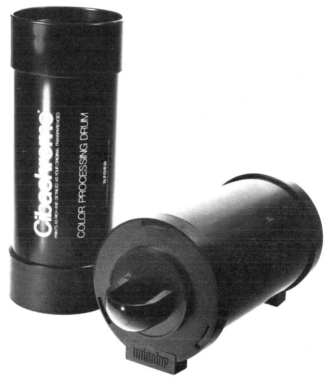

Figure 7.2
Processing drums

A good thermometer and hot and cold water

An interval timer, or use your tape recorder

You don't need an analyzer

But you should have some sort of guide

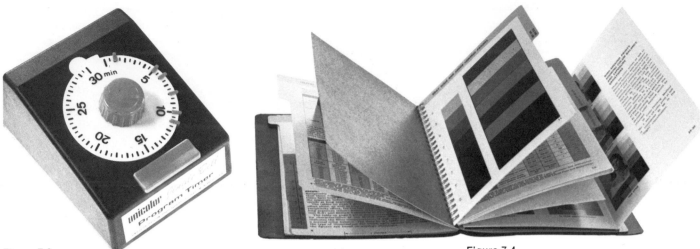

Figure 7.3
Jingle-Bell time

Figure 7.4
Color Dataguide

They're also economical to use and not very expensive to buy in the first place—all in all, a recommended piece of equipment.

You'll need a good thermometer. If you don't already have a reliable and accurate one that reads to at least 40°C (105°F), buy one before you start to work in color. I recommend the metal stem, dial-indicating type, such as the Weston.

A water-temperature control is useful, but by no means necessary for amateur use. You will need a convenient supply of hot and cold water, though, and a large pitcher or graduate (2-quart capacity) for tempered water will come in handy.

You'll appreciate a convenient and accurate interval timer. One inexpensive and ingenious model is supplied by Unicolor, Inc. Their Jingle-Bell timer is programmable so all the intervals in any process can be preset. Simply push the "start" bar to begin a timing cycle; the bell will ring and the timer will stop when the preset interval is up. The next cycle will begin, at your convenience, when the "start" bar is pressed again. You can use your tape recorder as a timer, too, if you want to. Just record the processing instructions in detail, including such reminders as "turn off the lights" or "rinse your hands," and fill in the blank times with music.

Color analyzers are fascinating toys which can simplify color filter selection and save you time and materials, but unless you plan to go into the color printing business, don't buy one (at least not at first). Inexpensive ones aren't worth having and good ones are expensive. The prices are almost certain to come down, though, as new electronic miracles keep appearing, and it's probable that really functional analyzers will eventually be priced within reach of the average photographer. In the meantime, there are several ways of estimating filter requirements. One approach is to buy Kodak's *Color Dataguide* which contains a "standard" color negative and print (so you can see what it's supposed to look like) plus several dial calculators and a set of viewing filters, all designed to help you make a visual comparison of color balance alternatives.

Another good approach to the problem is to use a *color matrix* of some sort. One typical device is the Unicolor Mitchell Duocube, which is described and illustrated on pages 193–198. There are several similar devices available; all are useful and relatively inexpensive.

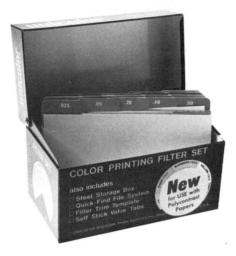

Figure 7.5
Unicolor filter set

You'll need a set of printing filters

Or a color head on your enlarger

Four methods of making color prints

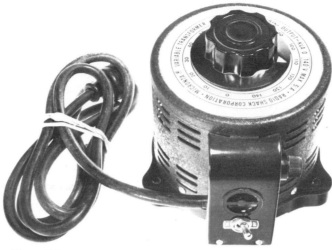

Figure 7.6
Voltage regulators

In the past, most authorities have insisted that you should equip your enlarger with a heat-absorbing glass for color printing. This is now being questioned. The present attitude seems to indicate that dichroic infrared filters are desirable but that ordinary heat-absorbing glass screens may not be. My recommendation is to start out without one, unless your enlarger generates enough heat to damage your negatives.

You will need a set of printing filters. Kodak's CC or CP filters in values of 025, 05, 10, 20, and 40 in cyan, magenta, and yellow, plus an ultraviolet filter, Wratten 2B or CP2B, will make a reasonable starter set. Get the CP (acetate) filters if your enlarger has a *filter drawer* above the condensers. Get the CC (gelatin) filters if you must use the filters under the lens in the image light path. Both kinds are available in several sizes. Buy the smallest CPs that will work in your enlarger; the 2″ square gelatin filters are large enough for almost any under-the-lens application. Other manufacturers also supply printing filters in sets and they may be less expensive than the Kodak product.

If you like equipment and have the money to spend, buy a color enlarger or a color head for your present enlarger. Modern color enlargers feature efficient, fade-resistant dichroic filters which can be introduced into

the light path by means of external levers or dials to provide stepless filtration of 200 or more. They have several advantages—greater range of filtration; high intensity printing light; convenient, repeatable filter settings; built-in ultraviolet and infrared filters; and excellent heat protection for the negatives. In addition, some models offer voltage stabilization (for uniform light color) and have companion analyzers with matching filter characteristics. Nice, but certainly not necessary.

If you live in an area where the electric power drain is irregular or poorly regulated, you may want to buy a voltage regulator for your enlarger light. An automatic regulator will keep the lamp voltage fairly constant, regardless of supply variations (within reason), which, in turn, will keep your enlarger light white. Regulators are fairly expensive and come in several sizes, rated, usually, in volt-amperes which means about the same thing as watts. If you buy one, be sure its V/A rating is the same as, or slightly higher than, the wattage of your enlarger lamp. Don't buy a much larger one than you need, even if it happens to be a bargain; regulators don't regulate very well unless they're loaded close to capacity.

If you need some voltage control but can't afford an automatic regulator, you can buy a variable autotransformer, and a voltmeter. You can monitor the line voltage on the meter, then adjust it manually. Actually, except for color-matching or scientific purposes, line-voltage fluctuations may not be much of a problem. My recommendation is to start out under the assumption that the line voltage is going to be reasonably stable, and work without any sort of voltage control until it's apparent that you need it. Plate 9 illustrates the magnitude of color shift you can expect if your line voltage varies from its typical maximum to a typical minimum without correction. Most variations will be less obvious than these.

There are presently four well-known and widely used methods of making color prints—prints from color negatives by exposure and color-forming development of color-sensitive paper; prints from color slides or other positive transparencies by exposure and color-forming reversal processing of color-sensitive paper; prints from slides on Cibachrome (a direct positive, dye-destruction or dye-bleach process); and, finally, the venerable old dye-transfer process which can be made to produce beautiful prints from either positives or negatives, but in such a devious, painstaking, and expensive manner that it is out of the question for most amateurs. A fifth way to "get" color prints (rather than "making" them) is to use a Polaroid or Kodak instant-color camera, but this approach is so simple that it hardly needs description.

Although Cibachrome is one of the most expensive color materials on the market, it offers unique advantages for the amateur—it is simple, relatively foolproof, relatively safe, and nonpolluting. It is capable of dazzlingly brilliant, saturated colors and it has no equal for detail rendering and sharpness. Additionally, it employs dyes of better-than-average stability and is considered to be one of the most durable and permanent of the color processes.

Some people object to its plastic appearance but that is a matter of personal taste. Its main photographic disadvantage, aside from cost, is its rather high contrast characteristic.

As a *positive-to-positive* process, Cibachrome shares with Kodak's Ektachrome paper type 1993 the distinct advantage of being suitable for use with color slides. For beginners in color work, particularly, this is good because slides are easy to appraise for image content, composition, and color balance. Negatives are much harder to judge. Working from slides is also simpler, at first, because the slide image serves as a convenient reference for color balance, and print filtration is relatively easy to determine when you can compare the print directly with the original color image. For these reasons, and its other advantages, Cibachrome is a good "first process."

You can buy the paper and chemical kit as separate items or you can purchase an introductory "discovery kit." You'll probably find this starter kit inadequate for any serious amount of experimentation and practice and I'd recommend getting the half-gallon P-12 chemical kit and a 20-sheet package of 8″ × 10″ type A paper.

Cibachrome is easy to process in its own special drum, but it can also be processed in other types of drums if you prefer. Liquids poured into the top of the Cibachrome drum while it is standing on end are retained in a cup built into the cap; at the same time, the used solution in the drum drains out of a vent at the bottom. The new solution is released into the drum when the drum is laid down on its side and the fluid then spreads over the paper surface as the drum is rolled back and forth on a level surface. This drum design is fast and convenient for this process but is a little more likely to cause uneven development, particularly on large print sizes, than the horizontal-filling design, such as Unicolor's Unidrum II.

The Unidrum cylinder is larger in diameter than the Cibachrome tube and is equipped with plastic channel guides which permit its use with from one to four 4″ × 5″ prints, one or two 5″ × 7″ prints, or one 8″ × 10″ print. Solutions are poured into an end spout while the drum is resting on its stubby feet in a horizontal position. The solution flows into the drum immediately but lies in a trough at the bottom and doesn't touch the paper until the drum is rolled. Drums of this design can be completely filled with water for either pre-rinse or washing operations but they are not as easy to drain as the Cibachrome drum is. Investigate both types and see which one strikes your fancy. My recommendation is to buy the Cibachrome drum if you plan to do only Cibachromes, but buy the Unidrum (or equivalent) if you plan to do other sorts of prints as well as Cibachromes. You can do all sorts of prints in either drum type, but the Unidrum type is more versatile and probably the best compromise.

Cibachrome Printing

Put on your rubber gloves, then follow the package instructions for mixing the chemicals and prepare one-quart volumes of the working solutions at first. Save the remaining chemical concentrates for later. Store the working solutions in clean glass or plastic bottles and label them clearly. Be careful of the bleach chemicals; pour the powder slowly to avoid raising too much dust and don't inhale any of it. If you spill any of the powder or the mixed solution, neutralize it with baking soda before you mop it up or before you flush it down the drain. The bleach is a strong and corrosive acid which is potentially harmful to you as well as to metal utensils and your darkroom plumbing.

The solutions are reasonably stable but they will work best when they are fresh. Try to use up the working solutions within a week or two at the most; the unused concentrates will keep for a month or two in partially full bottles. Very old chemicals will not produce good color results and are likely to cause mottled tones, degraded whites, streaks, and stains.

When you are ready to begin printing, stand the bottles of working solutions in a large tray of warm water (try about 30°C to 32°C or 85°F to 90°F at first) to bring them up to temperature. Cibachrome is remarkably tolerant of processing temperature variations, but it's wise to pick a convenient temperature within the acceptable 18°C to 30°C (65°F to 85°F) range, and stick to it. The recommended temperature is 24°C (75°F) and, since that's easy to maintain, you should probably try to work with it. By the time you're ready to process your first print, the chemicals in the water bath should have arrived at about the right temperature.

Cibachrome works best with fully exposed, low-contrast transparencies. Heavily dense or contrasty images are not suitable and should not be attempted. Select a transparency; clean it carefully with a soft brush or compressed air (not canned air or freon) and put it into your enlarger. Cleaning is especially important with positive processes because dust spots show up in the print as black marks which are almost impossible to remove.

Adjust the image size, focus carefully, and stop the lens down to f/11. Then consult the back of the paper package for the *basic filter pack* recommendations. If you have a color head on your enlarger, you can simply dial in the recommended filtration; otherwise, select individual CC or CP filters to add up to the recommended totals and insert them into the enlarger—CP

filters up in the condenser system somewhere, above the negative; CC filters below the lens, in the image light path. Although it is not specified in some recommendations, *always* use the Wratten 2B filter (or some equivalent UV filter) in any filter pack to exclude ultraviolet. You may be able to ignore this if you have a color head; it may already be in there.

Color filter selection can get confusing, and it will be discussed in more detail shortly. For now, remember that you can add filter numbers to arrive at the value you want (you can make a 30Y, for example, out of three 10Ys, or a 20Y and a 10Y, or any other similar combination). Also, remember that as a general rule you should not have more than *two* filter colors represented in any filter pack unless you are deliberately trying to reduce light intensity; all three primaries add up to *neutral density*. More about this later.

Check your developing drum to be sure it's clean and dry and lay it out with its cover so you can get at it in the dark. Turn out the lights and open the paper package. Cibachrome paper is protected by two envelopes, the inner one made of paper-covered plastic, and by a sheet of heavy cardboard on each side of the paper stack. You will probably find it easiest to slip the entire stack partway out of the envelope so the paper sheets can be separated, rather than trying to extract a single one from the package with your fingernails.

After removing one sheet of paper, reclose the plastic envelope and replace it in the cardboard package, folded end first. Then identify the emulsion side of the paper sheet by rubbing it lightly with a dry fingertip, first on one side, then the other. The emulsion side is glassy smooth and will make almost no sound when stroked; the back side has a fine matte texture and will make a light "whispering" noise as it is rubbed. Place the paper in the easel, emulsion side up, and make a conventional geometric test strip (see page 131), beginning with an exposure of about 10 seconds @ f/11 and doubling the exposure total each time until it reaches 80 seconds. Then use the next larger aperture (f/8) at 40 seconds, and, finally, f/5.6 @ 40 seconds to complete the series of six steps. In other words, expose: Step 1, f/11 @ 10 secs; Step 2, f/11 @ 10 secs;

Figure 7.7

a. Cibachrome is relatively tolerant of temperature variations but, for best results, work at about 24°C (75°F). Wear protective gloves when mixing the chemicals, and set the bottles in a water bath to maintain temperature.

b. Be sure the drum is clean and dry. Set it out in a convenient location so you can find it in the dark.

c. Dust the transparency carefully, using the enlarger light to reveal the dust and lint.

d. Adjust the image to size and focus.

e. Stop the lens down to f/11.

f. Make up the recommended filter pack and insert it into the filter drawer. Now turn out the light and work in total darkness, no safelight.

g. Remove a sheet of Cibachrome paper from its protective package and place it in the easel. Be sure the emulsion side is up. See text.

h. Make a geometric test strip as described in the text.

i. Locate the drum and load it. The paper emulsion side must be inside the curl so the processing solutions can flow over it easily.

j. When the drum is loaded and the end caps are closed securely, turn on the room lights and pour out 3 ounces of each solution, using the plastic cups provided with the kit. They are clearly marked; don't mix them up. Set them back in the water bath to maintain temperature.

k. Stand the drum on end and pour the developer into the funnel opening. The solution flows into a cup in the end cap and will not contact the paper until the drum is laid down on its side.

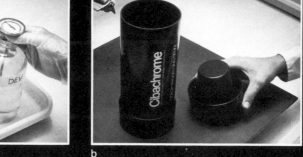
a

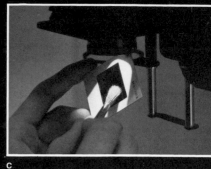
c

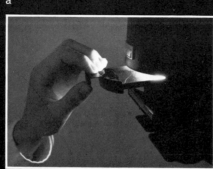
f

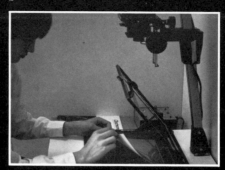
g

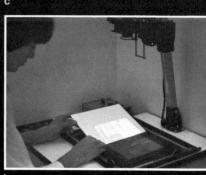
h

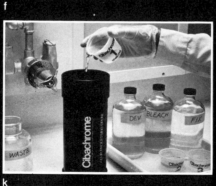
k

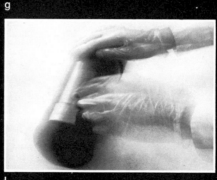
l

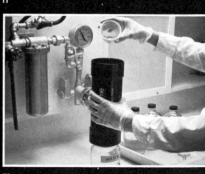
m

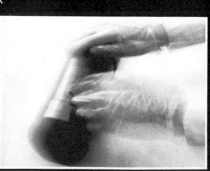
p

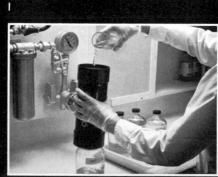
q

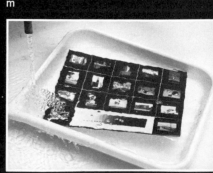
r

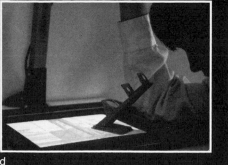

d

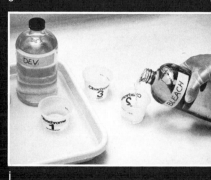

e

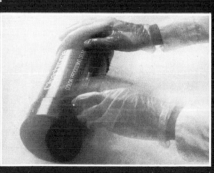

i

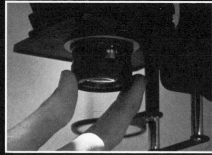

j

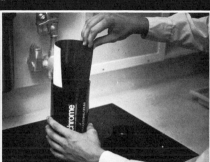

n

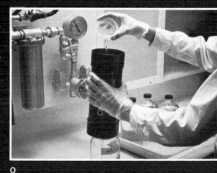

o

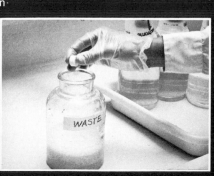

s

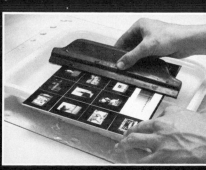

t

l. Set the timer for 2 minutes, start it running and immediately lay the drum down on a flat, level surface and roll it back and forth continuously during the developing period. Be sure to roll the drum far enough each way to make a little more than one complete revolution, otherwise the print may not develop evenly. You can use an automatic agitator if you have one.

m. About 15 seconds before the end of the development time, stand the drum on the waste container so the developer solution can drain out while you are pouring the bleach bath in at the top. Let the drum drain until the timer rings, then set the timer for 4 minutes and immediately lay the drum on its side again and . . .

n. . . . agitate as before, continuously.

o. At 3:45, dump the bleach into the waste container while you pour the fixer into the funnel top of the drum. Let the bleach drain until the timer rings, then set the timer for 3 minutes and immediately lay the drum on its side and . . .

p. . . . agitate as before, continuously.

q. Fix for the full 3 minutes, then, when the timer rings, stand the drum on the waste container to drain and pour in a few ounces of water as a rinse. Roll the tank back and forth a few times, then remove the end cap, take out the print and slip it into a tray of clean water.

r. Wash the print for 3 minutes in running water.

s. While the print is washing, clean the drum, rinse the utensils, and add two of the neutralizing tablets to the waste liquid. This step is necessary to prevent possible damage to your drainage system and contamination of the environment.

t. Squeegee the finished print lightly and hang to dry. The color will be somewhat magenta while the print is damp. Wait until it dries to appraise color balance and exposure.

Synopsis **Process Steps, Cibachrome P-12 Chemistry in Drum**

Developer (at 22°C to 26°C or 72°F to 78°F). Use 3 ounces and develop with rolling agitation for 2 minutes (including drain time). At 1:45, drain developer into a glass or plastic waste storage container. At 2:00, pour in 3 ounces of

Bleach (same temperature range). Roll tank to agitate for 4 minutes. At 3:45, drain bleach into waste storage container. At 4:00, pour in 3 ounces of

Fix (same temperature range). Roll to agitate for 3 minutes. At 3:00, drain fix into waste container and pour in about 4 to 6 ounces of water. Agitate briefly and drain. Remove print from drum and place it in running water to

Wash at about 24°C (75°F) for 3 minutes. Wash out the tank thoroughly and dry it with a clean towel. Add two neutralizing tablets to the used solutions in the waste container. When the wash time is up, wipe or squeegee the print surfaces carefully and hang the print to dry. Warm, moving air will hasten drying, but avoid excessive heat.

Check solutions temperatures; pour in the developer

Develop for 2 minutes

Bleach for 4 minutes

Fix for 3 minutes

Wash for 3 minutes; wash the drum and other utensils

Step 3, f/11 @ 20 secs; Step 4, f/11 @ 40 secs; (total 80 seconds); Step 5, f/8 @ 40 secs; Step 6, f/5.6 @ 40 secs. This procedure will reduce errors due to reciprocity failure. (See plate 12.) Load the paper into the drum cylinder, emulsion side in, put on the drum cover, and turn on the lights.

Check the solution temperatures and adjust them, if necessary, by setting the bottles in hot or cold water and stirring the contents, one after the other, with the thermometer stem until they are correct. Be sure to rinse off the thermometer before going from one solution to the next; contamination is fairly serious in color processing.

When the temperatures are suitable, pour three ounces of each chemical solution into the plastic cups provided in the kit. Each cup is clearly marked and should be used only for its own chemical. Set the filled cups in a shallow tray of 24°C (75°F) water to maintain temperature. If you are using the Cibachrome drum, stand it on end and pour the developer from the cup into the top opening. If you are using a Unidrum, stand the drum on its feet, horizontally, and pour the developer into the filler spout. Set your interval timer for two minutes, start it, and immediately lay the Cibachrome drum on its side on a flat smooth surface and begin to roll it back and forth, far enough to make at least a complete revolution on each pass. Agitate the Unidrum in the same way; knock it off its feet and roll it until it is stopped by the projecting feet, then roll it back

until it stops. Continue this agitation routine, briskly but not violently, with either drum type, for 1 minute and 45 seconds. Then, with 15 seconds to go in the developing period, hold the Cibachrome drum drain over a large glass or plastic container and turn the drum to a vertical position. It will begin to drain immediately and you can, at the same time, pour the bleach solution into the filler opening at the top. Rock the drum back and forth a little to facilitate the draining (don't overdo this or you'll spill bleach into the tank prematurely). When the timer goes off, lay the drum on its side again and resume the agitation, rolling the drum back and forth for 3 minutes and 45 seconds. (Drain the Unidrum into the waste container through the filler spout, then set it on its feet to refill.)

With 15 seconds (of the 4 minute bleach period) left, dump the drum as before, collecting the used bleach with the developer in the waste container. Pour in the fixer while the bleach is draining and, when the time is up, lay the drum down and begin the agitation of the fixer. Fix for 3 minutes, then drain the fixer into the waste container and pour a few ounces of water into the drum. Agitate it briefly, dump, then remove the cover and take out the print. Put the print into a tray of running water for 3 minutes, then wipe both sides lightly with a damp chamois, a soft squeegee, or a viscose sponge and hang it by one corner to dry. Wash out the drum thoroughly and wipe it dry. Rinse out the chemical cups and invert them over their respective bottle caps.

Neutralize the waste chemicals

Inspect the dry print for color balance and density

This is a positive process; filter accordingly

There are two ways of using the viewing filters

Filter changes may require changes in print exposure

The used chemicals must be neutralized before they are discarded. Add two of the neutralizing tablets (supplied in the kit) to the waste container and let them fizz. You can continue to accumulate chemical waste in the container until you're through printing (or until it's full) if you remember to put in two tablets for each 3 ounces of used bleach that is added. After the last tablets have been in the waste liquid for half an hour or so (they will probably have disappeared), it is safe to pour the used chemicals down the drain. If you run out of tablets for some reason, use baking soda—adding it until the liquids stop fizzing.

This procedure should give you good results, but you may notice what the Cibachrome instructions describe as "an unpleasant odor" during or after the bleaching action. It is not likely to be a problem if the developer is well drained before the bleaching begins, but it can be avoided by using a brief water rinse after the developer. Three or 4 ounces of water, agitated for about 10 seconds just before adding the bleach bath, should solve the problem. You're more likely to need this with the Unidrum than with the Cibachrome drum; the Unidrum is harder to drain completely and will probably retain more of the used chemical solutions in each step.

The prints will dry rapidly, especially in warmed, moving air. When your test print is dry, you can inspect it for exposure and color balance. (See plate 10.) The range of exposures sampled should certainly include a usable one and you should also be able to see the effects of extreme under- and overexposure. Remember, this is a direct positive process; overexposure will lighten the print and underexposure will darken it. Find the step or steps which seem closest to normal density and estimate an exposure for the next trial; then examine the color. Make exposure corrections by adjusting the aperture, if possible, to avoid reciprocity failure effects.

If the print appears strongly tinted with color, it may need a filter correction of 30 or more. If the tint is obvious, but not excessive, try about 20. If it is noticeable, but not obvious, try 10. A correction of less

than 10 is harder to estimate without direct comparison with the original transparency colors.

Because this is a positive process, the print will react directly and positively to filter colors—for example, adding magenta to the filter pack will add magenta to the print and removing a yellow filter from the pack will reduce the yellow saturation in the print image. You can get some idea of the necessary correction, therefore, by viewing the print through various filters to see which one seems to balance the color most satisfactorily. This is a rather subjective and haphazard procedure, but, with practice, you'll develop some skill at it. (See plate 11.)

There are two ways of using the viewing filters— if you hold the filter to your eye and look at the print through it, you will see a relatively subtle color shift; if the filter is laid in direct contact with the print surface, the color shift is apparently greater. With Cibachrome, and also with Ektachrome 1993, holding the filter at the eye is the best way to appraise the probable effect of adding *that* filter to the filter pack. If you like the effect you see when the filter is lying on the print surface, you'll have to add a filter of *twice* its strength to the filter pack to get the desired correction. For example, if holding a 10M filter to your eye causes a pleasing effect, then add 10M to the filter pack. If it looks better when the 10M filter is lying on the print face, add 20M to the filter pack.

If you make substantial changes in the filter pack, you'll probably have to adjust the exposure to compensate, but exact calculation is practically impossible. As long as there are only one or two colors in the pack, the filter values can be combined and used as a rough guide for exposure estimation. Adding or subtracting yellow filters will not affect the total exposure substantially, regardless of their apparent density, so you need only concern yourself with changes in magenta or cyan filtration. As a very general guide, consider each 10 value in either magenta or cyan to be worth about 1/5th stop, then increase the exposure an additional 10% for each filter *sheet* added regardless of color. For example, if you add 10Y and 20M (to a pack which con-

Wet prints will appear slightly magenta; judge them dry

You can reduce contrast a little

By modifying development

But don't overdo it: paper is expensive

Use a cardboard mask to make small prints on large paper

tains *no cyan),* ignore the added yellow filter factor; then, if the original exposure had been 30 seconds, the magenta factor (2/5 stop) would raise it to about 42 seconds and the two filter sheets would increase that further by 20% for a final exposure of about 50 seconds.

Your next print, using the filter correction and exposure time estimated from the test, should be better, but will probably not be perfect. Process the print as before, and let it dry before appraising it (wet prints appear more magenta than they will when dry). Estimate the corrections again, if necessary, and make another print; this one should be nearly perfect. If it is not, review the previous instructions and try again. When you arrive at a satisfactory filter pack, record it for future reference. It will be valid for other prints made from similar transparencies on that particular batch of paper.

It is not usually wise to deviate very far from the manufacturer's instructions in the use of any material, and, of course, you do so at the risk of wasting your time and some expensive material. Still, if you have good control of the process and are a sensitive worker, you can manipulate Cibachrome to some extent. Its excessive contrast, for example, can be reduced a little, without serious loss of other qualities, if the development is reduced somewhat. Don't attempt to do this by reducing the time alone, however. It's better to weaken the developer by giving the paper a preliminary rinse with plain water for about a minute. Dump it out, add the developer and continue normally. You can, if you prefer, dilute the developer with up to about equal parts of water and develop normally or for a little longer time. A third alternative is to use a milder developer, such as D-76 (any ordinary black-and-white developer will produce an image of some kind on Cibachrome) for 4 minutes or more. All these modifications will necessitate some increase in exposure, reduce contrast, and result in a color shift which is generally correctable by filtration. If carried to extremes, however, reduced development will result in muddy colors, uncorrectable color shifts, and, worst of all, putty-colored highlights which are unacceptable. (See plate 13.)

One other deviation from the recommendations may be possible. If you are careful to level your working surface, you may be able to process the materials satisfactorily in less than the recommended 3 ounces of each chemical solution. A preliminary water bath will help prevent uneven development streaks. Obviously this is not the best procedure, but if economy is an overriding concern it may be worth a try. Weigh the possible savings in chemicals against the possible waste of paper, however. A single sheet of paper is worth more than the chemicals it's processed in.

You can make small prints with the Unidrum by cutting the paper into 4″ × 5″ or 5″ × 8″ pieces before exposure, but the Cibachrome drum will not process these small pieces reliably. It's not difficult to make multiple prints on a single sheet, however, and you'll find this a convenient way to compare the filter requirements of two or more transparencies.

A simple cardboard mask (fig. 7.8) fastened to the easel margins will permit exposing a quarter or half sheet of paper at a time. Focus and compose the image in the mask opening, then before putting the printing paper into the easel, clip one (for instance, the upper right-hand) corner to identify its position. Make the first exposure in the mask opening, then (if you want more than one copy of the same image) turn the paper around so the clipped corner is in the lower left. Make the exposure, then remove the paper to a lightproof place

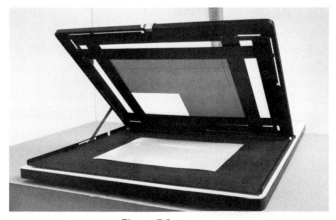

Figure 7.8
Cardboard mask on easel

and turn on the lights. Turn the cardboard mask over to shift the position of the mask opening, and recompose the image (or a new one) in the new position. Turn out the lights, insert the paper with the clipped corner in the upper right and make the exposure. Turn the paper around and make the fourth exposure with the clipped corner in the lower left. Process the print and you should have four small prints, neatly spaced on the sheet.

After you have gained some experience, you should be able to make useful first tests of new transparencies by simply contact printing them, cardboard mounts and all. (See plate 14.) This is an excellent way to estimate exposure and filtration for the individual prints. It will be most useful if the enlarger is used as the printing light and is set at the right height and the right aperture for the prints you will make by projection, and if you can use a previously tested filter pack for the exposure.

Although this may sound complicated, you will find the process quite simple after you've tried it a few times. Keep notes on all details of exposure and filtration and on any other process details which you feel may influence the results. Work logically; if something goes wrong, try to find out the cause and correct it before going on.

Printing from Negatives: Unicolor R-2

If you plan to do very much color printing from negatives, you should probably buy one of the *color matrix* subtractive color calculators marketed by Omega, Beseler, or Unicolor. Unicolor's Duocube is typical, easy to use, and effective. You should also get a horizontal-filling drum like the Unidrum, mentioned previously. Similar products are available from a number of other manufacturers. A convenient (but not necessary) addition is a motor agitator unit which twirls the drum for you during processing. Again, several similar models are available; Unicolor's product is called a Uniroller. You probably don't really need a safelight, and it's safer not to use one; but if you think you must have one, get the Wratten #13, which is recommended for Ekta-

color type 74 paper. It can also be used, with reasonable care, with Unicolor paper (but not with Cibachrome). Finally, of course, you'll need to buy a chemical processing kit such as Kodak's Ektaprint 2 (for type 74 paper) or Unicolor's R-2 kit which will process their own RD paper or Kodak's type 74.

Before mixing the working solutions from your chemical concentrates, check them to be sure they have not crystallized (from being chilled or frozen in transit or storage). If crystals are present in any of the solutions, loosen the bottle caps, place the bottles in a warm water bath (about 32°C or 90°F), and stir the contents occasionally until the crystals redissolve. Plan to use up the partially used concentrates within a month or two for best results. Don't deliberately freeze color chemicals to preserve them; they'll keep well in full bottles, protected from air and excessive heat.

With all-liquid chemistry, it is easy and advisable to make only as much working solution as you will use within a few days. Unicolor's R-2 kit makes this easy by including mixing instructions for as little as 8-ounce volumes of each solution. Smaller volumes than this are probably not advisable because of the difficulty of measuring accurately the very small amounts required of some of the concentrates. You should, of course, wear some sort of hand protection when mixing any color chemicals. Follow the instructions carefully and store the working solutions in very clean glass or plastic bottles of the appropriate size. Clean any chemical spills and wash all utensils and your hands, after the chemical preparation.

When you are ready to begin printing, set the bottles of working solution in a water bath to bring them to the recommended temperature. Although tray development is possible, drum processing is easy and economical and allows most of the work to be done in full room light, a real convenience. My recommendation is to use trays only for very large or odd-size prints that won't fit into your drum.

If you are using the Unicolor materials (other processes are generally similar but will differ in detail), bring the working solutions to about 24°C (75°F). The actual temperature of the individual solutions is not partic-

Figure 7.12

a. The temperature of the Unicolor solutions is not very critical because the drum will be hot when they're poured in and the small volumes involved will be warmed almost immediately; nevertheless, it's wise to standardize on a starting temperature of about 24°C to 26°C (75°F to 80°F). Be sure the drum is clean. You can leave it in the sink if you plan to load it "wet" (Unicolor representatives recommend this procedure).

b. If you plan to load the drum "dry," be sure it is dry inside and out, and set it out in a convenient location so you can find it in the dark.

c. Clean the negative as previously described.

d. Adjust the image size and composition and focus.

e. Tape the cardboard mask onto the easel so it will provide four equal test areas. Move the easel so the mask opening is directly under the enlarger lens.

f. Make up the recommended filter pack or dial in the filtration if you have a color head.

g. Stop the lens down one full stop from maximum aperture. Now turn out all the lights and work the next four steps in total darkness.

h. Put a sheet of paper in the easel. Either Unicolor or Kodak papers are suitable. Notch one corner of the sheet so you can tell which exposures are which.

i. Place the Duocube on the paper. It will fit neatly into the cardboard mask opening. Expose through the plastic diffuser which is supplied with the Duocube kit. The enlarger shown here has a diffuser built-in. After the first exposure, turn the paper around and expose the second test. Then remove the paper to a lighttight place and turn on the lights.

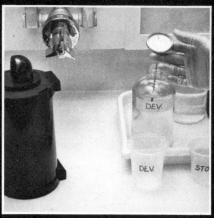
a

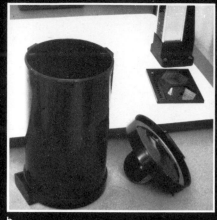
b

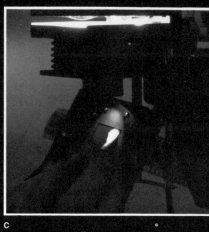
c

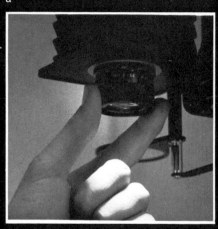
g

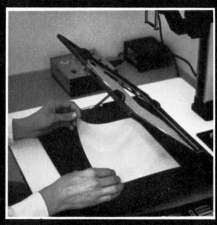
h

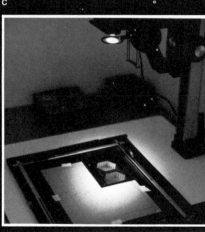
i

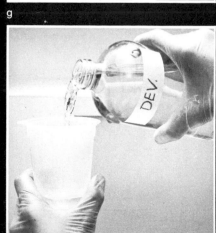
m

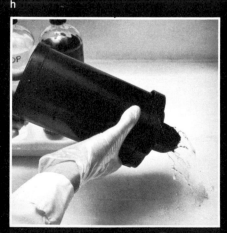
n

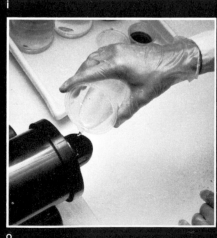
o

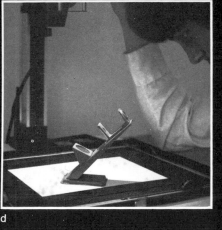

d

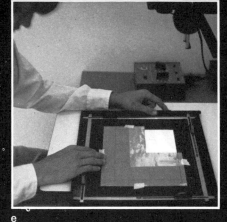

e

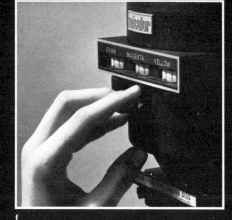

f

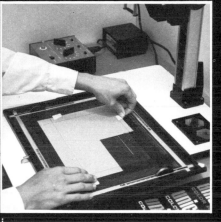

j

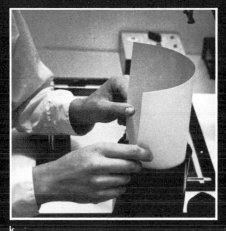

k

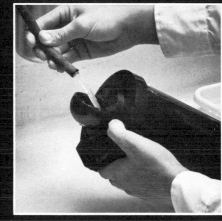

l

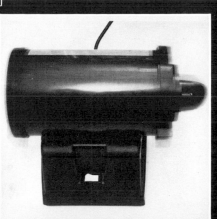

p

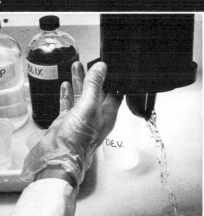

q

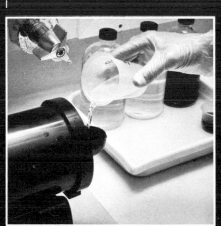

r

j. Turn the cardboard mask over and retape it to the easel so you can expose the other two quadrants of the paper. Turn out the lights again. Replace the paper and the Duocube and make the final two exposures. The notched corner will help you identify the location of each exposure.

k. Still in complete darkness, load the drum. If you prefer the "wet" method, tuck the exposed paper away out of the light while you fill the drum with water at about 41°C (105°F), then turn out the lights again and load the drum. With either method, be sure the end cap is on and securely seated before turning the lights on.

l. If you loaded the drum "dry," now is the time to fill it with 41°C water for the presoak step.

m. While the paper is presoaking, measure out 2 ounces of developer. Presoak for 1 minute.

n. Dump out the presoak water . . .

o. Set the drum on the agitator (or on its feet if you don't have an agitator) and pour in the developer. In this tank design the solutions flow into a trough below the print and will not contact it until the drum is rolled.

p. Set the timer for 4 minutes, start it and the agitator. If you don't have an agitator, simply knock the drum off its feet and roll it back and forth until the feet stop it, continuously. Be sure the surface is flat and level to avoid uneven development.

q. While the development is proceeding, measure out 2 ounces of stop. At about 3:45, dump out the developer and drain until the timer rings.

r. Then pour in the stop, set the timer for 30 seconds and start it. Start the agitator at the same time.

(continued)

s. Agitate the stop for the full 30 seconds.

t. Then dump the stop and drain thoroughly.

u. Pour in 2 ounces of Blix, set the timer for 2 minutes and start both timer and agitator.

v. Agitate the Blix for the full 2 minutes.

w. Dump out the Blix and agitate the drum a few seconds with several ounces of water. Then remove the print and slip it into a tray of running water.

x. Wash the print for 2 minutes.

y. Soak the print in a tray of stabilizer for about a minute.

z. Squeegee the print lightly and hang to dry. Wait until the print is dry before attempting to judge color balance or exposure.

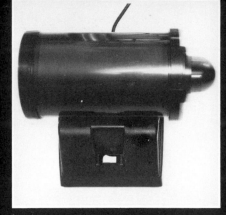

s

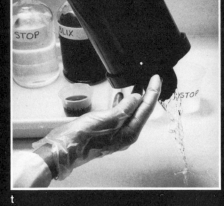

t

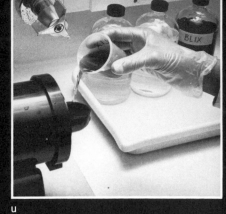

u

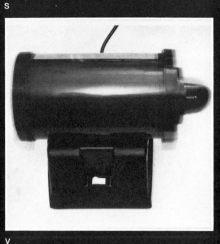

v

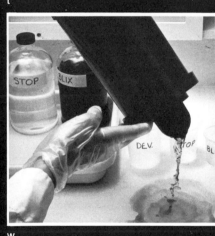

w

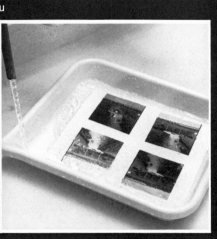

x

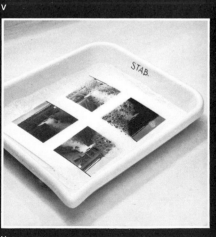

y

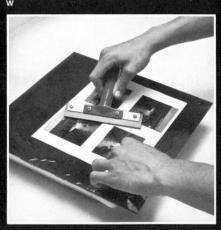

z

Synopsis **Process Steps, Unicolor R-2 Chemistry in Drum**

Presoak paper in Unidrum by filling drum with about 2 quarts of water at about 40°C to 43°C (105°F to 110°F), allowing drum to stand on end for at least 1 minute. Then dump, and add 2 ounces of

Developer at about 21°C to 27°C (70°F to 80°F) and agitate by rolling drum for 4 minutes. Drain drum and pour in 2 ounces of
Stop bath at same temperature range as developer. Agitate stop bath for 30 seconds to a minute. Drain drum and pour in

Blix at same temperature range and agitate for 2 minutes. Drain drum and pour in about 8 ounces of
Water at same general temperature range. Agitate, drain and refill every 15 or 20 seconds for at least 2 minutes—minimum of 6 times. Remove print and treat in a tray of

Stabilizer solution, at same temperature range, for 30 seconds to a minute, with agitation. Remove print; wipe or squeegee surfaces very gently and hang or lay out, emulsion up, to dry. Clean up drum, utensils, and sink area, and wash your hands. Wipe drum dry for next use.

Look up the filter pack recommendation

Select a good, average negative and clean it

In the dark, expose the Duocube; use the diffuser

Print all four quarters of the paper; load the drum

ularly critical in drum processing, because of the very small volumes used; the drum temperature itself is more important, and that is established by a hot water presoak step immediately preceding development. While the chemicals are warming up, check your drum to be sure it's clean and dry and set it and its cover in a convenient spot for loading in the dark.

Consult the manufacturer's literature to find the recommended basic filter pack for the kind of negative film you are printing (different types of films require different filtration) and for the paper in use. For example, if you are planning to print a Vericolor II negative on Unicolor RB (resin-base) paper, the recommended filter pack is UV + 50Y + 40M. The UV filter is similar to the Wratten 2B used in the Cibachrome pack; they can be used interchangeably, but be sure to include *one* of them in the pack. You will probably notice some filter *color correction numbers* stamped on the back of the color paper package. Ignore them, temporarily; we'll discuss them later.

For your first test, select a well-exposed negative which contains an average mix of color and density, such as an outdoor group or street scene. Clean your negative carefully and insert it into the enlarger, being sure that no white light can leak past it to dilute the color of the projected image. Focus and compose the image at the desired size, then either make a test strip similar to the one recommended for the Cibachrome test (page 187) or, preferably, use your Duocube (or equivalent) subtractive color calculator. If you have the

Duocube, proceed as follows (follow manufacturer's instructions for other brands).

Install the cardboard mask (fig. 7.8) on your easel and position the easel so the mask opening is directly under the enlarging lens. Don't worry about the image position or composition at this point. Stop the lens down one stop from maximum aperture.

Turn out the lights, place a sheet of RB or type 74 paper in the easel, and place the Duocube matrix on the unmasked quarter of the paper emulsion. Hold the diffuser (supplied) under the enlarger lens to integrate the image colors into one more-or-less neutral tone, and make a 10-second exposure. Reverse the paper sheet under the mask to reveal a new quarter of the sheet and make another contact print of the Duocube, this time using a 20-second exposure.

Tuck the paper sheet away in a lightproof container; turn on the lights and turn the mask over so it will expose the other two quarters of the paper. Re-center the mask opening under the lens and turn out the lights. Insert the paper in the easel and make a Duocube print through the diffuser, as before, with an exposure of 40 seconds. Repeat on the last quarter of the paper, for 80 seconds. Load the paper into the drum and install the lid; this will take a firm twist if the the sealing gasket is new. Check it by feeling the position of the drum feet. If they are not aligned, the cover is not seated properly. Correct it before turning on the lights.

In room light, check temperatures and presoak the paper

Develop 4 minutes

Stop bath for 30 seconds

Blix 2 minutes

Wash 2 minutes

Stabilize 30 seconds, wipe lightly and hang to dry

Appraise the Duocube image with the gray comparator

Adjust the filter pack and the exposure as indicated

In full room light again, check the temperature of the solutions. If they are not within the permissible 20°C to 27°C (70°F to 80°F) range, raise or lower the temperature of the water bath and stir the developer in its bottle until it is approximately 24°C (75°F). Then, fill the Unidrum with water at about 40°C (105°F) by holding the drum at about a 45° slant and pouring water into the spout until it runs over. This will take about two quarts of water. Stand the drum on end and let it soak for a minute. While you are waiting, pour out 2 ounces of developer in a small graduate or plastic cup.

Dump the water out of the drum and shake it a few times to be sure it's empty, then set it down on its feet (or on the Uniroller motor agitator, if you have one) and pour the 2 ounces of developer into the drum spout. Set the timer for 4 minutes, start it, and immediately turn on the agitator or begin manual agitation by rolling the drum back and forth until its feet hit on a level surface. Continue the agitation for 3 minutes and 45 seconds. Dump the developer down the drain and, when the timer rings, pour 2 ounces of stop bath into the drum and agitate for at least 30 seconds. Dump the stop bath, add 2 ounces of Blix, and agitate for 2 minutes. Dump, and pour in about 8 ounces of water at about 21°C to 27°C (70°F to 80°F); agitate briefly and drain. Repeat this rinse-and-drain procedure at least five more times over a period of at least 2 minutes; then open the drum and remove the print. Rinse it briefly once more in a tray of clean water, then slip it into a clean tray containing at least 8 ounces of stabilizer solution and agitate the print for 30 seconds or so. Then wipe the print surfaces *gently* with a damp chamois or soft squeegee and lay it faceup to dry. Alternatively (and in my opinion preferably), wipe gently and hang by one corner in a film dryer. Return the stabilizer to its storage bottle and save it for future use. Discard the stabilizer when the other chemical solutions in that working set have been used up.

When the print is dry, you should have at least two or three usable test images of the Duocube color matrix to work with. Below the left-hand array of each set of color patches, you should be able to discern a row of blue-green squares. Select a sample image which shows from three to five squares (count the squares as visible if you can see all four corners), then lay the gray comparator card (supplied in the kit) over the left-hand color matrix and locate the color patch in the array which seems most nearly neutral gray, as compared to one of the gray comparator sections. Use a light gray section to match a light color patch and a darker gray section to match a darker color patch so tonal differences won't interfere with your color perception. (See plate 15).

None of the color patches will be a completely neutral gray, but you should be able to locate a "most nearly neutral" patch without too much difficulty. Identify this patch on the filter correction chart; let's assume it's patch D 10Y 15C, near lower left center of the left-hand array. This indicates that you should add 10Y and 15C filters to the existing filter pack in the enlarger before you make a print.

Now, suppose you have selected the test image which received the 20-second exposure and you can count 4 blue squares under the left-hand matrix. Consulting the exposure correction chart for patch D and square 4 leads you to the information —1f 1.0. This means that, after adding the recommended filters to the pack, you should reduce the lens aperture by one stop and multiply the exposure time by 1.0—in other words, don't change it; use the 20-second exposure which you used for the test.

Adding the new filters to the existing pack may produce some neutral density. In the illustration given, for example, the basic pack contains UV + 50Y + 40M and the new filters will make the pack UV + 60Y + 40M + 15C. Because there is at least 15 of each primary color in this new pack, it contains 15 neutral density which will simply reduce the enlarger light intensity without doing anything to the color balance. Normally we would remove 15C + 15Y + 15M from the pack, leaving UV + 45Y + 25M; but, when using the Duocube system, *leave all the filters in place*. The appropriate exposure increase, necessitated by the neutral density, is included in the exposure correction recommendations.

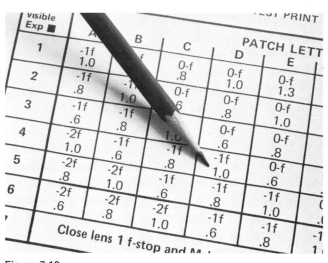

Figure 7.10
Duocube correction chart

Filter Pack Adjustment

Using the complete new filter pack, the reduced aperture, and the 20-second exposure time, make a print of your negative and process it. When it is dry, inspect it carefully for density and color balance. (See plate 16.) If the print is much too dark, it has probably received more than one stop *too much* exposure (remember this is a *negative* process); if much too light, it will need a stop or more increase in exposure. If the color balance is improved when the print is viewed through a 10 filter of some color, held at the eye, *remove half that value (05) of that color* from the filter pack, or add 05 of *the complementary color* to the pack. If the correction is best when the 10 filter is laid in contact with the print surface, adjust the filter pack by 10. (See plate 17.) If a 10 filter is not sufficient correction, even when in contact with the print surface, you will need to alter the filter pack by 15 or more (highly unlikely).

For example, the print seems best when a 10B filter is laid on its surface. This indicates that the print image needs 10 more units of blue which, in other words, means that we must *remove 10B from the negative* image or *add 10Y* (the complement of blue) *to the*

negative image. Except when using the Duocube calculator, it's always advisable to remove filters from the pack rather than adding them (if you can) so extract 10B from the pack. Again, the existing pack consists of UV + 60Y + 40M + 15C.

There's apparently no "blue" in this pack, but remember that blue is a mixture of magenta and cyan (just as green is a mix of cyan and yellow and red is a mix of magenta and yellow). Furthermore, although the hue changes when you blend two different filter colors, the numbers don't add up (for example, 05Y + 05C = 05G, not 10G; and 10M + 20Y = 10R + 10Y, not 20R + 10Y or 30R). To remove the 10B from the filter pack, therefore, we must first dissect it into its component pigment primary colors; 10M + 10C. Now it's easy:

$$\begin{array}{r} \text{UV} + 60\text{Y} + 40\text{M} + 15\text{C} \\ - 10\text{M} - 10\text{C} \\ \hline \text{UV} + 60\text{Y} + 30\text{M} + 05\text{C} \end{array}$$

Now, since we're beginning to make intuitive corrections in the pack, we really should remove the neutral density by taking out all of one of the colors and equal amounts of each of the other two. Cyan is present in the smallest amount, so out it goes, followed by equal amounts of magenta and yellow:

$$\begin{array}{r} \text{UV} + 60\text{Y} + 30\text{M} + 05\text{C} \\ - 05\text{Y} - 05\text{M} - 05\text{C} \\ \hline \text{UV} + 55\text{Y} + 25\text{M} \end{array}$$

Now we must include some exposure compensation for the filter changes. There are several ways to estimate this, and they don't all produce the same results. The charts and dial calculators in the *Kodak Color Dataguide* offer what are probably the most accurate methods of estimation. But, lacking those, you can use the rule of thumb given earlier—ignore the yellow filter factors entirely (but count them as "sheets") and assume that a value of 10 in either magenta or cyan is equivalent to 1/5th stop; then make an additional adjustment of 10% for each filter added to or subtracted from the old pack.

Make a new print and check it for color balance and density

Now you can remove the neutral density from the pack

And adjust the exposure

This print should be good

A new package of paper may require filter adjustments

Make your own standard negative for calibration

Work carefully and keep records and you'll get good results

For example, if we ignore the yellow filtration, the new pack differs from the old by —15M —15C. Together this represents about 3/5ths of a stop *less* density and indicates, therefore, that the new pack will require less exposure. The original exposure was 20 seconds so the new one should be about 14 seconds, approximately 3/5ths of a stop less than 20. If we assume that the two filter packs contained the same number of filters, there is no "filter sheet" correction to apply. If the new pack contains, say, one fewer filter than the old, a further 10% exposure reduction to about 12.5 seconds is in order. This method is obviously rather approximate, but it will serve reasonably well in the absence of a better one.

Make another print and check it carefully. It should be reasonably good, but if it needs further correction, review the previous instructions and try again. (See plate 18.)

When you have arrived at a satisfactory filter pack for the negative type and paper lot that you're using, it should be satisfactory for other negatives of the same type, printed on paper from that emulsion batch. The emulsion number is printed on the paper package. Get the same emulsion number, if you can, when you buy your next supply.

Although you may have arrived at your present working filter pack by personal trial, it will include some filtration necessitated by the paper balance itself. A new paper lot will probably be somewhat different. You can compare the old paper with the new by checking the filter recommendations on both packages. Then, remove from your working pack the filters recommended for the old paper lot and add to the pack the filters recommended for the new paper. A single print on the new paper will probably be sufficient to appraise the color balance and make a satisfactory adjustment in the working filter pack.

There are many approaches to color printing control but most workers would agree that it is important to proceed methodically and consistently and to keep careful records of details like filter packs, exposure times, paper characteristics, and so forth. It will help

a very great deal if you have a "standard" negative, preferably one containing some neutral grays and some relatively pure colors. You can make your own standard negative or you can buy one. A useful one, with matching reference print, is included in the *Kodak Color Dataguide*. (See plate 19.) Comparing your print with the reference print will give you a quick and accurate check of color balance.

Although only two methods of color printing have been covered in any detail, the basic principles discussed will apply to others, as well. You do not need lots of expensive equipment or extensive experience to "do color." Simply follow the instructions for the process you select; use reasonable care in handling the chemicals and other materials; use fresh materials; work from good original slides or negatives; study the effects of filtration until you understand the principles involved; and keep careful and complete records of your procedures. Good results are sure to follow!

Summary

The absence of all light color is black; the absence of all pigment color is white. Blending light primary colors can produce other colors or white light; blending pigment primaries can produce other colors or black. The light and pigment primaries are complements of each other. Colors in photography are reproduced by separating the subject colors into their light primaries by filtration to form a negative record; recombining them in pigment primaries produces a positive image. Color films accomplish this by employing three separate emulsion layers, each sensitive to one of the light primaries. Color-negative films must be printed on color-sensitive paper to produce the color-positive image; color-positive films produce the color-positive image in a two-stage process in the film itself.

Color films are less tolerant of exposure errors than black-and-white films and they permit very little contrast control. Fast films are more grainy and less sharp, in general, than slow films. Color films record colors objectively and most are balanced for some specific white standard. If exposed to light of some other color, they record it as a tint. Color balance is expressed in Kelvin degrees as color temperature. Daylight films are balanced for 5500°K; tungsten films are either 3200°K or 3400°K. Light of nonstandard color can often be adjusted by filtration.

Conversion and light-balancing filters are intended to adjust color temperature in the blue-orange range. Computing filter correction in Kelvin degrees is mathematically awkward; mired correction is easier to deal with. Positive mired numbers indicate warming filters; negative numbers indicate cooling filters. Color temperature can be measured with a special meter. For most accurate results, all three primary colors must be measured.

Color-compensating filters are logically calibrated and identified by the prefix "CC" and a number indicating the filter strength. They are available in six colors in several densities. They are useful for both camera work and printing. For color printing, however, many workers prefer dichroic color enlargers which provide a greater range of stepless control over color balance.

Color films suffer from reciprocity failure, just as black-and-white films do, and react by exhibiting signs of underexposure and color shifts. Special negative color films are available for long (L) and short (S) exposure times to minimize reciprocity failure effects.

Developing color films is simply a matter of following instructions carefully. It is not economical to do yourself unless you use up the chemicals completely. Printing, however, is interesting and well worthwhile.

In addition to the normal black-and-white darkroom equipment, there are a few desirable equipment items; among them, controls for water temperature and line voltage, printing filters or a color head for your enlarger, and some device for estimating print exposure and filtration. There are four common color printing methods: color negative, color positive (dye-forming), color positive (dye-bleaching), and dye-transfer. Cibachrome is a dye-bleach procedure and a good first process.

It is convenient to use the Cibachrome drum for processing. Mix the chemicals carefully and use them fresh. Follow the process step instructions carefully and produce a test print. Collect the processing chemicals in a large plastic container and add the indicated number of neutralizing tablets to the mixture before pouring it down the drain.

View the dry print through the various CC filters to to see which seems to produce the best color balance; then add that filter to the filter pack for the next print. Some exposure compensation may be necessary.

Cibachrome contrast is normally high. It can be modified somewhat by reducing development, but there is danger of excessive color shifts and muddy highlights if this is overdone. Prints smaller than 8″ × 10″ can be made in the drum by printing several images on one paper sheet, using a cardboard mask in the easel.

Color negative printing requires special chemicals and paper but drum processing is convenient. The Unicolor (or similar) drum is easy to use, and a motorized agitator is helpful. A color matrix calculator, such as the Duocube, will simplify testing.

Mix the solutions carefully and use them fresh. Follow manufacturer's filter pack recommendation and make a Duocube test, as described. A safelight is neither necessary nor desirable; work in total darkness. Process the test as instructed and view the dry print through the viewing filters. The filter color which seems to provide the best visual balance should be *subtracted* from the filter pack, or its complement *added*. Some exposure adjustment will probably be required; follow the instructions for refining the filter pack and calculating exposures. Printing from different negative material or using a different emulsion lot of paper will require filter pack adjustment.

Outline

8 Special Camera Techniques

There is a revival of interest in large-format photography

View and field cameras must be used on tripods

They use sheet film

View and Field Cameras

In recent years there has been a considerable revival of interest in large-format photography and a substantial number of people have turned to the field camera as a reasonable compromise between the image quality of the view camera and the portability of the hand camera. Field cameras are basically view cameras, with somewhat restricted capability, very lightly constructed, usually of wood, and designed to fold up very compactly for carrying. The lightest models in the 4″ × 5″ size are not very much larger (in their folded state) and no heavier than some full-size 35mm SLRs.

Like view cameras, field cameras must be used on a tripod or other firm support. Most of them will accommodate wide-angle lenses or moderately long-focus lenses without difficulty and will provide enough bellows extension to permit life-size close-ups. Although they don't provide as great a range of adjustments as view cameras do, and cannot be adapted and added onto to anywhere near the same degree, they handle most view camera chores very adequately and are much more convenient to carry and use outside the studio.

Although some models can accept rollfilm holders, both view and field cameras use sheet film primarily. As the name implies, sheet film (occasionally called cut film) is usually supplied in boxes of twenty-

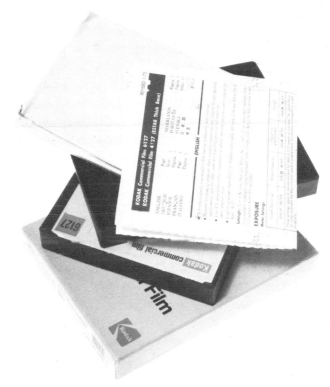

Figure 8.1
Opened film box

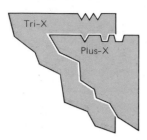

Figure 8.2
Notches in the corner of each film sheet identify the film type and indicate the emulsion side.

Sheet films must be loaded into holders

Shiny side, fresh film; black side, exposed film

Holders each contain two sheets of film

five or more sheets. The stack of sheets is typically wrapped and sealed in a vinyl-foil envelope, then enclosed in a box composed of three interlocking "halves," which seal out the light entirely. After the envelope has been opened (in the dark, of course), it can be discarded and the unused films can be stored in the box without any other protection. Almost all sheet films are so sensitive that they must be handled entirely in the dark until they have been developed and fixed. They must also be handled with considerable care to avoid damage to the sensitive emulsion surface. You can identify the emulsion side of a film sheet by code notches (fig. 8.2) which are cut into one of the short sides of the sheet. When you hold the sheet with the long sides vertical and the notches are found in either the upper right or the lower left corner, the emulsion side is facing you. For simplicity, remember to hold the film vertically; the emulsion faces you when the notches are in the upper right-hand corner.

The number and shape of the notches are a clue to the identity of the film. For example, Tri-X pan film sheets can be identified by three closely spaced V-shaped notches. Plus-X film sheets are marked with one V-shaped notch, a space, then two closely spaced nearly square notches, reading from left to right. These notching codes are printed on the bottom of the film boxes and on the information sheets which are included in the film boxes. Save the sheets for reference. You must know who made the film before it can be identified by the notches, but the position of the notches does identify the emulsion side of the sheet, regardless of the manufacturer.

For use in view or field cameras, sheet films are loaded into sheet film holders (fig. 8.3). Holders must be loaded in total darkness. But first, clean them thoroughly in the light. Arrange the holders on a clean, dry table surface in the darkroom, with the slides pulled out far enough to clear the entire front opening (but don't remove them entirely). Remove and insert the slides a few times to clean any dust out of the light trap slot and dust the holder interiors thoroughly. Remove possible chemical traces with a dampened cloth.

Don't let any moisture get into the light trap and let the holders dry completely before proceeding.

It is conventional to insert the slides into the holder before loading the film, in such a way that the silver-colored, or shiny, top margin of the slide faces out. The other side of the holder clip is painted black. The shiny side is also identified by a deep notch or a row of embossed dots or lumps, a feature which makes it possible to tell which side is which in the dark. As a general rule, a closed holder with the shiny side of its slide showing should contain fresh, unexposed film. If the dull or black side of the slide shows, the holder may contain exposed film or it may be empty.

Film holders are equipped with simple latches which can be swung over the closed slides to keep them in place. Some photographers consider a holder empty if its latches are open, regardless of the color of its slide clips. This is a more elegant code, and entirely feasible if you pay attention to detail. If there is any doubt in your mind, it is prudent to check the contents of a holder in the darkroom.

Holders are designed to contain two sheets of film at a time, one on each side, in separate lighttight compartments. The film sheets are inserted from one end so the edges of the sheets slip under narrow metal guides at the sides of the compartment (fig. 8.3). When the sheet is pushed all the way in, the entering end slips under a similar guide, and the trailing end of the film is held in place by a hinged flap which closes the end of the holder and seals it against light leakage. Then a dark slide, held in slots just above the film surface, is slid closed, and as it interlocks with the end flap, the film chamber is made lighttight. It is good practice to load the film into the holder so the notches on the short edge of the film sheet lie under the holder flap. If this is done, it is easy to check the notches without unloading the film if the emulsion type must be identified.

If their various specialized adjustments are set at the neutral position, view cameras and field cameras are relatively simple to operate. For ordinary work, the lensboard and the camera back should be centered and parallel to each other, and the unused adjustments

Figure 8.3

a. Clean the holder and position its slides, silver side out, like this. Hold the film by the edges, lightly, to avoid fingerprints. The film notches in the upper right-hand corner of the sheet indicate that the emulsion is facing you.

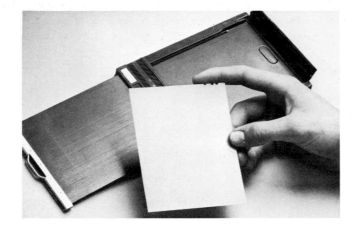

b. Place your thumb and fingertips over the ends of the film guides. When you feel the film slip under your fingers you can be sure it is entering the guides properly.

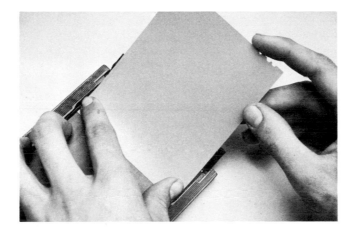

c. Push the film sheet all the way into the holder. If it is not all the way in, the end flap will only close with difficulty, if at all, and the slide may not close completely. If the film is loaded properly the end flap and the slide will interlock easily to seal the holder against light.

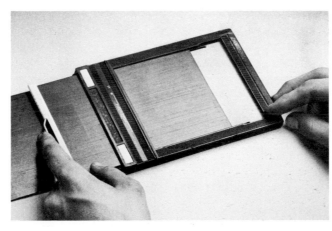

should be locked. The camera should be mounted straight on the tripod head so tilting the head forward and backward will not deflect the image horizon. Both front and back standards of most view cameras are equipped with focusing knobs (most field cameras have only front-focus controls) and they should be adjusted if necessary to balance the camera on the tripod. Be sure to lock all adjustments securely, but not so tightly that they bind.

Adjust the tripod height by lengthening or shortening the legs. A minor change in height may be made with the tripod central column, but it is risky to operate a view camera on a column extended more than just a few inches because of probable vibration.

Point the camera in the general direction of the subject. Open the shutter by using the Time setting or the press-focus lever and open the diaphragm fully. Cover your head and the camera back with a black focusing cloth and look at, not through, the groundglass. The image will appear on the groundglass upside down, backwards, and in full color.

Loosen the tripod head controls slightly and move the camera as necessary, while watching the image on the groundglass, to adjust the composition. Image size can be adjusted by moving the camera toward or away from the subject. When the composition is satisfactory, lock the tripod head controls firmly.

Adjust either the front or back focusing controls until the image is in focus or sharp. You may find that it is not possible to get all of the image in focus at one setting. If this is the case, focus the most important area. Lock the focusing controls.

Close the shutter and set it on the desired speed. Cock the shutter if necessary. Set the diaphragm pointer on the selected aperture number. Insert the film holder in the camera back being careful not to move the camera out of position. Pull out the front dark slide. Shade the lens. Press the cable release to make the exposure. Insert the dark slide, with the black side showing to indicate exposed film. Remove the holder from the camera and mark the exposed side if desired.

Figure 8.4

a. Open the camera shutter. Here the press-focus button is being used. You can also use Time.

b. Open the diaphragm fully. This makes the visual image bright and reduces depth of field for most critical focusing.

c. Point the camera at your subject, focus and compose. You can use either the front or rear focusing controls in normal situations. The dark cloth or focusing cloth shields the groundglass image from extraneous light.

d. Stop the lens down to shooting aperture. Some lenses may exhibit some focus shift when they are stopped down. For extremely critical work it is wise to check the focus at the shooting aperture with a magnifying glass. This will not usually need to be considered.

e. Close the shutter and, if it is not already cocked, cock it now.

f. Pry (don't pull) the spring back open and insert the holder. Be sure it is seated properly to avoid light leaks.

g. Pull out the front darkslide. Don't pull the rear one or you'll miss your picture and fog your next film.

h. Use the darkslide to shield the lens from light and make the exposure. Be sure to leave some slack in the cable release to avoid jarring the camera as you press the plunger.

i. Replace the darkslide. Be sure that you have turned it around so the black side of the metal end clip is facing out.

j. Pry the back open and remove the holder. It will interlock with a shallow groove in the camera back; pull it back slightly before you try to lift it out. Store your holders in the shade or, preferably, in a closed case in the shade. Most holders will leak a little light in direct sunlight and heat is not good for the film.

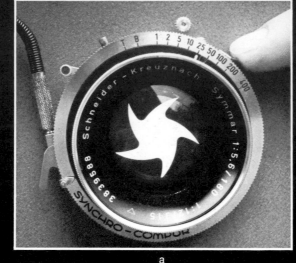

a

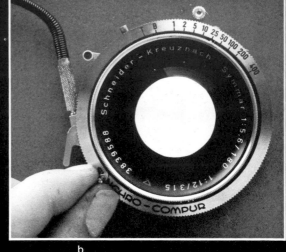

b

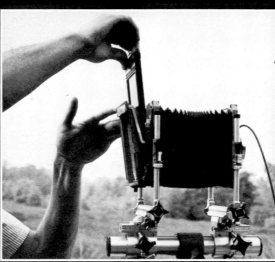

f

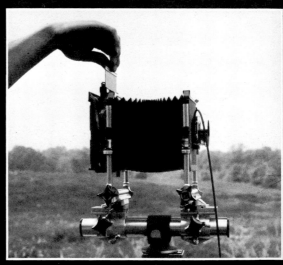

g

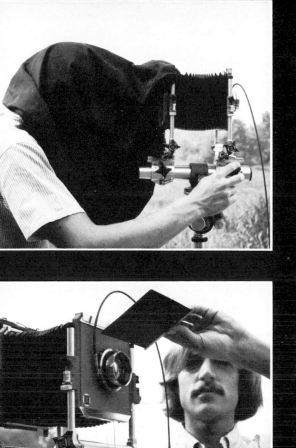

c

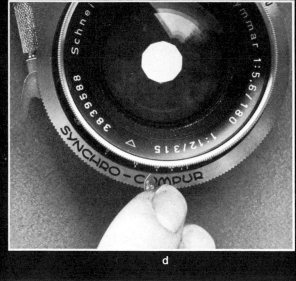

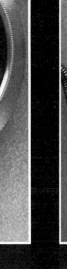

d

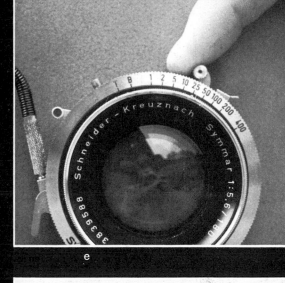

e

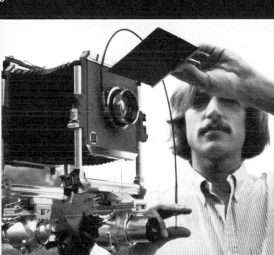

h

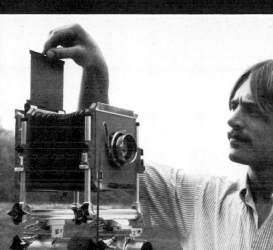

i

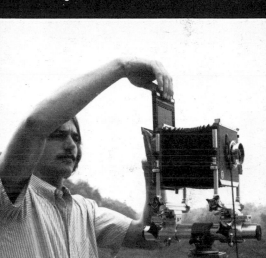

j

Processing Sheet Film in a Tray

Tray development of sheet film is convenient and economical for batches of up to about six sheets at a time (although you'd better not try to do more than two or three at a time at first). For larger quantities of film, done day after day, tank processing may be preferable. Tray development aerates the developer so thoroughly that it cannot be reused but the volume required is relatively small and the cost-per-sheet is fairly low. Tank development requires a much larger volume of solution and one-shot use of the developer would be prohibitively expensive. Tank developers, therefore, are almost always replenished after use and are protected from oxidation during storage by "floating lids" which do, literally, float on the surface of the solution.

Tank agitation is intermittent and must be carefully done to avoid problems of streaking and uneven development. Hand agitation is usually accomplished by lifting the film hangers out of solution several times, and tipping them in alternate directions as they drain briefly. This is done for about 5 seconds every minute during the development interval. Some older commercial installations agitated the various solutions by introducing bursts of inert gas, frequently nitrogen, through perforated pipes laid in the bottom of each tank. Most of these *nitrogen burst* systems have now been replaced by complex automatic processing machines. For amateur work, tank processing is probably more trouble and expense than it's worth. Tray processing is at least as fast and cheaper and will produce negatives of excellent quality when it is done competently. It will take practice but you can learn to do it.

Tray processing requires constant agitation because the films are stacked up in the tray and the solutions can't work on them until they're separated. Using spoiled film and plain water in the tray, practice the agitation technique in normal room light, then try it in the dark until you feel confident. You'll soon work out ways of handling the sheets so they don't cut each other with their sharp corners and so you don't gash them with your fingernails. When you've reached that point you can work with real pictures.

Since tray processing is done in total darkness, you must set up the three main solutions—developer, short-stop, and hypo—and adjust their temperatures, before you turn out the lights to unload the film. Set the interval timer for the proper developing time, too, so you can start it quickly as soon as the film is in the developer. Arrange the trays from left to right (developer, stop, hypo), and be sure you can locate them accurately when the lights go off. You may find it convenient to turn the stop bath tray at right angles to the others so you can identify it, as the middle tray, by touch. When you're set up and oriented, dry your hands, stack your film holders where you can get at them, and be sure the table surface, where you'll be handling the film, is clean and dry. Turn out the lights.

Remove the film sheets from the holders, one by one, and stack them carefully emulsion up on the table surface. Don't remove the holder slides completely as you do this, just pull them out about halfway. (Not all slides are interchangeable and they may get mixed up if you remove them from their holders.) Then pick up the stack of films, touching the emulsion sides as lightly and as little as possible, and fan them out in your left hand like a hand of cards. Count the corners to be sure you have them all and that they are not stuck together. With your right hand, locate the developer tray; then, as quickly as possible, take the films with your right hand, one at a time, and place them flat, emulsion up, on the surface of the developer solution and gently push them under. Your right hand will get wet, of course, but if you work quickly and avoid heavy or prolonged pressure on the emulsion, the films will not be damaged.

As soon as the last film is in the developer, start the timer with your dry left hand, and immediately get both hands into the developer to begin the agitation. Speed is important here; if the films are allowed to lie in a pile in the developer for more than just a few seconds they will begin to stick together as the gelatin softens and swells. Using just the balls of your fingertips, herd the films into a loose stack in one corner of the tray, lifting them individually to free them if they seem to be sticking. As soon as this has been accomplished, begin the agitation routine. Lift the edge of the stack

Figure 8.5

a. Holding the films lightly like a hand of cards, count the corners to be sure you have them all and that they are separate.

b. Keep one hand dry. Insert the first film into the developer solution and pat it down to be sure it is completely immersed.

c. Place the other sheets, one at a time, on the surface of the developer and pat each one down to wet it thoroughly before adding the next.

d. Herd the sheets into one corner of the tray, gently, then . . .

e. . . . commence the agitation by sliding the bottom sheet out from under the stack and laying it, carefully, flat on the surface of the solution.

f. Pat it down and extract the next sheet from the bottom of the stack. Continue this sequence throughout the development time.

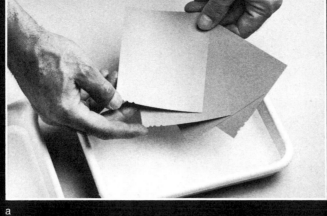

a

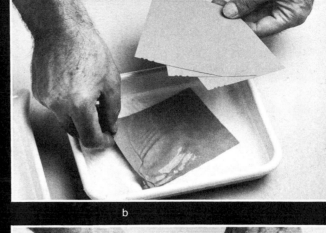

b

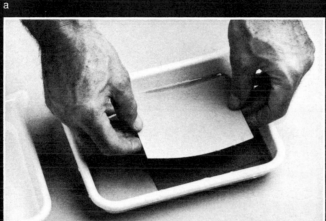

c

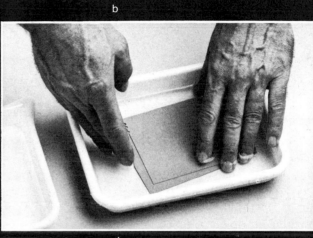

d

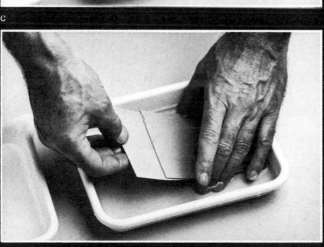

e

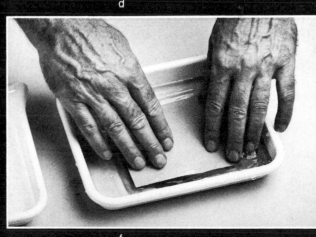

f

off the tray bottom far enough so that you can slip your fingers underneath, and slide the bottom film out from under the stack. Lift it out of solution, drop the stack, and place the film flat on the surface and pat it down lightly. Repeat this operation, gently and deliberately, throughout the developing interval.

To avoid uneven development, turn the entire stack around in the tray from time to time and vary your hand positions so the warmth of your fingers will not cause local patterns of overdevelopment. Don't try to slide the films back together if the stack floats apart. Re-build it, film by film, and don't touch the film surfaces with your fingernails. Support the sheets on your fingers, don't lift them by pinching a corner. The wet gelatin is quite soft and very susceptible to cuts, scratches, and finger pressure.

Watch the timer (it should have luminous hands and numbers) and prepare to remove the films to the stop bath so as to complete the transfer just as the time is up. In the stop bath continue the agitation procedure through three or four cycles, then transfer the sheets to the hypo bath. Agitate the sheets in the hypo for several cycles, then let them lie quietly and rinse and dry your hands. Turn on the lights and inspect the films to see if they have cleared. If so, give them another minute or two in the fix, with agitation, before removing them. If they are not clear, time them and leave them

in the hypo for twice their clearing time, whatever it is, with periodic agitation.

When fully fixed, the films should be rinsed briefly in a tray of gently running water, adjusted to approximately the temperature of the processing chemicals, then placed in the clearing bath. Agitate constantly for the recommended time, then transfer to a large tray of slowly running water or a tank-type film washer. A tray siphon or print siphon is a handy washing device which will provide simultaneous fresh water flow and drain while maintaining a constant water level in the tray. Adjust the water flow so the films move slowly and separate them by hand from time to time to insure good water circulation around them.

The washed films should be treated in a wetting solution, using the same precautions that apply to roll-films. Soak them for about a minute in the solution, then pick them out individually. Attach a film clip to one corner of each and hang them up to dry in a dustfree place. If you have not used a wetting solution, or if your wetting solution was mixed with very hard water, you should wipe the films, especially their backs, with a damp, folded piece of chamois skin. Gently!

Store the dry negatives in individual envelopes or use the punched storage sheets which fit standard notebooks.

Synopsis **Sheet Film Developing Process Steps**

Total darkness

1. Developer: Kodak HC-110, dilution *B*, 20°C (68°F). Use no less than 4 ounces of solution for each 4″ × 5″ sheet of film, a minimum of 8 ounces total. Agitate continuously. Discard after use. Developing time as recommended. Other developers may be used; follow the instructions supplied.
2. Short-stop: 1% acetic acid, as for printing, 20°C (68°F). Agitate continuously for about 30 seconds. Discard after use.

3. Fixing bath: Rapid fix, prepare as recommended for films, or use Kodak F-6 solution at regular strength, 20°C (68°F) for twice the clearing time. Agitate at intervals. Save after use. Discard when clearing time reaches about 5 minutes.
4. Water rinse: 16°C to 24°C (65°F to 75°F) for 30 seconds or more with continuous agitation. Discard.

5. Hypo-clearing bath: About 21°C (70°F), dilution, time, and agitation as recommended. Save if desired. Discard when hypo is discarded (unless the manufacturer gives other instructions).
6. Wash: Running water, with occasional agitation, at about 21°C (70°F), for time as specified on hypo-clearing bath package. If hypo-clearing bath is not used, wash must be for at least 30 minutes.

7. Wetting agent: Photoflo solution at about 21°C (70°F), prepared according to package instructions. Soak for about a minute. Distilled water may be advisable if tap water is "hard."
8. Dry: Suspend each film sheet by one corner using film clips or wooden spring clothespins. Hang in a dust-free place or in a film drying cabinet, if available.
9. Keep the dry negatives in negative envelopes for protection from dust and fingerprints.

Figure 8.6

a. The movements of the view camera lens and back are easy to describe but their effects on the image are not so simple. In general, movements of the back affect perspective primarily, and movements of the lens affect depth of field by displacing the plane of focus; but these adjustments interact to a considerable extent. It is usually safest to move the back first. Avoid extreme swings and tilts of the lens, or image sharpness will suffer. Your best guide to using the view camera adjustments is simply to watch the effect of the movements on the image and don't use any more drastic adjustment than is absolutely necessary to accomplish your desired result. Here is a view camera in its neutral position.

b. Both standards can be "swung" in either direction, together or separately.

c. The standards can also be "tilted" forward or backward. Tilts and swings of the front standard are risky because they move the image circle away from the film plane. Back swings and tilts alone are much safer.

d. Displacing the standards laterally, while keeping them parallel, is called shifting. Here the back is shifted left and the front is shifted right, effectively displacing the film off-center in the image circle. You must have a lens of wide coverage and fine quality to produce a useful image with a shift like this.

e. The back and lensboard can be raised or lowered. These are shift adjustments, but the vertical movements of the lensboard are referred to as the rising (or sometimes falling) front. Again, in using any of the adjustments, be careful not to let the film get too far off the lens axis or you'll be disappointed by the image quality.

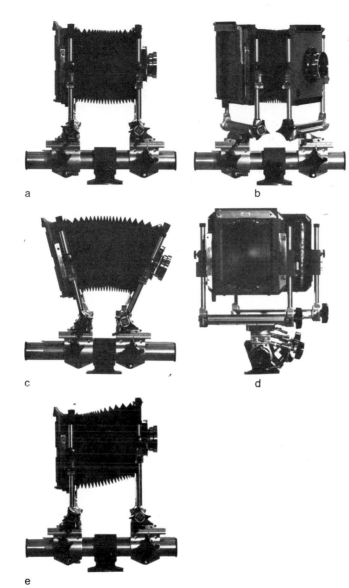

a

b

c

d

e

View Camera Adjustments

An ordinary camera sees objects in perspective just as the eye does. It will record the sharp convergence of railroad tracks receding into the distance and will picture tall buildings as tapering into the sky. In pictures of this kind the perspective effect may be distracting or the depth of field of the lens may be inadequate to record the subject area sharply because the subject cuts through it at an angle rather than lying parallel.

A view camera has adjustments designed to help solve these problems. They are called the shifts and swings and refer to movements of the front and rear standards of the camera which make it possible to change the normal alignment of the lens and film. The *shifts* are movements of either standard, either vertically or laterally, which keep the lensboard and film plane parallel to each other but decenter the lens with respect to the film. The vertical shift of the lensboard is referred to specifically as the *rising front*. The *swings* allow the standards to pivot around either a vertical or horizontal axis. The rotation around the horizontal axis is often referred to as a *tilt*.

The shifts are often used to reduce or eliminate the normal effect of converging lines in perspective and are particularly effective in architectural photography. The shift adjustments are also valuable for making slight changes in composition of the groundglass image, eliminating the need to move the entire camera. Both of these uses are possible because the image formed by the lens at the film plane covers a much larger area than the film itself, and the film can be positioned to record any portion of it.

The perspective convergence of a building, for example, is caused by the fact that the building top is farther from the camera than the building foundation is, and since distant objects are normally seen as smaller than close objects, the top must appear smaller than the bottom. But this is true only when the camera is tilted back to look up at the building. If the camera is pointed horizontally so as to look perpendicularly at the building front, there is no convergence, but the top of the building is out of the picture.

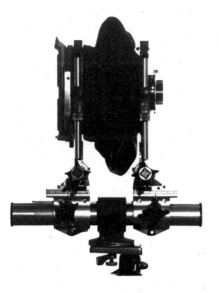

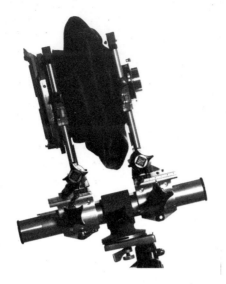

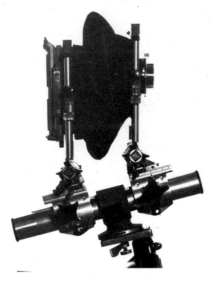

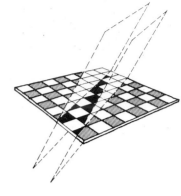

Figure 8.8
Chess game

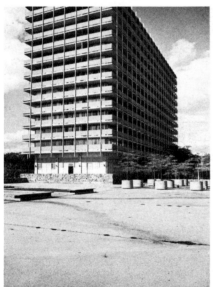

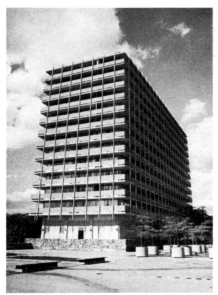

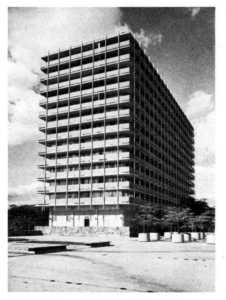

Figure 8.7
a. When photographing a tall building you may not be able to include the top when the camera is level.

b. Pointing the camera up will allow you to include the whole building but the verticals are converged in sharp perspective.

c. If the camera back and front standards are tilted forward until they lie in a vertical plane, the building can be included entirely without perspective convergence of the verticals. You can accomplish this same result by leaving the camera bed-tube level and using the rising front adjustment to raise the lens above its normal position.

Figure 8.9
a. No swings used, lens wide open; depth of field is very shallow.

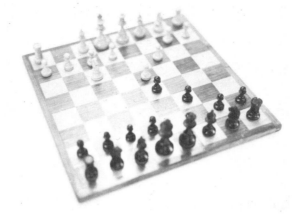

b. Back swung to coincide with image plane in space; lens stopped down only one stop for adequate depth of field but image is strongly foreshortened.

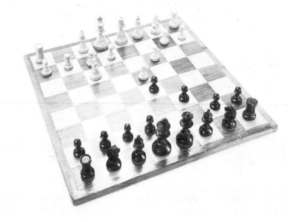

c. The original perspective can be closely approximated by "swinging" the enlarger easel and negative carrier.

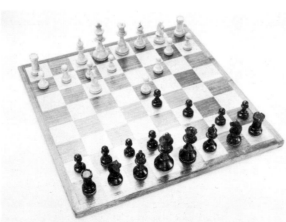

To maintain the parallelism of the verticals, but include the top of the building too, the camera is adjusted to face the building squarely, specifically so the *camera back is parallel to the subject plane,* which insures against perspective convergence, and the rising front is raised until the building is composed on the groundglass as desired. As long as the camera back and subject plane are parallel, the subject will be devoid of perspective convergence. If the lensboard is also parallel, the depth of field will cover the subject plane most efficiently. If the reduction of perspective effects is not of primary importance, it is sometimes possible to use the swings to make better-than-normal use of the available depth of field. For example, suppose you are trying to photograph a chess game from a 45° angle and at fairly close range. You will probably find that with the camera in its neutral position the depth of field will be inadequate to cover the width of the board even with the lens stopped all the way down.

Now consider the position of the board image in space near the film plane. The near point of the board must be imaged behind the film and above film center, while the far point of the board must be imaged in front of the film and below center.

By swinging the film plane to coincide with the plane of the image in space, you can get the entire board into sharp focus without having to stop down at all, but the effect of perspective distortion (convergence) will be emphasized.

If the perspective must remain nearly normal, it may be possible to tilt the lensboard forward far enough to include the subject in the depth of field without adjusting the back, but the image will then be formed on the very edge of the lens field, and sharpness and illumination of the image may not be adequate. The best procedure is to swing the back first to coincide with the image in space, accepting the distortion, then adjust the lensboard for best sharpness by observing the groundglass image with a magnifier. Then stop the lens down a little farther than seems to be required for excellent depth of field coverage. The resulting negative will be sharp, and the distortion can be compensated for (restituted) by adjusting the en-

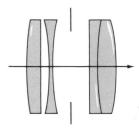
Figure 8.10
Tessar lens

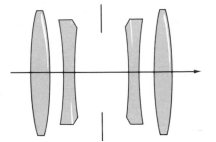
Figure 8.11
Goerz Artar

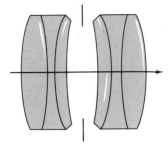
Figure 8.12
Goerz Dagor

There is more than one way to adjust the camera

Adjust the back first, then the lensboard

View camera lenses should be well corrected for a wide field

Some fine old lenses were convertible

larger during printing. The final print will be both un-distorted and sharp if all is done well—a clear case of "having your cake and eating it too."

Most efficient use of the lens field in this application will be achieved when the respective planes of the subject, camera back, and camera lensboard, suitably extended, meet at a common point in space.

In practice it will be found that there is more than one way to adjust the camera to achieve the various results described above. For example, it is possible to correct for building convergence by tilting the camera up to cover the subject first, then tilting the back and lensboard forward until they are parallel to the subject plane. The ultimate effect is identical to that attained with the rising front; that is, the lens and back are parallel to the subject but vertically decentered. Either method of adjustment is effective and proper. They are not different adjustments, merely different methods of arriving at the same end.

In setting up the view camera to deal with problems which are not as obvious in their solution as those above, much fumbling with the controls can be avoided if you will remember to *adjust the camera back first, then adjust the lensboard.* All significant control of perspective is accomplished with the back shifts and swings, as are some gross adjustments of the depth of field coverage. Save the lens shifts and swings for relatively minor refinements of the image.

It should be obvious that the lens used for these adjustments should be capable of forming an extensive image area on an essentially flat plane in space, and that the sharpness of the image should be adequate out to its edges. The lens, in short, should be very well corrected for the various aberrations, and should, in addition, cover a fairly wide field even at maximum aperture.

Although good lenses of four-element Tessar-type construction (fig. 8.10) are suitable for view camera use in normal focal lengths and at moderate apertures, they do not, as a rule, provide sufficient coverage to permit more than modest adjustments without some loss of image quality. Lenses of more nearly symmetrical construction (fig. 8.11) are probably preferable, since they are likely to provide better coverage and are more likely to maintain their correction at close subject distances.

Some fine lenses, such as the old Protars, the original Schneider Symmars and Goerz Dagors (fig. 8.12), combine good correction, wide coverage, and moderate speed with the added virtue of being *convertible;* that is, one component can be used alone as a long focal length lens of fairly good quality, satisfactory for many purposes when stopped down. This feature has been eliminated from most of the newest designs to permit better correction and enhanced performance for the complete lens.

The swings possible with wide-angle lenses will be limited by the inflexibility of the compressed camera bellows as well as the restricted image area available. Some cameras provide recessed lensboards or special bellows units for use with short lenses to allow for some bellows movement, but the swings and shifts should be used with caution with wide-angle lenses. Even in "neutral," the lens field is likely to be only slightly larger than the film area, and deterioration of image quality near the edges of the field will be rapid and extreme. For the same reason long lenses of telephoto construction will permit only moderate swings, since their image circle is deliberately restricted. Long lenses of conventional construction will permit extreme adjustment without much loss of quality.

The Exposure-Development Relationship

One of the oldest adages in photography is the classic "expose for the shadows and develop for the highlights." This means, of course, that sufficient exposure must be given the film so it can record the darkest portions of the subject; then the development must proceed no further than is required to produce useful negative density corresponding to the brightest areas of the subject. This relationship between exposure and development, and the corresponding relationship between negative density and contrast, is an extremely important one. If you hope to control the medium of photography in any sort of predictable way, you must understand these relationships thoroughly.

An excellent way to investigate the effects of exposure and development is to make a series of negatives which illustrate their possible combinations. Nine negatives will demonstrate the possibilities adequately and the test is easily done. Find a stationary subject of normal contrast in an adequate light condition, and focus and compose it satisfactorily. The camera should be fixed in position so it will not move significantly during the test; nothing should change except the camera exposures. Meter the subject carefully in your usual manner and select a moderately small aperture (for good depth of field) and the appropriate shutter speed.

If you are using sheet film, set the camera controls for normal exposure and expose three films, identically.

Then set the camera controls to overexpose the subject by two stops and expose three films. Finally, set the camera to underexpose the subject by two stops and expose three more films. Be sure to mark the holders so you can identify the individual films during processing.

If you are using rollfilm, the procedure must be done differently. Either use three separate rolls of film, exposing one-third of the frames on each normally, overexposing one-third of the frames by two stops and underexposing one-third of the frames on each by two stops; or vary the exposures on a single roll in a repetitive sequence (under, normal, over; under, normal, over; under, normal, over; etc.) until the roll has been used up.

In the darkroom, set up a process line of fresh chemicals for film developing and adjust them to the proper temperature. If you are using sheet film, take one normally-exposed sheet, one overexposed sheet, and one underexposed sheet and develop them together for *half* your normal developing time. Similarly, develop the next set of three sheets in fresh or replenished developer for your normal time. Finally develop the remaining set of three in fresh solution for twice your normal developing time. Fix and wash the films as usual and hang them up to dry.

If you have used three rolls of film for the test, each roll will contain some underexposures, some normal exposures, and some overexposures. Develop one roll for half normal time, one for normal time, and one for twice normal time, using fresh or replenished volumes of developer for each roll. If you have made all the exposures on a single roll of film, develop it in an open tank in the dark. At half the normal developing time, remove the roll from the developer and snip off about one-third of its length with scissors. Put the cut-off piece of film into the short-stop bath and return the rest of the roll to developer. At the end of the normal developing time, snip off another third of the roll and put it into the short-stop with the first piece. Continue developing the remaining third of the roll until you have doubled the normal developing time. Add the last film section to the short-stop, then transfer all three pieces to the hypo. Agitate them briefly (wash your hands) and turn on the lights.

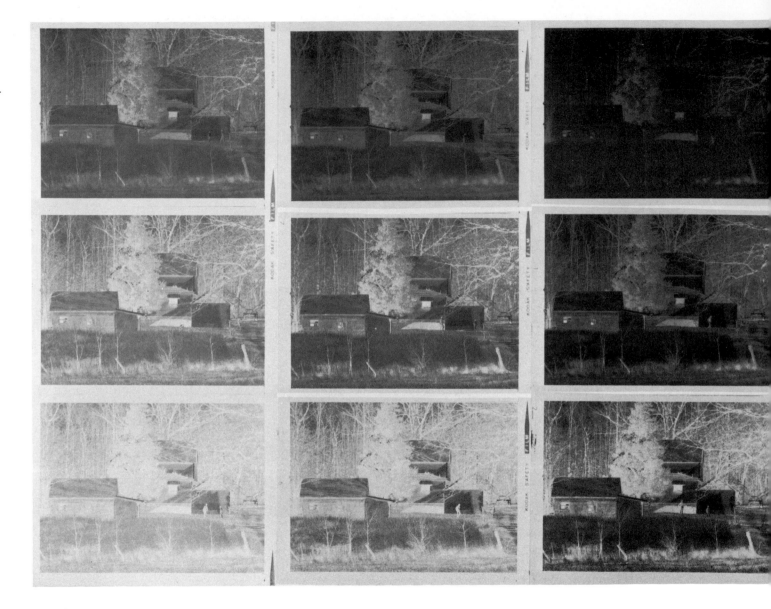

Figure 8.13
The nine-negative array. Overexposed negatives in top horizontal row; normal exposures in middle horizontal row; underexposures in bottom horizontal row. Underdeveloped negatives in left-hand vertical row; normal development in center vertical row; overdevelopment in right-hand vertical row.

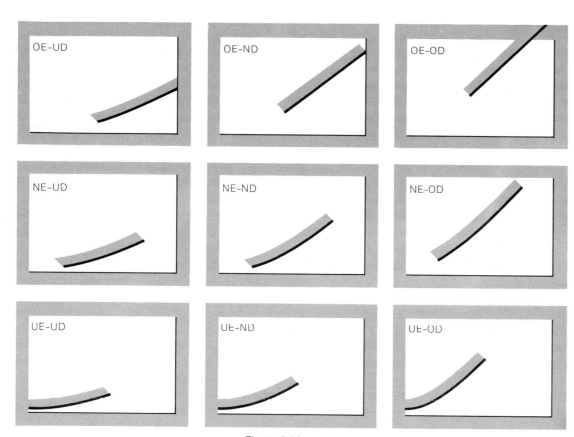

Figure 8.14
Exposure-development diagrams

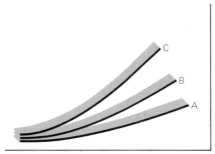

Figure 8.15
Three curve film family

If you have carried out the test properly, you should now have nine different negatives. Arrange them on a light box in a three-by-three array with the normal negative in the center, as shown in figure 8.13. With a little study, you should be able to identify the significant characteristics of each. With more experience you will be able to look at any negative and determine whether it is "normal" and, if not, whether exposure or development was at fault. In general, the negative shadow areas will provide clues to film exposure—thin shadows indicate underexposure; dense shadows indicate overexposure. Contrast is usually a reliable clue to film development—low contrast probably indicates underdevelopment; high contrast probably indicates overdevelopment. Exposure and development interact to some extent and not all films will react in the same way, but these tendencies are usually dependable, at least for preliminary analysis.

If you are unfamiliar with "bad" negatives, try printing this group of nine. In all probability you'll discover that, while most of them are printable, the normal negative will print easily and yield a fine image with the least fuss. You may get good results from some of the others, too, but you'll probably have to change paper grades and work at it a little. It's very likely that the two extreme examples, underexposed/underdeveloped and overexposed/overdeveloped, will be unprintable. Take a good look at them and try not to make any more like them *ever!*

These exposure-development relationships can be displayed graphically in *characteristic curve* diagrams as illustrated in figure 8.15. Here the horizontal axis of the graph represents values of exposure, such as might be caused by variations in subject illumination or subject value or by changes in either exposure time or aperture setting. On this axis, exposure values increase from left to right. The vertical axis of the graph indicates values of negative density, which result from film exposure and development and increase from bottom to top. Each curve stands for a specific developing time.

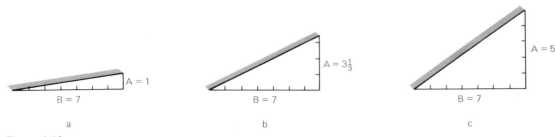

Figure 8.16

a. Normal subject (7 stops), gentle slope (underdevelopment), flat negative (1).

b. Normal subject (7 stops), moderate slope (normal development), normal negative (3⅓).

c. Normal subject (7 stops), steep slope (overdevelopment), contrasty negative (5).

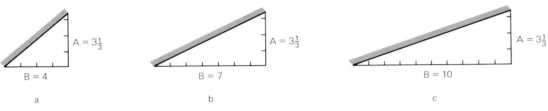

Figure 8.17

a. Flat subject (4 stops), steep slope (overdevelopment), normal negative (3⅓).

b. Normal subject (7 stops), moderate slope (normal development), normal negative (3⅓).

c. Contrasty subject (10 stops), gentle slope (underdevelopment), normal negative (3⅓).

Development can be varied purposely for contrast control

Curves for three development conditions are shown. Here curve *A* represents underdevelopment, *B* is normal, and *C* represents overdevelopment. Notice that the slope of the curves changes with development—less-than-normal development produces a gentle slope; overdevelopment results in a steep slope; and normal development produces a moderate slope. (See the curves that correspond to the nine test negatives in fig. 8.14.)

The actual meaning of the curves is easier to explain if they are drawn as straight lines, converting the graphs to simple triangles. In figure 8.16 this has been done, using a base line *B* seven stops long in each case. Seven stops has been chosen as the length of the exposure axes because it represents the range of subject luminance which is considered to be "normal." In other words, the brightest textured highlight area of a normal subject is seven stops lighter than the darkest useful shadow value of the subject.

Now it is apparent that if *B* is held at constant length and the slope of the curve is changed, the negative contrast, line *A*, must also change. A steep curve slope, corresponding to longer-than-normal development, produces extended negative contrast, while a gently sloping curve results in a negative of short density range. Similarly, if *A* is constant and the curve gradient changes, *B* must vary.

From here it is only a short step to a graphic demonstration of how development can be varied purposely to compensate for abnormal subject contrast. Assuming that a negative range of 3⅓ stops is desirable for printing on normal paper, figure 8.17 illustrates several different subject contrasts, translated into "normal" negatives by different development curve slopes or gradients.

Interpreting the Technical Literature

In technical literature the degree of development, or curve gradient (G), is indicated by the number found by dividing density range (DR) by subject brightness (more correctly, luminance) range (SBR).

When the film curve is actually a straight line, as it has been represented in the demonstration triangles, the number thus found is called the *gamma* number (fig. 8.18). Gamma is not used much anymore, however, because modern films' curves are *really* curves and you can't draw a respectable triangle with one curved side. To deal with this problem we sometimes select two points on the film curve which represent useful limits and simply connect them with a straight line to

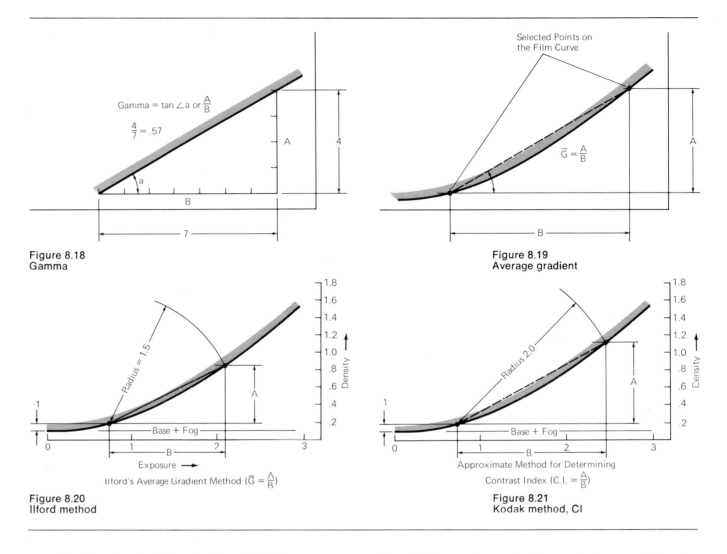

Figure 8.18
Gamma

Figure 8.19
Average gradient

Figure 8.20
Ilford method

Figure 8.21
Kodak method, CI

complete the standard triangle (fig. 8.19). The gamma number computed this way is called an *average gradient* number. Most manufacturers publish film developing information based on some form of average gradient measurement. Eastman Kodak calls their method *contrast index;* Ilford, using a more direct approach, describes theirs simply as average gradient and lets it go at that.

Ilford's procedure (fig. 8.20) involves locating a point on the film curve which represents negative den-

sity of 0.1 over base-plus-fog or background density; then, using that point as a center, drawing an arc of 1.5 radius to intersect the curve and establish the second point. Connecting the points establishes the average gradient and completes the triangle. Kodak's contrast index procedure is much more complicated than this, but a close approximation can be obtained by following the Ilford method, using a radius of 2.0 rather than 1.5 (fig. 8.21).

Notice the calibration numbers on these two graphs. They are common logarithms (logs to the base 10) of the actual values of subject luminance and negative opacity. Actually, you don't have to know very much about logarithms to use them effectively in photography. The most important information about them is that the $\log_{10}$ equivalent of the number 2 is 0.3. Therefore, 0.3 is equivalent to 1 stop and 0.1 equals ⅓ stop. The number of stops equivalent to any range of luminances or densities can be found by dividing the log range by 0.3; thus, Ilford's 0.1 over base-plus-fog represents a negative density ⅓ stop greater than the film background density, and the arc radius of 1.5 is equivalent to 5 stops. Similarly, Kodak's arc radius of 2.0 defines a section of the film curve which is 6⅔ stops long.

Table 8.1 is a brief list of regular numbers, compared with their $\log_{10}$ equivalents and the intervals in stops between them. Actually, the logs are not exact equivalents of most of the numbers given—the $\log_{10}$ of 8, for example, is closer to .90309 than it is to .9—but these are near enough for our purposes. The log values for 1 and 1000 are correct, and you may be interested to know also that the log of 10 is 1.0, $\log_{10} 100 = 2.0$, and $\log_{10} 1,000,000 = 6.0$ exactly.

Table 8.1
Comparison of numbers with their log equivalents and intervals in stops

Numbers in geometric sequence	$\log_{10}$ equivalents	Stops
1	0.0	1
2	.3	2
4	.6	3
8	.9	4
16	1.2	5
32	1.5	6
64	1.8	7
125	2.1	8
250	2.4	9
500	2.7	10
1000	3.0	

One final bit of information will help you interpret the published film curves—*positive* logs refer to numbers greater than 1; *negative* logs indicate decimal fractions less than 1. Thus, 2.0 is the log of 100 but minus 2.0 (frequently written as −2.0 or $\overline{2}.0$) is the log of 1/100 or .01. You will frequently see negative log numbers on the exposure axis of film curve graphs because the unit of exposure used in calibration (meter-candle-second) is too large for most film materials and they must be exposed to fractions of the basic unit (fig. 8.22). Most printing papers, on the other hand, are slow enough so the basic exposure unit is not sufficient to affect them at all. Their characteristic curves are calibrated in positive logs indicating multiples of the basic exposure unit (fig. 8.23).

Now let's review briefly. The film characteristic curves display the relationship between values of exposure, film development, and the resulting negative densities. These three variables, graphed simply, form a right triangle (fig. 8.24)—the values of the subject luminance range (from lightest highlight to deepest shadow) fall along the base of the triangle; increments of negative density (from the clearest negative shadow area to the densest highlight) lie along the triangle altitude; and the triangle hypotenuse slope represents the degree of development which the exposed film must receive to produce the desired negative density range or contrast. Development contrast can be identified by a number which compares the negative DR with the subject luminance range, in either stops or $\log_{10}$ numbers. For example, if a negative has only half as much range (contrast) as the subject had, its development contrast number is 0.5. Under some test conditions this number is called gamma, but more usually it will be referred to as contrast index (CI) or, sometimes average gradient ($\overline{G}$):

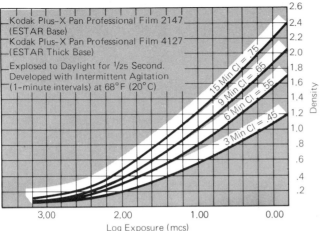

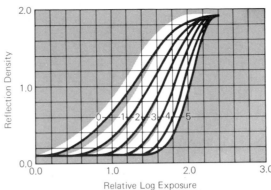

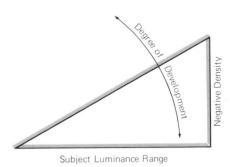

Figure 8.22 ▲
The sensitometric curves and data in the publication from which these curves were taken (Kodak publication no. F-5) represent current product under normal conditions of exposure and processing. They are averages of a number of production coatings and, therefore, do not

apply directly to a particular box or roll of film. They do not represent standards or specifications which must be met by Eastman Kodak Company. Kodak reserves the right to change and improve product characteristics at any time. (Reproduced with permission of the Eastman Kodak Company.)

Figure 8.23 ▲
Sensitometric curves which represent approximately the characteristics of various grades of Kodak papers with a glossy, ferrotyped surface. Reproduced with permission of the Eastman Kodak Company.

Figure 8.24
Exposure-development triangle

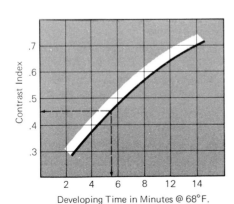

Figure 8.25
CI chart with development time

Using Average Gradient Information

In practice, you know (or can estimate—see the appendix, page 310) the negative density range which prints best for you on normal paper and you can measure the subject range with your meter. Divide the negative DR (it will be given in log numbers) by the subject range (convert stops to log numbers by multiplying stops by 0.3) and you will get the required average gradient number. For this illustration, you can consider this number to be a contrast index and, by consulting the film manufacturer's published charts, you can find the developing time required to translate the latent film image into a negative of normal contrast. Let's consider a typical example.

Suppose you discover that your favorite paper and your printing conditions require a negative DR of about 1.1. Suppose also that your measurement of the luminance range (SBR) of your subject turns out to be 8 stops. Convert 8 stops to a log by multiplying by 0.3,

which gives you a subject range of 2.4. Divide 1.1 by 2.4 to get .458, call it .46; this is your contrast index. Consult a contrast index/developing time chart (fig. 8.25) to find the appropriate developing time for your subject, in this case 5½ minutes. Be sure to observe the temperature and agitation instructions accompanying the CI chart; proper negative contrast depends upon close control of all development variables.

By definition, CI can only be measured between the points on the film curve defined by its intersections with the 2.0 radius line (fig. 8.21). If your subject tones occupy more or less of the film curve length than this, the average gradient can be determined but it is not contrast index. In spite of this fact, you can use the procedure above in most situations without much danger of error. There will be some discrepancy between your average gradients and published CIs with films which have strongly curved curves (like Tri-X) and there will be greatest chance for error with subjects of extreme contrast, either high or low, but you're not likely to get into serious trouble even in these cases.

Exposure-development systems are simple with sheet film

But not much help with rollfilm

Incident meters measure illumination accurately

Base the exposure on the low light reading

And use the appropriate film speed setting

To make this contrast control system workable it is only necessary to devise some method of determining subject range with reasonable accuracy. Of course, there must be some provision made for developing the exposed films individually if the subject contrasts are not all the same. This last requirement is no problem with sheet film which can be developed, sheet by sheet, in a tray, but rollfilm exposures are a different matter. The best procedure is to commit a whole roll of film to subjects of similar contrast—relatively easy to do if you have several camera bodies or accessory backs for your camera, but impractical, generally, for long rolls of 35mm film. If this isn't feasible, be sure that none of the frames on the roll are underexposed and develop for either the average contrast or specifically for the most important pictures on the roll, letting the others do what they will. Probably all, or most of the negatives will be printable but some of them will probably require paper of other than normal contrast.

You can determine subject contrast in several ways. The most accurate method requires the use of a spotmeter to read the luminance values of the subject tonal extremes. You can try reading the extremes with an ordinary reflectance meter, too, but the highlight and shadow accents will be difficult to measure and you'll have to estimate their actual values.

With whatever reflectance measurement of the subject range, it is usually safe to assume that an average of the two extreme luminance values can be used as the basis for determining the camera settings. Alternatively, you can take the actual exposure reading from a gray card placed in an average light condition in the subject. If the subject is very contrasty, both of these procedures may lead to underexposure, however, and it's wise to increase the indicated exposure by a stop or two when the subject luminance range exceeds 8 or 9 stops.

An Incident Metering System

Another method which can produce good, consistent results is based on the use of an incident meter. Although incident readings don't include any information about the subject color or value, they do give accurate measurements of illumination. Also, an incident reading, like a gray card reading, provides camera settings which are appropriate for a subject of any color or value in the measured light condition.

The procedure makes two assumptions, which sound rather arbitrary but are usually valid—first, that the average subject range is 7 stops; second, that 5 stops of the 7 typically result from local variations of subject color or value and that the other 2 stops are due to local variations in illumination resulting from shade or shadows or from glaring surfaces. Presumably, then, a typical subject in a totally uniform light condition, without either surface glare or shaded areas, will have a maximum range not exceeding 5 stops. If a portion of the subject is shaded and a portion left in full light, the total subject range is the basic 5 stops *plus* the illumination contrast, whatever it is. Since the incident meter is ideally suited to measuring lighting contrast, the rest is easy; simply meter the illumination in the shadows, then measure the brightest illumination level in the subject space and count the stops between these extremes. Add 5 stops and you have an approximation of the subject luminance range.

For example, suppose you measure the subject shadow illumination with your Luna-Pro (in incident mode) and get a reading of 10. Then, measuring the highlight illumination gives you 14. The illumination range is 4 stops; add the basic 5 for the subject values and you get 9, the subject luminance range (SBR).

You'll get reasonably good results most of the time with this method, if you base your camera settings on the incident reading of the shadow areas. For greater precision, however, it's necessary to adjust the exposures somewhat for subjects of very long range or very short range because these subjects require abnormal development. Less-than-normal development will

Figure 8.26
The illumination difference between the sunlit and shaded areas of the table top is 3 stops. The gray scales each represent a 5-stop range. The total range of this subject area is, therefore, at least 8 stops. If holding detail under the table is important, the range must be considered to be even greater.

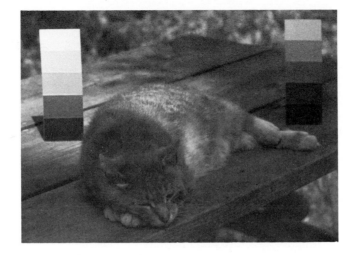

Figure 8.27
Subjects of abnormal contrast (luminance range) require compensating development to produce normal contrast negatives. This, in turn, requires exposure compensation if the negatives are to maintain normal density. This chart will provide appropriate film speed settings for subjects of varying contrast and will be effective for all general purpose films developed in the usually available developers. For use, calibrate the chart by labeling the "ASA normal" line with the official film speed of the film you plan to use. Then mark the vertical lines at left with speeds of decreasing value and the lines at right with increasing values. For example, if you are using Plus-X film, mark the "ASA normal" line "125." The left-hand lines would then be labeled "100, 80, 64, 50, 40, and 32"; and the right-hand lines would be labeled "160, 200, and 250."

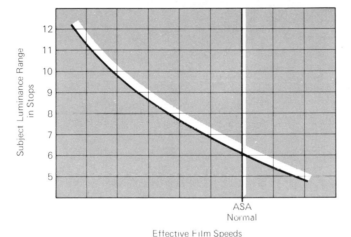

effectively reduce the film speed and greater-than-normal development will increase it. The ASA setting of the meter can be changed to compensate for this effect—by using a lower ASA number than normal (to overexpose) when the subject range is long and development is correspondingly reduced; by using a higher ASA number (to underexpose) when the subject is low in contrast and will require more-than-normal development. Although films and developers are not all alike, the chart shown as figure 8.27 suggests film

speed compensation which will be useful with most films under all but the most extreme conditions.

Using the chart information adds only one short step to the normal metering process. The meter ASA setting is adjusted *after* the subject range readings are made but *before* the camera settings are determined. Here is the procedure—with an incident meter read the subject shadow illumination; similarly read the highlight illumination. Subtract the low reading from the high one to get the illumination range in stops. Add this to 5 to find the subject luminance range (SBR). Consult the chart to find the appropriate ASA compensation and adjust the meter ASA setting. Reset the meter dial to the subject shadow reading and consult the meter scales for the camera settings. Take the picture and record the subject range so the film can be developed for an appropriate length of time.

Back in the darkroom, determine your desired negative density range and divide it by the subject range (both ranges must be in the same form, either stops or logs) to find the average gradient desired. Consult an appropriate contrast index/development chart to establish the proper time, and develop the film. With a little practice you'll find that this method gives good results and is more consistent than the usual, uncompensated procedures.

The Zone System

Over the years there have been numerous procedures proposed for the control of image quality by manipulations of film exposure and development. A very comprehensive system, and by far the best-known, is the Zone System which was originated by Ansel Adams and Fred Archer many years ago. It is a remarkably ingenious approach to image control and one which has been well publicized. Adams himself has explained it thoroughly in his various writings and numerous other authors have published their own versions. Today the Zone System is taught, more or less authentically, in a large number of schools and colleges and has become a photographic tradition.

The details of the usually recommended empirical testing and calibration procedures required to suit the Zone System principles to individual use are too well known and too extensive to justify further publication. Ansel Adams's book, *The Negative,* and the *New Zone System Manual* by White, Zakia, and Lorenz are the usual recommended references.

The Zone System is based on the principle of *previsualization,* which means that the photographer, before exposing his film, will analyze the subject tonality visually to determine which areas of dark and light he wishes to preserve with adequate detail and what effect of contrast he wants to achieve in the final print. In other words, he attempts to "see" the print in the subject before the negative is made. He then measures with a light meter the tones in the subject which he judges to be significant and determines from these meter readings both the proper exposure for the film and its subsequent development conditions, based on extensive previous testing and experience with these specific materials and processes. If all goes well, he produces a negative which will print easily to reproduce his previsualized image in tangible form.

The system gets its name from the fact that certain tones of gray in the subject have been labelled as Zones and numbered for easy identification and convenience in calculation. Zone V (Roman numerals are always used for Zone numbers) is identified as middle gray, for example, while a subject value 1 stop brighter than middle gray would be called Zone VI. Zone IV is 1 stop darker than Zone V; Zone III is 2 stops darker than Zone V.

Minor White's explanation of the Zone System limits the range from Zone I to Zone IX, inclusive, and defines the Zones approximately as follows.

Zone I	Maximum photographic paper black
Zone II	First printable separation of tone
Zone III	Very dark gray
Zone IV	Dark gray
Zone V	Middle gray
Zone VI	Light gray
Zone VII	Very light gray; textured white
Zone VIII	Untextured, but still toned white
Zone IX	Maximum photographic paper white

These definitions are descriptions of print values which will result from proper *translation* of subject Zones into print tones. The actual reflection density difference between these values on the print itself will not be mathematically uniform, nor will the nine zones represent a 9-stop range of print densities (print *reflection* densities can rarely exceed a total range of about 7 stops even under the best conditions). This is a source of some confusion in many descriptions of the Zone System.

Application of the Zone System principles, as they are usually explained, must follow extensive testing to determine the minimum film exposure required to produce the first useful printing density (used to determine the working film speed), the developing time required to produce a printable representation of the nine Zones, as previously described, and variations in development which will effectively *expand* or *contract* the density range of the negative to compensate for unusual subject luminance ranges. Expansion refers to greater-than-normal development; contraction means less-than-normal. A final field test is recommended to verify these experimental conclusions.

Careful metering is essential to the success of this system. In essence the exposure meter is used as a reflection densitometer to measure the luminance of subject areas individually. It is almost imperative, therefore, that a spotmeter be employed. No ordinary wide-field averaging meter can supply the accurate small-area readings which the system demands.

Meter scales are designed to deal with average readings. To use them with the Zone System it is convenient to modify them to display the Zones themselves as areas of graded gray. This can be done as indicated in figure 8.28. In this homemade scale, the pointer of the calculating dial, which is usually aligned with the

If we place the same subject light value opposite the Zone V mark (Zone System users call this "placing the value *in* Zone V"), we will get a middle gray area in the print. Likewise placing some subject tone in Zone VIII will tend to reproduce it in the print as an untextured white. Placing a reading in Zone III is the same as underexposing it by 2 stops, and this provides a convenient method of working with meters which are not equipped with Zone scales. Since the normal pointer on the meter scale is equivalent to Zone V, setting the pointer 1 stop higher than any given luminance reading will effectively place that subject value in Zone IV. Setting the meter pointer 3 stops above the reading places it in Zone II; setting it 2 stops below the reading will place it in Zone VII; and so forth.

If the subject contrast or luminance range is normal (by Zone System definition), placing some subject value in its proper Zone will automatically position all the other subject tones in their proper Zones, too. Under these conditions the recommended development is "normal." For abnormal conditions of subject contrast it is customary to identify the subject value which we want to render as a very dark gray and place it in Zone III on the meter dial. Then we measure the luminance of the area we wish to render as a textured white (Zone VII in the print) and see where that value falls on the meter scale. If the reading falls in Zone VIII it is too high so the range must be contracted by underdevelopment. In this case, since the error is one Zone, the development recommendation would be "normal, minus one" or "N − 1." If the high value had fallen in Zone VI, it would suggest that the range should be expanded by 1 stop and the proper development would be N+1. Other high-value reference Zones are sometimes suggested.

One of the shortcomings of the Zone System, as it is usually explained, is its failure to compensate for expansion or contraction (extended or shortened) development by appropriate changes in the effective film speed. This is probably the reason why many Zone System users place their detailed blacks in Zone III or even Zone IV, on occasion. Experience has taught

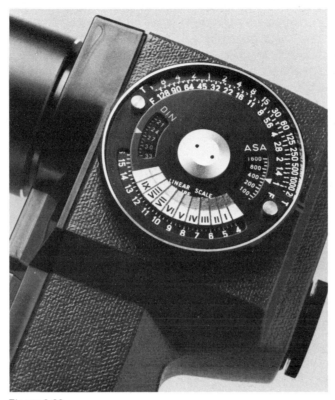

Figure 8.28
A homemade Zone Scale applied to a spotmeter dial.

Placing values in their Zones

Other values fall

Expansion and contraction development affect film speed

meter light reading, is replaced by the Zone V area and the other Zones are arranged appropriately on either side of it. The placement of the Zone V gray at the normal pointer position acknowledges the fact that an average gray in the subject, properly exposed and developed, will produce a medium density in the negative which can then be made to print as a middle gray.

The other Zones can be used similarly. For example, suppose we place some subject luminance reading opposite the Zone III mark on the meter dial. The resulting exposure recommendations will tend to produce an area of very dark gray (Zone III) in the print.

Ideally, each film-developer combination should be calibrated

Calibrate this chart for your own use

And plot your personal test results on this one

them that if they don't they'll get unprintably thin negatives when dealing with contrasty subject matter. It's a fact of photographic life that reduced development results in loss of effective film speed. Ignoring this loss will lead to underexposure and loss of shadow details (in Zone II at least, and Zone III in extreme cases). But, if the film speed is adjusted to match the development condition, the lower Zones can be adequately and predictably detailed under any subject condition.

Ideally the necessary exposure compensation should be computed for each film-developer combination used. But, since it does not vary greatly from one film type to another and since exact calculation requires the use of a densitometer (which is not available to most students), the charts in figures 8.29 and 8.30 are recommended for use with any film. Although they will not provide exact compensation, their use will improve the quality of negatives made of contrasty subjects and provide a more consistent minimum density than Zone System negatives often exhibit.

To calibrate the effective film speed chart for your own use, label the ASA line with the actual published speed of the film you use. The spaces to the left, then, should be labeled with lower speeds; higher speeds go to the right. Each single space is equivalent to one film speed number in the standard sequence (⅓ stop). Every third line is equivalent to a full stop in the sequence. For example, if you are using Plus-X film, label the ASA point with the number 125. The successive lines to the right will then be labelled 160, 200, 250, 320, and 400. To the left of the ASA point the numbers should read 100, 80, 64, 50, 40, 32, 25, 20, and 16.

The other chart, figure 8.30, is provided for your own calibration of developing time versus N-numbers. From your personal test results fill in the developing times required for the various expansions and contractions, and connect the points with a smooth curve. This will provide an accurate indication of the times required for fractional values of expansion and contraction.

To use these charts, proceed as you normally would to read the subject values with a meter, and place the shadow reading in Zone III. Then read Zone

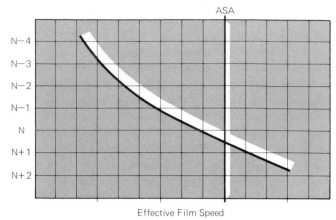

Effective Film Speed

Figure 8.29
N-numbers vs. effective film speed

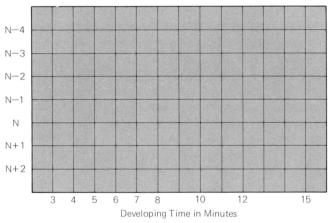

Developing Time in Minutes

Figure 8.30
N-numbers vs. development time

VII tones and see where they fall to determine the expansion or contraction required. When this has been determined consult the effective film speed chart (fig. 8.29) to find the appropriate film speed, set it into the meter (replace the shadow reading in Zone III if necessary), and compute the exposure settings. Make the picture using these settings (modified by such filter, bellows, and reciprocity factors as are appropriate) and mark the holder with the N-number for identification. Back in the darkroom, develop for the time indicated in figure 8.30. Practically speaking, this is not greatly different from normal procedure but it does require the extra step of film speed determination. This compensation will tend to assure adequately detailed shadows and will make Zone II a useful and reliable Zone under all conditions, eliminating any necessity for intuitive "fudging" in the placement of the low values. This procedure is based on the Zone III and VII readings only. If you read other Zones for the determination of exposure and development data, you will not get entirely reliable information from the charts as they are given here.

If you have not completed a personal test of your materials, you will have to rely on the manufacturers' data. The published charts do not include any Zone System information as such, but you can derive developing times for the various subject range conditions from contrast index data. These data are not universal, however; you must use the film and developer specified and follow the chart instructions for temperature and agitation.

CI Charts

First take luminance readings of subject Zones III and VII and count the number of stops between them. If the total is less than the normal 4 stops, subtract it from 4 to get a *plus* N-number. For example, Zone III reads 10 on your Luna-Pro meter and Zone VII reads 13, a difference of 3 stops. Subtract 3 from 4 to get I. The N-number is N+1.

Figure 8.31
This chart relates subject contrast (stated either as luminance range in stops or indicated by Zone System "N-number") to contrast index or average gradient. It assumes a desired negative density range (DR) of 1.1—a typical average value. The dotted lines demonstrate that a subject luminance range of eight stops (equivalent to N-½) requires development to a contrast index of about .46 to produce a negative DR of 1.1.

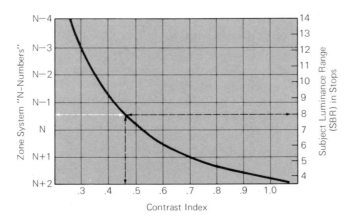

If the difference between the readings is greater than 4, subtract 4 from the difference and call it a *minus* N-number. For example, Zone III reads 12 and Zone VII reads 18. The difference is 6 (stops). Subtract 4 from 6 to get 2. The N-number is N−2.

When you have determined the N-number (calculate it to within ⅓ stop if possible), consult the chart (fig. 8.31) to find the appropriate contrast index (development condition) for that subject range. Then, on the manufacturer's contrast index/developing time chart for the film and developer in use, find the correct developing time, temperature, and agitation. Charts for most Kodak films and their recommended developers are to be found in the Kodak *Professional Data Book* number F-5, available at most camera shops or directly from the Eastman Kodak Company, Rochester, New York. Other useful CI information can be determined from the charts given in the appendix, pages 308–309.

Much of the work done with a view camera involves filtration, close-up focusing, or very long exposure times, and all of these will necessitate increasing the film exposure beyond the normal calculations. The exposure factors required by filtration and bellows extension are explained on pages 151 and 231. Reciprocity failure due to long exposure times or, more precisely, weak exposing light, varies with the kind of film in use. A very general guide can be given, however, and the chart on page 306 in the appendix will supply information to help you compensate for reciprocity failure by adjustment of both exposure and development. Lacking a more specific guide, this can be used for all normal films with good results.

Notice that the exposure factors are not the same for aperture and shutter speed compensation. This is because opening the diaphragm for compensation brightens the exposing light and tends to nullify the cause of the reciprocity failure. Prolonging exposure *time,* if anything, simply aggravates the problem, although compensation will eventually occur. Reciprocity correction should be the last factor applied to the exposure calculation. Don't forget to apply it if it's needed, however. It affects both negative density and contrast.

Close-up Photography

When it is necessary to produce an image on film, larger than about one-tenth the subject size, special equipment or techniques may be required.

Most small cameras will not focus close enough to allow for greater image size than this without special lenses or accessories, and some are not particularly satisfactory for close-up photography even when modified. Single-lens reflex cameras can usually be adapted rather easily and are generally excellent for the purpose if the relatively small image is not a drawback. When larger film sizes are desirable, the view camera is the obvious choice.

A great deal of confusion has surrounded the terms which are used to describe photography of objects at close range. It is quite common to hear the terms *photomacrography* and *photomicrography* interchanged with *macrophotography* and *microphotography*. Lenses designed for precision work at close range are often described as *macro-* or *micro-* lenses and are recommended for *close-up* work.

In the interests of standardization we will follow the lead of the Kodak technical writers and define these terms as follows. Close-up photography covers the range from the minimum focusing distance of the basic camera to a distance about equivalent to two focal lengths from the subject, at which range the subject is being recorded at life-size. Accessory lenses, extension tubes, or bellows units may be required.

Photomacrography overlaps this range and more specifically refers to the recording of subjects which would normally be examined visually under magnification, such as is provided by a reading glass, pocket magnifier, or a low-powered, simple microscope. Extra long extension tubes or bellows are required, special lenses are necessary for best results, and magnification may range from $1\times$ to perhaps $50\times$.

Photomicrography refers specifically to photography through a compound microscope, a procedure which involves highly specialized manipulation and lighting techniques. Magnification may run from as low as about $20\times$ to more than $2000\times$. Electron microscopes overlap this range and extend it to an incredible $200,000\times$ or so.

The term microphotography is used to describe the techniques of producing very small images as, for example, in making patterns for electronic integrated circuitry. This is a highly specialized field in which exotic sensitized materials and meticulous control of processing conditions are required to maintain satisfactory definition in images which are literally invisible to the naked eye. The term macrophotography is assigned to the making of very large images, such as photomurals.

Meter readings of close-up subjects must be taken with extreme care. Incident readings can be difficult to obtain if the camera-to-subject distance is very short or if the subject is likely to be disturbed. Incident readings cannot be relied on if the meter cell is not placed quite precisely in the subject plane and in a typical light condition. Conventional luminance meters are not much better for this purpose. Because of the small subject area and the proximity of the camera, accurate coverage of the subject field is difficult, and the meter will probably cast a shadow which will affect the accuracy of the reading. If the camera has a built-in through-the-lens meter, the problem is made much simpler and very accurate readings can usually be obtained.

When a subject is at infinity, the image is formed as close to the lens as it can be under any circumstances, and the distance approximately from lens to focal plane is called the focal length of the lens (fig. 8.32a). In ordinary photography, the focal distance is rarely very much greater than the focal length of the lens; in fact, most popular cameras are designed to prevent much focusing adjustment.

Although there is some increase in focal distance as the subject approaches the camera from infinity, the percentage of increase, compared to the normal focal length, is insignificant until the subject reaches a point about eight focal lengths in front of the lens (fig. 8.32b).

From this point on, as the subject approaches still closer, the focal distance increases very rapidly until, when the subject has reached a point two focal lengths

Unit magnification

Close-up focusing can become confusing

Subject and image must be at least four focal lengths apart

Film illumination is affected by focal distance changes

in front of the lens, the image is formed two focal lengths behind the lens. At this point, the subject and the image are identical in size (fig. 8.32c), and we refer to this as the condition of *unit magnification.*

If the subject is brought still closer to the lens, the image will recede at an accelerating pace (it is now larger than the subject and growing rapidly) until, when the subject reaches a distance equal to one focal length in front of the lens, the image is formed at infinity and is infinitely large (fig. 8.32d).

Focusing a camera is a simple enough procedure when the object is some distance away. At distances approaching unit magnification, however, it is sometimes a very confusing task. At near unit magnification you will probably find that moving the *lens* to focus will become ineffective and it will become necessary to adjust the image sharpness by moving the whole camera or the subject itself. If you are using a view camera, it may be feasible and effective to use the *back* focusing adjustment. The problem becomes most perplexing when the subject plane and film plane are just a little more or less than four focal lengths apart. If a little more, there will be some position of the lens which will produce a sharp image, but if a little less, no adjustment of the lens will result in good focus. It will be close enough, though, to keep you working at it. The only way out of this dilemma is to increase the subject-to-film distance to four focal lengths or more. A sharp image is impossible at shorter total distances.

As you will recall, the f/numbers marked on the aperture scale of the lens are derived from the relationship between the aperture diameter and the lens focal length.

$$f/ = \frac{\text{focal length}}{\text{diameter}}$$

From this you can see that if the focal length value is changed and the aperture is unchanged, the marked relative apertures are no longer reliable.

This is what occurs in focusing on a very near object. The lens must be racked out to bring the image into sharp focus, and in so doing, the distance from

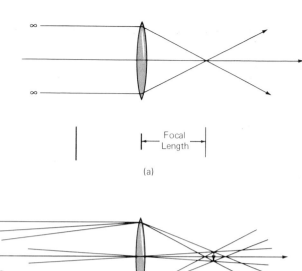

(a)

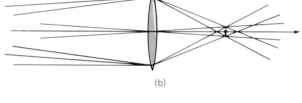

(b)

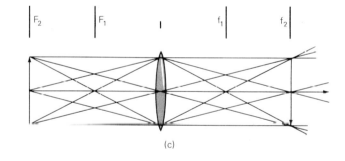

(c)

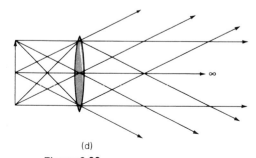

(d)

Figure 8.32

Here's an example

And a working procedure

Another method for calculating the exposure increase

lens to focal plane (focal distance) is increased. This in turn reduces the illumination on the film surface which, unless compensated for, will cause underexposure of the film.

An example should clarify this relationship. Imagine a lens of 6″ focal length with an aperture diameter of ½″. According to the formula above, the lens has a relative aperture of f/12. When this lens is focused on an object close enough so the distance from lens to film measures 10″, the effective relative aperture is f/20, although the aperture pointer on the lens mount will still indicate f/12! If the same lens is focused on an object 12″ away, the image will also be 12″ behind the lens, since this is the condition of unit magnification, and the effective relative aperture will be f/24. Under this condition, if the exposure is based on the marked aperture of f/12, the film will receive only one-fourth the illumination it requires, and the negative will be seriously underexposed. Clearly something must be done to compensate for these errors.

There are several methods of computing the required exposure adjustment but the simplest and most convenient method is perhaps this one. (Use of the macro-exposure computer scales, in the appendix, will save some mental arithmetic.)

1. Focus and compose the image as desired.
2. Stop down for adequate depth of field coverage and and note the aperture which you have selected.
3. Measure the focal distance (from the approximate plane of the lens diaphragm to the film plane).
4. Divide this measured distance by the lens focal length (printed on the lens mount in inches or millimeters).
5. Square the resulting number. This is the exposure factor.
6. Take an exposure meter reading of the subject and note the shutter speed which is indicated for use with the aperture you have selected (but don't use this shutter speed).
7. Multiply this shutter speed by the exposure factor from step 5. Use this new shutter speed to make the exposure.

For example, after focusing, composing, and stopping down you find that you have a bellows extension (total length) of 10″ and the aperture scale reads f/22. The lens focal length is indicated to be 100 mm, about 4″, so:

$$10 \div 4 = 2\frac{1}{2}, \text{ which squared is } 6\frac{1}{4}.$$

This is the exposure factor. The meter indicates that an aperture of f/22 will require an exposure time of 1/125 second, but this must be multiplied by the factor just found.

$$1/125 \times 6\frac{1}{4} = 25/500 \text{ or } 1/20 \text{ second}$$

Use the nearest marked speed on your shutter, favoring the longer interval in preference to the shorter one. In this case, if the shutter can be set for 1/15 second, this is the speed that should be used. If the shutter calibrations provide only 1/10 and 1/25 to choose from, the 1/25 speed will probably be adequate, but the 1/10 is a little safer. If you have time and plenty of film, take one shot at each setting since an extra negative is better than none.

Here is another method using simple proportions to achieve the same ultimate result but working with the aperture numbers to affect the exposure increase.

Effective aperture: Marked aperture =
Focal distance: Focal length

Using the same values as in the last illustration we substitute:

$$x : f/22 = 10 : 4 \text{ then,}$$
$$4x = 220 \text{ and } x = 55 \text{ or } f/55.$$

Set the camera aperture scale for f/22 but select the shutter speed which the meter indicates for f/55 or the closest marked aperture. An obvious difficulty with this method is the fact that most meter scales do not extend past f/32 or f/45.

Most close-up photographs are of still-life material, and movement is not as much of a problem as is depth of field. Occasionally, though, it is necessary to specify some shutter speed and then determine how to set the lens to provide the proper exposure. Use of the proportion above will also make this possible. If the selected shutter speed requires an effective aperture of f/8, how must the aperture scale be set to achieve this? Using the 4″ lens working at 10″, as above, we substitute:

f/8 : x = 10 : 4 then,
10x = 32 and x (the marked aperture) = 3.2

Use your selected shutter speed, but set the aperture scale at f/3.2. The effective aperture, because of the extended bellows, is f/8.

You can modify these procedures, or perhaps even ignore them, if you are using a single-lens reflex with through-the-lens metering. Most cameras of this type compensate automatically for increases in focal distance because the light intensity is diminished on the meter cells to the same degree that it is on the film surface. In some SLR metering systems the sensitive cell is included in the mirror coating or it may be inserted into the light path at some point ahead of the film. In these meters the light on the meter cell is not diminished quite as much as the actual film image light is and the meter readings may tend to underexpose the film if some compensation is not calculated. Practical experience is the best guide for coping with this condition. Cameras which meter the image light on the groundglass will usually provide almost perfect compensation for any macro-situation.

Because close-up photographs often require long exposure intervals, it is quite likely that the effective sensitivity of the film will be reduced by failure of the reciprocity law (see page 85). As a rule of thumb, it will be a good idea to double the calculated exposure if it is greater than one second, and double it again if it exceeds about ten seconds. Since films vary in their susceptibility to failure, it will be wise to bracket the exposures or make a preliminary test if the picture is important and cannot be repeated.

The focal length of a lens can be defined as the distance between the image plane and the rear nodal point of the lens when the lens is focused at infinity. In simple terms this rear nodal point is a hypothetical point in space which represents the intersection of light rays as they pass through the lens toward the film plane. It is a point, in other words, around which the lens may be pivoted slightly without displacing the focused image of an object at infinity.

In most lenses of conventional design, the nodal points, front and rear, are actually contained within the lens structure, and the diaphragm is placed between them. The position of the diaphragm, therefore, serves as a convenient and fairly accurate point from which to measure the focal distance in computing close-up exposure compensation.

Although the focal lengths of telephoto and retro-focus lenses cannot be measured from the diaphragm position, because the nodal points are nowhere near it, the diaphragm position will still indicate the approximate source of light illuminating the film surface and may be used with fairly accurate results as the reference point in computing the bellows extension exposure factor. Simply consider the diaphragm-to-film distance at infinity focus to be the *focal length* of the lens. Measure again after focusing on the object and call it the *focal distance*. Then proceed with the normal calculation. This is admittedly a rather haphazard method because the position of the diaphragm is not easy to establish with any real precision. It will not work, either, with lenses which focus with floating elements. In most cases, though, it is sufficiently accurate to keep you out of trouble. If this, or some similar compensation is not made, retro-focus lenses will tend to overexpose and telephotos will tend to underexpose when used for close-ups.

If the exposure increase is computed from the image magnification ratio, it will also have to be modified for use with these lenses. Exact compensation involves finding the ratio of the diameters of the lens *entrance and exit pupils* and use of a formula which is given in the appendix on page 302. In practice it's unlikely that a very serious error will occur even without this special compensation because neither lens type is particularly easy to use for extreme close-ups. Many retro-focus lenses in particular will actually touch the subject before they will focus a life-sized image.

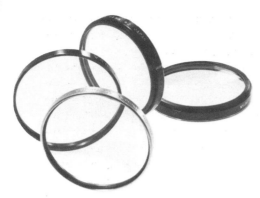

Figure 8.33
Close-up lenses

Macro-lenses are best for close-up work

Close-up lens attachments don't require exposure compensation

They are calibrated in diopters

Bellows units and extension tubes are useful with some cameras

Some extension tubes may cause serious flare

Neither ordinary telephoto nor retro-focus lenses can be expected to produce as good results in close-up work as do normal lenses, and it is unwise to use them in this way if image quality is of critical importance. A number of manufacturers of small cameras produce special lenses for close-up photography which are intended to provide superior correction of the various aberrations in this rather critical range. They are often referred to as macro-lenses, and the prefix sometimes appears in the name of the lens. Such lenses for view cameras are not labelled as macro-lenses as a rule but are simply called *process* lenses and are often designated in addition as *apochromats* to indicate that correction of the color aberrations has been carried out to an unusually high degree. There are also some *macro-zoom* lenses featuring ingenious optical or mechanical refinements which permit moderate close-up focusing and provide good macro-correction.

Cameras which do not focus closer than eight or ten focal lengths can be adapted for close-up work by the use of close-up lens attachments, sometimes inappropriately called portrait attachments. These lenses are generally just simple positive plano-convex lenses of low power designed to slip over the camera lens, and thereby effectively shorten its focal length. The lens then works as if it were a shorter lens *racked out* (working at focal distance greater than its focal length) which is the condition necessary for close-up focusing.

Since neither the lens-to-film distance nor the actual aperture diameter is changed by the addition of a close-up lens, there is no light loss of any consequence, and no close-up exposure compensation is required. The only real disadvantage of the close-up lens attachment is the generally slight loss of image quality due to the addition of the aberrations of the supplementary lens to those already existing in the normal lens system and the addition of some flare light from the two extra glass surfaces.

Close-up lenses are often sold under the designations plus 1 or plus 2 and so forth. These numbers refer to the lens focal length in *diopters,* a term usually used by optometrists, and not often encountered in photography. A focal length of one diopter is equivalent to one meter or about thirty-nine inches. Two diopters implies a focal length of one-half meter, three diopters means one-third meter, and so forth. If the lens is positive, the description includes the word *plus;* negative lenses are designated *minus.*

Negative supplementary lenses are not as popular as the positive ones, but they are useful as focal length extenders for long lens or telephoto effects, if the camera can be physically extended enough to bring the converted image into focus. By lengthening the focal length, minus lenses convert a normal lens into a long one and reduce its speed, since the aperture is not changed. The effective relative aperture must be computed to avoid underexposure.

Some manufacturers provide accessory bellows units for their cameras (see fig. 3.23). These units are fairly common for 35mm cameras, and some are available for rollfilm cameras as well. They can only be used on cameras whose lenses can be removed and are only practical for use on single-lens reflex cameras since focusing and framing of the image are extremely critical at close range.

Bellows units usually replace the normal lens in the camera body, and the lens is attached to the front frame of the unit. The camera can no longer be focused at infinity, using its normal lens, because of the irreducible thickness of the bellows, but extreme close-ups are possible.

Extension tubes provide another means of close focusing. Supplied in sets of three or four rings of different lengths, they can be interposed between camera body and lens, alone or in combination, to provide more or less continuous coverage of the range from infinity to unit magnification.

They are cheaper than the accessory bellows units and allow for moderate close-ups, which the bellows cannot accommodate, but they are awkward in use because of the number of pieces involved and the difficulty of interchanging them. They can, of course, be used in combination with a bellows unit for greater magnifica-

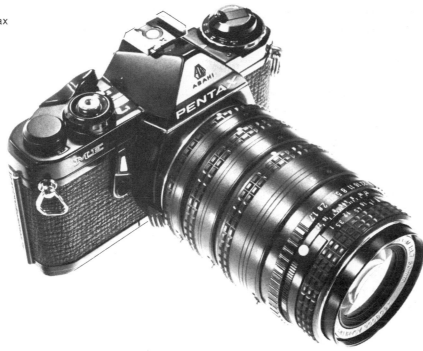

Figure 8.34
Extension tubes on Pentax

tion of the image, and if really extreme blowups are desired, supplementary lenses can be added, too. Image quality is likely to suffer considerably, however.

A potentially serious problem of flare light can be caused by extension tubes, especially the cheaper varieties, and it is a problem which is seldom mentioned in discussions of close-up photography. The flare results from light reflecting from the smooth interior surfaces of the tubes. The resulting image degradation can be disastrous (fig. 8.35). If you plan to do much serious close-up work with small cameras (this problem is rare with bellows-type cameras), check the entire camera interior for flare-producing shiny areas by pointing the camera toward a fairly strong light source and inspecting the interior surfaces through the shutter opening (fig. 8.36). A good camera repairman can usually improvise extra baffles to eliminate the reflection or apply matte black lacquer or flocking to reduce it. You may be able to treat the surfaces of extension tubes yourself but it is best to let a professional work on the camera body if it needs extra baffling.

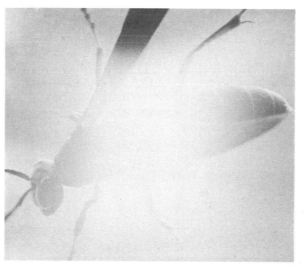

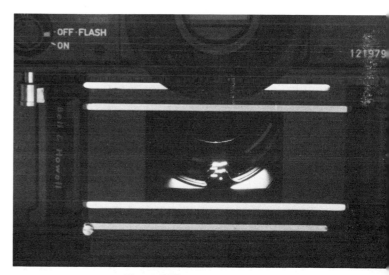

Figure 8.35
a. A hornet on a windowpane, shot again the light with well-designed extension tubes.

b. Same hornet, same windowpane, shot with "bargain" extension tubes.

Figure 8.36
Although the inside surfaces of these extension tubes were blackened during manufacture, they still reflect enough light to cause the disastrous flare in figure 8.35b.

Figure 8.37
Reverse adapter

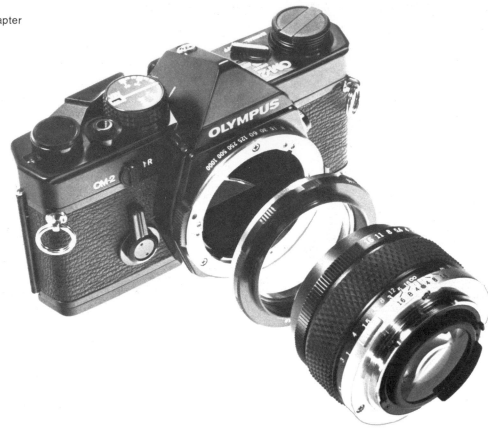

It is one of the unpleasant facts of optics that lens aberrations are not uniform in any given lens at various object distances, and the changes become extreme and particularly troublesome in the unit magnification range where the image and object relationships are subject to considerable variation. For this reason, a lens which is superbly corrected for all the aberrations at infinity may be poorly corrected at 1:1 (unit magnification) and vice versa.

Because the corrections are made for rather specific conditions of image-object relationship, it is sometimes possible to improve the performance of an ordinary lens at close range by reversing it in its mount. If it is designed to work best with a large object distance and a short image distance (infinity condition), it will probably work better at extremely close range, when the image is larger than the object, if the front of the lens faces the image. Some manufacturers suggest this practice and supply special adapters to make it possible. Reverse adapters offer no improvement in image quality unless the image is magnified, although they may permit an advantageous increase in the lens-to-subject distance. The lens will probably give better image quality in its normal position until unit magnification is reached.

One of the aberrations which is most troublesome at close range is field curvature. If the lens provides a flat field for objects at infinity it is quite likely not to at close range. It is for this reason that the use of ordinary camera lenses on an enlarger is not advisable since, of all the possible virtues of a lens, flatness of field in enlarging is most important.

This quality is so necessary in the design of high-quality enlarging lenses that at least one famous manufacturer produces two separate premium-quality enlarging lenses which are corrected for different magnification ratios. If used for image magnifications outside their intended range, these lenses are still very good but no longer considered superb. Within their intended magnification range, incidentally, enlarger lenses can be used as camera lenses with excellent results.

Which you may not be able to see in the viewfinder

Reversing your lens may help

Enlarger lenses make fine close-up lenses

It's worth mentioning that the flare light from these shiny surfaces is not usually apparent in the viewfinder image, especially when the surfaces causing it are part of the camera body itself. It's quite possible, therefore, to see the subject in the finder quite clearly with excellent visual contrast and still find that the film itself has been badly fogged.

Exposure compensation is necessary with both bellows units and with tubes since both increase the focal distance of the lens without affecting the aperture. The procedures for computing exposure are identical with those outlined for use with the view camera.

Figure 8.38
Here is a simple, but effective method for making photocopies from books or magazines. Here the book pages are held flat by a large clip and the book is held open by fastening the vertical half to a brick with a large rubber band. When the camera is positioned so the finder image shows the lens reflection in the center of the mirror and the range-finder prism circle (in the center of the groundglass) is centered in the lens reflection, the camera is centered over the copy and is facing it squarely. For best accuracy of exposure, replace the mirror with a standard gray card for metering. The single light is sufficient here because the vertical book page acts as an efficient reflector. This is the set-up used to make the copy in figure 1.16.

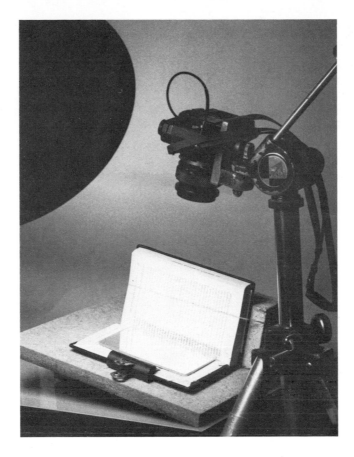

Close-up lighting is not particularly difficult

Copying is a typical close-up activity

Use black paper under the copy to prevent print-through

Lighting the subject well is not particularly difficult in close-up photography in spite of the limited space available. Bright light, which is usually desirable, both for groundglass focusing and for making the exposure, is relatively easy to provide because the light sources can be placed close to the subject without much danger of unevenness. If the subject is likely to be harmed by high temperature, it may be necessary to focus and arrange the composition by subdued light, turning the bright lights on only for a final focus check and the actual shooting. In extreme cases the subject can be protected by shields of heat-absorbing glass (available from Edmund Scientific Company, Barrington, New Jersey). Electronic flash is also an excellent cool light source, but focusing will have to be done with conventional illumination.

Copying Techniques

Copying material from books or magazines is a typical close-up activity. It's easy to get good results too, if a few precautions are taken. If the page to be copied can be laid out flat and if it is heavy, dull-surface paper, the problems are minimized. Simply position the camera so the lens axis is perpendicular to the page and arrange a pair of lights, one on either side, to shine on the page at an angle of about 45°. This is important because, if the camera does not face the page squarely, the copy may be distorted and, in extreme cases, a portion of the page may go out of focus. An easy way to get the camera into correct position is to lay a small mirror in the center of the subject space and observe it through the viewfinder. When you can see the reflection of the camera lens in the viewfinder image of the mirror, the lens axis is centered and perpendicular to the subject plane. Focus carefully and stop down to a moderately small aperture to insure best definition and adequate depth of field.

If you are using an SLR with a built-in metering system, it is best to take the meter reading from a standard gray card, placed temporarily over the page. Be sure that the gray card is large enough to cover the entire field of the meter and that it is evenly illuminated. If a gray card is not available, you can meter a white card and increase the indicated camera setting by 2½ stops. In any case, it's advisable to bracket your exposures on the first roll, to be sure everything is working properly. Lock the mirror up (if you're using an SLR) and use a cable release or the camera's self-timer mechanism to make the exposure. This will reduce vibrations and help to insure sharp images.

If the book or magazine can't be opened flat without breaking the binding, open it only halfway and support the opened half with stationer's clamps (fig. 8.38). Stretch the page to be copied as flat as possible and clamp it in place, too. If the printing on the other side of the page shows through (with thin papers this is a real problem), insert a sheet of black paper under the page. This will darken the paper very slightly but practically eliminate any print-through in the photograph.

Use glass only if necessary

Polarizing filters may be necessary

Color slide film is good, even for black-and-white

Black-and-white reversal processing is not easy to control

Tent lighting is excellent

Axial lighting can be bounced from a white card

Use only a single light for this set-up but position it with real care. Again, direct the light at the page at an angle of about 45°, and keep the light far enough away so there is no sign of any hot spot. Angle the light up slightly so some of it strikes the vertical pages of the half-opened book; they will serve as an efficient reflector and take the place of a second light source. With a little adjustment and careful observation, you should be able to provide uniform illumination on the page to be copied.

If the page cannot be made to lie flat by itself, it may be necessary to hold it down with a sheet of glass. Do this as a last resort because it is awkward to manage and the glass surface is very likely to show bothersome reflections, usually of the camera itself. To eliminate them, keep the camera out of the light and surround it with black paper or cloth.

If the copy page is lustrous or shiny, be sure that the lights are not reflected in its surface. If any sign of glare is apparent, lower the lights until the glare disappears. If the glare can't be controlled this simply, as may be the case if the subject consists partly of acetate overlays, for example, it may be necessary to use a polarizing filter over the camera lens or over the light sources, or (very probably) both.

Color slide film is excellent for copy work if the light is suitably balanced by filtration. Even black-and-white originals are reproduced well on Kodachrome or Ektachrome, as a rule, but there is usually a slight color cast and the contrast may be too high for some purposes. Good black-and-white slides can be made by photographing the original on High-Contrast Copy film (for line copy or type) or Panatomic-X (for continuous-tone originals like pencil or wash drawings) and printing the negatives on Fine-Grain Positive film. This process is made simpler if you have a *slide copier* attachment for your SLR or have access to a Repronar or Illumitron copy machine. In either case, the negatives can be fed through the copier and rephotographed on Fine-Grain Release Positive film which is available in 35mm size in 100-foot rolls. This procedure is more complicated than the frequently recommended reversal

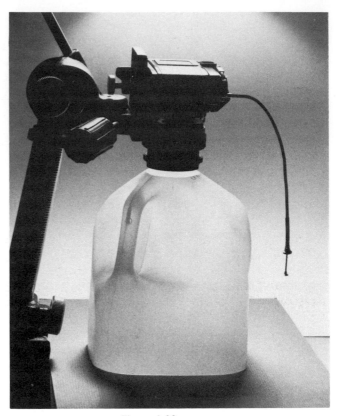

Figure 8.39
Plastic jug tent

processing of Panatomic-X film, but the results are excellent. The reversal process itself is not an easy one to control and one of the chemicals (the fogging developer) has been notoriously unstable.

Three-dimensional subject matter is a little more difficult to handle than flat work. Depth of field will become a major problem and the lighting will have to be arranged with great care to bring out the form and surface texture of the subject.

There are numerous techniques for lighting close-up subjects. Simply directing a light at the subject from beside the camera will suffice for some purposes but it is frequently necessary to use more than one source or to use reflectors to reduce the contrast and control the surface rendering. Don't overlook the possi-

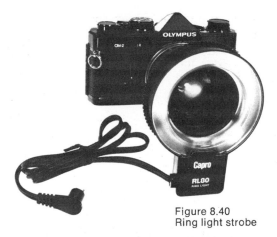

Figure 8.40
Ring light strobe

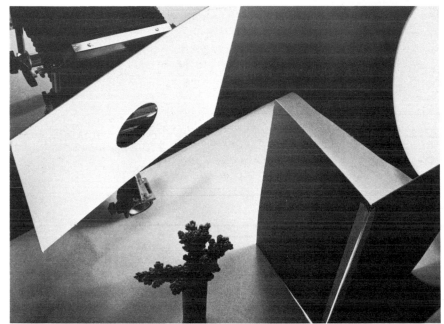

Figure 8.41
One method of achieving axial lighting. The angled white card in front of the lens shields the lens from light and bounces diffused light toward the subject. The subject is protected from direct light sources by a cardboard shield.

bility of tent lighting; a paper cone tent will provide excellent light for many sorts of close-up subjects. A semipermanent tent of this sort can be constructed by cutting off the neck and bottom of a large white plastic jug; set it over the subject and poke the camera lens in through the neck hole. Illuminate it from the outside with any sort of light and the subject will glow with a soft brilliance. For more contrasty lighting, cut off a portion of one side to let some direct light in.

Small objects can be separated from their own shadows by placing them on a sheet of glass suspended over some suitable background material. With this arrangement the relative values of subject and ground can be controlled easily and the subject can even be lighted from behind, if desired, to show up some edge details or to dramatize some effect of translucency or transparency. Reflections from the glass surface may cause problems but they can usually be eliminated by surrounding the camera lens with black paper or by tilting the glass slightly to avoid the reflecting light. If necessary, raise the object off the glass surface an inch or more on a little concealed pedestal of wood or wire. This will throw the glass surface completely out of focus and subdue the reflections.

For some purposes it is desirable to use *axial lighting,* flat frontal lighting which appears to shine onto the subject from the camera lens itself. This is not as difficult to arrange as it might seem to be. There are *ring light* flash tubes available for several brands of electronic flashguns, and one of these, fitted around the camera lens, will provide shadowless illumination. Their high-speed, high-intensity, negligible heat output and good daylight color balance make ring lights especially suitable for medical and dental work where the camera must frequently be hand-held and operated quickly, and where it is sometimes necessary to photograph hard-to-illuminate spaces such as the interior surfaces of the mouth. For these same reasons, the ring light is an excellent light source for some sorts of nature photography.

In the studio, still-life objects can be photographed with axial lighting by bouncing light onto the subject from a white card surrounding the camera lens. Be very careful not to shine the light directly into the lens. If this arrangement provides too large a source of light for the subject or if flare light is entering the camera, move the camera behind the card a few inches and shoot through the central hole. This will allow you to concentrate intense light on the card without spilling any into the lens itself.

Sometimes these methods are unsatisfactory for use with shiny objects because the image of the lens is reflected as a dark blob in the objects' surfaces. This effect can be reduced, and sometimes eliminated, by shooting through a piece of plate glass angled at about 45° to the lens axis. The subject can be illuminated with genuine axial light in this case because the light source is directed at the glass from the side so its reflection obscures the lens and the light parallels the lens axis. To be effective the glass must be flawless and very clean; any dust or lint spots on its surface will glow strongly in the light and may show up as light blobs or simply cause general flare in the image. It's a good idea to cover the camera with black cloth and keep it out of any direct light to avoid possible reflections, but this is not usually a serious problem. There is a possibility that the angled glass may cause some loss of sharpness in the image but this, too, is usually tolerable.

And so you see close-up photography is not simply a matter of pushing the button. If excellent results are required, the lens must be of fine quality, well corrected for close-up work, focusing must be precise, and depth of field accounted for. Both subject and camera movement must be avoided; illumination must be adjusted, light readings must be taken with particular care, and compensation made for the bellows extension if it is required. Anything less than precision at every stage of the operation will show up in the print as a flaw.

Summary

View and field cameras use sheet film, which must be loaded into holders in total darkness. The film type is identified by notches which appear in the top right-hand corner of the sheet when the film is held vertically and the emulsion faces you. Each holder contains two sheets of film, protected from light by dark slides. Fresh film is indicated when the shiny side of the slide end shows; after exposure the slide is turned over to show the black side.

A view or field camera must be used on a tripod or other firm support, but the operation is straightforward; follow the instructions given.

Processing sheet film can be done in tanks, automatic processors, or by hand in trays. Tray processing is most practical for small batches of film but requires skill and practice for good results. Practice with spoiled film before attempting to work with important pictures. Follow the detailed instructions and be careful to avoid cutting or scratching the delicate film surface.

View cameras have adjustments called shifts and swings which permit some control of image placement on the film, image perspective, and depth of field. All three controls can be exercised by moving the camera back; perspective is not affected by movements of the lens. In general, move the back first, then refine the image with lens movements if necessary.

View camera lenses should be of good quality and should cover a fairly wide field if the shifts and swings are to be used effectively. Camera movements will be restricted if the image circle is small or if the camera bellows is compressed, as is likely if the lens is a very short one.

The exposure-development relationship is a very important one which can be demonstrated by a nine-negative array combining the effects of under-, normal, and over-exposure and development. Follow the instructions carefully. Although there is some interaction, negative density is determined by film exposure and negative contrast is determined by development. These relationships can be expressed by characteristic curve diagrams which demonstrate that film development can be varied to produce useful negative contrast from any practical subject. Gamma, average gradient, and contrast index are all terms used to describe negative contrast as it is affected by development.

In these curve diagrams, exposure and negative densities are expressed in $\log_{10}$ values. The log of 2 is .3 and is equivalent to one stop. Other values are given in the chart. You can find the appropriate developing time for film exposed to any subject range by determining the contrast index required and consulting a CI chart for your film and developer. Subject range can be measured fairly accurately with a spotmeter or it can be estimated. One useful method is to take the difference between incident meter readings of the illumination extremes in stops and add five. If the total is other than the normal 7, some exposure adjustment will be required to compensate for the abnormal development required. Consult the charts for recommendations.

The Zone System is a well-known system of exposure and development control incorporating the principle of previsualization. The print density range is divided into seven identifiable tones of gray, plus black and white, each assigned a Zone number. Zone V is considered to represent middle gray, with Zone I maximum black and Zone IX maximum paper white. In using the Zone System, the photographer measures the luminance values of significant areas of the subject and tries to visualize how they will appear in the print, comparing them mentally with his concept of the standard Zone values. Scene contrast is usually estimated by measuring the difference between subject areas which are to be rendered in the print as Zones III and VII. If the difference is less than the normal 4 stops, the subject requires N-plus or expansion treatment; if more than 4 stops, development is considered to be N-minus and is contracted from normal. Exposure should be adjusted to compensate for abnormal development; see charts. Zone System information can also be derived from CI charts, as illustrated. Don't forget to apply compensation for reciprocity failure if necessary.

Close-up photography, as distinguished from photomacrography, photomicrography, macrophotography and microphotography requires some special equipment and techniques. SLR cameras with built-in metering systems are very convenient to use, and most will compensate automatically for the exposure increase required by the lens extension. For other cameras the bellows factor must be calculated. One method is to divide the focal distance by the lens focal length, square it, and increase the exposure time by the factor so found. There are other methods, and a dial calculator pattern is provided in the appendix. Telephoto and retro-focus lenses are not recommended for close-up work although some modern zooms offer good correction at close range.

Special macro-lenses are best but ordinary lenses can be used with close-up supplementary lenses, bellows units, or extension tubes. Flare may be a problem with extension tubes. Some lenses perform better at close range if they are mounted in reverse, and special mounting rings are sold for this purpose. Enlarging lenses are excellent for this work if they can be mounted for camera use.

Lighting for close-up work is not particularly difficult but will require some care. If the lights are too close the subject may be damaged by heat.

Copying material from books or magazines is not difficult. Hold the page flat with clamps and back it up with black paper if the print shows through. Use the facing pages of the half-opened book as a reflector and meter with a gray card or use an incident reading. Color film can be used for either black-and-white or color originals but black-and-white slides of excellent quality can be made on the Fine-Grain Positive film from good negatives.

Tent lighting is good for small three-dimensional objects. They can be effectively backlighted by supporting them on glass. Axial lighting will provide shadowless illumination and is often effective for medical, dental, or nature photography. A similar light effect can be achieved by bouncing the light from a white card surrounding the lens or from an angled glass in front of the lens. The reflection of the camera itself can be subdued by draping the camera with black cloth. Careful attention to detail will result in good work.

Outline

9 Special Darkroom Techniques

Process Manipulations

Most of our photographic efforts are directed toward the production of images which document the subject and represent it more or less accurately. Frequently we will dodge or burn-in some areas of the print to adjust the tonal balance or to influence the mood of the picture, and occasionally we'll use a little Farmer's reducer to accent some highlight area. Finally, many photographers tone their prints, either for visual effect or for greater permanence. All these manipulations can be considered normal if the photographer's intent is to represent the original subject without obvious distortion. Many fine images are made this way, but there are other ways to use photographic techniques—ways which can modify, distort, dramatize, or depart completely from the original subject matter.

Practically speaking, any violation of the normal procedures of negative making or printing will result in an unusual image of some sort but simply blundering around in the darkroom will not usually produce very interesting pictures. Some knowledge of process is definitely helpful and some sense of craft and control is necessary in even the most destructive distortions of the normal processes, if they are to result in images to be taken seriously.

Images can be altered in a number of ways. The images' shapes and outlines can be distorted by optical manipulation in the camera or during the printing process. Tonality can be distorted by increasing the contrast dramatically or by decreasing it until the image is barely discernible. The image can also be distorted by partial or complete reversal, either overall, or affecting only a portion of the image area. The sense or identity of the pictured objects can be distorted by juxtaposition or superimposition of other image forms, either photographically or by handwork. Colors or textures can be incorporated into the image and photographs can be printed on a variety of surfaces and materials by several methods. The photographic image can be included as a motif or element in painting, collage, silk screen, etching, weaving, or even three-dimensional arts like sculpture and ceramics. Finally, of course, we are all so familiar with the surreal photographic effects in films and on television that we no longer even think of them as distortions.

Dropouts, High-Contrast Techniques, Posterization

The easiest and most direct way to depart from photographic reality, which all these processes are intended to do, is to load your camera with a very high-contrast

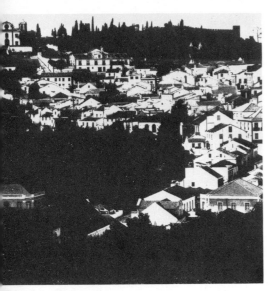

Figure 9.1
High-contrast dropout

You can dissect the image into tonal separations

Project one image and trace it as a registration guide

Make a test strip to determine gray exposures

film, such as Contrast Process Pan, High-Contrast Copy film, or Kodalith, and simply take pictures with it. The film will reduce the subject tonality to black-and-white pattern and the image will resemble a brush drawing in ink, practically devoid of any gray tones (fig. 9.1). Because the grays have been *dropped out* of the photograph, all high-contrast images of this sort, however they're done, are called *dropouts.*

Kodalith will work well in the camera in bright light but it is a very slow, orthochromatic material (a panchromatic variety is available but not common) which is better suited to printing. It can be handled safely in a light red safelight (series 1A) and is slow enough so that it can be treated like a fast projection paper. It requires its own special developer for highest contrast results but it can be developed in almost any developer if less-than-maximum contrast is desirable. One caution—the film is effectively more sensitive to light when developed in ordinary developers and it may be necessary to reduce the safelight intensity to avoid fog.

Kodalith (or any of the other similar "litho" films on the market) is extremely useful for dissecting images: by printing an ordinary negative onto successive sheets of Kodalith and changing the exposure a little each time, different patterns will be formed, each of which divides the image tones into black-and-white areas of different proportions. These *tonal separations* can be printed individually as simple dropouts, or they can be combined in various ways by multiple printing techniques to produce *posterizations,* in either black-and-white or color.

To make a simple black-and-white posterization, you should have at least two tonal separations and three are probably better. Four or more may produce a final image so similar to a regular continuous tone print that the effect will be minimized or lost entirely.

You can work from the original subject, by making the separations in the camera, or you can begin with either a black-and-white positive transparency or a black-and-white negative. You can use color slides, too, but since Kodalith is red-blind it may be difficult to predict the patterns that will be formed. Usually the process begins with a black-and-white negative.

Expose the negative by either contact or projection onto each of two or more sheets of Kodalith, varying the exposures to produce distinctly different patterns. If three separations are to be used, one should be almost entirely black except for a few small accents of clear film; one should be approximately half black and half clear; and the third should be mostly clear with some black accents. These are all positive images. Print these images on Kodalith (by contact, preferably) to produce negatives. These negatives should be small enough to fit into your enlarger negative carrier for projection.

Select the negative which shows the most image detail and put it into your enlarger. Bring the image to the desired size, focus it on a clean sheet of white paper in the easel and move the easel as necessary to compose the image the way you want it. Carefully trace the image outlines on the focus paper with dark pencil or felt-tipped pen. This tracing will serve as a registration guide for the projected images. Stop the lens down to its smallest aperture and remove the negative from the carrier. Remove the focus paper but leave the easel in place.

Now make a test strip on the printing paper you intend to use, to find out how much exposure is required to produce several shades of gray and a satisfactory black tone. Make the test in your usual manner but remember that because there is no negative in the carrier the light will be quite intense in spite of the small aperture. Suppose, as a result of the test, you discover that it takes 3 seconds to produce a nice light gray, 8 seconds to produce a pleasant dark gray, and 30 seconds to reach a convincing black. Jot these times down.

Replace the focus paper in the enlarging easel and select the negative which is most clear (least black image). Put it into the enlarger carrier, check the focus, and be sure that the lens is set at the same aperture used for the test strip. Move the easel, if necessary, to register the projected image with the drawn outlines. Turn off the enlarger light and, being very careful, now, *not* to move the easel (tape it down if necessary), remove the focus paper and lay it aside temporarily.

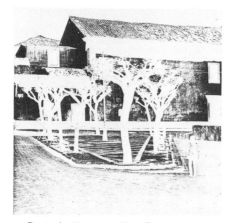
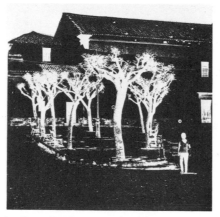
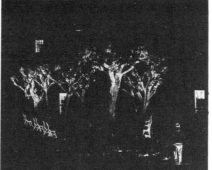

Figure 9.2
Black-and-white posterization

a. Posterization negative #1   b. Posterization negative #2   c. Posterization negative #3

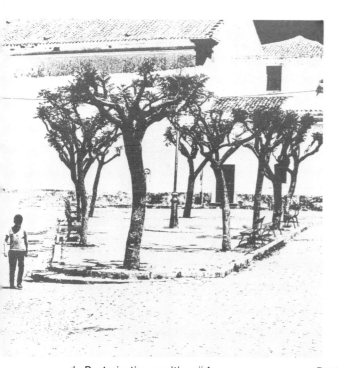
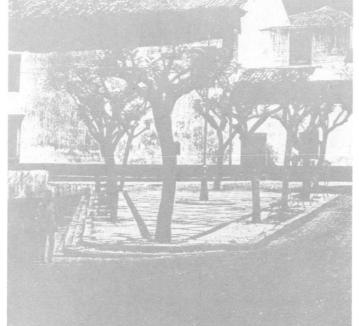
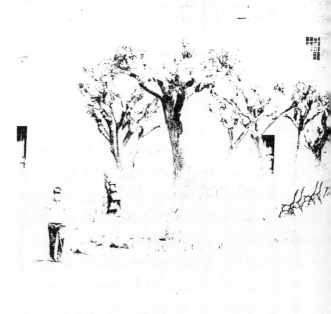

d. Posterization positive #1   e. Posterization positive #2   f. Posterization positive #3

g. The three positives combined to make the posterized print.

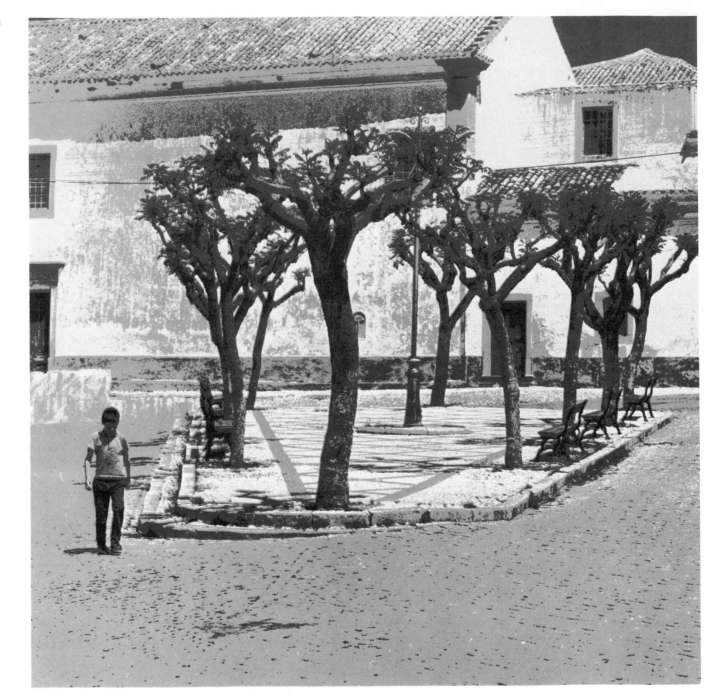

Print the first image; mark the paper

Print the second image; don't move the easel

Then print the third

Printing controls won't affect a Kodalith image usefully

Make a positive; register it with the negative

Put a sheet of printing paper in the easel, positioning it against the edge guides in such a way that it can be removed and replaced exactly. This first negative will provide the light gray tone for the finished image, so it should be given the 3-second exposure. Then (carefully!) remove the printing paper from the easel and immediately turn it over and mark it lightly on the back with pencil to identify the top of the latent image. Tuck it away out of the light.

Leaving the easel in place, replace the focus paper and project on it the second negative image (half black, half clear). If the images are not in perfect register, move the negative carrier or move the negative in the carrier until the registration is as close as you can get it, then improve it, if you can, by moving the easel *slightly* (moving it very far may change the image size). Remove the focus paper.

This second negative will provide the dark gray areas of the print which, according to the test, will require 8 seconds; *but* the paper has already had 3 seconds exposure over the entire area which this negative will affect, so this exposure should be 5 seconds. Carefully replace the printing paper, being careful to get it oriented correctly, and make the exposure. Remove the paper to a safe place and register the third negative image with the focus paper, as before, then remove the focus paper.

The third negative is mostly black so it will protect most of the previously exposed areas of the print and provide exposure only for the image black tones. They require 30 seconds, but somewhat more won't hurt. The paper has already had a total of 8, so this exposure must be at least 22 seconds. Replace the printing paper and make the exposure. Process the print normally and you should have a posterized image consisting of black, dark gray, light gray, and white.

If the image tones are satisfactory but the picture doesn't look right, it may be because the original Kodalith positives were not exposed correctly to abstract the essential outlines or details of the subject. With a little experience you should be able to select a set of positives which break the image down into a coherent pat-

tern of grays. Don't waste your time trying to correct the Kodalith *negative* exposures, however; the Kodalith positives they are printed from are so contrasty that they won't respond usefully to any printing controls.

Masking, Tone-Line, Solarization

Negatives can be *masked* to alter their printing characteristics. If a weak positive image is made from a negative by contact printing (so the image sizes are identical) and then registered with the negative, the two can be printed together, as a negative of reduced contrast. If the positive image mask is more contrasty than the negative, the final print may show a partial reversal in the shadows with drastically reduced shadow contrast and density and near-normal highlights. If the mask is much less contrasty than the negative, but still dense enough to function, the effect will be more even throughout the tonal range.

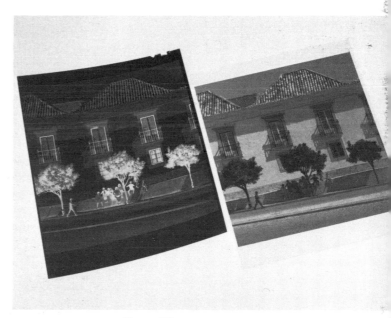

Figure 9.3
Negative and positive mask

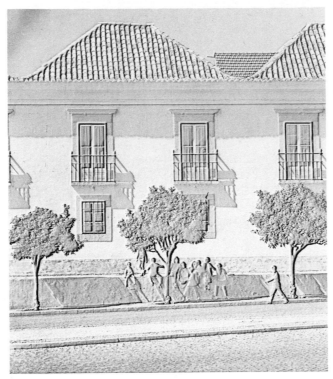

Figure 9.4
Bas-relief

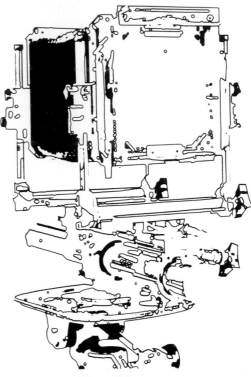

Figure 9.5
Tone-line print

If the negative and positive images are similar in density and contrast, their combined density will be high and nearly uniform over the entire picture area; the contrast will have been cancelled, in other words, and the image will no longer be printable in the normal way. If the images are slightly misregistered, however, a bright outline will appear around one edge of all the image forms and the opposite edges will be shown as a dark outline. This negative-positive "sandwich," printed heavily, will produce a simulated *bas-relief* image of light and dark outlines on a uniformly gray ground (fig. 9.4).

The outline can be made to resemble a pen drawing if the images are registered exactly, back to back (rather than emulsion to emulsion) so the image layers are separated by the two thicknesses of film base material. Viewed straight on, this sandwich will appear uniformly dark, but seen from an angle of, say, 60° or so, a thin line of light will appear along all the image edges. If this sandwich is printed by contact in a very diffused source of light or, better, if a direct light is allowed to strike the printing frame from an angle while the frame is rotated on a turntable of some sort, a complete outline image can be produced on Kodalith film. If this first line image is reprinted, again on Kodalith, the image will be "cleaned up" considerably and a negative image will result. It can then be printed on almost any sort of paper to produce what Kodak refers to as a *tone-line* print. Some photographers call these images *spin dropouts* or *spin-outs*.

Flashing film can produce the Sabattier effect

Mackie lines may appear

The effect is not entirely predictable

So it's best not to solarize an original negative

High-contrast films work best

Most films can be made to mask themselves, partially, if they are *flashed* (reexposed briefly to light) about midway through the negative development step, then allowed to develop further in the dark. This flash exposure must be sufficiently strong to fog the clear areas of the negative image (shadows) but not strong enough to penetrate the relatively dense areas of the negative which correspond to the image highlights. In effect, this procedure prints the partially formed negative image back on its own film emulsion to produce a latent positive image. Further development acts on both images and the result is a negative which is part positive. This process is frequently called *solarization* (which it is not) but is correctly known as the *Sabattier effect.*

With most films, treated in ordinary developer in the usual way, this partially reversed image simply looks like a badly fogged negative, but under some circumstances the negative and positive areas of the image are separated by distinct light lines which can be quite delicate and precise, or broadly smeared, or a combination of both. These are called *Mackie lines* and they result from the fact that the immediate border of an actively developing image area is contaminated by the bromide released by the developing action and is therefore inhibited from development itself. The formation of Mackie lines, a highly interesting feature of the Sabattier effect, is encouraged by *still* or *stagnation* development (no agitation) and by the use of a developer type which is both readily oxidized and easily restrained by bromides in solution. Dektol or D-72, diluted 1:2, is usually satisfactory.

Solarization (to use its common name) is not an entirely predictable effect, which, of course, is one of its principal charms. It is most likely to be successful with fairly contrasty films—High-Contrast Copy film, Professional Copy film, Contrast Process Ortho or Pan films, or even Kodalith. The developer should be partially exhausted, for best results, and should be used without much agitation after the reversal exposure. The timing and extent of the reversal exposure is critically important to the success of the process. If the film is flashed too early in the development, the negative image will not have had time to form sufficiently to serve as a mask and the entire emulsion is likely to be disastrously fogged. If the flashing occurs too late, the positive image will be confined to the shadows of the image only and may not have time enough to develop into a useful density. Too much flash exposure will simply fog the film or produce a very dense positive image; too little will leave it looking like a spoiled negative.

Although it is possible to solarize films that have been exposed in the camera, the relatively unpredictable nature of the process makes this a risky and time-consuming procedure. It's better to make the negative normally, then print it on either film or paper and solarize the print. Any film can be used for the original negative but the print film should be a high-contrast material, as mentioned above. Kodalith and Contrast Process Ortho are preferable to Pan films because they can be developed by inspection in a red (series 1) safelight. Fine-Grain Positive film would be even more convenient to handle but it does not usually solarize well.

You will have to experiment to find the proper exposure times, but in general, the print film should be slightly underexposed, developed just until the image is clearly visible but not fully formed, then flashed to dim white light for a brief period while still in the developer. Then continue the development until the reversed image nearly matches the original image in density. Typically the reversal exposure can be given at about one-third to one-half the normal developing time and about a one-second exposure to indirect room light will probably be a reasonable first guess. Don't cut the development short; solarization will reduce the image contrast considerably and (on any film but Kodalith) the images will tend to be too flat.

A paper print from a well-solarized negative will display the best full tonal range and preserve the best highlight whites that are possible, but solarizing the prints themselves is so easy and so fast that it is probably the most satisfactory method of producing these

Figure 9.6
a. Print solarization. First exposure slightly less than normal, flash exposure 1 second to dim room light.

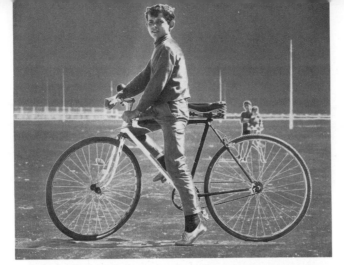

b. First exposure 90% of normal, flash exposure about 2 seconds.

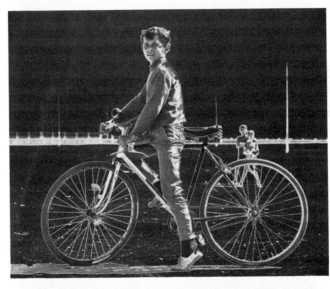

c. First exposure 75% of normal, flash exposure about 5 seconds.

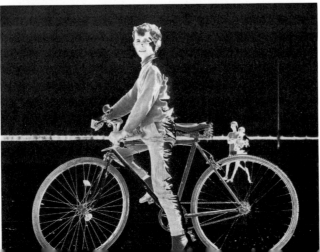

images. The routine is simple—use a very high-contrast paper such as Brovira #6 and print in your usual way, underexposing the print slightly. Negatives of normal or low contrast are usually best, but high-contrast negatives will sometimes produce attractive effects. Develop the print in an ordinary MQ print developer (some other types will also work well), such as Dektol, diluted normally, until the image is visible but not fully formed. Flash the paper to white light (a 15-watt bulb, about 4 feet from the developer tray is probably adequate) for about ½ second and continue the development until the time is up or the image seems to have stabilized.

The quality of the final image is dependent on the amount of original print exposure, the time and extent of development before the flash exposure, the extent of the flash exposure, and, to some degree, the extent of development after the flash exposure. Low-contrast papers do not work well. The formation of the Mackie lines is facilitated if the developer is nearing exhaustion or if a little quantity of potassium bromide is added to the working solution (try about ½ gram per quart at first).

The process is made even easier and more predictable if the prints are developed in Solarol, a special product (Solarol Co., Box 1048, El Cerrito, Ca.) available in some camera stores. Solarol produces better contrast and allows better control than ordinary developers do. Follow the procedure outlined above, but increase the flash exposure to about 3 or 4 seconds for the first trial. Best results seem to be obtained if the print is developed about 40 seconds before the flash, and about 1 to 1½ minutes after the flash exposure. Agitation can be continuous and the developer should be used at at least 68°F to avoid possible streaking.

Screening

In the normal photographic process the image tones are *continuous* from black to white, through an infinite range of grays. When photographs are printed in magazines or newspapers, or, for that matter, when

High-contrast papers work well, try #6 Brovira

And old, worn-out developer

Or Solarol

Normal photographic tones are continuous

Magazine illustrations are not; they've been screened

Unscreened ink images automatically drop out the grays

Autoscreen film will produce a regular dot pattern

Printing through matte acetate produces random dots

printmakers employ photographic imagery in their lithographs or etchings, the gray tones are not truly continuous. Instead, they are simulated by patterns of tiny dots of ink, too small for the eye to resolve individually, and the illusion of continuous gray tone occurs. These *halftone* grays are produced in the graphic arts media by *screening* the image to break it into the halftones. If the screen pattern is fine enough to be invisible, we perceive the gray tones as smooth and continuous; if the screen is coarse, as it is in newspaper reproduction, we are conscious of the dot texture but are not usually offended by it.

Screened images are occasionally used in photography for graphic or poster effects but they are more frequently employed in silk screen, photolithography, or photoetching. If the images are not screened in these processes the midtones are automatically dropped out by the process itself and become simple dark and light patterns.

Commercial screens are usually regular patterns of lines or dots, but for some purposes *random dot* screens are preferable because they simulate a natural, rather than a mechanical texture. For ordinary photographic purposes it is not necessary to work with these commercial screens. They are cumbersome and expensive and unnecessarily precise for most simple visual purposes. Relatively inexpensive *replica* screens (printed from the original glass screens on Kodalith) are satisfactory, and an even more convenient technique involves the use of Kodak's Autoscreen film. Photographic images printed on this material are automatically screened in a regular dot pattern, suitable for immediate use. The coarseness of the final image screen pattern is controllable by enlargement; if the screened image is used at same size, the pattern has approximately 125 lines per inch. Enlarging the screened image, obviously, will reduce the number of lines per inch and make the texture more apparent.

Random dot effects, approximating a *mezzotint* screen appearance, can be obtained by printing the photographic image onto Kodalith film through groundglass, matte acetate, or the nonglare glass used for

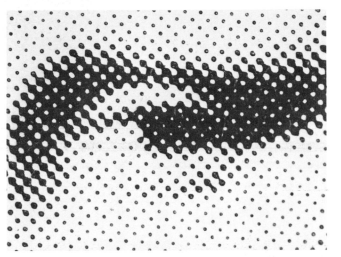

Figure 9.7
Enlarged autoscreen image

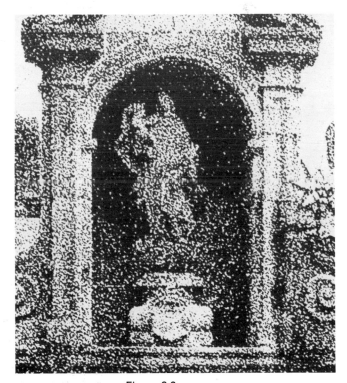

Figure 9.8
Detail of nonglare glass screen pattern.

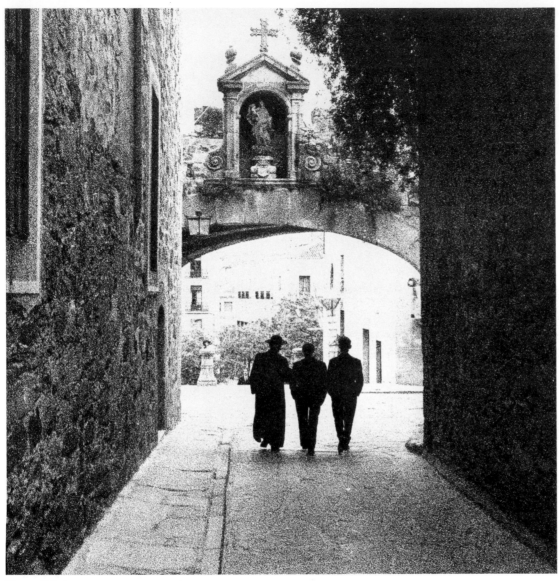

Figure 9.9
Print screened with nonglare glass

picture-framing. Replace the glass in your printing frame with nonglare glass, then place the negative and a sheet of Kodalith, emulsion to emulsion, in a printing frame and expose through the negative under your enlarger. The best exposure can be determined by trial, and it should produce an image which contains detailed areas of tone in both the near-blacks and near-whites. The contrast of the image can be controlled to some small extent by varying the *area* of the light source —a small lens aperture (on the enlarger) will tend to reduce contrast and emphasize the screen texture; larger apertures tend to *block-up* the light and dark tones and the image will begin to approach a simple dropout in appearance. The same effects can be achieved by projection. Put the negative in the enlarger and enlarge it to the desired size on a sheet of Kodalith which is held by itself in the printing frame with the emulsion side against the nonglare glass. Be careful to clean the glass. Dirt particles between the glass and the Kodalith will result in unsightly dark blotches in the image.

Color Manipulations

Many of the techniques just described can be worked in either black-and-white or color but, in color, they are somewhat complicated. Solarization is a case in point. Just a few years ago when color prints were normally developed in trays, it was fairly easy to flash and partially reverse the color image using either white or colored lights for various effects. Now, with color printing done in drums or in special processors, and with the developing times abbreviated by the high temperatures involved, it is very awkward to get the print out of the processor, flashed, and back into the developer in any sort of reasonable time. Tray processing is still possible, but it is relatively wasteful of chemicals and clumsy because of the necessity of working in the dark (or near-dark) wearing rubber gloves.

Color posterization is relatively easy, however, and is done just as it is in black-and-white. It's easiest with Cibachrome. Start with the recommended filter pack for the paper you're using. Set the enlarger at the necessary height and focus it. Stop the lens down to a small enough aperture so an exposure of a second or two will still produce a good black (remember, this is a *positive* process) and, with nothing in the enlarger carrier, make test strips on each of the four quarters of the paper using different colors of filtered light, any colors you're interested in. Use the cardboard mask described in chapter 7 to make these four exposures on the same sheet of paper.

Since this is a positive process, use the Kodalith positives, rather than negatives, to produce the posterization. Proceed as in black-and-white (page 242), using the selected filter colors for each exposure and dividing the exposure times, as indicated by the test strips, so the last (most dense) positive image supplies enough light to produce a white highlight tone. Develop as usual and you should have a posterized image in brilliant color. Remember, in this process the color is *additive*: red light applied over green light will make yellow; red and blue make magenta; and blue and green make cyan. The accumulated exposures will be lighter in value than the individual colors, too. A little experimentation will lead to some fascinating discoveries about color formation and, no doubt, produce some interesting images.

You may have a little difficulty figuring out the proper times of exposure for the various filters, since the filters will probably not all have the same printing densities (factors) and will produce any given gray tone at different exposure times. To take a simple example, let's suppose your red filter test indicates that 2 seconds is an adequate black exposure and that the times required for dark gray, light gray, and white are 4, 7, and 16 seconds respectively. For a similar range of tones the green filter requires 3, 6, 11, and 25 seconds. Say the red filter is printed first, for 4 seconds, to form black and dark gray areas. If the next exposure were also to be made with the red filter, the total required (4 plus 3) would be 7 seconds to make light gray. But, the

green filter will require more; if used alone it would have required 6 seconds to form dark gray. But dark gray has already been formed; regardless of *how* it was formed, the green filter needs 5 seconds more (than dark gray) to make light gray. In other words, consult each color test strip to find the appropriate exposure time to move from one selected gray to the next *for that filter,* disregarding the previous exposure times and the accumulated total.

Posterization with color negative papers is a little more complicated mainly because of the heavy original filtration required and the fact that the filter colors will be reversed in the print. Use the Kodalith negatives on this paper and keep in mind that accumulated exposure produces *black*. The filter factors and exposure times can be determined as outlined above. Try to keep some control of the exposures; the temptation is strong to simply experiment wildly. This sometimes works out well, but more often it will simply waste quantities of expensive paper and lots of time.

You can produce experimental posterization effects in great variety if you photograph the Kodalith separations on color film rather than projecting them onto color paper. You will have somewhat less control of the colors and the exposures are a little more difficult to arrive at, but the process is relatively cheap and fast and is capable of truly bizarre imagery.

Begin by making a series of separations from some positive or negative original, using Kodalith for dropout effects and Fine-Grain Positive if you wish to preserve some grays. Positive and negative separations can be combined and printed to produce simulated solarization effects and these, in turn, can be combined and reprinted to abstract the image still further. When you have dissected the image into interesting fractions, select four (at first) and register them on a light box, taping each one to the glass along a different edge so each can be photographed separately or can be folded over each other and photographed in combination. Set up your camera on a tripod and focus carefully on one of the films, using a close-up lens if necessary to fill the image area.

Calculate the exposure as well as you can

Use T or B and a locking cable release

And make the exposures by switching the light

Be sure to exclude light from outside the image area

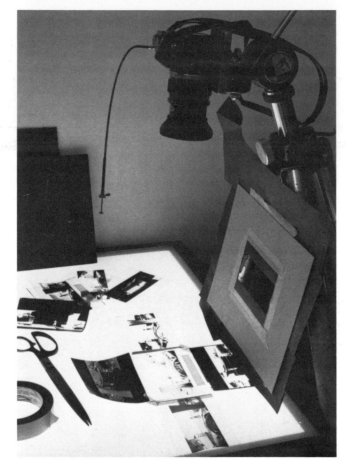

Figure 9.10
Camera set up over masks

Reduce the light intensity in the light box by using a low-wattage bulb or by covering the bulb with layers of translucent material until a meter reading of the raw light indicates an exposure of ⅕ second or longer. The basic exposure, then, will be about five or six times longer than this because the meter reading, if followed as given, will render the light as a medium gray. Overexposure of at least 2½ stops is necessary to record the light as white.

The actual exposures used will have to be estimated and several factors must be taken into account. If there are to be four exposures, and if each of the separations is transparent in a common area, the basic exposure will have to be divided by four so the accumulated total will add up to white. Furthermore, since each of the exposures will be made through a color filter (to add color to the posterization), each exposure will have to be increased by the factor of the filter used.

For example, suppose the corrected meter reading of the light box indicated an exposure of 1 second @ f/16 for the color film in use. Each of the four separations would then require exposures of about ¼ second @ f/16 if no filters were used. But if the four filters had factors of 2x, 3x, 5x, and 10x respectively, the final four exposures would be ½ second, ¾ second, 1¼ seconds, and 2½ seconds respectively.

Sequential exposures on a single frame of 35mm film are impossible with some cameras, and awkward and unpredictable with others. You'll find it easiest to do the actual photographing in very dim room light, or none at all, controlling the exposure times by turning the light box on and off while the camera shutter stays open on *Time* or *Bulb*. A locking cable release will hold the shutter open on Bulb if the camera is not equipped with a locking release of its own.

The actual procedure is simple enough—flip one of the separations into the camera field of view, dim the room lights, hold the chosen filter over the lens, and open the camera shutter and lock it. Turn the light box light on for the necessary time and turn it off. Flip another separation into place, use another filter, and repeat the operation, leaving the shutter open. Do the same with the third and fourth, then close the shutter and wind the film.

The process can be much more complex than this example. More separations can be used and they can be overlapped in various combinations to isolate or emphasize small areas. The exposure times will become very difficult to calculate under these circumstances but film is relatively cheap (compared to paper) and you can afford to bracket. Remember that the exposures will accumulate if they overlap, but will not if they don't. One precaution—if direct white light from outside the image area is allowed to strike the lens, it will almost certainly produce a high fog level in the image; it is wise to mask the area around the subject with black paper, especially if more than two or three exposures are used.

Color slide film is recommended for this kind of posterization. When the film is processed you can either project the slides or print them on Cibachrome or one of the reversal papers.

In the last few years there has been increasing interest in *machine art* of all sorts and quite a number of contemporary photographers have experimented with such things as computer graphics, holograms, and other forms of *generated* images. Although some of these techniques require exotic equipment, one useful machine, the Xerox copier, is generally available. Xerox pictures, especially in color, are interesting transformations of the normal photographic image, ranging from almost representational reproduction to extreme distortion, at the whim of the operator. Although Xerox prints are limited in size and are fairly expensive to produce, they offer an appealing alternative to the usual photographic derivations (see "Portfolio").

Introduction to Nonsilver Processes

The early photographic processes offer another exciting alternative and are a rich field for exploration. If you are interested in the print as an artifact rather than a mere picture of something or if you are offended by the plastic predictability of the popular RC printing papers, you should investigate the "old processes."

There are, in general, three categories—one in which some salt of silver is used as the sensitive emulsion ingredient and forms the image in metallic silver; one in which some nonsilver light-sensitive compound is used as a sort of catalyst to form a dye image or precipitate some image metal; and one in which some sort of "bichromated colloid" is employed as the sensitive material.

The early silver processes include the daguerreotype, the calotype, the ambrotype, and the albumin prints as well as many other types. Some of them are

capable of images of exquisite quality—a good albumin print is as fine as any contemporary image form—but they are not intrinsically different enough from modern silver print images to be of more than technical interest or novelty to most of us. They are, additionally, not easy to work with and the images are subject to staining and fading to an even greater extent than modern silver prints.

There are a number of interesting and relatively easy processes in the second category. Here the most common and useful sensitive material is an iron compound, such as ferric oxalate or ferric ammonium citrate. In most instances the final print image is composed of some metal, usually either silver or platinum, but in one case a dye image is formed. This last process, cyanotype or blueprint, is one of the easiest of the old processes and is a good one to begin with.

The third category is the largest and most versatile of the group. The bichromated colloids can be used to produce images in a variety of forms, including ink, pigment, dye, or ceramic glazes. The materials are cheap, generally accessible, relatively safe to handle and very stable, and the images are generally as permanent as the material they're printed on. The colloids usually used are gum arabic, gelatin, casein, and various organic glues; the processes include gum printing, photogravure, photoetching, silk screen, carbon, oil and bromoil, and woodburytype, among others.

All of the old processes involve materials of very low sensitivity to light and can only be worked by contact-printing methods. It is necessary, therefore, to produce original negatives large enough to print directly or to make enlarged negatives from small original ones. Negative quality is rather critical. Overly dense negatives are unsuitable for all the processes because of the excessively long exposure times that they require. The contrast of the negatives is also important; some processes, like multiple gum, work best with negatives of quite low contrast if continuous tone and representational imagery are desired. Others, like platinotype and cyanotype, work best with negatives of high contrast.

Making Enlarged Negatives

The easiest way to produce enlarged negatives is to project color slides onto sheet film (in total darkness, of course) and develop for the desired degree of contrast. Use panchromatic film if you want to reproduce the colors in normal shades of gray or if you are interested in making color separations for gum or carbon printing. Tri-X film is good because of its extended highlight contrast but you may have to reduce the enlarger light intensity (neutral density filters are useful for this) to avoid exposure times of fractions of a second. These short times may not be a problem if you have an electronic timer for your enlarger or if you can fit a BTL shutter to the enlarger lens, but the average mechanical timer cannot cope with exposures of less than a second or so.

Make a test strip on the film, just as you would on paper, being sure to include the deepest shadow tones of the image on the test strip. The exposure must be sufficient to produce useful detail in shadow areas; film development will control the highlight density. If you want a soft negative, develop the sheet film in some good film developer, like D-76, for about two-thirds the recommended "normal" time. Even this may be too much if the transparency is unusually contrasty. For contrasty negatives, suitable for cyanotype or platinum, develop for somewhat more than normal time.

The final negative should show detail in the shadows but not have any unnecessary shadow density. The highlights, for the gum negative, should be thin enough to read through when the negative is placed in contact with a magazine page but should appear generally quite dark. Cyanotype negative highlights should obscure the type completely. If you have a densitometer available for measurement, the gum negative should have a shadow density of about .25 and a highlight density of about .9 or 1.0. Cyanotype negatives should range from about .25 to about 1.6 minimum.

If you need to make enlarged negatives from existing small ones, you have at least two alternatives. You can project the original negative onto Kodak SO-015 film, or you can make an intermediate positive transparency and print that on film to make the final negative.

Kodak Professional Direct Duplicating film, SO-015, is convenient but expensive and somewhat limited in range. It is also a fairly unstable material which should be used fresh. Because it is a *direct reversal* material, it will produce a *negative* image from the original negative. Keep this firmly in mind. If you've had much experience in photography, it will be difficult to believe that *more* exposure is required to make an image *lighter;* but, with this material, it's true.

Make a test strip (including exposures of up to at least 2 minutes) in the usual manner and develop in Dektol, 1:1, for 2 minutes, using a light red (series 1A) filter in your safelight. Fix the film as usual and, after a brief wash, inspect it carefully in good light to appraise the densities. If the strip is too light, make another and reduce the exposure; if too dark, increase exposure. Contrast is controllable by development; to increase contrast, increase developing time; to lower contrast, reduce development time or dilute the developer, or both. Under ideal conditions, SO-015 will yield good duplicate negatives, usually with a somewhat greenish image tone, and with a fairly high background density level. Old film is likely to produce foggy, low-contrast images.

Making duplicate negatives from intermediate positive transparencies is less convenient and more time-consuming than using the direct duplicating film, but it permits greater control and usually produces negatives of good quality with minimum fog density. The positive image can be made by either projection or contact, but, in the interest of saving material, it need not be as large as the final negative. It's probably best to make it by projection, large enough to handle easily but still small enough to fit into the enlarger carrier for final projection onto the negative film. Fine-Grain Positive film is a reasonable material for this positive image; but, for critical work, something like Gravure Positive film, or Professional Copy film (both of which will enhance the shadow contrast of the positive) may be more suitable.

**Make a test strip;
work for murky highlights**

**You have some control of contrast at
this stage**

**And still more when you make the
negative**

Fine-Grain Positive film can be handled in the light of an OA or OC filter and has about the same printing speed as Polycontrast paper. The film has no backing dye so it can be exposed from either side, but it is generally preferable to expose the emulsion side. You can identify the emulsion side by the code notch (in the top right-hand corner of the sheet, when the emulsion is facing you) or by its very slightly dull appearance compared to the back. The sheets usually curl toward the emulsion, too, but don't count on it.

Make a normal test strip and develop in Dektol (or other standard print developer), diluted normally, for 2 minutes. Select the time which produces distinctly grayed highlights; this positive is not intended to be an attractive image itself and it must have unusually well-defined highlight details if they are to be retained in the negative. Contrast can be varied to some extent by development but the practical range is not great. Development for less than 45 seconds (with constant agitation) will yield weak shadows and probably result in uneven or mottled tones. Extending development beyond 7 or 8 minutes will not result in a useful increase in contrast.

As a rule of thumb, if the original negative is contrasty (needs a #1 paper to print well), develop the transparency in Dektol, 1:1, for 45 seconds or in D-76 for about 4 minutes. If the negative is normal develop the positive about 2 minutes in Dektol; if the negative is flat (needs a #3 or #4 paper to print well), develop 4 to 8 minutes in Dektol. Development will influence the effective film speed to some extent. Adjust the exposure to obtain the necessary "grimy" highlights if the development is unusually long or short.

Contrast can be modified still further, if need be, in making the negative. Project the positive image onto any standard sheet film or, preferably, Kodak Commercial film or Professional Copy film, both of which can be handled in red safelight. If the transparency contrast appears to be about normal (for a print image) when viewed against strong light, develop the negative film to a contrast index of about .4 for low-contrast results and about .7 or more for negatives suitable for

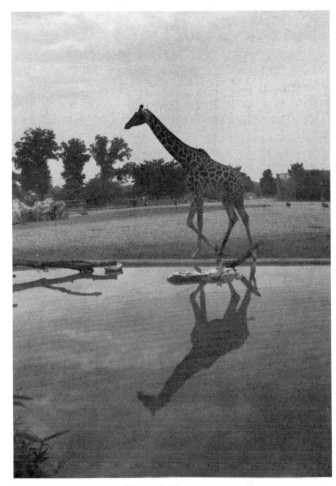

Figure 9.11
Transparency with grayed highlights

cyanotype. (See discussion of contrast index, pages 219–221 and appendix charts on pages 308–309.)

You can use Commercial or Copy film for both the positive transparencies and the final negatives, if you want to, with very fine results. Try developing both negative and positive films in Dektol, 1:1, for about 2 to 4 minutes. If the final negative contrast is too high, reduce development time in either or both steps. If too low, increase it.

When very large negatives are required, it is almost prohibitively expensive to use regular camera film like Tri-X, Plus-X, or Super-XX; in fact, it is now almost impossible to get large sheets of these films even on special order. One alternative which can be quite satisfactory is to use one of the less well-known litho films, which are relatively inexpensive and can often be obtained from graphic arts supply houses. Ordinarily these materials produce extremely high-contrast images, but they can be made to yield negatives of fairly normal characteristics if they are developed in relatively mild film developers. If you try this, be sure to use a safe safelight; ordinary developers enhance the speed of these films and may produce fog if the safelight is too bright. D-76 is a good developer to start with, either straight or diluted if still lower contrast is desired. For bold, posterish effects, of course, use the film as it is intended to be used and it will give you its natural dropout images.

The Cyanotype Process

The cyanotype process is probably the easiest "old process" there is. It is also versatile, attractive for some purposes, and remarkably stable. Aside from the chemicals involved, there is nothing new to buy; you will need a few trays, a printing frame, a good bright light source, rich in ultraviolet (a sunlamp will work pretty well or you can use sunlight), some paper or cloth to sensitize, and a flat brush of appropriate size to spread the sensitizer fluid with. A natural bristle fan-blender, about #6, is fine for prints of moderate size. Here is the simplest formula I know.

Solution A
ferric ammonium citrate	25 gms
water	100 mls

Solution B
potassium ferricyanide	9 gms
water	100 mls

Store the solutions in separate brown "dropper" bottles if you will be making only small prints. If you plan to work on cloth or make very large prints on paper, make larger volumes of both solutions and store them in plain brown bottles.

For use (in dim room light), mix equal parts of the two solutions together in a glass or plastic container and spread the mixture thinly on paper, brushing it back and forth gently until it is even and no longer fluid. Hang the paper in a dark place to dry and hasten the drying, if possible, with gentle heat or air movement, or both. When dry, the paper is ready to print. Place it under a negative and expose to direct sunlight until the coating which is visible around the edges of the negative has changed from its original yellow-green color to a distinct bluish-gray (or some other dark tint).

When the paper is removed from the printing frame, there should be a fairly distinct printed-out image visible but its intensity is not an absolutely reliable guide to exposure.

Development couldn't be simpler; slip the print into a tray of cool water and agitate it gently. The image will form in a few seconds and progress to a deep, rich blue color. Further washing in several changes of water is all that is really necessary to fix the image but it will be more stable if it is rinsed in a weak solution of hydrochloric acid (commercial Muriatic Acid is all right)—just a few drops in a quart of water will be sufficient. *Caution*—hydrochloric acid is poisonous and corrosive. Read the warning label and handle it with extreme caution.

The color of the image will be altered to greenish-blue by this acid treatment. It can be turned into an intense purplish-blue by immersion in a weak solution of ammonium hydroxide (household ammonia will do as well)—again, just a few drops in a quart of water will do. *Caution*—ammonium hydroxide is a strong base with suffocating vapors. Handle with care in a well-ventilated area. If the ammonia is too strong the image will be lightened and perhaps destroyed, but if the process has not gone too far it can be reversed in the acid bath. The alkaline purple color is elegant, but probably not as stable as the normal blue-green.

Figure 9.12

a. Cyanotypes are simple and inexpensive to make. Blend the two ingredients in a glass beaker or ceramic cup; don't use a metal container or you may have staining problems.

b. Spread the mixture on the paper rather generously. On some papers two coats may be required to produce a good image. The brush shown is a fan-blender. Its metal ferrule has been lacquered to prevent possible rust stains which would show up as blue streaks. Coating can be done in ordinary room light but avoid direct sunlight or bright fluorescents.

c. Hang the coated paper in a dark place to dry. Quick drying is beneficial and moderate heat can be used. The coating is a light yellowish-green at this point.

d. When the paper is thoroughly dry, put it in a printing frame with your negative, emulsion to emulsion. Contrasty negatives will give the best results.

e. Expose to a bright light, rich in UV. Daylight is usable but may be variable. This bank of fluorescent tubes is a fine fast source. The exposure will be long—at least several minutes.

f. There will be a strong printed-out image when the exposure has been sufficient, as demonstrated by the undeveloped section of the print in the model's right hand. Development in plain water is almost instantaneous. Acid water gives greenish tones, alkaline water produces purplish tones and will eventually reduce the image density. Strong alkalis will destroy it. No fixing is required. Rinse the paper until no more blue color is discharged, then hang the print up to dry.

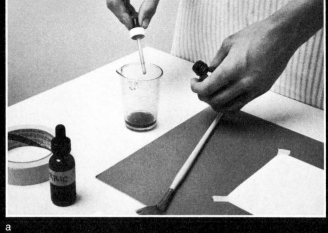

a

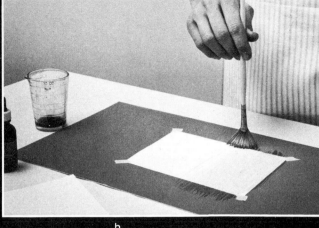

b

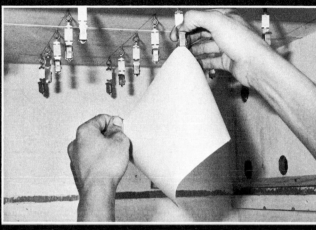

c

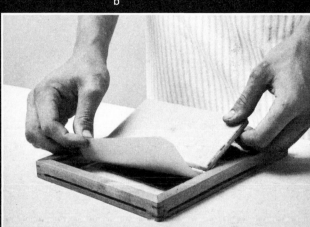

d

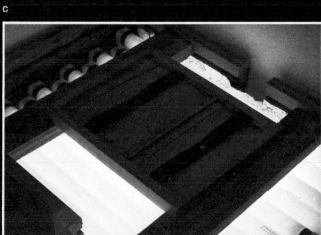

e

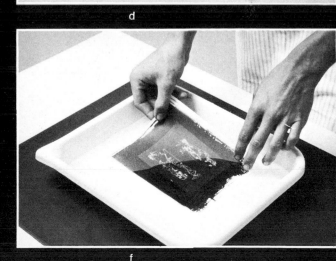

f

Cyanotypes can be made on cloth

Watch out for rust contamination

Gum produces pigment images in black-and-white or color

Equipment and materials are minimal

The pigments, and especially the paper, are very important

Cyanotypes can be made on cloth almost as easily as on paper. Small pieces of cloth can be dipped in the solutions and squeezed dry before hanging them in the dark for final drying. Larger areas can be sensitized with a large sponge well charged with the sensitizer. Spread the cloth out on papers to protect the table or floor, and wet it as uniformly as possible with the sponge. Too much sensitizer is better than too little. The image will use what it needs and the rest will simply wash away.

The cyanotype process is usually quite trouble-free but a few difficulties may arise. Like most of these old processes, the paper used is an important factor in determining the quality of the image. Problems of weak or mottled tones, local variations in color, grayed or glazed-over dark tones, and obvious coating streaks in the image may all be due, at least in part, to the paper itself. The best papers are firm, smooth long-fiber papers with good wet-strength. Rag stationery is usually good and so are many good-quality drawing papers, watercolor papers, and some art papers. The real test of paper, however, is actual use. Try a sample and see what happens. If the image is satisfactory, the paper is good. Cyanotypes are quite permanent in normal handling but launder cyanotype-printed cloth as infrequently as possible and avoid strong soaps or bleaches. Alkaline solutions will destroy the dye image.

Chemical contamination is an occasional problem. Blue streaks may form in the coating before development if particles of rust should happen to fall into the sensitizer or if the coating brush has a rusty metal ferrule. It's better to avoid metal ferrules, if you can, or at least to seal them from the sensitizer with lacquer or clear nail polish. For the same reason, don't mix or store the sensitizer solution in any sort of metal container; use plastic or glass.

The Gum-Bichromate Process

The gum-bichromate process, and the similar *casein* and *glue processes,* all produce pigment images. Any color pigment can be used, and the images can be monochromatic or multicolored. The processes are capable of reasonably good photographic representation as well as broad, flat-tone effects and there is plenty of opportunity for hand-modification of the image if that is desired.

The equipment required is minimal. You'll need a coating brush, such as the fan-blender previously mentioned, a printing frame, two or three trays a little larger than your print size, and some exposing light—a sunlamp or the sun itself will do. The chemicals are gum arabic (sometimes called gum acacia) and either sodium or potassium or ammonium dichromate (the same chemical used to be called *bi*chromate). Of these, potassium dichromate is the least satisfactory but it will work if that's all you can find. Ammonium dichromate is usually recommended and is available from graphic arts suppliers and, especially, silk-screen supply houses. Sodium dichromate is as good as ammonium dichromate for these processes but is slightly more expensive to use and a little less common. All three are inexpensive chemicals and the quantities used are so small that the cost is almost negligible.

You'll need some pigment colors and some paper. Watercolor pigments (not casein or acrylic colors), either in tubes or in dry form, are generally good; get tube colors at first to simplify mixing and measuring. The earth colors, such as umbers, siennas, and ochers, are generally good. Ivory black usually works well and some people like lamp black. The modern synthetic colors are generally good, too. Don't get the cheapest "student" grade colors; some of them contain dye rather than pigment and dyes don't work well, as a rule. Start out with ivory black or burnt umber or burnt sienna.

The paper must have good wet-strength so it should be at least part rag and quite well-sized. Watercolor papers are generally usable as are some drawing papers. Avoid soft papers at first; they have a tendency to stain. Very hard or glazed papers will have the opposite effect; they'll tend to give you high-contrast, dropout type images, and the image may flake off in unsightly patches. Try several types of paper and see which works best for you.

**Prepare the gum solution;
it will have to stand**

**Prepare the dichromate solution;
use care**

**Store the solutions in dropper bottles;
measure by squirts**

Mix the ingredients thoroughly

Test for pigment strength

Begin by preparing these two solutions:

Solution A

first dissolve	mercuric chloride	3 gms
in	hot water (125°F)	300 mls
then add	cold water	300 mls
and stir in	gum arabic (powder)	250 gms

Mercuric chloride, used here as a preservative for the gum solution, is a dangerous poison and must be handled with extreme care. Avoid contact with the powder; don't breathe the dust; and wash your hands and utensils thoroughly after handling this material. It dissolves with difficulty even in hot water. Be sure it is completely in solution before adding the cold water and the gum. The gum will not dissolve immediately. Stir it until it has been thoroughly wet, then let it stand in a covered wide-mouth bottle for a day or two. It will gradually go into solution and turn into a tan-colored, syrupy liquid. Keep it covered to prevent evaporation and it will keep indefinitely. (If mixed without the mercuric chloride, or some other preservative, the gum solution will sour within just a few days.) Be careful to clean off the top of the bottle before screwing the cover on; the gum mixture is an excellent adhesive and is capable of gluing the bottle cap on firmly. If this happens to you, run hot water over the bottle cap until the dried gum is softened, then remove the cap and clean it thoroughly.

Solution B

| ammonium dichromate | 150 gms |
| water | 600 mls |

or, alternatively (and my personal preference),

| sodium dichromate | 300 gms |
| water | 600 mls |

If only potassium dichromate is available to you, prepare a saturated solution and use it in place of these as solution *B*. Store the dichromate solution in a brown bottle to protect it from strong light. It will keep indefinitely. *Caution*—dichromates are poisonous and can be absorbed through the skin to cause painful and dangerous dermatitis. They can be handled safely with reasonable precautions, but be careful not to inhale the dry chemical dust or allow the crystals or their solutions to remain on the skin. Rubber gloves will offer complete protection, but a silicone barrier cream rubbed into the skin before contact will probably be adequate. If no hand protection is used, try to avoid prolonged or repeated contact with the chemicals, and wash your hands immediately and thoroughly after each use.

For use, pour small quantities of solutions *A* and *B* into separate dropper bottles and measure the working quantities by "droppersfull" or "squirts." Fasten a piece of your selected paper down on a clean washable (or disposable) surface using small bits of tape at the corners of the sheet. In an old ceramic coffee cup, or other similar container, measure out 2 "squirts" of the gum solution and add to it a 1-inch long section of the pigment "worm" squeezed from your tube of, say, burnt umber. Dampen the fan-blender brush with plain water and slap it as dry as possible against your hand or a towel; then stir the pigment and gum with the brush until the pigment lump is apparently dispersed. Finally, holding the brush vertically in the pigment mixture, twirl the handle rapidly between your palms until the gum mixture is whipped into a fine froth and check to be sure none of the pigment is clinging to the brush hairs.

In moderately dim room light, add 2 squirts of the dichromate solution and stir briskly until blended. Then, after pressing most of the gum mixture out of the brush against the side of the container, paint a small patch on one corner or edge of the paper, spread it out, and brush it back and forth lightly until the brush begins to drag a little. The area should be thoroughly covered but not obviously wet with the liquid. Label this patch "4 squirts." Now add 2 more squirts of gum (and 2 more of dichromate), blend thoroughly and paint another patch, labelled "8 squirts." Continue this process, adding measured amounts of gum and sensitizer, blending, coating, and labelling, until you have a total of, perhaps, 20 squirts of solution, and have six or eight patches on the paper. Hang the paper in a dark place to dry. Use warm moving air to hasten drying, if you can.

Figure 9.13

a. To make the pigment test, as described in the text, measure the pigment "worm" to determine quantity. This much is plenty for the entire test.

b. Whip the pigment into the gum solution alone, then when it is thoroughly blended, add the dichromate solution and blend again. Be sure there are no particles of raw pigment clinging to the brush hairs; they'll leave streaks in the image.

c. Press the brush almost dry against the side of the mixing container, then paint a small patch on the paper. Brush it out until it shows no tendency to run, then add a measured quantity of gum and dichromate to the mixture and paint another patch. Repeat, diluting the mixture each time by some known amount, until you have produced a series of patches, ranging from dark to very light tone. Judge the tone by pigment content only, if you can; they'll all be strongly stained with dichromate yellow.

d. Hang the test strip up to dry in a dark place. Strong light will invalidate the test.

e. Don't expose the test strip. Simply take it out of the drying cabinet when it is completely dry and immerse it in cool water. After a few moments the pigment will begin to loosen. Float the paper facedown on the surface of the water and let it stand quietly for a half hour or so. Be sure there are no air bubbles trapped under it while it's developing.

f. When the paper no longer drains any appreciable amount of pigment, consider it fully developed and hang it up to dry. When it is completely dry, pick out the patch that shows just the faintest trace of pigment stain. That mixture is the maximum strength that you can use for printing without risking stained highlights.

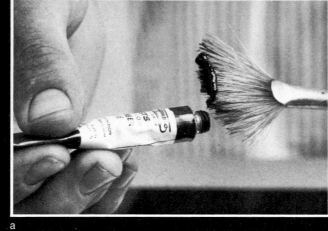

a

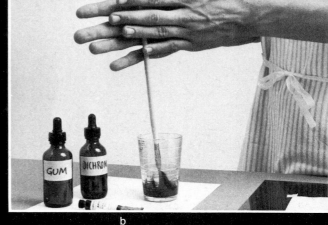

b

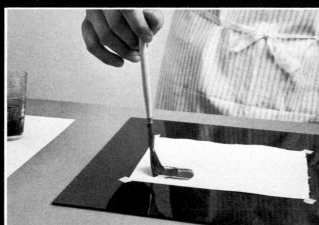

c

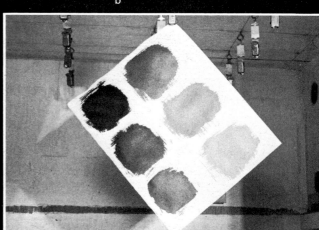

d

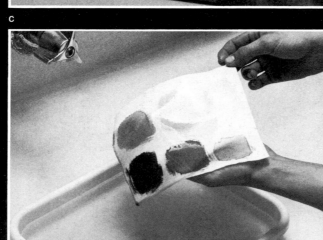

e

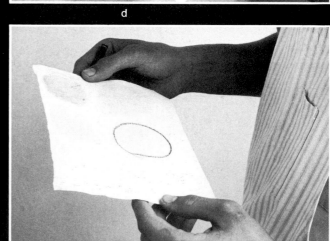

f

g. Mix a batch of the selected emulsion and spread it rather briskly, brushing it out until the brush marks stop blending readily and begin to show. Then, with much lighter strokes, whip the surface gently with just the bristle tips to blend the marks away. The emulsion will begin to feel a little tacky—a sign that it's ready to hang up to dry.

h. Dry the coated paper in the dark.

i. Put it into the printing frame.

j. Expose it. You'll have to determine the exposure time by trial. Gum is faster than cyanotype but the exposure will still be timed in minutes. Tungsten lamps are a poor source of light for these processes; they produce too much heat and not enough UV. Fluorescents are good if you can get enough of them together. Sunlamps are usable.

k. Develop. Don't handle the print after it begins to drip pigment, unless you want granular tones and unsubtle gradation. For best tonality float it until all soluble pigment has been discharged.

l. Multiple-gum is capable of full tonal range and good gradation. Here is a three-layer print in a black and burnt umber mixture.

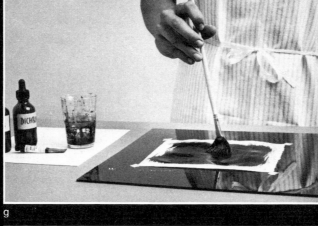
g

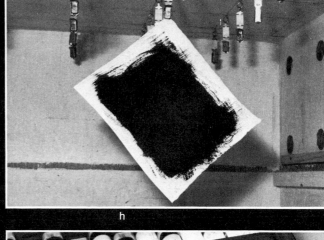
h

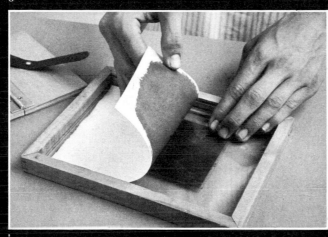
i

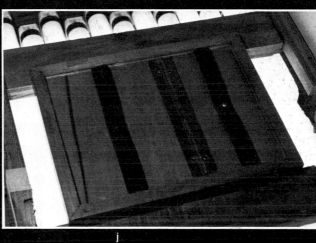
j

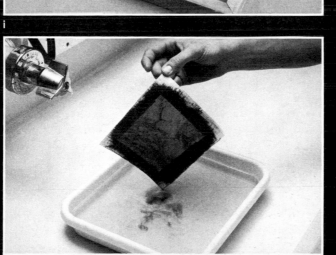
k

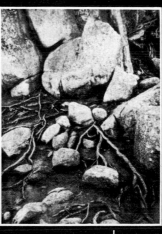
l

Float the paper facedown on plain cool water—carefully

Each paper and each pigment may give different results

Make a print

Then another, and another, and another

Every gum print is unique

When the paper has dried thoroughly (*don't* expose it to bright light), slip it into a tray of cool tap water, faceup, and immediately pick it out by one corner to let it drain. The dichromate will dissolve almost instantly and drain off in a yellow stream. Reimmerse the paper and drain again and repeat this procedure until you see some indication that the pigment is beginning to loosen. As soon as this occurs, gently place the paper, facedown this time, on the surface of the water, being careful not to trap a bubble of air under it, and let it float quietly for a half hour. Then rinse it *very* gently in a tray of clean water and let it drain dry, hanging from one corner in a film dryer or on an open line.

When the paper is completely dry, the pigment patches (if there are any left) will be durable and you can handle the paper freely. Inspect it in good light. If the test has been successful, one or more of the pigment patches will have disappeared but some will probably still be visible and perhaps even quite dark. This procedure is designed to test the maximum amount of pigment which you can use and still retain reasonably "white" highlights in the image.

Let's suppose the ½-inch patch is almost colorless but the ¾-inch patch shows a distinct tone; this indicates that ½ inch of *this* pigment, mixed into 10 squirts of gum-dichromate mixture (equal parts) and spread on *this* paper, is an optimum mixture. Other pigments may permit greater concentration or may require less; other papers may stain at lower concentrations or wash clean at much higher ones. If you're interested in predictable control of the medium, you should probably run this sort of test with each pigment and each paper you plan to use.

When you have arrived at a paper and pigment combination that pleases you, coat a whole sheet with the optimum mixture and dry it thoroughly. Then expose it, under your (fairly low-contrast) negative, to the printing light and make a conventional test strip exposure series with times running from about 1 minute to about 10 or 15 minutes. You should be able to see a faint image resulting from the exposure but it is not a reliable guide.

Wet and drain the print until the color starts to loosen, then float it, image down, in clean water for the half hour, changing the water once or twice if it becomes badly discolored. Handle the wet print *very* gently; the gum image is extremely delicate and fragile at this stage.

Select the best test section and make another print using the indicated time. If all goes well, it should be acceptable. If not, make another, and another, and another. . . .

If you are after normal photographic tonality in your gum prints, you will probably be unhappy with most of them because of their very low contrast. This is an inherent characteristic of the medium and can't be cured by any such apparently logical moves as using more contrasty negatives or adding more pigment to the mixture. If you want better contrast and richer dark tones than a single layer of pigment can provide, you'll have to resort to *multiple-gum printing*. As the name implies, this involves coating the dry print with another layer of pigmented gum, registering the negative over the existing image, developing it, and drying it. If the contrast is still not good enough, do it all again. Some of the old Pictorialists have been reported to have gone through as many as seventeen printings to get a single image but that seems rather extreme.

For satisfactory contrast in a monochromatic image, using good paper and a good pigment (avoid gouaches or "designers colors" for multiple-gum printing), three printings is usually sufficient.

Although this sounds tiresome, consider what you may have when you finish. If all goes well, the print will have a long scale of tones from near-white to a rich velvety dark; it will have a pleasantly soft definition which emphasizes tonal masses rather than edges and textures; it will preserve much of the intrinsic surface quality of the paper it's printed on; it will be one of the most permanent of photographic images; it will testify to your skill as a craftsman; and it will be unique, because no two multiple-gum prints can possibly be identical in every detail. Although this medium is certainly not appropriate for every type of photographic

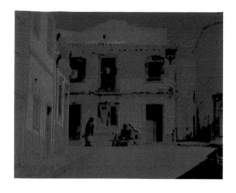
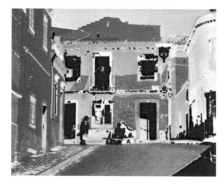
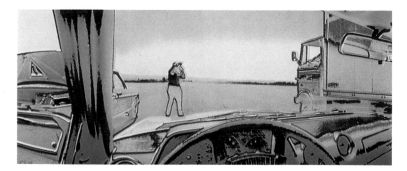

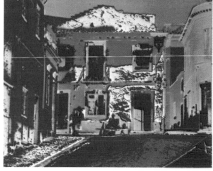
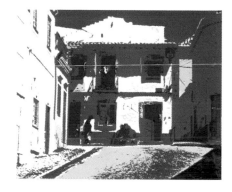
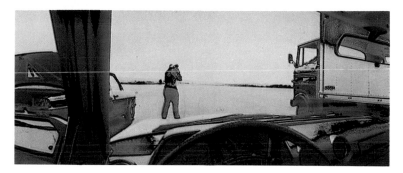

Colorplate 20
Simple posterizations like these are
easy to make on Cibachrome. The colors
can be any that you choose and can be
made brilliant or muted by controlling
exposures.

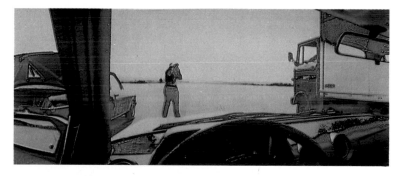

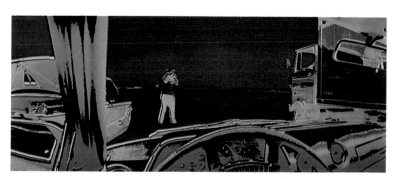

Colorplate 21

Colorplate 22

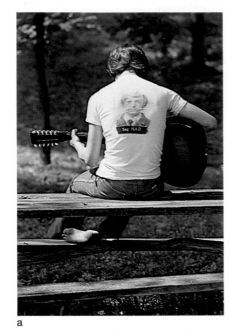

a

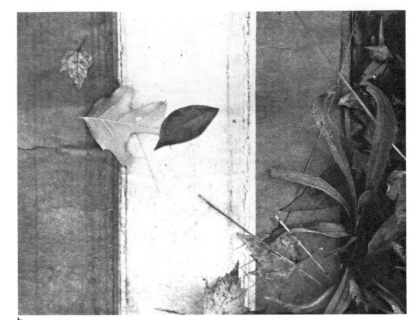

b

Colorplate 23

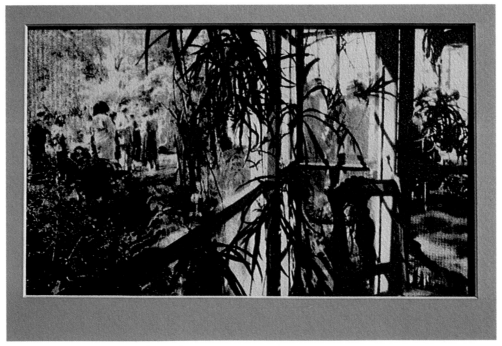

Natural or arbitrary color can be achieved

Registration is difficult

But you don't have to register if you don't want to

Gums and cyanotypes can be dry-mounted

This has only scratched the surface

image, it is very suitable for some and will certainly attract attention.

Multiple-gum prints can also be made in either natural or arbitrary color. Full-scale prints in natural color will, typically, require six or seven printings, two for each pigment primary color and a final one of a dark neutral shade to accent the blacks. The negatives can be made conveniently from any color slide by direct projection on panchromatic film, using the usual color separation filters (Wratten #s 29, 61, 47B). No color correction masks are necessary. The only requirements are that the negatives be of suitably low density and contrast and that they be approximately matched. As in dye-transfer printing, the red-filter negative (#29) prints cyan (thalo blue) pigment; the green filter negative (#61) prints magenta (alizarin crimson); and the blue filter negative (#47B) prints yellow (cadmium yellow light). They are usually printed in sequence (yellow, magenta, cyan; yellow, magenta, cyan), with a final coating of Payne's gray or ivory black.

Registering the images for multiple-gum printing is one of its most difficult aspects. Because the existing image is practically obscured by each fresh coating of sensitizer, it's almost impossible to register the negative visually. In my opinion, the best (nonmechanical) method of registration is the one outlined by Paul Anderson in the old Henney and Dudley *Handbook of Photography,* published by Whittlesey House about 1939. He suggests scribing register lines on the negative margins and using paper sheets *smaller* than the negative so the register lines can be transferred to the *back* of the print when it is first printed. For subsequent printings it is only necessary to place the coated paper on the negative, facedown, and match the register lines, a relatively simple and foolproof procedure (fig. 9.14).

Of course, it isn't necessary to register the images at all if you don't want to, and most contemporary gum-printers don't. Gum is an excellent technique for doing color montages or for incorporating a photographic image into a drawing or watercolor painting. The images can also be produced on some other materials, too, including cloth. It is, in fact, a very versatile and interest-

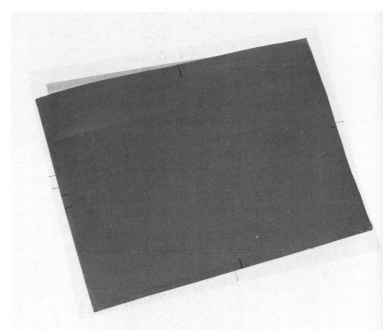

Figure 9.14
Seen on a light box, this gum print appears dark gray as it lies facedown on its negative. The registration marks on the negative and the print permit accurate repositioning of the print for each new exposure.

ing technique but one which will never be widely practiced (except in its crudest forms) because of its difficulty.

Gum prints and cyanotypes, and, for that matter, almost all of the old process prints, can be mounted and matted in the same way conventional silver prints are handled. Either high- or low-temperature mounting tissues may be used but you should be especially careful to dry out the mounting press. Gum prints can be spotted with regular watercolor pigments of the appropriate color.

This relatively brief description of two old processes should give you enough information to get started; but it has only scratched the surface. There are many other ways to produce photographic images using these basic materials and each method has certain unique characteristics. There is, fortunately, a great deal of published information available and, if these image forms interest you, you should have no trouble finding formulas and instructions for the technique of your choice. You will find a few readily available reference book listed in the bibliography on pages 331–332.

Summary

The normal photographic process represents the subject without obvious distortion, but there are many ways to manipulate the process for dramatic effect. One way is to drop out the image gray tones by using a very high-contrast film material, such as Kodalith—a slow, ortho material which requires a special developer for greatest contrast. By using Kodalith as a print material and varying the print exposures, an image can be separated into several different areas of flat tone and recombined to form a posterization.

Negatives can be masked by printing them on film, then registering the positive with the original negative. Masking reduces image contrast and may alter it selectively. Misregistering the images allows a thin outline to form which can be printed as a bas-relief. By slightly separating the registered images a similar outline can be produced which resembles an ink line drawing and is called a tone-line image.

A somewhat similar effect can be obtained by exposing a partly developed film or paper image to dim white light, briefly, then continuing the development. When properly executed, this flash exposure partially reverses the image, causing it to mask itself, and forms white Mackie lines around contrasting forms. This Sabattier effect is commonly called solarization (which is something else entirely) and is frequently interesting.

Screening the image allows it to be printed in silk screen, etching, or lithographic techniques by breaking the tones into tiny dots of pure black and white. The visual illusion of gradation still exists if the dots are small enough. If the image is enlarged, the screen pattern becomes visible as a texture or pattern which

may be decorative. Random dot patterns can be produced by printing an ordinary negative or film positive on Kodalith through nonglare glass or some similar material.

Color solarization is possible but rather unpredictable. Color posterization is fairly easy on Cibachrome. Proceed as in black-and-white, but use positive masks, and test for color and exposure. Remember, colors will be additive and filter factors must be applied to the exposures.

Posterization is awkward with negative papers but it can be done on color film by successively photographing different image separations on a light table, through various filters. The separations can be either high-contrast or continuous-tone, positive or negative, or combinations, and may be registered or not. The process is fast and easy once set up, and bizarre effects can be produced. The finished transparencies can be printed, if desired, on Cibachrome.

Machine art and generated images are currently popular. Xerox black-and-white copiers are widely available and widely used. Color Xerox copiers offer and appealing alternative to the usual color processes.

The old processes are becoming increasingly popular. There are three general categories—silver-sensitive systems, iron-sensitive systems, and bichromated colloid systems. All of the old processes are slow and will usually require brilliant printing light and contact-printing procedures.

You can make the necessary large negatives for these processes by projecting color slide images onto regular sheet film and developing to the appropriate degree of contrast. Cyanotype negatives should be quite contrasty; gum negatives (for continuous tone results) should be quite low in contrast. To duplicate existing negatives, you can use Kodak SO-015 but you'll get better results by making an intermediate positive on film and printing it to final size, again on film. Very large negatives can be made on litho film, developed in mild developer for normal contrast results.

The cyanotype process produces deep blue images on almost any material including paper and cloth.

The entire process can be carried out in dim room light and the materials are relatively cheap and available.

Gum-bichromate prints are pigment images. They can be made in any color or combination of colors and can be manipulated very easily. Equipment and material needs are minimal. You will have to experiment to find a paper and a procedure that works for you. Use good quality watercolor pigments at first and follow the chemical preparation and testing instructions carefully.

Full-color photographic quality gum prints are the most difficult to make. Work from low-contrast color-separation negatives and use the recommended pigment colors. Registration is difficult; nonrealistic, non-registered color is much easier. Gum prints are easy to combine with painting or drawing techniques and every print is unique.

10 What Is a Good Photograph?

A good photograph for you is any photograph you like

Much significant art has derived from self-expression

But don't consider this as license to do your own thing

What is a good photograph? That depends upon whom you ask and what criteria are being used to make the judgment. In the opinion of the gallery-owner, a good photograph is one he can sell easily and at a good price. The scientist considers a good photograph one which displays the visual information he wants, clearly and succinctly. The advertising art director and his client call a photograph good if it will glamorize the product and make it appealing to the purchaser. Your photography teacher may call your photographs good if he sees in them some sign of visual awareness, technical ingenuity, or personal expression. To your mother, any photograph of you is good, especially if it shows you smiling. A good photograph, for you, is any photograph you like, whether anyone else likes it or not.

The definitions above relate to the judgment of the consumer of photographs; as a producer of photographs, your criteria of what is "good" should be quite different. Logically, an artist can consider his work good if producing it is an engrossing and gratifying experience and if the finished work measures up to or exceeds his expectations. The process of *making* and his satisfaction with the result reflect the artist's taste. The success or failure of the work in the marketplace reflects the taste of the consuming public.

You should consider carefully the difference between these two criteria. Although a great deal of "fine art" of the past was commissioned by wealthy patrons, much of the work that we consider to be significant or seminal in the history of art reflects the desire of the artist for *self*-expression. It seems unlikely that Picasso's *Guernica,* for example, could have resulted from a commercial assignment. Julia Margaret Cameron's magnificient portraits of the great men of her time resulted from her feeling that photographing them was "the embodiment of a prayer." By comparison, her contrived allegorical illustrations of literary and biblical themes are unremarkable and, in some cases, insipid and silly. More recently, the commercial work of Avedon, Arbus, Davidson, and Michals, although skillful and ingeniously effective for its purpose, is much less interesting and inspiring than their personal work. It seems clear that the "best" work done by any artist is the work he does to please himself solely, unmindful of the opinions or criticisms of others.

You shouldn't, however, consider this as license to "do your own thing," regardless of consequences. Only relatively mature and sophisticated individuals who have mastered their craft are equipped to produce work of much lasting significance. Furthermore, as human beings we can't operate in total isolation; communication, sharing of ideas, and approval are all important to us. The work of an inexperienced, unskilled artist, however gratifying it may be for him, will probably seem naive and crude to a sophisticated public, and this re-

Without the guidance of personal taste, work becomes trendy

Taste differences are not serious

But wishful seeing is

The photographic process is predictable

And the hand of the photographer is well concealed

Selection and organization are the essence of straight photography

jection can be a painful experience. Far too many young artists react to this rejection by subduing their own instincts and trying to cater to what they perceive to be "public taste." This can only lead to mediocrity. Without the intuitive guidance of personal taste, their work must necessarily mimic that of others and become derivative and "trendy." The better course, by far, is to work harder to develop your own taste and improve your skills until your work merits attention. Then you'll get the approval you deserve.

Although you shouldn't accept other people's pronouncements of what is "good" and "bad" without question, you should consider their reactions to your work carefully and as objectively as you can. By showing your work, you are both asking for approval and risking criticism. If you get criticism rather than approval, it is obvious that your critic's taste differs from yours or that the fine qualities which you see in the photograph are not apparent to him. If approval is important to you (and if you're human, it certainly is), you must find out what the problem is and try to correct it.

Simple differences in taste are not particularly serious. Your critic can express lack of interest in your work but concede that it is well conceived and well executed for what it is. The more serious problem is a difference in perception of the work and this is something that you should consider very carefully. If you are a beginner in photography, you may still be so charmed by the mere mechanics of image formation that *any* picture is a triumph. On an intermediate level you may feel that you have entered the ranks of the Friedlanders and Winogrands with a series of "street photographs" which your critics see as rather pointless snapshots. Even mature photographers can fall into the trap of "wishful seeing" and fail to recognize in their pictures flaws which are distractingly evident to another person. Like a person singing in the shower, exulting in the beauty and resonance of his melodious tones, we all tend to see in our own photographs just those fine qualities that we *want* to see; and just as the singer's efforts may sound, to a person outside, like the bellowing of a wounded moose, so may the inadvertent flaws in our work be distressingly obvious to viewers.

Take criticism seriously, then, but not personally. Good criticism can indicate to you the success or failure of your efforts to share your ideas and emotions. It should not be interpreted as an attack on you as an individual. Criticism can help you grow; learn to deal with it objectively.

Photography is a complex mechanical medium governed to a very large extent by physical and chemical principles which are reliable, predictable, and inflexible. Because of this, it is fairly easy to become technically competent; all that is required is comprehension of the principles, respect for the materials, and careful workmanship. But this same technical rigidity makes photography a difficult medium of personal expression. Unlike the other visual arts, which permit the gradual building up of a work, constantly subject to review and modification at the artist's whim, photography allows almost no opportunity for review or change during the actual process of image formation. The image can be modified, to be sure, by subsequent manipulation, but it is initially a record of what the lens "saw" at the instant of film exposure.

In this sort of medium the hand of the artist is well concealed. There are no telltale brushstrokes, no personal idiosyncracies of line, perspective, or color, and very few possibilities for useful "accidents" such as the natural blending of fluid color in a wash drawing or the spontaneous crazing of a ceramic glaze. Accidents, in most photographic processes, are disastrous rather than decorative. "Creativity" in photography is, therefore, limited to the organization or selection of subject matter and manipulation of the image after it is formed.

Selection and organization of subject matter is the essence of "straight" photography. The choice of camera position, lens focal length, depth of field, exposure interval, film type, filters or other lens attachments, light condition, and development will contribute to a certain quality of image which will reflect, to some degree, the taste and sensitivity of the photographer. The work will be still further personalized by the choice of print materials and the presentation style of the finished image. The degree to which a photographer's style is recognizable will depend partly upon the degree to

Don't be fooled by this medium

You are programmed to see what you want to see

Is it any wonder that your friends fall asleep?

Your pictures must be coherent

And well organized

which his personal taste and judgment are involved in making these various selections and decisions. It will also depend upon the extent of his commitment and the lengths to which he'll go to achieve "perfection." Don't be fooled by the apparent simplicity of this medium; technically, it's easy to master; artistically, you'll find it a formidable challenge.

One of your first problems, as a beginning photographer, will be learning to see things as the camera will record them, and there are a few fundamental differences between human vision and camera vision that you will have to become accustomed to. In the first place, your eyes really see sharply only very small areas of any subject at any given moment. Your visual impression of things you look at is assembled mentally from a series of fragments which you perceive in very brief, scanning glances. Added to this is a general visual orientation of the entire area of the subject obtained by your very wide-angle but unfocused peripheral vision. You use the peripheral vision to establish the relative position of objects in space, then glance at the areas that seem to need more complete analysis with your precise central vision.

This is generally a very brief, totally unconscious act. Your eyes leap from point to point without being willed to do so, and your brain pieces the visual bits together. At the same time, your brain computer is operating to make the impression intelligible. It automatically emphasizes things which it knows will interest you and suppresses things which you have programmed it, by experience, to classify as insignificant.

In addition to the purely visual impressions that you receive, your computer circuits may supply you with some information from your other senses. All of these bits add up to a general impression of the total experience. If you are paying attention, you will experience some sort of reaction, usually a mild one, of interest or boredom, pleasure or displeasure. If you experience pleasure while you are looking for photographic subject matter, you will probably take a picture of the object or scene that prompted it; and if it is done casually for so trivial a reason, it will probably be a rather trivial picture.

The reason is not complicated. The camera simply does not record what your brain recorded. Your snapshot photograph really does little more than confirm the fact that you were present at the subject area when the picture was taken. It will emphasize none of the points which interested you, suppress none of the areas which bored you, illustrate a very small area of the total subject space which your peripheral vision described to you, and will display the whole distorted mess in smaller-than-life scale, confined within artificially described boundaries, in two dimensions and, perhaps, in black and white. Obviously there can be no hint of any of the extravisual perceptions which you experienced and which contributed to your total impression.

Is it any wonder that your friends fall asleep when you show your vacation slides? *You* can enjoy them because they help you to relive the whole enjoyment of your trip. They serve for your memory the same function that a prompter serves for an actor who has forgotten his lines. But no amount of prompting can help an actor who has not learned his part, and no amount of simple visual reminding can be of much use or much pleasure to a person who has not had the experience to remember.

If you want to communicate your own impressions to others (and what photographer doesn't), you must supply them with complete, coherent pictures. In very simple terms of straight photography, this means that your print must display clearly, sharply, and without confusion of background details all those areas of the subject which your eye examined with pertinent interest. By the same token, your print must eliminate or subdue those areas of the subject detail which your brain classified as irrelevant or uninteresting. Every visible feature of the print will affect the viewer in some way, and if you supply him with the wrong elements or present them to him in confusion, he will not get your message.

Another very important factor is the composition or visual arrangement of the image forms for the sake of the design itself. Consider it this way. The photographic print is a picture of something which conveys

You may employ symbolism

Some photographers manipulate the image

And some work in old processes

It frees them from mechanical naturalism

It's hard to explain the fascination of image making

real information about the subject, and which, with luck and skill on your part, may suggest something of the way you related to the subject while making the picture. In addition to this symbolic aspect, the print is physically a piece of paper coated with gelatin, containing irregular areas of black, white, and gray. Even if they represented nothing at all, these areas of tone create a pattern which nearly everyone can appreciate, to some small degree at least, for its own sake. In fact, whether he is consciously aware of it or not, virtually every viewer will be at least subtly influenced by the abstract design of the image tones and textures.

As your skill and vision improve, you will probably begin to appreciate the less obvious, more subtle uses of photography. You may want to experiment with visual symbolism to convey part of your message. This may be as direct as presenting the image of a loaf of bread in such a way that it stands for "food," or it may be so personal and complex a symbol that only you will know that it exists in the picture.

Whether you plan them that way or not, people may occasionally claim to recognize symbols in your pictures. This is probably good. It indicates at least that you have managed to avoid being too specific with your imagery. Symbolism is a difficult problem to deal with photographically because of the inherent realism of the photograph. It is very easy to take a picture which means "this is what Billy looked like on his tenth birthday." It's much more difficult to make Billy an anonymous symbol for "boyhood" without getting obvious or corny.

In the last few years, there has been a renewed interest in the manipulated image. These pictures take many forms, their common characteristic being that they all depart from naturalism. The most common manipulated images are the simple dropouts, solarized images, and screened images of various sorts. Some workers retain the photographic gray scale but distort the imagery in some way. "Weegee" (Arthur Fellig) did it by printing through warped plastic sheets. Uelsmann cunningly combines parts of two or more photographs in one print by multiple printing techniques. Some photographers use simple cut-and-paste techniques to pro-

duce photocollages, then work on the prints with dyes, and pencil to enhance the effects. Others work with the Xerox process or other "generative" systems and some are investigating electronic imaging systems and holography.

At the same time, there has been a revival of some of the very early techniques. George Tice and others are exhibiting platinum prints, an exquisite method of printing which was popular around 1900. A few photographers have experimented with daguerreotypes and calotypes. Scott Hyde is known for his composite images done in a modern version of the old gum-bichromate process, and Betty Hahn and others combine the older, more traditional methods with hand-work to produce very unusual and exciting contemporary images. Todd Walker has experimented with many of the old processes and has produced some elegant solarized nudes in gum-bichromate and in the more modern offset lithographic techniques. He and a few others have also worked in collotype, the beautiful but difficult gelatin equivalent of stone lithography.

The purpose of all these procedures seems to be to free the photographer from the mechanical naturalism of the straight photographic image and the cold, machine-perfect surfaces of the commercial papers. These departures from the straight tradition should not be thought of as dishonest or bad or nonphotographic even though, at first appearance, many of them are startling and even ugly if judged by conventional camera club standards. Consider them as paintings or prints if that will help you appreciate them. In many cases, it is really difficult to classify them; they are truly mixed-media expressions that can be both fresh and exciting.

It's hard to explain the fascination of image-making to a nonartist. The physical act of photography is a relatively simple procedure which anyone can learn to do passably well if he puts his mind to it. It only becomes really difficult, and engrossing, when the image itself begins to capture your imagination. Then the differences between "good" and "bad" pictures become so important to you that it's hard to think of much else. Where you go from there is up to you.

Look at the work of other photographers

We inevitably influence each other

You must involve your mind as well as your trigger finger

Photography will give you your money's worth

Your own interest may stop at the snapshot. That's not a bad place to be if you do it well (look up the photographs of Jacques Henry Lartigue to see how intimately delightful a family album can be). Or you may find that the straightforward documentation of your own environment is worth your attention. Look at the straight, beautifully detailed interiors of Walker Evans and the views of Paris that Atget did so naively and with such obvious affection.

Perhaps you will be attracted to social commentary. There is a great deal of material to draw on here— from John Thomson, Jacob Riis, and Lewis Hine, through the incredible FSA record of the depression to the present and people like Gordon Parks, David Douglas Duncan, Bruce Davidson, and Diane Arbus. A more subdued approach to photojournalism, combined with strong visual design, is exemplified by Kertész and, later, by Henri Cartier-Bresson.

Look at Weston and Adams for their reverence for form and light. Look at the powerful, brooding photo-essays of Eugene Smith; the cool professional elegance of the work of Irving Penn; the subtle romantic Polacolor studies of Marie Cosindas. Inspect the composite images that Rejlander and Robinson produced in the 1850s and 1860s and the more recent surrealistic compositions of Uelsmann. Look at the cameraless images of Man Ray, Schad, and Moholy-Nagy, and the bitterly satirical montages of Heartfield.

Investigate the work of the Photo-Secession group, a marvelously varied and skillful group of photographers. Follow the birth and growth of photojournalism from Salomon to the present day. Look at the industrial photographs of Weston, Bourke-White, and d'Arazien and study the portrait styles of Newman, Halsman, and Karsh.

As photographers, we inevitably influence each other and this is a healthy thing. Make the most of this interchange of ideas and inspiration and use it as a springboard for your personal expression. It is far more constructive to plagiarize, to deliberately imitate someone whose work you admire, than to wait, without *doing* anything, for the spontaneous arrival of an idea

which no other photographer has ever had, or a subject which no one else has ever dealt with. These things simply will not happen.

I believe sincerely that it is impossible to copy anyone else's style for very long even if you try to do it seriously. Your own personal vision will certainly intervene and you will gradually find your own expressive form in spite of yourself if you work at it. You can't become a great photographer, or even a good one, by simply thinking about pictures. It's also true, though, that you'll have to involve your mind and your emotions as well as your trigger finger if you want to amount to very much.

You'll find, in fact, if you take it seriously, that working at photography will demand as much from you and involve you as totally as anything you have ever done. In return, it will give you more than your money's worth in profound, personal gratification.

Portfolio

This photograph of an open window and the scene beyond was done in 1896 by Frederick Evans. It is disarmingly ordinary at first glance; so ordinary, in fact, that it can easily be overlooked or ignored unless it is pointed out as worthy of attention. Studied perceptively it is still a simple image, but a charming one. It can be appreciated for its clean, economical design, its delicate rendering of light and atmosphere, and the interesting tones and textures of the handsome old buildings and courtyard seen partly through, and partly reflected in, the glass of the open casement window.

It is easy too, to identify with the photographer; to sense the shadowy atmosphere of the old house and the soft glare of the outdoor light. Is it foggy or misty? Is there a hint of stable smell and the scent of wet grass in the air? Are there bird songs? An active imagination can supply the missing ingredients of a complete scenario, and each viewer will project himself into the situation in a way which relates to his own sensitivity and experience.

For some persons the photograph may function as an "equivalent," evoking in some mysterious way an emotional response quite unrelated to the reality of the objects pictured. For others it may simply trigger recollections of past experiences, old friends, or episodes from childhood.

Any photograph can function on at least two or three levels: graphic (its two-dimensional design), representational (what it depicts, real or surreal), and evocative (what response it arouses in you); but before it can function at all, you must give it a chance by really looking at it—not casually or out of simple curiosity, but with genuine intent to perceive. The burden of communication is borne equally by the image-maker and the image-viewer!

On the following pages—and worthy of your careful attention—are examples of the work of a number of serious and dedicated photographers. Most of these men and women are well known and in many cases, the choice of images was theirs. This portfolio has no theme. It is intended to suggest some of the vast variety of work that has been done and, although it is by no means a complete summary , I hope you will find it instructive, enjoyable, and inspiring.

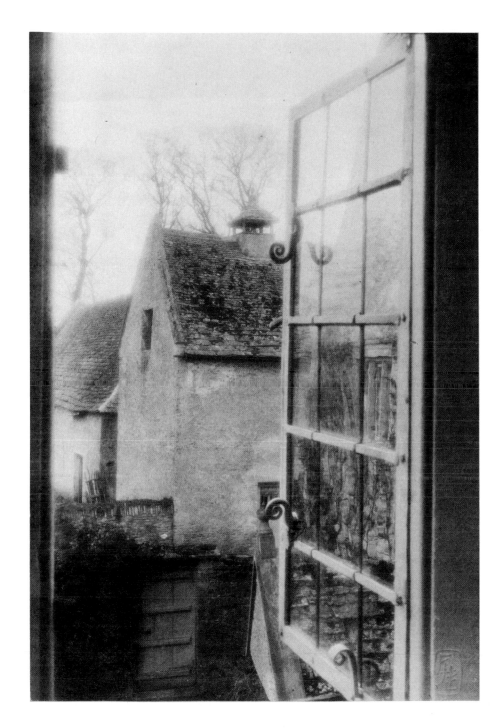

Frederick H. Evans. *Kelmscott Manor:*
Thro' a Window in the Tapestry Room,
1896. (Courtesy of George A. Tice)

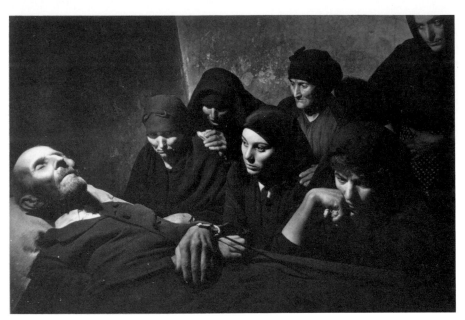

Eugene Smith. *Wake,* from the series *Spanish Village.* (Courtesy of the photographer)

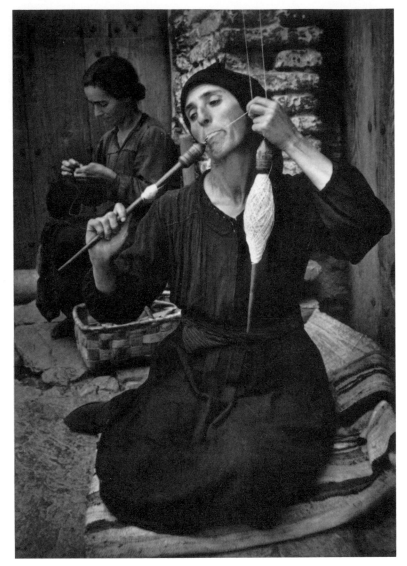

Eugene Smith. *Spinner.* (Courtesy of the photographer)

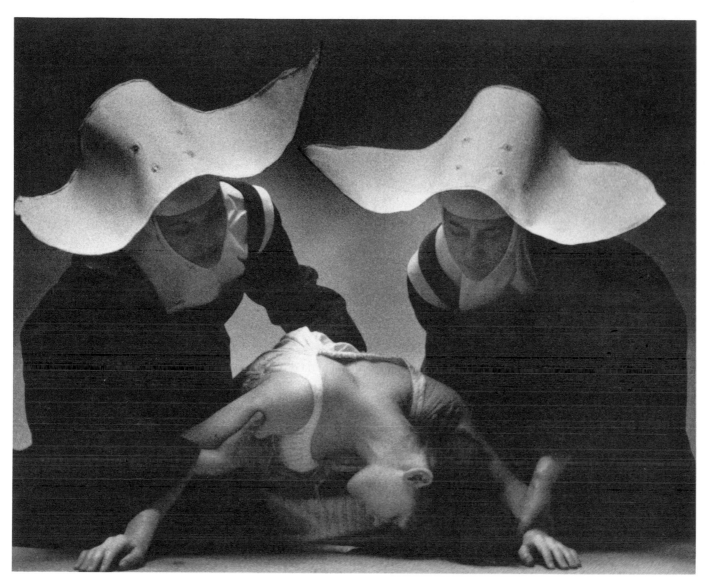

Max Waldman. *Marat / Sade.* (Courtesy
of the photographer)

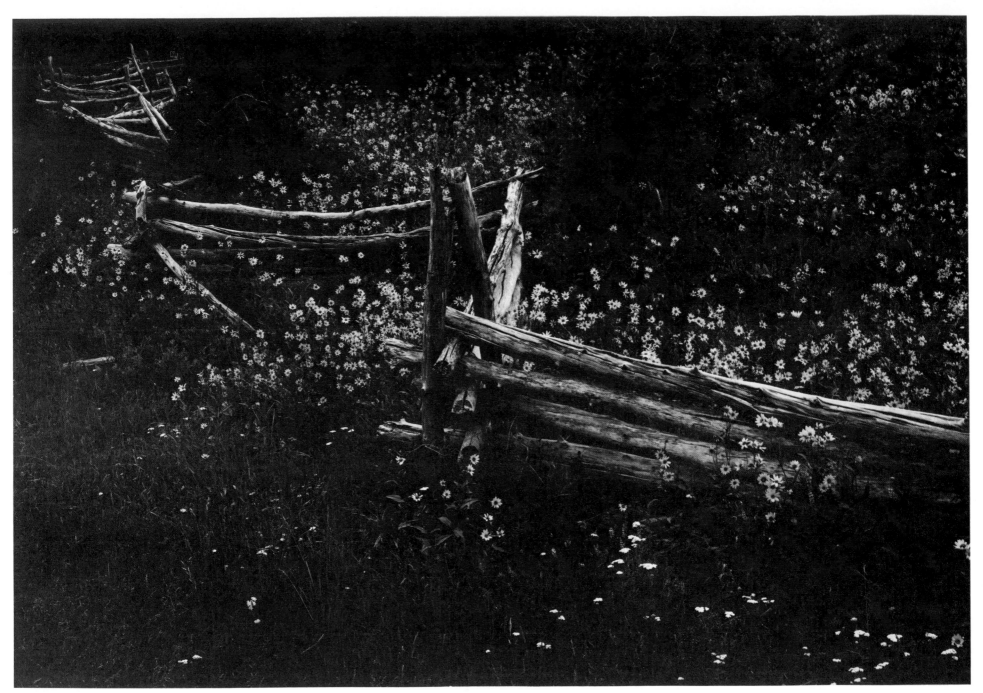

Dick Arentz. Untitled. (Courtesy of the photographer)

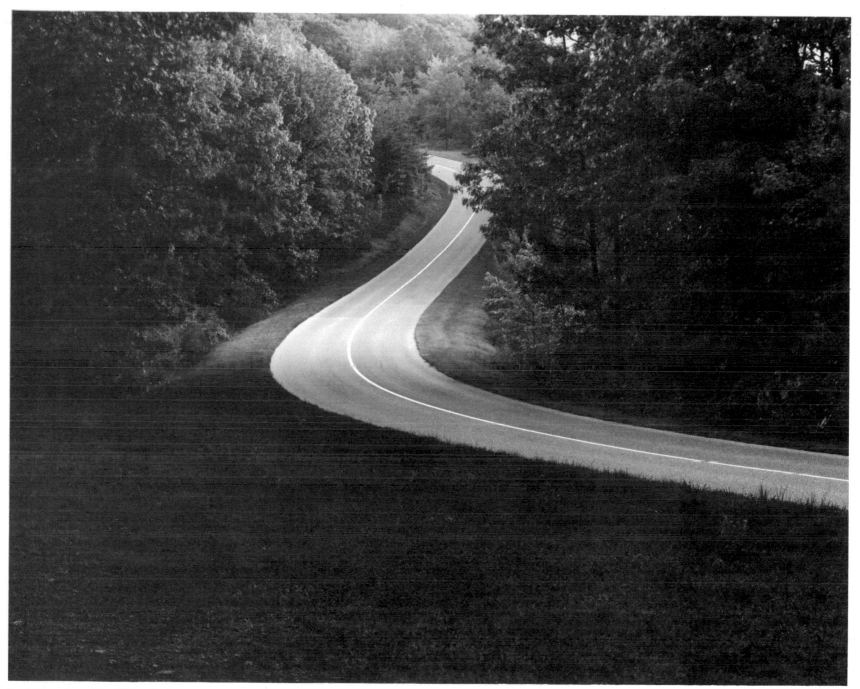

Paul Caponigro. *Blue Ridge Parkway.*
(Courtesy of the photographer)

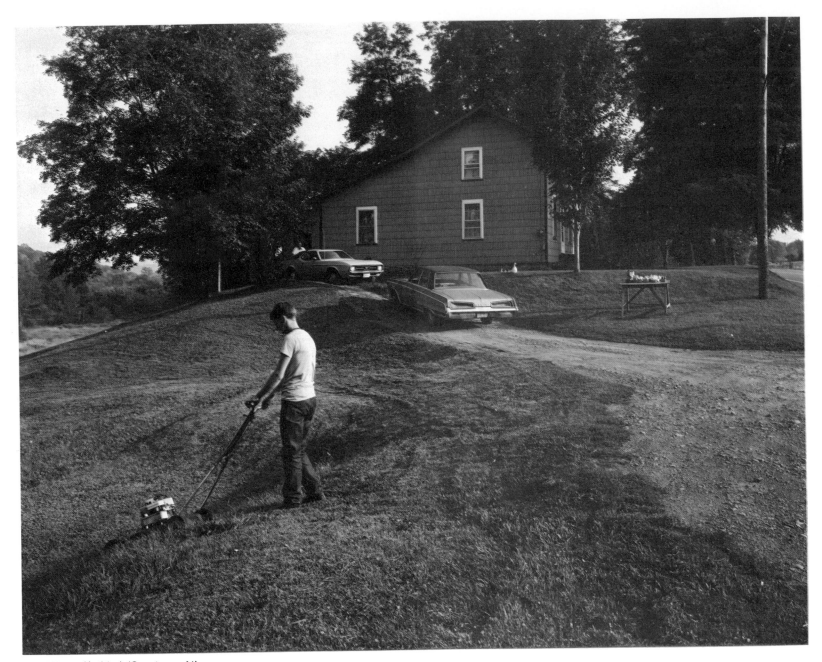

Nick Nixon. *Untitled.* (Courtesy of the photographer)

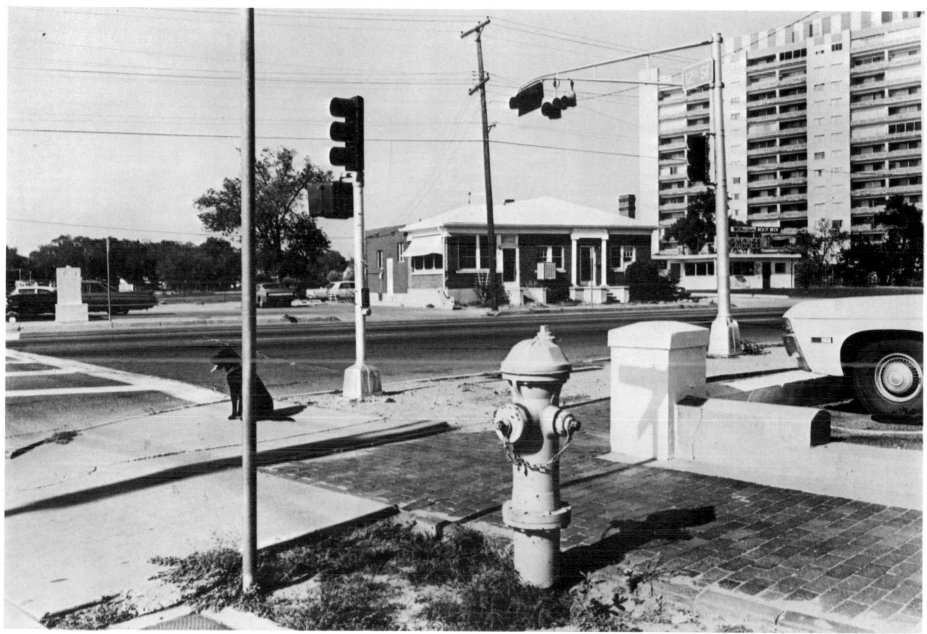

Lee Friedlander. Untitled. (Courtesy of
the photographer)

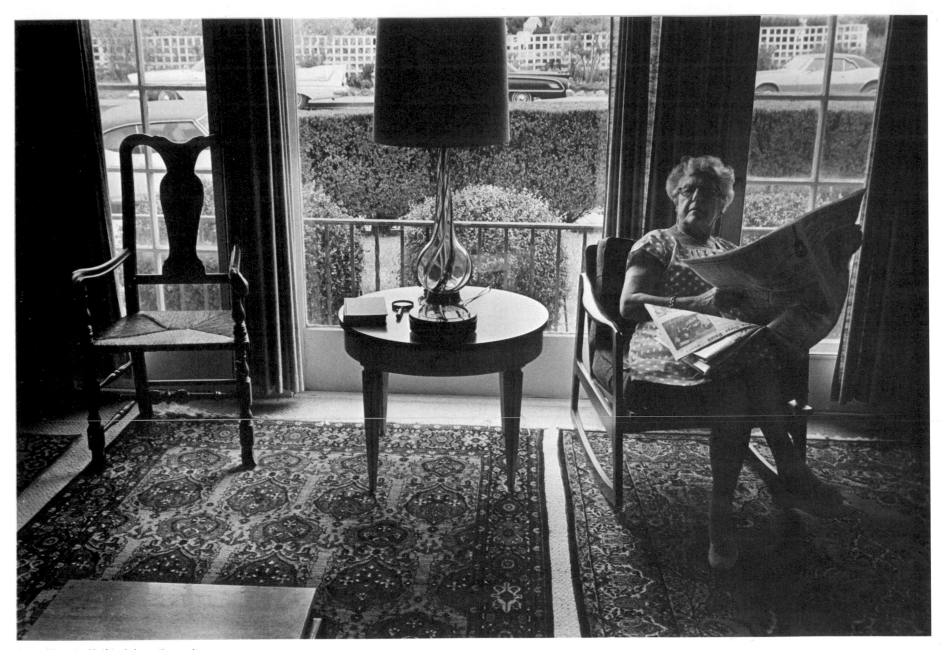

Anne Noggle. Untitled, from the series
Agnes, 1970. (Courtesy of the photographer)

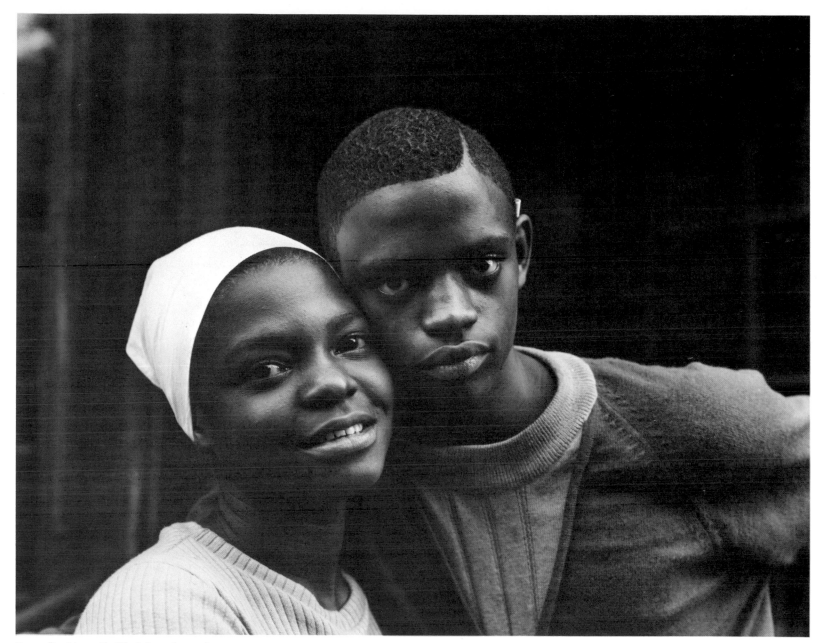

Bruce Davidson. Untitled, from the series
East 100th Street. (Courtesy of Magnum
Photos, Inc.)

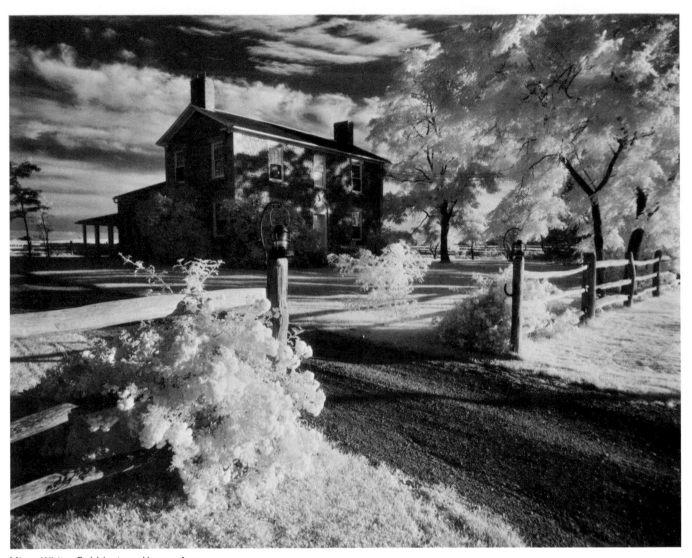

Minor White. *Cobblestone House, Avon,
New York, 1958.* (Courtesy of the Minor
White Archive, Princeton University)

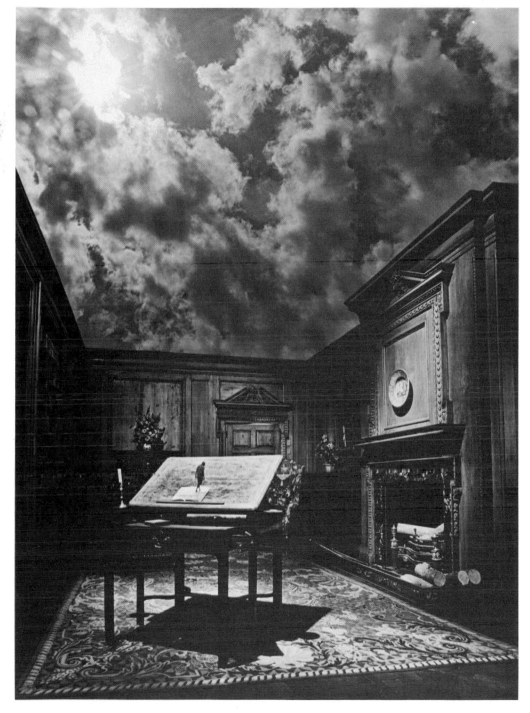

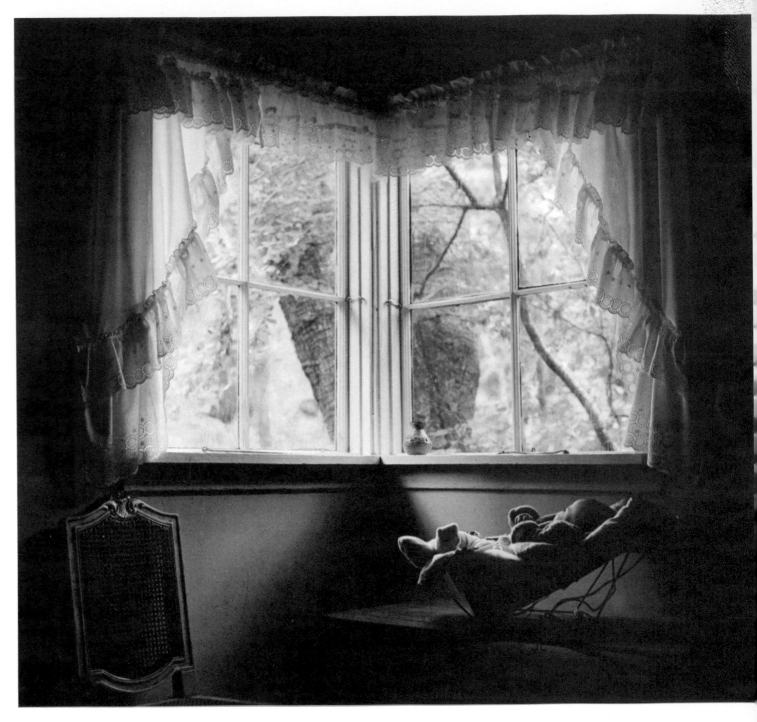

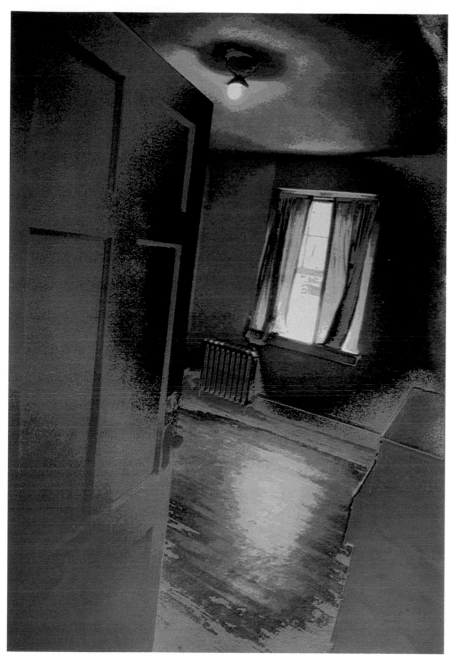

Todd Walker. Untitled, silkscreen print.
(Courtesy of the photographer)

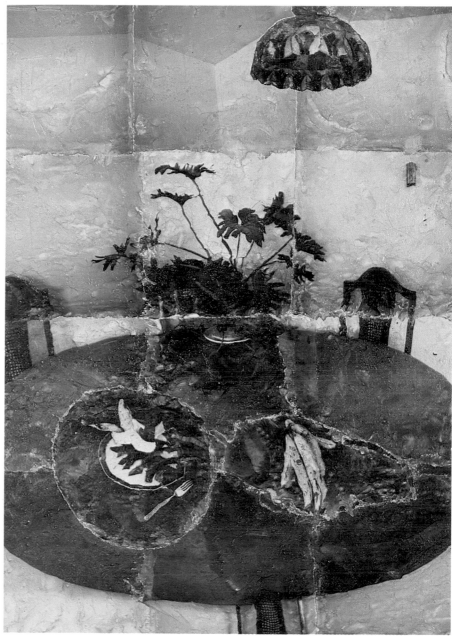

Ardine Nelson. *Banana Table, 1978*, SX-70 Transfer, 9" × 12". (Courtesy of the photographer)

Jill Lynne. *Madam Lorraine and the Pea-cock Feathers*, Xerograph. Copyright Jill Lynne. (Courtesy of the photographer)

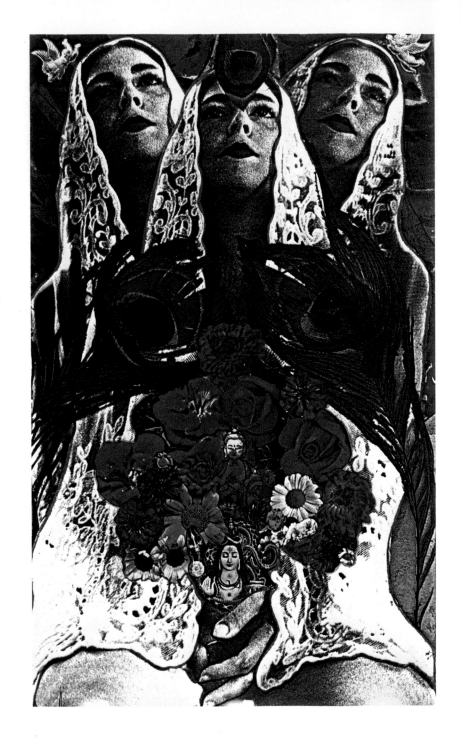

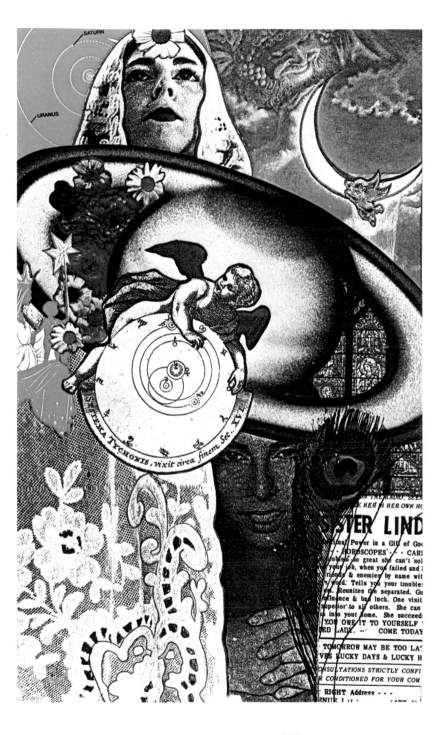

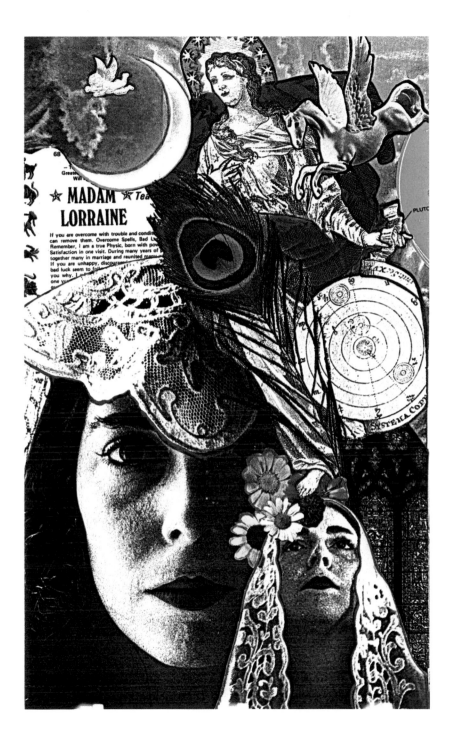

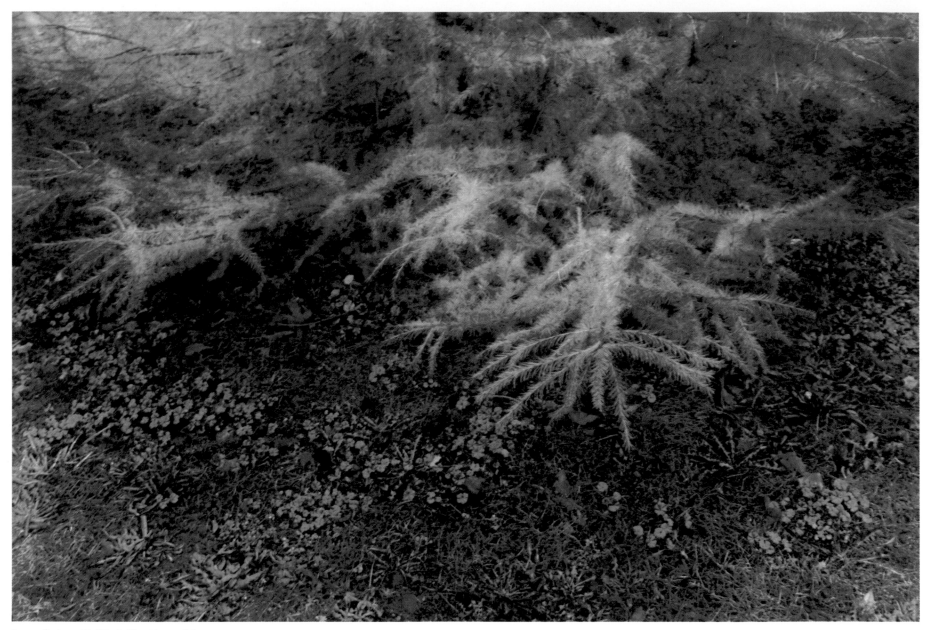

Joyce Culver. Untitled. (Courtesy of the photographer)

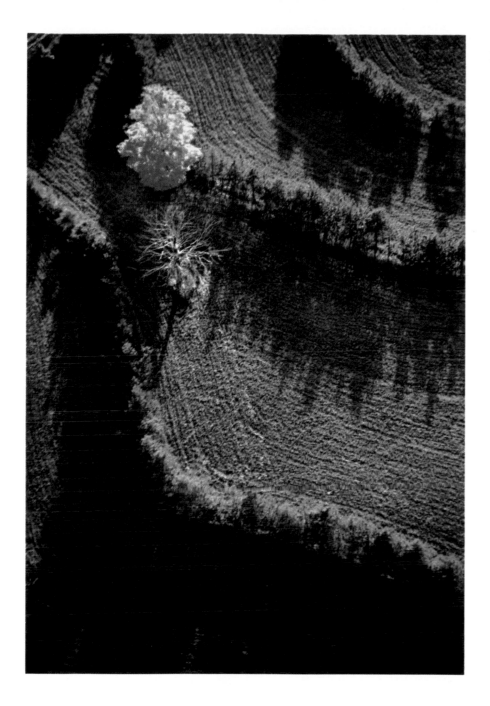

William Garnett. *Northern Michigan Farm in the Fall*, aerial photograph. (Courtesy of the photographer)

Betty Hahn. *Sunset,* from the series *Who Was That Masked Man? I Wanted to Thank Him,* cyanotype print with watercolors, 18″ × 22″. (Courtesy of the photographer)

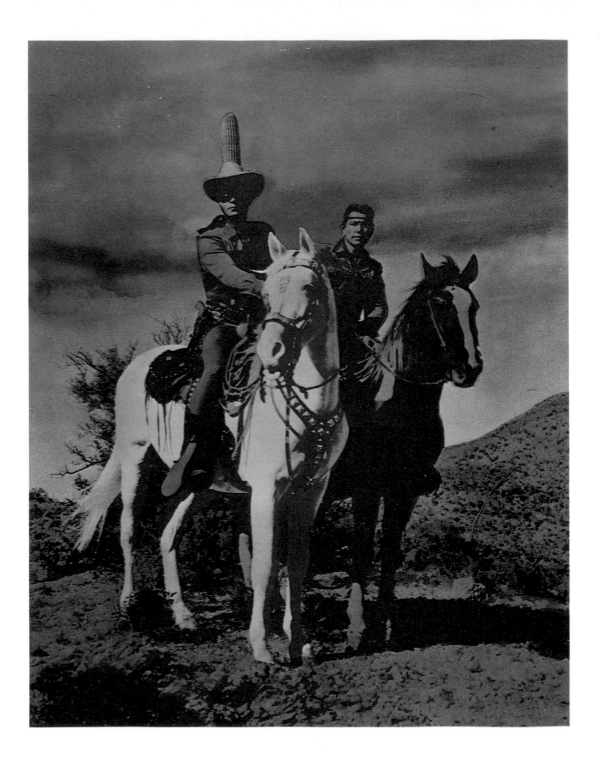

Appendix

The reference material and formulas contained in this section have been compiled from a number of sources and are believed to be accurate at the time of publication. Specific product information will change as the products themselves are modified or replaced on the market. It is wise, therefore, to consult the product manufacturer's latest technical data sheets for the most reliable information. Lacking these, the information given here will be useful and will keep you out of serious trouble.

1 Table A.1
Currently Available Films and Their Characteristics

Film Manufacturer and Name	Sizes Available				Speed	Contrast	Sharpness	Color Sensitivity	Grain	Recommended Uses
	Sheets	Rolls	35mm Cart.	35mm Bulk						
Kodak										
High Contrast Copy			x	x	64*	High	Very High	Pan	V. F.	Line and halftone copies
Panatomic-X and Panatomic-X Prof.	x		x	x	32	Medium	Very High	Pan	V. F.	General purpose use in good light, where maximum sharpness is desired
Plus-X Pan Plus-X Pan Prof. Plus-X Pan Prof. 4147	x	x	x	x	125	Medium	High	Pan	V. F. V. F. Fine	General purpose, especially in daylight. Especially studio.
Tri-X Pan Tri-X Pan Prof. Tri-X Pan Prof. 4164	x	x x	x	x	400 320 320	Medium	High	Pan	Med. Fine	General purpose daylight or studio; available light
Recording Film 2475			x	x	1000	Medium	Low	Pan C	Coarse	Available light; science
Verichrome Pan		x†			125	Medium	High	Pan	Fine	General purpose
Ektapan Film 4162	x				100	Medium	Medium	Pan	Med.	Studio flash; portraiture
Royal Pan 4141	x				400	Medium	Medium	Pan	Med.	General; studio flash
Kodalith Ortho Film	x			x	8‡	Ex. High	Ex. High	Ortho	V. F.	Line copy, dropouts
Fine Grain Positive	x				Low	Med. High	Very High	Blue	V. F.	Transparencies
High Speed Infra-red	x		x	x	Varies	Medium	Low	UV & IR	Coarse	Medical, scientific, unusual visual effects
Ilford										
Pan F		x	x	x	50	Medium	Very High	Pan	V. F.	General purpose, for maximum sharpness
FP-4	x	x	x	x	125	Medium	High	Pan	V. F.	General purpose
HP-4	x	x	x	x	400	Medium	High	Pan	Med. F.	General purpose, for available light (to be discontinued)
HP-5			x		400	Medium	High	Pan	Med. F.	Available light

*Tungsten light rating
†Includes some obsolete sizes as well as 110 and 126 cartridges
‡In Kodalith developer; 25 in D-19

2 Currently Available Photographic Papers and Their Characteristics

Photographic papers come in a wide variety of brands, surfaces, weights, contrast grades, image tones, base materials, and speeds. RC (resin-coated), RD (rapid dry), and similar plastic-laminated papers permit very short processing times, dry quickly in room air, and require low-temperature mounting tissues for dry-mounting. Glossy plastic-laminated papers dry to a mirror-smooth finish without special treatment and should not be ferrotyped. Plastic-laminated papers of all varieties are convenient to use but are not yet considered suitable for archival storage.

Fiber-based or baryta-coated papers require much more thorough washing than plastic-laminated papers but, when suitably treated, are considered safe for archival storage. These papers are supplied in greater variety than the plastic laminates and are generally easier to tone and spot. Glossy baryta-coated papers must be ferrotyped to achieve a mirror finish; if dried in air, they produce a slightly textured, highly lustrous surface. All fiber-based papers show a pronounced tendency to curl while drying and in response to humidity changes. They can be dry-mounted using either high- or low-temperature tissues.

Table A.2 lists some of the printing papers on the market; papers with similar specifications are roughly comparable in appearance and performance, but there are individual differences which will be apparent to the careful printer. For a more comprehensive listing consult the various manufacturers' literature.

Key to Kodak Surfaces

F White, smooth, glossy. Single and double weight.

N White, smooth, lustre. Single and double weight.

A White, smooth, lustre. Lightweight.

J White, smooth, high lustre. Single and double weight.

M Warm white, smooth, matte. Double weight.

E White or warm white, fine-grained lustre. Single and double weight.

G Cream, fine-grained lustre. Double weight.

K Warm white, fine-grained high lustre. Double weight.

R Cream, tweed lustre. Single and double weight.

Y Warm white or cream, silk, high lustre. Double weight.

X Cream, tapestry lustre. Double weight.

Table A.2

Currently Available Photographic Papers and Their Characteristics

Brand Name	Image Tone	Surface Texture	Weight	Contrast Grades
Plastic-Laminated Papers (RC, RD, etc.)				
Kodak, Kodabrome RC	Neutral black	F, N	Medium	Soft to ultra-hard
Kodak, Polycontrast Rapid RC	Neutral black	F, N	Medium	Variable; 1–4 filters
Ilford Ilfospeed	Neutral black	Glossy, semi-matte, silk and pearl	Medium	0, 1, 2, 3, 4, 5
Ilford Ilfospeed Multigrade	Neutral black	Glossy and pearl	Medium	Variable; 1–7 filters (Equivalent to grades 0–4)
Unicolor B&W Resin-coated	Neutral black	Glossy (F) Pearl (P) Fine Grain (J) Matte (N) Silk (Y)	Medium	1, 2, 3, 6 1, 2, 3, 6 2, 3 2, 3 2, 3
Luminos S-ST RD (adhesive backed)	Neutral black	High gloss, velvet matte	Medium	2, 3
Luminos Bromide RD	Neutral black	Gloss, matte, silk	Medium	1, 2, 3, 4
Fiber-Based (Baryta-Coated) Papers				
Kodak Medalist	Warm black	F (White) F, J, E (White) G, Y (Cream)	Single Double Double	1, 2, 3, 4 2, 3 G: 2, 3, 4 Y: 2, 3
Kodak Kodabromide	Neutral black	F (White) N, E (White) A (White) G (Cream)	Single, Double Single, Double Light Double	1, 2, 3, 4, 5 2, 3, 4 2, 3, 4, 5 2, 3, 4
Kodak Polycontrast	Warm black	F, N, J (White) A (White) G (Cream)	Single, Double Light Double	Variable; 1–4 filters Variable; 1–4 filters Variable; 1–4 filters
Kodak Portralure	Brown black	M, G, Y (Warm White) R (Cream)	Double Double	Variable; 1–3 filters Variable; 1–3 filters
Agfa-Gevaert Brovira	Neutral black	#1 White Glossy #111 White Glossy #119 White Matte	Single Double Double	1, 2, 3, 4, 5, 6 1, 2, 3, 4, 5, 6 1, 2, 3, 4, 5, 6
Agfa Gevaert Portriga Rapid	Warm black	#111 White Glossy #118 White, Fine-Grain Semi-matte	Double Double	2, 3, 4 2, 3, 4
Ilford Ilfobrom	Neutral black	Glossy Semi-matte Glossy; velvet stipple Semi-matte, matte Rayon	Single Single Double Double Double	0, 1, 2, 3, 4, 5 1, 2, 3, 4 0, 1, 2, 3, 4 2, 3, 4 1, 2, 3
Luminos Bromide	Neutral black	ZF Glossy FF Glossy; N semi-matte C Matte J Crystal, lustre	Single Double Double Double	1, 2, 3, 4, 5 1, 2, 3, 4 2, 3, 4 1, 2, 3
Luminos Portrait	Brown black	G Cream-white, fine-grain lustre E White, fine-grain lustre Y White silk	Double	1, 2, 3

3 List of Metol-Free Developers

Although, strictly speaking, all developing agents are capable of causing some sensitizing or toxic effect on susceptible individuals, most can be considered safe to handle in normal use if simple precautions are taken to avoid prolonged or repeated contact with the dry chemical or its concentrated solutions. Silicone protective handcream, applied before contact, will help prevent skin irritation. After contact with any photographic chemical it is advisable to wash your hands, or other affected area, thoroughly.

Whether or not you are troubled by common allergies, you may be affected by some developers, notably those containing the reducing agent p-methyl-aminophenol sulfate, or Metol—also known as Elon, Pictol, Rhodol, and other common names. This chemical is included in almost all developers manufactured by the Eastman Kodak Company and in many developers formulated by other manufacturers. If you notice any sign of skin irritation, other than simple reddening or drying, after working with standard Metol or MQ (*Metol-Hydro-Quinone*) developers, you should stop using them immediately or wear rubber gloves while handling them.

The developers listed in table A.3 by their manufacturers contain no Metol. While their use will not guarantee freedom from toxic or allergic reactions, they are presumably less likely to be troublesome than formulas containing Metol.

Table A.3
Film Developers

Edwal Scientific Products Corp.

FG-7	Fine-grain formula for roll and cartridge film.

Acufine, Inc.

Acufine	Fine-grain formula for roll and cartridge films.
Diafine, 2-bath	Compensating formula for roll and cartridge films.
ACU-1, one-shot	Fine-grain formula for roll and cartridge films.

Agfa-Gevaert, Inc.

Rodinal	High acutance formula. Avoid contact with liquid concentrate.

Ilford, Inc.

Microphen	Fine-grain formula for roll and cartridge films.

Eastman Kodak Co.

HC-110	Avoid contact with liquid concentrate. For all films.
D-8	Very high contrast formula, not suitable for general use.
*DK-93	For films or papers.
*D-32	Lantern slide developer.
*D-51,	containing Amidol, and *SD-1, containing Pyro, are Metol-free, but are at least equally hazardous. Not recommended for users who are sensitive to photochemicals.

*Developer formulas must be mixed from bulk chemicals; not available in prepared form.

Table A.4
Paper Developers

Acufine, Inc.

Posifine 16	Neutral tone. For all papers.

Ethol Chemicals, Inc.

LPD	Neutral tone. For all papers.

Ilford, Inc.

Bromophen	General purpose paper developer, neutral tone.
Ilfospeed 2	Liquid concentrate for Ilfospeed RC papers, and others.
Multigrade	Liquid concentrate for Multigrade papers, and others.

Eastman Kodak Co.

Ektaflo, type 2	Liquid concentrate for all papers; warm tone.

4 Formulas

The formulas given here are typical and useful for the purposes indicated. In all cases when mixing chemical formulas from bulk materials, follow the instructions carefully and mix the chemicals in the order given. In general, each chemical should be dissolved before the next one is added. Use clean paper on the scales for each new formula to avoid contamination. Also, avoid skin contact with dry chemicals or their liquid concentrates and don't breathe chemical dust or fumes. Wash your hands and all utensils thoroughly after chemical mixing.

Developers

Adapted from Kodak formula D-72, developer printing papers and for vigorous development of sheet films. This is a stock solution.

Water (52°C or 125°F)	500	ml
Elon or Metol	3	gms
Sodium Sulfite (desiccated)	45	gms
Hydroquinone	12	gms
Sodium Carbonate (mono-hydrated	80	gms
Potassium Bromide	2	gms
Cold water to make	1	liter

For use with papers, dilute 1:1 or 1:2 and develop 1 to 3 minutes.

Adapted from Kodak formula DK-50, developer for sheet films.

Water (52°C or 125°F)	500	ml
Elon or Metol	2.5	gms
Sodium Sulfite (desiccated)	30	gms
Hydroquinone	2.5	gms
Kodalk (or sodium meta-borate)	10	gms
Potassium Bromide	.5	gm
Water to make	1	liter

For conditions of use, see contrast index charts, page 309.

Adapted from Kodak formula D-76 or Ilford formula ID-11

Water (52°C or 125°F)	750	ml
Elon or Metol	2	gms
Sodium Sulfite (desiccated)	100	gms
Hydroquinone	5	gms
Borax (decahydrated)	2	gms
Cold water to make	1	liter

For conditions of use, see contrast index charts, pages 308–309.

Stop Bath

To prepare a standard acetic acid stop bath stock solution (28%) from glacial acetic acid (99.7%), mix 3 parts of glacial acetic acid into 8 parts of water. See page 96 for detailed instructions. *Caution*—glacial acetic acid can cause severe burns and may be fatal if swallowed. Do not get the liquid on the skin or in the eyes; do not breathe the vapor. Keep away from heat or open flame and store at temperatures above 16°C (60°F) to avoid freezing.

To prepare a working solution of stop bath for films, add 30 ml of 28% stock solution to 1 liter of water (1 ounce/quart). For papers, add 45 ml stock solution to 1 liter (1½ ounces/quart).

Fixing Baths

Nonhardening fixing bath for use with papers to be toned in gold or selenium; also recommended for clearing bath, following dichromate, permanganate, or iodine bleach solutions.

Water (52°C or 125°F)	500	ml
Sodium Thiosulfate (Hypo)	250	gms

Stir until hypo is dissolved and solution has cooled to room temperature, then add

Sodium Bisulfite	25	gms
Water to make	1	liter

Stir until dissolved. Potassium metabisulfite may be substituted for the sodium bisulfite in equal amounts.

Kodak formula F-6, acid hardening fixing bath, for general use.

Water (52°C or 125°F)	600	ml
Sodium Thiosulfate (hypo)	240	gms
Sodium Sulfite (desiccated)	15	gms
Acetic Acid (28%)	48	ml
Kodalk Balanced Alkali	15	gms
Potassium Alum	15	gms
Water to make	1	liter

Dissolve hypo completely, then add remaining ingredients one at a time and dissolve each before adding the next.

Hypo Test Solution

Water	100	ml
Potassium Iodide	2	gms

Mix and store in a dropper bottle. Add one drop to the fixing bath; if a yellowish cloud forms in the solution the fixer is nearing exhaustion. For archival purposes discard the fixer if any sign of cloudiness appears in this test.

Hypo Eliminator

Kodak formula HE-1, for prints processed to archival standards.

Water	500	ml
Hydrogen Peroxide, 3% solution	125	ml
Ammonia solution	100	ml
Water to make	1	liter

Ammonia solution is prepared by adding 10 ml of ammonium hydroxide (28%) to 90 ml of water. *Caution*—prepare solution immediately before use and keep in an open container; do not store the mixed solution, evolved gas may break a stoppered bottle.

Treat well-washed prints in HE-1 for about 6 minutes at 20° (68°F). This bath will soften the print emulsion so be careful not to damage the prints by rough handling. Wash the treated prints for about 10 minutes, and dry carefully. Drying between blotters or facedown on screens may damage the emulsion; use care.

Toners

Gold Toner, for protection of the silver image or for producing bluish-gray tones on most papers.

Solution A

Gold Chloride	1	gm
Water, distilled	100	ml

Solution B

Sodium or Potassium Thiocyanate	10	gms
Water, preferably distilled	1	liter

For archival protective toning, add (with vigorous stirring) 1 ml of solution A for each 8″ × 10″ print to be toned, to 500 ml of B. Immerse thoroughly washed prints, one at a time, in the toning bath and agitate until a barely perceptible darkening or cooling of the image is apparent. For blue toning, use 2 ml solution A for each 8″ × 10″ print and tone until color change is satisfactory. Wash toned prints for at least 10 minutes and dry as usual. Prints must have been thoroughly washed and preferably treated with HE-1 before toning in this solution, to avoid possible yellowing of highlights.

Sepia Toner for brown tones on most papers

Solution A

Water (52°C or 125°F)	700	ml
Potassium Ferricyanide	50	gms
Potassium Bromide	10	gms
Sodium Carbonate, mono-hydrated	20	gms
Water to make	1	liter

Solution B

Sodium Sulfide, desiccated	5	gms
Water to make	500	ml

Cool solution A to room temperature and agitate the well-washed print in it until the image bleaches out to a yellowish-tan color. Rinse the print in running water until the yellow ferricyanide color is gone; then re-develop in solution B for a minute or two, until the image is restored. Wash the toned print thoroughly in running water (30 minutes or so), not above 20°C (68°F), and air-dry. This toner softens the print emulsion; it is, therefore, advisable to harden the toned print, before washing it. After removing the toned print from solution B, rinse it for several minutes in running water, then immerse it in a hardening bath compounded as follows:

Water (52°C or 125°F)	500	ml
Sodium Sulfite, anhydrous	15	gms
Acetic Acid (28%)	40	ml
Potassium Alum	15	gms
Water to make	1	liter

Dissolve chemicals in the order given and cool to room temerature for use. Harden print for about 5 minutes, then wash in running water for 30 minutes and dry on screens, clean cloth, or blotters.

Reducer

Farmer's Reducer, for correcting over-exposed negatives; also local reduction of print images.

Solution A (stock solution)
Sodium Thiosulfate (hypo)	12	gms
Water, warm	100	ml

Solution B (stock solution)
Potassium Ferricyanide	4	gms
Water	100	ml

Store solutions in separate bottles. For use add one part *A* and one part *B* to 18 parts water. Use less water for faster action; more water to slow it down. Soak films to be reduced in plain water for several minutes, then immerse in solution and agitate constantly until image appears sufficiently lightened. Rinse films in water to stop reducing action, then treat in hypo-clearing bath and wash as usual. Mixed solution of reducer will not keep; mix it fresh for each use. Stock solutions will keep indefinitely in normal storage conditions. For use on prints see pages 135–136.

Bleach Baths

Iodine Bleach for removing dark spots from prints. Use ordinary tincture of iodine, obtainable from any drugstore, or mix the following:

Water	25	ml
Iodine, crystals or scales	.5	gm
Potassium Iodide	2.5	gm

The iodine is virtually insoluble in plain water but will dissolve slowly in the solution of potassium iodide. Store in a small stoppered bottle. It will keep indefinitely. For instructions for use, see page 136.

Permanganate Bleach, for total removal of print image density.

Solution A
Potassium Permanganate	1	gm
Water, warm	200	ml

Solution B
Water, cold	200	ml
Hydrochloric Acid	20	ml

These solutions will keep in separate containers, but working solutions should be mixed fresh for each use. For very rapid action use equal parts of *A* and *B*. For milder action add one part *A* and one part *B* to two parts water. *Caution*—hydrochloric acid is dangerously corrosive and poisonous. Avoid skin contact and don't breathe the fumes. If spilled on the skin, flood with water then apply baking soda solution and get medical attention. See instructions for use on page 136.

5 Metric Conversions and Equivalents

Temperature Conversion Formulas

To convert Fahrenheit to Celsius degrees, subtract 32 and multiply by 5/9. For example,

$$68°F - 32 = 36 \times \frac{5}{9} = 20°C$$

To convert Celsius to Fahrenheit degrees, multiply by 9/5 and add 32. For example,

$$100°C \times \frac{9}{5} = 180 + 32 = 212°F$$

See figure A.1.

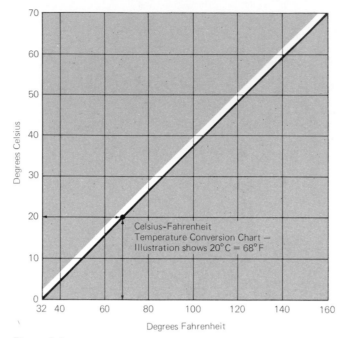

Figure A.1
Celsius-Fahrenheit temperature conversion chart. Illustration shows 20°C = 68°F.

Linear Measurements

To convert inches to millimeters, multiply by 25.4. For example,

$$6'' \times 25.4 = 152.4mm$$

Similarly, divide millimeters by 25.4 to find inches:

$$127mm \div 25.4 = 5 \text{ inches}$$

See figure A.2.

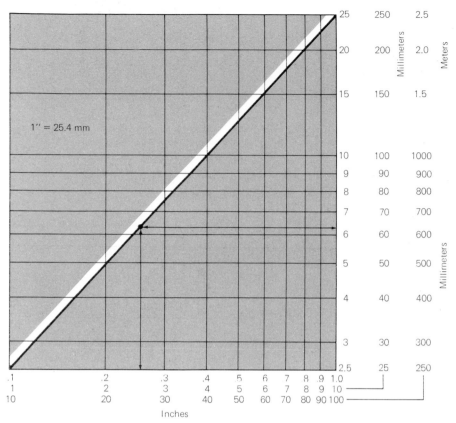

1" = 25.4 mm

Figure A.2
Inches-millimeters conversion chart.
Read matching scales. Illustration shows
¼" (.25) = 6.35mm or 2.5" = 63.5mm or
25" = 635mm.

Weights

The common Avoirdupois weight units are the pound (lb.), ounce (oz.), and grain (gr.); common metric units are the kilogram (kg) and the gram (g).

1 pound = 16 ounces
 = 453.6 grams
1 ounce = 437.5 grains
 = 28.35 grams
1 grain = .0648 grams
1 kilogram = 1000 grams
 = 2.2 pounds
1 gram = 15.43 grains

Liquid Measure

Our common liquid measurement units are the gallon (gal.), the quart (qt.), the pint (pt.), and the fluid ounce (oz., or fl. oz.); metric units are the liter (l) and the milliliter (ml). The cubic centimeter (cc) is, strictly speaking, a measure of volume but, since it is virtually identical with the milliliter, it is frequently used interchangeably with milliliter in liquid measurements.

1 gallon = 4 quarts = 8 pints
 = 128 ounces = 3.785 liters
1 quart = 2 pints = 32 ounces
 = 946.4 milliliters
1 pint = 16 ounces
 = 473.2 milliliters
1 fluid ounce = 29.575 milliliters
1 liter = 1000 milliliters
 = 1.057 quarts = 33.82 ounces
1 milliliter = .0034 fluid ounces

6 Close-up Exposure Correction

A fairly simple method of exposure compensation, based on the increase in lens focal distance required for close-focusing, is explained on pages 230–231. You can also calculate the correction factor by working from image magnification. Find the image magnification by dividing some image dimension by the corresponding subject dimension,

$$M = \frac{\text{Image dimension}}{\text{Subject dimension}}$$

then apply the formula

Exposure Factor $= (M + 1)^2$

For example, some image dimension is found to be .8 inches and the corresponding subject dimension is .5 inches. The magnification (M) is:

$$M = \frac{.8}{.5} = 1.6$$

The exposure factor (EF) is

EF $= (1.6 + 1)^2$ or 2.6^2 or 6.76

The factor found this way is useful for lenses of normal construction but for lenses of telephoto or reversed telephoto (retro-focus) construction, the *pupillary magnification* of the lens must be considered. To find the approximate value of pupillary magnification, divided the apparent aperture diameter, as the lens is held at arm's length, and viewed from the rear (the *exit pupil* diameter) by its apparent diameter as seen, similarly, from the front (the *entrance pupil*).

Pupillary Magnification (P) $=$
$$\frac{\text{Diameter of Exit Pupil}}{\text{Diameter of Entrance Pupil}}$$

then use the formula,

$$EF = \left(\frac{M}{P} + 1 \right)^2$$

For example, if the exit pupil measures 12 mm and the entrance pupil measures 18 mm, the pupillary magnification is

$$P = \frac{12}{18} = .67$$

if the image magnification is 1.6 (as in the illustration above) the formula is,

$$EF = \left(\frac{1.6}{.67} + 1 \right)^2$$

or $(2.39 + 1)^2$ or 3.39^2 or 11.5

Figure A.3▶
This macro-computer will help you find the amount of exposure increase required for close-up photography if you have trouble with formulas and mathematics. Since it contains both inch and millimeter scales, it can also be used for metric conversions if desired. For example, find the measurement in inches (larger numbers) on either dial and read its equivalent in millimeters (small numbers) on the same dial. Thus, 7″ is seen to approximate 180mm, 4″ is slightly more than 100mm. Reading the other way, 350mm is about 13¾″.

To use the computer for close-up exposure calculations, set up the camera, compose and focus on the subject, then measure the distance from lens-to-film in either inches or millimeters. Find this distance on one of the outer scales. Now move the inner scale until the lens focal length (either inches or millimeters) is aligned with the focal distance just located. Both exposure compensation and image magnification can now be read through the windows. For example, suppose you are using a 100mm lens, extended to a total distance (lens-to-film) of 13″. Set 100mm on the movable scale opposite 13″ on the fixed scale. The image is found to be about 2⅓ times larger than the subject and the exposure can be compensated by either opening the lens about 3½ stops or by multiplying the shutter speed by 11.

If measuring the focal distance is not convenient, and if the image size can be measured fairly accurately, you can determine the exposure compensation by setting the subject-to-image size ratio in the inner window. For example, if some subject dimension is found to be ½″ and the same dimension of the image measures 2½″, the ratio is 1:5. Set this number (5) in the inner window and read the exposure compensation in one of the other windows. Either open the lens five-and-a-fraction stops or increase the exposure interval by 36 times. This method is convenient if you are using a view camera with inch or millimeter markings on the groundglass.

Copy these scales on Kodalith film and print them to convenient pocket size. Mount them on thin, stiff cardboard, such as Bristol board, and cut them out neatly. You can color the white central area of the larger dial, if you want to, using a light-colored felt-tipped pen or marker; yellow is probably best for visibility. Mount the smaller disc on the larger one, so it is free to turn, by using a single rivet, grommet, or paper fastener through the center.

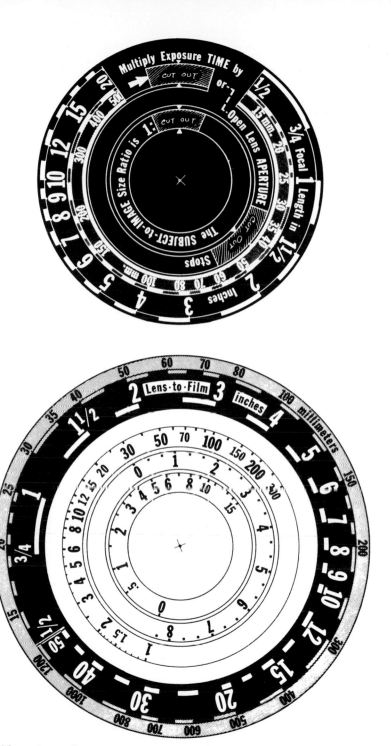

7 Flashbulb and Electronic Flash Guide Numbers

A guide number represents the product of a lens f/ number multiplied by the subject distance in feet. For example, the guide number "240" indicates that proper exposure will be achieved with the film and flashbulb specified if an aperture of f/8 is used with a subject distance of 30 feet, or f/2 is used at 120 feet, etc. Figure A.4 supplies guide numbers appropriate for the flashbulb types and film speed indicated. This chart applies to single flashbulbs, used at or near the camera position, and pertains to the flashbulb-to-subject distance, not the camera-to-subject distance, if they are not the same. If two similar bulbs are fired together from the same location, multiply the guide number by 1.4. For bounce flash calculation, estimate the total distance the flash light must travel from the bulb to the reflecting surface and then to the subject, calculate the f/ number and increase the exposure further by one stop if the reflecting surface is white, two or more if the surface is gray or a dark color. For more specific information consult the information sheet packed with the film in use.

Electronic flash exposure can also be estimated if a regular guide number is known. In some cases electronic flash units are rated in *effective candlepower seconds* (ECPS) or, more usually, in *beam candlepower seconds* (BCPS). Figure A.5 will give you guide number information for various film types if you know the BCPS rating of your flash unit. Since amateur flash units are frequently rated as having a certain guide number "for Kodachrome" or "for Tri-X," you can use this information to determine the BCPS of your unit. For example, if your unit has a guide number of "240 for Tri-X," the chart indicates its BCPS to be 2800, and, with this information, it is easy to calculate guide numbers for use with other films.

Film Speed

		25	32	64	125	400
Flash Cube	*1/30	48	60	85	120	195
	1/60	32	40	55	80	125
	1/125	27	34	48	68	100
#5B	*1/30	105	135	190	270	400
	1/60	95	120	170	240	380
	1/125	80	100	140	200	320
#22B	*1/30	135	170	240	340	540
	1/60	120	150	210	300	480
	1/125	100	125	180	250	400

Figure A.4
Flash guide numbers for use with "M" synch, (or "✕" synch* at 1/30th or less). This chart is based on the use of efficient reflectors with #5B and #22B bulbs.

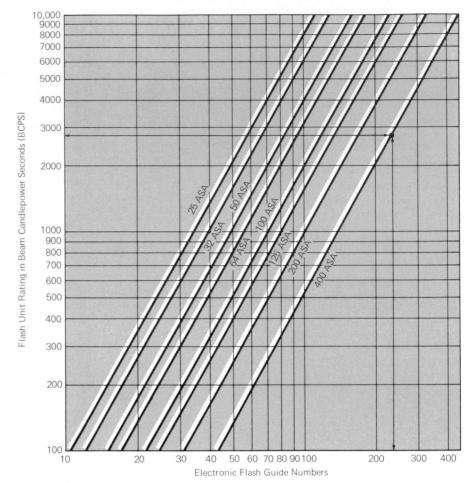

Figure A.5
The arrows on the chart show that a guide number of 240 for Tri-X film (ASA 400) is appropriate for a flash unit rated at 2800 BCPS.

8 Color Temperature

Color temperature is expressed in Kelvin degrees, since it follows the absolute centigrade scale named after the famous British physicist, Lord William Thompson Kelvin. A few common light sources and their approximate Kelvin temperatures are given in table A.5.

Table A.5
Common Light Sources and Their Kelvin Temperatures

Candle flame	1900°K
40-watt bulb	2650
75-watt bulb	2800
100-watt bulb	2900
Professional photographic flood	3200
Amateur "photoflood"	3400
Clear flashbulb	3800
Noon sunlight	5400
Photographic standard daylight (Kodak)	5500
Typical electronic flash (uncompensated	6100
Light from north sky 15,000 to 20,000 or more	

9 Kelvin Temperature and Filtration Calculator

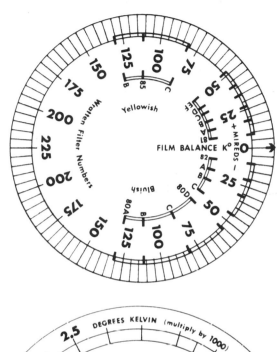

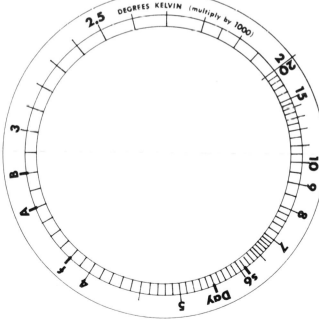

10 Table A.6
Filter Factors for Black-and-White Photography

Wratten Filter Number	Filter Color	Panchromatic Film		Orthochromatic Film	
		Daylight	Tungsten	Daylight	Tungsten
8	Yellow (K2)	2	1.5	2.5	2
11	Yellow-green (X1)	4	3	4	3
15	Deep yellow (G)	3	2	5	3
25	Red (A)	8	6	—	—
58	Green (B)	8	8	8	5
47B	Blue	8	16	6	8
29	Deep red (F)	25	12	—	—
61	Green (N)	12	12	—	—

Figure A.6 ◄
The Kelvin Temperature Scale: This scale will help you determine the necessary filter correction whenever the existing light color is not correct for the type of color film you are using. Set the "Film Balance K°" arrow opposite the appropriate film type on the Kelvin scale. The three normal emulsion types are labelled "Day" (5500°K), "A" (3400°K), and "B" (3200°K). Next, on the Kelvin scale, find the color temperature of the existing light. The filter required for proper color rendition will be found opposite this temperature, on the mireds scale. For example, suppose you are using clear flashbulbs with Kodachrome II, type "A" film. Set the pointer on "A." Opposite the small "f" (flash) at the 3800°K mark read the required correction: plus 30 mireds. The appropriate filter is the "81B" (plus 27 mireds). Slightly warmer results will be obtained by using the "81C" (about plus 35 mireds). The small letter "s" at 6100°K indicates the approximate color balance of unfiltered electronic flash tubes.

Copy these scales on Kodalith film and print them to convenient pocket size. Mount them on thin, stiff cardboard such as Bristol board and cut them out neatly. Mount the smaller disc on the larger one so that it is free to turn by using a single rivet or grommet or paper fastener through the center.

11 Development vs. Temperature Chart

Figure A.7
Development vs. temperature chart for finding development times for temperatures other than normal. Example shows that, if 5 mins. is correct developing time at 68°F, then the proper time at 62°F is 7 mins. Read up from known developing time to appropriate temperature line (horizontal) then diagonally up or down to desired temperature; then straight down to find new developing time.

Chart for Finding Development Times for Temperatures Other Than Normal

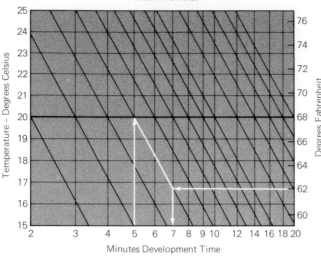

12 Suggested Reciprocity Failure Compensation

Figure A.8
Suggested reciprocity failure compensation for all general-purpose black-and-white films.

Compensation for reciprocity failure cannot be determined with real precision. Kodak's published recommendations seem rather extreme in practice and this chart will suggest compensation which differs from the official information. You should use the data which work best for you. To use this chart, lay a straightedge across it so as to connect the reference point *A* with the indicated exposure time in seconds on scale *B*.

The straightedge will then indicate the suggested exposure compensation on scales *C* and *D*. If you wish to adjust the aperture to make the compensation, open the lens up by the number of stops indicated on scale *C*. If you wish to compensate by increasing *exposure time,* use the exposure time in seconds indicated on scale *D*. Do *not* make *both* adjustments; use one or the other. The dashed line shows that an indicated exposure time of 8 seconds (scale *B*) will require exposure increase of one stop (scale *C*) or an exposure time of 19 seconds (scale *D*). With either setting the *normal* developing time for the film should be *reduced* by 7%, as indicated on scale *E*.

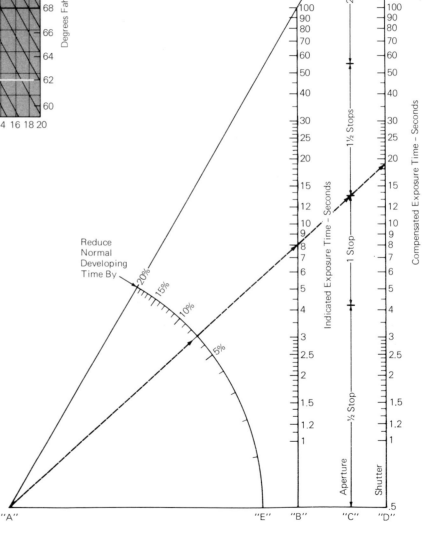

13

Table A.7
Equivalent Lens Focal Lengths For Various Camera Sizes

Angular Coverage of Horizontal Field*

Image Size	100° mm.	81°	65°	55°	45°	39°	24°	15°	10°	5°	3.4°	1°
35 mm	15	21	28	35	43	50	85	135	200	400	600	1030
1⅝" × 2¼" 4.5cm × 6cm ⎫ 2¼" × 2¼" 6cm × 6cm ⎬	22	32	42	52	65	76	127	205	308	615	910	1545
2¼" × 2¾" 6cm × 7cm	28	39	52	63	80	93	155	250	377	750	1110	1890
2¼" × 3¼" 6cm × 9cm	34	48	64	78	100	115	192	311	469	940		
3¼" × 4¼" 9cm × 12cm	45	63	85	103	128	150	250	402	605	1210		
4" × 5"	53	74	100	122	152	180	295	478	720			
5" × 7"	75	104	140	171	210	251	418	676	1015			
8" × 10"	107	149	200	244	300	359	597	965	1450			

```
          very
        ←—wide—→  ←——— wide ———→  ←—"normal"—→  ←——long——→  ←—————very———————→
                                                                    long
```

* Lens coverage is usually given for the image diagonal (corner-to-corner) measurement—an unrealistic statistic. This table indicates the useful coverage along the *long dimension* of the image. Focal lengths are given in millimeters.

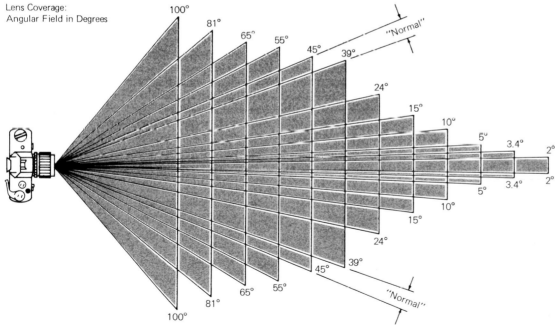

Lens Coverage:
Angular Field in Degrees

Figure A.9
Lens angular coverage chart

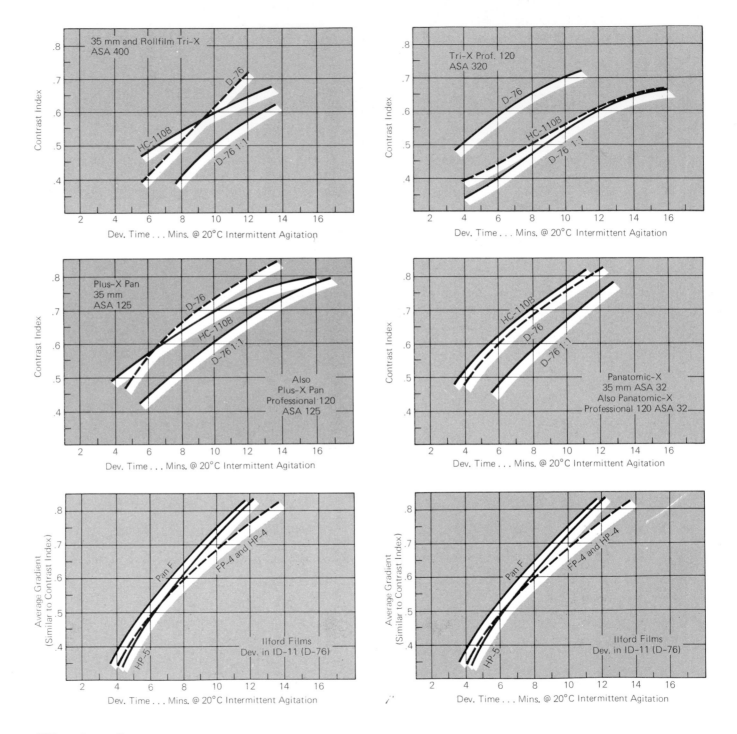

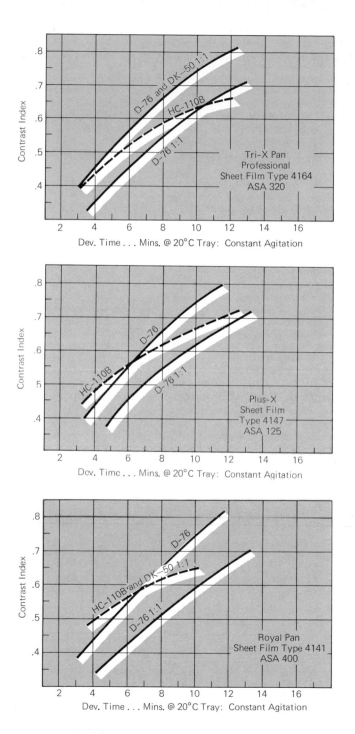

Tri-X Pan
Professional
Sheet Film Type 4164
ASA 320

Dev. Time . . . Mins. @ 20°C Tray: Constant Agitation

Plus-X
Sheet Film
Type 4147
ASA 125

Dev. Time . . . Mins. @ 20°C Tray: Constant Agitation

Royal Pan
Sheet Film Type 4141
ASA 400

Dev. Time . . . Mins. @ 20°C Tray: Constant Agitation

15 Matching Negative Density Range to Paper Contrast Grade

Paper contrast grades are neither as consistent nor as stable as film characteristics. Contrast is apt to vary from emulsion batch to emulsion batch and it generally decreases with age. The contrast grade suitable for any given negative contrast is also dependent upon the type of enlarger used and on such correctable problems as old or exhausted developer, dirty enlarger lens, etc. With these disclaimers in mind, use table A.8 to estimate the negative density range you need to print satisfactorily on your favorite paper type and grade. These data are derived empirically but should serve as a starting point, assuming that your enlarger is average in contrast. Condenser enlargers may require less contrasty negatives than indicated; diffusion enlargers may require negatives of higher contrast for best results with any given paper grade.

Table A.8
Negative Density Range

Paper Types	Negative Density Range Suitable for Paper Contrast Grade													
	1.6	1.5	1.4	1.3	1.2	1.1	1.0	.9	.8	.7	.6	.5	.4	.3
Kodak Graded Papers		0		1		2		3		4	5			
Polycontrast Regular and Rapid				1	1½	2	2½	3	3½	4				
Kodabrome RC				Soft			Medium		Hard			Extra Hard		Ultra Hard
Ilfobrom		0			1	2		3		4		5		
Brovira			1		2	3		4		5			6	
Portriga					2		3		4					
Unicolor					1	2		3				6		

Glossary

Aberrations   The several defects of a lens, inherent in its design, material, and construction, which, by deforming the image points in various ways, limit the sharpness of the focused image.

Accelerator   Same as **Activator,** which see.

Acetic Acid   A relatively mild acid used, in highly diluted form, as the rinse bath (short-stop) which follows the developer in the normal film and paper developing processes. The acid in vinegar.

Achromat   A lens which has been corrected for two colors thus partially eliminating the effects of chromatic aborration.

Acid   A hydrogen compound having a pH value less than 7. Most acids will combine readily with certain metals to form salts. Typically an acid solution feels gritty when rubbed between the fingers and has a sharp sour taste. Acid solutions neutralize alkaline solutions and turn blue litmus paper red. The stronger acids cause severe burns and are dangerous to handle.

Activator   The chemical ingredient of a developer solution which stimulates the reducing agent to begin its work and accelerates it. The activator in most developers is an alkaline salt such as sodium carbonate or borax. Also called the **Accelerator.**

Adapter Rings   Narrow metal rings, outside-threaded to fit most popular lenses, and inside-threaded to accept accessories of other than the nominal lens diameter. *Step-up* rings adapt a lens for use with larger-than-normal accessories; *step-down* rings permit the use of slightly smaller accessories than the lens will normally accept.

Additive System   A name for the principles of color mixing using the light primaries. Mixtures of light colors are brighter and lighter in tone than the individual colors were, and the three light primary colors, red, green, and blue, produce white light when blended.

Agitation   The process of stirring, swirling, or otherwise causing a liquid to move freely over the surfaces of film or paper during processing.

Air-Bells   Tiny bubbles of air which are apt to cling to a dry surface which is immersed gently. In developing films or papers, an initial vigorous agitation is usually recommended to dislodge air-bells so as to avoid pinholes.

Air-Spaced Elements   In a compound lens, those elements which are not cemented together.

Albumin   Commercially, simply dried egg white. Used in the preparation of printing paper emulsions from about 1850, it was replaced by gelatin in the 1880s. The old spelling is albumen.

Alkali   A compound whose pH value is greater than 7. Alkaline solutions typically feel slippery or soapy when rubbed between the fingers and are difficult to wash off, especially in soft water. They neutralize acids and turn red litmus paper blue. The stronger alkalis can cause severe burns and are dangerous to handle.

Ambient Illumination   The light condition existing at the subject location.

Ambrotype   A silver image on glass, popular in the 1860s and 1870s, and made by coating a weak collodion negative with black lacquer. Viewed by reflected light the image appears as a grayish positive. Ambrotypes were usually mounted in plastic or leather cases, like **daguerreotypes,** and were frequently hand-tinted.

Anastigmat   A lens which has been well corrected for all the aberrations specifically including astigmatism and curvature of field.

Angular Coverage   The field of view seen or covered by the lens, expressed in degrees.

Anhydrous   Without water; dry. Used to distinguish the dehydrated form of a compound from its crystalline form which might normally contain a substantial amount of water of crystallization while still appearing to be completely dry. When chemical measurements are made by weight, less of the anhydrous than the crystalline form will be required.

ANSI   American National Standards Institute. The present title of the organization which used to be called the American Standards Association (ASA).

Aperture   Opening, specifically of the lens, and expressed as a fraction of the focal length. The f/ number. See **Relative Aperture.**

Apochromat   A lens which has been corrected for three colors, thus reducing the chromatic aberrations to negligible amounts. Apochromatic lenses sometimes include the prefix "Apo-" in their names, e.g., Apo-Tessar, Apo-Lanthar, etc.

Archival Processing   Procedures followed during film or print processing to produce a stable image, free from harmful residual chemical compounds and resistant to attack by environmental contaminants.

ASA The American Standards Association, now the American National Standards Institute. A system of film speed rating now standard in the United States.

Astigmatism One of the common aberrations of photographic lenses and the human eye, characterized by the lens's inability to bring into common focus lines which are radial and those which are tangential to the image circle.

Available Light The light condition which the photographer finds existing at the subject position. The term usually implies an indoor or nighttime light condition of low intensity requiring fast film, large lens aperture, and slow shutter speed.

B See **Bulb.**

Back That portion of a camera which contains the film; specifically, the complete assembly attached to the rear standard of a view camera (and usually removable) which includes the focusing screen, and which accepts the film holders.

Back Focus The distance from the rear surface of the lens to the focal plane when the lens is focused at infinity.

Backlight Illumination from a source beyond the subject, as seen from the camera position, which tends to silhouette the subject. See **Rim Light.**

Barrel Distortion One of the forms of the aberration, **Distortion,** which is characterized by a bowing-out of lines near the edges of the image. See **Pincushion Distortion** and **Rectilinear.**

Baseboard The large, flat board, usually plywood, to which the enlarger column is attached, and on which the enlarging easel is normally placed.

Base The transparent sheet material, usually acetate or polyester, upon which film emulsion is coated.

Base-Plus-Fog Density The density of an unexposed area of a developed film (negative or positive).

Bas-Relief A picture printed from the slightly misregistered images of a negative and its positive mask. The print usually resembles the linear shadow pattern of the subject as it would be seen in low relief in strong slanting light.

Bellows The center section of a view camera which connects the front and back standards. The bellows is usually made of leather, cloth, or plastic, is accordion-pleated for flexibility, and is, of course, lighttight.

Bellows Extension A term often used to refer either to the total bellows length or to the additional extension of the bellows (beyond that required for infinity focus) necessary for focusing at close subject distances.

Belt The endless canvas strip which carries prints through a motorized or manual drum dryer. Sometimes called an **Apron** or **Blanket.**

Between-the-Lens Shutter A shutter designed to operate in a space between the elements of the lens. See **Leaf Shutter** and **Focal Plane Shutter.**

Bichromate Also, and preferably, **Dichromate.** Refers to the chromium salts of sodium, potassium, and ammonium which are used in various bleach baths and in the numerous variations of the **Gum** and **Pigment Printing Processes.** They are poisonous and can be absorbed directly through the skin to cause painful dermatitis and ulcers.

Black Body A hypothetical, unreflecting source of pure radiant energy.

Blade Arrestor Old term for device similar to **Press-Focus Lever,** which see.

Bleach A chemical bath or treatment which converts the silver image into a less visible form, or which removes it entirely. See **Reducer.**

Bleed An image edge trimmed without a border; as, "the picture bleeds top and bottom."

Blind An emulsion not sensitive to certain colors; colorblind.

Block-Up Refers to an area of the negative image so overexposed, and therefore dense, as to obscure textures and details.

Blotter Book A number of sheets of pure white blotting paper, interleaved with nonabsorbent tissue sheets, and bound at one edge to form a large book. Used for nonglossy drying of relatively small prints.

Blue-Sensitive The sensitivity of an ordinary silver emulsion; red and green blind.

Bounce To reflect light; specifically, light directed away from the subject toward some nearby light-toned surface so as to reach the subject diffused by reflection.

Bracket To make a number of exposures (some greater and some less than one considered to be "normal") in addition to the "normal" one, with the intent of getting one near-perfect exposure.

Bromide Any salt of hydrobromic acid but commonly used as a shortened form of potassium bromide.

Bromide Paper A printing paper sensitized principally with silver bromide.

BSI British Standards Institution. A system of film speed ratings used in Great Britain and essentially similar to the ASA speeds.

BTL See **Between-the-Lens Shutter.**

Bulb A marked setting (B) of most shutters which permits the shutter to be held open for an indefinite period by continued pressure on the shutter release. See **Time.**

Burned Out Describes an area of the print image in which highlight detail has not been recorded, usually because of severe overexposure of the negative. See **Block-Up.**

Burning-In The process of allowing some relatively small image area to receive more than the normal exposure by shielding most of the printing paper surface from the light. See **Dodging** and **Flashing.**

Cable Abbreviation of **Cable Release.**

Cable Release A long flexible cloth or metal braid-covered plunger which screws into a special threaded socket on the shutter or camera body. Compressing the plunger with thumb and finger pressure will release the shutter without much danger of camera movement or vibration.

Cadmium Sulfide Cell A light-sensitive (photoconductive), solid-state device which is widely used in exposure meters.

Calotype The ancestor of modern photographic processes, invented by William Henry Fox Talbot in about 1840. The camera exposure was made on sensitized paper and developed out. The prints were made by contact on salted paper, printed out, and fixed. The process came to be known as talbotype and was quite popular. It would probably have been much more widely used if Talbot's patents had not been so restrictive.

Camera Literally, *room* in Latin. The instrument with which photographs are taken, consisting, at least, of a lighttight box, a lens which admits focused light, and some device or provision for holding the film in position.

Camera Obscura Latin for *dark room.* Ancestor of the photographic camera; probably originally an actual room in which observers could watch the images of outside subjects formed by light rays entering the room through a small aperture and passing directly to the opposite wall. The camera obscura eventually evolved into a portable box, equipped with a lens and viewing screen, which was used for viewing and sketching, and finally, after the invention of suitable sensitized materials, for actual photography.

Carbon Process A method of making prints or transparencies, using carbon (or some other pigment) suspended in gelatin, as the image material. The process is extremely flexible and versatile and is capable of excellent photographic quality. It was popular with the Pictorialists but is rarely practiced now because the materials are no longer readily available commercially and are difficult to manufacture at home.

Carrier The negative holder in an enlarger.

Carte-de-Visite A popular image form of the 1860s and 1870s, they are albumin prints mounted on cards about 2½″ × 4⅛″, usually depicting individuals or small family groups. They were sometimes used as visiting cards but portraits of famous men and women were also collected and exchanged as novelties and keepsakes.

Cartridge The disposable metal or plastic container in which lengths of film are sold and used. Sometimes called a **Cassette.**

Cassette A metal container (usually designed to hold lengths of 35mm film) which can be used repeatedly. Of ingenious design and construction, cassettes are made specifically for a particular camera and will not normally work in any other brand. Sometimes referred to as a **Cartridge.**

Catadioptric Lens A lens system comprised of both reflecting and refracting elements.

Cats Slang term for catadioptric lenses.

CC Filters Color-compensating filters, intended for use in color photography to modify the overall color balance of the image. They are available in six colors and several degrees of saturation.

CdS Cadmium Sulfide

CdS Meter An exposure meter which employs a cadmium sulfide cell as its light-sensitive element.

Cemented Lens A lens composed of two or more individual glasses whose adjacent surfaces are ground to fit accurately and bonded together with some transparent adhesive. Most photographic lenses contain some cemented components as well as some air spaces.

Characteristic Curve Another name for the **D log E Curve.**

Chloride Paper Printing paper sensitized principally with silver chloride. A term which is seldom used any more.

Chromatic Aberration A general name for the inability of a lens to bring all the light colors of an object point to a common point of focus in the image plane. Chromatic aberration causes simple blurring of the image in black and white, and color fringing of the image in color photography. Two forms are described, lateral and axial or longitudinal, and the effects are most severe near the edges of the image area.

Circle of Confusion The tiny, but not necessarily the *most* tiny, blurred circle of light which a lens will form as an image of a point of light at the subject position. It has no significance as a measure of lens accuracy or precision, but is measured and discussed simply as a means of defining tolerable sharpness of the image, and therefore the acceptable limits of depth of field.

Clear The appearance of a negative after the fixing bath has removed all visible traces of undeveloped silver halides.

Clearing Time The length of time required to clear a negative. It depends on the strength, temperature, and agitation of the fixing bath and the kind of emulsion being fixed.

Click Stops Detents in the diaphragm or shutter scale of a lens which produce a tactile indication and an audible click to mark the significant scale settings.

Close-Up Lens A positive supplementary lens which, when placed over a camera lens, shortens its focal length and thereby permits closer-than-normal focusing.

Close-Up Photography The techniques and practice of using supplementary lenses, extension tubes, bellows units, etc., to take pictures at closer ranges than the normal focusing adjustment of an ordinary hand-camera will allow. Refers to image magnification ratios of up to, perhaps, 2×, and therefore overlaps **Photomacrography,** which see.

Coating The thin film of magnesium fluoride, or other material, deposited on the surfaces of the lens glasses which gives photographic lenses their characteristic magenta or amber color by reflected light. Its purpose is to reduce the intensity of flare light within the lens which in turn increases the brightness and contrast of the image.

Cocking the Shutter Winding or tensioning the shutter mainspring prior to making the exposure.

Cold Tones Bluish or greenish tinge in the black-and-white image.

Collodion A thin, clear, slightly syrupy solution of pyroxyline in ether and alcohol. It was used in the preparation of wet-plate emulsions, a procedure described by Frederick Scott Archer in 1851.

Collotype Process A printing process, similar to lithography, which uses a plate of selectively tanned gelatin, dampened and inked, to produce photographic images in ink on paper. Unlike other ink processes, collotype plates produce halftones without screening. Although capable of exquisite quality, the process has been superseded by faster, cheaper printing methods.

Color-Compensating Filters A special family of filters, available in calibrated strengths in red, green, blue, magenta, yellow, and cyan, intended for use in color photography. Each is identified by the prefix CC, followed by a number which represents its density (multiplied by 100) for light of its complementary color, and a final letter which identifies the filter color. For example, CC 20Y designates a yellow filter whose density for its complement (blue) is .2.

Color Fringes The rainbowlike outlines caused by lateral chromatic aberration of the lens that surround dark areas of the image and are particularly apparent in areas of high contrast near the edges of the image.

Color Head An enlarger light source containing adjustable dichroic filters which can be set to provide light of any color for color printing.

Color Temperature A standard for defining the color of light based upon its similarity to the light color emitted by a black body heated to a known temperature. Color temperature is expressed in degrees Kelvin, or "Kelvins," and is only appropriate for the description of continuous spectrum light such as is emitted by the sun, tungsten filament bulbs, etc.

Coma An aberration of the lens which causes marginal light rays from a subject point off the lens axis to fail to converge at a common image point. The effect is most severe near the edges of the lens field and can usually be eliminated by stopping the lens down. It is a common defect of high-speed lenses.

Compaction Same as **Contraction,** which see.

Compensating Developer A developer whose activity tends to be inversely proportional to image density. It therefore is self-limiting, working relatively vigorously in areas of underexposure, and slowing down in the overexposed areas as density increases. No practical developer is outstanding in this respect, but those containing the reducing agent, Pyrocatechol, or two-solution Metol formulas, are sometimes recommended. Almost any developer will tend to be more compensating in action if it is highly diluted, and if it is used with only occasional and gentle agitation.

Complementary Colors Any two colors in the subtractive system which, when mixed in the proper proportion, produce black or dark neutral gray. In the additive system, any two colors whose mixture results in white light.

Completion That state of development when essentially all of the exposed silver halides have been reduced to metallic silver; that is, when further development will produce no more image density.

Concave Hollowed out. The side of a spherical surface seen from the center of the sphere.

Condenser Enlarger An enlarger employing condenser lenses to provide uniform illumination of the negative.

Condenser Lens A positive lens used to concentrate light rays. Condensers are used in many enlargers to collect the light from the bulb and direct it through the negative into the enlarger lens.

Contact Paper A printing paper, usually sensitized with silver chloride, which is intended for use in contact printing.

Contact Printing A method of printing in which the negative is placed in contact with the printing paper, emulsion to emulsion, and held in that position in a **Printing Frame.** The exposure is made by exposing the frame to raw light so that the paper emulsion is exposed by light passing through the negative densities. Contact printers, machines which contain a controllable printing light, are also used.

Contact Screen Type of engraving screen in which the dots are not sharply defined but, rather, are surrounded by individual haloes of decreasing density. These screens will form excellent halftone negatives by simple contact printing methods. At least two types are used, gray screens for color work and magenta screens which permit control of image contrast in black-and-white work. Also sometimes called **Halo-Dot Screens.**

Continuous Spectrum Light which contains an appreciable amount of all the visible wavelengths or colors. See **Discontinuous Spectrum.**

Continuous Tone Describes an image containing a gradation of grays as well as black-and-white extremes. See **Dropout.**

Contraction In the Zone System, reduced development which compensates for high subject contrast so as to produce normal contrast in the negative. Some photographers prefer the word **Compaction.**

Contrast Density difference, usually of adjacent areas of the image.

Contrast Grade A number or descriptive term assigned to a particular printing emulsion which identifies its contrast characteristic. In the range from 0 through 6, a normal contrast paper is usually considered to be 2, with the lower numbers indicating a tendency toward lower contrast and higher numbers indicating higher contrast. Printing filters for use with variable-contrast papers are numbered similarly. In some cases paper contrast is indicated by such terms as "soft," "medium," and "hard," instead of numbers.

Contrast Index The numerical expression of the relationship between the negative density scale and the subject luminance range when, simply, the minimum useful image density is considered to be about .1 above base-plus-fog and the useful curve length is assumed to be 2.0. It might be called the average gamma under the stated conditions.

Converter An optical unit which can be interposed between the camera body and lens to effectively double or triple the lens focal length; usually, but not always, with some loss of image quality, and always with a substantial loss of lens speed. Sometimes called an **Extender.**

Convertible Lens A lens whose two major components can be used either together or separately. They were once called "double anastigmats" because each half is separately corrected. When used together the two components yield the "normal" focal length, and a relative aperture of about f/5.6 or f/6.3. When used separately the components work as long lenses—about 1.2 to 2.5 times the normal focal length—at reduced aperture. Performance and correction of the complete lens is excellent. The individual components are fair to moderately good.

Convex Bulging. The opposite of **Concave.** The surface of a sphere seen from outside the sphere.

Correction The design and construction refinements of a lens which tend to minimize the aberrations. A practical photographic lens usually consists of several simple lenses (or glasses) since adequate correction normally requires a variety of types of glass and lens shapes, and meticulous spacing of the elements.

Coverage The area of the image (formed by a lens) which is of useful quality. Also, the area of the subject which the lens can record as an image of useful quality.

Crop To trim, or sometimes to cover, the borders of an image for any reason, but usually to improve the composition.

Cross Light Light striking the subject from one side.

Curtain Shutter A shutter variety in which a slit or opening in a strip of metal or cloth is made to travel past the film surface to effect the exposure. See **Leaf Shutter.**

Curvature of Field The tendency of a simple lens to form its image on a spherical, rather than flat, plane.

Cut Film Another name for **Sheet Film.**

Cyanotype Process An iron-sensitive process which produces an image in bright blue dye. The blueprint process.

Daguerreotype Generally recognized as the first practical photographic process, it was invented by Louis Jacques Mandé Daguerre and announced publicly in 1839. The image was formed on a polished silver plate, sensitized by fuming with iodine, and developed, after camera exposure, in the vapors of warmed mercury.

Dark Slide The black plastic or fiber sheet which is inserted into a film holder through a lighttight slot to seal the film chamber against light.

Daylight Sunlight or skylight or any mixture of the two. For the purposes of color photography, daylight is considered to have a color temperature of from about 5500°K to 6000°K and this condition is likely to exist when the sun is high and slightly overcast. Under other conditions the color of daylight is likely to be quite different from the "norm" and must be filtered if "normal" color rendition is desired.

Decamired Ten mireds. See **Mired.**

Deep Tanks Commercial film processing equipment in which large volumes of processing solutions are agitated by nitrogen burst, and controlled replenishment maintains the solutions at optimum strength throughout their life.

Delay In synchronized flash photography, the interval between the application of the firing current to the bulb and the opening of the shutter. The delay interval is controlled by the shutter. See **M, F, X.**

Dense Descriptive of a negative which is dark overall, or of an area of a negative which has a heavy silver deposit and therefore transmits only a little light.

Densitometer An instrument designed to measure the amount of light transmitted by individual small areas of a negative, thus appraising the density of the areas.

Density The common logarithm of the reciprocal of transmission. That characteristic of the image silver deposit which absorbs (or which prevents it, for any reason, from transmitting) light. Transmission density refers to the absorption of transmitted light, as by areas of a negative. Print tones are described as reflection densities, since they are seen and measured by reflected light.

Density Range The range of densities represented by, for example, a negative image. It is found by subtracting the lowest density value from the highest and is expressed numerically. Also called **Density Scale.**

Density Scale Same as **Density Range.**

Depth of Field The region of acceptably sharp focus around the subject position, extending toward the camera and away from it, from the plane of sharpest focus. The boundaries of the depth of field are referred to as the near limit and the far limit.

Depth of Field Scale A calibrated scale, ring, or chart, often a part of the camera lens mount, on which the depth of field for any distance and aperture setting is indicated.

Depth of Focus The little zone including the focal plane of the lens through which the film can be moved, toward and away from the lens, and still record an acceptably sharp image.

Desiccated Dried. Describes a substance from which at least some water has been removed. Not necessarily **Anhydrous,** which see.

Developer The solution which produces the silver image in the normal photographic process. It ordinarily contains a reducing agent, a preservative, an accelerator, and a restrainer in water solution. A practical developer must develop only the exposed silver halide grains in the emulsion, leaving the unexposed grains unaffected. Such a developer is called clean working. A solution which develops an appreciable quantity of unexposed halide is said to produce chemical fog.

Developing-Out. The photographic process in which relatively brief exposure produces a latent image which is made visible by subsequent development. See **Printing-Out.**

Diaphragm The assembly of thin metal leaves, usually incorporated into the lens barrel or shutter assembly, which can be adjusted to control the size of the lens aperture. Same as **Iris Diaphragm.**

Dichroic Filter A filter, usually of glass coated with a thin film of some durable material, which has the unique ability to transmit certain colors while reflecting the rest of the spectrum. Because the transmitted and reflected colors are complementary the filter appears to change color in certain lights, hence the name "dichroic." Dichroic filters are highly resistant to heat and fading and are therefore especially suitable for use in color printing applications.

Diffraction The tendency of light rays to be bent around the edge of an obstruction.

Diffusion Of light, the random scattering of rays as by transmission through a turbid medium or by reflection from a matte surface.

Diffusion Enlarger An enlarger which employs diffused light to illuminate the negative.

DIN Deutsche Industrie Normen. The German system of film speed determination.

Diopter An optician's term which identifies the power of a lens. It expresses the reciprocal of the lens focal length in meters and is usually preceded by a plus or minus sign to indicate whether the lens is positive (converging) or negative (diverging). Thus, a close-up (positive) lens having a focal length of 50 cm ($\frac{1}{2}$ meter) would be labelled a $+2$ lens.

Discontinuous Spectrum Light radiation from which certain wavelengths (colors) are missing or present in negligible amounts.

Dispersion The separation of a light ray into its component colors as by a prism.

Distortion Sometimes referred to as llinear distortion or curvilinear distortion, it is an aberration of the lens which is characterized by variable magnification of the image. The effect increases toward the edges of the image area and will cause straight lines near the edges of the subject field to be formed near the image margins as curved lines. Two forms are identified, **Pincushion** and **Barrel Distortion.**

D log E Curve The graphic presentation of the relationship between exposure and density when development is a constant. When several conditions of development are expressed the result is a "family of curves."

Dmax Maximum density.

Dmin Minimum density.

Dodging The practice of shading a relatively small area of the image in printing to prevent it from becoming too fully exposed, and thus to render it, in the finished print, as lighter in tone than it would otherwise have been. See **Burning-In.**

Dodging Tool Any device used in dodging. Usually, a thin wire handle on which is mounted a piece of cardboard trimmed to match the shape of the image area to be dodged.

DR Density Range, which see.

Dropout A photograph from which certain tones—usually the grays—have been eliminated.

Drum Dryer A machine for drying paper prints. It typically consists of a heated drum or cylinder of metal and an endless canvas belt which holds the prints in contact with the drum surface. The larger models are motorized for continuous operation.

Dry-Mounting A method of mounting prints on cardboard or similar sheet materials. **Dry-Mounting Tissue** placed between the print and mount board is softened by the heat of a **Dry-Mounting Press** to effect the bond.

Dry-Mounting Press A machine for dry-mounting prints. It has a large flat metal pressure plate which can apply uniform pressure and thermostatically controlled heat on the prints to be mounted.

Dry-Mounting Tissue A thin tissue paper impregnated with shellac or some similar material, which, when heated sufficiently, softens to become an effective adhesive for paper.

Dry Plate Term used in the 1880s to distinguish gelatin-coated glass plates (dry plates) from the previously very popular collodion-coated plates which had to be sensitized immediately before use and inserted into the camera while still damp.

DS Density Scale. Same as **Density Range,** which see.

Dye Transfer A method of making very high-quality color prints, in which the final full-color image is produced by separate printings (transfers) of the three primary dye images, cyan, magenta, and yellow, from individual film matrices to a single sheet of prepared paper.

Easel The device, usually a frame of metal with adjustable metal masking strips, which holds printing paper flat for exposure under the enlarger, and permits adjustments of the width of the picture borders.

Electronic Flash A photographic light source which produces a brilliant flash of light by the discharge of electricity through a gas-filled glass or quartz flash tube. The flash duration is very short, usually less than 1/500 second and there is no firing delay. Most flash tubes produce a light which approximates daylight in color and only minor filtration is required for use with daylight color films. Electronic flash is commonly referred to as **Strobe,** an inaccurate nickname derived from stroboscope, a related but different device.

Element Of a lens, one of the unit structures. A term rather loosely used to refer to a single glass unit, a cemented unit of one or more glasses, or even a complete component of several air-spaced and cemented glasses; as, ''the front element (component) of a convertible lens.''

Elon Eastman Kodak's brand of p-methylaminophenol sulfate, most familiarly known as ''Metol'' which is itself a trade name (GAF, Agfa, Hauff etc.). See **Metol.**

Emulsion The light-sensitive coating on photographic film or printing paper.

Enlarger A printing machine designed to project the image of an illuminated negative onto a sheet of sensitized paper. While all enlargers can be adjusted to make prints larger than the negative image, most can also be adapted to make prints reduced in scale as well, so the name is somewhat misleading.

ES Exposure Scale, which see.

EVS A system intended to simplify the determination of exposure. It assigns the EV numbers, 0 through 12, to the shutter speeds, 1 second through 1/1000 second, and the EV numbers, 1 through 12, to the relative apertures, f/1.4 through f/64. Similarly, Additive Speed Values (ASV), 0 through 10, are assigned to ASA Indexes, 3 through 3200, and Light Value Scale (LVS) numbers, 0 through 10, are assigned to illumination levels of 6 footcandles through 6400 footcandles. In use, the sum of film speed (ASV) plus light intensity (LVS) yields a number which must be matched by the sum of a shutter speed EV number plus an aperture EV number. The system has not elicited much enthusiasm.

Expansion In the Zone System, extended development which compensates for low subject contrast so as to produce normal negative contrast.

Exposure (1) The act of subjecting a photosensitive material to the action of light. (2) The accumulated effect of the action of light on a sensitized material.

Exposure Factor A number (multiplier) indicating the exposure increase required when, for example, a filter is used. The factor for a condition requiring, for example, four times the normal exposure would be written 4×.

Exposure Index A number indicating the relative effective light sensitivity of a given film, as determined by any methods other than those proposed by the ANSI or similar organizations.

Exposure Meter An instrument used to measure the illumination level at the subject position or the brightness of the subject, and to equate this information with the film speed to indicate appropriate camera aperture and shutter speed settings.

Exposure Scale The range of exposures (usually the range of light intensities with exposure time a constant) required to produce, after suitable development, the useful range of densities which a given emulsion can produce. The term is relevant specifically to paper emulsions.

Extender See **Converter.**

Extension Tubes A set of three or more (usually) rings or tubes of varying lengths, intended to be interposed between the body and lens of a small camera, so as to permit focusing the lens on subjects very close to the camera.

Factor A number by which the duration or effect of some action or process must, for some reason, be multiplied.

Failure of the Reciprocity Law Refers to the fact that sensitive emulsions, when subjected to extremely intense or extremely dim exposing lights, require more total exposure than would be predicted by the Reciprocity Law. See **Reciprocity Law.**

Farmer's Reducer A water solution of potassium ferricyanide and sodium thiosulfate, proposed in 1883 by E. H. Farmer as an effective reducing solution for the silver image. It is still popular.

Fast A term used to describe lenses of large relative aperture or films of high sensitivity. Sometimes also applied to unusually sensitive papers.

Feathering a Light The technique of evening the illumination across a set by directing the bright central beam of a light toward the farthest objects, thus allowing the nearest objects to be illuminated by the less intense margins of the beam.

Ferrotype One name for the tintypes. They were also called the melainotype. They were made on small polished and varnished sheets of iron, hence the name *ferro*-type.

Ferrotype Tins After gelatin-coated printing papers became popular, prints were sometimes dried by squeegeeing them, emulsion down, on a Japanned (varnished) iron sheet or ferrotype tin. Prints so treated dried with a high gloss and the technique of glossing a print came to be known as ferrotyping. Nowadays glossy prints are dried on chromium-plated brass or plastic sheets or chromium or stainless steel drum dryers, but the term ferrotyping persists.

Fiber-Based Paper Printing paper whose base material is high-quality paper, usually coated with a thin layer of barium sulfate (baryta). The term is clumsy but frequently used to distinguish plain paper-based materials from **Resin-Coated Papers,** which see.

Field Camera A simple view camera of special light-weight construction, intended for use outside the studio. Field cameras are usually built of wood and are designed to fold up compactly for carrying.

Field Curvature See **Curvature of Field.**

Fill Light Light directed into the shadow areas of the subject to reduce the lighting contrast.

Film Generally, the familiar light-sensitive material used in cameras in the practice of photography. It normally consists of a flexible, thin, transparent sheet or strip of acetate or polyester plastic coated on one side with a light-sensitive emulsion, and on the other with a dyed layer of gelatin to reduce curl and halation.

Film Clip   A spring clip of metal, plastic, or wood designed to hold the film securely as it hangs in the film dryer.

Film Holder   Thin container of plastic, metal, or wood, usually black, designed to hold two sheets of film in separate compartments, back to back. Film is loaded into the holder in the darkroom and is protected from light by the dark slide. The film is positioned so accurately in the holder that, when it is inserted into the camera and the slide is withdrawn, the previously focused image falls precisely on the film surface, insuring that the photographer will actually get the picture he saw on the groundglass.

Film Pack   A metal container of several sheets of film, so designed that when the pack is loaded properly into the camera, an exposed sheet can be removed from the focal plane into a lighttight compartment and a fresh sheet positioned for the next exposure by simply pulling a paper tab protruding from the end of the pack. After all the films are exposed, the pack can be removed from the camera, but must be unloaded in the darkroom. Film packs are not normally reusable.

Film Speed   A number indicating the relative light sensitivity of a given film, as determined by some official body such as ANSI or the BSI. The ASA film speed.

Filter   (1) To pass light through some material which absorbs selected wavelengths or colors or polarized portions of the light. (2) A sheet or disc of plastic, glass, or other material, usually colored, which can be used to absorb selected components of transmitted light.

Fingernail Marks   Slang term for little crescent-shaped gray, black, or occasionally translucent marks which appear on negatives, resulting from pressing or crimping the film before development, as, for example, when loading rollfilm (inexpertly) onto a tank reel. The emulsion may be either effectively exposed or desensitized by physical violence of this kind, and the marks are authentic parts of the developed silver image. They will almost always be seen to coincide with a visible crease in the film base. They cannot be removed.

Fisheye Lens   A type of super wide-angle lens, or lens attachment, capable of covering a field of about 180°. Fisheye images are circular, if the whole image appears on the film, and are notable for their barrel distortion.

Fix   To make the film insensitive to further exposure to light, usually by bathing the emulsion with a solution containing hypo or some other effective silver halide solvent. Such a solution is called a fixing bath.

Flare   That extraneous light, not part of the controlled image light, which passes through the lens to the film. Flare light resulting from diffusion of the normal image light by dirty lens surfaces, reflections from scratches or chips in the glass, or reflections from bright metal surfaces inside the camera usually causes a more or less general fogging of the film. Actual patterns, usually the out-of-focus images of the lens aperture, are caused by multiple reflections of strong light between the various lens surfaces.

Flash   General name for any photographic light source which produces a very brilliant, very brief pulse of light.

Flashbars   An array of several small flashbulbs, each with its own reflector, mounted side-by-side on a common base, and designed to permit sequential firing. Flipflash is a similar device.

Flashbulb   A light source, similar in appearance to an ordinary electric light bulb, but containing a quantity of combustible wire and some priming material in an oxygen atmosphere. When a suitable electrical connection is made to the bulb terminals, the primer fires, igniting the wire which in turn burns very rapidly with a brilliant flash of light. Typically, the flash reaches useful intensity about fifteen milliseconds after the application of the firing current, with the peak intensity occurring at about twenty milliseconds. Total effective duration is in the order of ten to thirty milliseconds. A flashbulb can only be used once, of course.

Flashcube   Small, cube-shaped assembly of four tiny flashbulbs, each with its own reflector, in a common housing. A special base design fits the flash socket of certain specialized cameras and permits the flash units to be fired in quick succession. Coupled with motorized film transport, flashcubes can be used to make four synchronized flash pictures in just a few seconds. Now obsolescent.

Flashing   The technique of darkening an area of a print image by exposing the sensitized paper to raw white light. Flashing fogs the image unlike **Dodging** and **Burning-In,** both of which modify the effect of the image-forming light itself.

Flash Synchronization   The adjustment of the timing of the application of firing current to a flashbulb and the actuation of the shutter release so that the peak flash intensity occurs while the shutter is open.

Flat   (1) A large, free-standing, movable wall or panel, usually painted white, and used as a reflector or background in studio photography. (2) A term used to describe a low-contrast image, usually in reference to a print; it implies that the contrast is *too* low.

Floating Elements   A glass or group of glasses in a lens, designed to move independently during focusing so the lens spacing is optimized for all subject distances.

Flood   A photographic light source which is designed to illuminate a wide area with light of relatively uniform intensity. Almost without exception, it implies an incandescent or fluorescent source, but flood reflectors are also available for use with flash sources.

f/Number   The numerical expression of the aperture diameter of a lens as a fraction of the focal length. See **Relative Aperture.**

Focal Distance   The distance from the lens to the plane of the focused image. In practice, it is usually measured from the plane of the lens diaphragm.

Focal Length   Loosely, the focal distance when the lens is focused on infinity; more accurately, the distance from the rear nodal point of the lens to the image plane when the lens is focused on infinity. See **Nodal Point.**

Focal Plane Shutter   A curtain or blade shutter operating in the camera body just ahead of the film (or focal) plane.

Focus   To adjust a camera, for example, so that an image is formed precisely on the film plane. Also a term applied to the adjustment of instruments such as binoculars and microscopes so as to provide a visual impression of sharpness in the image. Generally, the adjustment of any positive lens system so that light rays passing through it converge at a desired point. The convergence of light rays to a point.

Focusing Cloth   Sometimes also called dark cloth. A large square or rectangular piece of black material, usually cloth, used by photographers as an aid in focusing the image on the groundglass screen of a view camera. It is used to enclose the camera back and the photographer's head, thus excluding outside light and making the image appear bright and clear.

Fog   Any tone or density in the developed emulsion which was caused by extraneous light or chemical action, not related to the normal formation of the image.

Forced Development Development deliberately prolonged considerably beyond the normal time. See **Push.**

FP Shutter See **Focal Plane Shutter.**

Frame (1) To adjust the position and angle of the camera with respect to the subject for the purpose of containing or composing the image within the boundaries of the viewfinder. (2) The useful area and shape of the film image; the picture.

Frame Numbers Numbers printed on the paper backing strip and along the edges of rollfilm, and outside the perforations of 35mm film strips which can be used to identify the individual pictures (or frames).

Freckling Slang term describing a common flaw in ferrotyped prints. Groups or areas of tiny dull spots in an otherwise highly glossy surface.

Frilling The detachment (and wrinkling) of areas of the emulsion layer along the edges of the film or paper base during processing. Likely to occur with, and for the same reasons as, reticulation. See **Reticulation.**

GaAsP Chemical symbol for gallium arsenide phosphide, the compound from which gallium photo-diodes are made. Familiarly known by the initials, GAP.

Gallium Photo-Diode A solid-state photo-conductor, characterized by fast response time, freedom from memory effects, and relative insensitivity to infrared; used as a light sensor in some camera meters. Also known by the initials GPD.

Gamma A numerical expression of the gradient of the straight-line portion of the film characteristic curve, it can be defined as D log E. Loosely, an indication of the contrast of the image as influenced by development. See **Contrast Index.**

Gelatin A complex protein substance made from animal hides and hooves which is used as a chemical-bearing medium and binder in the manufacture of photographic emulsions. Its many unique properties make it especially suitable for use in silver halide emulsions, but it is also an essential material in some nonsilver techniques such as the collotype and carbon processes.

Gelatin Filter Squares Thin sheets of dyed gelatin of high optical quality, available in various sizes and colors, and intended for use in the image light path for the selective absorption of color or control of light intensity.

Glacial Acetic Acid The concentrated (99%) form of acetic acid. It is a transparent, colorless, dense liquid with a sharp, powerfully penetrating odor. It freezes at about 16°C (60°F); it is an effective solvent for some plastics; and its vapors are flammable. It burns the skin painfully on brief contact and should be handled with caution. See **Acetic Acid** and **Short-Stop.**

Glossing Solution A bath in which prints are soaked briefly before being ferrotyped. It is intended to reduce freckling, prevent sticking, and generally improve the luster of the print surface.

Glossy Describes a printing paper with a smooth surface suitable for ferrotyping. A print with a mirrorlike luster such as is produced by ferrotyping.

GPD **Gallium Photo-Diode,** which see.

Gradation Variation in tone. Tonal range or scale.

Gradient Slope, specifically the slope of a film characteristic curve or some section of one.

Graduate A container, usually glass, enameled steel, stainless steel, or plastic, which is calibrated in fluid ounces or milliliters, or both, for use in measuring liquid volumes.

Grain The visible granular texture of the silver image, caused by apparent clumping of the individual silver particles, not usually apparent until the image is enlarged or viewed under magnification.

Gray (1) Any of the intermediate tones of a black-and-white image. (2) Describes a print image which is without extremes of tone and is unpleasantly low in contrast. See **Flat.**

Gray Card A card of known reflectance, usually 18 percent, intended to be placed in the subject area and used as a meter target in the determination of exposure. Also used in color photography to establish a neutral reference for the adjustment of print color.

Gray Scale (1) The gradation of an image. (2) A strip of film or paper displaying individually uniform areas of density ranging from light to dark in a series of steps. Also sometimes called step tablets, they are used in testing the sensitivity and contrast characteristics of photographic materials.

Gross Fog Density Same as **Base-Plus-Fog Density,** which see.

Groundglass A general name for the focusing screen in a reflex or view camera.

Gum Process Also **Gum Bichromate Process.** A method of printing in which the sensitized surface is a coating of gum arabic, a pigment, and a dichromate. The emulsion is rendered insoluble by exposure to bright light, and the image is ultimately composed of the areas of pigment which are not washed away during development in plain water.

H and D Curves Film characteristic curves, specifically those plotted by F. Hurter and V. Driffield who published their procedure in 1890.

Halation The fringe or halo which sometimes occurs around very heavily exposed image points as the excess light, penetrating the emulsion layer, is reflected back into the emulsion from the surfaces of the film base. It is reduced in modern films by dyeing the film base material itself or by the application of a dyed gelatin layer, called the antihalation or antihalo backing, to the film back.

Halftone Printer's and engraver's term for an image which has been screened so as to produce the effect of continuous tone. This is accomplished by breaking up the image into halftone dots in a regular pattern too fine to be visually resolved under normal conditions. Tones of gray are identified by percentage numbers which indicate the total area of ink in a given area of the image. Thus a 10 percent gray would imply that the dots composing it were 1/10 as large in area as the area of the white paper separating them.

Halides Metallic compounds of the halogens, namely the elements fluorine, chlorine, bromine, and iodine. The chloride, bromide, and iodide of silver are the light-sensitive materials upon which most photographic processes are based.

Halo-Dot Screen **Contact Screen,** which see.

Hand Camera Little-used term to identify any camera that can be carried and used without a tripod. Also "hand-held" camera.

Hangers The frames, usually of metal or plastic, in which sheet films are placed for processing in deep tanks.

Hard Term occasionally used to describe high contrast in images or lighting arrangements. Harsh.

Hardener A chemical solution for tanning or toughening the emulsion. Hardeners may be used as separate baths or they may be included in some other solution.

Harsh Implies an unpleasant lack of subtlety of gradation or light distribution. Contrasty, glaring.

Highlights The brightest light accents in the subject. Also, the areas in the image corresponding to the subject highlights. In the negative, of course, the highlights are the most dense areas.

Highlight Mask A deliberately underexposed, high-contrast black-and-white negative of a color transparency which records only the highlight areas of the transparency and which is bound in register with the transparency while the principal color correcting masks are being made. Its purpose is to increase the highlight contrast of the final color print image in the dye transfer process. Highlight masks are also useful in black-and-white photography.

Holder See **Film Holder.**

Hot-Spot An undesirable concentration of light on the subject in studio photography. The brilliant area of illumination produced by the concentrated central beam of a flood or spotlight. An area of unusual brightness in the projected light from an enlarger or projector.

Hydroquinone Common name for p-dihydroxybenzene, a reducing agent in many popular developers. Its fine, needlelike crystals are white, lustrous, and fairly soluble in plain water and in sulfite solutions. It keeps well in dry form, but only fairly well in solution. It is a high-contrast developer, especially so when accelerated with the caustic alkalis such as sodium hydroxide. It is normally nonstaining but must be heavily restrained to prevent fog. In general use, it is almost invariably teamed with Metol or Phenidone—combinations which not only exhibit the best features of each ingredient, but have some additional desirable characteristics of their own. See **Metol** and **Phenidone.**

Hyperfocal Distance The distance from the camera to the near plane of the depth of field when the lens is focused on infinity. Also the distance from the camera to the plane of sharpest focus when the far plane of the depth of field is at infinity.

Hypo The common nickname for the chemical sodium thiosulfate, which was originally called sodium *hyposulfite* by Sir John Frederick William Herschel who discovered it in 1819 and recommended its use to Talbot in 1839. It is still considered to be one of the best of the few practical solvents for the silver halides and is the major ingredient in almost all of the general-purpose fixing baths. The term hypo is commonly used to refer not only to the chemical itself but also to fixing baths compounded with it, and even to those which are made with ammonium thiosulfate—the so-called rapid fixing baths.

Hypo Eliminator A bath for films and papers, recommended for use following the fixing bath and intended to convert the chemical products of fixation into compounds more readily soluble in water, thus facilitating washing and increasing the stability of the silver image. Most such baths are more properly called hypo-clearing baths since they do not really eliminate hypo but do aid in its removal.

Image The photographic representation of the subject photographed. The visible result of exposing and developing a photographic emulsion.

Incident Light The light reaching the subject from any and all sources.

Incident Meter An exposure meter designed, or adapted, for the measurement of incident light intensity, or illuminance.

Infinity For photographic purposes, that distance from the camera beyond which no further focusing adjustment is required to maintain a satisfactorily sharp image of a receding object. It varies with the focal length of the lens, the aperture, and the photographer's standard of sharpness, but for most purposes infinity can be considered to be anything beyond a quarter of a mile or so from the camera.

Infrared Name assigned to an extensive band of invisible, long wavelength electromagnetic radiations which continue the spectrum beyond visible red light. We can perceive a portion of the infrared spectrum as heat, and some special films are capable of making pictures by infrared light.

Inspection A method of determining the extent of development by observing the image under dim safelight illumination.

Intensifier A solution used to increase the density or contrast of the silver image, usually to improve the printing characteristics of underdeveloped negatives.

Interchangeable Lens A lens which can be removed from the camera body as a complete unit and replaced by another.

Interference The cancellation or reinforcement of light waves, resulting from phase shifts such as may be caused by reflection between surfaces spaced apart by some appreciable fraction of the light wavelength. The effect is frequency-selective and often results in colors or patterns such as those visible in soap bubbles, oil films on water, and lens coatings.

Interval Timer A device for indicating the end of a selected period of time, usually by ringing a bell or sounding a buzzer. It is used to time development and other procedures which must be carried out in darkness or where a conventional clock cannot be seen.

Inverse Square Law A statement to the effect that "illumination intensity on a surface will vary inversely with the square of the distance from the light source to the illuminated surface."

Iris Diaphragm See **Diaphragm.**

Kelvin Temperature Temperature on the absolute Celsius (or Centigrade) scale. In photography, another name for **Color Temperature.**

Lantern Slide A transparency mounted in a cardboard or metal frame or bound between glass plates for projection. Usually implies the 3¼″ × 4″ slide size used in large auditorium projectors. See **Slide.**

Latent Image The invisible impression on the sensitized emulsion produced by exposure to light in the developing-out processes. Development converts the latent image to a visible one.

Leader A strip of film or paper, attached to and preceding the useful film area of rollfilm, provided for threading the film into the camera, and in some cases, for protecting the unused film itself from light during storage and handling.

Leaf Shutter A type of shutter, usually operating in the space between the major lens components or immediately behind the lens, consisting of a number of thin metal leaves or blades, arranged concentrically around the lens axis, pivoted so they can either form an opening for the passage of light or overlap to block it. An associated mechanism controls the movement of the leaves and the duration of the exposure interval.

Lens   A disc of transparent glass, plastic, or other material whose opposite faces are ground into (usually) spherical, nonparallel surfaces (one face, but not both, may be plane) having a common central axis, and capable of forming either a real or a virtual image. If the center of the lens is thicker than its edges, it will form a real image and is called a positive lens. If the center is thinner than the edges, only a virtual image can be formed and the lens is termed negative. A single lens is usually referred to as a simple lens and is used for picture-taking in only the cheapest cameras. In photography, the term "lens" usually refers to the complex composite structures of two or more glasses as used in a camera. See **Correction.**

Lens Barrel   The metal tube in which a lens is mounted. It usually also contains a diaphragm assembly. A barrel-mounted lens does not have an integral shutter.

Lensboard   The wooden or metal panel on which a view camera (or other) lens is mounted.

Lens Hood   A device for shielding the front element of a lens from direct light from outside the subject area so as to prevent or reduce flare.

Lens Mount   That portion of the camera body which holds the lens in position.

Lens Shade   Same as **Lens Hood.**

Lens System   A group or series of lenses assembled for purpose of controlling light.

Lens Tissue   A special soft, lintless tissue used for cleaning lens surfaces.

Light Meter   An instrument which measures light intensity. If supplied with a suitable computing scale, it becomes an **Exposure Meter.** The term is commonly used interchangeably with exposure meter.

Light Primaries   The three light colors —red, green, and blue—which, when mixed together, produce a color we recognize as white. None of these colors can be produced by mixtures of any other colors, but appropriate mixtures of the primaries can make any color desired.

Lighttight   Describes a container, room, or space which light cannot enter or leave, or a door or baffle or aperture which light cannot penetrate.

Light Trap   A device (such as, for example, a maze) which will permit the passage of air or water or objects, but will exclude light.

Long Lens   A lens of longer-than-normal focal length. Most accurately applied to lenses of conventional construction, but also commonly used to refer to telephoto lenses as well.

Luminance   Light reflected from, or produced by, a surface.

Luminance Meter   A meter which measures luminance. Also sometimes called reflectance meter or reflected light meter.

LVS   Light value scale. See **EVS.**

Mackie Lines   The light-toned lines typically formed around areas of heavy image density in the **Sabattier Effect,** which see.

Macro-Lens.   Also occasionally **Micro-Lens.** A term used to describe lenses especially corrected for use at short subject distances and generally applied only to those supplied for small cameras. The prefixes *Macro* or *Micro* often appear in the lens name.

Macrophotography   The process of making very large photographic images; for example, photomurals. See **Microphotography.**

Main Light   The light in a studio setup, usually the brightest one, which establishes the light and shadow pattern on the subject and thus describes the forms. Also sometimes called the modelling light.

Masking   The process of blocking out portions of the image area or its borders with opaque tape or paint. Also, the technique of modifying image gradation by registering negative and positive versions of the same image and printing them together to produce a new version.

Mask   A negative or positive transparency made for the purpose of masking the original image.

Mat   A wide-bordered frame, usually of cardboard, placed over a picture to define the composition, isolate the image area, and improve the appearance for presentation.

Mat-Knife   A short-bladed knife with a large handle and, usually, replaceable blades, intended for cutting cardboard. In use it is generally guided by a straightedge metal ruler.

Matte   Dull, unreflective, nonglossy; referring to surface texture.

Matrix   In dye transfer printing, the final positive film image. The matrix image is in gelatin relief, and it is used to make the actual transfer of dye to the print paper surface. Three matrix images are required, one for each of the pigment primary colors. The plural is matrices, but professional printers call them simply "mats."

Maximum Aperture   The largest useful opening of the lens. Wide open.

Meniscus   In photography, describes a simple lens, one of whose faces is convex, the other concave.

Metol   Most common name for the reducing agent p-methylaminophenol sulfate. Also known as Elon, Pictol, Rhodol, Photol, etc. It has low staining tendencies, is easily accelerated by mild alkalis, and produces little fog. It is supplied as a white or slightly grayish powder which turns yellowish or brownish with age and oxidation. It keeps well in powder form, but oxidizes quite rapidly in solution. It works very rapidly, producing an image of neutral tone and very low contrast. It is considered to be a strong sensitizer and will produce an irritating and painful skin rash on those unfortunate photographers who are susceptible. It is generally used in combination with hydroquinone which complements its characteristics very satisfactorily.

M, F, X   Markings found on some shutters indicating the flash synchronization settings for use with different flash sources. M, medium peak, for use with regular wire-filled bulbs, provides a delay of about twenty milliseconds. F, now rarely seen and intended for fast peak bulbs which are obsolete, provides a delay of about five milliseconds. X, zero delay, is recommended for use with electronic flash units and makes the flash contact when the shutter blades are fully open.

Microphotography   The photographic production of extremely small images, as in the preparation of masks for electronic microcircuits.

Microprism   Descriptive of the structure of a type of focusing aid incorporated into the groundglass viewing screen of some miniature cameras. Consisting of a multitude of minute three- or four-sided transparent refracting pyramids arranged in a regular pattern, and placed in the center of the viewing screen, it functions as an area of rather coarse-textured groundglass for viewing, but provides a more sensitive indication of image sharpness than ordinary groundglass does.

Millimicron One millionth of a millimeter, one nanometer; formerly, and still occasionally, used to describe wavelengths of light. Equivalent to ten Angstrom Units. See **Wavelength.**

Mired Pronounced "my-red," it is a contraction of *micro-reciprocal de*grees. It is a value found by multiplying the reciprocal of a color temperature by 1,000,000. The expression of color temperatures in mireds rather than the usual Kelvin degrees simplifies considerably the problem of filter selection for color photography in unusual conditions of light color.

Mirror Lens Optical system which employs a (usually) spherical mirror surface, rather than a positive glass lens, to form a real image. Most such lenses for photographic use incorporate one or more glass lenses in addition to the main mirror element to improve the system performance. These composite systems are called catadioptric systems.

Monobath Processing solution, usually for use with film emulsions, combining the functions of developer and fixing bath.

Monohydrate The stable form of sodium carbonate, and the one commonly specified in formulas calling for this chemical. If either the anhydrous or crystalline form is used in place of the monohydrated form, the amount, by weight, must be adjusted. See **Anhydrous.**

Motor Drive A battery-powered accessory which, when attached to a camera, permits automatic film advance for single-frame exposures as well as continuous rapid sequence exposures at the rate of several frames per second.

MQ Nickname for developers compounded with the reducing agents *M*etol and (Hydro-) *Q*uinone. Also sometimes called MH, for *M*etol-*H*ydroquinone.

Multicoating An improved method of lens coating, employing more than one coating layer on one or more of the lens surfaces.

Negative Any photographic image in which the subject tones have been reversed. Specifically, the reversed-tone image resulting from the simple development of the film exposed in the camera in the conventional process of taking a picture.

Negative Carrier The frame of glass or metal which holds the negative in printing position in the enlarger.

Negative Lens A diverging lens, thinner at the center than at the edges, which can produce only a virtual image.

Neutral Density Filter A thin sheet or disc of glass, plastic, or gelatin, having plane and parallel faces, toned to some uniform and specific shade of gray, and intended to be used over the camera lens during exposure for the purpose of reducing the intensity of the exposing light without changing its color. Sometimes called ND filters, they are available in accurately calibrated densities from 0.1 to 4.0.

Nodal Point A point on the axis of a lens around which the lens can be rotated slightly without displacing the focused image of an object at infinity. Specifically, the point from which an accurate measurement of the lens focal length can be made.

Normal Lens Any lens whose focal length is approximately equal to the diagonal measurement of the film frame. See **Frame,** 2. The angular coverage of a normal lens is usually about 55° across the film frame diagonal. See **Angular Coverage.**

Notches Specifically, the notches which film manufacturers cut into one of the short edges of a sheet of film which identify the type of film by their number, shape, and position, and the emulsion side of the film sheet by their placement.

Object The thing photographed. Often used interchangeably with subject, but usually applied to inanimate things. See **Subject.**

Objective In optics generally, the lens or lens assembly which faces the object. The objective normally forms an aerial image which (in a microscope, for example) is then viewed through the eyepiece or ocular lens. In photography, the term objective is sometimes used to refer to a camera lens.

One-Shot Developer A developing solution, usually compounded and stored in very concentrated form, intended to be highly diluted for one-time use, then discarded.

Opal Bulb Electric light bulb having an unusually dense, translucent envelope of white opal glass, intended for use where uniform diffusion of light is important, as for example, in an enlarger.

Opaque (1) Incapable of transmitting light. (2) A special fine-ground tempera paint, usually brick-red or black, for use in blocking out (opaqueing) unwanted areas of the negative image prior to printing.

Open Flash Method of taking pictures with flash in which the shutter is opened on *Time* or *Bulb* and the flash is fired manually.

Opening Refers to lens opening and is used, loosely, to mean either aperture or relative aperture.

Ordinary Refers to emulsions whose color sensitivity has not been extended beyond visible blue light. Ordinary films are not really ordinary any more. The vast majority of available film types are now Panchromatic. See **Orthochromatic.**

Orthochromatic Type of emulsion which is sensitive to visible blue and green, but not to red. See **Panchromatic.**

Overexposed Refers to a photographic image which has received too much light.

Oyster Shelling A defect in glossy prints dried on flat ferrotype tins, which shows itself as a series of concentric rings or ridges of torn or strained emulsion, caused by uneven drying. Not common in prints dried on glossy drum dryers.

Pan (1) Abbreviation of **Panchromatic.** (2) To swing a camera during the exposure to follow a moving object, and thus to render the object sharp against a blurred background.

Panchromatic Describes an emulsion sensitive to blue and green and some, or all, of the red region of the spectrum. See **Type A,** 2; **Type B,** 2; and **Type C.**

Paper The sensitized paper used in making photographic prints.

Paper Negative A negative image on a paper base, prepared either by exposing the paper directly in a camera or by printing from a positive transparency. The term implies that the image is not in its final form, and that another printing step will follow. If the image is finished for presentation as a negative, it would more likely be referred to as a negative print.

Parallax In photography, the differences in both the framing of the subject forms and their spatial relationships between the image seen by the camera viewfinder and that recorded on the film. Sometimes referred to as the parallax error.

PC Lens See **Perspective Control Lens**

Perspective Control Lens Typically for SLR cameras, a moderately wide-angle lens in a special mount which allows the lens to be decentered with respect to the film, thus providing image controls similar to those obtainable with the rising front and lateral shifts of the view camera.

Phenidone Ilford's trade name for 1-phenyl-3-pyrazolidone, a reducing agent becoming increasingly popular as a substitute for Metol, especially in combination with hydroquinone. PQ developers can be prepared and stored for long periods as highly concentrated liquid stock solutions and their working solutions are highly active, clean-working, and relatively stable. Phenidone is not significantly affected by bromide and must usually be restrained by benzotriazole. It is not considered to be as strong a sensitizer as Metol and is generally tolerated well by persons who are susceptible to "Metol poisoning."

Photoflood A type of incandescent light bulb of high efficiency but limited life, designed to burn at 3400°K. Formerly popular with amateur photographers because of their small size, modest cost, and low current requirements. They are now being superseded by quartz-halogen lights.

Photogram A shadow image made by simply placing objects on the sensitized surface of a sheet of photographic paper and exposing it to light. If the light is sufficiently intense and the exposure long enough, the exposed portions of the paper will turn dark, and the image is a light-toned record of the shadow pattern on a dark background. This is called printing-out the image. Relatively brief exposure to light will form a latent image which can be developed-out like a conventional print image. Developed-out images are more neutral in tone and more contrasty. Both types must be fixed to be preserved for any great length of time.

Photogravure A process in which the image, etched into the polished surface of a grained copper or zinc plate, is filled with soft ink, scraped or wiped to clean the surface, and printed in a press.

Photomacrography The photography of objects under some magnification, usually employing accessory bellows units, extension tubes, supplementary lenses, or simple microscopes. Image magnification may range from about life-size (1:1) to perhaps $50\times$.

Photomicrography Photography through a compound microscope.

Pigment Primaries The primary colors in the subtractive color system, normally considered to be red, yellow, and blue, but in photography specifically magenta, yellow, and cyan.

Pincushion Distortion One of the two forms of curvilinear distortion in which image magnification is disproportionately greater near the edges of the field than near the center. Thus, for example, the image of a large square, placed concentric with the image center, would assume the shape of a pincushion. Barrel distortion is the other, and opposite, form.

Pinhole (1) A very small aperture in the front panel or lensboard of a modified or contrived camera for the purpose of forming an unfocused but useful image on the film. (2) A small transparent spot, usually circular, in a negative image, marking the position of an air-bell which, by shielding the emulsion from the developer, prevented the formation of silver in that area.

Plane of Focus The position of the focused image in space; the image plane, as distinguished from the film plane which will usually, but not necessarily always, coincide with it. Actually, the term is misleading, since the image of any three-dimensional subject closer to the camera than infinity is not plane but three-dimensional—and even the image of a flat subject is plane only under unusual conditions, usually being warped into one or more spherical curves.

Plate A sheet of glass or occasionally metal, coated with light-sensitive emulsion and usually intended for exposure in a camera.

Platinotype Another name for *platinum print*. An iron-sensitive process which produces an image composed of platinum metal on paper.

Polarized Light Light waves which have been caused to vibrate uniformly in, or parallel to, a particular plane.

Polarizer A transparent material such as certain natural crystals and some plastics, capable of polarizing transmitted light.

Polarizing Filter A lens accessory designed to transmit polarized image light.

Pola-Screen Eastman Kodak's trade name for their line of polarizing filters.

Portrait Attachment An old term (and a rather inappropriate one) for a close-up lens. See **Close-up Lens.**

Portrait Lens A lens designed to produce soft-focus images, and popular with portrait photographers. See **Spherical Aberration.**

Positive An image in which the tones or colors are similar to those of the subject.

Positive Lens A converging lens; one which has relatively thick center and thin edges and which can focus light to form a real image.

Posterization Popular name for a printing process in which the image gradation is arbitrarily limited to two or three tones of unmodulated gray (or color) resulting in a simplified posterlike pattern.

PQ Refers to mixtures of *Phenidone* and hydroquinone, as used in developer formulas.

Preservative The ingredient in a developing or fixing solution which tends to prevent or retard spoiling, usually sodium sulfite.

Press-Focus Lever A device incorporated in many leaf shutters which permits opening, or holding open, the shutter blades regardless of the speed setting. On some old shutters this was called a "blade arrestor."

Primary Colors Those fundamental colors, in light or pigment, which cannot be created by mixing any others. See **Light Primaries** and **Pigment Primaries.**

Print In photography, the term is generally used to identify an image on paper, produced by photographic means. It is usually understood to mean a positive image and implies a final image rather than an intermediate one in some longer process.

Print Finishing The process of producing a permanent, presentable photographic print, sometimes including treatment in the fixing bath and the final wash, but certainly referring to drying, spotting, cropping, mounting, and matting and related operations.

Printing Frame A shallow, rectangular frame of wood or metal equipped with a removable front glass and a separate folding back which can be fastened to the frame with leaf springs so as to hold a negative and a sheet of printing paper against the glass smoothly and tightly. In use, light is allowed to shine through the front glass and through the intervening negative to reach the printing emulsion. Also called a contact printing frame. See **Contact Printing.**

Printing-Out A method of photographic printing in which a visible image is formed by the action of light directly, and without subsequent development.

Printing Paper Photographic printing paper. Any paper coated with a light-sensitive substance, to be used for making photographic images, but generally in reference to commercially manufactured papers coated with gelatin emulsion containing silver halides as the sensitive materials.

Print Quality This term refers to the craftsmanship of the print and whatever evidences there are of the photographer's technical understanding and competence (or lack of them). But there are often intangibles involved which influence the viewer in ways difficult to explain, and these factors, whatever they are, must be included in the term. Print quality is unrelated to pictorial content.

Prism-Reflex A type of camera, usually small, in which the viewfinder image is focused, right-side-up and correct from left to right, on a groundglass screen, and viewed through a magnifying eyepiece. The optical system which accomplishes this includes both a mirror and a pentaprism, hence the name.

Process (1) To subject photographic films or papers to chemical treatment, such as, for example, development. (2) The sequence of chemical steps required to produce the desired image or result.

Process Lens A photographic lens especially designed and painstakingly constructed for the purpose of producing images of the highest quality at object distances of only a few focal lengths. Usually nearly symmetrical in construction and corrected apochromatically, these lenses are exceptionally free from distortion, of relatively long focal length, slow, and very expensive. They are used almost exclusively by professionals in industry and the graphic arts. The nearest equivalent for the small-camera user is the *macro*-lens.

Projection Print Any print made by projection, rather than by contact. Usually interpreted to mean an enlargement.

Projector In photography, usually a machine used to project enlarged images onto a viewing screen, such as a slide projector or movie projector.

Proofing The process of making test exposures, frequently of an entire roll of negatives in a printing frame, to obtain a record of the images and aid in their selection.

Push To prolong the time of development of film in an effort to compensate for underexposure. Also, to underexpose a film deliberately with the intention of attempting compensation in development. To force, but moderately. See **Forced Development.**

Pyro Common contraction of pyrogallic acid or 1, 2, 3-trihydroxybenzene. One of the first organic reducing agents to be used as a photographic developer, it is usually in the form of white prismatic crystals of irregular size and shape. It is a very active developer. It keeps well in dry form or in suitable stock solution, but oxidizes very rapidly in most working dilutions. It is usual to prepare the stock as three separate highly concentrated solutions: Sol. *A* containing the pyro, the restrainer and a substantial quantity of an acid sulfite as a special preservative; Sol. *B* containing the normal preservative; and Sol. *C* containing the accelerator. Pyro developers of this kind typically produce a heavy yellowish stain image and also tan or harden the image gelatin as they work so that the final image combines silver, stain, and gelatin relief. Pyro stains the hands and utensils badly and the usual handling cautions should be observed.

Quartz Light Also quartz-iodine light or quartz-halogen light. An incandescent electric light of small size and high efficiency employing a tungsten filament burning in an atmosphere of iodine or bromine vapor and enclosed in a quartz envelope. Characterized by long life, exceptional resistance to blackening or dimming with age, and uniform color temperature.

RC Papers **Resin-Coated Papers,** which see.

Racked Out Referring to the bellows of a view camera, the term means extended.

Rangefinder Primarily refers to an optical device consisting of a system of lenses and beam-splitting prisms, which, viewing the subject through two slightly separated objective lenses, presents the images together in the viewfinder. When the two images are made to coincide by turning a dial, the subject distance can be read from a calibrated scale. Now also used to refer to a simple arrangement of two small prisms incorporated into the viewing screen of some single-lens reflex cameras as a focusing aid.

Rangefinder Camera A camera featuring a built-in, coupled, optical rangefinder, usually incorporated into the viewfinder and linked mechanically with the focusing mount of the lens so that bringing the rangefinder images into coincidence also focuses the lens.

Raw Light Unfocused light.

Real Image An image which can be projected on a surface and seen with the unaided eye. See **Virtual Image.**

Reciprocity Law A law which states that exposure varies uniformly with changes in either time or intensity.

Rectilinear Free from linear distortion.

Reducer A solution of chemicals capable of dissolving the developed silver image, thereby reducing its density.

Reducing Agent In chemistry, a substance capable of reducing the positive charge of an ion by supplying electrons. Many reducing agents are capable of reducing silver halides to metallic silver, but only a few are appropriate for use as photographic developing agents. See **Developer.**

Reel The metal or plastic spool featuring parallel spiral flanges (sometimes adjustable) on which rollfilms are wound for small tank processing.

Reflectance Describes the ability of a surface to reflect light.

Reflectance Meter **Luminance Meter,** which see.

Reflection The rebounding of light from a surface, especially a plane polished surface. Also the image seen by reflection, such as the image "in" a mirror.

Reflector A surface used to reflect light. Photographic reflectors are usually sheets of cardboard, plywood, masonite, or stretched fabric, painted white or covered with metal foil.

Reflex Camera A type of camera in which the viewfinder image is formed by a lens and reflected by an inclined mirror onto a groundglass screen mounted in the top of the camera body. See **Single-Lens Reflex** and **Twin-Lens Reflex.**

Refraction The bending of light rays as they pass obliquely through the interfaces of transparent mediums of varying or different densities.

Register To superimpose one image on another of identical outline so that the forms and edges coincide.

Relative Aperture The relationship between the diameter of the lens opening and the focal length of the lens. It is found by dividing the focal length by the diameter and is, strictly speaking, the number so found—as distinguished from the aperture which includes the prefix *f*. This is a niggling distinction—photographers use the terms interchangeably.

Replenisher A solution of chemicals, similar in composition to a developer but usually more concentrated, intended to be added in measured quantities to a developer after each use for the purpose of restoring the strength of the developer and extending its useful life.

Resin-Coated Papers Printing papers employing a special base material, treated during manufacture with a plastic "Resin Coating" which, by limiting water absorption, allows for very rapid processing and reduces drying time.

Restrainer An ingredient in a developer solution intended to inhibit the development of unexposed halides. In most solutions which contain one, the restrainer is potassium bromide.

Reticulation The pattern of tiny wrinkles or tears in the emulsion of a negative which sometimes results when the film is subjected to temperature extremes or harsh chemical treatment during processing. In extreme cases, the emulsion may be detached from the film base in large patches. See **Frilling.** Mild cases of reticulation are often overlooked or confused with the image grain. See **Grain.**

Retro-Focus Lens A type of wide-angle lens, supplied for reflex cameras, which has a back focus greater than its focal length. This is made possible by special reversed telephoto design and provides clearance for the reflex mirror.

Reversal (1) The transformation of the original tonal scale from negative to positive or vice versa, which occurs whenever a conventional photographic emulsion is exposed and developed. (2) A special process by which exposed film is made to produce a positive image of the original subject. Actually a double reversal of the subject tones, the film is first developed to form a conventional negative image which is then bleached out of the emulsion. The remaining unexposed silver halides are then fogged by exposure to raw light or chemical treatment and developed to form the final positive image.

Rim Light Backlight which illuminates the edges of the subject, producing a bright outline.

Rising Front One of the shifts of a view camera, this refers to that adjustment of the camera lensboard which permits vertical displacement of the lens while allowing the lensboard to remain parallel with the film plane.

Rollfilm Film supplied in rolls rather than sheets, but especially those films protected from light by paper leaders rather than those supplied in protective cartridges of metal or plastic.

Sabattier Effect The partial reversal of image tones caused by exposure of the emulsion to light during development, usually after the image has been partially formed. Named after Armand Sabattier who first described the effect in 1862. Commonly referred to as solarization which is a misnomer. See **Solarization.**

Safelight Illumination, used in various darkroom processes, which is of a color and intensity which will not appreciably affect the emulsions being handled. Blue-sensitive emulsions can be handled in a yellow safelight and orthochromatic emulsions are generally unaffected by orange or red safelight. Image density resulting from excessive exposure to safelight, or to an inappropriate safelight color, is known as safelight fog.

Salted Paper Photographic printing paper such as was described and used by Talbot in his calotype process. It can be prepared by soaking a sheet of good-quality paper in a weak solution of salt, then coating it with one or more layers of a silver nitrate solution. The halide formed is silver chloride. The paper is used for printing-out and the image is an elegant purplish tone which, unfortunately, changes to brown during fixation.

SBC **Silicon Blue Cell,** which see.

SBR See **Subject Brightness Range,** for which this is a contraction. "Subject Luminance Range" is preferred.

Scale Focusing A method of focusing a camera by measuring or estimating the subject distance and adjusting the focusing controls to align the appropriate mark on the footage scale with the fixed reference mark on the camera or lens body.

Scattering Loss of intensity of light in passing through a turbid medium. The shorter wavelengths are typically absorbed most readily, causing the transmitted light to appear yellowish or reddish. This is the atmospheric effect which is responsible for the warmth of color in late afternoon sunlight and in sunsets.

Screen (1) The surface upon which images are projected for viewing. Usually made of special fabric painted white, or covered with tiny glass or plastic beads, or metallized for maximum reflectance. (2) The sheet of glass or film containing a fine pattern of lines or dots, through which films are exposed in the production of halftone printing plates. See **Halftone** and **Screened Image.** (3) Occasionally used to refer to the groundglass of a camera, as the viewing or focusing screen.

Screened Image A photographic image composed of minute dots which vary individually in size in proportion to the intensity of the light which formed them. Photographs or other continuous-tone images must be screened for reproduction by letterpress or offset techniques in order to preserve the gradation of the original subject. See **Halftone.**

Secondary Colors Colors which result when approximately equal parts of any pair of primary colors are mixed together.

Sensitivity In photography, the susceptibility of an emulsion to alteration by light energy.

Sensitometry The science of the measurement of the sensitivity, and related characteristics, of photographic materials.

Separation (1) The visual quality of any image area which makes it visible against its background. (2) The process of recording, on individual black-and-white films, the extent and intensity of each of the primary color components of a photographic subject or image.

Shadow Area Any region of a photographic image which corresponds to an area of shade or shadow in the original subject. Loosely, any dark area of a positive or light area of a negative image.

Sharpness The subjective impression of clarity of definition and crispness of outline in the rendering of the detail and texture of the photographic image.

Sheet Film Film supplied in individual pieces; also called cut film.

Sheet Film Holder See **Film Holder.**

Shifts and Swings The various adjustments of the front and rear standards of a view camera, provided for the purpose of facilitating framing, control of perspective, and the efficient use of the available depth of field. See **Rising Front.**

Short Lens A lens of less-than-normal focal length; a wide-angle lens. See **Wide-Angle Lens.**

Short-Stop Old term, still occasionally used, to describe an acid stop bath.

Shoulder The upper, diminishing-gradient portion of a film characteristic curve, which represents the region of overexposure.

Shutter The mechanism, sometimes electronically controlled, which opens and closes to admit light to the film chamber of a camera and control the length of the exposure interval. See **Leaf Shutter, Focal Plane Shutter,** and **Between-the-Lens Shutter.**

Shutter Release The lever or plunger which, when pressed, allows the shutter mainspring to operate the shutter mechanism and make the exposure.

Shutter Speed (1) The duration of the interval of exposure. (2) The marked settings on a shutter dial. The numbers represent the denominators of fractions of which 1 is the numerator.

Silicon Photo-Diode A solid-state photo-conductor device used in many modern cameras and meters as a light sensor. It is characterized by fast response time, freedom from memory effects, and sensitivity extending well into the infrared. Abbreviated as SPD.

Single-Lens Reflex A reflex camera in which the viewfinder image is formed by the camera lens and reflected to a top-mounted viewing screen by a hinged mirror normally inclined behind the camera lens. During exposure of the film, the mirror flips up to seal the groundglass opening, allowing the image light to pass through to the film chamber. In most designs, a focal plane shutter is employed.

Slide (1) A transparency mounted in cardboard, metal, plastic, or glass, for projection onto a screen for viewing. (2) A shortened name for the dark slide of a film holder. See **Dark Slide.**

Slow A term used to describe the longer exposure intervals provided by the shutter, as "one-half second is a slow speed." Also applied to relatively insensitive emulsions, as a "slow film."

SLR Abbreviation for **Single-Lens Reflex,** which see.

Sodium Thiosulfate One of the few chemicals which, in solution, can dissolve the silver halides, and one of a still smaller group which is suitable for photographic use. It is the principal ingredient of ordinary fixing baths and is somewhat less active, but also less prone to attack the developed silver image, than is ammonium thiosulfate which is used in the so-called rapid fixing baths. Available in both anhydrous and crystalline form, the crystals are generally used and are sometimes sold as hypo-rice. See **Hypo.**

Soft (1) Describes an image which is not sharp; that is, one which is blurred, diffused, or not accurately focused. (2) Photographic emulsions, specifically printing papers, which tend to produce images of lower-than-normal contrast; for example, the paper grades 0 and 1, and some others of similar characteristics, are called soft papers.

Solarization Originally, the reversal of image tones occurring in the early printing-out processes resulting from extreme overexposure; now almost universally used to describe the Sabattier effect. See **Sabattier Effect.**

Spectrum A complete and ordered series of electromagnetic wavelengths, usually construed to mean the band of visible wavelengths which we perceive as colors. The visible spectrum consists of wavelengths of from about 400 to 700 nanometers, a band which represents a gradual color transition from deep violet, through blue, green, yellow, orange, and red. The spectrum colors can be displayed by dispersing white light with a prism. A natural example, resulting from the dispersion of sunlight by raindrops, is the rainbow.

Spherical Aberration The tendency, inherent in any simple positive lens whose surfaces are spherical, to focus light rays passing through the peripheral areas of the lens at points closer to the lens than the focal point of the central rays. This results in a zone, rather than a plane of focus, and produces a film image which is generally well defined, but overlayed and blended with a kind of ethereal diffusion. It is a common and troublesome defect in fast lenses, but can be greatly reduced by stopping down. It is deliberately left uncorrected in lenses intended for portraiture so as to produce a pleasing softness of image.

Spin Dropout Slang term for Kodak's **Tone-Line Process,** which see.

Split-Image Rangefinder A variety of rangefinder in which the opposite halves of the image are displaced along a dividing line when the instrument is not properly focused. Correct distance is indicated when the image halves are adjusted to match. See **Rangefinder** and **Superimposed Rangefinder.**

Spotmeter An exposure meter which measures reflected light, or luminance, over a field of only a degree or two. The portion of the subject being read is outlined on a viewing screen to facilitate accurate appraisal of the individual luminances of small areas of the subject.

Spotone Trade name of a popular spotting dye available in several shades of warm, neutral, and cool colors to match almost any black-and-white print image tone.

Spot Reading A measurement of the luminance of a small area of the subject; specifically, a reading made with a spotmeter.

Spotting The process of bleaching or painting out blemishes in the print image for the purpose of improving its appearance.

Spotting Colors The dyes and especially the pigments used in spotting.

Spring Back The entire assembly attached to and usually removable from the rear standard of a view or press camera, which includes the ground-glass viewing screen and the frame and springs which secure the film-holder in position.

Stabilization The process of rendering the unexposed halides in the developed image resistant to further visible change by the action of light. Stabilized prints are not permanent and they are heavily contaminated with chemicals, but the process is a valuable one for many purposes because it is fast and convenient. It does, however, require a special machine called a stabilization processor and uses special papers and chemicals.

Stain Colored or toned area, generally of a print, caused by chemical oxidation or contamination and not usually stable, permanent, premeditated, or desirable. The exceptions are the stain images, formed by such developing agents as pyrogallic acid, which have certain virtues.

Star Filter A glass disc etched or scratched in a regular pattern, intended for use over the camera lens for the purpose of producing radiating streaks around the highlights of the image. A square of shiny window-screening or a stretched piece of nylon stocking will produce a similar result.

Step Tablet A gray scale composed of regular areas of density increasing in incremental progression. Film step tablets are intended for use with transmitted light; paper step tablets are used with reflected light.

Stock (1) The base or support material such as paper on which sensitized photographic emulsions are coated. (2) The concentrated form of a photographic chemical solution which is commonly diluted into the working solution for use.

Stop (1) Originally a metal plate, centrally perforated, and intended for insertion into a slot in the barrel of a lens for the purpose of limiting the amount of light passing through the lens. Sometimes referred to as Waterhouse stops (after James Waterhouse, who devised the system in 1858), these stop plates were supplied in sets with apertures of different sizes. (2) The aperture or f/number of a lens. (3) A change in exposure, from any cause, which doubles or halves the preceding one. For example, changing the shutter speed from 1/25 second to 1/100 second, other things being equal, is said to reduce the exposure by two stops. (4) Contraction of short-stop, the acid rinse bath which commonly follows the developer.

Stop Bath A mildly acid solution (typically about 1% acetic acid) in which films or prints are treated immediately after their removal from the developer. By neutralizing the developer alkali the stop bath halts development and prolongs the life of the fixing bath.

Stop Down To reduce the size of the aperture of a lens.

Straight Line Portion The central length of the D log E curve, between the toe and the shoulder, which represents a progression of image densities which are uniformly proportional to their corresponding increments of exposure. The portion of the curve exhibiting uniform gradient.

Strobe Contraction of the word strobo-scope. A special form of electronic flash unit capable of firing repeatedly and automatically at rates which can be varied from a few flashes per second to hundreds. This term is applied inaccurately, but almost universally, to ordinary photographic electronic flash units which usually require several seconds to recharge after each flash and do not flash repetitively. See **Electronic Flash.**

Subject The thing or view photo-graphed. There is some implication that the term subject refers to animate things, and that object refers to inani-mate things, but the terms are gen-erally used interchangeably.

Subject Brightness Range See **Subject Luminance Range,** a preferable term.

Subject Luminance Range The numer-ical difference between the light in-tensities of the shadows and highlights of a subject as expressed in arithmetic or logarithmic terms, or in terms of the number of stops represented. Some-times called "Subject Brightness Range."

Subtractive System The system of color mixing involving pigments or dyes in which the primaries represent the most intense and brightest colors available and any mixture of them must necessarily be darker and less intense. Pigments and dyes are seen to be colored because they reflect that color of the incident white light, absorbing the remaining wavelengths. The absence of all pigment color is assumed to be white, as represented by the untouched ground or surface which reflects light without selective absorption. Since each of the three pigment primaries absorbs one of the three light primaries, a mixture of the three pigments will absorb virtually all of the incident light, providing, the-oretically, the visual effect of black. See **Additive System** and **Pigment Primaries.**

Superimposed Rangefinder A type of rangefinder in which the two images appear to overlap. One is usually slightly tinted for easy identification, and the instrument will indicate the correct subject distance when the im-ages are adjusted to coincide by superimposition. See **Split-Image Rangefinder.**

Supplementary Lens A simple lens or lens system to be used over a camera lens for the purpose of altering effec-tive focal length.

Surface A term relating to printing pa-per, referring specifically to the tex-ture of the emulsion coating.

Swings and Tilts Another name for the adjustments of a view camera. See **Shifts and Swings.**

Synchronizer The device, usually in-cluded in the shutter mechanism, which fires a flash unit at the precise moment required to provide peak light intensity during the instant that the shutter is open.

T Time, which see.

Tacking Iron A small, electrically heated, thermostatically controlled tool used to tack or attach dry-mount-ing tissue to the back of a print or to the mount board, so as to hold it in place while the print is being trimmed and heated in the dry-mount press.

Taking Lens The lens which forms the film image in a twin-lens reflex camera, as distinguished from the viewing lens which forms the viewfinder image.

Tank A small, lighttight container, usu-ally of plastic or metal, in which film is placed for processing. Also the larger rectangular containers of hard rubber, plastic, or stainless steel used in sheet-film processing and some-times called deep tanks.

Tanning Developer A developer solu-tion which hardens the gelatin of the emulsion in the same areas and at the same time that it develops the silver image.

Telephoto A type of lens constructed in such a way that its physical length is unusually short in relation to its focal length. Telephoto lenses are usually more compact, and sometimes lighter in weight, than conventional lenses of similar aperture and focal length. They are invariably used as long lenses, since their angular cov-erage is inherently restricted, and they are more likely than are conventional lenses to suffer from distortion and chromatic aberrations.

Tessar A modified and improved ver-sion of the Cooke triplet lens, in which the rear element of the triplet was re-placed by a cemented pair. Designed by Paul Rudolph for Zeiss in 1902, it was enormously successful and is still considered to be an excellent design for lenses of normal coverage and moderately wide aperture. It has been widely copied, and virtually every lens manufacturer in the world now has a few Tessar-type lenses among his offerings.

Test Strip A piece of paper or film which is subjected to a sequence of regular and cumulative exposures and controlled development, so as to sample the estimated range of useful exposures in an effort to determine the optimum one.

Thin Describes the appearance of a transparency image (usually the nega-tive) of low overall density.

Thin-Emulsion Film One of a group of modern roll and 35mm films coated with an unusually thin layer of silver-rich emulsion and capable of pro-ducing images of high resolution, relatively fine grain, and brilliant grada-tion. They are typically of medium or low speed and tend to produce high contrast unless specially processed.

Time One of the marked speeds on most shutters. A shutter set on *Time* will open when the shutter release is pressed and will remain open until the release is pressed again. It is a convenient setting for exposure in-tervals of more than a few seconds. See **Bulb.**

Time-and-Temperature The method of controlling film development, when the film is processed in small tanks or in total darkness in large tanks or trays, by maintaining the process solutions at a known temperature and limiting the duration of development to a se-lected interval. See **Inspection.**

Time Exposure Specifically, a camera exposure made by setting the shutter dial on *T,* but generally used to refer to any exposure, timed manually, of longer than a second or so.

Timer A mechanical or electronic de-vice used to terminate an exposure in-terval or ring a bell or otherwise indi-cate the end of some selected interval of time.

Tintype Common name for the Ferro-type or Melainotype. Tintypes are col-lodion images on Japanned (black varnished) iron sheets. Exposed in the camera and treated to appear as posi-tive images, each tintype is unique. They were relatively inexpensive and extremely popular in the 1860s and 1870s.

TLR See **Twin-Lens Reflex.**

Toe The lower segment of the D log E curve, characterized by its progres-sively increasing slope or gradient. Its lowest extreme represents the region of underexposure of the emulsion.

Tonal Scale The range of grays or den-sities of a photographic image. Grada-tion.

Tone-Line Process A method of pro-ducing a photographic image which resembles a pen-and-ink drawing. It includes a step in which a high-contrast film material in contact with a fully masked negative is exposed to slanting light while being rotated on a phonograph turntable, and is, therefore, sometimes called the spin dropout process.

Toner Any solution of chemicals used to alter the color of the silver image, either during development or, usually, as a postdevelopment treatment.

Trailer The length of opaque film or attached paper which follows the useful image area of the film strip and, when wrapped in several layers around the exposed film roll, serves to protect the image exposures from raw light.

Translucent Describes a diffusing material which will transmit light, but not focused light.

Transparency An image which is viewed by transmitted light. Specifically a film image, usually positive, and often in color, intended for projection.

Tray The shallow, rectangular, open containers in which prints, and sometimes films, are processed. In England they are called dishes.

Triplet A lens of three elements, specifically the three-glass lens designed in 1893 by H. D. Taylor and known as the Cooke Triplet. It was considered a breakthrough in lens design and is the ancestral prototype of a great many modern lenses.

Tripod A three-legged stand, usually adjustable in height and provided with a tilting and swivelling head, on which a camera can be fastened for support and stability during use.

TTL Through-the-lens; describes a type of exposure meter, incorporated in the structure of a camera, which reads the intensity of the image light transmitted by a lens.

Tungsten Light Generally, the light emitted by a heated tungsten filament such as is contained in conventional electric light bulbs. Sometimes used to refer specifically to the light of special photographic tungsten-filament bulbs which are designed to burn at either 3200°K or 3400°K. Also often used loosely to apply to artificial light in general, as distinguished from daylight.

Twin-Lens Reflex A type of reflex camera which uses separate but similar lenses in separate compartments of the camera body for the individual functions of viewing and recording the image. See **Single-Lens Reflex.**

Type A (1) Refers to those color films which have been balanced or specially sensitized for use in tungsten light of 3400°K. (2) Very occasionally refers to panchromatic emulsions whose sensitivity to red light is minimal.

Type B (1) The group of color films intended for use in tungsten light of 3200°K. (2) Commonly, the designation of panchromatic films whose red-sensitivity approximates that of the human eye.

Type C Panchromatic films whose red-sensitivity exceeds that of the human eye.

Ultraviolet The common name for the band of short wavelength, high-frequency electromagnetic radiations which border the visible spectrum beyond visible violet light.

Underexposed Refers to a photographic image which has received too little light.

Unit Magnification The formation by a lens system of an image identical in size or scale with the subject.

US Uniform system. The name of an obsolete system of lens aperture scale marking which expressed, inversely, the arithmetic relationship of the light transmission of the various apertures. In the system, the number 1 was assigned to the aperture f/4.0, 2 was equivalent to f/5.6, 4 equalled f/8.0, 8 equalled f/11.0, etc.

Variable-Contrast Paper A type of printing paper coated with a mixture of two emulsions which are separately sensitized to (usually) green and blue light. Since one emulsion has a high-contrast characteristic and the other low, the overall contrast rendition of the paper can be controlled by varying the proportions of green and blue in the exposing light. With most such papers, green light will produce an image of low contrast, while high contrast will result from exposure to blue light. Light color—and therefore image contrast—is controlled by filters, each numbered to indicate the paper grade it corresponds to.

View Camera A type of camera in which the image is viewed and composed on a groundglass screen placed precisely at the film plane. The viewed image is therefore identical to the one presented to the film during exposure. After the image has been focused and composed, the groundglass is replaced by the film in a suitable holder and the picture is made. Most view cameras provide for considerable adjustment of the relative positions of the lensboard and film plane. They are typically designed to accept sheet film in the larger sizes and must be used on a tripod, or other firm support. See **Shifts and Swings.**

Viewfinder The aperture or optical device, usually an integral part of the camera, through which or in which the subject can be seen, appraised, and composed.

Viewing Lens In a twin-lens reflex camera, the lens which forms the viewfinder image. See **Taking Lens.**

Vignetted Describes an image whose edges or corners have lost density, definition, or contrast. Print images are sometimes vignetted purposely to eliminate or subdue unwanted detail. Vignetting can also occur in the camera if the lens used cannot cover the film area adequately or if lens accessories, such as filters or sunshades, restrict the lens's angular coverage.

Virtual Image An image, such as is typically formed by a negative lens, which can be seen in the lens or as an aerial image, but cannot be formed on a screen.

Warm Tones In photography, shades of red or orange (browns) in the black-and-white silver image. Generally, similar shades in the color or tone of any material.

Washed Out A term to describe a pale, lifeless, gray print image, usually implying loss of highlight detail, such as might typically result from underexposure of the print.

Wavelength The distance from crest to crest, or trough to trough, of adjacent, cyclic waveforms. The completion of a single waveform, including crest and trough, is called a cycle, and the number of cycles which are completed in a second of time is called the frequency (of vibration) of the waveform. The traditional units of wavelength measurement in light are the Angstrom Unit, abbreviated "A" and equal to 1/10,000,000 of a millimeter, and the millimicron, equivalent to 1/1,000,000 of a millimeter. The preferred unit is now the "nanometer" which is equivalent to the millimicron. The unit of frequency is the Hertz, cycles per second.

Weak Describes an image which is not fully formed or which is unpleasantly low in contrast or density. Pale, gray, lifeless.

Wedging The deviation of a light ray in passing, for example, from air through a glass plate with plane, but not parallel, faces. Also sometimes used loosely to describe the lateral displacement of an image being projected through a thick glass or plastic filter which is slightly tilted in the light beam.

Weight The thickness of printing paper stock.

Wet-Mounting   Methods of attaching prints to their mounts by means of liquid, especially water-based, glues or adhesives. •

Wet-Plate Process   Another name for the collodion process, in which glass plates coated with a thin film of salted collodion were sensitized in a solution of silver nitrate and immediately loaded into the camera for exposure while still damp. The process was popular from about 1850 until about 1880 when it was largely superseded by gelatin-coated dry plates.

White Light   Generally used (as distinct from safelight) to refer to any light which is capable of exposing an emulsion. Also, in color photography, it describes light of a Kelvin temperature suitable for use with a particular emulsion type. Thus, white light for daylight film is considered to be of about 5600° K, while for "Type A" film white light is 3400° K, etc.

Wide-Angle Lens   Describes a lens whose angular coverage is substantially greater than that of a "normal" lens. Also sometimes called "wide field."

Winder   A battery-powered camera accessory, similar to a motor drive but intended primarily for single-frame operation. Some winders are capable of automatic sequence photography at speeds of up to about two frames-per-second.

Working Solution   Any solution used in photographic processing, as distinguished from stock or storage solutions which are usually more concentrated for better keeping qualities. Stock solutions are almost invariably diluted for use, to make the working solution.

Zone   In the Zone System a specific subject tone as it will be rendered in the print. Seven to nine Zones are usually described as covering the useful range of print tones and each is assigned a number; thus, Zone III is considered to represent very dark gray or textured black in the print, Zone V is middle gray, Zone IX is maximum paper white, etc. In the subject the Zones are defined as being luminances and the interval between adjacent Zones of a "normal" subject is one stop.

Zone Focusing   Adjustment of the camera controls to achieve depth of field between selected near and far limits in the subject space. Often done in anticipation of the sudden or brief appearance of some subject whose position or movements can be predicted only generally.

Zone System   A method of exposure and development determination advanced by Ansel Adams, and later propounded by Minor White, which involves analysis of the luminances of the significant areas and the tonal extremes of the subject and the previsualization of their translation into print densities. It is a logical theory, but one which tends to become pseudoscientific, if not actually intuitive, in practice.

Zoom Lens   A type of lens of very complex structure which can be adjusted in use to provide a continuous range of focal lengths within its design limits. They are very popular with cinematographers and are also widely used in still photography with small cameras.

Bibliography

The following bibliography lists only a few of the books available which treat the subject of photography in words or pictures. It is not intended to be a definitive list but does represent a selection of titles which would form a fine reference library. I am sure there are many valuable books which are not included and, no doubt, some of these selections could be contested but within this listing there should be something of interest for almost any photographer, regardless of his background or specialty. The bibliography emphasizes picture books and books of historical interest because, it seems to me, these are major sources of inspiration for students. The relatively few instructional books listed are basic; extremely technical or specialized scientific works have not been included.

Picture Books

Abbott, Berenice. *The World of Atget*. New York: Horizon Press, Inc., 1964.

Abbott, Berenice, and McCausland, Elizabeth. *New York in the Thirties*. Unabridged republication of 1939 edition (formerly titled *Changing New York*). New York: Dover Publications, Inc., 1973.

Aldridge, James. *Living Egypt*. Photographs by Paul Strand. New York: Horizon Press, Inc., 1969.

André Kertesz, Photographer. Intro. by John Szarkowski. New York: The Museum of Modern Art, 1964.

The Appalachian Photographs of Doris Ulmann. Intro. by John Jacob Niles. Pennland, N.C.: The Jargon Society, 1970.

Barbara Morgan Monograph. Foreword by Peter Bunnell. Hastings-on-Hudson, N.Y.: Morgan & Morgan, 1972.

Berenice Abbott, Photographs. Foreword by John Szarkowski. New York: Horizon Press, Inc., 1970.

The Best of LIFE. New York: Time-Life Books, 1973.

Brassaï. Intro. by Lawrence Durrell. New York: Museum of Modern Art, 1968.

Brown, Joseph Epes, ed. *Edward Curtis*. Photographs of the American Indian. Millerton, N.Y.: Aperture, 1972.

Bry, Doris. *Alfred Stieglitz: Photographer*. Boston: Museum of Fine Arts, 1965.

Bullock, Barbara. *Wynn Bullock . . . Photographs*. San Francisco: Scrimshaw Press, 1971.

Callahan, Sean, ed. *Photographs of Margaret Bourke-White*. Intro. by Theodore M. Brown, afterword by Carl Mydans. Greenwich, Conn.: New York Graphic Society, 1972.

Capa, Cornell. *The Concerned Photographer*. New York: Grossman Publishers, Inc., 1968.

――――. *The Concerned Photographer II*. New York: Grossman Publishers, Inc., 1972.

Capa, Robert. *Images of War*. New York: Grossman Publishers, Inc., 1964.

Carpenter, Edward. *They Became What They Beheld* Photographs by Ken Heyman. New York: Outerbridge & Dienstfrey, 1970.

Cartier-Bresson, Henri. *The Decisive Moment*. New York: Simon & Schuster, Inc., 1952. (Out of print)

――――. *World of Henri Cartier-Bresson*. New York: Viking Press, Inc., 1968.

Clark, Larry. *Tulsa*. New York: Lustrum Press, 1971.

Curtis, Edward S. *Portraits from North American Indian Life*. Intro. by A.D. Coleman and T.C. McLuhan. New York: Outerbridge and Lazard, 1972.

Davidson, Bruce. *East 100th Street*. Cambridge, Mass.: Harvard University Press, 1970.

DeCock, Liliane, ed. *Ansel Adams Monograph*. Foreword by Minor White. Hastings-on-Hudson, N.Y.: Morgan & Morgan, 1972.

DeCock, Liliane, and McGhee, Reginald. *James Van Der Zee*. Intro. by Regina A. Perry. Dobbs Ferry, N.Y.: Morgan & Morgan, 1973.

Diane Arbus. An Aperture Monograph. Millerton, N.Y.: Aperture, 1972.

Dorothea Lange. Intro. by George P. Elliott. New York: The Museum of Modern Art, 1966.

Eisenstaedt, Alfred. *The Eye of Eisenstaedt*. New York: Viking Press, Inc., 1969.

Erwitt, Elliott. *Photographs and Anti-Photograph*. Greenwich, Conn.: New York Graphic Society, 1972.

Evans, Walker. *Message From the Interior*. New York: The Eakins Press, 1966.

The Family of Man. Intro. by Edward Steichen. New York: The Museum of Modern Art, 1955.

Feininger, Andreas. *Forms of Nature and Life*. New York: Viking Press, 1966.

Frank, Robert. *The Americans*. Photographs by Robert Frank, intro. by Jack Kerouac. New York: Grossmann Publishers, Inc., 1969.

Friedlander, Lee. *Self Portrait*. New York: Haywire Press, 1970.

Gernsheim, Helmut, ed. *Alvin Langdon Coburn, Photographer.* New York: Frederick A. Praeger, 1966.

Haas, Ernst. *The Creation.* New York: Viking Press, Inc., 1971.
The Hampton Album. Intro. by Lincoln Kirstein. New York: The Museum of Modern Art, 1966.
Harry Callahan. Intro. by Sherman Paul. New York: The Museum of Modern Art, 1967.
Hendricks, Gordon. *The Photographs of Thomas Eakins.* New York: Grossman Publishers, Inc., 1972.
Hughes, Langston. *The Sweet Flypaper of Life.* Photographs by Roy DeCarava. Philadelphia: Hill and Wang, 1967.
Hurley, F. Jack. *Portrait of a Decade.* Baton Rouge, La.: Louisiana State University Press, 1972.

Imogen Cunningham: Photographs. Intro. by Margery Mann. Seattle, Wash.: University of Washington Press, 1970.

Jerry N. Uelsmann. An Aperture Monograph. Intro. by Peter Bunnell. Millerton, N.Y.: Small, 1971.

Kertesz, André. *Sixty Years of Photography: 1912–1972.* New York: Viking Press, Inc., 1972.
Kirstein, Lincoln. *Eugene Smith, Photographs.* Millerton, N.Y.: Aperture, 1969.

Larry Burrows: Compassionate Photographer. New York: Time-Life Books, 1972.
Lartigue, Jacques Henri. *Boyhood Photos of J. H. Lartigue.* Lausanne, Switz.: Ami Guichard, 1966. (Out of print)
———. *Diary of a Century.* Ed. by Richard Avedon. New York: Viking Press, Inc., 1970.
Levitas, Mitchel. *America in Crisis.* Photographs by Magnum photographers. New York: Holt, Rinehart & Winston, 1969.

Looking at Pictures: One Hundred Photographs from the Collection of the Museum of Modern Art. Notes by John Szarkowski. Greenwich, Conn.: New York Graphic Society, 1972.
Lyon, Danny. *The Bikeriders.* New York: Macmillan Company, 1968.
———. *Conversations With The Dead.* Photographs by Danny Lyon, drawings and writings by Billy McCune. New York: Holt, Rinehart & Winston, 1971.
Lyons, Nathan, ed. *Aaron Siskind, Photographer.* Intro. by Nathan Lyons. Rochester, N.Y.; George Eastman House, 1965.
———. *Photography in the Twentieth Century.* New York: Horizon Press, Inc., 1967.
Lyons, Nathan; Labrot, Syl; and Chappell, Walter. *Under the Sun: The Abstract Art of Camera Vision.* New York: George Braziller, 1960. (Limited edition)

Manos, Constantine. *A Greek Portfolio.* New York: Viking Press, Inc., 1972.
McCarthy, Mary. *Portugal.* Photographs by Neal Slavin. New York: Lustrum Press, 1971.
Michals, Duane. *The Journey of the Spirit After Death.* New York: Winter House, 1971.

Natali, Enrico. *New American People.* Hastings-on-Hudson, N.Y.: Morgan & Morgan, 1972.
Newhall, Beaumont. *Frederick H. Evans.* An Aperture Monograph. Millerton, N.Y.: Aperture, 1973.
Newhall, Nancy. *The Eloquent Light.* A biography of Ansel Adams. San Francisco: Sierra Club, 1963.
———. *Yosemite Valley.* Photographs by Ansel Adams. Redwood City, Calif.: Five Associates, 1959.
Norman, Dorothy. *Alfred Stieglitz: An American Seer.* Millerton, N.Y.: Aperture, 1973.

Parker, Fred. *Manuel Alvarez Bravo.* Pasadena, Calif.: Pasadena Art Museum, 1971.
Paul Caponigro. An Aperture Monograph. New York: Aperture, 1967. Revised and enlarged, 1972.

Paul Strand: Photographs 1915–1968. Text by Alfred Stieglitz, Nancy Newhall, Paul Strand, and others. Millerton, N.Y.: Aperture, 1972.
Porter, Eliot. *In Wildness Is the Preservation of the World.* New York: Sierra Club-Ballantine, 1967.
———. *The Place No One Knew . . . Glen Canyon.* San Francisco: Sierra Club, 1966.

Sander, August. *Menschen Ohne Maske.* Luzern and Frankfurt: C. J. Bucher, 1971.
Steichen, Edward, ed. *The Bitter Years 1935–1941.* New York: The Museum of Modern Art, 1966.
Szarkowski, John. *The Photographer's Eye.* New York: The Museum of Modern Art, 1966.
———, ed. *The Photographer and the American Landscape.* Greenwich, Conn.: New York Graphic Society, 1972.

Tucker, Anne, ed. *The Woman's Eye.* Intro. by Anne Tucker. New York: Alfred A. Knopf, Inc., 1973.

Walker Evans. Intro. by John Szarkowski. New York: The Museum of Modern Art, 1971.
Weiss, Margaret R., ed. *Ben Shahn, Photographer.* Intro. by Margaret R. Weiss. New York: DaCapo Press, 1972.
Weston, Cole. *Edward Weston: Fifty Years.* Millerton, N.Y.: Aperture, 1973.
White, Minor. *Mirrors, Messages, Manifestations.* Millerton, N.Y.: Aperture, 1969.
Winningham, Geoffery. *Friday Night at the Coliseum.* Houston, Texas: Allison Press, 1971.
Winogrand, Garry. *The Animals.* New York: The Museum of Modern Art, 1969.

Instructional and Reference Books

Adams, Ansel. *Camera and Lens.* Hastings-on-Hudson, N.Y.: Morgan & Morgan, 1970.
———. *Natural Light Photography.* Hastings-on-Hudson, N.Y.: Morgan & Morgan, 1965.
———. *The Negative.* Hastings-on-Hudson, N.Y.: Morgan & Morgan, 1968.
———. *The Print.* Hastings-on-Hudson, N.Y.: Morgan & Morgan, 1968.

Dowdell, John J. III, and Zakia, Richard D. *Zone Systemizer.* Hastings-on-Hudson, N.Y.: Morgan & Morgan, 1972.

Eaton, George T. *Photographic Chemistry.* Hastings-on-Hudson, N.Y.: Morgan & Morgan, 1965.

The Focal Encyclopedia of Photography. New York: McGraw-Hill Book Company, 1969.

Gassan, Arnold. *Handbook for Contemporary Photography.* Athens, Ohio: Handbook Company, 1974.

Life Library of Photography. New York: Time-Life Books, 1970.
The Art of Photography
The Camera
Color
Frontiers of Photography
Great Photographers
Light and Film
Photojournalism
The Print
The Studio

Neblette, C. B. *Fundamentals of Photography.* New York: Van Nostrand Reinhold, 1970.
———. *Photographic Lenses.* Hastings-on-Hudson, N.Y.: Morgan & Morgan, 1972.
———. *Photography: Its Materials and Processes.* New York: Van Nostrand Reinhold, 1972.

Pittaro, Ernest M., ed. *Photo-Lab-Index.* Hastings-on-Hudson, N.Y.: Morgan & Morgan, 1972.
Procedures for Processing and Storing Black and White Photographs for Maximum Possible Permanence. Grinnell, Iowa: East Street Gallery, 1970.

Shipman, Carl. *Understanding Photography*. Tucson, Ariz.: H. P. Books, 1974.
Simon, Michael, and Moore, Dennis. *First Lessons in Black and White Photography*. New York: Holt, Rinehart & Winston, 1978.
Stroebel, Leslie. *View Camera Technique*. New York: Hastings House Publishers, Inc., 1967.
Swedlund, Charles. *Photography: A Handbook of History, Materials and Processes*. New York: Holt, Rinehart & Winston, 1974.

Todd, Hollis N., and Zakia, Richard D. *Photographic Sensitometry*. Hastings-on-Hudson, N.Y.: Morgan & Morgan, 1969.

Upton, Barbara and John. *Photography*. Boston: Little, Brown and Company, 1976.

Vestal, David. *The Craft of Photography*. New York: Harper and Row, 1975.

Wade, Kent E. *Alternative Photographic Processes*. Dobbs Ferry, N. Y.: Morgan & Morgan, 1978.
White, Minor; Zakia, Richard; and Lorenz, Peter. *The New Zone System Manual*. Hastings-on-Hudson, N.Y.: Morgan & Morgan, 1976.

Zakia, Richard D., and Todd, Hollis N. *101 Experiments in Photography*. Hastings-on-Hudson, N.Y.: Morgan & Morgan, 1969.

Aesthetics and Criticism

Brooke, James T. *A Viewer's Guide to Looking at Photographs*. Wilmette, Ill.: The Aurelian Press, 1977.

Coffin, Charles. *Photography as a Fine Art*. Intro. by Thomas Barrow. Hastings-on-Hudson, N.Y.: Morgan & Morgan, 1971.
Coke, Van Deren. *The Painter and the Photograph*. Albuquerque, N.M.: University of New Mexico Press, 1971.

Gernsheim, Helmut. *Creative Photography, Aesthetic Trends 1839–1960*. Boston: Boston Book and Art Shop, 1962.

Lyons, Nathan, ed. *Photographers on Photography*. Englewood Cliffs, N.J.: Prentice-Hall, Inc., 1966.

Scharf, Aaron. *Art and Photography*. Baltimore, Md.: The Penguin Press, 1969.
———. *Creative Photography*. New York: Van Nostrand Reinhold, 1969.
Sontag, Susan. *On Photography*. New York: Farrar, Straus and Giroux, 1977.

Books of Historical Interest

The following are titles from a recently issued collection of facsimile editions published by the Arno Press, New York, all dated 1973.

Anderson, A. J. *The Artistic Side of Photography*. Philadelphia and London, 1919.
Anderson, Paul L. *The Fine Art of Photography in Theory and Practice*. London, 1910.

Beck, Otto Walter. *Art Principles in Portrait Photography*. New York, 1907.
Bingham, Robert J. *Photogenic Manipulation*. Parts I and II. London: 1852.
Bunnell, Peter C., ed. *Nonsilver Printing Processes: Four Selections, 1886–1927*. New York: 1973.
Burbank, W. H. *Photographic Printing Methods*. 3rd ed. New York: 1891.
Burgess, N. G. *The Photograph Manual*. 8th ed. New York: 1863.

Croucher, J. H., and LeGray, Gustave. *Plain Directions for Obtaining Photographic Pictures*. Parts I, II, & III. Philadelphia: 1853.

Draper, John William. *Scientific Memoirs*. London: 1878.

Emerson, Peter Henry. *Naturalistic Photography for Students of the Art*, 3rd edition, including *The Death of Naturalistic Photography*. London: 1891; New York: 1899.

Fouque, Victor. *The Truth Concerning the Invention of Photography: Nicephore Niepce—His Life, Letters and Works*. Translated by Edward Epstean from the original French edition. Paris, 1867; New York, 1935.

Gillies, John Wallace. *Principles of Pictorial Photography*. New York: 1923.

Harrison, W. Jerome. *A History of Photography Written as a Practical Guide and an Introduction to Its Latest Developments*. New York: 1887.
Hartmann, Sadakichi (Sidney Allan). *Composition in Portraiture*. New York, 1909.
———. *Landscape and Figure Composition*. New York: 1910.
Hicks, Wilson. *Words and Pictures*. New York: 1952.

Jones, Bernard E. ed. *Cassell's Cyclopaedia of Photography*. London: 1911.

Lerebours, N. P. *A Treatise on Photography*. London: 1843.

Mortensen, William. *Monsters and Madonnas*. San Francisco, 1936.

Pritchard, H. Baden. *About Photography and Photographers*. New York: 1883.

Robinson, H. P., and Abney, Capt. W. deW. *The Art and Practice of Silver Printing,* American Edition. New York: 1881.
Robinson, H. P. *Picture Making by Photography*. 5th ed. London: 1897.

Sobieszek, Robert A., ed. *The Collodion Process and the Ferrotype: Three Accounts, 1854–1872*. New York: 1973.
———. *The Daguerreotype Process: Three Treatises, 1840–1849*. New York: 1973.
Sparling, W. *Theory and Practice of the Photographic Art*. London, 1856.

Tissandier, Gaston. *A History and Handbook of Photography*. 2nd ed. Ed. by J. Thomson. London: 1878.

Vogel, Hermann. *The Chemistry of Light and Photography*. New York: 1875.

Wilson, Edward L. *The American Carbon Manual*. New York: 1868.
———. *Wilson's Photographics*. New York: 1881.

Other books of historical interest

Andrews, Ralph W. *Picture Gallery Pioneers*. New York: Bonanza Books, 1964.

Braive, Michel. *The Photograph, A Social History*. New York: McGraw-Hill Book Company, 1966.

Camera Work: An Anthology. Millerton, N.Y.: Aperture, 1973.

Daguerre. Intro. by Beaumont Newhall. New York: Winter House, Ltd., 1971.
Doty, Robert. *Photo Secession, Photography as a Fine Art*. Rochester, N.Y.: The George Eastman House, 1960.

French Primitive Photography. Intro. by Minor White. Millerton, N.Y.: Aperture, 1970.

Gardner, Alexander. *Gardner's Photographic Sketchbook of the Civil War*. New York: Dover Publications, Inc. 1959.
Gernsheim, Helmut. *Lewis Carroll, Photographer*. New York: Dover Publications, Inc., 1970.
Gernsheim, Helmut and Alison. *A Concise History of Photography*. New York: Grosset and Dunlap, 1965.
———. *The History of Photography 1685–1914*. New York: McGraw-Hill Book Company, 1969.
Gutman, Judith M. *Lewis W. Hine and The American Social Conscience*. New York: Walker & Co., 1967.

Henney, Keith, and Dudley, Beverly, eds. *Handbook of Photography.* New York: Whittlesey House (McGraw), 1939.

Horan, James D. *Timothy O'Sullivan. America's Forgotten Photographer.* New York: Bonanza, 1966.

Hunt, Robert. *A Popular Treatise on the Art of Photography.* A facsimile edition with intro. and notes by James Yingpeh Tong. Athens, Ohio: Ohio University Press, 1973.

Lothrop, Eaton S., Jr. *A Century of Cameras.* Dobbs Ferry, N.Y.: Morgan & Morgan, 1973.

Mees, C. E. Kenneth. *From Dry Plates to Ektachrome Film.* Ziff-Davis, 1961.

Muybridge, Eadweard. *The Human Figure in Motion.* New York: Dover Publications, Inc., 1955.

Newhall, Beaumont. *The Daguerreotype in America.* Greenwich, Conn.: New York Graphic Society, 1961. Revised in 1968.
―――. *The History of Photography.* New York: The Museum of Modern Art, 1964.
―――. *The Latent Image.* Garden City, N.Y.: Doubleday & Co., Inc., 1967.

Newhall, Nancy, ed. *The Daybooks of Edward Weston, Vol. I, Mexico.* Millerton, N.Y.: Aperture, 1973.
―――, ed. *The Daybooks of Edward Weston, Vol. II, California.* Millerton, N.Y.: Aperture, 1973.

Pollack, Peter. *The Picture History of Photography.* New York: Harry N. Abrams, 1969.

Riis, Jacob A. *How the Other Half Lives.* New York: Dover, 1971.

Rinhart, Floyd and Marion. *American Daguerreian Art.* New York: Clarkson N. Potter, 1967.

Robinson, H. P. *Pictorial Effect in Photography.* Pawlet, N.H.: Helios, 1971. (A facsimile edition first published in 1869.)

Rudisill, Richard. *Mirror Image: The Influence of the Daguerreotype on American Society.* Albuquerque, N.M.: University of New Mexico Press, 1971.

Snelling, Henry H. *Art of Photography.* Hastings-on-Hudson, N.Y.: Morgan & Morgan, 1970. (Facsimile edition.)

Steichen, Edward. *A Life in Photography.* New York: Doubleday & Co., Inc., 1963.

Taft, Robert. *Photography and the American Scene.* New York: Dover Publications, Inc., 1964.

Talbot, William Henry Fox. *The Pencil of Nature.* A facsimile of the 1844–46 edition, with intro. by Beaumont Newhall. New York: DaCapo Press, 1969.

Thomson, John and Smith, Adolphe. *Street Life in London.* New York and London: Benjamin Blom, 1969. (Reissued)

Towler, J. *The Silver Sunbeam.* A facsimile of the 1864 edition, with intro. by Beaumont Newhall. Hastings-on-Hudson, N.Y.: Morgan & Morgan, 1969.

Index